POLITICAL CONFLICT IN PAKISTAN

Comparative Politics and International Studies Series
Series Editor: Christophe Jaffrelot

This series focuses on the transformation of politics and societies by international and domestic factors, including culture and religion. Analysing these changes in a sociological and historical perspective, it gives priority to trends from below as much as state interventions and the interaction of both. It also factors in dynamics at the interface of inter/transnational pressures and national tensions.

MOHAMMAD WASEEM

Political Conflict in Pakistan

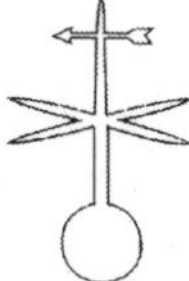

HURST & COMPANY, LONDON

First published in the United Kingdom in 2021 by
C. Hurst & Co. (Publishers) Ltd,
New Wing, Somerset House, Strand,
London, WC2R 1LA.

This paperback edition first published in the United Kingdom in 2025.

A Cataloguing-in-Publication data record for this book
is available from the British Library.

ISBN: 9781805264446

This book is printed using paper from registered sustainable
and managed sources.

www.hurstpublishers.com

For Raazia

CONTENTS

ACKNOWLEDGEMENTS

I have incurred various debts in the process of writing this book. I consulted the British National Archives and the British Library in London, the National Assembly of Pakistan Library and the National Documentation Centre in Islamabad, as well as the library of Lahore University of Management Sciences (LUMS). I must thank the staff in these institutions for their cooperation in locating the relevant material. I am grateful to my colleague in LUMS, Dr Asma Faiz, for reading the manuscript and for her valuable comments about linking ideas and arguments. I want to thank my friends and colleagues for waiting tirelessly for the book to be completed and for providing moral and institutional support, especially Dr Ali Khan. I thank Dr David Taylor for reading parts of the book and for suggesting improvements in both content and style.

The book draws heavily on my research in recent years that has focused on a reappraisal of politics in Pakistan. In this phase of my scholarship, my research gradually focused on the power play among various actors on the political stage belonging to different strata and communities. Parts of the present book draw on published articles and book chapters duly acknowledged in the text. However, a major part of the book is the product of my recent academic struggle to understand and interpret the persistence and sustainability of conflict at various levels of the state and society. In this endeavour, I brought to light the direct and, more significantly, indirect role of groups and communities, state institutions and political organizations, cultural frameworks and ethnic identities, which had long been part of my political imagination and academic pursuit but which have found fuller expression in the present book.

Finally, I must thank my publisher, Michael Dwyer, of Hurst Publishers for his understanding regarding the long wait for the manuscript of this book, which was delayed for various reasons during the Covid-19 pandemic that covered a major part of 2020. I am also thankful to Lara Weisweiller-Wu of Hurst, who was very patient with me with her gentle reminders as well as encouragement. My special thanks are reserved for Professor Christophe Jaffrelot for his encouragement in this endeavour and for his interaction with me at various points over the last quarter of a century. Ultimately, responsibility for the views expressed in this book lies with me.

LIST OF TABLES AND FIGURES

LIST OF ABBREVIATIONS

A-CII	Advisory Council of Islamic Ideology
AFP	Agence France-Presse
AIC	Asia Internet Coalition
AIML	All-India Muslim League
AISSF	All-India Sikh Students Federation
AL	Awami League
ANP	Awami National Party
APMSO	All Pakistan Mohajir Students Organisation
APNS	All Pakistan Newspapers Society
APP	Azad Pakistan Party
APPSF	All Pakistan Private Schools Federation
APPWA	All Pakistan Progressive Writers Association
APS	Army Public School
ARU	Asset Recovery Unit
ASR	Applied Socio-Economic Research Resource Centre
ASWJ	Ahl Sunnat Wal Jamaat
ATM	Automated Teller Machine
BAP	Balochistan Awami Party
BJP	Bharatiya Janata Party
BLA	Baloch Liberation Army
BNP-M	Balochistan National Party (Mengal)
BPC	Basic Principles Committee
BRA	Baloch Republican Army
BSO	Baloch Students Organization
BSU	Balochistan States Union
CCI	Council of Common Interests

LIST OF ABBREVIATIONS

CIA	Central Intelligence Agency
CII	Council of Islamic Ideology
COAS	Chief of Army Staff
CP	Central Provinces (India)
CPEC	China–Pakistan Economic Corridor
CPJ	Committee to Protect Journalists
CPNE	Council of Pakistan Newspaper Editors
CPP	Communist Party of Pakistan
CSS	Central Superior Services
DAC	Democratic Action Committee
DFID	Department for International Development
DYL	Democratic Youth League
EBDO	Elected Bodies Disqualification Order
ECL	Exit Control List
ECP	Election Commission of Pakistan
EUEOM	European Union Election Observation Mission
FATA	Federally Administered Tribal Area
FATF	Financial Action Task Force
FBR	Federal Board of Revenue
FC	Frontier Corps
FIR	First Information Report
FPTP	First-Past-the-Post (system)
FSC	Federal Shariah Court
GB	Gilgit-Baltistan
GCI	Global Competitive Index
GD	Ganatantra Dal
GE	General Elections
GIGA	German Institute of Global and Area Studies
GNC	General Nutrition Centres
HEC	Higher Education Commission
HM	Hizbul Mujahideen
HRCP	Human Rights Commission of Pakistan
IAS	Indian Administrative Service
IB	Intelligence Bureau
ICJ	International Commission of Jurists
ICS	Indian Civil Service
ICT	Information Communication Technology
IDEA	Institute for Democracy and Electoral Assistance

<h1 style="text-align:center">LIST OF ABBREVIATIONS</h1>

IDPs	Internally Displaced Persons
IHK	Indian-held Kashmir
IJI	Islami Jamhoori Itehad
IJT	Islami Jamiat Talaba
INGO	International Non-Governmental Organization
ISAS	Institute of South Asian Studies
ISI	Inter-Services Intelligence
ISIS	Islamic State of Iraq and Syria
ISPR	Inter-Services Public Relations
JCP	Judicial Commission of Pakistan
JI	Jamaat Islami
JIT	Joint Investigation Team
JM	Jash Muhammad
JSQM-A	Jiye Sindh Qomi Movement
JuD	Jamat ud Dawah
JUI-F	Jamiat Ulema Islam (Fazlur Rehman)
JUI-S	Jamiat Ulema Islam (Samiul Haq)
JUP	Jamiat Ulema Pakistan
JWP	Jamhoori Wattan Party
KK	Khudai Khidmatgar
KP	Khyber Pakhtunkhwa
LDA	Lahore Development Authority
LeT	Lashkar-e-Taiba
LJ	Lashkar-e-Jahngvi
MDI	Markaz Dawat-wal-Irshad
MEOs	Military Evacuation Organizations
MI	Military Intelligence
MIL	Movement for Islamic Literature
MIND	Movement in India for Nuclear Disarmament
MIT	Massachusetts Institution of Technology
MKP	Mazdoor Kissan Party
MMA	Muttahida Majlis Amal
MNA	Member of National Assembly
MPA	Member of Provincial Assembly
MQM	Muttahida (previously Mohajirs) Qaumi Movement
MRD	Movement for Restoration of Democracy
MYC	Milli Yekjehti Council
NA	National Assembly

LIST OF ABBREVIATIONS

NAB	National Accountability Bureau
NACTA	National Counter Terrorism Authority
NADRA	National Database and Registration Authority
NAP	National Awami Party (1957)
NATO	North Atlantic Treaty Organization
NDU	National Defence University
NFC	National Finance Commission
NGO	Non-Governmental Organization
NP	National Party
NPOs	Non-Profit Organizations
NPP	National People's Party
NRO	National Reconciliation Order
NSC	National Security Council
NWFP	North West Frontier Province
OBC	Other Backward Classes
PAP	Pakistan Awami Party
PAT	Pakistan Awami Tehreek
PATA	Provincially Administered Tribal Areas
PBA	Pakistan Broadcasters Association
PCCR	Parliamentary Committee on Constitutional Reforms
PCO	Provisional Constitutional Order
PDM	Pakistan Democratic Movement
PECA	Prevention of Electronic Crimes Act
PEMRA	Pakistan Electronic Media Regulatory Authority
PES	Post-enumeration Survey
PESA	Pakistan Ex-Servicemen Association
PFUJ	Pakistan Federal Union of Journalists
PIDC	Pakistan Industrial Development Corporation
PILDAT	Pakistan Institute of Legislative Development and Transparency
PIPFPD	Pakistan India Peoples' Forum for Peace and Democracy
PKMAP	Pakhtunkhwa Milli Awami Party
PMA	Pakistan Military Academy
PMDA	Pakistan Media Development Authority
PML-N	Pakistan Muslim League (Nawaz Sharif)
PML-Q	Pakistan Muslim League (Quaid-i-Azam)
PNA	Pakistan National Alliance
PNP	Pakistan National Party

LIST OF ABBREVIATIONS

PO	Presiding Officer
PODO	Public Offices Disqualification Order
PONM	Pakistan Oppressed Nations Movement
POPA	Protection of Pakistan Act
PPP	Pakistan Peoples Party
PPWA	Pakistan Progressive Writers Association
PRODA	Public and Representative Office Disqualification Act
PSP	Pak Socialist Party
PTI	Pakistan Tehreek-e-Insaf
PTM	Pashtun Tahaffuz Movement
PWA	Progressive Writers Association
RAW	Research and Analysis Wing
RCO	Revival of the Constitution Order (1985)
RMS	Result Management System
RO	Returning Officer
RSS	Rashtriya Swayamsevak Sangh
RTS	Results Transmission System
SAARC	South Asian Association for Regional Cooperation
SAFMA	South Asian Free Media Association
SAM	Sindh Awami Mohaz
SBPF	Sindhi Baloch Pushtoon Front
SDPI	Sustainable Development Policy Institute
SEAL	Sea, Air and Land Teams
SECP	Security and Exchange Commission of Pakistan
SGPC	Shiromani Gurdwara Parbandhak Committee
SHC	Sindh Hari Committee
SJC	Supreme Judicial Council
SMS	Short Message Service
SOAS	School of Oriental and African Studies
SSP	Sipah Sahaba Pakistan
TI	Tehrik Istiqlal
TJ	Tehreek Jafria
TLP	Tehreek Labbaik Pakistan
TLYRA	Tehreek Labbaik Ya Rasool Allah
TNFJ	Tehrik Nifaz Fiqh Jafaria
TNSM	Tehreek Nafaz Shariat Mohammadi
TTP	Tehrik-e-Taliban Pakistan
UDF	United Democratic Front

UG	Ustman Gul
UN	United Nations
UNHCR	United Nations High Commission for Refugees
UP	United Provinces
USAID	United States Agency for International Development
WAF	Women's Action Forum
WAPDA	Water and Power Development Authority
WP	Wrore Pakhtoon

INTRODUCTION

The central theme of this book is political conflict. Almost all scholarly research on the politics of Pakistan has dealt with conflict between the federal and provincial governments, Islamists and modernists, the religio-sectarian majority and minorities, the civil and military wings of the state, the judiciary and parliament and, though limited in time and scale, between industrialists and labour and between landlords and peasants. Often these conflicts have been studied as the outcome of a clash of interests and identities, expressed through public mobilization in pursuit of certain demands for change in the normal flow of social, cultural and political life. Sometimes, conflicts attained crisis proportions that made some bemoan 'a dream gone sour', others to live 'between dream and reality' and still others to draw a dreamy picture of Pakistan as a 'state beyond the crisis'.[1] Clash of institutions has become the name of the game. The study of conflict has focused increasingly on violence as a category by itself, as a spillover effect from the four-decades old Afghanistan war that cast a grim shadow on the country. Scholarly research has scarcely taken up the issue of conflict transformation, much less conflict resolution.

Lewis Coser analyses conflict as a way out of the stultification of a social system, which can open up new vistas of political innovation, challenge the status quo and operate as a precursor to transformation of the social and political hierarchy.[2] In other words, one can study conflict as both destructive and constitutive of the social order, which indeed is the story of Pakistan. At the heart of all politics lies conflict. One can trace two major clusters of states that provide for conflict resolution mechanisms: (1) where the institutional design of the state and the internal dynamics of the 'moral community' as a nation evolved concurrently, such as in the historical West; and (2) where, typically, self-governing traditional states and statelets, such as those from the Arabian Peninsula, effectively contained and managed the conflict without any reference to constitutional safeguards.

However, conflict is almost endemic in postcolonial societies, essentially because of the distance between the modern state and traditional society. This contradiction is brought out in terms of the post-independence reformulation of the political system characterized by a gradual encroachment of tradition over modernity through the route of cultural nationalism. At one end, the colonial state in its pristine form transplanted European ideas and the institutions of the rule of law, rational-legal bureaucracy, the judiciary and public finance. The new state apparatuses were increasingly operationalized by the modernist elite couched in a Western educational and professional ethos and a relatively 'liberal' cultural framework. In this context, the 'local' bureaucracy operated as a stakeholder at the district and sub-district levels. At the other end, the patterns of social hierarchy were consolidated even further in the framework of a 'collaborative mechanism',[3] which emerged as a guarantee of political stability. If we follow Lapidus's view of two kinds of social formations in Muslim countries — one which has a modern, 'secular' and rational–legal state apparatus along with a traditional society, and the other which incorporates a composite traditional framework of social and political authority — then Pakistan as a postcolonial state clearly falls in the former category.[4] In this model, the state represents a continuum from colonial times as a bureaucratic polity. In its new incarnation from the mid-twentieth century to the first quarter of the twenty-first century as a legal state, the Western tradition of law and philosophy constantly grappled with the resurgent Islamic jurisprudence. Under colonialism, the two worlds — modern and traditional — ran parallel to each other, till the modernists were able to mobilize wider society in pursuit of the nationalist agenda of independence. The former included Gandhi, Nehru, Jinnah and scores of others in British India in pursuit of the goal of self-determination. The force of nationalism pushed colonial power out but led to a permanent conflict between the state and society, between a 'Western' framework of authority and Islamic norms and practices, and between management of the present and planning for the future at one end and ambition for re-living the past at the other.

This book deals with political conflict in Pakistan in the context of four clusters of themes, as mapped by Figure I.1.

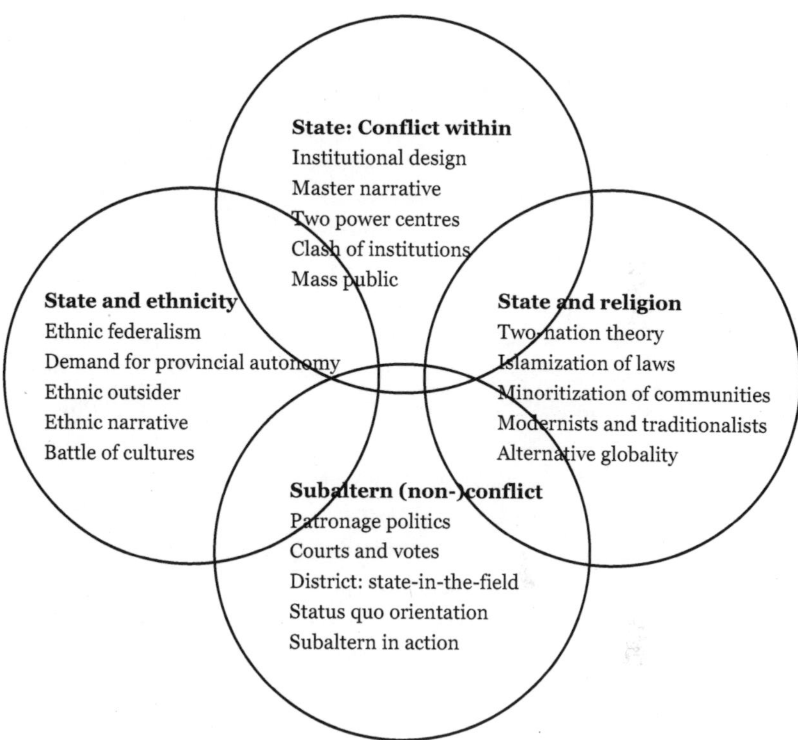

Figure I.1 Political conflict in Pakistan

The first cluster deals with conflict within the state. One of the basic arguments of the book is that the institutional design of the state plays a crucial role in determining the nature and scope of the conflict. I shall focus on the constitutional dynamics as the centre of conflictual activity surrounding the issues of parliamentary sovereignty, the federal project and the Islamic project. The state's narrative as the master narrative re-makes history and re-charters a vision of the future in pursuit of defining the national destiny. This exercise runs into conflict with alternative narratives, which are by no means extinct. In the process of nation-building, Pakistan experienced the emergence of two power centres, the middle class and the political class, which were diametrically opposed to each other in their political vision. These power centres defined the mega conflict between the civil and military organs of the state. A clash of institutions ensued not only between the (military) establishment and parliament, which often resulted in a coup or dissolution of assemblies or dismissal of prime ministers, but also between parliament and the judiciary.

Away from the state institutions, I bring in the role of the mass public in a variety of modes of operation, ranging from intellectual debates to street demonstrations. I discuss the role of civil society, education and the media in the framework of 'new publicness', which, however, remains yet to be achieved. One of the key sources of clash continues to be the design and practice of federalism, which remains at the heart of the debate about distribution of legislative powers and financial resources between the centre and the provinces. All provinces other than Punjab proclaimed their demand for autonomy in making policy and taking action within what they considered their legitimate sphere of activity. While these provinces developed their own narratives, reflective of their ambitions and aspirations as 'outsiders', Punjab and Urdu-speaking migrants (Mohajirs) represented the insiders, along with the army as the core insider. I look at the insider–outsider dichotomy in ethnic terms, from the perspective of the Punjabization of the country. I discuss how the federal and ethnic forces sought to re-shape the cultural landscape, the former writing the big text over the small text written by the latter.

In the domain of conflict between religion and state, I draw on the grand legitimizing potential of the two-nation theory, which has provided the ultimate ideational sanction for the ambitious project of Islamization of laws, morals and manners. I analyse how Islamization led to a division between modernists and traditionalists, which pushed the two sides into a permanent tug of war even as both have undergone change in the process. I shall define today's modernists as less modern than their predecessors three generations back. Meanwhile, traditionalists also moved forward in adopting extra-constitutional – including militant – means to achieve their ends. Religious minorities struggled to find a place for themselves in an increasingly inhospitable land. I want to explore the extent to which Pakistan has been struggling to exit from the perceived world order and develop its own globality based on a parallel world-of-Islam perspective. I analyse micro-level (non-)conflict in Pakistan inasmuch as it brings out the element of the status quo in the power structure as the foundation of politics defined by patron–client relations. Here, the state-in-the-field in the district is hand-in-glove with local stakeholders who get facilitated through access to the local bureaucracy and the courts. In this context, vote politics plays a politically conservative role since patronage politics gets authenticated through the ballot. I wish to analyse the way the subaltern classes keep depending on those who speak for them. However, I shall also discuss the continuing low-intensity class-based consciousness and its expression at various times and places, although its structural dynamics gradually diminished in power and influence. This is a reflection of the gradual decline of the left from the first quarter of the century after independence.

I discuss the four clusters represented in Figure I.1 in a contextual rather than sequential way and I follow a thematic scheme rather than a chronological order for my observations in this book.

Conflict can be destructive in the context of loss of peace, prosperity and life, but also constitutive of a new social and political order. One can point to the growing gap between the 'alien' and gradually de-legitimized institutional design of the state and the popular nationalist forces of various shades which demand an overhaul of the system along the indigenous pre-colonial framework of public life. Indeed, Dr Ambedkar found in the institutions of the modern state the requisite power to contain the ascendency of traditional norms and practices that would have blocked the growth of democracy.[5] In that sense, constitutionalism provided 'congenial spaces' for articulating the conflictual demands through a rights-based regime that set the juridical equality of citizens in postcolonial society against the established social hierarchies.[6] One can point to various sources of conflict rooted in the slippage from design to practice: the emergence of a discourse about community rights in India; emergency provisions that strengthened the regulative and manipulative machinery of the state; and cultivation of the transcendental goals of the majority communities at the cost of minorities.[7] Conflict within the state is an outgrowth of developments such as the inability of the legislature to safeguard its autonomy vis-à-vis the executive; the expansion of judicial review that caused the continuing functioning of parliament to be left hanging in the balance; and the new confrontation between the written word of the constitution and the mass mandate of an elected government. British India had moved from a century-old model of administrative decentralization to a federalist arrangement for distribution of power via the 1935 India Act. Later, the executive in India and Pakistan periodically overruled the legislature and dismissed provincial governments in pursuit of the centralization of power. Unlike India, Pakistan did not carry out any provincial reorganization programme that would have met the ethnolinguistic demands of the federating units. Provincial autonomy at the heart of the federalization project remained in limbo for several decades. The postcolonial state continued to display certain contentious features of the colonial state, such as public policy remaining off the desk of public representatives. The same holds for the corruption-accountability nexus in South Asia as a whole. There has been a 'non-accountability pyramid', with the political class occupying its large base, the bureaucracy a middle position, the judiciary near the top and the armed forces at the very top.[8] This situation has opened a Pandora's Box in Pakistan because of the common belief that the 'establishment' continues to hold public representatives accountable and exercise various options ranging from coercion to co-option, while it enjoys immunity from accountability itself.

Democracy has been studied in both quantitative and qualitative frameworks. The former maintains that political power is closely related to the satisfaction of a 'winning coalition' of the 'selectorate'. With the expansion of the winning coalition, the leaders are expected to shift from a policy of distribution of private goods to one of distributing public goods, thus effecting a move from a coterie of loyalists to a relatively open-ended constituency, signifying the emergence of a popular democracy.[9] However, in Pakistan's case, the winning coalition, in the form of the establishment, has typically operated from outside the system. The essence of representative democracy is the role of political agency, i.e. a parliament which arrives at political decisions on behalf of its principal, the citizen. But, in the case of postcolonial societies, representative legislatures emerged only under late colonialism. Political agency in the form of political parties and parliament owes its origin not to citizens but to the two erstwhile superordinate entities, the British government and the political dynasties at the macro and micro levels respectively.

Postcolonialism has recently emerged as the new mantra for modernists, who got indigenized after the 'colonial' sources of inspiration for their cultural, legal and institutional outlook lost their overt role in shaping their life world. At the other end, traditionalists learnt to operate through the 'modern' ways of organizational activity, use of the print and electronic media and re-defining religion as a complete code of life. Both modernists and traditionalists changed in a qualitative sense and, in this book, these terms are used with this important caveat. Indeed, the gap between the two sides has not only persisted but also expanded. They could no more be neatly identified simply with reference to modernity and tradition. The newly ascendant modernist forces operated at cross purposes, with traditionalists defined in terms of caste, ethnicity, language and religion. The emerging pattern of 'meshing' of identities was underscored by efforts to change the intellectual configuration of the past. As a seceding state, imbued with a promise to live according to Islamic principles, Pakistan has been in conflict with the British Indian legacy ever since partition.

The basic premise of postcolonialism is that colonialism fragments society, breaks things, destroys cultural unity and inflicts fear on the native population. Not surprisingly, the decolonization project influenced vast sections of the public in their effort to return to one's 'native' land, which symbolized 'pastoral, folk, innocent, utopian, productive wholeness'.[10] However, Houston Baker and others argue that the cultural goods have always been 'fragmented, pluralistic, socially constructed, historically indeterminate' in the form of 'foibles, idiocies, hubris and general lack of capacity to share space'.[11] Partha Chatterjee focused on the role of community in the Indian peasantry, which is tied by the pre-existing bonds over and above the individual interests as opposed to the bourgeois consciousness that focused on individuals, along with societies as their aggregates.[12] Chibber, in his critique of subaltern studies, questioned their premise that metropolitan 'capital abandoned its universalising mission once having arrived on Indian shores'.[13] He brought out the contradiction between anti-colonial nationalism and what he considers as Chatterjee's orientalist understanding of a division between the West and the East, representing rationality and objectivity and its absence respectively.[14]

In this book, I shall discuss postcolonialism essentially in the context of a resurgence of tradition, rejection of colonial modernity and the 'return of the native' as a persistent – even growing – sentiment that has informed several domains of public and private life. I shall discuss Islamic scholarship as part of what is sometimes euphemistically presented as postmodernism, as part of a broad and comprehensive framework of postcolonialism.

What makes conflict endemic to postcolonial states such as Pakistan? My argument is that the state remains a key factor in the emergence of conflict, not as agency – not as what is understood as the 'outermost structure' encompassing the institutional–constitutional conundrum operating at will[15] – but rather as the condensate of official policies focusing on state-building. After nationalism transformed a colonial–administrative unit into an independent state, the ruling elite felt it mandatory to weld together what was considered a mosaic of potentially autonomous regions and fiefdoms. The construction of a nation out of several non-nations previously identified as provinces under direct rule or as princely states under indirect rule – merged together such as in India, Pakistan, Tanzania, Uganda and Nigeria – has been at the heart of the conflict. Nationalism often brought the pre-colonial past alive as a reference point in certain crucial ways, such as the revival of religion – Islam, Hinduism and Buddhism in Pakistan, India, and Sri Lanka respectively.

The diagnosis of conflict should not necessarily focus on breakdown of the political system. Instead, conflict should be conceived as a product of the state-building project itself, spearheaded by the ruling elite.[16] The literature on conflict focuses on causes, ideological or ethnic, external or internal, global or domestic.[17] This line of argument ignores the 'systematicity' of the conflict. Pakistan inherited a strong institutional design inasmuch as British imperialism was the most developed imperialism of the twentieth century. However, it has been put into practice by a weak state in terms of low compliance of citizens with the law, low public participation in the business of the state, low operation of a service structure and low maintenance of legitimacy.[18] After partition, two competitive forces were already in the field in Pakistan: the state bureaucracy, the army and the higher courts at one end and the landed elite along with elements from the professional elite represented on the floors of elected assemblies at the other. This book deals with them in terms of their social foundations and as recruitment bases for the middle class and their engagement with public life for the political class respectively. The idea is to move beyond the conventional wisdom of relying on the state institutions as the focus of enquiry and, instead, to analyse the sociology of elite formation.

The Constitution in Pakistan, as in other postcolonial societies, operates as the final ideational sanction for the state-in-action. Not surprisingly, it is often resented by the state managers. For example, the constitution provides for: formal spaces to underprivileged sections of the people by way of ethnicity, gender, sector, caste and tribe; a regime of rights based on equality for citizens; accountability of the government to public representatives; a federalist arrangement for distribution of power; and civilian supremacy over the military. Political conflict in Pakistan has drawn massively on the gap between design and practice. This has applied to religious minorities, ethnolinguistic communities, women in public and private life, military intervention in politics, and loss of parliamentary sovereignty in terms of both dissolution of elected assemblies and legislation through presidential ordinances. The conflict has been rooted in the gross imbalance between the federal and provincial governments and the functioning of the courts as a triadic entity heavily tilted in favour of one party at the cost of the other in a dyadic conflict. Over time, the institutional apparatuses of the state reflected the increasingly conservative ideological and policy orientations of the expanding middle class. In a parallel development, the political class declined in power and privilege. The middle class represented the power structure dispersed through institutions responsible for making policy on issues ranging from public finance, environment, education and health to art, literature, music, dance, and film. The master narrative in Pakistan is ultimately the middle-class narrative. The political class formally represented 'agency' but not the substantive, meaningful and sustainable structure of authority.

The political expression of the two dominant classes through the state institutions often led to a clash of institutions that befuddled democracy. However, we need to distinguish between institution and class. Institutions are characterized by hierarchy, command structure, esprit de corps and clear policy orientations. Classes, on the other hand, are not purposive communities per se. In Pakistan, the middle class is the custodian of the state ideology, the policy structure and the master narrative as expressed through education and media. The middle-class narrative focuses on the national interest, but the political class's idiom focuses on the public interest. Ethnically, the middle class is dominated by the province of Punjab and by the Urdu-speaking migrants from India (Mohajirs). Their narrative is based on Islamic ideology, all-Pakistanism, perceived Indian belligerency and a world-of-Islam perspective. The political class, especially from smaller provinces, is less ideological in the context of the Islamization of politics and more responsive to demands based on identity, culture, language, and economic equality. The conflict between these worldviews, one based on ideology and security and the other drawing on sub-national identities and interests respectively, brings out the discursive modalities for understanding politics in Pakistan.

The first quarter of the twenty-first century promised to bring about a new publicness in the context of civil society's input into the public agenda, and the expanding outreach of the electronic and social media and educational institutions in the private sector. This book focuses on the mass public as an arena for cultural battles, competition for resources, and expressions of anger by groups and communities over issues ranging from faith to inflation. Civil society has been engaged in pursuit of 'progressive' causes such as women's social, economic, and cultural uplift, elimination of child labour and bonded labour, poverty alleviation and digital rights. However, the conventional wisdom that civil society is the route to democracy is not tenable because of its relatively non-political agenda. The donor community's input into electoral democracy in Pakistan focused on the mechanics of elections rather than the formation of governments based on genuinely polled votes.[19] Apart from civil society, this book seeks to build on the burgeoning literature on education and the media as the breeding ground of a narrative of conflict that shaped the new political currents flowing in the direction of right-wing populism led by Imran Khan (prime minister, 2018–).

As an ethnic federation, Pakistan remains a fractured democracy in the context of centre–province relations. While the centre has most typically sought to concentrate power in its own hands, the provinces other than Punjab have constantly demanded autonomy ever since partition. The 2010 18th Amendment took a great leap forward in pursuit of provincial autonomy, but its implementation was far from ideal. Punjabization of the state represented the mono-ethnic tendency in the power structure that has all along functioned as a source of ethnic conflict.[20] In this book, I shall dwell on the ethnic idiom at length and bring out the discourse surrounding the political dynamics of the relatively intractable centre–province conflict. In 2020, the centre and the province of Sindh were at loggerheads with each other on various issues ranging from the management of law and order in Karachi to the appropriation of two islands off the shore of Sindh by Islamabad through a presidential ordinance. The federating units of ethnically plural Pakistan produce a variegated pattern of reactions ranging from participating in the available public space in the educational, professional, and political life to cynicism and, in some cases, to guerrilla warfare in the mountains. While the Baloch represented tribal violence on a limited scale after the loss of the elder statesman, Akbar Bugti, in 2006, the Mohajir violence (1992–5) was most lethal in terms of both strategic planning and cost of human life for both the Muttahida Qaumi Movement (MQM) and the law enforcement agencies.[21]

At the other end, religious conflict is rooted in the two exclusive cosmological systems that have been transformed into distinct discursive patterns of social and cultural interaction as cognitive modalities and essentialisms.[22] In this book, conflict is not understood as an upsurge in the smooth waters of political life; indeed, the pre-conflict 'peace' should be defined as a process rather than the status quo, beset with multiple micro-conflicts. Conflict emerges when the popular and legitimate intellectual framework of ideas and events is challenged by a new paradigm of rights and demands often bound by the transient nature of the issue at hand and the number of people involved.[23] This happened, for example, with Sunni-based Islamization and Bengali ethnic nationalism. The state's role as adjudicator in a conflict, as per the institutional design to protect the right of citizens to profess and practise their religion via Article 20 of the constitution, was compromised by its own project of nation-building based on a faith-bound commitment. Provisions for Islam as the state religion, separate electorates (1979–2002) and the exclusion of Ahmadis from the pale of Islam (1974) turned religion into a contested territory. The exercise in re-creating an Islamist past was bound to seek its epicentre either in the classical Islamic lands or sometimes in the Mughal empire in India, whose epicentre lay outside the territorial boundaries of present-day Pakistan. More Islam meant less territory as a source of identity and legitimacy, which engendered a potential for conflict between Islamists and ethnic nationalists. On parallel lines, 'divination of political landscape' hardened the boundaries between religious and sectarian contenders for power.[24]

All along, conflict has been culturally coded. After a generation of slow-paced Islamization of the master narrative, it was gradually elevated to a fully-fledged political movement against Z. A. Bhutto's government in 1977, when industrialists and the middle class in general used Islamic elements as cannon fodder. Zia's Islamization project was meant to create a divine source of legitimacy to counter the constitutional source of legitimacy that would have brought Bhutto back to power. Islamization under Zia effectively steered the nation towards piety as policy, and morality as law. The history of Pakistan can be divided between pre-Zia and post-Zia periods, or more specifically before and after the 1985 8th Amendment that indemnified the martial law ordinances, including those relating to the Islamic crime and punishment regime. Reacting to public cynicism about the use of Islam as a cliché spread over a generation, the state chose to focus on performance of rituals and constitutionalizing Islam. Three international sources of Islamization in Pakistan can be outlined in this context: Afghan resistance against the Soviet incursion that was couched in an ideological war against atheism; the great economic pull of the petrodollars in Saudi Arabia and other Gulf countries that led to export of Salafism to Pakistan; and the 1978 Iranian revolution along with its spillover into the Shia community that in turn led to the emergence of anti-Shia terrorist groups and activities. Beyond its sectarian backlash, the enhanced Islamic fervour pushed the socially underprivileged religious minorities to a high level of alienation and vulnerability. The Christian, Hindu and Ahmadi minorities experienced social exclusion (being barred from entry into shops), cultural and religious apartheid through ghettoization and separate electorates, and attacks on their places of worship. The majority's gain was the minority's loss in terms of protection of law, social privilege and equal citizenship. National life was increasingly bounded within ideological borders, as public values were reinterpreted by denying a role to the international human

12

rights regime in court cases dealing with minorities.[25] Pakistan moved towards an alternative globality that stepped out of the minimum international consensus on public behaviour sanctioned by the state.[26]

The general perception about the control of the army over all other state institutions can be analysed with reference to 'state capture'. This concept was first developed in the context of post-Soviet Eastern Europe to describe the 'mega-corruption' that regulated the state institutions and the relevant laws and procedures. In 2017, a state capacity research project reported that the ruling party in South Africa had lost its role as the real maker of strategic decisions about the economy.[27] State capture symbolized erosion of democracy, election-rigging and an agenda for social and economic transformation. State capture amounts to 'the hollowing out of state institutions'.[28] Tom Lodge discusses state capture as a regulatory mechanism in terms of 'bribing parliamentarians', 'inducing political parties', 'subversion of public interests' and 'formulating rather than breaking rules'.[29] He analyses militarization of politics in terms of state capture.[30] In Nieuwkerk's view, South Africa presents a case of sovereignty within a sovereignty, an 'imperium in imperio'.[31] He discusses the phenomenon of the deep state in 'democracies' such as Russia, Turkey and Egypt, where the military, along with intelligence agencies, private business and criminal gangs, subverts political leadership.[32] Since the deep state operates under the surface, where the real power, and thus policy, is located across different party-based governments, it is often brushed aside as the product of a conspiracy theory.[33] In several cases, it is the electoral process itself that is captured by 'encoding' the rules.[34] In this regard, patronage politics provides the captors with the role of gatekeepers.[35] This book explores the phenomenon of state capture by the deep state through constitutional engineering, manipulation of elections and management of the party system in Pakistan.

The question is: what has kept the social fabric intact and the political status quo far from crumbling in the face of incessant crises? Barring a political movement that could destabilize the structures of power and privilege, such as Bhutto's populist wave in the 1970s, society in large parts of the country has kept intact the pattern of electoral victories for 'local dynasts', both old and new.[36] Close proximity between vernacular bureaucracy at the sub-district level and local stakeholders has kept the influence of the political elite intact in the context of vote politics. A major source of their influence is the reward-in-waiting in the form of membership of the national and provincial assemblies that promises access to district courts as well as to police and revenue departments along with an outreach to the provincial secretariat. There is a strategic relationship between courts and votes, i.e. between the mechanism of dispensation of justice and the exercise of political influence over the judicial proceedings and judgments. Citizens have no direct access to the state's regulatory and adjudicatory machinery. Most typically, they find themselves up against the wall. Elected representatives provide the route to the state's authority. Ali Cheema, along with a group of researchers, brought out the reciprocal but essentially unequal transactional relationship in the Sargodha District of Pakistan as it was investigated over a generation.[37] Here are 'subalterns' as a class-in-itself tied to an apparently free and optional bond which is territorially localized and transactionally personalized in the context of the periodically activated electoral politics. Conflict between electoral heavy-weights is rationalized through several modes of access to the state's resources, such as the winning party/losing candidate, losing party/winning candidate and the winning party/winning candidate. These models are operationally underscored by a cluster of lateral relationships based on marriage, family ties and *biraderi* that keep cross-party links of the political class intact.[38]

Relations with the district administration, both civil servants at the top and the vernacular bureaucracy at the bottom, provide an additional variable in determining the capacity of the electoral hopefuls to maintain and enhance their power. The local government elections only supplement the hold of the 'dynasts' in terms of fielding their lesser kith and kin into the electoral arena and keeping it all within the family. The military governments of Ayub and Musharraf put together electoral systems of local government that sought to connect the centre directly with the district, thereby bypassing the province which was considered to be the stronghold of the political class. Ayub pursued the project of de-politicization of people through disenfranchisement by introducing a two-tier system of elections whereby the common voter was denied the right to vote for presidential and parliamentary elections. Musharraf introduced the system of elected district officers called *Nazims* at the top of the district administration as all-powerful non-party leaders. Both aimed at undermining the political class and thus the electoral dynamics. The net effect of these local government elections was two-fold: to create a source of legitimacy at the bottom by putting in place elected officials in the district, and to provide a sense of political participation for people without involving policy or transfer of power. Of course, the narrative surrounding the local government was couched in the idiom of 'government at the doorstep, local nature of demand for services and nursery for democracy'. The donor community generously obliged.

In all this, customary law played a passive, low-intensity and almost invisible role in maintaining stability at the level of family, village, tribe, caste/*biraderi* and locality in the name of culture. In Pakistan and other countries of South Asia and beyond, custom plays the role of the ultimate guardian of the prevalent hierarchies based on ethnicity, gender and generation. Culture has been upheld by public activists as a source of inspiration across the political spectrum, ranging from the rightists, as a code of ethics, to the leftists, as the dignity of the subaltern classes. While the human rights lobby and the 'liberal' intelligentsia criticized several customary practices as repressive, 'culture' has typically operated as a bulwark against any reformist effort in this regard.

As opposed to the prevalent status quo orientation, one can point to at least three peasant movements: the Hari movement in Sindh in the 1950s and 1960s, the Hashtnagar movement in KP (Khyber Pakhtunkhwa) in the 1970s, and the periodically active peasant movement in Okara in Punjab in and around the military farm area. But these movements were generally confined to the region. Their 'class' dimension was not operational beyond a certain point. The reasons included: a high level of state oppression against the leadership by way of litigation, often involving imprisonment; barring media coverage; and a lack of willingness of political parties to take up the issue in the presence of the landed elite, which typically provided electoral heavyweights. While conflict is endemic in some parts of the body politic, intractable in its nature and all-encompassing in its scope, a situation of non-conflict exists at the district level where politics has been 'boxed' into units of cooperation between the local bureaucracy and the political leadership. The industrial labour movement had its heyday during the anti-Ayub movement of 1968–9.[39] However, during and after the Bhutto years, trade unions lost their organizational and agitational power.[40]

I propose to take a sociological approach to the two power centres represented by the two dominant classes – the political class and the middle class – that collide, collaborate or clash with each other insofar as they represent distinct ideological and policy orientations. Especially, I shall focus on the peculiar but much less researched input of the middle class in shaping the politics of Pakistan. Fernandez and Heller, dealing with India, brought out the hegemonic aspirations of this class in the framework of prioritization of policy.[41] Yogendra Yadav discussed the middle class in India as a force operating outside democratic goals and procedures.[42] In Pakistan, the middle class has a predominant role in shaping not only ideology and policy but also the master narrative of the nation. In this context, I shall dwell on Lyotard's postmodern critique of Habermas's view of a well-integrated, rational and consensus-based social order.[43] The concept of master narrative itself has lost its prescience and global appeal that was prevalent in the nineteenth century. However, it is still relevant inasmuch as it provides the grand intellectual postulate that underscores Pakistan's self-perception. As opposed to the 'life-narrative' based on individual and personalized accounts of social and political experience,[44] the master narrative reflects the 'general will' if you will.

I want to explore how the master narrative has transcended the temporal and spatial dimensions of the communication that has carved non-dialogical spaces in recent decades. I shall look at the mediated messages across the territorial boundaries within a globalist framework of exchange of news and views.[45] The idea is that the role of local media has created a sophisticated public in Pakistan in terms of access to the world media. My argument is that this connection represents globalization far more than Westernization, technological breakthrough far more than attitudinal transformation, and bland information far more than reflection on the leading ideas of master intellectuals of different times and places. The civil society of Pakistan has surrealistic 'humanitarian' aims and objectives that are not supported by the cultural predilections of the people, basically due to its dependence on the donors' understanding of the zero point from where to start. The slow growth of home-grown social, cultural, artistic, legal, literary and rights-based organizations points to a non-political and therefore

16

non-democratic input of civil society into the body politic. The new publicness carries an ambitious agenda of catapulting the people into the modern age of rights and duties but misses out on the requisite level of freedom from the bondage of traditional values and practices.

Beyond the media and civil society, education has produced a new form of publicness which has undermined the 'public' from within. This happened by making the youth inward-looking, taking them in the direction of rudderless individual career-making away from community orientation, especially in the institutions of higher learning in the private sector, and focusing on piety which is wholly personal. The public sphere in the sense of Habermas, which would typically create ideals, norms, views, originality and creativity, has been severely constrained by a series of educational policies and hate-based messages processed in the name of education. All this has created a conflicted mind. Over decades, Pakistan has moved from a state in pursuit of development to a reactive state engaged in meeting the competing demands of social and institutional contenders for power. This has led to rival, even contradictory, interpretations of the constitution – such as, for example, the 18th Amendment – and of the national interest, such as Pakistan's India policy. The formal rhetoric about change is in substance a manifesto for the status quo. All this has destroyed the merit of the spoken or written narrative of the stakeholders across the board.

I shall look at the two populisms of the left and the right, symbolizing the governments of Z. A. Bhutto (1971–7) and Imran Khan (2018–) respectively. Bhutto mobilized people in the teeth of opposition from the establishment. Imran Khan's populist movement was based on his build-up by the establishment itself as a party leader to counter the two mega political parties, the Pakistan Peoples Party (PPP) and the Pakistan Muslim League-Nawaz (PML-N). The military establishment was able to cultivate a constituency for Imran Khan by mobilizing the middle class, including youth, as well as overseas Pakistanis, and by shifting the electables from other parties to the Pakistan Tehreek-e-Insaf (PTI).[46] This book will analyse this model of populism, somewhat parallel to Modi in India and Rajapakse in Sri Lanka. Critics of populism find that it is opposed to human rights, which are meant to protect people, and that populists deny these rights in the name of the people.[47] Xenophobia, Islamophobia, intolerance of the opposition reflected through scapegoating and a perception of media criticism as anti-national, are some of the leading examples of the populism of the right.[48] The populist's agenda is to first make people into a herd and then shepherd them. Numbers supersede rights.

Finally, I would mention the 'India syndrome' as the ultimate reference point in shaping foreign policy as it is presided over by the army.[49] Stephen Cohen and Robert Wirsing have given the impression that Pakistan's India policy was a pathology.[50] The central point of this policy is the decades-old Kashmir dispute. Having lain dormant for fifty years, Kashmir was catapulted into the news when Prime Minister Modi of India scrapped Article 37 of the Indian Constitution in August 2019 and thus put an end to the largely rhetorical but hugely symbolic profile of the autonomy of the state. A regime of political repression of the people of India-held Kashmir followed, along with a deterioration in Indo-Pakistan relations. After the attack on Pulwama in Kashmir in 2019, the Indian Air Force carried out a 'surgical attack' on Balakot in Pakistan that led to a dogfight between Indian and Pakistani aircraft, the downing of one Indian warplane, and the return of its pilot to Delhi after he had bailed out in Pakistan. After more than a year of cross-border firing along the ceasefire line in Kashmir, the two countries agreed to control it in early 2021. Commentators on both sides welcomed what they considered a new dawn of peace. Soon after, the PTI government decided to import sugar, cotton and cotton yarn from India on 31 March 2021 but then took a U-turn within twenty-four hours in the absence of a meaningful move towards peace.

Pakistan has anthropomorphized India as the ultimate 'other'. There exist deeply internalized public perceptions about Indian bellicosity. The passage of the Citizenship Act 2019 offered Indian citizenship to illegal immigrants from neighbouring countries 'belonging to Hindu, Sikh, Buddhist, Jain, Parsi or Christian community', but not to Muslims.[51] The liberal view within and outside India condemned the move as religious apartheid. A senior Congress leader, Shashi Tharoor, declared that the Act had ensured that Jinnah was right in his demand for a separate state for Muslims.[52] These developments were part of the 'ideological baggage' on both sides after parting as foes in 1947.

South Asia is a region without regionalism.[53] The SAARC (South Asian Association for Regional Cooperation) has kept bilateral issues outside its scope. India has enjoyed pre-eminence in the region, where it shares land or sea borders with Pakistan, Nepal, Bangladesh, Sri Lanka and the Maldives. However, Pakistan has no neighbours in South Asia except India. In this context, the latter-day entry of Afghanistan into SAARC from outside the region remains problematic.

No two countries have had worldviews more different than India and Pakistan. India was a status quo power. Pakistan wanted change, especially in Kashmir. India followed a confidence building measures (CBM) approach, while Pakistan adhered to a conflict resolution approach. India pursued a bilateral solution of issues, with no external interference – a Monroe Doctrine of its own. Pakistan wanted that there was a role for an external 'equalizer' such as the USA, which took it into CENTO (Central Treaty Organization) and SEATO (Southeast Asia Treaty Organization). India operated through a politics of introversion, utilizing history for ideological mobilization. Pakistan looked outside and developed a mini clash-of-civilizations perspective based on the Hindu–Muslim dichotomy. India was at the heart of the South Asian region bounded by smaller countries that served as its territorial limits. However, Pakistan sought to operate at the global level in the context of the Cold War through military alliances and through Islamic bloc-ism, which reached its high point in the 1974 Islamic Summit Conference. Nearer home, it turned its back to South Asia after the emergence of Bangladesh and entered the Middle East in diplomatic, economic, and strategic terms. The rise of religion in both countries converted nationalism into pre-destinationism.

In Pakistan, conflict with India led to the emergence of a national security dilemma as a seceding state coping with a successor state next door. This changed enormously the institutional imbalance and contributed to the eventual rise of the military to the position of the establishment. Perceptions about India included the country being seen as a strategic threat, a source of gruesome memory of communal riots in 1947 and – for migrants – nostalgia for their loss of homes and hearths as well as history and geography. Nationalism in Pakistan was the codified version of anti-Indianism. Research into the common cultural heritage of the two countries was considered heretical. Writings that highlighted differences between the two countries in religious, cultural and historical terms were rewarded. Over time, the establishment assumed the responsibility and legitimacy to declare dissident politicians, peace activists and 'liberal' intellectuals as traitors.

Ranging from Sohrawardy, A.K. Fazlul Haq, G.M. Syed, Abdul Ghaffar Khan, Samad Achakzai to Z.A. Bhutto and Mujibur Rehman onwards to Benazir Bhutto, Asif Zardari and Nawaz Sharif, scores of politicians were condemned for their 'close' relations with India.

The first generation of Hindus, Muslims and Sikhs after independence had known each other as human beings – good, bad and ugly. After three generations of cross-demonization, people on both sides were fighting ghosts in the dark churned out by education textbooks, media messages and the political discourse in general. Now, there were human agents on this side and an army of ugly, aggressive, and evil robots on the other side.

The Indo-Pakistan conflict was played out by proxy in Afghanistan. Here, India was in, Pakistan was out as a friend before 1979. Pakistan was in, India was out under the Taliban (1996–2001). Under NATO, India was in, Pakistan was out (2001–2021). After the Taliban's second coming in 2021, Pakistan was again in and India was again out. In Pakistan, the conflict outside massively shaped the contours of the conflict inside.

This book analyses Pakistan as a unique country with specific characteristics such as being a new state on the world map born out of cultural nationalism as opposed to the more common territorial nationalism. It also brings out the resilient patterns of rule in postcolonial states. Some of the shared dimensions of this rule include: institutional imbalance; inability to manage ethnic and tribal pluralism; tempering black letter law with customary law; and identity construction at the sub-national level in a combative mode of thought and action vis-à-vis the superordinate entity of the state. Other sources of political conflict include manipulation of discordant voices, corruption as a route to interest articulation, conspiracy as the prevalent worldview, as well as rampant poverty underscored by a galloping population increase. There is need to focus on the nature of political conflict in postcolonial societies as the source of a permanent crisis of governance. This book is an attempt to put together an analytical framework for the study of political conflict in a postcolonial state such as Pakistan.

1

SEVENTY YEARS OF PARTITION

Introduction

This chapter deals with a subject that has been covered copiously by scholars: partition. Mainstream South Asian historiography imagined partition as a relatively smooth affair, given its heavy reliance on the transfer of power documents relating to constitutional debates, official correspondence and the statements of political leaders and parties.[1] However, research in recent decades has highlighted the mobilizational aspect of the process of conversion of Muslims to the cause of partition and of their faith-based identity that distinguished them from the Hindu majority.[2] My argument is that this composite heritage of partition, based on ideology as a mission-mantled agenda and identity as an exclusionary commitment to faith, carved out a huge public space that emerged as a battleground for rival contenders for power in Pakistan. In this book, partition is discussed essentially as a blueprint for the political conflict in Pakistan.

Partition made religion a defining variable for evaluating the role of the elite and the masses, past and present, culture and politics. It produced a robust sense of predestination whereby people felt they had arrived in the promised land. Partition made India a lasting grief for Pakistan, just as it had made Pakistan a lasting grief for India.[3] Apart from the archival history of the constitutional negotiations that led to partition, one finds emotionally charged and highly subjective accounts of partition that can be grouped together as partition exotica. In India, this approximates the 'vivisection syndrome', while in Pakistan this has been elevated to a war between Islam and Hinduism. On both sides, 'sacrifice syndrome' became a source of sanctifying violence, especially in Punjab where demobilized soldiers had recently returned from the war.[4]

Communal violence raises some interesting questions about the nature of the political leadership of Gandhi, Jinnah and Nehru, among others. These Anglicized, modern and charismatic leaders mobilized the traditional public and delivered it from colonial rule by the strength of their command over the public will. However, the fact that these leaders were totally helpless in the face of violence, which assumed colossal proportions during partition, rendered them mere spokesmen of their respective communities in British India rather than their 'representatives'. While deeply immersed in the high politics of constitutional wrangling, they did not share, much less participate in, the religious hatreds at the bottom of the society that had percolated down from the cultivation of religiously coded propaganda. Once belligerent identities moved from high politics to low politics, the political initiative shifted away from the hands of the leadership and created mayhem in the locality.

The basic argument of this chapter is that nationalism arrived late in India, sometime around the turn of the twentieth century, whereby the Hindu, Muslim and Sikh elites heralded the process of an exclusive faith-based nationalist upsurge in their respective communities. India's nameless and faceless humanity developed religious boundaries that eventually provided the basis for a separate nationhood for Muslims. This chapter also locates the pattern of an exclusive reliance on religion for building a Muslim nation across the future borders of Pakistan that has great potential for explaining the country's divergent path vis-à-vis India in the context of parliamentary democracy. There is a need to look at the specific nature of the two migratory movements across the emergent borders in terms of the number and share of refugees in the host countries. In Pakistan, this gave rise to a new ethnic hierarchy by turning it into a 'migrant state', while India had its political imagination firmly rooted in the soil. Most scholarship focuses on the politics of partition in the context of the emergence of two states and the concomitant processes of migration, communal violence, refugee resettlement and nation-building projects. There is a significant gap in the sociology of partition by way of the ruralization of communities after the loss of their urban sectors – such as in the case of Sindh and East Bengal – the loss of the multicultural syncretic society that was built over a millennium in these provinces as well as Punjab, the brutalization of social and cultural attitudes towards the new 'other' in the partitioned provinces, and the rise of religion as a maker and shaper of the national destiny first in Pakistan and a generation or two later in India.

Moment of Partition

In 1947, Pakistan got out of India. But India did not get out of Pakistan. That has made all the difference. India continued to be part of Pakistan in various ways. Apart from Pashtu and the languages of the northern areas, the languages of Pakistan are essentially Indian languages, including the national language, Urdu, along with Punjabi, Sindhi and some minor linguistic varieties.[5] The Indian calendar, Indian dress, Indian cuisine, Indian medicine, Indian wedding rituals and Indian customary laws have continued to operate in large parts of what became Pakistan. The name for Sunday (*Itwar*) is derived from the Hindu sun god, Aditya; similarly, the names for Monday (*Somwar*) and Tuesday (*Mangalwar*) belong to the Sanskrit, while the name for Wednesday comes from Buddha.[6] Several superstitious practices, including the witchcraft among Muslims of Pakistan, are essentially Hindu practices. While the Muslim Ashraf was largely influenced by the British rulers, organized according to a pattern of one man/one wife, monogamy was typically carried into life after conversion to Islam, even though polygamy was not unknown among Hindus. Not surprisingly, the Pakistan project aimed at creating a divide between the two communities, by giving an identity to Muslims that was explicitly separate from their non-Muslim street neighbours, friends, colleagues, employees, and employers. This exercise followed both a vertical approach from the elite downwards and a horizontal approach across regions throughout India. The genesis of the first major conflict in Pakistan can be traced to the mandatory requirement for Pakistan to de-Indianize itself, a constant pursuit ever since partition. This is a conflict between the cognitive 'self'— the deep-rooted social attitudes, cultural mores and linguistic and behavioural patterns at one end — and the new national identity that subsumed the post-partition ideological context at the other.[7] General Zia expressed it succinctly: if Turkey or Egypt did not project Islam, they would remain Turkey and Egypt.[8] But if Pakistan did not pursue Islam aggressively, it would become part of India again. This fear became part of the national psyche.

The Partition of Indian Society

Pakistan has always felt obliged to take the agenda of partition forward in order to inject meaning into the existence of a country separate from India. The Hindu–Muslim conflict has been at the heart of the meta-narrative in Pakistan. According to this, Indian history was beset with conflict between the two faith-based communities, called 'nations' according to the two-nation theory.[9] My argument seeks to question the periodicity of conflict between the two nations of Hindus and Muslims spread over the centuries. India before and under the Mughal Empire was, of course, a scene of internecine warfare. But Hindu and Muslim generals and soldiers jointly fought for Akbar against Chand Bibi, for Aurangzeb against the descendants of the Bahmani Sultanate in the Deccan, for the Sikh Maharaja Ranjit Singh against the Durranis in what later became North West Frontier Province (NWFP), and against Nawab Muzaffar Ali Khan of Multan, and for Tipu, Sirajuddaula, Wajid Ali Shah and Bahadur Shah Zafar against the British. Most typically, people fought for region, not religion, for the ruling dynasty, not an ideological agenda, and for territory, revenue and prestige rather than for a transcendental goal or racial superiority. Conflict defined the breaking point of relations among the stakeholders from different faiths as well as among co-religionists playing on the chessboard of the Indian subcontinent. Those around the Muslim courts of various kingdoms conspired, planned and strategized warfare around conflict between the followers of Tariqa and Sharia, between Shias and Sunnis, between liberals who allowed music and dance and conservatives who did not, and between loyalists of the kingdom and dissidents, including potential or actual rebels be they Hindu, Muslim or Sikh.

I. H. Qureshi and a whole generation of scholars before and after partition argued that Hindus and Muslims had existed as separate entities for a millennium.[10] They took religious boundaries for granted as these existed in the twentieth century. But conversion to Islam was a prolonged process, spread over six hundred years in what can be called a pre-identity construction phase. The idea of conflict between the two 'nations' in a context where boundaries between religions were hardly demarcated was superimposed on the emergent pattern of conflict between the Hindu and Muslim elites struggling for space in British India. In a peasant society such as India, as the British administrators of the population census discovered, faiths were deeply intermingled. As Harjot Oberoi has discussed, many among the Meherat Rajputs from Ajmer and its vicinity who considered themselves descendants of Prithvi Raj Chauhan identified themselves with Islam, practised *nikkah* and buried their dead. More than a million Sikhs in Punjab declared themselves Hindus in the 1891 census, while 200,000 people in Gujarat registered themselves as Mohammadan Hindus. Bengali Muslims used the name Iswar for the Creator. A seventeenth-century Muslim scholar, Umaru Pulavar, wrote about the early Islamic history based on local Tamil tradition.[11]

Much has been written about the causes of the conversion to Islam in India: the spread of Islam through the sword; liberation from caste-based inequality; intermarriages between Muslims and non-Muslims; acculturation through service in the Moghul administration, such as among Kayasthas; upward social mobility; and the teachings of Sufi saints, among others. What concerns us here is the life and times of the converted Muslims who were not part of the power play at the top. Their identity was indistinct, muddled and blurred for generations, even centuries. In Peter Hardy's view, even the Europeans took time to acknowledge their existence as an entity separate from the Muslims of non-Indian origin who ruled India.[12] While the latter were remembered as Tartars, the former were termed 'Moors'.[13] Indeed, the educated and sophisticated Muslim professionals and landlords discovered the large mass of converted Muslims through the colonial censuses and gazetteers. The masses now acquired a new relevance for them as an electorate after the constitutional reforms of 1919.[14] The elite was now attracted essentially to the number of Muslims that would become handy with the expansion of franchise.

British administrators such as Ibbetson found slow change in Muslims after conversion, because they considered religion a matter of social belonging rather than a creed or a code of life.[15] One finds a deliberate effort at using faith-based icons for proselytization purposes. In East Bengal in the mid-nineteenth century, the low-caste Bediyas were converted to Islam but they did not join the mainstream for a considerable time. Indeed, Ibbetson found a Muslim in East Punjab carrying a baggage from before conversion, whereas a Hindu across the Indus was considered 'almost as the Musulman'.[16] Richard Eaton identifies conversion to Islam in India with accretion, i.e. 'adding new deities or superhuman agencies to their existing cosmological stock',[17] without involving exclusion or distinction from the village community's practices of propitiating a local goddess or performing devotion to Krishna's avatar.[18] A Bengali poet, Syed Sultan, used the word Isvara in the late sixteenth century; one Shaykh Mansur similarly used pre-conversion names for divinity.[19]

As per the 1901 census, some Bengali Muslims indulged in religious activities, which were alien to Islam.[20] An interesting example of inter-mingling of faith-based groups is the Meo community which lives in the vicinity of Delhi. Shail Mayaram refers to several narratives of Muslim bards, poets and storytellers. For example, Shamsuddin Pathan started his story with a tribute to a local divine figure. Mufti Jamaluddin of Alwar claimed Surajwansi descent – lineage from the sun – while seeing no contradiction in it with his own faith. Qadiri Sufi Shah Abdurrazak enjoyed the theatrical rendering of the story of Narsimha Avatar and Krishna. Syed Rasul Shah became a Peshwa of a gypsy tribe. Abdul, an old Mirasi, praised God for showing the right path, but also attributed his inspiration to a local celestial figure.[21]

The overlapping nature of religious identities often drew on a shared worship of saints and of pilgrimages to their shrines. For example, the Muslim saint, Sakhi Sarwar, was one of the most popular saints among Sikhs in the nineteenth century, with a following registered at around 80,000 at the turn of the twentieth century. Sakhi Sarwar's shrine in Dera Ghazi Khan and the sub-shrines devoted to him in Gujranwala, Lahore and elsewhere attracted Hindu, Sikh and Muslim devotees. Oberoi has argued that the unlettered masses from all communities faced physical as well as mental ailments and took recourse to 'spiritual' healing that crossed religious boundaries.[22] Shrines – far more than Sufis, who have been accredited with the task of conversion in the literature for generations – were the real agents of conversion.[23] In death, Sufis became larger than life as their miracles became popular myths. The blending of Hindu–Muslim faiths comes out clearly in Mohammad Mujeeb's monumental work, *The Indian Muslims*: for example, the Hindu cult of the river Indus among Sindhi Lohanas; Darya Panth becoming the worship of Khawaja Khizr; and the cult of the crocodile, which was still visible in Mangopir in Sindh. He also mentions Hussaini Brahmins, devotees of Khawaja Ajmer, who were Hindus but wore Muslim dress, performed fasting and gave burial to the dead.[24] These local and disparate communities were travelling along different routes of a long-range conversion process when British India presided over the new moral universe of the subcontinent after 1857. In other words, conflict alone did not define the vast humanity living across India. Far more pervasive were the patterns of cooperation, co-optation, compromise, collaboration, partnership, co-existence, concurrence, fusion, reciprocity, symbiosis, fraternization, rapport, concord and communion. The shrine-based Sufi orders played a significant role in synergizing Muslim beliefs and practices with local conditions. The shared sacred places were indeed the breeding grounds of a large section of humanity pursuing divinity in multiple ways around Muslim shrines and elsewhere. Intermarriages across religious boundaries, especially during the Mughal period, emerged as a visible symbol of inter-faith harmony. The most famous literary work of Punjab, *Heer Ranjha,* was a love story, not an epic. Common bards such as Kabir sang songs of peace not war. The Muslim divine, Mian Mir, laid the foundation stone of the Golden Temple in Amritsar, and Baba Farid's *kafis* were included in the Granth Sahib. No major Hindu or Muslim revivalist movements took place from the thirteenth to the eighteenth century. Micro-conflicts did not generally destabilize the hegemonic framework of the locality.

British India changed all that. The second half of the nineteenth century saw the end of thuggee,[25] the establishment of public peace of some kind, the spread of railways 'connecting Calcutta to the North-West Provinces',[26] and the emergence of public space where all communities could project and profess their cultural, religious and artistic expressions.[27] The Sikh, Hindu and Muslim elite revivalists sought to join hands across large distances and founded the Singh Sabha,[28] Arya Samaj,[29] and Shuddhi and Tabligh movements[30] in pursuit of their respective renaissances. Muslim elites from the presidencies of Calcutta and Bombay, *talukdars* and *zamindars* from United Provinces (UP) and Bihar, and Shia and Sunni intellectual, professional and commercial elements discovered not only each other but also the large Muslim peasantry which was a new factor to consider. Urdu literature, Islamic historiography and Muslim educational foundations and philanthropic activities, which financed social, religious and later political causes, served the crucial purpose of community formation.

As the legislatures emerged and the electorate expanded, the separatist sentiment of the Muslim elite that emerged from the fear of being smothered by the Hindu elite in the event of a British withdrawal was mobilized for making a nation out of a multitude of Muslim communities. The latter lived in various ethnic, regional, linguistic and sectarian groups, some close to their faith's moral obligations, others far from them, some eclectic in their approach to the divergent beliefs and rituals of their co-religionists, others declaring certain groups within the fold of their religion to be infidels. The Muslim League faced a tremendous task of identity construction by differentiating all these Muslims from Hindus of all persuasions. A discourse of 'difference' shaped the agenda of Muslim nationalism in British India by crystallizing a narrative of conflict between the two 'nations' over a millennium.[31]

Partition attached tremendous power to religion to define leadership, communities and the state. Jinnah was criticized by his Indian counterparts for leading a communalist party – the Muslim League – and for implementing a communalist agenda of creating a nation on the basis of religion. He was re-evaluated decades later as a secularist by a 'liberal' Pakistani, Justice Mohammad Munir, and by a 'communalist' Indian, L. K. Advani.[32] Partition gave the Indian Muslim minority the status of a nation and rendered Pakistani non-Muslims a minority. Jinnah's oft-quoted speech of 11 August 1947 was a grand qualifier in the words of *The Pioneer* as a shift 'from Jinnah the partisan to Jinnah the statesman'.[33] However, it is hard to miss the real message: that partition was a landmark in an inexorable march of the partitioning of hearts and minds. Partition made Pakistanis think in terms of a religious framework that would soon be a challenge to the state as a rival source of legitimacy. Was partition, then, a 'closure', a 'rupture' whereby one social and political order collapsed as the other was struggling to emerge?[34] Was the 1949 Objectives Resolution that laid the Islamic foundation of the constitution a 'closure' for religious minorities as well as for mainstream liberals and modernists? Defined as ethnic cleansing, 'nationalist fratricide' and 'genocide', partition often reflected a partisan attitude on the part of the two states' law-enforcement agencies.[35] The communal violence drew a blood line, thick and visible, that was fated to be a defining variable for individual and collective perspectives on the past and its relevance for the future. It became an unconscious and instinctive commitment to living with the new 'other', mainly across, but also within, the borders. In this sense, partition created a grand new subjectivity, a new framework for looking both inside and outside oneself and a new agenda that ultimately found its niche in a mini clash of civilizations in the form of deteriorating relations among religious communities of South Asia.

The majority's faith-based identity as the new currency in Pakistan has been thinning out, downgrading and disestablishing the other religious communities by turning them into constitutionally defined minorities. Pakistan moved from a pre-1947 social and political order characterized by relatively un-problematized communal groups engaged for centuries in a series of micro-conflicts under some locally defined socio-cultural hegemonic power, to an emerging order drawing on a new paradigm formed by extra-local belligerent identities shaping the national destiny.[36] By injecting a politics of exclusion at the local level, partition pushed people away from their micro-level linkages and commitments to a vision defined by the macro-level cleavage. The mainstream current of religious identity pushed the local identities of village, caste and profession off the screen of people's political imagination. The story of post-independence Pakistan's nation-building effort draws on symbols and icons developed during the tumultuous partition years. This story was defined by a sense of achievement that drew on a feeling of predestination along with its antithesis as 'otherization'.

The process of making Muslims different from Hindus – socially, politically and culturally – brought into action the transcendental appeal of religion. The Islamic campaign led by the Muslim elite superseded ethnic, linguistic, sectarian and cultural differences among Muslims across India in order to create a grand dichotomy between the two faith-based communities. In Jinnah's strategy, religion played a boundary-creating role that defined Muslim nationalism. After partition, while India followed a politics of identity based on the culture and language of the land and the people, and reorganized provinces on that basis, Pakistan followed a model of culture as vision, agenda and mission to establish the rule of Islam. Unlike India, one of the most comprehensive and pervasive sources of conflict in Pakistan is the gap between the reality on the ground in linguistic, cultural and social terms at one end and the ideational sanction of Islamic culture, which was supposed to be the raison d'être of the new country, at the other end.[37] In this way, a mission-mantled state felt obliged to de-acknowledge the cultures and languages of the constituent parts of the country.

The two countries adopted different sources of political legitimacy. In India, language was in, religion was out. In Pakistan, religion was in, language was out. Adeney has pointed to religious politics after partition as a force against regional or linguistic identities as part of a federal project. Unlike India, linguistic parties were unable to become the building blocks of the federation of Pakistan.[38] Religion contributed to the formation of a transformative state in Pakistan, at least by its goal orientation and public deliberation. This function was constantly propelled into action riding the wave of Muslim nationalism that conflicted with the English-based modern and secular state. This led to conflict between modernists, who wanted to keep the constitutional state system intact, and traditionalists, who wanted to replace it with an Islamic state based on Sharia.

The general reliance of partition analysts on Jinnah, the Muslim League and the two-nation theory runs the risk of focusing on 'agency' at the risk of ignoring structure,[39] i.e. the huge reservoir of symbols, icons, daily rituals, theological doctrines and physical, moral and spiritual shapers and makers of the 'collective unconscious' of the Muslims of British India.[40] Pakistan is most essentially and comprehensively a legatee of the Indo–Muslim civilization, which incorporated both Indian and Muslim characteristics. Its heartland lay in UP, where it excelled in architectural monuments ranging from the Qutb Minar to the Taj Mahal. Its expressions of art, culture and literature included miniature paintings, musical *ragas* from Khusro onwards, Kathak dance appropriated by Muslim rulers, and the rich Persian and Urdu languages and literature. At the same time, however, UP was a Hindu province par excellence. It contained the leading religious symbols of the River Ganges, the Himalayas, Banaras and Ayodhya, among others. The perceived Hindu renaissance, increasingly couched in the majoritarian context of a democratic framework, led to Muslims' self-perception as a minority. Indeed, the phenomenon of decline had already set in as the 'Islamicate' culture started to lose ground in various fields of public activity such as Bombay films and theatre,[41] the rise of Hindi as the language of education and the courts,[42] and social and cultural life in general. The activity around shrines gradually shrank as the Muslim mind embarked on a journey from past glory to present insecurity, from the spiritual zone to the material world, and from the syncretic tradition of Sufis that merged identities to the scriptural tradition that made identities explicit and exclusive. Those upholding Indo–Muslim civilization felt obliged to opt out of the cartographies of Indian nationalism. Their history did not match their geography anymore. They ended up with a demographic solution to the emergent civilizational conflict by relying on Muslim majority provinces, according to the 1941 census. Demography rather than geography laid the foundations of the new country. Nostalgia for Indo–Muslim civilization permeated deep into the psyche of the nation, ingrained in the memory of the lost glory when Muslim rule had a pan-Indian profile.[43] Partition, followed by the emergence of Bangladesh, reduced Pakistan to a residual nation as a self-proclaimed legatee of Indo–Muslim civilization.

Partition Exotica

In India, partition was translated into a conceptual construct largely rooted in 'the great divide' of Indian civilization.[44] One can take up the argument with Samaddar, whose views acquired exotic proportions about partition, underscored by a sense of rupture, dissension, division, conspiracy, unnatural divide in an organic whole, and a clash of belligerent identities whereby a 'nation dies and re-emerges'.[45] Partition is analysed from the perspective of a participant observer who is depressed over the impasse in the dialogue between the two main contenders for power prior to partition, which imposed an exit option on one of them. Partition is thus conceived as transgression, as 'excess', 'as an infamous event', as the 'other' of the nation, geared to producing 'molecular partitions' such as neighbourhood partition, village partition, city partition, community partition, family partition, gender partition, and even partition of political parties and organizations.[46]

Samaddar argued that, as opposed to a short partition that could have led to re-unification, the long partition created a permanent other.[47] The politics of partition is thus conceptualized as an antithesis to the politics of accommodation. In other words, partition is a source of permanent grief. The argument runs like this. The idea of sovereignty tends to descend on the identities of the two emergent units through nation-forming violence that establishes a right to have a state of one's own. Fatality is midwife to the birth of a new community.[48] Since the 'other' is required to be eliminated, partition symbolizes 'the division of humankind', inasmuch as India was 'doomed to be partitioned'.[49] In this process, *demos* was transformed into *ethnos*, almost as an explication of the clash of civilizations thesis.[50] These reconstructed communities tend to shed their 'common past' on their way to learning a one-dimensional history, whereby they produce the 'other' and distinguish themselves from it, because the latter is imagined as a parallel ethnicity.[51] However, as Yasmin Khan argues, the meaning of partition has differed over half a century among different sections, classes, sectors, provinces and localities, and these differences have been deliberately submerged in the 'unified' grand narratives proclaiming one dominant theme on each side of the border.[52]

For Samaddar, however, the power of discourse is reflected through its long-term deterministic influence over the worldview of a community. He studied partition as the endgame of confrontation between constitutionalists led by Jinnah, speaking for a reconstructed national community of Muslims at one end, and 'republicans' – Gandhi, Nehru and others – operating through grand politics at the other.[53] According to this formulation, Jinnah's lack of initiative in making the latter tolerate internal bargaining finally precipitated partition. At the same time, this line of reasoning is followed by an abrupt condemnation of partition as a territorial solution to an otherwise inescapable bind. He argued that the composition of the Punjab Boundary Commission itself reflected 'the communalisation of deliberations' by giving representation to the Muslim, Hindu and Sikh communities of the province. The irrationality of violence is thus claimed to be a necessary attribute of the rationality of partition.[54] Samaddar sees in it a combination of ethno-politics and geopolitics, the internality and externality of the nation, whereby democracy as characterized by differentiation of the masses according to various identities encouraged partition. The 'dark glass of partition' is then a 'broken nation' and the act of breaking goes down to the level of the village, as well as from rationality to irrationality, including 'the absurdity of the geography'.[55] There is no doubt that partitions throughout the world represent a series of otherness-creating phenomena. This leads to the question of whether partition is a solution to the conflict or a breeding ground of the conflict itself, especially if partition is seen as a reflection of the dominant geopolitical will of the great powers.[56] These observations point to the surreal aspects of the grim reality of partition in the world of Indian scholarship, at least on the margins of mainstream archival history.

The argument is that partition was an elite project, that three negotiators around the table influenced the fate of millions and that this was a logical conclusion of the colonial policy of defining communities along cultural and religious lines. Nehru confessed:

> We were tired men… Few of us could stand the prospect of going to prison again and if we had stood out for a united India…, prison obviously awaited us. We saw the fires burning in Punjab and heard of the killings. The plan of Partition offered a way out and we took it.[57]

Sanjay Chaturvedi looks at partition as an 'imperial spatial formation' via 'reflexive otherness'.[58] Ishtiaq Ahmed has traced the origins of partition to the British security need for the employment of the western-orientated state of Pakistan for military engagements.[59] The idea is that 'the supremacy of territoriality' in thinking about the other's hegemony is rooted in the 'state logic' that confers identity on a territory.[60] Thus, partition is seen as excessive geopolitics that presides over the transition from 'topophilia' to topomania.[61] Since the ultimate decision of dividing India was taken by the political leadership from both sides, partition was rooted in 'elitist mental maps seeking popular mandate or legitimacy'.[62] As for the map, the British had embarked on drawing cartographies of India as part of the 'imperial knowledge systems' very early after taking over.[63] Partition was, it is claimed, a continuation of the British policy of cultivating a cultural understanding of the political space and spatial demands that led to the construction of Hindus and Muslims as two community-based identities and entities. The instruments of manipulation included mapping, census, constitutionally sanctioned representation of communities, and devolution of power, thus bringing about division of people in various categories. In Chaturvedi's view, while Jinnah insisted on the existence of two cultural nationalisms in India, he found it difficult to identify them with their respective 'geo-bodies'.[64] Gradually, 'communalized geographies' led to a politics of difference in a big way. As opposed to these observations, one can maintain that faith-based activities had already produced a series of partitioning agendas among Muslim, Sikh and Hindu communities that delineated boundaries between them.[65] In all this, one can look at the emerging conflagration along cultural, religious and class lines that provided the ultimate fault lines for partition.[66]

It is instructive to look at the central features of this series of arguments emanating from some of the Indian sources, which, however, should not be attributed en masse to Indian scholars. These features include: the factor of division in an organic body; the state of impasse, both constitutional and ideological; reconstruction of parallel communities out of a shared past; violence as a maker and shaper of identity; and partition as an elite project based on cultural nationalism promoted by the British and reformulated by the political leadership on the Muslim side. These features point to a putative Indian perspective that grossly impacted the national narrative in Pakistan. The framework of a composite Indian civilization was comprehensively challenged by the two-nation theory, which claimed that Indian unity was more imagined than real, at least for one-quarter of the Indian population. The story of partition hinged most conspicuously and problematically on two contrasting paradigms: one was based on a shared past, such as in India; the other was based on two nation-like, faith-based communities in conflict with each other for centuries, such as in Pakistan.

In the Pakistani version of the partition exotica, Jinnah's definition of India's constitutional problem[67] as an impasse that eventually led to an exit strategy was later defined in supra-constitutional terms. For some, it became a battle of faiths between Hinduism and Islam far beyond a constitutional problem. Others were engaged in a quest for identity based on a recently discovered Indus Civilization that existed on the territory of (West) Pakistan 4,000 years ago. Similarly, K. B. Sayeed described Pakistan as 'a creation of art' by Jinnah.[68] Pointing fingers to the 'other' stood for analysis. For Hamid Khan, 'a good part of the blame for the carnage in Punjab lies with Mountbatten';[69] Jinnah faced 'an intolerant and arrogant Hindu majority';[70] and riots were started by Sikhs and Rashtriya Swayamsevak Sangh (RSS).[71] There was a cyclical meaning attached to partition in terms of freedom from Hindu exploitation: the British exploited Hindus, who got them out of India; Hindus exploited Muslims, who jumped the ship and got Pakistan.[72] In this context, violence has been elevated to a sacrifice syndrome on both sides of the border, essentially as freedom's price. This belies the fact that the British government had announced its plan to leave India as early as 3 June 1947, and the real mayhem started after people found themselves on the wrong side of the border as per the Radcliff Award announced on 17 August 1947. The question is: while partition left a deep scar on the national psyche of Pakistan, why has there been no concerted effort to keep the memory of the tragedy alive in civil society, media or textbooks relating to the various disciplines of history, sociology and anthropology? One can suggest that the first generation suffered through the gruesome violence and struggled to adjust to it by way of rehabilitation of refugees. It was the second generation that really picked up on the colossal loss of human life as the national tragedy, for which the 'other' across the border was held responsible. Nationalism turned the catastrophe into sacrifice as if it was deliberate and voluntary. Lately, there has been a small-scale initiative of the Citizens Archive of Pakistan in this direction.[73]

Parting as Foes: Communal Violence and the Destruction of Pluralism

Second only to 'high politics', communal violence has been covered extensively by historians, political scientists, sociologists, feminists and human rights activists. I focus on communalization as the way to partition, starting with its institutional design, its fallout on the concerned communities, and its assumption of a larger-than-life character in terms of paving the way for a gruesome journey from a pluralist 'culture' to an exclusivist 'identity' in Pakistan. While the oral cultures of the past represented a dispersion of identity where politics was dialogic in nature and fluid in character, the printed texts introduced in colonial times were fixed in time and space, underscored by linearity and totalization.[74] I will examine the mechanics of partition as per the Radcliffe Award and the transfer of power. I will then deconstruct the gruesome act of committing maximum violence on rival communities and explore the translation of faith-based hatred into the inter-state hostility that has persisted to this day. The two nations graduated from community to state, from culture to identity and from pluralism to bigotry while they pursued their separate nationalist projects. In the process, violence was internalized by people as sacrifice, as a source of power and as a worldview based on war rather than peace. I will analyse the role of those leaders who partitioned India, and who were now called upon to deliver. Their role is the stuff of which the policy, ideology, and code of public behaviour of the modern state of Pakistan is made. Finally, I will discuss partition as contestation, as the material for erecting the edifice of conflict over generations and recasting the classic notion of 'national interest' into an ideological mould that defined the regional and global frameworks of international behaviour.

The Mechanics of Partition

Mountbatten's partition plan of 3 June 1947 included provision for the partition of the two provinces of Punjab and Bengal. Muslims did not want partition of these provinces, where they were in a majority, but Hindus and Sikhs vehemently demanded it.[75] As Mountbatten aptly remarked, the Congress used the same argument for demanding partition of the provinces as the Muslim League used for demanding the partition of India. The idea was that neither Muslims nor Hindus nor Sikhs wanted 'to live against their will under a Government in which another community has a majority and the only alternative to coercion is partition'.[76] Not surprisingly, members of the Punjab Assembly representing Muslim majority districts voted against partition 69 to 27, while those representing non-Muslim majority districts voted for it 50 to 22. Similarly, members of the Bengal Assembly belonging to Muslim majority districts rejected partition 106 to 35 while their counterparts from Hindu majority districts voted for it, 58 to 21.

The Radcliffe Award on the partition of Punjab, announced three days after partition, shocked public opinion in Pakistan. Earlier, a 'notional' award was contained within the Second Schedule of the Indian Independence Act that had actually allocated Muslim majority areas such as Gurdaspur district to Pakistan. The Radcliffe Award was widely condemned in Pakistan as partisan and 'a deliberate perversity of justice'.[77] This led to a permanent sense of grief in Pakistan at the hands of Lord Mountbatten and Sir Cyril Radcliffe, as well as the Indian authorities in general, who were perceived to have manipulated the Radcliffe Award in their own favour.

The Pakistani sense of injustice over the rendering of certain Muslim majority areas to India was compounded by the fact that these areas provided access to the state of Jammu and Kashmir and thus involved issues relating to larger factors operating outside Punjab. It has been suggested that Radcliffe was presented with a fait accompli by Lord Mountbatten and his assistant V. P. Menon to announce an award which was more geopolitical than judicious in nature.[78] The fact that India and Pakistan entered into a bitter dispute over Kashmir immediately after partition points to the extra-local nature of the controversy about the Radcliffe Award. Books written on Kashmir typically carry a discussion of the Radcliffe Award and the way it was widely understood in the strategic context of linking India with the Himalayan state.[79] In turn, Kashmir and the defence of Pakistan have been closely linked in the national consciousness of Pakistan.[80] In other words, it was not merely a Punjab question. The Radcliffe Award was perceived to have put the country at a disadvantage vis-à-vis its stand on Kashmir. After seventy-two years, when Modi's Bharatiya Janata Party (BJP) government annexed the valley and took over its administration in 2019, Pakistan's loss was translated from a mere territorial dispute to the collapse of a legal fiction, even as it was mediated all along through an external agency such as the United Nations.

It is instructive to compare the argument of Muslim majority as the foundation of Pakistan with the Sikh claims of its distinct identity based on non-demographic factors. Sikhs did not constitute a majority in any district and did not exceed 14 per cent in the Punjab. They focused on 'other factors' such as their substantial role in the agricultural life of canal colonies, the relatively high ratio of land revenue paid by them – 46 per cent in the Lahore division alone, and their role in the army.[81] Justice Teja Singh, the Sikh representative on the Punjab Boundary Commission, stressed 'the necessity of preserving the solidarity and integrity of the Sikh community and the situation of their shrines'.[82] He pointed to the 'special circumstances of [the] Sikh community in the Punjab' which needed to be taken into account in addition to the factor of population as per the terms of reference of the boundary commission.[83] The Sikhs had over the years projected a distinct political profile separate from the two communities of Hindus and Muslims. They had floated the idea of 'Azad Punjab' in 1942 and Sikhistan in 1944. Later, they demanded constitutional guarantees for Sikhs in case India was not divided, but an independent Sikh state if it was partitioned.[84]

It has been suggested that 'the Sikh problem' was always kept in mind when Mountbatten communicated with Radcliffe, the Governor of Punjab Evan Jenkins, and other colleagues on such issues as the inclusion of the Ferozepur and Zira *tehsils* (which contained a large Sikh minority) in Pakistan, postponement of publication of the Radcliffe Award till after the transfer of power for fear of the anticipated hostile reaction of the Sikhs, and the need to show more generosity to Pakistan in Bengal, where there was no Sikh problem, than in Punjab.[85] As a consequence, the Punjab Boundary Commission produced an award that was far more controversial than the award about partition of Bengal, despite the controversy about the transfer of the district of Murshidabad and certain parts of Nadia and Jessore to India. On the other hand, the Chittagong Hill Tracts with a predominantly Buddhist population were included in Pakistan because the area was completely isolated from West Bengal and depended for its economic survival on East Bengal.[86] Criticism of the Radcliffe Award on the partition of Bengal related to the unsocial and ugly line of demarcation passing through historically established localities. However, it was nowhere close to the national outcry over the Punjab partition in terms of both intensity of feelings in the short run and potential to shape political attitudes in the long run.

Apart from the controversy about demarcation, the partition of Punjab involved a high level of organized violence, unparalleled elsewhere in India, including Bengal;[87] violence as a push factor related to migration, involving arson, murder and rape. Accounts of vandalism, attacks on trains carrying refugees across the border, and grossly uncivil behaviour of one community against the other, reflect partisan views depending on whether the victims were Hindus, Sikhs or Muslims. There is no doubt that all communities were ready to perpetrate violence on their perceived enemies given the opportunity and resources.

The level of communal violence in Punjab was much higher than elsewhere. Around a quarter of a million people died during the few months surrounding partition. The pattern of violence in Punjab, especially in the form of attacks on refugee trains, was characterized by 'the use of military tactics', 'the methodical and systematic manner', 'a high degree of planning and organisation' and 'military precision with one half of the gang providing covering fire while the others entered the train to kill'.[88] Political agency was lost in pursuit of transcendental goals translated into communal violence. In the following decades, the net result of mixing faith with politics was the emergence of a religiously defined majoritarian state in Pakistan. Religious minorities paid a heavy price for the national leadership's attachment of a premium to the majority's faith.

The fact that Punjab was the premier recruitment area for the army in British India was responsible for the selective militarization of its society. At the beginning of the Second World War, 48 per cent of the Indian army comprised men from Punjab, meaning that 1 out of 3 able-bodied men between the ages of 17 and 30 in Punjab, and 1 out of 2 in Rawalpindi district, belonged to the army.[89] A relatively high level of group solidarity in a situation of confrontation characterized communal strife in Punjab, especially on the side of Sikhs. The 1919 Montagu–Chelmsford Reforms had ensured that the 'martial castes' of Punjab constituted a majority of the electorate in the recruitment area for the army in British India and, as a consequence, filled patterns of leadership in the locality.[90] At the end of the Second World War the large, demobilized soldiery of Punjab, mainly belonging to the Sikh and Muslim communities, perpetrated violence of all kinds on each other. Many ex-servicemen carried weapons with them, which enhanced their power to inflict damage on others because of their professional training in the use of such weapons and their relatively recent experience on the war front. Attacks on non-Muslims in Attock district were reportedly led by retired Muslim army officers.[91] The Darbar Sahib Committee based in Amritsar similarly employed ex-soldiers.[92] It was observed that Sikhs were generally well-organized in their attacks on the departing Muslims. Akali *jathas* were organized in many districts. An Akali *fauj* was also recruited and organizations like Shahidi Dal, the Shiromani Gurdwara Parbandhak Committee (SGPC), Fauji Guard, Tarna Dal, Budha Dal, Dashmesh Dal and Naujawan Singh Sabha mushroomed in an effort to prepare for civil war.[93] Similarly, the Muslim National Guards were involved in organized acts of communal violence.[94] As the army was divided along communal lines, religion pushed Muslim soldiers to Pakistan and non-Muslim soldiers to India.[95]

A closely related phenomenon in Punjab was the deep commitment with which religious minorities were harassed and pushed across borders by religious majorities, thus putting an end to the religious pluralism that had operated for hundreds of years. The partition project created a vision of a society based monolithically on religious identity. In Punjab, the three revivalist movements of the Arya Samaj, 'the militant strand from which, in particular, Hindu nationalism would spring forth',[96] the Singh Sabha among Sikhs, and Ahrars and others among Muslims, led to reification of identities through such actions as *shuddhi* (purification), *gurdwara* reform and *tabligh* (proselytization) respectively. Sikh revivalism displayed a quantum of political dynamism that was unrivalled by other communities, not least because the relatively egalitarian structure of the Sikh community provided a greater scope for collective action.[97] The acute minority status of Sikhs in both parts of the divided province led them to apply this potential for organized violence to a strategy of consolidating their position in East Punjab with the ultimate goal of establishing a federation of Sikh states and districts under the leadership of Patiala state.[98]

The official view on the Pakistan side was that the killing of Muslims at the hands of Sikhs in August was part of a plan to liquidate the entire Muslim population of East Punjab and bring in Sikhs from West Punjab in order to stake a claim for the formation of a Sikh state adjoining the states of Patiala, Faridkot and others.[99] The Punjab Governor, Evan Jenkins, claimed to have noticed a similar commitment among Muslims of West Punjab, especially in the Rawalpindi division, to exterminate non-Muslims from these districts.[100] This tendency on both sides led to a pattern of complete migration of religious minorities. This model differed from the pattern in Bengal where minority communities continued to live in the shadow of majority communities, although communal hatred led to killings on both sides and pushed migrants across the border in steady waves. The partition initially left 42 per cent of the non-Muslim population of Bengal, i.e. 12 million Hindus, on the Pakistan side.[101] The two partitions had different consequences. In Punjab, it became a national tragedy because it provided India with the route to Kashmir. In Bengal, it was relatively non-controversial, with only a local fallout characterized by sporadic violence and selective migration. This was reflected in the difference between the political attitudes of Muslims in Punjab and Bengal vis-à-vis Hindus in the context of policy towards India and intercommunal harmony at home.

The deep sense of injustice among Pakistanis vis-à-vis the Radcliffe Award added to the legacy of hatred against India. The Mountbatten–Radcliffe performance in drawing the new international boundaries between India and Pakistan was indeed reflective of the way the colonial powers in their scramble for Africa had drawn lines across the continent at the Berlin Conference in 1885. Not only did the exercise take place on the map and not on the ground in both cases, but also the human element – characterized by identities, communities and habitats – was missing altogether. The 1941 census in India served as the foundation for determining the majorities and minorities at the district and sub-district levels. New definitions of citizenship relating to migration, the disposal of properties and the fulfilment of certain criteria as proof of loyalty to one state or the other were described as 'bureaucratic violence' in procedural terms.[102] The two political centres at Delhi and Karachi were de-Muslimized and de-Hinduized respectively, along with other cities and towns, most notably Lahore.

Leaders: From Mobilizers to Deliverers

Once the dust had settled and people's physical and emotional involvement in the whole process of transition was routinized, the question emerged as to how could only a few people – Gandhi, Jinnah and Nehru among others – decide the destiny of millions of people.[103] Closely related to this is the strategic question as to why Gandhi, Nehru and

Jinnah — who enjoyed unrivalled legitimacy and authority over their followers' hearts and minds and who actually struggled to stem the tide of communal killings — were totally helpless in the face of this carnage? This is not to deny the fact that the state, typically if not in every case, struggled to control both communal violence and its aftermath in the form of destruction of property and displacement of people by rising above the ideological frenzy and taking up what is understood as a 'transcendental' role.[104] The history of the transfer of power places the leaders at the centre of negotiations both amongst themselves and with the outgoing British office holders. They come out clearly as makers of history. However, their role is minimized when the 'other history' is considered, with human life at its core, characterized by more than a million people running, screaming, burning, killing, looting, raping and jumping to death in utter desperation.

Remarkably, the failure of the charismatic leadership to deliver interfaith harmony has not been the subject of any detailed scrutiny. Most dramatically, Gandhi — the greatest apostle of Hindu–Muslim harmony during partition — failed to stop the mayhem and eventually fell to an extremist Hindu assassin's bullet. The Hindu idiom of Gandhi's strategy of mass mobilization, including *satyagraha*, *maran barat*, Swadeshi movement and *ahimsa*, unleashed forces that were beyond his capacity as a politician to control, despite his saintliness in an era of communal frenzy. The masses were impervious to the constitutional idiom of their leaders. Instead, they were deeply engaged in constructing boundaries against other faith-based communities. The political vocabulary of Gandhi and Nehru fully embraced secularism as an ideology rather late in the day, in the 1940s.[105] Meanwhile, Jinnah and his team were fully engaged in the task of Muslim identity construction. Both during and after partition, Jinnah was similarly unable to stem the tide of Muslim acts of violence, rape and arson against Hindus and Sikhs.

It looks as if there are two parallel histories. In one history, leaders are given full credit for winning independence for their people, along with a new state in the case of Jinnah. In the other history, they are clearly absolved of all responsibility for plunging the two countries into the darkest period of recent times in terms of brutality and the number of fatalities. This raises an interesting question about the nature and potential of the national leadership. For one thing, these leaders typically belonged to the Anglicized elite of British India that was deeply immersed in the British legal and constitutional tradition. It spoke the idiom of citizens' rights, electoral politics, human rights, legislative powers, national self-determination and parliamentary democracy. However, an overwhelming majority of their followers did not operate through that idiom, given their traditional lifestyle that was not geared to participation in an English-based state system. Still, they had immense faith and trust in the leadership, without any real communication between the two. My argument is that the charismatic leadership did not represent society in terms of the latter's traditional morals and manners, religious and sectarian commitments, caste and tribal loyalties and the customary framework of thought and practice. They were 'spokespersons' far more than representatives of their respective communities.[106] This leadership had a relatively modern and liberal approach to life that considered violence based on caste and creed an abhorrent phenomenon. Typically, it did not adhere to the oppressive authority systems operative in the spheres of family, tribe and community. The differential in the quantum of religiosity, morality and exposure to the West between the two sides could not have been greater.

Was it, then, the case that the more like an Englishman you were the more privileged and influential you were to deal with the British proper? Did Jinnah's laudatory references to the Spaniards, French, German, Italian, English and Dutch in postcolonial America contributing to nation building, and to his commitment to the security of Hindus and other minorities in Pakistan and to various acts passed by the legislatures, ranging from provincial assemblies in British India to Westminster in London, reflect the genius of his nation?[107] If not, can this persistent disconnect between the leader and his followers be analysed in terms of the 'unconscious' belief in the innate superiority of Westernism as a value per se that characterized the leadership, be it in the sphere of English education, professional excellence or capacity to communicate with its alter ego — the British rulers? Was it, then, the old paternalism born anew, a local *mai-baap* (paterfamilias plus materfamilias) in lieu of the outgoing British *mai-baap*? Of course, the charismatic leadership acted as 'agency' for the birth of independent India and Pakistan. But beyond that, it also represented the principle of structural continuity rather than change. In Pakistan's case, the new set-up was actually termed the 'viceregal system' after the British viceroy was gone.[108] Was, then, the charismatic leader both a harbinger of change in the form of independence and a custodian of the status quo by keeping the legal-institutional structure of the colonial state intact? Perhaps the latter role would have been even stronger in the case of a mere transfer of power to a continuous entity without the intervening variable of religion such as in India. Yet, partition initiated a colossal change by way of mobilization. While the charismatic leadership struggled to manage the new 'moral community', it acutely suffered from the deliverers' dilemma on various counts.

On the one hand, people expected a lot by way of the reward of freedom, especially escape from poverty, illiteracy, unemployment, lack of health facilities, rampant social insecurity, as well as deliverance from oppression, such as in the context of caste inequality that was identified with the heroic leadership of Ambedkar.[109] On the other hand, the leadership in the two countries often focused on moral, ideological and subjective goals such as destiny, national integration, state-building and projection of past glory. This is not to discount Nehru's Fabian Socialism, which led to land reforms that put him in conflict with the higher judiciary. The fact remains that the two countries embraced an increasingly opaque idiom of national vision couched in a utopian framework. As partition changed the leaders' role from mobilizers to deliverers, it also changed the role of society as a force operating from outside the colonial state to the one pursuing its demands from within as a 'mass public'. Mitra has described the meaning of independence for people in terms of a transition from subjects to citizens.[110] I want to argue that, in practical terms, they actually moved from objects of a 'high politics' of nationalism that vowed to take them to the 'promised land', through extra-local 'ideological' input, to objects of a 'low politics' concerned with protection of interests based on ethnic, caste-based and tribal identities.

In Pakistan, the leadership struggled to keep people tied to larger-than-life objectives, such as introducing Islamic law at home and consolidation of the Muslim *umma* abroad. At the same time, the new postcolonial public reverted to paternalistic politics in the locality for redress of their grievances after a sojourn in the ideological universe led by supra-local political actors. Not surprisingly, periodic mass mobilization in pursuit of relatively unattainable goals in the context of elections spread cynicism far and wide. The postcolonial state shied away from establishing a devolutionary framework of government. It sought to rule by discretion, often by stretching the constitutional provisions ad nauseam in favour of the centre. Micro-politics was first sucked into the mega-politics of partition in the process of state-making and then pushed back to the district where it has been boxed for decades.

In this context, one needs to mention reification of the project of Pakistan at the hands of the UP Muslims, who were never far from the history of Muslim ascendancy in late medieval India. They had tried to stem the tide of Marathas, Jats and the British aspirants to take over India in the eighteenth and nineteenth centuries. They were now clueless about what their fate would be in a Hindu-dominated united India after independence.[111] This reality was made rudely clear after a foretaste in the form of the Congress government in UP (1937–9), when Muslims experienced what they considered belligerent 'Hindu' rule after several hundred years. The Muslim League was able to provide the fullest media coverage of the alleged atrocities in Bihar committed by the Congress government there. The other option was Pakistan, a distant land that carried some hope. The die was cast. This option – based on a remote unknown area in the backwaters of the British Indian empire in cultural, historical, geographical and linguistic terms – was hazy, uncertain and unpredictable. At that stage, religion as a political resource made it possible for Muslims to decide in favour of what many considered a mere illusion in preference to the perceived adverse reality at home.

The political leadership of the Pakistan project located in UP and other Muslim minority areas belonged to the landed and professional elite that emerged as the principal advocate of the Muslim separatist agenda.[112] The Hindu–Muslim question had reflected 'the newly-minted identities' among the educated middle class that dextrously projected them, even as these identities were not to be confused with the religious practice that would have disqualified quite a few leaders.[113] The middle class engaged itself in the 'nation-building' project after partition and paved the way for understanding one's nationalism in terms of the other.[114] Partition soon brought the middle class to the top of the state machinery of Pakistan. In particular, elements from the migrant middle class were considered to be qualitatively better than their compatriots from the Pakistan areas proper, especially in the context of higher education.

Partitions as 'Contested Arrangements'

At one end of the spectrum, the view against partition sees Pakistan as a country that was increasingly at war with itself. It was claimed that the whole Pakistan project was indeed insufficiently imagined,[115] an observation that — seen from the perspective of nations being considered 'imagined communities' — casts a shadow on the bona fides of Pakistani nationalism. At the other end, Radha Kumar finds Indian partition as the most successful of all partitions in the twentieth century.[116] It was a relatively smooth affair in legal and institutional terms, barring a few hiccups in terms of settlement of the division of assets and the contentious issue of the accession of princely states to India or Pakistan. Both countries officially recognized each other. They have had ongoing diplomatic relations for more than seven decades except for short periods during and after wars or warlike situations. They operated through the regional organization, the South Asian Association for Regional Cooperation (SAARC), even though it has lost its initial promise in recent decades. Individual migrants on both sides of the border naturally showed nostalgia for their areas of origin for a generation. But Pakistan did not produce any elite or mass movement that would mobilize people to re-join India. Similarly, after the establishment of a pro-Indian government in Bangladesh under Sheikh Mujibur Rahman, there was no move for a merger of the new country with India. In other words, partition is holding up in the Indian subcontinent, in contrast to the desire to be united from relevant quarters in the two Irelands, the two Koreas and previously the two Germanys. The emergence of Pakistan reflected the culmination of a process of social, economic, cultural and political partition under late colonialism. For the independence generation, history shaped geography. For the following generations, geography continuously sought to redefine and rediscover history. 'Spatial partitioning' increased the complexity of the political situation on the ground in terms of social and cultural partitioning.[117]

Brendan O'Leary discusses partition and migration in the following terms: 'right-sizing' the state, i.e. contraction, and 'right-peopling' the state, i.e. keeping within borders those with a shared but problematic sense of nationality.[118] Borders 'which encompass willing potential co-nationals' are considered ideal.[119] By the mid-1940s, a vast majority of Muslims in India had been sufficiently mobilized to opt out of the envisioned borders of post-independence India and seek partition. By the same token, the Congress, as representative of the majority Hindu community – a profile that its leadership denied because it would have limited its supra-communal secular mission – finally adjusted to the idea of getting rid of their unwilling co-nationals by conceding territory to the Muslim League. O'Leary argues that partitions are executed by Great Powers and that there is always one party that finds partition 'an imposition, a violation'.[120] Therefore, partitions are at best 'contested arrangements'.[121] Kaufmann maintained that India opposed partition on the plea that it bred violence and led to large-scale population transfer as a result of mass mobilization by communalist elite groups.[122] He took a different position: that it was the potential withdrawal of the state in British India from exercising its authority and fulfilling its responsibility to keep law and order that created security dilemmas for the emergent minorities in the new dominions.[123] He argued that population exchange actually resolved security dilemmas for Hindus of Pakistan and Muslims of India in the immediate post-partition period. In his view, the Kashmir conflict remained unresolved due to the very fact that partition did not go far enough to include that area. He also maintained that, since there was no provision for a Sikh homeland, it created a problem later on, considering that Sikhs represented a powerful community in terms of wealth and political influence.[124]

The question of whether partition was inevitable has been answered differently in the two countries. Several Indian analysts tend to focus on the mishaps, missteps and mistakes on the part of the Congress during the last decade of the colonial rule, which gave Jinnah his chance to push for the ultimate step of partition. One of the leading examples of such 'freak' developments was the Congress's refusal to establish a coalition ministry in UP after the 1937 elections, which left the powerful Muslim landed elite and the educated middle class out in the cold.[125] A second example was the famous refusal of Nehru to countenance the Cabinet Mission Plan's provision for the right of provinces to opt out of the federation, that made Jinnah withdraw his acceptance of the plan, whereby the last chance of keeping India united was gone.[126]

This understanding of partition as an aberration made possible by the follies of statesmen at the top is, in one sense at least, problematic. It omits the ongoing intellectual, political, social and cultural expression of alienation of the largest minority in India. A quest for 'security' in a united India emerged as the most robust concern of the Muslim stakeholders in the form of demands for irreversible guarantees, such as institutional–constitutional arrangements. The archival history focuses on negotiations and communications at the official level at the expense of the fiercely assertive articulate sections of the Muslim population. Hamza Alavi found in the archival record an imaginary construct of state and society.[127] Hindu icons, symbols, linguistic expressions and slogans used by the Congress in meetings, banners and posters – often attributed to the influence of the Hindu Mahasabha in the party ranks – created negative feelings among Muslims.[128] The archival historian typically sees partition as a failure of the project of Indian nationalism. However, Farzana Shaikh found the Muslim mind of the mid-twentieth century struggling with the normative aspects of religious and political life, searching for a clue about the 'right' conduct for Muslims and gradually moving from the logic of parity with Hindus to separatism.[129] Christophe Jaffrelot makes an interesting point about the genesis of the Muslim League that led 'a defence movement for a minority fearful of the majority rule (a principle on which democracy is built)'.[130] In other words, it was the fear of democracy, rather than a passion for it, that underscored the Pakistan project. Since democracy meant Hindu rule, the Muslim elite chose to mobilize its co-religionists around Islamic ideology. The Muslim League's success lay in making Muslims – living next door to Hindus, and in Punjab also to Sikhs, and interacting with them in a thousand ways on a daily basis – conscious of their distinct cultural identity. This process pierced through people's local, regional, cultural and linguistic contexts, which were now massively redefined by the religious context.

The basic difference between the narrative of 'high politics', which delved into the complex and dense tripartite negotiations surrounding partition, and the narrative of the public at large, which experienced communal violence and its gruesome memory for a lifetime, is the former's use of the idiom of law. Never before, since black letter law started to operate in India after the colonial takeover, did it play such a negligible role in public life in the context of maintaining communal peace. At the time of partition, the state typically withdrew from the public scene and virtually stopped performing its three important functions: maintenance of law and order; bringing criminals to justice; and establishing the supremacy of law over and above faith-based identities. The state's withdrawal from action effectively rendered the written word on the statute book infructuous. In this context, transformational ideologies sought to re-shape the existing territorial, demographic and administrative entities, especially in the case of Muslims and later Sikhs in Indian Punjab. These two communities went into state-formation mode, one after 3 June 1947 and the other – learning from it by way of creating a Sikh majority in East Punjab – for its future Khalistan project. The new wisdom was that you first create a majority and then demand a state of your own.

Partition put a seal on what had been happening by way of an ideological divide among neighbours, friends, colleagues, co-followers of religious shrines, as well as the middle-class literary writers, artists, journalists, professors, doctors, engineers and businessmen from the Hindu, Muslim and Sikh communities. Muslim League propaganda operated as an agency to deliver a Muslim 'moral community'.[131] It did so by isolating and then insulating the large Muslim population in India from its Hindu compatriots. The transcendental route to achievement of this unmistakably political goal left a deep imprint on future generations of Pakistan. This religious fervour was operationalized through contestations in public life expressed through riots and the tension surrounding elections, cultural activities, religious festivals and the popular press that together shaped the public arena.[132]

Chaturvedi sees the current times as the 'partitioned times'.[133] The idea is that partition becomes a contested phenomenon because it provides an easy way out of various ethno-political conflicts within states and then contributes to instability and friction instead of peace and harmony. The partition of India led to different commitments in the two emergent states. One was loathsome for the idea of religion as a basis of nationalism in the case of the broadly defined successor state of India. The other showed an everlasting commitment to partition as the very genesis of the seceding state of Pakistan. This factor was destined to play a role in cultivating a transcendental vision in the latter's case, even as the modernist elite upheld religion mainly as principle rather than practice.[134]

The fear of further partitions in the two countries led to a ferocious centralization of power. This book deals with the fear of disintegration in Pakistan that became a source of conflict both directly in the ethnic context and indirectly by relying on religion as a conflict resolution mechanism. But this mechanism, far from its impugned function, created an endless series of clashes among adherents of various religious and sectarian denominations. In Pakistan, the present shaped the past, which in turn shaped the future by way of setting successive generations to grow firmly apart from India. In this process, Pakistan experienced a regional transition by opting out of South Asia after the secession of Bangladesh. This process of opting out affected the cultural, economic, diplomatic and ideological domains of public policy.[135]

Partition is a depreciating currency insofar as it is progressively pushed back into history with each new generation. As opposed to India, where a collective sense of political tragedy attracted a lot of attention from civil society, especially from the feminist groups, in Pakistan partition is remembered as the genesis of a Muslim homeland. The urban-based middle class that had transformed Muslim interests into an Islamic ideology as part of the Pakistan project soon made it to the top decision-making positions. Refugees from India were potentially de-territorialized in the process of migration. They felt obliged to reconstruct their identity on the basis of religion to carve out social, cultural and ideological space for themselves in their land of migration. For more than seven decades, the Islamic idiom remained essentially an urban middle-class phenomenon. This development corresponded to the loss of political initiative on the part of the parliament and the political class in general, which drew essentially on the local electoral dynamics defined in terms of caste, village, shrine, tribal affiliation and sectarian ties. It typically found the Islamic agenda a source of national identity rather than a vote-catching strategy. No major Islamic legislation emanated from the political class except the 1974 2nd Constitutional Amendment.[136]

Violence as the other face of partition has attracted scholarly attention for decades. In 2011 Ishtiaq Ahmad's book, *The Punjab*

Bloodied, Partitioned and Cleansed, made available detailed accounts of violence, as narrated by their perpetrators, victims, witnesses and chroniclers in both East and West Punjab.[137] Two things distinguish this book from others. One, it is a compendium of real stories from life about dying, butchering, rape, escaping and sometimes discovering lost family members after two generations. Two, it is a testament to the grim reality on the ground based on what religion meant in terms of the violence that erected boundaries among people of different faiths.

As noted earlier, violence in Punjab was attributed to its position as a military recruitment area.[138] Like the demobilized army of Iraq after the Second Gulf War in 2003 that carried out resistance against the US-led occupation forces, the Indian returnees from the battlefront after the Second World War picked up their weapons against their respective religious enemies. Violence has been studied as 'sacrifice, as revenge and as an instrument of revenge', often accompanied by a sense of victimhood.[139] Ian Talbot and Gurharpal Singh consider five characteristics of the partition violence: ethnic cleansing; contestation for power; brutality, especially in the case of female victims; transition from public violence to private oppression; and military-level planning and sophistication.[140] A notable feature of this violence was the absence of state machinery to control it. This related to the blatant partiality of state officials, who typically did not file cases against killers, arsonists and rapists, and the collapse of the British will and capacity to rule, arbitrate, adjudicate and administer. Communalization of the Indian and Pakistani armies followed. Members of the Military Evacuation Organisations (MEOs) and the Punjab Boundary Force struggled to save their respective co-religionists. On both sides of the border, the state was perceived as 'agency' for security of their faith-based compatriots far more than a neutral and judicious entity. The figure of the citizen was lost in this process. Only religiously defined perpetrators or victims of violence emerged as the agenda of the state, prompting restraint on the former and providing shelter, food and security to the latter. Once the horrendous scale of communal violence in Punjab became clear, the two states sought to evacuate refugees safely across the border. However, in Bengal the situation was far less forbidding, and therefore the large-scale transfer of people was not necessarily on the official agenda.

Migration and Refugee Resettlement

While Jinnah had mentioned the possibility of a mass exchange of population across the new border in the case of partition being part of the official agenda, no serious action or policy followed.[141] As an unforetold and unforeseen development outside the framework of high politics, migration represents low politics in its pristine form, whereby the state in British India suddenly withdrew the use of its administrative muscle and conceded space to the mob. The collapse of the government's will in the face of communal riots prior to partition has yet to be fully analysed. What concerns us here is the way the two dominions picked up the process of the resettlement of refugees, largely keeping their original social status in mind. For our purposes, the migration of eight million Muslims from India to Pakistan represented a phenomenon that can be described as 're-peopling' the state, as a consequence of 're-sizing' the state.[142] For hundreds of years, people had moved from the periphery in the south, west and east of India to the centre of the Mughal empire and – during its later part – the British empire, in and around UP and Delhi in search of patronage, jobs, businesses and careers in culture, art and architecture. Partition led to a reverse movement of Muslims, from the centre to the periphery, i.e. from UP and other Muslim minority provinces as well as Hyderabad Deccan and other princely states to northwest and northeast India.[143]

Both Jinnah and Liaqat, and the higher echelons of the Muslim League – the architects of the Pakistan project – belonged to non-Pakistan areas. Pakistan emerged as a 'migrant state' par excellence. It included the two-thirds of the Muslim Indian Civil Service (ICS) officers who opted for Pakistan, three-quarters of the business class, and a large majority of intelligentsia crossing over the border far beyond their ratio in the local population.[144] A large part of the migrant elite was socially, culturally and linguistically alien to its land of migration. Therefore, the elite–mass distance was far greater and more forbidding in Pakistan than in India. The pattern of refugee settlement generally enhanced the class basis of the migrants because they were allotted Hindu evacuee property that outvalued the Muslim evacuee property in India by a large margin, i.e. almost double for agricultural land and three times for urban property.[145]

All this created a new ethnic hierarchy, with Urdu-speaking migrants (Mohajirs) at the top, followed by those from East Punjab. More than seven decades later, Pakistan is still, in the eyes of Sindhis, Pakhtuns and the Baloch, just as for East Bengalis before 1971, a Mohajir–Punjabi state. Migrants accounted for 20 per cent of the population of (West) Pakistan as compared to 1 per cent in India.[146] With migrants accounting for every fourth household in Punjab and every second household in Karachi after partition, 're-peopling' the state was a political phenomenon with gruesome consequences. Sindh developed two rival nationalisms: Mohajirs who had lost their initial pre-eminence in politics, bureaucracy and business after 'the indigenous revival' in the 1970s, and Sindhis who feared the grim prospects of turning into a minority in their own province after migration from across the border. The two communities remained at daggers drawn after three-quarters of a century. The military carried out operations against Sindhi and Mohajir nationalists in 1983 and 1992–5 respectively at the peak of their agitation. Demographic nationalism underscored the two movements in pursuit of their respective claims to jobs and businesses that made the census a dubious exercise in their eyes as per Punjab's alleged design to dwarf the population of Sindh.[147]

The high quantum of violence, contentious routes to refugee resettlement, and the emergence of ethnic movements as a result of migration have all attracted scholarly attention.[148] One needs to explore the regional patterns of refugee resettlement in order to deconstruct the holistic picture of migration by raising up a comparison between Punjab and Bengal, between Punjab and Sindh and between West and East Punjab. The purpose is not to take a break from macro-history and dwell on micro-history. Instead, the idea is to look for reasons behind the emergence of different patterns of discourse and policy orientation according to different patterns of resettlement. The partition of Punjab turned out to be politically far more significant than the partition of Bengal inasmuch as it determined political attitudes towards India, the composition of the governing elite at the top, and commitment to the cause of Kashmir. Demographically speaking, 73 per cent of migrants from India landed in Punjab alone while only 9 per cent of them went to East Bengal. That meant that the emergent political attitude of West Punjab was different from its counterpart in East Bengal.

Table 1.1 Partition and migration in Punjab and Bengal

Punjab	Bengal
Controversial	Non-controversial
National tragedy	Local problem
Organized violence	Sporadic violence
Total migration	Selective migration

Migration was not only a movement of people across the border. In Pakistan's case, it was the migrant elite that itself had championed the agenda of state formation. The first governor general, the first prime minister, a majority of members of the council of the All-India Muslim League (AIML) and its central working committee, and a dominant part of the industrial–commercial elites, the civilian bureaucracy and the intelligentsia – mainstream, Islamic and leftist – were all migrants. Public policy remained the preserve of the migrant elite, as did the national discourse that left an impact on the nation's hearts and minds for generations to come. The leading ideas of Pakistan in the first quarter of the twenty-first century bore a clear imprint of the migrant elite that steered the nation through the muddy waters of post-partition politics.

Nostalgia for the 'lost' part of the Muslim nation, i.e., the Indian Muslims, lasted for a generation in the context of the divided family syndrome, but then gradually declined.[149] Only the 'lost' part of society in Punjab, Sindh, East Bengal and elsewhere – comprising Hindus and Sikhs – was not bemoaned at all. The make-up of the new society in Pakistan replaced a centuries-old plural society that had been couched in a syncretic framework of belief and practice across religious boundaries with overlapping dimensions of cosmology, morality and custom.[150] The recurrent patterns of conflict had been typically, if not in every case, contained by a configuration of power in the locality dominated by scions of Sikh, Hindu or Muslim aristocracy. The question is: what really happened when an integral part of the cultural ecology defined by religion, sect, caste, sub-caste and class disappeared from the scene? After all, the plural and syncretic character of society in what became Pakistan had been engraved on the collective memory and practices of people for a thousand years by way of linguistic expressions, common proverbs, shared understanding of human nature about gender and family life, and frequent references to the Indian calendar as a trajectory of time, especially for the purposes of agriculture, weather and weddings. These communities shared various shades of anti-colonialism, ranging from street agitation to militant action, and heroes such as Abdul Majeed Sindhi, Bhagat Singh and hundreds of people who died in the Jallianwala Bagh massacre in 1919. After partition, the incoming Muslim refugees who were brutalized by Hindus and Sikhs in East Punjab, Delhi, West Bengal and elsewhere lent a new character to society, which conceived religion in terms of a transformative agenda based on a silent war with history and culture. Anti-Indianism, understood as anti-Hinduism, both under military-led dispensations and weak civilian governments, never allowed the earlier spirit of syncretism to resurface. The leading agenda of the new ruling elite theologized 'cultural signifiers' into boundary-creating principles as part of the national project.[151]

Resettlement of Refugees: Punjab and Sindh

Our first point of departure is the difference between the two provinces of Punjab and Sindh. Migrants from East Punjab and surrounding areas spread their exclusionary framework of political imagination to the whole of Punjabi society on the western side of the border. However, in Sindh, Mohajirs were not able to spread the same message to Sindhi society because the latter had not been similarly brutalized by communal riots. Typically, Hindus were not keen to leave Sindh nor did Sindhi Muslims actively struggle to push them out of the province. The syncretic tradition of Sindhis was able, to a large extent, to keep the social fabric safe from penetration of the agenda of war against Hindu and Sikh 'infidels'. Sindhi nationalists proudly claimed that their society was not communal like Mohajirs or Punjabis.[152] After arrival in Pakistan, middle-class refugees excelled over others in the process of starting a new life, due to representation of their kith and kin in bureaucratic positions, their own educational qualifications, their credentials for loans, and their lobbying for allotment of evacuee property. To a large extent, the pre-partition model of social stratification was saved.[153] Overall, the sufferings of refugees were woven into the surge of nationalism as people told horrendous stories of sacrifices for at least a generation. On both sides of the border, killings by one community were remembered as sacrifices by the other. Partition has continued to surface in India and Pakistan through textbooks, celebrations of independence days, memorials erected for martyrdom, and the artistic, literary and scholarly rendering of various aspects of the gruesome event.[154] However, this is indeed a story of diminishing interest and importance along with the tragic loss of life and the divided family syndrome that merged into the new realities of independent nationhood, marginalization of religious minorities, and emergence of ethnic movements. West Punjab presents a unique example of the assimilation of a huge migrant community into the host society within a relatively short period of time. It experienced immediate and en masse migration as a direct result of the breakdown of communal relations, whereas migrants continued to come to Sindh from various non-partitioned provinces of India for a generation through a slow-moving, selective and voluntary process. Migration in Punjab directly related to the issue of the physical security of Muslims in East Punjab when they found themselves on the wrong side of the border.[155]

As opposed to this, migration to Sindh (or more precisely to Karachi, Hyderabad and other urban centres) from UP, Bombay and other minority provinces was essentially due to ideological and political reasons, as well as the pull of new job opportunities. The two cases of Punjab and Sindh represent the two models of assimilation and non-assimilation respectively. The Punjab accommodated 5.3 million refugees, which accounted for 25.6 per cent of its population in 1951.[156] Thus, every fourth person in West Punjab was a refugee. It was a classic case of what O'Leary describes as 're-peopling the state'.[157] Refugees were rehabilitated in villages, towns and cities. They profoundly influenced the political attitudes of the local population in terms of a heightened sense of insecurity vis-à-vis India and a relatively enhanced consciousness about Muslim identity that was the reason for their migration in the first place. This process was facilitated by the fact that both migrants and locals shared linguistic and cultural traditions.

The place of origin of refugees in India was a significant factor in their prospects of assimilation into the host society. In Punjab, 97.5 per cent of refugees came from the 'north-west zone', comprising essentially East Punjab, along with Ajmer, Delhi, Rajputana states and Jammu and Kashmir.[158] But the migrant community of Sindh was totally non-Sindhi in ethnic, linguistic and geographical terms. It spoke a variety of other languages including Urdu, Punjabi, Gujarati, Marathi, Tamil and Kutchhi among others. This represented a radical break with the situation in Punjab. In Sindh (excluding Karachi), out of 540,278 refugees, 30 per cent came from East Punjab, 21.7 per cent from UP and 25.6 per cent from Rajputana states, along with small pockets from Ajmer, Bombay, Delhi, Central Provinces (CP) and Bihar.[159] Similarly, out of 616,900 refugees in Karachi, 35 per cent came from East Punjab and adjacent areas, 32 per cent from UP and 19 per cent from Bombay and Western India, in addition to 8 per cent from the central zone (CP, central Indian states and Hyderabad state).[160]

The single largest ethnic community among refugees in Sindh belonged to East Punjab. Indeed, Punjabis had been coming to Sindh from the 1890s onwards when canal irrigation was initiated over vast areas and commercial agriculture flourished in the form of the cultivation of cash crops. The completion of the Sukkur Barrage in 1932 led to a fresh influx of Punjabi peasant proprietors that elicited a hostile reaction from Sindhis.[161] After independence, especially after the establishment of One Unit in 1955, the perceived 'Punjabization' of Sindh was reflected through the allotment of land to civil and military officers, a majority of whom were Punjabis, and through recruitment to jobs and the establishment of industries.[162] In this way, Urdu-speaking elite bureaucrats, Gujarati-speaking businessmen and Punjabi-speaking elite farmers and civil servants together occupied large parts of the social, cultural, administrative and economic space available in Sindh. Refugees defied assimilation because of their linguistic, cultural and historical remoteness from the local population. In Sindh, 63.9 per cent of refugees lived in urban areas, 86.16 per cent in Hyderabad district and 71 per cent in Sukkur.[163] In Karachi, there were only 14.28 per cent speakers of Sindhi as opposed to 58.7 per cent who spoke Urdu as their mother tongue.[164] While migrants in Punjab settled in both rural and urban areas, migrants in Sindh emerged as an urban community pitted against Sindhis, who were overnight relegated to the position of a rural community after the largely urban-based Hindu Sindhis migrated to India.

This was bound to reflect in a lack of integration between the two communities. A crucial factor in the relatively successful integration of migrants with locals in West Punjab was the relative balance of power between the two sides. Migrants had an edge over 'locals' in education and jobs in selective fields, but the 'locals' dominated electoral politics, commercial agriculture in the canal colonies, as well as the army. This situation indirectly paved the way for assimilation because no real clash of interests developed along sectoral, class, professional or institutional lines. The 'ruling' dispensation in Punjab led by the Unionist party for two decades prior to independence comprised Muslim Rajput landlords and Sufi *pirs* from the western part of the province who were politically ascendant in the Muslim League at the time of partition.[165] On the other hand, East Punjab was typically represented by Muslim *biradaris* of peasant proprietors.[166] Outgoing Hindu officers and professionals from West Punjab were replaced in many cases by their Muslim counterparts from East Punjab.

As opposed to this pattern, the pre-partition exercise in political coalition building in Sindh continued to present an extreme case of faction-ridden politics.[167] Here, the migrant elite at the top represented the new state to the virtual exclusion of Sindhi leadership. In 1948, it pushed the latter out of Karachi to Hyderabad, which became the capital of Sindh. The most prosperous region of Punjab in terms of commercial agriculture lay in the canal colonies and central districts that fell on the Pakistan side. As opposed to this, Sindh typically lacked a progressive peasantry. Overnight Mohajirs dominated the political, administrative and cultural life of Sindh, especially in the capital cities of Karachi and Hyderabad, while Sindhis looked upon them as land grabbers and imperialists.[168]

Many migrants who came to Punjab after partition were settled on agricultural land in the form of large communities. The government tried to keep whole communities belonging to the same area of origin together in the process of rehabilitation.[169] The idea was to preserve group identity and familial bonds amidst the anarchic situation prevailing at that time. Refugees who came from East Punjab, Delhi and Jammu and Kashmir were largely accommodated in West Punjab districts. Almost half the refugees from East Punjab, i.e. 2.6 million, were agriculturists, of whom 2.25 million had already been rehabilitated by July 1948.

A similar pattern of refugee rehabilitation operated across the border. Delhi believed that refugees from West Punjab should ultimately be settled in East Punjab and their migration to Delhi, UP and other areas should be discouraged. Only refugees from non-Punjab areas such as

Sindh, KP, and Balochistan were likely to be settled in areas east of Punjab.[170] Following the policy of settlement of whole communities in specific places, refugees from the canal colony districts of West Punjab were settled in the original areas from where they had initially migrated half a century ago. Similarly, refugees from Lahore *tehsil* were settled in Ajnala *tehsil*, those from Sialkot in Gurdaspur, those from Rawalpindi division in parts of Ambala division, and Sikhs were settled in the riverine areas of Ferozepur, Fazilka, and so on. On both sides of the border, the governments thought that rehabilitation should be on a communal basis. The idea was that individuals should be safeguarded from the devastating effects of a breakdown of support structures such as family, tribe and community. The pattern of resettlement of urban refugees from India, however, remained anarchic because of the non-availability of large, compact property in cities as well as the relatively spasmodic nature of the flow of refugees in urban areas.

Immediately after partition, the issue of refugee resettlement became a bone of contention between India and Pakistan. The two governments formally reached agreement on the methodology to handle the matter of evacuee property and established institutions for that purpose, such as the Custodian of Refugees Property and the Inter-Dominion Refugee and Evacuee Council to resolve conflicts. But both countries often arbitrarily and unilaterally redefined the parameters of these agreements and categories of evacuees after gradually losing hope of coming to an understanding with each other for a comprehensive solution to the issue. Of course, the illusion that migration was temporary in nature and that the two countries would be reunited kept the two governments from taking up the matter of evacuee property on an emergency basis, at least up until 1950.[171]

The definition of an evacuee fell a victim to the ambition and agenda of respective governments to grab evacuee property one way or the other. This included the making of new laws, extending the scope of the existing laws to apply to additional areas and provinces, and practically nullifying the rights of property owners to sell, transfer, or exchange property in their absence, or even during their presence. As per the 1948 Bombay Refugees Act, Muslim properties could be placed at the disposal of the custodian, the state government or the Government of India. This had the potential to unleash another exodus of Muslims to Pakistan in the event of their being dis-appropriated. For this purpose, a category of 'intending evacuees' was devised. Both India and Pakistan made laws to appropriate the property of both evacuees and intending evacuees.[172]

The two countries continued to take a different line on the issue of devising the value of evacuee property and thus coming to some agreement about compensation for the difference. Indian sources claimed that evacuee property left by Hindus and Sikhs in Pakistan amounted to more than 8 million acres of land in West Punjab, augmented by land in Sindh and other provinces, as opposed to evacuee land vacated by Muslims in East Punjab and surrounding states, amounting to 4 million acres.[173] This translated into Rs 38.1 billion for Hindu–Sikh property left in Pakistan against Rs 3.8 billion for Muslim property left in India.[174] Not surprisingly, India took the position that the situation called for a government-to-government approach whereby the debtor country – in this case Pakistan – should pay the difference to the creditor country, i.e. India.[175] Pakistan, on the other hand, emphasized the role of the evacuees themselves to dispose of their property, because the full data were not available and a comprehensive and collective approach was not feasible at all.

In the final event, the two governments settled down with whatever they had got by way of evacuee property. When the two governments were unable to agree on the mechanism to decide about the actual price of the evacuee property and the way to compensate for the difference, both Delhi and Karachi went ahead and allotted property to claimants and provided legal space for refugee claims for the property abandoned on the other side of the border. These claims were not only mostly exaggerated but also part of the large-scale corruption, spread over a decade, that involved self-serving bureaucrats and politicians as well as migrants as litigants.[176]

The Liaqat–Nehru Pact of April 1950, following the communal riots in East and West Bengal, sought to put an end to the process of forced migration that would involve loss of property.[177] It was decided that property would be restored to returnees from the neighbouring countries and the logic of expropriation of evacuees that operated immediately after partition would not hold anymore. That one single progressive step forward virtually stopped the process of forced migration, because the agreement provided for the reclaiming of property owned by the migrants before crossing the border. In this way, 189,240 Muslim returnees in West Bengal out of 234,450 got their land back, while 30,893 out of 31,660 Hindu returnees to East Bengal got their land and houses back.[178]

A new principle was set. Unlike during the volatile situation of partition, now Muslims and Hindus were acknowledged as citizens of their respective countries, where their co-religionists were in a minority but where they had full rights to property as citizens irrespective of faith. Also, it sent a message to those given to communal frenzy that the 'victims' from across the boundaries of faith were no longer considered aliens within the country of their residence. Partition was undone at least in the context of stopping the practice of appropriating the possessions of the forced evacuees. The two states decided to give citizenship rights to people according to their location in territorial terms. The new property considerations came to the rescue of minorities who could no longer be dis-appropriated simply on the basis of their faith. The territorial state, along with its citizenry, finally took over in both India and Pakistan.

(West) Punjab enjoyed a pivotal position in post-Independence Pakistan. Some wondered if the country should be called Punjabistan inasmuch as that province functioned as the power base of Pakistan.[179] Initially, Hindu and Sikh evacuee property was selectively occupied by neighbours from the locality. Later, the property was allotted to refugees, which created antipathy towards them.[180] It was not uncommon to see local – Mohajir conflict in various localities. The large settler communities in Sargodha, Faisalabad, Multan, Jhang and Sialkot districts, as well as Bahawalpur state, evoked a negative reaction from the local population after the initial euphoria of helping the calamity – ridden refugees had subsided. However, the two sides belonged to overlapping tribal, caste and sectarian communities, especially in the absence of different sources of identity such as language, history and culture.

The only area where linguistic differences could have triggered such a reaction was south-western Punjab. Here, an incipient Siraiki movement emerged, first as a move to make the erstwhile Bahawalpur state a province and then as a campaign to create a Siraiki province with its epicentre at Multan. Siraiki activists showed resentment toward the allotment of 600,000 acres of local land to non-Siraikis, the neglect of Siraiki-speaking people in the quota system, and hurdles in the way of growth of a Siraiki culture through the print and electronic media.[181] However, the Siraiki language took three decades to grow beyond a mere dialect of Punjabi and to get Siraiki acknowledged as a language separate from Punjabi, at least for the purpose of census.[182] On that basis, it now demanded a province of its own in south Punjab. Over time, the Siraiki movement outgrew its initial opposition to settlers and refugees, and even adopted the region of south Punjab beyond the Siraiki language area as a basis of their demand for a new province. Asma Faiz points out that the Siraiki-speaking political elite generally sought to operate at the level of Punjab as a whole and not limit itself to the 'poorer' region of south Punjab.[183]

The scene in Sindh presented a different model. Here, refugees came from all over India, speaking different languages and representing different cultures. Furthermore, they did not come en masse. Instead, their arrival extended to the 1965 war, with a small trickledown continuing. Most crucially, the political and administrative machinery handling refugees in Punjab was itself dominated by migrants from East Punjab and elsewhere in India. This facilitated the process of rehabilitation tremendously.

As opposed to this, the Sindh government had to deal with refugees who were non-Sindhi. Not surprisingly, the process of refugee rehabilitation in the alien geographic, cultural, and social milieu of Sindh created considerable mistrust between refugees and Sindhis. Indeed, it forced many to go back to India. Karachi blamed the Sindh government for not doing enough for refugees and thus forcing them to return to their places of origin across the border.[184] In Punjab, claims to evacuee property were filed and disposed of in a relatively smooth way, especially as the governments of India and Pakistan cooperated with each other in the matter of exchange of information about property, leading to the allotment of 350,000 acres of evacuee land to incoming Muslim refugees within a short time.[185]

The performance of Sindh differed in the matter of disposal of property claims, especially as the distinction between 'agreed' and 'non-agreed' areas arose for determining the legal status of evacuee property. The areas 'agreed' for disposal of evacuee property were essentially West and East Punjab on the two sides of the border. Following agreement, revenue records of agricultural land were exchanged between the two governments, followed by verification of claims by a Central Record Office. Out of a total of 1,143,102 disposed claims, 95 per cent belonged to Punjab.[186] Refugees from 'agreed areas' were therefore allotted land on a provisional permanent basis. This pattern of handling claims to evacuee property led to the emergence of at least a majority of refugees as a more or less propertied class, especially in cities, where they acquired a relatively middle-class status. Having passed through a bloodbath of migration that enhanced their sense of insecurity, migrants behaved as a constituency for the military and as a lobby for Islamic right-wing parties.[187]

On the other hand, refugees in Sindh who hailed from 'non-agreed areas' were allotted land only on a temporary basis and on a smaller scale. This led to major misgivings among the Mohajirs of Sindh. The issue resurfaced thirty years later from the platform of the MQM, which projected it as a gross injustice done to Mohajirs. The process of refugee rehabilitation in Karachi and Sindh generally remained far from satisfactory. Even in 1954, seven years after partition, no less than 240,000 out of a total of 750,000 refugees in Karachi were still to be rehabilitated.[188]

The two models of refugee rehabilitation in Punjab and Sindh thus turned out to be radically different. Punjab settled the issue quickly: 90 per cent of refugees were settled by July 1948. They got provisional permanent allotment of property and were dispersed all over Punjab in both rural and urban areas. Sindh was delayed in the settlement of refugees and 30 per cent were still not settled by 1954. They were given temporary allotment of property. Refugees were concentrated in Karachi and other urban centres.

Table 1.2 Refugee resettlement in Punjab and Sindh

Punjab situation	Resettlement: smooth; quick	90% settled: July 1948	No returnees	Refugees dispersed all over	Permanent allotment
Sindh situation	Problematic; delayed	30% not settled: 1954	Returnees to India	Convergence on Karachi	Temporary allotment

The trauma of migration in Punjab that involved sacrifice of life and property created three dominant patterns of political thinking:

securitization of the national vision, deification of the state, and an Islamic agenda. A fixation with leadership led to a preference for presidentialism at the cost of parliamentarianism. The migrants' political attitudes carried extra weight because of their presence in cities in large numbers. Lahore city was 43 per cent migrant, Multan 49 per cent, Gujranwala 50 per cent, Jhang 65 per cent and both Faisalabad and Sargodha 69 per cent.[189] The fact that migrants in Punjab who were brutalized in the process of crossing the border were increasingly assimilated into the wider society made their influence non-distinct and relatively diffuse. Also, northern Punjab was the traditional recruitment area for the army units that had been deployed along the border area in Punjab for the evacuation of Muslim refugees from India as well as along the ceasefire line in Kashmir, where they fought with Indian forces alongside the mujahideen. All this meant that there was no major difference in the anti-Indian sentiments of locals and migrants in Punjab. The pattern in Sindh was, however, different. Here, Mohajir attitudes, which were based on anti-Indianism and a commitment to the centralization of authority, were resented by Sindhis, who took an opposite stand on issues such as the demand for provincial autonomy, the denial of a political role for the army, and a relatively neutral foreign policy orientation towards India. The migrants' assimilation in Punjab rendered the potential sources of conflict between locals and migrants ineffective.

Amazingly, one does not find an analysis of the way that the protection of the class structure of migrants in their land of resettlement emerged as the common agenda of the two governments. The state showed a high level of ingenuity in retaining class-based identity, status and sources of income and in putting in place a support system for people to earn a living through soft loans to start their businesses. While the issue of evacuee property has come up in several scholarly works, relating to the way it was allotted on the basis of the proven or claimed property left behind, there is hardly a discussion of the huge project of reconstruction of the class structure itself. Both India and Pakistan exchanged information about property in the so-called 'agreed areas', which continued to be redefined. This provided the yardstick for the allocation of property that was seldom the same as claimed. It could be more or less as per the availability of evacuee property to be distributed, the level of corruption in the context of high claims supported by mostly dishonest witnesses, as well as the favourable attitude of the bureaucrat settlement commissioners belonging to the same area, same caste or same family as the petitioners. Locals grabbed half the evacuee houses and one-third of the shops.[190]

Corruption in the allotment of evacuee property to refugees involved the rehabilitation machinery along with the revenue administration, and the Punjab Muslim League leaders including Chief Minister Mamdot.[191] There followed a discourse of corruption whereby the political class was considered corrupt per se.[192] On their part, refugees filed massively fraudulent claims to their property abandoned in India.[193] Property emerged at the heart of the resettlement process. Sindhi nationalists accused the Mohajir-led government of grabbing property in the name of the resettlement of refugees.

Apart from property, jobs became the other means of reproducing the migrant class status in the new country. This applied to those officials who were 'transferred' to Pakistan from India and those who somehow managed to cross the border on foot after walking hundreds of miles as part of refugee marathons or who travelled by ship or by whatever means available. After reaching Pakistan, they were accommodated in jobs and services on the basis of documentary evidence or the demonstrated competence of individual officials.

Lower down, such arrangements as the 'Guzara Scheme' kept the allocation of landed property at the minimal production level, often at 12.5 acres of irrigated land or its equivalence.[194] The focus on property set the pattern for reconstruction and maintenance of the middle class in Pakistan, especially as 75 per cent of urban immovable property belonged to Hindus in pre-partition days. A large beneficiary of this largesse was the relatively enterprising section of migrants from Jallandhar, Amritsar, Ludhiana, Ambala, Hoshiarpur, Gurdaspur and other cities of East Punjab. The same pattern operated in urban Sindh, where migrants from UP, Bihar, CP and other areas from northern India obtained urban property left by the relatively prosperous Hindu professional and commercial middle classes. These migrants were able to start new businesses, expand the transactional network of commercial activity and install industry with the help of the development-orientated ruling elite of Pakistan.

West Punjab and East Punjab

One can understand post-partition West Punjab even better in comparison with East Punjab, which became part of India. East Punjab represented the antithesis of all that West Punjab symbolized. It was marginal not central to the state of India, with a population not exceeding 2 per cent of the national total as opposed to West Punjab at 38 per cent in Pakistan, and later 54 per cent after Bangladesh. The territory of East Punjab was reduced to one-fifth of the original province in British India after the creation of the two new provinces of Haryana and Himachal Pradesh. The obvious gain from the migration for the Akali movement was concentration of the Sikh community in northwestern districts of East Punjab, which could provide it with a demographic support base. However, the more the Akali Dal focused on the demand for a separate Punjabi province, the more Hindu communal organizations such as the Jana Sangh and Hindu Mahasabha became hostile and the greater became the inter-communal divide. Thus, unlike the West Punjab scenario, where the grand communal divide disappeared after the migration, East Punjab was given to a situation of bipolarity immersed in communal hostility. The two traditions of Congressite politics and Sikh revivalist Akali Dal politics competed for influence. In the face of the former's domination over state politics for a quarter of a century, the latter resorted to upholding the cause of state autonomy. That culminated in the Anandpur Sahib Resolution of 1973, which further sharpened the divide between the two communities.[195] It has been suggested that the green revolution led to economic competition between the two communities and alienated the educated unemployed among Sikh youth, who then formed the All-India Sikh Students Federation (AISSF).[196] One is reminded of the All Pakistan Mohajir Students Organisation (APMSO), which drew upon the alienated Mohajir youth of Karachi for its support and which similarly embraced political violence as a strategy in pursuit of nationalist goals.

The East Punjab situation deteriorated from the early 1980s, punctuated by Operation Bluestar in June 1984 and the assassination of Indira Gandhi in October 1984, followed by anti-Sikh riots and a series of repressive counter-insurgency measures for a decade. There is more to the Sikh nationalist movement in the 1980s and 1990s than what is described as the failure of a democratic governance that could have channelled the potential volatility of participant groups into constructive behaviour.[197] The Sikh movement ultimately failed to delegitimize the federal government in Delhi, which crushed it in a low-intensity war although at the cost of the militarization of Punjab.[198]

From East Punjab's perspective, India represented an ethnic democracy because it upheld 'a form of pan-Indian ethnicity' represented by Hinduism.[199] Nostalgia for Lahore-based Sikh rule in the late eighteenth and early nineteenth centuries generally provided inspiration for East Punjab's assertion of identity that was, however, incommensurate with the prevalent political and demographic realities of India. As opposed to the linguistic agnosticism of West Punjab, it was the Punjabi-based linguistic nationalism that represented the Sikhs' political vision and agenda. The Sikhs of East Punjab operated in the multiple identities of religion, ethnicity and state – Sikh, Punjab, India – which often conflicted and which were, even at the best of times, hardly as harmoniously integrated as the trio of Muslim, Punjab, Pakistan in West Punjab.

Table 1.3 Refugee settlement in East and West Punjab

West Punjab	Heart-land of Pakistan	Unity of community	Linguistic agnosticism	Concentric identities	Centralist/ unitarian
East Punjab	Rimland of India	Bipolarity	Linguistic nationalism	Conflicting identities	Provincial-ist/separatist

It is interesting to see how the ethnic profiles of certain communities in India and Pakistan got reversed after cross-migration. West Punjab continued to be the least ethnically conscious province of Pakistan, whereas a fierce ethnic movement was launched in East Punjab in India. Conversely, ethnic consciousness was least developed in UP in India, whereas the third generation of Mohajirs, a majority of whom belonged to UP, developed a militant ethnic movement in Pakistan. We can argue that the ethnic profile of a community was essentially defined by its positioning vis-à-vis the state as well as such vital sources of identity and legitimacy as language, geography and demography. Identification with the perceived all-Pakistan lingua franca, Urdu, neatly fitted with the ethnic sentiment of Punjab, as we shall discuss in Chapter 2 in the context of linguistic agnosticism. Similarly, Hindi in India not only served the ethno-national identity of its home state UP but also had a constituency spread over the Hindi belt and the rest of India. In geographical terms, UP in India and Punjab in Pakistan have a self-image of being the heartlands of India and Pakistan respectively, while Sikhs in East Punjab and Mohajirs in Sindh felt that they had been pushed to the periphery.

Nativization of a Migrant State

Pakistan initially operated as a migrant state until an indigenous revival took place in 1970.[200] The daunting challenge of settling 6.3 million refugees in West Pakistan spread dissatisfaction, frustration and anger among various sections of refugees. And yet no refugee group in modern history enjoyed more goodwill and material help in a more substantive sense than the Muslim refugees from India. Until 1947, both refugees and locals were co-nationals belonging to British India and co-ethnics in the case of Punjab. It was virtually an 'internal' migration. The secure position of refugees depended on the fact that the government was itself dominated by migrants. In December 1947, when the All-India Muslim League (AIML) Council met in Karachi, delegates from India accounted for 160 out of 300 members, along with 13 out of 23 members of the All-India Muslim League Working Committee.[201] The AIML's Central Parliamentary Board, which selected candidates for election to various provincial assemblies and later the Constituent Assembly of Pakistan, comprised three persons, all of them Mohajirs: Liaqat Ali, Khaliquzzaman and Sir Hussain Imam. The migrant-dominated central government distrusted provincial leaders because of their perceived anti-Muslim League stance before partition. The Muslim leadership of Punjab was converted to the Pakistan cause as late as 1946 when it shifted from the Unionist Party to the Muslim League. KP (then named North-West Frontier Province) came to the fold of Pakistan even later, through a controversial referendum held in July 1947. So did British Balochistan, where a controversial *jirga* was reportedly held for that purpose. That explains the suspicious attitude of the Mohajir-dominated Muslim League high command towards the party leaderships in the provinces that now constituted Pakistan.

However, the migrant leadership was acutely conscious of its inherently insecure position in Pakistan in terms of electoral politics. Prime Minister-designate Liaqat Ali Khan was not, at this stage, even a member of the Constituent Assembly. He and five other legislators were 'elected' in place of six members from East Bengal who vacated their seats for them. The message was clear: the migrant leadership could hardly be excited about the prospects of general elections. Their erstwhile constituencies had eroded with the disappearance of separate electorates in post-independence India.

The central government, led by migrants of both Mohajir and Punjabi extraction, chose ways and means of bypassing the Constituent Assembly, which had been elected by the Muslim members of the legislative assemblies of the majority provinces comprising Pakistan, and which therefore represented 'locals'. In this way, a dichotomous model of state authority came into being, with a party hierarchy and state bureaucracy dominated by migrants of both Punjabi and Mohajir extraction pitched against a local-dominated parliament. Out of 95 Indian Civil Service officers who opted for Pakistan, roughly two-thirds were Mohajirs and one-third Punjabi with a sprinkling of others. Mohajirs, who were only 3 per cent of the population, occupied 21 per cent of the jobs. The Mohajir youth generally took to bureaucratic careers in disproportionately high numbers. However, while Mohajirs occupied 33.5 per cent of higher positions in the federal bureaucracy in 1973 and 20 per cent of the Secretariat group in 1974, their share came down to 18.3 per cent in 1986 and 14.3 per cent in 1989 respectively.[202] The decline in Mohajir representation in the higher bureaucracy significantly contributed to discontent in that community.

The third major area of Mohajir domination was that of business and industry. There has been a lot of scholarly research about the mercantilist–industrialist class that was taking root in the new country.[203] Gujarati-speaking migrants from Bombay in India, especially from the Memon, Bohra and Khoja communities, were in the vanguard of the process of industrialization in Pakistan. Several leading businessmen had enjoyed Jinnah's confidence in Bombay and helped finance the Pakistan movement during the decade before partition. In turn, Jinnah played a role in mobilizing them to form Muslim chambers of commerce and later 'nation-building' companies for building the new state of Pakistan, including a Muslim airline.[204]

Regular contact between these businessmen and the Muslim League government in Karachi, both dominated by Mohajirs, played a significant role in shaping market dynamics in Pakistan. The policy initiative in the field of economic management of the new country lay firmly in the hands of the Mohajir-dominated bureaucracy to the exclusion of any legislative measures from parliament that would have favoured 'locals'.[205] The government also took up industrial projects under the Pakistan Industrial Development Corporation (PIDC) and then sold them to the private sector, thus diverting the start-up costs of private industrialization mostly to the public sector. In this way, the government heavily subsidized the national bourgeoisie led by Gujarati-speaking Mohajirs who controlled seven of the twelve largest industrial houses, followed by other industrial families who came from Delhi, Calcutta and Lahore.

The Mohajir-dominated bureaucracy and bourgeoisie made common cause with the Punjabi-dominated army in bringing about a 'bureaucratic polity' in Pakistan during the first quarter of a century after independence.[206] The 1970 election campaign targeted the so-called '22 families', a number popularized by the chief economist, Mahbubul Haq, who had criticized their amassing of wealth in the industrial, insurance and commercial sectors.[207] But in 1972, when the Bhutto government nationalized industry in the ten leading sectors, including electrical engineering, petrochemicals, iron and steel as well as rudimentary automotive assembly plants, the Mohajir bourgeoisie of Karachi was dealt a severe blow. (The cotton industry, which was located mainly in Punjab, was not nationalized.) Not surprisingly, while the business community in general turned against the Pakistan People's Party everywhere, Mohajir businessmen were particularly incensed about the colossal loss of their assets and the continuing insecurity in the commercial enterprise throughout the Bhutto period. Combined with nationalization, the labour reforms of the PPP government hit the business community hard. The Mohajir industrial elite shared with its non-Mohajir counterpart the overall insecurity at the hands of the 'socialist' PPP regime (1971–7). In 1972, it allegedly tried to wean industrial labour in Karachi away from the PPP by using the Urdu–Sindhi controversy to divide it along linguistic lines.

The 1970 election results justified the worst Mohajir fears of the regionalization of politics, augmented by the ascendancy of 'local' forces operating from leftist and ethnic platforms in West and East Pakistan respectively. Mohajirs were clearly out of touch with the popular currents of politics. After the military operation started in East Pakistan in March 1971, Mohajirs in both wings of the country generally identified themselves with the army. They desperately sought security against Bengalis by keeping the Awami League away from power in Islamabad and Dhaka, as well as against Sindhis by undermining the prospects of PPP from coming to power in Karachi. The PPP government grossly alienated Mohajirs, who saw it as a sons-of-the-soil movement of Sindhis. In 1977, Zia's martial law was welcomed because it 'delivered' Mohajirs from what was perceived as Sindhi rule. However, the Zia regime caused an influx of Punjabi military officers and employees in government departments, especially in the police. Mohajir fears of the prospects of the PPP's electoral victory in Sindh tied them to Zia, especially after the Movement for the Restoration of Democracy (MRD) launched agitation in 1983. Not surprisingly, the emergence of the MQM in 1984 led to widespread speculation about Zia's role in its creation.[208]

Mohajirs interpreted the two-nation theory in the context of the right of Indian Muslims to migrate to Pakistan. They were deeply involved in the fate of their own kith and kin across the border. They were acutely sensitive to the latter's need to get jobs and tried to help them migrate to Pakistan. Extra-territorial rather than land-based sources of identity shaped the Mohajir personality in Pakistan. In British India, the Muslim elite had comprised absentee landlords, who were essentially city-based amidst a large Hindu peasantry. Similarly, their language – Urdu – remained an urban phenomenon amidst a plethora of local Hindi dialects spoken in the large rural hinterland. A parallel can be drawn with Mohajirs after partition who lived in urban areas amidst a largely agrarian society of Sindh, and who spoke Urdu in the midst of a large Sindhi-speaking community. The Mohajir middle class lent its identity to all Mohajirs, both culturally and socially. Even after the loss of a major presence in the state machinery, Mohajirs still had a predominantly middle-class self-image. Indeed, Mohajirs became the epitome of the middle class, even though not supported by income, education, consumption patterns, social conservatism, and ideological orientations commensurate with that status in many cases.

The UP Muslims' espousal of the two-nation theory in British India was non-commensurate with the territorial foundations of their cherished goal of Pakistan. After partition, this territorial agnosticism took a leap forward. Mohajirs were neither identified with a specific territorial unit in Pakistan nor keen to develop such an identity. One can argue that the emergence of the 'migrant state' in Pakistan, followed by the 'indigenous revival' a generation later, brought about cataclysmic changes in terms of a shake-up of political attitudes and behaviour patterns. As opposed to the local Sindhi population, which was 'structured' in and around the family, village, district and province for generations (even centuries), Mohajirs came from towns and cities from north, central, east and west India, spoke different languages, practised different customs and traditions and came with different expectations for their new homeland. In the process, they were 'atomized' inasmuch as their familial, tribal, caste and sectarian ties broke down. This also put them in contrast with the other much larger community of refugees in Punjab who were re-settled as communities by keeping their agnate associations intact. This phenomenon of the 'atomization' of the Mohajir community contributed to the emergence of violence.[209] Migration sowed the seeds of conflict along ethnic lines by putting Mohajirs at the top and grossly alienating Sindhis, followed by the alleged 'appeasement' of Sindhis under the PPP governments in Islamabad and Karachi from the 1970s onwards.

Conclusion

In this chapter, I have covered partition as the maker and shaper of conflict across the broad spectrum of political life in post-independence Pakistan. I have argued that, unlike the conventional wisdom relating to the two-nation theory, Hindus, Muslims and Sikhs had lived in a pluralistic, syncretic and tolerant society along with their intermingled faiths for hundreds of years. It was only in the late nineteenth century that the emergent elites of these communities launched their respective revivalist movements that defined their exclusive faith-based political agendas. Partition — conceived by religion, delivered through violence, and commemorated by sacrifice — initiated an all-encompassing partitioning agenda. What was described by Jinnah as a constitutional problem of India morphed into a mini clash of civilizations, as the initiative slipped from the communities to the states proper. First, macro-level politics, defined by charismatic leadership and state ideology, penetrated micro-level politics during and after partition. Gradually, the macro-level leadership became distant, opaque and utopian, indeed regional and even global in ambition and imagination. The ideologies of secular India and Islamic Pakistan became a thorn in the side of the three generations of non-delivering ruling elites in the two countries respectively. The Muslim League high command in British India, which established the 'migrant' state in Pakistan, gave way to an ascendancy of the local elite in the 1970 elections. Punjab replaced UP as the power base of the new Muslim entity in the region. Migrants of both Punjab and Mohajir extraction shaped the national narrative for the following generations in terms of the perceived Hindu bellicosity next door.

I have discussed the two communities of Sindhis and Mohajirs as developing a sons-of-the-soil movement and a movement for nativization of a migrant community, respectively. The peculiar nature of the Mohajir community, which typically migrated as individuals or as nuclear families but not as whole communities, made it susceptible to recruitment into the militant cadres of the MQM. This chapter has analysed the turmoil in the domain of ethnic hierarchy, construction of ideology and projection of the national narrative in pursuit of the agenda of state-building. Partition and migration were no longer household words in Pakistan in the twenty-first century. And yet the nation lived in the eighth decade of its independent existence as conceived, produced, conjured-up, socialized and indoctrinated by those who made Pakistan three generations ago.

2

MASTER NARRATIVE

Introduction

Edward Said has mentioned that nations are in essence narrations because they narrativize their perceived destiny and seek to block other narratives from becoming rival sources of inspiration.[1] There has been a tendency amongst historians in recent times to revive the 'grand narrative' tradition. These 'positivist master-narratives' of history remain relevant insofar as they provide a mega-picture.[2] The concept of master narrative as used by Lyotard, more as a critique than an affirmation, refers to grand idea systems carrying 'unconscious effectivity' or simply the 'political unconscious'.[3] The idea is that a master narrative totalizes the plurality of events and gives a meaning to them, and thus makes sense of history. Master narratives are exclusive in nature because they belong to specific societies. For example, the Indian master narrative is inherently different from, and on various points diametrically opposed to, the Pakistani master narrative. Typically, the master narrative is a big story that encompasses small stories in its fold and lends authenticity to them. The study of master narrative provides a clue to the absolute minima of the intellectual self-expression of a nation. In Pakistan, as elsewhere, this narrative is played out on 24/7 television, in the daily press and through the educational curricula, political debate, street demonstrations and diplomatic activity.

Over time, it has transformed certain ideological and policy orientations into 'givens', such as the establishment of Pakistan in the name of Islam, Kashmir as the lifeline of the country, and language politics being detrimental to national integration per se.

The master narrative of Pakistan is steeped in conflict. Racine has pointed to the country's preponderant conspiratorial perspective – the 'India syndrome' – rooted in fear and insecurity.[4] In the early years after partition, the Hindu–Muslim dichotomy underscored the nation's regional perspective. After Bangladesh, Pakistan moved away from looking at India face-to-face to developing back-to-back relations with that country. It moved into the Middle East in a big way in pursuit of jobs, businesses and professions.[5] There has been a grand 'Arabist shift' in terms of moving from the centuries-old Iranian and Central Asian Islam to Wahhabist Islam.[6] Saudi extremism combined with jihadism in the context of the Afghanistan war after 9/11 massively pushed the country to a world-of-Islam perspective couched in a clash of civilizations thesis. Pakistan moved from Westophilia in the 1950s to Westophobia from the 1990s onwards in the context of various regional conflicts where Muslims were perceived to be in the position of underdog, such as in Bosnia, Chechnya, Kosovo, Afghanistan and Iraq. At home, a battle of cultures ensued after the state-sponsored national project sought to unify the nation by promoting Islamic culture. After Bangladesh, the Indus civilization was defined as a putative territorial foundation of the state for (W) Pakistan. However, the quest for identity with a little known pre-historic people failed to attract many adherents. The leftist narrative that emerged from the platform of the Progressive Writers Association (PWA) and the Pakistan Communist Party faced a nationalist fervour that would not allow space for a discourse projecting Hindu–Muslim unity, issues of class and gender, and tolerance across social and cultural divisions. In Pakistan, bellicosity towards India is not only a foreign policy 'given' but also a sentiment incessantly cultivated and preserved as state policy.[7] At the other end, despite close ties with the USA, which peaked during the strategic military alliances under Ayub, Zia and Musharraf, people generally adopted a hostile attitude towards the USA especially after 9/11. Public discourse changed its dynamics in response to external stimuli as and when it impinged on the people's primordial commitments. At home, various doctrinal currents of opinion have been driven by faith-based hostility against other religious communities. I plan to dwell on those aspects of the master narrative that play a significant role in providing a direction to the nation in matters of self-perception and producing a collective sense of agenda.

Shaping the National Discourse

The phrase 'master narrative' became popular to describe the leading discourse of a nation that shapes people's minds, attitudes and policies. It found a cultural expression in various forms ranging from literary writings to performing arts and research scholarship. It includes a long gestation period of ideas and thoughts that not only predates the current discourse but also determines its ideological contours. It provides the social and political contexts for defining the nation's historical legacy, cultural framework and future vision. Frost considers history as narrative in terms of its use of time – both static and changing – as a plot, as the principle of storytelling and as a sequence of events linking causes and effects.[8] The master narrative includes 'memory texts',[9] which can include iconic photographs, museums and commemorations of significant days.

Of course, the very expression 'master narrative' connotes that there are other narratives as well. The latter do not carry the potential for wide acceptance as compared to the master narrative and are often opposed to it. In Pakistan, as elsewhere, the master narrative is not simply the official discourse on policy and ideology; indeed, it is possible to have in power governments, elected or otherwise, that do not fully circumscribe to this narrative. For example, the Pakistan Peoples Party (PPP) government of Z. A. Bhutto (1971–7) often transgressed the chartered path of the 'establishment' in pursuit of its 'socialist' agenda, which appeared on the party pamphlets, in daily and weekly papers and in posters carrying the message: 'East is Red'. The Bhutto government's 'socialist' idiom and radical educational, labour, administrative and land reforms extended beyond the ideological framework of the state defined by an Islamist and status-quo orientation. At the other end, the ulema parties of various persuasions, which formed the Muttahida Majlis Amal (MMA) government in Peshawar (2002–7), went beyond the doctrinal approaches and behavioural patterns of Islamic modernists who had always been the custodians of ideology and morality of the state. In 2006, the MMA government passed a Hasba Bill that provided for 'moral policing' along Islamic lines by giving enormous powers to the provincial Ombudsman. It was a kind of Pakistani edition of the Taliban's vice and virtue department.[10] President Musharraf filed a Reference in the Supreme Court under Article 186 against the revised Hasba Bill 2006, with the plea that it would create a parallel judicial system. The Supreme Court invalidated the bill.[11] For its part, the Musharraf government passed the Women's Protection Bill in November 2006, which relaxed various provisions of the Hudood Ordinances by shifting them to the Pakistan Legal Code. While ideology conceived the nation, and demography acted as midwife, the task of building a credible cartography of nationalism emerged as an interminable exercise in identity construction.

Territory may have arrived late on the scene but the new states faced the perceived challenge of geopolitics. After the Second World War, the use of the term 'geopolitics' was discarded for a generation for its fearsome connotations of German justification of domination over Europe. Henry Kissinger seemed to revive the term 'geopolitics' in an indirect way as a defining variable of foreign policy.[12] However, the language of geopolitics became a constant reference to the emergent national boundaries that led to a zero-sum view of the world, whereby identity was tasked with the ominous mission of serving as the boundary against 'constructed dangers'.[13] Identity, or more precisely the cultural discourse, presented the worldview in a microcosm that was based on a framework of inclusion and exclusion as part of a system of knowledge production.[14] The pursuit of a national discourse in Pakistan, as elsewhere, involved: a projection of the 'naturalness' of the national territory drawing on antiquity; homogeneity of the national culture; a mission transcending the borders by fostering a cultural zone, such as the world of Islam; and a 'geopolitical code' that would provide a list of friendly and non-friendly nations.

The Civilizational Metaphor

It is instructive to follow the discussion in a colloquium organized for Radio Pakistan Lahore in 1954, which brought forth the essential components of the debate that dominated the cultural narrative for decades to come.[15] One comes across some major and recurring themes that point to the emergent intellectual capital of the new state. The colloquium focused on Islamic civilization, which generally and rather ironically transcended specific references to the territorial state of Pakistan, except for some lone voices. Khalifa Abdul Hakim claimed that Islamic civilization was not only the legatee of the achievements of human civilization spread over thousands of years but that it also produced intellectuals better than Aristotle and Plato, such as Ghazali, Rumi, Farabi and Bu Ali Sina. Another claim was that Islam introduced democracy, which was its special gift to mankind.[16] Others were not so sure about the achievements of Islamic civilization because its basic tenets were soon forgotten and it had been overtaken by dynasticism, capitalism and a life of luxury. When the Islamic world, including the Mughal empire, was at the pinnacle of its glory in terms of music, painting and architecture, that would have been rendered un-Islamic by the pious caliphs.[17]

The colloquium experienced some awkward moments when participants discussed questions about the institution of slavery under Muslim rule, a point raised by the chairperson, Justice S. A. Rehman.[18] Opinions ranged from extreme cynicism to acute moralization. One of the leading literary figures, Jamil Jalibi, saw life in Pakistan suffering from a crisis of insecurity and an inferiority complex that characterized religion, philosophy, politics, economy, morality and both individual and collective life. In his view, the crisis of meaninglessness had extinguished the creative spark and sense of humour, whereby selfishness, and irresponsible behaviour had taken over. Muslims lost their traditional ideas, mores and manners, but did not enter a new set of ideas and norms. Thus, they were in a no man's land.[19]

Jalibi's instinctive orientation towards a worldview based on a dichotomy between Islam and the West – which was shared by most of his contemporary intellectuals – led to his calling 'our' culture normative and visionary as opposed to Western culture, which was profoundly this-worldly in its essence. In Jalibi's view, Sir Syed had sought to interpret our normative culture through the scientific perspective of the West. Thus, after independence Pakistan had been caught between the old and the new, between the traditional and the modern, and between the normative vision and scientific enquiry.[20] Participants generally believed that Pakistan was born out of a cultural vision and that, even if Muslims were not a nation before 1940, they had developed a cultural sense of being distinct from other Indian people. Accordingly, Indo-Iranian culture, known in common parlance as the Mughal heritage, provided the essence of the culture of the new nation.[21]

But what would happen if Pakistan defined its culture in terms of aspirations and expressions emanating from within its territory? Would Mir and Hali, the two great poets of Urdu literature, have to be disowned, simply because they did not belong to the areas now included in the country?[22] Ibadat Barelvi narrated the religious and cultural origins of Pakistan, dotted with such names as Shah Waliullah, Syed Ahmed Barelvi, Shah Ismail Shaheed, Sir Syed, Iqbal and Jinnah.[23] Thus, in his reckoning, these — one religious scholar, two 'Wahhabi' martyrs in jihad against the Sikh rule in Punjab in 1832, an Anglophone reformer, a pan-Islamist poet and a modern political leader — were all considered part of the legacy of the Pakistan movement.

Dr Wazir Agha pointed to culture as a collection of concentric circles surrounding a person, a family, a region within two rivers or mountains, provinces, the nation such as Pakistan, South Asia, Asia, and then the world, that would look different from the cultures of other planets to other inhabitants.[24] Agha represents the duality of the modern Pakistani cultural perspective. While he is happy that Western civilization has been breaking the fossilized Pakistani culture, he is also happy about the quest for the religious and spiritual sources of Muslim inspiration that was originally and comprehensively started by Iqbal. Indeed, he welcomed the process of 'regression' that carried the prospects of a cultural renaissance.[25]

Saleem Ahmed also addressed the need for the formulation of an intellectual strategy as a response to the perceived onslaught from Western civilization. He gave a critique of Iqbal, who had argued in favour of reconstruction of religious thought through innovation on the one hand and positive engagement with Western science, based on empirical, rational and inductive method — that he had deemed to be close to the spirit of Islam — on the other. Saleem Ahmed found the whole logic of cohabitation between Islam and Western science belaboured.[26] He interpreted it as the modernists' greatest dilemma in Pakistan. They had recently mobilized a comprehensive Islamic identity in the form of the two-nation theory, but they also belonged to the most Westernized section of the population, which was exposed to the dynamics of the larger intellectual, scientific, literary and artistic achievements of the West.

In this context, one can refer to Muhammad Hasan Askari, who typically reflected on the dominant themes of the national culture during the first quarter of a century after independence. As an Urdu literary writer, a master intellectual and a freewheeling journalist, Askari commented on cultural aspects of the new nation from the 'liberal' perspective, even though he took the followers of the PWA to task for not being cognizant of the mission and reality of Pakistan as a Muslim homeland. In his view, there were three categories of intellectuals who dilated on the culture question under Muslim suzerainty.

First, there were those who were in favour of Arab culture as it had existed at the time of Islam's emergence in the sixth century. They wanted Arabic to be the national language of Pakistan and even wanted people to wear the Arab dress. Askari believed that this shortsighted view of Islam was against the spirit of religion. Askari argued that there was no Muslim architecture per se, because Muslims borrowed from Roman, Egyptian, Iranian and Hindu architectural traditions.[27] Elsewhere, Askari talked about the architectural borrowings, such as the minaret from Byzantine buildings, the dome from India as well as the use of the specific Indian symbol of the lotus on top of the dome.[28] The second cultural perspective was rooted in the Indo–Muslim civilization, epitomized by Mughal architecture and the Urdu language. Muslims all over India had responded to this perceived common heritage that led to the Pakistan project. The third category of cultural activists comprised the regional intelligentsia. They wanted to define the national culture in terms of various ethnic cultures. In the end, Askari argued for keeping the window open to Western culture. In the twentieth century, he argued, it was not possible to avoid Western leadership if we wanted to develop an energetic culture of our own.[29]

A persistent theme that underscored this discussion was the shared cultural legacy of the Indo–Muslim civilization over and above the local cultures. Askari maintained that Muslims from the Muslim minority provinces had supported the Pakistan movement and rendered sacrifices essentially for the preservation of pan-Indian Muslim culture.[30] In Anwar Sadeed's words, those Muslims who actively participated in the Pakistan movement but stayed on in India rendered unfathomable sacrifices, and Pakistanis were deeply indebted to them.[31] In this way, Indo–Muslim civilization continued to be the supreme source of inspiration for the first generation of the intellectual and political elite after partition.

The foundation stone of the two-nation theory was laid not by geography but by history. Some sections of the Urdu-speaking migrant elite harked back to what was described in nostalgic terms as Ganga-Jamuni culture as a microcosm of the UP culture in pursuit of their ethnic and linguistic identity.[32] In Mohammad Taqi's view, geography did not fit into the scheme of things.[33] Jalibi also argued that Pakistan was born out of historical rather than geographical consciousness.[34] Some found in the Indus thesis an attempt to undermine the two-nation theory by projecting pre-Islamic civilizational artefacts and thus sanctifying the Dravidian and Indo–Aryan civilizations.[35] However, the perceived requirement for cultivating a separate territorial identity for Pakistan as part of a state-building project, especially after Bangladesh, kept the Indus civilization thesis from being pushed to oblivion. Indeed, many stretched their imagination to link the Muslim ascendency in India historically with the territory of Pakistan. S. M. Ikram mentions Akbar's birthplace in Sindh, his ministers Adual Fazal and Faizi belonging to Sindh and a later minister, Saadullah, to Punjab, a leading academic Abdul Hakim to Sialkot and architects Ahmed and Hamid to Lahore, all located in (West) Punjab.[36] The intellectual narrative sought to separate the 'true spirit' of Islamic civilization from the mundane practices of the Indo–Muslim civilization, whereby the former had provided for knowledge, pursuit of wisdom and personal enhancement through scientific thinking whereas the latter fell short of it due to not being Islamic enough.[37] At the other end, the intelligentsia tried to resolve the perceived anomalous situation of belonging to regional cultures of Pakistan whilst at the same time being part of the collective Islamic 'nation', and sought to justify both.[38]

Muhammad Askari to a high degree represented the mainstream elite's thinking about the unity of the Muslim world, in fact even about an international Muslim government. In his view, what blunted this ambitious agenda were the selfish motives of kings, tribal lords, and capitalists, all of them traitors.[39] The undercurrent of this thinking was that Muslims were now placed in a very important position on the chessboard of global politics, because of the Arab oil reserves and the emergent Muslim bloc, and that this 'opportunity' must not be missed.[40]

One finds a raw version of Gunder Frank's theory of underdevelopment of the Third World in Askari's claim that Europe's prosperity owed a great deal to the Eastern, especially Muslim, countries.[41] However, the same writer reacted sharply to an editorial in *Dawn* (Karachi) that lambasted Governor General Ghulam Mohammad for appreciating the Hindu holiday of Dussehra as a symbol of war between good and evil. He forcefully reminded *Dawn* and the like, of the intellectual borrowings of Muslims from other cultures. He regretted that, in Pakistan, a thinking mind itself was considered un-Islamic.[42] At the same time, he argued that European orientalists had been engaged in disfiguring Islam – in fact all the Eastern religious traditions – either consciously or unconsciously, since the eighteenth and especially the nineteenth century onwards.[43] Among other recurring themes taken up by the intelligentsia were the claims that Islam was spread not by sword but by the teachings of Sufis.[44] Hafiz Mahmud Shirani developed a thesis that Urdu had its origin in Punjab purportedly to prove that this language had an affinity with the territory of the new state; however, this claim was repudiated by several scholars.[45] This meta-narrative massively represented the emergent 'constructed ideological edifice of a unified Muslim moral community'.[46]

The left in Pakistan represented a ramshackle movement after partition because it lost ground in the face of the strident and triumphalist ideology of the two-nation theory. Its relatively weak participation in shaping the new discourse in post-partition politics has been attributed to a kind of brain drain, as the prominent Hindu and Sikh Marxists had left for India.[47] The Communist Party of Pakistan (CPP), led by Sajjad Zaheer, launched its publication *Naya Zamana* to increase party funds. Such publications, along with literary journals linked to the Progressive Writers Association (PWA), such as *Sawera*, *Adab-e-Latif* and *Naqush*, were often banned for their alleged 'anti-state' message. The PWA was founded by young students and activists in England in the 1930s who were inspired by the Russian revolution. Back in India, they operated under the umbrella of the Congress, which was the leading 'left' wing force at that time.[48] They wished to rescue their culture from decadent feudal elements, foreign imperialism and capitalism. The idea was to broaden the horizons of the writers' imagination.[49]

Sajjad Zaheer believed that CPP workers should be part of the study circles of the new All Pakistan Progressive Writers Association (APPWA).[50] The 1949 manifesto of APPWA criticized 'non-progressive' writers for towing the official line, for lack of social consciousness and the inability to raise their voice against the ruling classes. It opposed followers of the ideology of art for art's sake and those who claimed to write 'Pakistani literature' that spread hatred against India, as well as Islamic writers who wanted to establish Sharia rule.[51] Over time, writers such as Manto, who wrote about perverted sexual behaviour among other issues, were dubbed escapists who possessed a sick mentality and who avoided the real problems of the people.[52] One of the critics of the APPWA, Muhammad Hasan Askari, felt that the progressives were alienated from their own Muslim culture and were not loyal to the idea of Pakistan. He attacked Sajjad Zaheer and other stalwarts of the movement for distorting Muslim culture and supporting India.[53]

The weakness of progressive politics constrained the options for continuing to operate in public life as 'a viable socio-political alternative'.[54]As the legatee of a relatively dynamic leftist movement in British India, the remainder of the left in Pakistan comprised ex-members of the Communist Party of India led by urban-based intelligentsia,[55] and political workers and professionals operating through trade unions and peasant associations.[56] Leftist groups, including CPP, Azad Pakistan Party (APP), Mazdoor Kissan Party (MKP) and Pakistan Socialist Party (PSP), looked at successive governments as pawns in the hands of American imperialism. They interpreted the power of the state in Pakistan in terms of the American superordinate role in shaping the framework of politics and foreign policy in the country.[57] The greater the perceived repression of a military government, the more severe was the criticism of the US policy of supporting military dictators in Pakistan. As critics of successive authoritarian governments of Pakistan, the leftists kept anti-Americanism alive in large sections of the mobilized public.[58] However, within a quarter of a century, mass discontent outgrew the ideological framework of the Marxism–Leninism espoused by the leftists of the independence generation. Trade unionists, public activists and progressive students and teachers overtook the relatively sophisticated urban intellectuals of the previous generation who talked through the idiom of 'scientific socialism'. The 1968–9 anti-Ayub movement was the high-water mark of 'leftist' politics even though it was not led by a communist or socialist party. Ayub and his colleagues in the army were dubbed American stooges. This profile mobilized millions of people against the ruling set-up.[59] The 'new' left in (W) Pakistan was represented by the populist leader Z. A. Bhutto, and by a large section of enterprising youth in his party struggling to enter the state system through the ballot. Under Bhutto (1971–7), the leading idiom of politics remained 'leftist' and anti-imperialist, though largely couched in the emerging framework of Third Worldism.[60]

Construction of the Hindu Demon

The master narrative of Pakistan has drawn massively on construction of the Hindu demon, personified as India after partition. If religion, as propounded from the AIML's platform, was to operate as the grand mobilizer of Muslims, the party needed two things. First, it needed to avoid intra-religious sub-identities that would involve not only variations and hostilities based on the creed but also contradictory practices in religious matters. Second, it needed to construct a demon and struggle to beat it, to escape from it, run away from it and, in the process, unite its own ranks to fight it.

Hindus provided the demon. The construction of the Hindu demon was taken up in earnest before and during the active pursuit of the Pakistan agenda. Jinnah called Gandhi the 'dictator of the Congress', a party that he understood 'as a fascist and authoritarian body' that was committed to 'the Hindu renaissance' and 'Hindu *raj* all over India'.[61] As Hindu revivalism represented the emergent narrative in British India, often linked with Hindu Mahasabha, Jinnah declared the Mahasabha and the Congress as two sides of the same coin.[62] The Muslim League championed the counter-discourse of Muslim nationalism that covered history, art, literature, language, icons, business activity, jobs and dress code. It made references to global Islam for seeking authentication of belief and practice and declaration of a common cause with the larger Muslim entity. It was claimed that the two nations – Muslims and Hindus in India – had always lived side by side as separate entities, sharing minimal cultural and political space.[63] This discourse found a fertile ground in Pakistan after partition. It was claimed that Hindus had masqueraded as faithful to Muslims but actually acted as traitors. They had tried to make Muslims fight with each other – for example, Babar with Ibrahim Lodhi in 1526. Hindus made brothers of Hamayun fight among themselves. They tried to convert Akbar to Hinduism but failed. They also tried the same with Jehangir and Shah Jahan but did not succeed. Finally, the British fulfilled the objective of Hindus by defeating the Muslims.[64] Most ironically, Dr Syed Abdullah followed a strange logic by holding the ruled (Hindus) responsible for discriminating against the rulers (Muslims). He criticized Hindus for not establishing social relations with Muslims, and for shunning employment under Muslim rulers up until Mughal times. In his view, the Hindu sense of distinctiveness turned into hostility against Muslims once the latter's hold over the government slackened.[65] Did the two communities live together, borrow customs, languages and traditions from each other and often fight the British rulers together – most prominently in 1857 – or was the division between the two communities always present in 'the collective unconscious' of Muslims that was now ignited by the prospects of withdrawal of British suzerainty?[66]

Most interestingly, the narrative of Jinnah's emissary to the Middle East, Sir Firoz Khan Noon, in the immediate post-partition period represented the ideas of the Muslim elite of the independence generation. In a write-up titled, 'The Position in Pakistan and India', which he circulated during his visit to Ankara in November 1947, Sir Firoz argued that Muslims wanted partition because 'they did not want to be slaves of Hindus'[67] who had 'been our slaves for over 1000 years'.[68] Now seething with 'a spirit of revenge',[69] Hindus wanted 'if possible to exterminate Islam'.[70] He claimed that Hindus under the British 'became richer and richer and started an economic strangulation of the Muslamans'.[71] Hindus 'had become accustomed to be a subject race'[72] under Muslim and then British domination. But 'the Muslims have been a free and conquering people and still have in their minds the value of freedom'.[73]

Early after partition, the master narrative of the country picked up on the indictment of Hinduism. In I. H. Qureshi's view, Hinduism 'had become a matter of superstition and ritual', and was thus the basic reason for the stagnation of Hindu society when Islam entered India.[74]

According to this narrative, the 'Muslim polemic against idolatry was unrelenting, merciless and vigorous'.[75] There was no possibility of assimilation between 'the austere beliefs of Islam and the ideas of the Varmamargis who indulged in sexual orgies as an act of worship'.[76] This narrative also revealed Muslims' fear at the possibility of their assimilation within the fold of Hinduism given the latter's tendency to accommodate diversity of opinion. Indeed, I. H. Qureshi enacted a dialogue between the two religions that put Hinduism on the defensive:

> Hinduism said to Islam: 'You have come with a philosophy which has considerable appeal for many of my adherents. I cannot win in this struggle ... I must save as many as I can from amongst those who are too enamoured of your way of thinking. You have already been stealing my sheep. I know you will steal many more; but I will save as many as I can by giving them in my own fold all that you have to offer'.[77]

Qureshi was not happy that Gandhi was described as an 'apostle of Christian values', and 'hailed as the most Christ-like man of his age'.[78] Gross reductionism that was bound to shape opinions about a persistent clash of two religions across centuries became the substance and style of the master narrative of Pakistan. This profoundly influenced the educational texts, which shaped the image of Hindus in an extremely negative way. The textbooks taught in schools before partition were not immediately and drastically changed: it took a generation to create a fully-fledged demon out of Hindus for students at a tender age. Especially under Zia's Islamization programme from the 1970s onwards, school and college textbooks smacked of hateful, spiteful and distasteful discourse about Hindus and Hindu civilizational artefacts such as temples. K. K. Aziz pointed to the negative portrayal of Hindus as a vocation. His critical examination of the school and college textbooks is now part of the classic literature on the subject. He quotes from the textbooks:

> The Hindus wanted to control the Government of India after independence. The British sided with the Hindus.[79] The Muslims came to this country bringing with them a clean and elegant culture and civilization .... The Hindus are indebted to Muslim culture and civilization today.[80] Hindus in order to wreak their vengeance for the partition of

the country … indulged in large-scale looting, raping, arson, murder and destruction.[81] The Hindu elements did not want any proper agreement between the two wings i.e., East and West Pakistan.[82] The advent of Islam in India reformed Hindu society…. Thereby Hindu religion of the olden times came to an end.[83]

A. H. Nayyar and Ahmed Saleem produced a revealing compendium of ideologically motivated discourses, *The Subtle Subversion*, that brought out hundreds of abhorrent descriptions of Hindus in the school textbooks. They quote:

> Hindus very cunningly succeeded in making the British believe that the Muslims were solely responsible for the [1857] rebellion.[84] … [T]he British announced political reforms. Muslims were not eligible to vote.[85] The Hindus who have always been opportunists cooperated with the English.[86] Hindus did not respect women.[87] Hindus worship in temples which are very narrow and dark places, where they worship idols. Only one person can enter the temple at a time. In our mosques, on the other hand, all Muslims can say their prayers together.[88]

As per these observations, Hindus were largely understood as co-conspirators with the British against Muslims, whereby the British showered all kinds of favours on the former, be it land, jobs or education. The textbooks directly attacked Hindus about their treatment of women or their places of worship. Hindus were held responsible for the exodus of Muslims (from India) without any mention of cross-migration.[89]

> The British confiscated all lands [from the Muslims] and gave them to Hindus.[90] The British, with the assistance of the Hindus, adopted a cruel policy of mass exodus against the Muslims to erase them as a nation.[91]

It is interesting to see Chaudhary Rahmat Ali writing about the Muslim empire in India in grossly speculative and visionary terms. Alyssa Ayres quotes him:

During the 11th century the Ghaznavid Empire comprised what is now Pakistan and Afghanistan. During the 12th century the Ghaznavids lost Afghanistan, and their rule came to be confined to Pakistan. ... By the 13th century, Pakistan had spread to include the whole of Northern India and Bengal... Under the Khiljis Pakistan moved further Southward to include a greater part of Central India and the Deccan... During the 16th century, 'Hindustan' disappeared and was completely absorbed in Pakistan.[92]

This is a weird depiction of Hindustan as Pakistan for hundreds of years, which is indeed unrealistic and historically totally anomalous. This preoccupation with the idea of Pakistan going back to late medieval India, and even to 'geological times', draws on Choudhary Rahmat Ali's visionary depiction of the existence of Pakistan moving from the eighth to the eleventh and thirteenth centuries – when it is called Pak Empire – onward to 1318, 1398, 1525, 1605 and 1700 when it covered almost the whole of India. The nomenclature for this 'empire' reverted to Pakistan in 1795 onward to 1933 and 1940 and to Pak Millat in 1942.[93] On a different note, as per the research of Bahuria and Shehzad, poet Amir Khusro of the fourteenth century was described as a 'lowborn Hindu slave' who had transferred all administrative powers to Hindus, who 'openly insulted Islam, dishonored mosques and used copies of the Quran as pedestals for idols'.[94] In reality, however, Amir Khusro belonged to the Turkish nobility born of an Indian mother. He has been one of the towering figures in the history of Indian music for 700 years. Mastery over his *ragas* has been considered the first step to maturity for all musicians and vocalists, Hindus and Muslims alike.[95]

The new nation moved towards a dichotomous worldview that had been substantively cultivated along a binary opposition between Muslim and Hindu identities. Previously, only powerful elite groups were defined in terms of their faith, while religious boundaries were opaque and non-functional for the general masses in the framework of everyday life. Now, religion defined the mass public itself in its mode of operation as an instrument of general mobilization against the community across the fence. Dichotomy became the instrument for understanding the self ever afterwards. In March 2016, the National Assembly of Pakistan (NA) passed a resolution to declare Holi, Diwali and Easter holidays for minorities. That came as a surprise to many

Pakistanis, who had forgotten the once pluralist and tolerant nature of the local society when non-Islamic holy days used to be celebrated as public holidays.[96]

'Paranoidistan'[97]

The US Afghan war and the involvement of Pakistan in it in an atmosphere of total mistrust made Washington wonder if it was dealing with 'Paranoidistan, a state that suspects that every US move is designed to weaken Pakistan for the benefit of a secret U.S. alliance with India'.[98] The conspiracy theory has established deep roots in the mindset of educated Pakistanis. It has been argued that conspiracy was the tool of the weak and the uninformed, who knew the effect but not the cause. Anderson makes a case that conspiracy theories 'deserve more respect'.[99] As the institutionalized discourse, these theories are 'self-sustaining, self-referencing, and self-evidencing'.[100] In Pakistan, political activists and intellectuals often criticize each other for following a conspiracy view of things. Intelligentsia from various backgrounds, including religio-sectarian, ethno-nationalist and leftist ideologues as well as the 'establishment' wizards, all have their respective conspiratorial worldviews. Husain Haqqani has covered the subject of conspiracy theory in Pakistan exhaustively.[101] Similarly, Huma Yusaf has expounded over conspiracy in detail.[102]

People selectively pick up 'facts' from international conferences, seminars and media to make and shape paranoia, whereby the world is perceived as an enemy out to devour Pakistan. Expatriate Pakistanis project and promote paranoia vis-à-vis Europe, the USA and the Gulf, and transfer it to their next generations. In Pakistan, conspiracy generally breeds fear and insecurity, whereby people are socialized into thinking that the military is the only saviour. Conspiracy theories help to divert attention from economic and political failures at home. Similarly, any kind of negative profile in the international community is described as enemy propaganda. There is a certain narcissist mindset that believes that 'Pakistan is simply too important in geostrategic terms to be ignored'.[103]

A cursory look at the public discourse reveals several examples of a mindset that feeds into a right-wing nationalist agenda. In this discourse, birth control is a Western conspiracy to reduce the population of Asia and Africa.[104] The brutal rape and murder of 6-year-old Zainab Ansari from Kasur in 2019 was attributed to women's 'provocative dress' that invited rape.[105] Violence against Ahmadis was justified because they were non-Muslims.[106] Pakistan's Nobel Prize physicist, Professor Abdus Salam, was accused of disclosing Pakistan's nuclear secrets to the USA since he was an Ahmadi.[107] In response to PTI worker Ayesha Gulalai's allegations of sexual harassment against the PTI leader Imran Khan in 2017, the party workers referred to an old British gazette that allegedly described the whole Gulalai clan as untrustworthy.[108]

In Husain Haqqani's view, conspiracy is a product of state ideology, public policy, or private instinct. Selective pieces of information, an agenda of war against the ghosts in the dark and rampant insecurity are intertwined and combined in a closed mind used by those ranging from the top decision makers to the people at the bottom.[109] Pursuit of conspiracy by the state or its agencies or by self-confessed defenders of the nation seeks to achieve a national objective which must, therefore, be justified in the noblest of terms.[110] The authenticity of the 'national cause' sanctifies conspiracy. Sometimes the supporters of a conspiracy theory later confess to the need for spreading false news or views in pursuit of the national interest. Conspiracy needs a devil against whom one can devise a conspiratorial narrative. It could of course be India or the USA or Israel, but also political adversaries at home such as Benazir Bhutto in 1990 or Nawaz Sharif in 2017. General Shahid Aziz saw conspiracy against Islam hatched by Freemasons and Zionists, amongst others.[111] The state propagates a situation of insecurity all around, which is infested with conspiracy underscored by the evil designs of the enemies. There is a logical step from conspiracy to treason. Thus, treasonable charges have been levied on people ranging from politicians to party workers, intellectuals, and bloggers who cross the Rubicon.

Various aspects of the nation's present, past and future provide conspiratorial narratives. The partition of Punjab provides an interesting example of paranoia. The writer of a regular column, 'Punjabi Themes', in *Dawn* builds a fantastic theory of an imperial design to cut Punjab to size in 1947 while building on the findings of one Lubna Saif's doctoral thesis about the province. His observations reflect the mindset of a 'progressive' Punjabi nationalist that is symptomatic of a common malaise among his counterparts from other ethnic and leftist activists and intellectuals. Drawing on Saif's research, the writer arrives at the following horrendous and totally false conclusions. Punjab was the target of the American, British and Pakistani spy agencies because it was the hub of what were considered subversive communist activities. Punjab's partition was carried out by the British in such a way that the two states should continue to fight permanently. Punjabis fought invaders from the West (Alexander) and the East (the British). The colonial government faced 'the wrath of Punjabis' such as in Jallianwala Bagh. The USA and the UK tried to further weaken Pakistani Punjab by dividing it whereby one British scholar, Professor Christopher Shackle, floated the theory of Siraiki being a separate language and not merely a dialect of Punjab. Since Punjab had demonstrated its anti-imperialist and anti-status quo orientations in the 1970 elections, and Bhutto had brought together most of the anti-American Muslim countries on one platform during the 1974 Islamic Summit, American imperialism toppled Bhutto's government. This finally led his successor, General Zia, to recognize Siraiki as a separate language. The teaching of Punjabi at the primary level will strengthen Punjab against American imperialism.[112] Many would find in it intellectual perversity of activists and writers pursuing various causes at the national and sub-national levels by indulging in an irrational discourse. Protagonists of conspiracy theory would in turn accuse them of being Western stooges.

Paranoia has taken deep roots in the mindset of the educated Pakistanis. There was a strong reaction against the publication of Malala Yusufzai's book, *I Am Malala*, in the form of another book, *I Am Not Malala*, written by one Mirza Kashif Ali, president of the All Pakistan Private Schools Federation (APPSF). This federation banned Malala's book in 173,000 of its affiliated schools and planned to move the courts to get the book banned officially. Mirza's book made staggering allegations against Malala as per the following observations. Malala was the creation of the CIA. She was an accomplice of Al-Qaida and ISIS. She was a 'double agent' and a traitor. She was a suspicious character because the 'timing' of the attack on her had coincided with an anti-US peace march. She was considered a Pakistani version of Bangladeshi author, Taslima Nasrin, in terms of her critique of the maltreatment of minorities in Pakistan. Her educational endowment, Malala Fund, was described as a move for secularizing education and 'modernising and westernising young minds' in Pakistan.[113] The youngest Nobel

Prize winner fell a victim to the conspiracies that sought to transform her into a villain. Right-wing commentators like Orya Maqbool Jan painted an extremely villainous portrait of Malala Yusufzai.

A Nation in Denial: History, Territory, and Language

In this section, I deal with a deep-rooted historical agnosticism in Pakistan. By this, I mean that the makers and shapers of the master narrative have muddled through the dilemma of what Anthony Smith calls territorializing the memory, by way of living in a place and appropriating it for identity formation.[114] In the case of Pakistan, the place in history that motivated and inspired the project of state formation is not the place that defines the state at present. Looking at it differently, the territory of Pakistan represents the Muslim majority provinces whereas the two-nation theory had applied to all Muslims of British India beyond numbers that would make it a nation.

Apart from history and territory, there is a third problematic area of identity formation, i.e. language, which has posed a great challenge to conventional wisdom about the process of nation formation, especially in the context of the historical West. In classical terms, language fashioned the nation, most significantly Hebrew in the case of Israel but also generally as the 'soul of the people' expressed through their mother tongue.[115] Pakistan faced the dilemma of its national language, Urdu, being the mother tongue of only 3 per cent of the population, which rose to 7.8 per cent after Bangladesh. In what can be considered a language non-policy, the state opted for the status quo in this regard. However, linguistic nationalism was soon to exert pressure on the body politic, first in East Bengal and then in Sindh, and later in the context of a demand for creating new provinces on the basis of language, such as in the cases of Siraiki in Punjab and Hindko in KP. I plan to discuss history, territory and language as the three sources of conflict that need to be understood vis-à-vis their input into the master narrative of the nation.

A Nation without History

Pakistan has generally lacked historical consciousness. At one end, there is the two-nation theory and its espousal by the spokespersons for the Indo–Muslim civilization. At the other end, there is the territorial state that emerged as the coveted Muslim homeland, distinctly away from the seat of Muslim ascendency for centuries in and around Delhi. History as it was told, written and learnt for several generations in British India was generally defined in terms of the 'outermost structure' of the country, which was typically divided into successive periods of Hindu, Muslim and British suzerainty. There were regional histories which included personal accounts of British officers operating in different areas, including the region that later became Pakistan.[116] There was an undercurrent of the subcontinental expanse in historical writings. The history of Muslim rule carried the stamp of conflict as well as co-habitation between Hindus and Muslims, reflecting a matrix of change in time and space. In British India, as history became a discipline in institutions of higher learning, it brought forth new patterns of contestation along racial and civilizational lines. For example, British historiography in India dwelled on essentialisms, such as the one defined by the 'effeminate Hindu' who had been subjected to rule by a succession of external rulers.[117] The Indian response, especially from early Bengali fiction writers such as Bankim and Dutt among others, focused on reordering the imagined 'facts' of the past into 'an empowering discourse'.[118] Such proto-nationalist historicism seemed to narrativize the 'other' as alien and therefore hostile, dig up antiquity in search of infinity, and claim spirituality in order to overcome the materiality of the subject position at present. It sought to appropriate the civilizational status by having a history of its own in the first place and providing a pre-history of nationalism long before the arrival of independence.[119] History fast became a handmaiden of nationalism.

Faisal Devji describes Pakistanis as 'a people without history'.[120] In his view, Jinnah had no patience for the history of Muslim rule in India, especially as a source of inspiration for the Pakistan movement, not least because he did not belong to northern India, the seat of the Mughal Empire.[121] He argues that instead of 'being tied to a language of historical and territorial integrity, therefore, nationality for Jinnah was a purely constitutional category, one crucial to the making of a social contract'.[122] This was so because Jinnah looked at the current Indian politics as a 'state of nature' where nation was 'little more than a negation of the minority'.[123] My argument is that history had already created a grand dilemma for active Muslim thinkers for two generations. The question was: how to own Indian history as a minority while the Hindu majority's commitment to the icons and artefacts of Indian civilization included the Himalayas, the Ganges River, the cities of Benares and Ayodhiya, the Sanskrit language and scores of other sacred landmarks that covered a period of more than two thousand years?

Devji's argument draws heavily on the statements of Jinnah. What I want to argue is that the process of opting out of Indian history, culture and identity started much earlier and away from politics, for example in the nineteenth century in the realm of Urdu language and literature. Urdu was understood to be Hindi or Hindavi written in Persian script, which was generally identified with Muslims.[124] The collapse of the Muslim princely states in succession continued with the upward mobility of the Hindu educated middle classes, who sought the status of official and educational language for Hindi in various parts of northern India.[125] This process led to the shrinking of public space for Muslims. The process of the elimination of Hindi words from Urdu, generally identified with the poet Imam Baksh Nasikh among others, had set in long before the symbolic collapse of the Red Fort in 1857.[126] However, there was a spurt of higher educational pursuits in Urdu in areas of residual Muslim ascendency such as Hyderabad. The famous Urdu–Hindi controversy in the late nineteenth and early twentieth century not only shifted Muslim cultural dynamism from supporting Persian as the symbol of cultural expression rooted in the old halcyon days of the Mughal empire but also pushed history itself to the recesses of the Muslim mind because of the need for adjustment to the new order. The symbols of Muslim landmarks of history shrank both in visibility and influence as the Hindu landmarks of history were exhibited and projected by a large and motivated Hindu intelligentsia in an all-embracing spirit of pre-destinationism. Correspondingly, the Muslim intelligentsia felt dispossessed as Indian civilization emerged as the territorial foundation of history in general.

The Muslim response was that it was a history of conflict par excellence. For them, conflict was the predominant metaphor for understanding Indian history, based on a continual process of fighting between Hindus and Muslims. Of course, the past was shared by various communities speaking the same language, wearing the same clothes, and eating the same food in different localities. The past was also dotted with a series of local micro-conflicts within the framework of a social, cultural, and economic hegemony of lineage, group or community, be it Hindu or Muslim. In this social order, historically charged religious identities were far from fully problematized, given the absence of massive extra-local input that now operated in the form of the message of national parties and leaderships. The twentieth century saw a fundamental shift from region to religion and from individual to community, especially for Muslims on the way to defining their identity that was now being activated from a position of weakness.[127]

The new history was littered with perennial conflict. The more the Muslim consciousness was constrained by cluelessness about the future, the more the past was defined in terms of Muslim glory and Hindu chicanery. The history of perceived conflict between the two hostile communities provided a rationale for the two-thirds of Muslims for exiting from India in the form of Pakistan. The pioneers and leaders of the Pakistan movement who migrated to Pakistan after partition experienced the loss of both history and geography. Indian Muslims had for centuries vacillated between the two commitments, one to the community of faith as part of the world of Islam and the other to the community of territory identified with India.[128]

After 1857, Muslims lost whatever vestiges of symbolic political leadership they had. One finds a surge of nostalgia for the glory of Islam in the framework of Muslim revivalist ambitions through literature, history and political treatises. The most famous example of this trend was Altaf Hussain Hali's long, elegiac poem *Musaddas*, which focused on a sense of lost glory.[129] At the other end, given the newly defined public spaces in British India, Muslim interests could be represented only through the new institutions, legal entities and representative bodies at various levels.[130] The Muslim elite, which struggled to carve out a niche for itself in the emergent legal and institutional infrastructure of the state, was obliged to cultivate the community of faith to compensate for its increasingly weak position as the community of territory. For decades, adherence to the Ottoman Empire as a symbol of Muslim ascendency along with Pan-Islamism as an ideology made the Muslim elite look towards the classical lands of Islam. Literary works included Hali's *Musaddas*, Shibli Nomani's history books about the Prophet and his companions, Iqbal's Persian poetry seeking to address the larger Muslim *umma*, Hafeez Jallandhari's

Shahnama-e-Islam and Nasim Hijazi's historical novels. The community of territory — led by the Indian Muslim elite — invoked the destiny of a community of faith as the supreme catalyst for the mobilization of Muslims for the exit option. Indian history was effectively undone in this process. After partition, calling the history of a bellicose India next door — studded with names ranging from Chandar Gupt Mauriya, Ashoka and Vikramajit to Akbar, Dara Shikoh, Gandhi and Tagore — as one's own was no more on the cards. Pakistan began its national life in a state of denial of 'Indian' history.

However, there was also another state of denial, which posed a grave challenge to the intellectual entrepreneurs of the new country. Writing about the history of the constituent parts of the new country was hardly countenanced as a genuine intellectual pursuit in the supreme national interest. The experience and knowledge of the upper layer of the Muslim leadership, which typically came from India, about the territorial units of Pakistan located in the northwest and northeast of the subcontinent were tenuous at best. Before partition, the provinces of Sindh, Punjab, KP, Balochistan and East Bengal were at the receiving end of policy, strategy and ideology churned out by the Muslim League high command. These peripheral areas became an object of will for the new political subject at the top. While the standard textbooks carried the story of the Pakistan movement as it had unfolded in the first half of the twentieth century, the focus was unmistakably on the Muslim-minority provinces. The pantheon of Muslim leaders ranged from Sir Syed Ahmed Khan, Nawab Muhsinul Mulk, Nawab Waqarul Mulk, Maulana Mohammad Ali Johar, Maulana Shaukat Ali, Sir Agha Khan, Mohammad Ali Jinnah, Liaqat Ali Khan, Raja Sahib of Mahmudabad and Khaliquzzaman, among a host of others. In K. K. Aziz's formulation, the Pakistan movement was often described as the Aligarh movement to the total exclusion of Bengal.[131] Political parties and leaders from the future Pakistan areas were hardly considered a substantive part of the struggle for Pakistan.[132] Their history under the British, and earlier as sovereign states of Sindh, Balochistan, Punjab and Bengal before annexation, remained far from being a central part of the collective memory of the nation.[133] As Jalal noted, instead of history, Pakistanis were given emotive lessons in ideology along with a compendium of selective facts, which instead of opening up minds parroted the 'truths' of hastily constructed national myths.[134] She also maintained that by 'devaluing history for political and ideological reasons, Pakistan has found it difficult to project a national identity that can strike a sympathetic chord with its heterogeneous people'.[135]

Thus, Pakistan was in a double bind at its birth. On the one hand, the history of India could not be the history of Pakistan anymore, while the history of the Pakistan areas was not yet the history of the new nation, nor has it become so even after three-quarters of a century. Islamabad considered this to be part of a conspiracy to encourage discourse about the various regions of Pakistan that allegedly reflected the centrifugal tendencies of non-Punjabi ethno-nationalists. To a lesser extent, the same even applied to Punjabi chauvinists hankering after their linguistic ties across the border, such as through joint international conferences held in Chandigarh, London, Delhi and Lahore.[136] As a great defender of the Punjab and the Punjabi language, Haneef Ramay considers this region a far greater victim of the state's oppression than Sindh, KP and Balochistan.[137] In an apologetic tone, he claims that Punjab has directly ruled the country only for 23 months during the first few decades after partition.[138] Of course, individual scholars and writers have produced works of history, literature, politics, sociology and Sufism pertaining to various provinces of Pakistan[139]. Academies and centres of excellence have produced much intellectual content relating to their respective areas and provinces. Against all this, the new geographical entity, at least its western wing, provided a source of contrived historical depth as part of an official project in the form of a book that talked of 5,000 years of Pakistan.[140] In the vacuum, Islamic ideology was cultivated to serve the cause of unity, a sense of destiny and an overarching identity to stymie the regional identities. The cumulative effect of living without history was the absence of a large pool of symbols, icons and artefacts that would have provided the social, cultural, linguistic, artistic and behavioural references. Without history, Pakistan's origins remained mythical, transcendental, overly ideological and therefore vague. All this created an impression that the county had fallen from the heavens like a bolt in 1947, instead of growing from within the territory of the state itself. In Pakistan, the past is another country — literally. The conventional wisdom is that history belongs to a place. In Pakistan, a lack of symbiosis between history and territory defined the way identity was externalized through constant ideologization of public life with reference to the larger world of Islam.

A State without Territorial Imagination

In British India, Muslim nationalism faced a great dilemma. It was the nationalism of a minority of the population that was spread throughout India at various levels of density. Therefore, one of the greatest sources of nationalist aspiration – in the form of identification with territory – was not available to the Muslim League, as opposed to the Congress that spoke for whole of India. The two-nation theory continued to exhibit territorial agnosticism as an ideological construct even after serving the cause of separation from India and even long after partition. In this endeavour, religion overtook not only history but also territory. Muslim nationalism was territorially agnostic because the two-nation theory identified Muslims throughout the subcontinent as one nation, pitched against Hindus, who were put together as the other mega-nation.

The leadership took pride in the fact that Muslims from different territorial regions had abandoned their local ethnic, linguistic and cultural commitments in favour of the envisioned Muslim homeland. As a minority, Muslims were devoid of a propinquity with Indian territory, in the way Hindus could identify themselves with Hindudesh, Bharat Varsh or Hindustan – the land of Hindus. Not surprisingly, the Muslim elite focused on Islamic ideology as the premium instrument for public mobilization. The subcontinental ethos of the Indo–Muslim civilization has operated as a supra-territorial influence on Pakistan ever since partition. Pakistan is a state without territorial imagination. After partition, the state managers concentrated on de-Indianizing the public imagination inasmuch as the purpose was to de-link the Pakistani mindset from the Indian territory from where the dominant political, bureaucratic, intellectual, commercial and religious elites had come. Instead of focusing on re-territorializing the political imagination of people in Pakistan with full force and commitment, the new state chose to embrace the agenda of ideologizing the political culture. While East Pakistan and West Pakistan were territorially distant from each other, no territorial vision of the new state was available for creating a new cultural, traditional, and ethnic imaginary. The two wings had different genealogies. East Bengal was a rural hinterland of the historically established political entity of Bengal Presidency. West Pakistan was historically never a distinct, united, and continuous political entity. All this made the task of defining national territory a formidable challenge.

In the political imagination of the new state managers, demography was uppermost whilst territory was secondary. In the face of the hundreds of thousands of migrants who converged on Karachi and turned it into a Mohajir city overnight, the territory was considered disposable and dispensable. The lack of sensitivity about the position of Karachi as part of Sindh – historically, politically, administratively, and culturally – reflected the all-pervasive territorial agnosticism. The 'migrant state' took away the most cherished and the richest part of the territory of Sindh. In Sarah Ansari's words, Sindhis felt 'effectively beheaded'.[141] The battle for the city was directly related to the issue of 're-peopling' the state by bringing in those who were left on the wrong side of the border and who needed a place in their new homeland. The federal government pushed the Sindh government from Karachi to Hyderabad against the prominent dissident voices of the Sindhi leadership.[142] The loss of Karachi was the most visible and hostile reflection of the federation's encroachment on the territory of Sindh. The Sind government's resolution against the separation of Karachi and the transfer of its jurisdiction to the federal government was overruled.[143] For two decades, this issue fed the Sindhi nationalist agenda among the increasingly mobilized sections of the mass public.

Political space in Pakistan was de-territorialized in several other ways, not least because determinants of the national idiom were borrowed from outside the newly bounded geography of the country. For example, the national language, Urdu, was among the leading defining variables of Pakistan before and after partition. But it was not the mother tongue of any region now included in the country. Like the two-nation theory that was steeped in the spirit of Indo–Muslim civilization, Urdu – as the leading mode of cultural expression for Muslims of northern India for centuries – had now turned into an extra-territorial input in the new state.

Urdu had established a strong footing in Punjab after its annexation with British India in 1849. In the following decades, this developed into a 'language paradox'.[144] After that, the literate sections of the Muslim population universally took to Urdu as the language of its educational, media, literary and intellectual activity. At the same time, Punjab retained its identity as a distinct linguistic, cultural, political and ethnic unit in British India that was underscored by the practice of bilingualism based on written Urdu and spoken Punjabi. By the time the partition of Punjab had led to the deconstruction of its territorial integrity, urban (W) Punjab had comprehensively appropriated Urdu as its own. Similarly, urban Sindh emerged as the Urdu-speaking part of a predominantly Sindhi-speaking province. In both provinces, territory was potentially undone by the Urdu language as a source of cultural, linguistic and political inspiration.

In the event of the ascendancy of the 'leftist' PPP to power in Islamabad in 1971, the emergence of rump Pakistan as a compact region led to cultivation of the Indus civilization as a symbol of the antiquity of the society living in this geographical region. Aitzaz Ahsen claimed that Pakistan had existed for more than 5,000 years and upheld its unique identity separate from India.[145] This seemed to produce a new spirit of territorial nationalism away from the tradition of territorial agnosticism. But the absence of a meaningful relationship of the 'Indus project' with present-day Pakistan in terms of language, religion, culture, race or ethnicity rendered it an artificial and, ultimately, a minor discourse at the national level. Islamically orientated scholars such as Dr Syed Abdullah disapproved of such ideas that linked Pakistan's culture with Mohenja-Daro and Gandhara art as authentic representatives of the culture of the land and the people. He also criticized the tendency to disown the history of Muslim India.[146]

Other developments, such as the Islamization drive of the 1980s, left their mark into the first quarter of the twenty-first century. Religion effectively superseded geography as a definitional category in the context of the mega-narrative. Even when an understanding of the new state's legitimacy is attempted from outside the framework of religion, one finds references to the racial composition of Muslims as a mark of their distinct identity. For example, I. H. Qureshi traced the foundations of the Muslim homeland in the imagined profile of a large part of the Muslim population belonging to the stock of Central Asia.[147] This is the idiom of Ashraf speaking in the face of an absolute majority of local Muslim converts. While the geographical partition from India was generally understood as the endgame of cultural partitioning spread over a long period of time, the emergent state all along struggled to eliminate the supra-state identity of Indian civilization from the national imaginary. Not surprisingly, apart from the defence of its territory, the armed forces under Zia assumed the role of defenders of the 'ideological frontiers' of Pakistan.[148]

The absence of new territorial identities can be located in the residual nostalgia of many Mohajir and Punjabi migrants for their areas of origin in India, ranging from UP (Lucknow, Allahabad, Aligarh, Moradabad, Meerath) and Punjab (Jallandhar, Amritsar, Ludhiana, Hoshiarpur) to east, west and south India (Calcutta, Bombay, Sholapur, Kolhapur, Surat, Hyderabad Deccan, Kerala and Madras). Their ethnic, cultural and linguistic socialization in their areas of origin along with their cultural landmarks such as Sufi shrines, periodical festivities (*melas*) and the peculiar patterns of class, caste and the religious composition of the local population, militated against their assumption of a new territorial imaginary during their lifetime. Theirs was a generation of 'sleepwalkers' who clung to the old territory at the subconscious level even as they had abandoned it for a 'superior' cause of migration to a Muslim homeland.[149]

It is understandable that there was no smooth transition from one territorial imaginary to another. Migrants settled in 'alien' lands representing different geographical and demographic set-ups. More than merely a shift from one territory to another, it was a shift from one ideological framework defined by Indian civilization to another framework defined by the Muslim homeland. A generalized and gradual process of de-culturation started in the case of migrants, grounded in their social, cultural and linguistic practices intermingling with those of local communities.

From the mid-1980s onwards, the gravitational pull of Saudi Arabia worked as a mission and agenda for the transformation of society along Islamic lines, which encroached upon the culture of the land and the people over time. The 'national project' to integrate various ethnic and tribal communities sought to override the primordial commitments to territory, language and tradition. All this created a landscape for national identity that was underscored by an extra-territorial system of inclusion and exclusion based on denominational identities that defined new majorities and minorities, new insiders and outsiders, new friends and enemies. Successive governments declared political activists of the provinces (other than Punjab) demanding autonomy, as enemies of the nation. The state generally denigrated a sub-national unit of territory as a source of identity since it carried the potential to operate as a platform for action in the name of one's own province and was thus condemned as parochialism. As a classic case of 'cultivation of hegemonic beliefs for territorial control',[150] this process led to the construction of a new subjectivity that transcended territory.

The absence of a historically continuous political entity identified with the territorial foundations of Pakistan posed a challenge to the state and society after 1971. It produced the Indus Saga, which argued for Indus civilization as a territorial symbol of the country's claim to antiquity. However, it was fortuitous at best. This pre-Aryan Dravidian civilization had no substantive bearing on the religious, racial, linguistic, customary, or administrative patterns of thought and practice of today's Pakistan. While Mohenjo-Daro, Harappa and Taxila flourished in this part of the world before recorded history, their purported civilizational context was never a part of the historical or cultural imagination of local inhabitants until these were discovered in the early twentieth century.

In the given political landscape of Pakistan, Islamists dismissed the 'Indus business' because it pointed to a pre-Islamic heritage of the country. On the other hand, this symbol has been often used by Sindhi nationalists, for whom Mohenjo-Daro became a valuable symbol of a distinct Sindhi identity. In 2015, the PPP leadership led by Bilawal Bhutto put together a grand show in Mohenjo-Daro for projecting the Sindhi nationalist vigour. Sindhis have been active in pursuit of the Indus civilization line not least because of their heightened territorial consciousness demarcated by the current boundary of the Sindh province. While facing the presence of millions of non-Sindhis on the soil of Sindh, including Mohajirs, Punjabis, Pakhtuns, Siraikis and the Baloch among others, and the MQM's on-again/off-again demand for division of the province, Sindhis demonstrated a highly emotional commitment to the preservation of their province as a united entity. Elsewhere in Pakistan, territorial consciousness along provincial lines has been hardly as visible as in Sindh.

KP changed hands from one dynasty to another for a millennium, along with shifting epicentres in Ghazni, Delhi, Kabul and Lahore. After North West Frontier Province (NWFP) — now KP — was separated from Punjab in 1901, there was no territorial nostalgia for Punjab left behind in Peshawar. The Pakhtun centre of gravity lay in Afghanistan, outside what became British India and later Pakistan. There was a residual irredentism about areas south of the Indus up to the Margalla Hills which, in the eyes of some Pakhtun nationalists, belonged to them. As far as Punjab was concerned, its dominant narrative was shaped by more than 5 million Muslim refugees from East Punjab and adjoining areas in India who had passed through a bloodbath along communal lines. The ethno-territorial bond between the two Punjabs was extensively destroyed by a faith-based cross-migration.

In the eighteenth century, Takht Lahore under Maharaja Ranjit Singh conquered vast territories including today's KP and south Punjab. Their annexation was too recent to become part of a territorial imaginary of Punjab as a whole. Indeed, Punjab remains the least territorially conscious province of Pakistan. Internally, it has at least three distinct regions. First, the Siraiki-speaking south has its epicentre in Multan, which produced an incipient Siraiki nationalist movement to carve out a new province. Second, central Punjab – the Majha region – has its epicentre at Lahore. Third, the Pothohari-speaking north has its centre in Rawalpindi, which has abounded with Punjabi-speaking people from central Punjab ever since Islamabad became the capital. Territory is a secondary defining variable for Punjabis, mainly for cultural, linguistic and administrative reasons.

In the case of Balochistan, Baloch nationalism has played out as a provincial nationalism, even as sizeable areas in the north down to Quetta are Pakhtun dominated. The Brauhi-speaking Mengal tribe has been owned by the Baloch for the purposes of their nationalist struggle against the centre. From the beginning of the Confederacy of Balochistan in the eighteenth century, dynastic, tribal and ethnic identities far more than territory have shaped local politics. Indeed, it was the Baloch dynasties that ruled the adjoining Sindh, among them Kalhoras and Talpurs, who thus spread their influence across the region. Far more than territory, Baloch nationalism has been defined in terms of the erstwhile Khanate of Kalat, the dominant Baloch tribes of Marri, Mengal and Bugti, the alleged exploitation of mineral wealth by the state and oppression of political activists. [151] Indeed, at least one faction of the Baloch Students Organization (BSO) had proposed to Governor Bizenjo in 1972 to get rid of the Pakhtun areas and reorganize the province of Balochistan on the basis of Baloch majority areas only. [152] There was a related but largely passive claim to the Baloch districts of D.G. Khan of Punjab and Jacobabad of Sindh. Overall, territoriality has remained a marginal commitment in provinces with the possible exception of Sindh.

Language Policy: A Blueprint for the Status Quo

The role of language in the politics of Pakistan attracted scholarly attention rather late. However, from the 1990s onwards, there have been several analytical studies relating to the power structure and social hierarchy in the country by way of ethnolinguistic movements, the official or national status of a language, and linguistic surveys.[153] The Center–Punjab nexus elicited negative feelings from all other federating units on the issue of language and various issues of provincial autonomy including economic disparity and a share in power in general. Urdu and Islam were the two leading symbols of the Pakistan movement.[154] Indeed, Baba-i-Urdu ('Father of Urdu'), Maulvi Abdul Haq, claimed that Urdu was the first brick in the foundation of Pakistan.[155] The lack of tolerance for sub-national languages and an insistence on the dominance of the national language is common practice among new states, such as Sri Lanka with its Sinhala Only policy. Even India under Nehru acquiesced to the demand for reorganization of provinces on a linguistic basis only after the initial resistance from Delhi. Israel is a major example of a language shaping the nation itself, far more than serving as a mode of communication among groups and communities, where the ancient language of Hebrew was revived and vernacularized through education, media, and literature.[156]

The dominant feature of the Pakistan project was the creation of a faith-based umbrella Muslim identity differentiated from the magnified identity of the Hindus. Regional identities were down but not out. These acquired a new significance as political resources after independence. The Bengali language provided an idiom of regeneration for community, which had been recently cut off from its ethnic cohorts in West Bengal and which felt grossly alienated by its religious cohorts in West Pakistan. The Bengali language, woven into the matrix of an organic culture – like other languages – served the purpose of 'magi-constructing a new nation'.[157] The contrast with the narrative of the ruling elite was indeed forbidding. The latter's iconography included the Mughal imperium, the Urdu language, the Perso–Arabic script of the languages of West Pakistan, and a condemnation of all language-based politics as anti-national. Indeed, Maulvi Abdul Haq claimed that 'neither Jinnah nor Iqbal had made Pakistan: rather Urdu made Pakistan'.[158]

East Bengal plunged into a language war between Bengali and Urdu. One finds this phenomenon in the 1920s in Europe, especially Germany, where Hebrew was promoted by Zionists for educational, unificatory and regenerative purposes, while Yiddish, as the vernacular of Jews in exile, lagged behind in community formation.[159] The language-based cultural nationalism of the former won the day. While the two cases belong to two different trajectories, in both cases language fashioned the nation by representing 'the soul of the people' expressed through the mother tongue.

For a hundred years under British rule, Urdu, which was generally known as Hindustani, served as a lingua franca. However, by the late nineteenth century, identification of Urdu and Hindi with Muslims and Hindus respectively was an established fact. Like other regional languages further south and east of India, Bengali operated in the grey area beyond the communal model of identification. After partition, there were efforts to create a binary opposition between a Hindu and a Muslim Bengali language.[160] On the eve of independence, the policy of making Urdu the language of instruction in Pakistan was termed by Bengalis as 'political slavery'.[161] Within months after partition, the demand for making Bengali a national language spread all around. Jinnah firmly believed in a one-nation-one-language formula as a guarantee of national unity, in step with men of his generation such as Nehru and scores of others who ruled over the new nations. On 21 February 1952, the tragic incident of the shooting and killing of Dhaka University students represented a milestone on the march of Bengalis in pursuit of national status for their language. The East Bengal Assembly passed a resolution to that effect against a background of province-wide turmoil in intellectual and activist circles. The massive defeat of the ruling Muslim League party in the 1954 elections in East Bengal finally paved the way to Bengali attaining the status of the national language. The demonstration of the influence and popularity of the cause contributed to a change of policy, with the purpose of keeping the ethnic outsiders inside.

The language situation in Punjab has directly contributed to disaffection between Punjab and other ethnic communities. When the British annexed Punjab in 1849, Urdu not Punjabi was declared the language of administration and education in the province. Urdu became a language of literacy, whereas Punjabi was never taught even at the primary level. As the language of Muslim nationalism in British India in the twentieth century, Urdu later served as a grand symbol of Indo–Muslim civilization, second only to Islam in political importance.

At the same time, the religious propinquity between the Sikh revivalist movement and Punjabi language kept Muslims at bay in the context of literary, scholarly, artistic and pedagogical engagement with Punjabi. The 'soft' boundary between the Urdu and Punjabi languages by way of a grossly overlapping vocabulary further helped blur Punjabi identity with respect to language. Various Punjabi revivalist forums such as Dulla Bhatti Academy, Punjabi Majlis and Khaddar Posh Trust continued to exert pressure in favour of restoring Punjabi to its rightful place.[162] Spread over a hundred years, this situation has converted Punjabis in Pakistan into linguistic agnostics. Not surprisingly, they have been generally impervious to the language-based demands of other communities as well as a relatively small number of Punjabi chauvinists. In the view of the ruling elite, linguistic identities were inherently centrifugal. The articulate sections of Punjabis all long identified themselves with Urdu rather than Punjabi. They defined Urdu-based Pakistani nationalism as the real legacy of the two-nation theory and the basic source of their political identity. Conversely, the absence of perceived linguistic boundaries between written Urdu and Punjabi has indirectly helped remove any hurdles in the way of expansion of the Punjabi folk culture, including songs, dances, films and *Qawwali*. The Punjabi idiom, style of life, worldview and career ambitions have expanded beyond the politics of linguistic realities. The issue of language has been thus de-politicized. In this context, commitment to Urdu has been surrealistic more than real, because an absolute majority of Punjabis continue to express themselves in their mother tongue.

Any move or movement for recognition or projection of a language other than the national language, Urdu, is considered heresy. In this regard, the past has continued to shape the present in the grand perspective of the success of the Pakistan movement riding the wave of Muslim nationalism across various ethnolinguistic groups, ranging from Sindh, Punjab, UP, Bihar and Bengal, to Bombay, Madras, Kerala and Hyderabad. Moving away from Urdu would have been as heretical as abandoning Islam as the supreme source of identity for the new state of Pakistan.

While in India language was finally acknowledged as a legitimate source of identity that could provide a territorial identity for the purpose of provincial reorganization, in Pakistan it was understood as the source of a centrifugal tendency that would cause the country to disintegrate. This prevalent cult of unity militated against the emergence of a sub-national language as a source of identity. Non-Punjabi migrants from India, even though speaking different languages from the north, west, south, and east of India, gradually developed a meta-identity as Urdu-speaking migrants, called Mohajirs. Similarly, the literate population of Punjab could read and write only in Urdu and was therefore alienated from the written shape of their spoken tongue.

After the annexation of Punjab in 1849, the British found it expedient to move away from Punjabi in order to contain the influence of the Sikhs.[163] There followed a hundred years of literary production in Urdu in Punjab. Over time, Punjab produced Iqbal, the virtual poet laureate of the future Pakistan, followed by a generation of poets led by Faiz, by three out of four of the leading Urdu short story writers – Manto, Krishan Chandar, Bedi – and Ismat Chughtai. After partition, Karachi and Lahore became the major centres of Urdu literary production in poetry, fiction and literary criticism.

The symbiosis between Urdu and the Mohajir–Punjabi elite was an insider phenomenon. It faced two challenges: (1) from Bengalis for the status of Bangla as the second national language, which remained confined to one province; (2) from Sindhis for the status of Sindhi as the official language of Sindh under the PPP government in 1972. The subsequent Mohajir–Sindhi riots led to an understanding on the part of the ruling elite that sub-national languages have no role in the new country's march to national integration. Z. A. Bhutto skilfully postponed the whole issue to an unknown future date, even as the cultural 'goods' were distributed in a manner that left its scars on both the Mohajir and Sindhi communities. The National Awami Party (NAP) led the governments in Peshawar and Quetta, which declared Urdu their official language in 1972 instead of Pushto and Balochi respectively. That took care of language as a source of identity in the two communities in a general compromise between political expediency and ethnicity.

Apart from the symbolic and cultural significance of language, the establishment faced a demand for new provinces based on language. It showed willingness to create several new provinces on an administrative basis, such as divisions or districts, but not on the basis of language. The state was simply non-cognizant of identity politics.[164] This approach often led to the creation and encouragement of Islamic parties and groups to challenge the ethnolinguistic nationalists, for example in Balochistan, KP and Sindh. Part of the Islamization project in Pakistan can be attributed to a fear of language as a rival source of identity. The state responded to this fear by keeping the federation weak. The 18th Amendment that empowered the majority communities of the four provinces also created a demand for new provinces from their minority communities, namely Urdu-speaking, Siraiki-speaking, Hindko-speaking and Pushto-speaking people in Sindh, Punjab, KP and Balochistan respectively. Apart from some symbolic measures of decentralizing the Punjab administration with administrative secretariats in Multan, Bahawalpur and D. G. Khan, as announced in May 2020, the demand for language-based provinces was always likely to remain a dream. Sindh's struggle for separation from the Bombay Presidency on a linguistic basis in 1936 belonged to another era. Subsequent to partition, language as identity has been relegated to an abhorrent idea that would undermine the 'national project'.

Islam: Modernists and Traditionalists

As the Pakistan movement progressed from creating 'Muslim con-sciousness' for shaping the political imagination of individuals and communities to charting out a legal and institutional framework for the new state, politics and religion became intertwined in several ways. In a Pakistani diplomat's view, Pakistan heard two *azans* (calls to prayer) recited in its ears at birth. One was secular and national about a state defined by geographical boundaries and history. The other was religious. It said: 'You are a Muslim... and it is your destiny to follow the divine will.'[165] The Muslim League leadership was, in the words of the celebrated Indian historian Irfan Habib, not orthodox but 'communal'.[166] In Pakistan, this duality found an expression through a dichotomy between modernists – the architects of the Pakistan project – and traditionalists, who wanted to Islamize this project.

Modernists and Traditionalists

A long line of individuals – ranging from Sir Syed, Hali, Shibli, Agha Khan, Jinnah, Raja Sahib of Mahmudabad, Iqbal and Mashriqi to Hafiz Jallundhari and Zafar Ali Khan – who injected consciousness about the Muslim destiny belonged to what can be safely described as modernists. Not being the product of madrassahs, they took the 'political route' to securing Muslim interests in India rather than the 'religious route' taken by the ulema. The latter hailed from the two leading madrassahs from Deoband and Bareilly, except in the case of Maulana Maududi and Allama Mashriqi. Modernists gambled on using the Islamic card, mobilized the public along separate identities of Hindus and Muslims, enlisted the support of *pirs* belonging to future Pakistan areas for securing the votes of their followers, and promised the rule of Sharia to whomsoever wanted assurance in this regard.

The Muslim League leadership and a large section of the educated and professional middle classes employed a civilizational metaphor to project their vision of a Muslim homeland where they could live a life without Hindu domination both politically and culturally. The buzz word for modernists was Hindu domination. The buzz word for traditionalists was Sharia. This dichotomy was interwoven in the very movement for Pakistan. The former's political objective relied on the latter's co-option as a means to an end.

The conflict between the narratives of the modernists and traditionalists has continued for three generations. In 1970, an advertisement published in the Urdu weekly, *Lail-o-Nehar*, brought out interesting facets of this debate. [167] It claimed that back in 1938, the Muslim League leader, Raja Sahab of Mahmudabad, bemoaned the fact that certain issues relating to the period of thirteen and half centuries ago were being raised to create discord among Muslims and those who were called Maulanas were destroying their followers. The advertisement pointed out that a Muslim League pamphlet from that time had claimed that the ulema had already destroyed Afghanistan, Turkey and Iran. It claimed that once the Muslim League got into power, it would hang the ulema and that it wanted to bring women into public meetings to attract people. It declared that Jinnah's position as Ithna Ashari (Shia) *Rafizi* Khoja disqualified him as a true Muslim. While modernists claimed that a blueprint of an Islamic state already existed, traditionalists argued that such a system was nowhere to be found.[168] Modernists believed that the traditionalists' influence had to be contained without 'open confrontation', i.e. without allowing them to go to the street.[169] That has remained the official policy for the following seven-and-half decades.

While the makers of Pakistan were proud that a shared religious agenda had brought together Muslim ethnolinguistic communities from across British India, this new 'social contract' was based on religion in the broadest sense. Indeed, Farzana Shaikh has argued that Islamic ideology as an instrument of mass mobilization functioned largely in lieu of consensus among Muslims.[170] The more difficult part, in fact the riddle, was the leadership role of Jinnah, who was a Shia. In and around 1936, a battle of *fatwas* broke out against the issuance of the Muslim League tickets for elections crossing the sectarian boundaries for electoral candidates, including Jinnah himself.[171] Since Jinnah had converted from an Ismaili Shia sub-sect to Ithna Ashari Shia, who in turn considered the former infidel, he barely escaped from being branded doubly infidel. How could a Shia leader defeat Sunni ulema and a vast terrain of Sunni political leadership and capture the leadership of Muslims who were 84 per cent Sunnis? Nothing in Jinnah's personal life would have endeared him to the conservative Muslim public at large. This included his Western attire and preference for communication in English, his marriage to a non-Muslim lady who converted to Islam, and his daughter's marriage to a non-Muslim. Jinnah belonged to a Gujarati-speaking family that originally hailed from Karachi in Sindh, i.e. a peripheral region as compared to the heartland of the Pakistan movement in UP. What kind of commitment was it that worked like magic to put in motion Muslim nationalism without letting the internal divisions along regional, sectoral and tribal lines stand up and rock the boat?

Faisal Devji has brought to light a forgotten page of history when the Shia elite was dominant in the early part of the nationalist stirrings rooted in southwestern India.[172] The Shia leadership lent a relatively 'liberal' broad-based character to Muslim awakening, especially as it represented a 'bourgeois' and modern flavour as opposed to what the

Congress dismissed as the 'feudal' setting of the Muslim leadership in north India.[173] In Devji's view, religion was an abstract notion orientated towards a modern public life that was minimalist in its ritualistic expression, and functioned as an instrument in the hands of a secular leadership.[174] The phenomenon of the mosque–military alliance in Pakistan at the expense of various ethnic groups came half a century later.[175] Incessant moves of Sunni-based Islamization led to the emergence of anti-Shia hostility in the wider public, especially after the 1978 Iranian revolution, not least through official patronage of militant Sunni organizations such as Sipah Sahaba Pakistan (SSP). In two generations, Jinnah's community was declared infidel in his own country by many Sunni ulema, with the tacit support from some official quarters.

It is interesting to see how foreign observers pointed to the tradition/ modernity dichotomy in the immediate post-independence period, and clearly hoped that modernists would prevail over orthodoxy. One of the periodical diplomatic reports warned that Muslims were 'religious and fanatical', that religion was invariably used as a means to an end, and yet there was no immediate danger of the leadership 'allowing the maulvi influence to get out of hand'.[176] Another periodical communication mentioned the attacks in the vernacular press of KP on the 'emancipated' wives of the air force officers 'for not observing *purdah*'.[177] One diplomatic message claimed that there were leading personalities 'working against the *mullahs*, such as Mr. Jinnah, Ms. Fatima Jinnah, the premier Liaqat Ali Khan and his wife, and locally the Chief Minister'.[178] British diplomats seemed to be concerned with the emerging bipolarity between modernists and traditionalists. However, both modernists – Khaliquzzaman, Ghazanfar Ali, or Begum Liaqat Ali Khan – and traditionalists used the overlapping idiom of establishing Islam in the country. Only the former used various caveats to define their own vision of Islam, for example, that first there should be social justice and only then Islamic punishments should be made part of the law. Begum Tasadduq Hussain's statement that she would introduce a bill that would ban cosmetics if prohibition had been implemented was labelled a 'stupid stunt' in another diplomatic message.[179]

The expression of modernists in Pakistan has been an amalgam of a queer logic, references to Western authors, divinity, morality, spirituality, globalism and disapproval of whole communities by looking at them through one's own religious lens. A leading lawyer, A. K. Brohi, harked back to the time when a 'carpenter's work had a religious, not a mere economic, orientation',[180] or when a shoemaker – he quotes Spanish philosopher Unamuno – becomes 'a serviceable means for the embodiment of Divine purpose and in such a state he is worth, nay more than, the whole universe'.[181] In Brohi's view, it is fine to wage war on poverty but obedience to moral law, which is a 'transcendental law',[182] necessarily creates 'material progress'.[183] He dismisses 'all this sickly talk about "raising the standard of people"'.[184] He maintains that Americans were beginning to realize that their prosperity was rooted in the 'great puritanical revolution' and 'the almost religious sense of earnestness with which they mastered a hostile continent'.[185] At the other end, he sees Communism 'at war with harmonies of human life'.[186] Brohi sees the life of ancient Jews and Hindus 'in terms of racial nexus'.[187] Since both are non-proselytizing religions, they lack internal elasticity and are therefore 'intolerant communities'.[188] Modernists from Brohi's generation onwards were increasingly lost to opacity, inscrutability, incomprehensibility, abstruseness and indeterminacy.

One can argue that the ulema were somewhat clearer about the end in prospect in the form of an Islamic state, even though their sectarian differences militated against a consensus about its specific shape. The agenda of making the learning of Arabic compulsory for students has been a regular demand which, however, did not take off for various reasons.[189] The ulema initially opposed but then manipulated the Islamic clauses of the constitution to establish what Western scholars would call theocracy.[190] The Objectives Resolution and the Principles of State Policy became legal instruments in the ulema's arsenal.

At the other end, modernists spelled out widely different and wildly imaginative approaches to what they meant by making Pakistan a most liveable, peaceful, harmonious and prosperous Islamic state. They put together their selective, half-baked ideas, often profusely and confusingly borrowed from Western thinkers. In their view, an absolute majority of people living in the rural areas of West Pakistan were traditional, while the rest living in urban areas were under the modern influence. Modernity would 'eclipse' the traditional way of life, essentially because the power and authority were held by those who received modern education. Modernists sought to eradicate the most glaring problem of conservatism among the 'ruralists who had been neglected for centuries'. They attributed to themselves a role of Platonic proportions whereby the 'villagers would find philosophical support for taking initiatives' in their realm of 'fatalism and blind faith'.[191] At one end, as Gregorian argued, Islamists saw democracy as being wholly incompatible with a Muslim society because it seemed too individual-centred or focused on the 'temporal materialistic world'.[192] At the other end, modernists were not ready to render the initiative into the hands of those whom they wanted to help. Indeed, they attributed the creation of Bangladesh to democracy itself in the context of the 1970 elections that weakened the process of nation-building.[193] The modernists' case for Pakistan was typically couched in the idiom of attaining freedom from Hindus. It focused on escaping 'from isolation, powerlessness and deprivation experienced in the Hindu social system based on rigidly fixed inequalities' and portrayed Pakistani society – in a spirit of unbelievable naivety – as 'classless and egalitarian'.[194]

The divide between modernists and traditionalists continued to shape the contours of the discourse. The former claimed that Islam was a religion of peace. The latter embraced the idiom of war against the West after a generation of slow upward growth in their political strength, characterized by the Afghanistan war of resistance against the Soviet Union in the 1980s. In Iftikhar Malik's view, the ideological vacuum that was left as a result of the futile attempts of the modernizing elite to alleviate inequality, opened up an interesting option for the lower middle-class elements in the form of the clergy's offer of a 'reductionist version of Islamic panacea'.[195] He maintains that the manipulation of Islam at the hands of modernists along with the retrogressive nature of the ulema allowed a discourse of Islamic 'reconstructionists' to emerge.[196] The question remains whether what has happened by way of Islamization from the 1970s onwards has, in any identifiable sense, reconstructed the faith, ideology, community or nation that has put Pakistan on the way to progress.

While modernists carried the day in terms of production and projection of the master narrative, Islamic parties re-emerged after the initial years of partition to assert their role in defining the ends and means of the national agenda. Between the two large Sunni sects, first the Deobandis were ideologically mobilized and then the relatively inchoate and quietist Barelvis set foot on the way to militancy. The archetypical religious agitation was of course the 1953 anti-Ahmadiya movement that set the debate between modernists and traditionalists about the goals and means of exercising ideational sanctions of the state. The 1953 movement became the symbol of the street power of the ulema.[197] Apparently it failed to achieve its target, i.e. the dismissal of the Ahmadi foreign minister Sir Zafarullah.

Two decades later, Z. A. Bhutto would not take the risk of Islamic mobilization in the country on the issue of declaring Ahmadis as infidel, especially as there was a sizeable number of Islamic Members of National Assembly (MNAs) who exerted their pressure against Ahmadis.[198] Bhutto went ahead with the Second Amendment that declared Ahmadis beyond the pale of Islam in 1974. The 1977 anti-Bhutto agitation adopted the agenda of establishing *Nizam-e-Mustafa* (the Prophet's system) highlighted by midnight *azans* to put an end to the apocalypse that was Bhutto's regime in the eyes of the industrialists, the landed elite, the bureaucrats, the army and the ulema.

Not surprisingly, successive governments tended to shun the grim prospects of an Islamic movement that could get out of hand and thus destabilize the system. Gurharpal Singh argues that India's policy of secularism based on adoption of a neutral policy vis-à-vis all religions, has had a negative effect because it overlooked religious differences among people and thus did not provide a political platform to address them.[199] In his view, an 'ethnic democracy' such as India will almost always give power to the dominant group by way of majority rule. The dominant group can then abuse its power and use other groups to its advantage. This 'hegemonic control' could work in liberal democracies where it brought together the idea of force and consent.[200] In Pakistan, modernists did not exercise a secularist agenda as policy or practice: instead, they sought to co-opt the traditionalists in the system. However, it created an unforeseen result of rendering the legitimacy of the state system itself into the hands of the Islamists.

Islamic parties have been able to resist the successive governments of Benazir Bhutto, Nawaz Sharif and Pervez Musharraf from carrying out reform in the controversial provisions of certain Islamic laws, especially in some procedural aspects of the Hudood Ordinances and the Blasphemy Law. The ulema formed the Milli Yakjehti Council (MYC) in the 1990s and thwarted all attempts in this regard under the threat of a countrywide agitation. A quarter of a century later, a new Barelvi outfit, Tehreek-e-Labbaik Ya Rasool Allah (TLYRA), under the leadership of the cleric Khadim Hussain Rizvi, aimed at punishing the PML-N government, especially its law minister Zahid Hamid, for using a nuanced expression about confirming the finality of prophethood in the new election bill instead of keeping the original oath. Islamists carried the day after they forced the government to agree to the minister's resignation through the good offices of the army.[201] It was followed by their April 2018 agitation from the platform of their party, Tehreek Labbaik Pakistan (TLP), against the acquittal of a Christian woman, Asia Bibi, in a blasphemy case. Islamists practically barred the way to successive government initiatives for reform in the current body of Islamic legislation.

I have argued elsewhere that the formidable Islamic parties, groups and media operated like an 'establishment' even without any organizational unity and internal hierarchy.[202] A major stronghold of the ulema are the Islamic madrassahs controlled by five federations, four of them formally based on sects.[203] Whenever successive governments, most prominently the Nawaz Sharif government (2013–17), declared a policy of action against the perceived militant activities of some madrassahs, especially under the 2014 National Action Plan, the madrassah federations demonstrated complete defiance, whereby the government was obliged to retract its initiative.

However, Islamic parties have no control over Islamic legislation or Islamically-sanctioned social, cultural and moral practices. So while Islamist movements appear to be strong, they have not had the requisite electoral support to come to power. This led to the official policy of their co-optation, depending on the nature of the regime.[204] The ulema opposed the 1961 Family Ordinance for six decades because of its allegedly un-Islamic provisions for disallowing a man from divorcing his wife by simply declaring his intent three times, and for putting constraints on polygamy. Even the most 'Islamic' regime of Pakistan, the Zia government, did not abrogate the Family Ordinance. In recent times, the 2016 Protection of Women against Violence Act passed by the Punjab Assembly was vehemently opposed by the ulema under the threat of mass agitation. But this law remains on the statute book. However, the shyness of successive governments from pursuing a policy that could provoke the ulema to go to the street is now part of the political strategy.

A majority of people in Pakistan belong to two Sunni sub-sects, the Deobandis and the Barelvis, who are followers of madrassahs located in UP in India. The mainstream narrative in Pakistan provides a glossy view of the two madrassahs that formally promoted humanitarianism, cosmopolitanism and liberation.[205] During the last three-quarters of a century, these sub-sects have carried on an internecine war on the soil of Pakistan, drawing on their differences of creed and rituals. Some Deobandis came under the influence of Wahhabism via Saudi Arabia and Islamic militants fighting the Afghan jihad in the 1980s and again after 9/11. A generation later, Barelvis also moved to street violence after the assassination of Governor Punjab Salman Taseer at the hands of one Mumtaz Qadri. How to explain the prevalent mood of asserting street power in yesterday's Sufi-orientated community? We need to understand it with reference to the changing social, cultural and ideological matrix of the Pakistani mindset.

The Sufi shrines and *pirs* typically represented the peasant society of Punjab, Sindh, and elsewhere. Rapid urbanization removed their followers from their quiet, uneventful and relatively non-combative life patterns and exposed them to urban insecurities. Urbanization spread over three generations has produced an 'atomized' society in the provincial capitals, vulnerable to economic insecurity and cultural alienation. In the absence of a mechanism for articulating their interests to the 'system', this lower middle-class section, supported by madrassah students and followers of Sufi orders, developed a street power of its own. In Zaigham Khan's formulation, the TLP is the poor man's PTI in terms of its Islamic populism.[206] Similarly, the educational textbooks draw essentially on a worldview based on a war vector rather than a peace vector.[207] Ideologization of mind indiscriminately hit people across all sects and sections. Indeed, the vast network of close association between the followers of the Barelvi sect and the bazaar, including Karachi,[208] Lahore,[209] and other cities, provided them with a financial base and a social support system. During the twentieth century, the new icon for Islamic mobilization has gradually moved upwards from sectarian beliefs and practices to the exalted personality of the Prophet himself in the framework of legislation and public activity about blasphemy. On 1 January 2020, the Punjab Assembly unanimously passed a resolution asking the federal government to make new laws or to improve the existing laws to punish blasphemers strictly.[210]

One of the biggest challenges facing 'moderate' Muslims is the presence of deep-seated internal schisms preventing a broader democratization of Muslim societies.[211] On the one hand, Javed Ahmed Ghamidi has been celebrated in the liberal English press for denying fixity of meaning within the Qur'an, even as the word of the Qur'an and its system of laws and prohibitions remain central to his argument.[212] On the other hand, hard-line Islamic groups such as Jamaat Islami (JI) and the more radical Islamist groups, remain uncompromising on social and political issues.[213] Further down the ladder there are militant outfits such as Jamat ud Dawah (JuD) and Markaz Dawat-wal-Irshad (MDI), which carried out indigenization of Salafi thought through homogenization (complete replication) or hybridization (leaving room for modification) of ideas imported from Saudi Arabia and the Gulf.[214] Two prophecies were popularized by Islamic militants at the turn of the century, which turned into a full-blown mythology: a Khorasan army would join the Mahdi to champion the forces of good against evil; and Ghuzwa-e-Hind (holy war of India) would take the Islamic army into India as ordained by the Prophet. Islamic organizations such as Al-Huda, JI, Jaish-e-Muhammad, Lashkar-e-Jhangvi (LJ), Tehreek-e-Taliban Pakistan (TTP) and similar organizations used Qur'anic texts for construction of a master narrative with 'agentic capacities'.[215] The violent jihad narrative has been popularized by JI, LeT (Lashkar-e-Taiba) and JuD. Their activism in support of Islamic womanhood in Pakistan was meant to produce ideal, modest and pious Muslim women as a counter-narrative to modern feminism.[216] Some argued that the Ghuzwa had already happened, which had led to Muslim rule in India.[217] In sum, Pakistan was deemed to be a state that would accommodate any militant non-state actor who would apply for patronage to fight against the Hindu demon across the border. Haqqani blames such theological foresights for producing Don Quixotes who are tilting at foreign policy windmills as Islamabad's 'national security experts'.[218]

Construction of an Alternative Globality

Dietrich Reetz has talked about alternative globalities among groups, communities and nations.[219] The history of the territorial state in

Pakistan has been grossly mixed with the history of Islam in the Middle East. For example, one book on Pakistan covered topics ranging from Islamic teachings, early Islam, major philosophical currents, individual Islamic philosophers, the fall of Baghdad (1258 AD), Muslim rule in India, and a scholar from late medieval times, Mujadid Alif Sani, to intellectual stalwarts of the nineteenth and twentieth centuries. But it hardly touched Pakistan.[220] With a streak of inbred narcissism, the writers generally considered it a duty of Pakistan to 'show to the world how much Islam is able to play a decisive role in international affairs', with its 'fifth position among the world kingdoms'.[221] The belief that Muslims abandoned their ethno-regional and linguistic commitments throughout the length and breadth of India 'to be one political entity' shaped the cult of unity that characterized the overly ambitious national project.[222] It was argued, in a bland and extremely unreflective way, that Rome was a civilization based on material wealth but that it had no culture, i.e. no 'foundational ideology'. Christianity had culture but no civilization. Islam had both, as reflected through unity of religion and state.[223] There is a feeling that Islamic activism is a response to the failure of the national project. In the 1970s, Bhutto invoked the glory of Islam as part of a developing world-of-Islam perspective. He declared that 'we are not barbarians', and referred to Umar's mosque in Jerusalem, Badshahi mosque in Lahore, and Qutb Minar in Delhi in one breath.[224] This general anti-imperialist posturing made even the British government cautious as it sometimes shied away from contacts with political leaders of Pakistan in order to avoid allegations of a 'London plot'.[225]

In recent decades, globalization – especially in terms of the communication and media explosion – through the internet and TV brought about a revolution in perceptions about encounters between Muslims and non-Muslims in various conflict zones. Public opinion in Pakistan, holding the USA responsible for the underdog position of Muslims in different parts of the world – especially in the heart of Islam in the Middle East – found a loud and striking voice in the 1990s. After the outcry over the creation of Israel in 1948, anti-Westernism began to take concrete shape after the 1956 Anglo–French attack on Egypt, the Algerian war of independence, the 1967 and 1973 Arab–Israeli wars, the 1979 Soviet incursion into Afghanistan, the American-led wars against Iraq in 1991 and 2003, the wars in Bosnia, Chechnya and Kosovo in the Balkans in the 1990s, and the US-led war against Afghanistan after 9/11.

Pakistan inherited a foreign policy perspective from British India. This was rooted in suspicion of the Soviet Union, which was allegedly searching for a warm-water port in Southern Asia.[226] From the perceived support of Moscow for successive Afghan regimes, along with the latter's Pashtun irredentism, up to Afghanistan under the Red Army (1979–89) and beyond, Pakistan remained steadfastly anti-communist and anti-USSR. Historically, Moscow's occupation of the classic Islamic lands of Central Asia for more than a century had provided a baseline for an ideational sanction against it and its 'atheist' philosophy of communism. As the Red Army withdrew from Afghanistan after the 1988 Geneva Accords, followed by the disintegration of the Soviet Union and the end of the Cold War, the lurking anti-Russian suspicions continued to prevent any real breakthrough in relations with Moscow, despite initiatives such as joint naval manoeuvres in 2016 and occasional exchanges of diplomatic goodwill in 2014 and 2018.

The story of Indo–Pakistan relations is different. As a bitter legacy of partition, anti-Indianism has been cultivated as a 'constructed primordialism'.[227] This comprises a series of hostile perceptions: that India never 'accepted' Pakistan; it was an aggressor in Kashmir, East Pakistan and Siachin; and its secularism was bogus and fraudulent and was responsible for regular discrimination against its Muslim minority.[228] Similarly, Pakistanis are anti-Zionist to the hilt. There is a popular belief that the West sought to wipe the Palestinian nation from the map of the world.[229] There was deep anguish over the two Palestinian intifadas (1987–93, 2000–5), along with the scenes of Israeli tanks shooting at stone-throwing young Palestinians and razing their houses, and the sprawling Jewish settlements appearing on the occupied lands. The Israeli bombardment of Hamas in Gaza (2009, 2014 and 2021) that killed men, women and children and destroyed schools, hospitals and houses, created widespread disgust for the Zionist state. People found Netanyahu's plan for annexation of East Jerusalem in 2020 contemptible. The media and Islamic elements often expressed their disgust over the alleged designs of Islamabad to recognize Israel, and thus put the government on the defensive, especially after the agreement in 2020 between the United Arab Emirates and Israel, followed by Israel's agreements with Bahrain,

Sudan and Morocco. In December 2020, Imran Khan's government in Pakistan strongly denied any agenda for recognizing Israel in the face of public outcry on this issue.

Since the 1990s, anti-Americanism has moved to the centre of the foreign policy narrative. In the post-9/11 period, the US approval rate in Pakistan was at 17 per cent in 2010, when six out of ten people thought of it as the enemy.[230] In Pakistan there are three major constituencies for anti-Americanism: the mainstream and anti-Indian groups; Islamists; and ethnic and leftist activists.[231] Pakistani perceptions of the USA are rooted in Islamabad's 'insecurity syndrome' not only as a hangover from the Cold War period but also as an essentially conflictual 'resurgent Islamic position'.[232] After 9/11, the question of whether the USA was for or against Pakistan was generally recast in broadly religious terms. Pakistan was a premier Islamic country that often linked itself to the destiny of the Muslim world. The public in Pakistan grew restive and cultivated suspicions of the USA in its capacity as the architect of the post-Cold War world. Indeed, there had been no direct war of any Muslim country with the USA up to the 1993 Gulf War against Iraq, which was professedly fought for a Muslim (Kuwaiti) cause. Thus, anti-Americanism never acquired the status of an ideology, unlike anti-Russian, anti-Indian and anti-Zionist perspectives.[233] Jalal wondered whether it was paranoia or denial or perhaps intellectual paralysis that not only Islamic extremists but also liberals joined hands in condemning American conspiracy to destabilize the country.[234]

The transcultural dynamics between the two universes of the 'West' and 'Islam' consist of the way in which a strongly internalized (Western) idea of religion exists against the less internalized and undifferentiated Muslim idea of religion.[235] The critical attitudes of the ruling elite have been issue specific, such as US sanctions against Pakistan's nuclear tests as opposed to the relatively stable and consistent pattern of pro-Americanism. In 2014–18, defiance against the US demand for stopping support for terrorist groups in Afghanistan, and President Trump's condemnatory remarks about Pakistan's alleged double-speak about its anti-terrorism agenda in 2019, elicited a fierce reaction against Washington. Of course, the major source of Pakistani perceptions about the USA relate to the way the latter addressed Islamabad's security concerns vis-à-vis India.[236] In the years 2020–1, anti-Americanism remained a rampant feeling amongst the public even as Islamabad continued to mend fences by way of facilitating the US-sponsored peace agreement with the Taliban in Doha. In other words, the public became increasingly anti-American in the larger framework of the world of Islam.[237] In particular, US policies were perceived to be hostile to Muslims in various regional conflicts.[238]

The world-of-Islam perspective has been a popular metaphor in Pakistan. The Muslim world is perceived as a mini world in the larger world. By way of comparison, one can argue that there is no Hindu world. The state of India comprehensively represents the world of Hinduism, with Nepal being the only other Hindu state and Bali being a remote Hindu island in Muslim Indonesia. There is no Buddhist world either, unless one puts together Thailand, Kampuchea, and Sri Lanka as building blocks of a faith-based community of states. Nor indeed is there a Christian world whereby countries ranging from the Philippines, Kenya and Tanzania to England, France, Germany, the USA, Canada, Mexico and Brazil would make a coherent bloc of countries bound by religious ties.

The world of Islam comprises fifty-six Muslim states, large historical Muslim minorities in India, China and Russia, as well as the expatriate Muslim community in Western countries. The Palestinian issue can be considered the oldest and most consistently frustrating Islamic cause in this regard. A series of Islamic causes followed: Kashmir, Afghanistan, Bosnia, Kosovo, Chechnya, Iraq, Syria and Yemen. The Nawaz Sharif government (1990–3) became part of the international coalition against Saddam Hussain in the First Gulf War in the teeth of opposition from an angry public. The Musharraf government's decision to join the US war against the Taliban and Osama bin Laden in 2001–2 ignited the anger of a large section of people. In all three cases of Suez (1956), Iraq (1991) and Afghanistan (2001), society at large reacted sharply against what it considered Western encroachment on the sovereignty and integrity of a fellow Muslim country. In each case, the government staved off a moral crisis and managed to survive in office.[239] The clue lies in the social and political milieu of Pakistan, which can be defined as an hour-glass society as opposed to a civil society.[240] There are very few channels of communication and pressure available to society at the bottom to influence and shape the policy at the top. Thus, it has been possible to have a pro-American state and anti-American society at the same time.

The 1971 war with India brought about an unexpected change in Pakistan's engagement with the world of Islam. Islamabad turned its back on South Asia, which was now for all practical purposes India's area of influence, and it turned to the Middle East in a big way.[241] This move could not have come at a more opportune moment. The post-1973 war boom in oil prices made this step increasingly more meaningful in financial, strategic and diplomatic terms. In this process, the 1991 Gulf War seems to be the turning point in the context of Pakistani perceptions about the USA. The traditional pro-Saudi Arabian Islamic parties such as the JI, as well as some officers in the army high command including Chief of Army Staff (COAS) General Aslam Beg, condemned the US-led attack on Iraq. The transnational Islamic networks that operated against the Soviet presence in Afghanistan in the 1980s now found a new adversary in the USA in the 1990s, as the latter made its presence in the Gulf noticed all around the Muslim world militarily, diplomatically and otherwise.[242] The master narrative of Pakistan in its pristine form symbolized exit from the larger world.

Postcolonialism: 'The Return of the Native'

Colonialism was not only part of the world capitalist system that transferred resources from the periphery to the centre[243] but it was also a system of transformation of local societies and cultures through Western influence via educational, cultural and religious reform, and institutionalization of state apparatuses.[244] It also symbolized racial superiority of the white man over indigenous populations. In Renan's words:

> The regeneration of the inferior or degenerate races, by the superior races is part of the providential order of things for humanity.... Regere imperio populos is our vocation. Pour forth this all-consuming activity onto countries, which, like China, are crying aloud for foreign conquest. Turn the adventurers who disturb European society into a ver sacrum, a horde like those of the Franks, the Lombards, or the Normans, and every man will be in his right role. Nature has made a race of workers, the Chinese race, who have wonderful manual dexterity,

and almost no sense of honour; govern them with justice, levying from them, in return for the blessing of such a government, an ample allowance for the conquering race, and they will be satisfied; a race of tillers of the soil, the Negro; treat him with kindness and humanity, and all will be as it should; a race of masters and soldiers, the European race.... Let each do what he is made for, and all will be well.[245]

Postcolonialism represents a visible strand of thinking in decolonized societies as the process of trying to grapple with the perceived negative effects of colonial rule after independence. This is part of the agenda of freeing the 'self' from the curse of alien rule. The colonial rulers considered the 'natives' as the 'other' by way of race, religion and culture. Now, postcolonial societies have found the West as the other, especially as the latter's domination continued to be a fact of life outside the colonial framework.

The emerging binary of Islam and the West has gained prominence in recent decades as two mega-constructs and essentialisms.[246] The struggle against colonial rule led to the construction of identity among the subject peoples, who developed state-forming ideologies, such as the two-nation theory in the case of Pakistan. Postcolonialism underscored nationalist aspirations with the idea that colonialism distorted and dehumanized the personality of the subject people. Franz Fanon and Ashis Nandy among others have explored the mental pressure exercised over the local population by the colonists in racial and cultural terms. Fanon opposes the way the colonized intellectual struggled to disprove the colonists' description of the pre-colonial people as barbaric, and instead glorified them.[247] In his view, this is like making a dead body alive. Fanon focuses on the role specification in colonial society in the context of relations between the white and the non-white, the master and the slave, the superior and the inferior. In his view, the lumpen proletariat, the class on the margins of colonial society and thus least touched by the colonial narrative of stratification, could be tapped for overthrowing the yoke of colonialism. Borrowing from Thomas Hardy, I describe the pursuit of the postcolonial intellectual who struggles to restore the nation's power and prestige through reviving and projecting the original pre-colonial sources of inspiration – religion, culture and custom – as 'the return of the native'.[248]

In Ashis Nandy's formulation, colonialism is symptomatic of 'the loss and recovery of self'.[249] Colonialists and their intellectual apologists self-consciously championed the march of non-Western societies to reason, maturity and rationality.[250] Nandi criticizes 'corrupt sciences and psychopathic technologies wedded to new secular hierarchies',[251] which destroyed major civilizations. Indeed, 'the second colonialism' started after decolonization proper, with a focus on capturing the mind so much so that the non-West itself became the creation of the West.[252] Nandy searched for 'an ethically sensitive and culturally rooted alternative social knowledge'.[253] Quoting Marx, he described the European profile of India as a land of 'small semi-barbarian semi-civilized communities',[254] and 'the childlike Indian', both innocent and ignorant.[255] For the colonized, the way out was Westernization.[256] Nandy finds the decolonized India struggling to take the West out from inside.

Here, I want to bring in the return of the native. How far can one realistically de-Westernize oneself? In what forms have certain people in India, Pakistan and elsewhere sought to discover their roots? In Hardy's novel the protagonist, Clym Yeobright, seeks and finds his identity in the landscape of Egdon Heath after returning from his sojourns in other places. The colonial native, in a postcolonial framework, seeks to outgrow the imperial narrative of evolution which has defined him in terms of a difference of genus.[257] The native was relatively invisible in the colonists' narrative except as part of nature all around.[258] For the colonist, knowing the landscape was the key to knowing the native. Later, this approach was turned upside down as anti-colonial nationalism appropriated the land by identifying it with the local people.[259] However, over time, a new native emerged out of the crisis of the nationalist project that led to migration to the mother country, a phenomenon known as 'the post-colonial migrancy'.[260]

At the other end, the revolt against the colonial state had been led by elements from the Westernized elite itself, which mobilized the masses in their cultural idiom, often couched in religion, history, language and custom. In British India, as elsewhere, this process was accompanied by the return of the native, who became the custodian of traditional culture. Nandy has sketched the profile of Arobindo Ghosh in detail. Here was a Bengali upper middle-class person who was raised as an Englishmen in Calcutta and later England, and whose relations with his mother tongue and his ethnic and cultural universe were tenuous at best. Later, he turned to his Indianness, became a revolutionary against colonial rule, which led to a jail sentence, and finally spent his later years as an ascetic in an *ashram* in the French colony of Pondicherry. Ghosh is a perfect example of 'the return of the native'. The phenomenon of the return of the native has been visible in varying degrees among political leaders in the twentieth century, ranging from Tilak, Lala Lajpat Rai and Gandhi to Jayaprakash Naryan and Vinoba Bhave. This search for roots in a pre-colonial era characterized to a huge degree the social, cultural, religious and political agendas of Indian intelligentsia.

In Pakistan, one hears the reverberations of the nativist sentiment far more in religious terms than in cultural, linguistic and customary frameworks. Here, the demand for 'return' took various forms: replacement of English by Urdu as the official language and the language of higher learning; religious and sectarian holidays; patronage of Sufi shrines; expansion of madrassahs; and condemnation of the phenomenon of Western skins/Islamic masks who ruled Pakistan.[261] A running theme is the critique of Western secularism, for which Talal Asad is most typically considered the master intellectual. His argument boils down to the failure of secularism, i.e. the secularist project of the West and by default the relevance of religion, in this case Islam. Asad negates the idea that democracy reflects 'the horizontal, direct-access character of modern society', because the modern elite uses secularism to transcend the identities of class and religion in order to create citizenship as the basic identity.[262] In his view, contrary to considering Islam as violent and secularism as the principle of civil harmony, 'the repeated explosions of intolerance' in the USA prove that secularism and violence can live together.[263] The demand for religious discourse to be prevented from entering public life, so as to save people from suffering, is built on a religious motive defined as the Freudian suppressed instinct of a fear of the unknown.[264]

Asad addresses Jose Casanova's thesis about the three elements of modernity: separation of religion from politics; privatization of religion; and the declining religiosity in society. He argues that since religion has penetrated various other spheres of life, so Casanova's first element – the separation between religion and politics – is undermined. With private religion having become public religion, the second element falls too. Finally, since religiosity cannot simply be measured by factors such as church attendance, the third element also falls. Thus, nothing remains of the secularization thesis.[265] Similarly, Asad addresses the secularists' fear of organized religion imbued with institutional authority by pointing to the travails of a deprived (minority) religion whose values are subjected to the already prevalent agreement among the concerned parties.[266] In this context, Asad mentions Islamic nationalism as a form of crypto-nationalism where religion and politics mix, drawing on a long history of their interaction with each other.[267]

One can find in these observations a persistent dichotomy between secularism and religion almost as a given binary, even as both generate and regenerate each other.[268] There is a relatively facile problematic of the modernist project of the emergent Muslim states as opposed to the analysis of the classical mode of transition to modernism in the historical West. One finds rather hasty conclusions about the fall of the theses relating to secularism. Asad's construction of secularism as the major revolution in the West that ushered in the era of modernity as well as his critique can be challenged in view of rival interpretations led by philosophers from Hobbes, Lock and Rousseau to Marx and Weber, and the colonial encounter that defined the modernist and nationalist projects.

Akbar S. Ahmed's thesis of Islamic anthropology is part of a larger project of producing Islamic social sciences. He operates through a purported framework of postmodernism but ends up delivering a hybrid pre-modern content through a modern research methodology. He is in line with the nineteenth-century apologists Sir Syed and Ameer Ali, who were engaged in the task of proving to the West that Muslims were not barbarians.[269] Ahmed represents the contemporary generation of Muslim scholars struggling to defend Islam, projecting and performing a corrective exercise in the domain of the Western scientific study of Muslims and reinventing the social sciences from an Islamic perspective. His project of Islamic anthropology self-confessedly 'defends a metaphysical position, advances an ideological argument and serves a moral cause'.[270] He takes the orientalists to task for offending Muslims by using the word Mohammadanism[271] for Islam and for making derogatory references to the Prophet and the Bedouin society of his time. He claims that Ibn Khaldun's findings are reflected through the works of Karl Marx, Max Weber, Pareto and

Ernest Gellner, and that Al-Biruni from the eleventh century – i.e. nearly a thousand years before Malinowski and Geertz – should be called the father of anthropology.[272] He defines Islamic anthropology as the study of Muslim groups by those who are 'committed to the universalist principles of Islam', which is conceived 'not as theology but sociology' or even as a 'social religion'.[273] He finds in Pakistan a symbol of 'a renascent Islam'.[274] As expected, his native instinct harks back to religion not to the land and people of Pakistan, as is usually the case with India. His narrative is underscored by a dichotomy of Islam and the West that draws on the clash of civilizations thesis rather blandly and unimaginatively. What Akbar S. Ahmed meant was that only Muslims (believers) were able to really analyse a Muslim society, hence the concept of Islamic Anthropology. This barred the possibility of non-Muslims being able to understand Muslims. Similarly, whether Pakistan represents an Islamic renaissance is an open question.

The return of the native takes a more radical spin in the case of Humeira Iqtidar, who characterizes the two widely known Islamic parties as agents of secularization in the country – the one, JI, as a 'fundamentalist party' and the other, JuD, which was proscribed as a terrorist party in Pakistan. Her reading of the politics of religion in Pakistan carries a strange logic in the form of not only peculiar questions that she poses to herself but also their uncanny answers. For example, she asks whether secularism in Pakistan is a failed experiment. This question dwells on a preconceived notion that Pakistan had experimented with secularism. Nothing in the relevant historical and political analyses ever suggested that the ruling elite had taken up a secularist project in earnest. All the milestones on the way – the 1949 Objectives Resolution, the 1952 Basic Principles Committee's Report and the 1956, 1962 and 1973 Constitutions along with the amendments – point to the opposite, known as the Islamic project. The question is grossly misleading. The next question – whether Pakistan can 'ever be a secular state'[275] – is again misconstrued because no such policy orientation or scholarly research has pointed to such a direction. Again, she traces a 'project of rehabilitating secularism in Pakistan', an assertion with no historical, political, sociological or cultural arguments to support it. Indeed, one finds what is described as a 'trinity' of Pakistan, Islam and fundamentalism, without a meaningful exercise in differentiating the latter two.

The target group for the author's argument remains the 'increasingly belligerent policy discussions outside of Pakistan'.[276] She maintains that Western scholarship on Pakistan is unpalatable and, like Ahmed, she seeks to fix it. This leads to wild assumptions: that 'secularism is a project';[277] that in Muslim countries, the state project of secularism will lead to 'secularization in the society';[278] that 'the self-proclaimed secularists were among the upper classes';[279] that Musharraf wanted 'to rid the nation of "fundamentalist" elements';[280] and that academia and the media were the focus of the 'success of such a state policy'.[281] The reality is otherwise. Islam rather than secularism was the project. Prime Minister Liaqat Ali Khan condemned the 'Frankenstein Monster which human genius has produced in the form of scientific inventions', which had ignored 'the spiritual values of life'.[282] Instead, '[I]t is God-consciousness alone which can save humanity'.[283] Indeed, Liaqat Ali Khan opposed the idea that the state should be 'a neutral observer wherein the Muslims may be merely free to profess and practice their religion', which would be the very negation of the Pakistan project.[284] The author claimed that the ruling elite was secular. However, the latter was instead reprimanded by Justice Munir as early as 1954 for constantly talking about Islam from public forums and thus raising the level of religiosity in the public.[285] In Musharraf's case, he actually supported the coalition government of six Islamic parties (MMA) in KP in 2002.[286] Iqtidar claims that Islamists are facilitating the process of 'secularization as rationalization of religion', defined as an attempt to conceive religion as 'a logical and cohesive whole'.[287] However, one finds an absence of both logic and cohesion in the two cases of JI and JuD, which were profoundly given to blind faith and to a sectarian rather than a consensus-based model of Islam.

I now turn to Saba Mahmood, whose work on the politics of piety among Muslim women focused on the mosque movement in Egypt, which is somewhat comparable to the Al-Huda movement in Pakistan.[288] Feminists generally looked critically upon the women active in the mosque movement who used the same Islamic discourse that had been instrumental in ensuring their subordination to patriarchal authority. Instead, Mahmood defines women's agency in the form of their 'embodied capacities and the means of their subject formation'.[289] She describes herself as a feminist, leftist and progressive from Pakistan in her younger days and harks back to her generation's intellectual enquiry into the Iranian revolution. Mahmood questioned whether the roots of Islamic resurgence lay in a lack of education, the influence of Saudi Arabia carried through migrant labour, or 'Zia's mimetic effects'.[290] She looked for a clue outside the domain of private belief, and began to question the perceived inferiority of solutions other than 'secular-left' politics.[291] In her later work, she criticizes colonialism for framing the dichotomy between the West and the patriarchal non-Western cultures in a way that continues to operate up until today.[292] She criticizes Western scholars for undermining (Egyptian) women's participation in Islamically motivated movements that pose a challenge to this framing and 'to an entire chain of equivalences associated with Islam'.[293] Mahmood holds 'modern sovereign governance', rather than Islamic concepts, responsible for exacerbating religious hostility by considering the faith-based majority fit for rule in Egypt but others such as Bahais unfit.[294] As in the case of Akbar Ahmed and Iqtidar, Saba's major concern is the negative way Islamism is understood in the Western discourse.[295] Away from the issues of representation, identity and rights, she finds the real stuff in what is the essence of ethical life expressed through 'the body, ritual observance and protocols of public conduct'.[296]

It is clear that Mahmood's journey from the left in Pakistan to her widely acclaimed scholarship in the USA led her from a critique of Islamism to its defence, on the way holding yesterday's colonialism and today's feminism responsible for creating a binary of the Western and non-Western worlds. She returned to her native religion during the interface with her land of migration. Her mode of analysis moved from consideration of gender from a social, economic and cultural subordination of women in a Muslim society to the perceived activated inner self of women cultivating piety. These characteristics portray a journey from a 'liberal' to a 'conservative' framework of thought after getting deeply immersed in Western scholarship. The 'native' reappeared with a vengeance.

Quite a few leftists, ethnic activists, social workers and progressive party cadres, whose public agenda relates to the downtrodden, the destitute and the depressed, also symbolize the return of the native. For them, the supreme value lies with the cult of the masses. This includes adherence to Sufism, folk culture incorporating arts, music and dance, shrines of saints, popular religious festivals, and the vernacular as the mother tongue. They are committed to local customs and ritual practices as the authentic expression of popular culture. Often the cult of the masses operated at the cost of women's well-being, if one includes honour killing, domestic violence, rape within marriage, preference for sons, burying women alive in sand, using women as compensation for killing or uncleared debt (*sawara*, *vani*), and the murder of women for adultery (*karokari*). The progressive profile of the subaltern's world misses out on worship of the living and dead saints. It is underscored by docility in the face of oppression of the state functionaries, ranging from the police to the revenue department, record keepers of the land, hospitals, dispensaries and schools in the public sector. War against the oppressive forms of culture is hardly present on the horizon of the mind of the left. To answer Gayatri Spivak's question, '[C]an the subaltern speak?',[297] one can only say 'No' for both subalterns themselves and their 'nativist' supporters.

Quest for a Cultural Paradigm

There is a battle of cultures in Pakistan that reflects a broad contestation about defining what is legitimate and not legitimate in the domain of everyday life. That in turn decides 'who is an "insider" and who is an "outsider"'.[298] In Pakistan, as elsewhere, the domain of culture both as a way of life and as a stylized expression of value and custom is shaped by the relative power of the dominant forces. It is necessary that we look at the changes in the cultural landscape both with reference to the everyday life pattern and literary and artistic expression. A cultural landscape is a battleground for rival frameworks of beliefs and practices. It represents the winners in the past contestations that shaped the ideological constructs of the present. One also finds dichotomous models of cultural precepts, national and ethnic, Islamic and liberal, indigenous and Western. The key variable is power, which seeks to capture the maximum cultural landscape defined by public space.

Cultural Landscape

For our analysis, cultural landscape is a conceptual and methodological approach to understanding culture. This represents a holistic picture – termed as 'phenomenology of landscape'.[299] Far more than a static and bland view of a geographical expanse, landscape at any given time represents the process of 'becoming', i.e. reconstructing the trail through the past to the present. Any landscape is a contentious product of negotiations between those who were imbued with the 'power to define' – for example, religion, the 'written' state or international organizations – and those who were at the receiving end, such as the underprivileged ethnic elites or religious minorities. As the beliefs and practices of the successive 'winners' in these contests, the cultural landscape displays the starkly ideological input of those at the helm of affairs by way of 'framing the social imaginary'.[300] The dominant forces adopt a series of symbols, icons and heroes – for example, in Pakistan's case, Islam, Jinnah and Urdu – that shape the ideological constructs and accredit meaning to the way people belong to a certain place. In Pakistan, the dominant elite used epithets such as unity, Muslim homeland, and the sacrifice syndrome as ideological constructs. However, Bengalis, Sindhis and the Baloch fell back on their ethnic identity, history, language and culture to mobilize their respective communities to exercise their political initiative under duress. In other words, 'power' is the independent variable in drawing the cultural landscape. Analysis of the landscape is tantamount to understanding the push factor, imbued with legitimacy conferred by the state, and the factor of resistance. The latter is often condemned as transgression, as questioning the unquestionable and as an abominable act of those who are designated 'outsiders', either by faith, i.e. Christians and Hindus, or by sect, i.e. Shias and Ismailis, or by ethnicity, i.e. Sindhis and the Baloch.

Landscape is a text written by those who have the power. The 'text', as a collection of historical meanings, cultural symbols, boundaries and innuendos, and allegories and colours – green in Pakistan and saffron in India – is writ large on the cultural landscape. Most predominant is the text from British India, including black letter law, democracy, human rights, writ jurisdiction, independent judiciary, citizenship, legitimacy, juridical equality, modern art and scientific education. Further along in history, the text drew on the Sikh period in Punjab, the Talpur period in Sindh, Mir Chakar Khan's reign in Balochistan, the Durrani and Sikh rule in KP and, further back, on the Mughal period and beyond. The big text and the small text, i.e. the national ideological orientation and the regional identities and cultures respectively, together shaped the cultural landscape of Pakistan. 'Culture wars', both past and present, show a measure of the 'power' of the contesting social and political forces. Culture is politics by other means. For example, the level and context of Islamization point to the assumption of power by a certain section of Islamic non-state actors who impinged on the power of the modern state as a formidable pressure group. It changed the meta-narrative from both outside the formal channels of opinion-making, such as the media and education, and from outside the political 'system' itself in a militant mode of action, such as the jihadi narrative imbued with the duty to eliminate evil, impose *jizya* (tax) on non-Muslims, and avenge the killing of Muslims.[301] As power changed hands from the civil to the military wings of the state, the sources of political imagination and legitimation also passed through a commensurate level of transformation, from the republican character of the system to Islamicate expressions of law and policy.

Cultural landscape is an indicator of the way micro-conflicts merge with macro-conflicts and small doctrinaire streams clash or coalesce with the meta-narrative. Conflict draws heavily on the landscape itself, its ingredients, its landmarks, its nodal points, its peripheral areas as well as the supply of 'power' or the lack of it for running the whole system.[302]

The general, if not universal, acceptance of the two-nation theory by the Muslims of British India reflected the fact that it was formulated as a broadly encoded Muslim culture.[303] Soon after partition, there were signs of deviation from this narrative, whereby a different set of symbols belonging to a different cultural matrix emerged in one community after another. Rival groups and communities, some dominant and others seeking freedom from domination, focused on culture as a significant arena for their battles. Partition was an inexorable march of the Muslim civilizational thrust, imbued with an identifiable set of values, symbols and customs.[304]

However, such a cultural schema, rooted in what Geertz described as a system of symbols,[305] complete with its coherent message, describes only the first part of the structure–agency dichotomy. One can argue that there is no agency in the formulation of a civilizational ethos in general. Culture, far from an automaton that reproduces itself across generations, can often be traced to a project whereby identity formation becomes a matter of strategy. This happened in late colonialism when cultural definitions of the political objective of partition were produced by Jinnah and the Muslim League in the form of ideologically conceived plans for the future. The Pakistan project bound Muslims together by making them a semiotic community,[306] with a shared sense of intelligibility and coherence of the message accruing from the national leadership, overriding local, regional, linguistic and ethnic identities. The power-wielding local elite continued to use the symbols and icons long after these had lost their magic.

The staple of the master narrative comprised accusations of chicanery and fraud against Hindus, anthropomorphization of India as evil, cultivation of Jinnah as saviour, and propagation of unity as the principle of survival and onward march to prosperity. General Yahya reinvented the two-nation theory as the ideology of Pakistan in 1970, to stem the rising tide of the anti-establishment vote. Under Zia, the need to follow the culture of Saudi Arabia as the true Islamic heritage became the official mantra. A large majority of the Muslim intelligentsia, ranging from Hali, Shibli, Deputy Nzir Ahmed, Maulvi Zakaullah and Iqbal, had written moral treatises, Islamic history and reformist Urdu literature for a century, and thus had dug up sources of Muslim identity and culture. More than a theatrical performance on the stage, more than a novel, a poem, a film or any other form of cultural expression, the term culture was increasingly used in the sense of a way of life, along with religion as a defining variable. 'Islamic culture' became the rallying ground for making the case for a separate Muslim homeland.

Stephen Lyon considered Pakistan a nation of 'border cultures', including such buffer zones as Attock district on the border of KP and Punjab provinces.[307] In the broader perspective, the mega-picture of Pakistan represented a hybrid culture where Indian, Middle Eastern and Central Asian cultures had frequently interacted in the past, and provided a constant reference point for the upper echelons of the Muslim elite.[308] In the twentieth century, its cultural expression included the classical art in the form of overarching Muslim visual narrative in South Asia symbolized by its leading contemporary practitioner Abdur Rehman Chughtai; Urdu and Persian poetry identified with Iqbal; and for the classical music some prominent Muslim *gharanas* (families) were widely known. The long list of Mughal architectural artefacts includes the Taj Mahal, the Red Fort, Fatehpur Sikri, Badshahi Mosque and Jehangir's tomb, among hundreds of other prominent symbols.

Similarly, it has poets ranging from Amir Khusrau, Urfi and Faizi to Ghalib, Hali, Iqbal and Faiz. This heritage was generally identified with high culture.[309] At the other end, one finds the folk literature of Bulleh Shah, Sultan Bahu, Khawaja Farid, Sachal Sarmast and Latif Bhittai. The regional heroes who once fought the Mughals, such as Dulla Bhatti of Punjab and Khushhal Khan Khattak of KP, were submerged in high culture inasmuch as the political elite was able to mobilize the larger public in pursuit of the Pakistan project.

Among the mainstream writers who thrived after partition were Muhammad Hasan Askari, Aziz Ahmed, Mumtaz Shirin, Dr Syed Abdullah, and a host of historians, political scientists, literary writers and journalists. Indeed, the whole gamut of intelligentsia, barring certain members of the APPWA, identified Pakistan with spiritual fulfilment, moral achievement and cultural autonomy.

Conceptualization of a separate Indo–Muslim culture that lived side by side with Hindu culture for centuries, most typically led to a fossilized binary opposition. According to this view, Muslims looked outwards, Hindus inwards. Muslim writers focused on human subjects, whereas Hindu writers focused on 'supernatural themes'. Similarly, Islamic culture was projected as cosmopolitan, especially as it established the subcontinent's cultural contact with the rest of the world including Central Asia, Turkey, Russia and Europe. It was claimed that Islam's Semitic origins and Indian Muslims' Aryan context produced an 'aptitude for synthesis'.[310] One of the common themes was that the British administration was based on the centralized Mughal administration. In Saadia Toor's view, linkage between culture and politics in the country was drastically affected by the Cold War that initiated McCarthyism in the USA, along with a 'liberal' anti-Communist policy, state repression of progressive politics and the subsequent elevation of right-wing pro-establishment groups among its allies such as Pakistan.[311]

Battle of Cultures

While Islam and Indo–Muslim civilization occupied a pivotal position in the cultural narrative, the counter-narrative of the culture of the land and the people continued to assert itself with reference to ethnolinguistic identities. The former projected culture as religion, ideology, vision and agenda; the latter upheld the values and practices of the people. The former doted on history, the latter on geography, even as both brought the other factor in as part of their narratives. The geographical approach was dictated by the idea that the envisioned past of the new political entity (W) Pakistan represented the Indus civilization as opposed to the Gangetic civilization. It was clear that the present dictated the past, because it was hard to distinguish the Indus civilization from its Indian counterpart simply in order to claim its separate character. After Bangladesh, 'progressive' Pakistani nationalism sought to de-ideologize the way nationalist sentiment was conceived in religious and historical terms. Dani focused on the unity of the Indus civilization and, therefore, the unity of Pakistan 4,000 years later.[312] Unlike Dani — who was not cognizant of the variety of ethnic cultures within the present political set-up based on the peripatetic territory of the ancient Indus civilization — others found the geographical, topographical, linguistic, literary and historical variations in today's Pakistan legitimate claimants for a 'place' in the patchwork of the new nation.[313]

The case for a geographical approach to the cultural and political entity of Pakistan was presented elaborately by Qudratullah Fatimi. He claimed that 'Pakistan' was at its zenith when Taxila 'University' was established in the sixth century BC, which spread Mahayana Buddhism all around, popularized Ayervedic medicine, and produced the Sanskrit grammarian Panini and the strategist Chanakiya — author of *Arth Shastra*. Fatimi sees the origin of 'urban-villages' in the typical habitat of the area currently known as Sindh.[314] The distinct character of the Indus civilization being the geographical foundation of today's Pakistan was also taken up by Aitzaz Ahsen, who argued for historical continuity of a cultural zone conceived in territorial terms.[315]

On the opposite side, two kinds of objection to the Indus civilization thesis emerged: first, that this was an arbitrary line drawn under the shadow of the Pakistan project largely in accord with the Radcliffe Award for the partition of Punjab; second, that historically there was non-Muslim dominance in both Sindh and Punjab. The pivotal character of the Indus valley culture in commercial, intellectual and professional terms was similar to the pattern operating elsewhere in ancient India. Curiously, if the Indus civilization had not been 'discovered' as a result of archaeological finds in Taxila, Harappa and Mohenjo-Daro, unearthed by a team led by John Marshall in the first quarter of the twentieth century, the whole argument would be redundant.

A major challenge to the framework of mainstream thinking came from the Progressive Writers Association (PWA), which was founded in 1936. This forum had mobilized literary writers, poets, novelists and others to shift the focus of their attention from the past to the present, from a visionary approach to history and politics to everyday life, from high culture to low culture, and from faith-based identity to issues relating to class, gender and justice.[316] The PWA was a forum for the production of literature following the principle of art-for-life's sake as opposed to art-for-art's sake. A large majority of writers in the Indian languages, especially Urdu, embraced the idea, and wrote about people who were destitute, morally depressed and economically exploited, including peasants, workers, prostitutes and a host of other socially marginalized individuals and families. The fact that the PWA was initially conceived by young Indian socialist students in London and was later established by leftist-orientated intellectuals back in India, led to speculation about its conspiratorial origins and alleged links with the Communist International. Similarly, the PWA was understood to be closely associated with the Congress's socialist wing led by Nehru. The leading figures of Urdu literature joined the movement, among them Josh Malihabadi, Maulvi Abdul Haq, Firaq Gorakhpuri, Sajjad Zaheer, Sibte Hasan, Ahmed Ali, Rashid Jehan, Faiz Ahmed Faiz, Ali Sardar Jafri, Zaheer Kashmiri, Sahir Ludhianvi, Krishan Chandar and Ahmed Nadeem Qasmi. They staked their claim as the conscience of India and later Pakistan, and espoused the causes of the eradication of poverty, injustice, communal hatred and class-based exploitation. The PWA clearly dominated a whole generation of Urdu writers before and after partition. It is no coincidence that the progressive writers' critique of mainstream writers for promoting hatred against India was subjected to a backlash in Pakistan.[317]

While the PWA operated along the 'liberal' lines of tolerance among faiths, castes and classes, the Pakistan movement had the opposite effect of creating an enhanced religious consciousness among Muslims couched in a clash of belligerent identities. PWA members and supporters either stood apart from the partition agenda or opposed it. After 1947, those who found themselves on this side of the border, by migration or otherwise, faced tremendous pressure from the protagonists of the Muslim nationalist agenda, who blamed them for being traitors. PWA writers wrote tragic stories of communal violence that involved loss of human life and the subjection of women to inhuman treatment, and they expressed disillusionment with the dawn of independence whose promise remained unfulfilled.[318] Not surprisingly, mainstream literary writers criticized the PWA affiliates for 'negation of the fundamental thought of Islam' and for their 'poetic camouflage to denounce the birth of Pakistan'.[319] In the overall, post-partition cultural framework, the decline of the PWA as an active literary movement was a foregone conclusion. The leading progressive literary journals such as *Adab-e-Latif* and *Savera* were put under surveillance. The involvement of progressive writers such as Sajjad Zaheer and Faiz Ahmed Faiz in the 1951 Rawalpindi Conspiracy Case clearly placed the PWA on the wrong side of the ruling hierarchy. Faiz, who was generally acknowledged as the master intellectual of his times, attempted to define Pakistani culture as a product of national, ethno-regional and international influences. His readiness to accept Western impact in certain fields of public life put him at odds with his contemporaries, who were swept by the wave of anti-Western imperialism.[320]

A 'battle of cultures' ensued. On the one hand, culture was conceived in ideological, visionary, and missionary terms as an independent variable operating on a given matrix of time and space. I argue that this meaning of culture can be traced to the two supra-cultural influences. At one end, religion was responsible for the genesis of the state in the first place. It acquired a quantum of legitimacy higher than other factors such as language, ethnicity, history, race, geography, sect and sector. At the other end, nationalism pressed the need for the projection of the idea of a unified culture for people living within the new borders. This view of culture was popular with the state elite and the educated middle class, especially from Punjab and the Mohajir community, along with their lesser compatriots from other provinces. Many of them were institutionally, professionally, or intellectually identified with the establishment. This vision of culture was shared by a whole range of ideologues, from the right of centre – including the so-called 'liberal' state elite and its modernist intellectual apologists – to the ultra-right elements committed to a divine agenda. Islamist groups were initially divided vis-à-vis the Pakistan project, with the

Ahrars and the JI opposed to it while the Jamiat Ulema Pakistan (JUP) factions, Sufis and *pirs* supported it.[321] State managers increasingly relied on Islamists to counter the demands from leftists and ethno-nationalists committed to safeguarding popular cultures.

On the other hand, the 'progressives' – including leftists and ethno-nationalists – conceived culture as a dependent variable, far from a transformative agenda. In their understanding, culture was inherently related to art, language, literature, gender, region, caste, class and tribe as rooted in the actual patterns of behaviour in public and private life. In other words, culture drew essentially and comprehensively upon the land and the people. The adherents of this view of culture included certain communities that additionally faced the dilemma of establishing the moral legitimacy of their ties with transborder co-ethnics. They included the Baloch in Iran, Pakhtuns in Afghanistan as well as Bengalis and Punjabis in India who shared cultural, linguistic and historical bonds with their compatriots inside Pakistan. The state was obviously more antithetical to cultural ties across the boundaries of faith, such as with Hindus and Sikhs in India, than it was to the faith community across the borders with Iran and Afghanistan.

In Punjab, the high quantum of violence perpetrated on rival communities of Muslims, Hindus and Sikhs had pushed the people from the two partitioned halves of the province poles apart. Moreover, in East Punjab it was the Gurmukhi script that developed Punjabi as the language of education, media and literature. In West Punjab, people used Urdu and not Punjabi as the language of literacy and, thus, as the language of literary, media and educational expression. Whatever written Punjabi was introduced by literary writers and intellectuals in Pakistan was in Shahmukhi, the Perso–Arabic script. That meant that any meaningful and regular communication across the border became virtually extinct, especially after the passing of the independence generation of Hindus and Sikhs in East Punjab, who had been educated in Urdu before partition. As mentioned earlier, the meagre efforts of Punjabi chauvinists in Pakistan to join hands with Indian Punjabis to organize cultural activities in India and Pakistan as well as in Europe and the USA remained marginal to the mainstream literary activities on both sides.

However, it was the challenge of shared cultural ties between East and West Bengal after partition that became a thorn in the side of the national project. Here, unlike Punjab, people on both sides spoke and wrote Bengali and used the same script. The difference between Hindu and Muslim Bengali was often brought up by supporters of the national project, who resorted to 'Islamizing' Bangla.[322] The Bengali language was considered 'Hindu'; it was not used on public artefacts ranging from postal stamps and coins to the curriculum for the elite civil services; and by extension, it was linked to the decline of Urdu in India, which shared the same fate.[323] In the face of Bengali nationalists in East Pakistan, who defied the cultural constraints imposed by Karachi – especially the denial of national language status to Bengali – official cultural policy was increasingly in the doldrums. Obviously, the state's agenda of cultural partitioning with India could not be successfully operationalized under these conditions. East Pakistan clearly presented a clash of the two prevalent opposite cultural approaches, one defined by religion and nationalism and the other defined by the land and the people.

Similarly, in the case of KP, Afghan irredentism and Pakhtun nationalism often joined hands to pull people's commitments away from the national bond cultivated by the state in Pakistan. However, unlike the Bengali situation, where the hub of cultural activity by way of art, language and literature lay across the border in Calcutta, studded by such names as Nobel Laureate Tagore and poet Qazi Nazrul Islam and institutions such as Shanti Niketan, the KP situation was far more complex. Afghanistan was in no position to attract Pakhtun nationalists en masse educationally, culturally and economically. From the 1980s onwards, Afghanistan plunged into a war that continued for more than four decades, with slim hope of peace after the 2021 US withdrawal from the country. The attraction of Kabul as the symbol of a land from where all Pakhtuns had come – both historically and mythically – to the areas now constituting Pakistan, gradually faded away. The debate about culture led to a quest for a formula that, in Faiz Ahmed Faiz's view, would meet the needs of a united nation while at the same time cater to the requirement for promotion and encouragement of regional cultures.[324] This debate overlapped with a parallel question about whether there was one nation or five nationalities – Bengali, Punjabi, Sindhi, Pakhtun and Baloch. Was Pakistan a nation or a multi-nation?

At the other end, a whole generation of migrant literary writers tried to come to grips with the horrors of partition and the pangs of nostalgia for their areas of origin in India. Joginder Paul in his scintillating novel *Sleepwalkers* described the way that UP migrants in Karachi lived in a make-believe world of their own where the street names, the style of greetings, the everyday idiom and the references in conversation pointed to the culture and places of Lucknow.[325] Several authors, among them Intizar Hussain, Qurratul Ain Haider and Ahsen Farooqi, set their stories in the context of a cultural milieu of pre-partition India that was no more, and in terms of the vicissitudes of the process of migration with all its hope, misery, instability, tension and fear of an alien land. Being at the top of the emergent ethnic hierarchy in their land of migration, Mohajirs allegedly displayed cultural snobbery vis-à-vis the local people of Pakistan, especially Sindhis with whom they had had no historical exchange culturally or linguistically. When Bengali was declared the second national language, Mohajirs demonstrated against it.[326] However, Punjab in Pakistan was far less given to nostalgia for the Indian Punjab even as migrants from Punjab and adjoining areas were twice as many as non-Punjabis – later called Mohajirs.

The trans-Indus provinces of Balochistan and KP, whose cultural ties with India were generally superseded by their historical ties with Iran and Afghanistan respectively, were no competitors for the Mohajir–Punjabi elite on the issue of preserving or challenging the national culture. However, Bengal and Sindh presented a different scene. Bengal was generally placed outside the traditional cultural framework of the dominant Muslim imperial tradition. Its elite had been historically related to Central Asia. However, the Muslim Bengali community at large had a weak urban-based intelligentsia of its own, and instead relied on the 'high culture' of the Hindu *bhadralok* community across the border. A continuing commitment of the East Pakistan intelligentsia to the cultural milieu of West Bengal grossly alienated the state managers of Pakistan, who had moved on from a mere geographical separation to an ever-expanding agenda of cultural partitioning from India. Nor was West Pakistan totally free of cultural ambitions that moved beyond the officially prescribed and defined limits of cultural expression. One legacy of the Sindhi nationalist agenda, along with its strong components of language, tradition, and commitment to the antiquity of its culture, was a crucial input of caste Hindus, who represented the intelligentsia, bankers, doctors, lawyers, and other professionals in the local society before they migrated to India.

Unlike Bengal and Sindh, Muslim Punjab had been a region of cultural fallout from the UP Ashraf after its annexation to British India in 1849. Inasmuch as the Punjabi language was too closely identified with Sikhs for the comfort of Muslims, the latter welcomed the official policy of the post-annexation British government to declare Urdu the language of education and administration. Today's KP, as part of Punjab for half a century, has similarly imbibed a strong influence of UP. While Pakhtuns have expressed a consistent anti-Punjab sentiment from the days of Ranjit Singh, they were not inimical to the current of religious sentiment per se. The neo-Wahhabist mission from Delhi that found its crescendo in the 1832 jihad against Sikh rule had been carried out in KP at Balakot. Nor indeed were Pakhtuns averse to the prevalence of Urdu language and literature that included a strong component of Islamic literature. This model differed from East Bengal where a vibrant Bengali culture from across the border remained a source of great inspiration, and the 'high culture' of Pakistan had to contend with an inborn, continuous, indigenous and authentic culture of Bengalis in East Pakistan.

The 1970 elections produced two mass movements that had strong cultural fallouts in rump Pakistan. First, there was the undoing of the ethos of migrant domination that was rooted in the Indo–Muslim civilization, thus leading to 'nativization' of the migrant state by way of erosion of the cultural domination of Mohajirs in Sindh. Second, there was the emergence of local identities such as Punjabi, Sindhi, Pakhtun and Baloch as legitimate political entities for operating on the political stage. Till then, the state had been benighted by a superior ideological framework that claimed inheritance from the vast Indian subcontinent and nurtured a pan-Islamic vision abroad. Now, in the aftermath of Bengali separatism, a new awareness emerged: that ethnic identity needed to be taken seriously and to be managed well, instead of being treated as frivolous and treacherous.[327]

In the 1970s, Pakistan entered the era of what can be called indigenous revival. There followed several coterminous developments in the realm of cultural identity. The Indus civilization that flourished 4,000 years ago in the parts of India that now constituted (W) Pakistan provided a new territorial base for the country as part of myth/ history whereby it established links with antiquity. This drift from an ideological mould of the nationalist idiom enshrined in the two-nation theory to a territorial identity based on the Indus valley indicated the potential for the emergence of a counter-discourse. This move from territorial agnosticism to territorial nationalism corresponded to the gradual loosening of cultural ties with India. Contrary to the geographically defined Indus civilization as coterminous with the borders of contemporary Pakistan, a discovery of ancient skeletons belonging to that civilization in Rakhigarhi in Haryana in India in 2014 challenged the current myth about the territorial expanse of their ancient heritage.[328] Another discovery of artefacts in Daimabad in Maharashtra, dated from two millennia BC, expanded the area of the Indus civilization far away from Sindh.[329] In addition, various migration theories thrived on the theme of the Vedic Aryans, as well as the Dravidian-speaking West Asians who left their remnants in Balochistan as speakers of a Dravidian language, Brahui, or even speakers of a dead language, Elam, from southwest Iran.

An important aspect of the indigenous revival was the acceptance of the idea of 'four cultures' represented by the four provinces. The annual Pakistan Day celebrations on 23 March commemorated the 1940 Lahore Resolution. These now included a mobile display of significant cultural symbols of these provinces on the road in capital cities and on a train across the country. The populist government of Z. A. Bhutto thus acknowledged the existence of four peoples, four nationalities and four cultures. This ideological reorientation would have been anathema to the first generation of rulers in Pakistan. The new quest for a cultural policy led to deliberations about a possible synthesis of the national and sub-national cultures. A new institution, the Academy of Letters, was established in Islamabad for the promotion of regional cultures and their representation in the national culture. It undertook the translation into Urdu of literary works written in regional languages, the publication of regional literatures, and cultivation of a dialogue across cultures. A sister institution, Lok Virsa (Folk Heritage), was established to bring together works of art, calligraphy, handicraft, music and various cultural artefacts from across the country. An annual exhibition, Lok Mela, has been the high point of its activities, which is attended by artisans, artists, musicians and others from the performing arts. Over time, this institution lost its vigour but not its relevance for projecting the cultural expression of people operating at the grassroots levels.

The focus on the four provinces highlighted the traditions of their respective majority communities, which led to alienation of their minority communities. In Sindh, the Mohajir community was left high and dry, out of this national display of culture. It felt disenfranchised from the whole exercise, especially after the Sindhi language controversy had grossly alienated it in 1972. The question was asked: Where does Mohajir culture belong? Remembered as 'Ganga-Jamuni culture', it had no territorial expression within Pakistan. Only Karachi was a Mohajir-dominated city, but after becoming the capital of Sindh in 1970 its Mohajir identity was submerged within the wider Sindhi identity. For two generations, one heard the expression 'Karachi and Sindh', which pointed to the Mohajir-dominated city of Karachi and the Sindhi-dominated area all around. Obviously, Sindhis did not countenance the idea of separating the two entities in public or in private communication. In August 2020, heavy rainfall brought down the infrastructure in Karachi and other cities of Sindh. Military contingents and rangers deployed for meeting the emergency mentioned 'Karachi and interior Sindh', thereby echoing the controversial expression of describing the province in dichotomous terms.

The indigenous revival in and around 1970 put Mohajirs on the defensive in linguistic, cultural as well as political terms. While they surpassed all other communities in terms of literacy rate and higher education, as well as representation in jobs and businesses proportionate to their population, the new openings for non-Mohajirs re-shaped the Mohajir psyche along the lines of acute disillusionment with their 'promised land'. Four decades after partition, the Mohajirs of Karachi, Hyderabad and Sukkur and other urban areas of Sindh started to perceive themselves as a separate cultural community. They fell back on their claim to cultural superiority and ethnic origins from outside the communities belonging to Pakistan. However, apart from Urdu as their mother tongue, which lent a distinct identity to them, but which was also spoken as a lingua franca by the large urban middle classes across the country, there was little to really put Mohajirs in a separate cultural category. In the beginning, the MQM MNAs and Members of Provincial Assemblies (MPAs) attended the sessions of the national and Sindh assemblies in their classical attire, comprising *kurta* and tight pyjamas along with a waistcoat from Lucknow of pre-partition days. That was a contraption that rendered them out of place and out of age and, not surprisingly, it was soon abandoned.

In terms of literature, writers from both Punjab and the Mohajir community from urban Sindh produced Urdu poetry and fiction. The two literary expressions were hardly distinct from each other along ethnic lines. The Mohajir espousal of culture as agenda, and identity as a mission opposed to the culture of the land and its people in Sindh, gradually developed a violent dimension. The migrants represented an atomistic society of individual families and people who came from various cities, towns and villages of the north, central, eastern, western and southern stretches of India. They left behind densely networked human relations that once provided sustenance of hierarchical patterns of moral authority within and outside the patriarchal family system. During migration, they passed through a process of deconstruction as a community. The host society of Sindhis, on the other hand, continued to remain stable in terms of its structural foundations in the family and the village community. The absence of strong community ties among Mohajirs bound by family, class, caste, area of origin and neighbourhood, later provided space for ethnic violence.

As an afterword before finishing this section, one needs to mention a conscious attempt to create 'Islamic literature' after partition. It was essentially the JI's offshoot, an initiative to counter the PWA. It was alleged that the progressives had taken literary writings in the direction of atheism, regionalism and even obscenity.[330] The leading JI intellectuals, ranging from Asad Gilani and Naeem Siddiqui to Tahir-ul-Qadri and A'asi Ziyaee, took up the task of establishing the branches of their organization, the Movement for Islamic Literature (MIL), in the country. They even tried to create an Islamic theory of literature that drew upon the concept of *fawad* (heart, the spiritual dimension) as well as *nafs* (instinct) along with its three stages of animal instinct, conscientious living, and the state of satisfaction with oneself.[331] The stirrings of Islamic literature reverberated outside the JI's party framework as well. For example, Dr Syed Abdullah of Punjab University Lahore took up the cause of Islamic literature. The movement soon dissipated because the requirements of aesthetics and strict moralism could not co-exist in the context of the creation of a genuine literary production.

Conclusion

This chapter has aimed at bringing out the leading features of the national discourse, most typically expressed through the written word. This narrative served the function of drawing a self-portrayal by cultivating a sense of the past and a vision of the future, and by connecting with the world at large. It has been largely defined in terms of an intractable conflict with India. Partition provided the means to a partial transition, from the Islamic heritage of Central Asia and Iran to Arabization, from Hanafi to Salafi schools of thought, and from South Asia to the Middle East as the pivot of the faith-based identity. The Islamic project increasingly defined the national project. Pakistan developed a dichotomous worldview based on Islam and the West. Its credentials as a legatee of Indo–Muslim civilization became a hotbed of controversy as the state took roots in the previously uncharted territory of present-day Pakistan. The country looked for an 'alternative globality' in the form of a world-of-Islam perspective in the international arena. As a gruesome legacy of partition, the master narrative of Pakistan created a Hindu demon as the 'other'. While feeling its way through the complexities of national and international life, the nation's strategic way out was to comprehend things as conspiracy. Thinking minds from the left, the right, the 'liberal' and Islamic categories of the political spectrum, continued to display paranoia about international conspiracies to pressure, bully, corner or undo Pakistan.

This chapter also brought out the three areas of historical, territorial, and linguistic agnosticism. Without being historically situated, with its territorial imaginary submerged in the ideological consciousness and with language not accepted as a legitimate source of identity for people, the potential for conflict continued to be high. The issue of religion at the heart of the master narrative has indeed been a story of unending contestation between modernists and traditionalists, the former rooted in the power dynamics of the state and the latter periodically resorting to street power, ballot power and bullet power. The master narrative has created a world-of-Islam perspective that draws on its underdog position within the wider world, which put it in a perceived combat position vis-à-vis the West. Postcolonialism has taken firm roots in the psyche of the nation, especially in the form of the return of the native, at the level of both a scholarly approach to religion and secularism and 'leftist' activism among the intelligentsia. I have used the concept of cultural landscape to bring out the process of narrativization of the prevalent fault lines across society. The current pattern of cultural landscape is the result of past contestations for framing the national imaginary along the symbols and icons selected by the dominant elite. The latter writes the big text while those from ethnic and religious minorities and the working classes in general write the small text, if at all. The master narrative duly reflects the relative power and privilege of the two power centres to which we turn in the next chapter.

3

TWO POWER CENTRES

Introduction

The central theme of this chapter is the persistent, perilous and devastating conflict between the two elite groups in Pakistan: the state elite and the political elite. The former is generally identified with the 'establishment', led by the army. The latter represents political parties and parliament, which draw on the constitutional edifice as the supreme source of legitimacy. This situation has led to a bifocal nature of state authority.[1] The two elite groups draw heavily on two power centres: the middle class and the political class, respectively. The first power centre draws massively on path dependence by way of institutionalization of civil bureaucracy and the military in British India. While institutional imbalance is a basic characteristic of postcolonial societies in favour of the state apparatuses, Punjab – the power base of Pakistan – was already a semi-military state in British India.[2] Sindh was a backward region of the Bombay Presidency in terms of developing representative institutions at the local level. Most of Balochistan was a region of indirect rule any way. After its accession to Pakistan, the Baloch princely states were brought together to form the Balochistan States Union, which provided a sense of administrative centralization. In this way, the territories that constituted (West) Pakistan had weak institutions of self-rule as compared to India.

The state elite has generally been known as the military–bureaucratic establishment and noted for its overbearing, deterministic and interventionist nature.[3] However, one can argue that there is no role for 'agency' in this model, i.e. for the political class that steers electoral politics, government formation, law-making and the execution of policy, indeed the whole gamut of governance. To put all one's eggs in the basket of what is now crystallized as the military establishment, also called miltablishment,[4] is to miss the role of the political class. Local electoral heavyweights, party cadres and workers, as well as the candidate/voter linkages, continued to be operative and relevant for government formation against all odds.[5]

At the other end, the state elite has been typically recruited from the middle class. Its institutional ethos has been geared to securitization of the national vision, centralization of power, control over policy, and manipulation of the mass public through education and the media. As a legatee of British imperialism in India Pakistan has firm roots in the British common law, court system, election system, rule of law and rule of public representatives. The political class, though divided along ideological and identity lines, has strong roots in the locality (district) and the region (province). As the constitutional tradition is upheld by the political class as the gateway to power, the much-touted goals of good governance, elimination of corruption and moral uprightness are the manifest ambitions of the middle class. In this chapter, I plan to draw profiles of the middle class and the political class as the two power centres.

The Middle Class: A Profile

My argument is that the state elite would not have been able to play the master's fiddle if it had not drawn on middle-class support. The middle class includes professionals, technocrats, lawyers, engineers, doctors, charted accountants, professors, journalists, architects, artists, literary writers, computer analysts, corporate managers and the business community. This class provides the catchment area for the state elite, i.e. civil bureaucracy, the military's officer cadre as well as the judiciary. It operates as the most stable, influential, and status quo-orientated segment of society. The institutional expression of this class is realized through the state apparatuses. The process of post-recruitment socialization in the form of the training of bureaucracy and army officers aims at merging their individual ambitions with an all-pervasive institutional ethos.[6] The middle class has a near-monopoly over higher education, professional expertise, scientific knowledge, artistic achievement and the cultural expressions of the nation. More than any other section of society, the middle class is ideologically orientated to the two domains of religion and nationalism. Religiously speaking, it adheres to scriptural Islam far more than syncretic Islam. It is more tolerant of the madrassah-orientated written tradition than the shrine-based oral tradition of religion.[7] It seeks the unity of the Muslim world and upholds a dichotomous worldview based on conflict between Islam and the West. Similarly, it pursues a nationalist framework of thought and expression, which is set essentially in an anti-Indian, anti-Western and anti-Zionist idiom.

Defining the Middle Class

The term middle class invokes gross definitional problems. While Marxist and Weberian models thrash out relatively clear profiles of classes and strata with reference to relations of production and educational, professional and status variables respectively, no overarching approach to the middle class was available for a long time. However, certain sociological variables have been widely used to describe middle-class orientations, especially with reference to 'public', such as public relations, public opinion and public sphere.[8] The middle class focuses on governance not government, performance-based legitimacy not entrance-based legitimacy,[9] managerial approach not representational ethos, result orientation of the executive not deliberations of parliamentary debates, and accountability not performativity.

The middle class has the self-image of a guardian, an imaginary supra-political entity overseeing systemic efficiency or the lack of it. In Pakistan, the role of guardian has been played by the civilian bureaucracy couched in the middle-class ethos as a legacy of British India. Later, the officer cadre of the army superseded the bureaucracy in the role of guardian. Yadav traces presidentialism in India as 'the middle-class fantasy of a benevolent dictator'.[10] For the middle class in Pakistan, the grass was always greener on the other side, especially in the USA with its presidential system, or in continental Europe with the proportional representation (PR) system considered to be a more representative electoral framework than the first-past-the-post (FPTP) system. Indeed, the middle class preferred to put democracy itself on hold.

One can trace the genealogy of the middle class to the state in British India. While the tribal and aristocratic elite was part of the 'collaborative mechanism' of colonial rule, the middle class was the very creation of colonialism. It soon served as a cog in the state machinery, comprising the new system of legal and administrative authority, the court system and the financial institutions. Over time, the collaborators became legislators under the patronage of the British state, from the district right up to the province.

The middle class expanded over a hundred years and became simply too large to be absorbed as 'Babus, Brahmans and Bureaucrats'.[11] Those who were not on the payroll of the government, including the intelligentsia, lawyers, public activists and professionals, were engaged in dozens of career pursuits. Together, they emerged as the middle class as we know it today. When analysing the middle class, what is often not taken into consideration is the mental infrastructure – moral, legal and philosophical – of the statecraft that groomed this class. The 'new left' typically looked at the postcolonial state in functional terms: as an instrument to control the masses and to 'mediate' between the contending classes from a potentially autonomous position.[12] The formative ideas of statehood, first formulated in Europe and then transplanted to British India as a template of colonial rule, have not been fully analysed as the right stuff for understanding the new state as well as its product in the form of the middle class in Pakistan and India.

Research about the middle class falls into four categories. First, there is the economic profile, which has social, cultural and political overtones.[13] Often, this profile is related to the larger context of urbanization.[14] Second, Sabiha Hafeez looks at this class essentially from a sociological perspective, i.e. as a class unto itself rather than a class-for-itself.[15] Third, this class can be understood as a catchment area for the institutional apparatuses of the state. Fourth, the middle class is seen as a political actor in its own right, such as in the 1977 anti-Bhutto movement,[16] and the Lawyers' Movement in 2007, and as Imran Khan's urban-based populist constituency in 2011–21.

In the following pages, I shall discuss the politics of the middle class essentially in a contextual framework beyond its understanding in common parlance. For delineating some of the leading characteristics of the middle class, we need to draw on Bourdieu's theory of social reproduction in the context of cultural capital that makes a definite contribution to the 'structural dynamics of class relations'.[17] In Bourdieu's understanding of the educational system, the distribution of cultural capital is far from a replica of economic capital; that in turn provides a justification for an ideology of meritocracy in the name of 'academic justice'.[18]

The role for a thriving, enchanting, overarching and intellectualizing middle class is most typically carved out of what Homi Bhabha calls 'in-between spaces'.[19] Fernandes and Heller have argued that the middle class in India was reacting against the upward thrust of the lower castes and classes.[20] However, their definition of the middle class in terms of an intermediary position between the two identifiable classes is both derivative and residuary in nature.[21] In my understanding, the middle class in Pakistan is autonomous in terms of its origins in cultural capital. The middle class has been in a dominant position all along except during the Bhutto period (1971–7) when 'the historical bloc' ruling the country was shaken up.[22] My argument is that, over time, the middle class has acquired a status, identity and privilege, which belies its 'middle' position by way of power and prestige. Both within the state as bureaucrats and technocrats, and outside the state as intelligentsia and professionals, the middle class played its distinct role by shunning politics and yet assuming a vigilante's role vis-à-vis the political class. Its self-image can be located in the modernization theory that considered it the repository of a forward-looking and progressive ethos in traditional societies.[23]

Fernandez and Heller argue that the economic opportunities of this class in India were not derived from property, which contributed to its rent-seeking character.[24] I want to argue otherwise: that property is at the heart of jobs and professional careers in Pakistan. The state in its capacity as the largest employer in the public sector – and more stridently in the security apparatus – has pursued a policy of allocating rural and urban land and housing property from the 1960s onwards. Indeed, during the initial phase of refugee resettlement in the 1950s, the migrant middle class set the pattern by getting evacuee property as its 'right' as citizens of its coveted homeland. By the turn of the twenty-first century, almost all government departments had pooled their resources, bought agricultural land from the peri-urban villages and developed housing schemes.

The middle class lives in gated communities in major cities. Since a lot of this property was acquired non-commercially, either by lottery or through buying 'files' prior to land development or as part of the retirement package, the salaried middle class – both civilian and military – is rent-seeking in nature. Similarly, the professional elite is interested in property buying and selling. In addition, remittances from the Gulf sent by doctors, engineers, bankers, chartered accountants, small businessmen, journalists, academics, and other professionals mostly went into buying property. The money that was frozen in property hampered the growth of capital accumulation. Unbridled consumer orientation further dampened the instinct for saving and investment. While the political class was enjoined to be engaged with the public through patronage, and periodically through elections, the middle class reproduced itself 'independently' through its cultural capital. The growth of a high-tech service sector further deepened this trend. Not surprisingly, the middle class's hatred for politics is legendary in Pakistan.

The concept of middle class continues to be a slippery one. Viewed in terms of income bracket, it leaves us with the urban and rural middle classes.[25] This is problematic because the middle class is defined by educational and cultural capital and its self-reproductive potential. Its city-based elitism, in terms of morals and manners, is underscored by cultural activities in the fields of art, literature, music, film, theatre and sports. Its near monopoly over academic excellence and physical and mental competence is the way to recruitment in the state apparatus. I want to argue that the middle class is quintessentially urban-based. The fluidity of its boundaries has kept the doors open for rural–urban migration and for upward mobility from the lower middle class, especially in the commercial sector.

A recent trend in research differentiated between the old and new middle classes with reference to the liberal and religio-conservative sections respectively in the specific context of Lahore city.[26] It has been argued that the new middle class in Pakistan gets frustrated in its consumption orientation, restricted by limited resources in the upwardly changing urban environment studded with shopping malls, multiplex cinemas, private school systems, the burgeoning fashion industry, parlours and fast food chains.[27] One wonders if this newness is in fact the generational transition per se. Barring those who entered the urban middle class laterally from the rural sector, an absolute majority of the middle class in the first quarter of the twenty-first century belonged to the generation that sent its children to English-medium schools (i.e. where English is the primary language of instruction) and provided them with a partial or full exposure to Western universities or the local variants of Silicon Valley.

In other words, a leap forward in income and consumption levels should be interpreted as a natural progression for an economy that thrives on rent-seeking, from the indirect state-supported accumulation of proprietary interests, largesse from the defence sector,[28] and remittances from the Gulf.[29] Imran Khan responded to middle-class ambitions of getting rid of the corrupt dynastic politics. However, he was able to capture political office in 2018 not through the active political participation of this class but through the army. The argument that the arrival of the new middle class led to a new political agenda couched in the need for political reform has become a cliché. One needs to go beyond the concept of 'newness', i.e. in the form of a new pressure for political reform after the entry of the middle class into the arena. The modern way of life in Pakistan as a behavioural or cultural expression is more 'global' than Western. This class is committed to maintenance of the 'system' as defined by centralization of power, militarization of authority and Islamization of the narrative. The view concerning the contradiction between modern and Islamic tendencies is not sustainable given the prevalence of the basic rules of the game operative within an urban middle-class household pertaining to the unsanctioned personal relations across gender, preservation of the traditional dress code for women, and patriarchy in letter and spirit. One also finds the argument unsustainable that, under Zia, religious and conservative elements of the middle class supported him whereas liberal elements opposed him.[30] There is no evidence that the middle class was divided along ideological and cultural lines. Indeed, a large part of this class was solidly behind Zia after the passing of the Bhutto period that had grossly challenged its interests and ideology.

155

Contrary to the grandiose claims about the progressive agenda of the middle class, one found rent-seeking and right-wing tendencies thriving under Imran Khan's government (2018–). His public discourse in office tilted away markedly from the 'liberal' rhetoric of his middle-class followers, in the direction of Islamism. In July 2020, the Punjab Assembly passed an Islamic law that symbolized a 'galloping religiosity' in terms of obliging Muslims to follow rituals stringently, at the risk of severe penalty, and was followed by the banning of almost a hundred textbooks that were not in line with the new Islamic provisions.[31] The PTI government formulated a new draft education policy in July 2020 for which an agreement was sought from the madrassah federations based on the four leading Islamic schools of thought. The progressive sections of civil society found in it a 'madrassafication' of the prevalent school systems, both public and private.[32] The middle class was poised to close itself off from the world, even as modern schools, colleges and universities had contributed to opening the doors to Western education for its prosperous sections for at least two generations. It thoroughly distrusted the judgement and the right of those they considered the uneducated, irresponsible, superstitious, and 'primitive' masses to exercise their vote, a vote that led to inefficient and corrupt governments. It lacked a social reformist vision and a public conscience in the context of mitigating poverty, facilitating public access to justice, and safeguarding the interests of religious, sectarian and ethnic minorities. With an enhanced awareness about the issue of corruption, the middle class found it very difficult to understand why people voted for 'corrupt' politicians. Its stock-in-trade was that elections were hijacked by landlords who were known in common parlance as 'feudals', that politicians were corrupt and inefficient, and that society was not yet ready for democracy. It failed to appreciate that the state structure, run by an administrative elite rooted in the middle class itself, barred people's access to the system of governance in various localities.[33] People could only manage to sneak through the gates of the remote, impersonal, English-based bureaucratic ruling mechanism with the help of elected politicians, 'corrupt' or otherwise.

The task of drawing estimates of the size of the middle class has been a difficult exercise. In various cases, it ranged from 60 per cent to zero per cent, if judged on the basis of economic indicators.[34]

Sridharan points to the extremely subjective estimates of the middle class in India, ranging from 50 million to 250 million people.[35] An early study of the growth of the urban middle class in Pakistan relied on income tax returns to determine the limits of its lower and upper income limits, even as it acknowledged the arbitrariness of the exercise in the face of categories of people exempt from tax. Those earning between Rs 6,000 and Rs 25,999 per annum and others from Rs 25,000 to Rs 49,999 were defined as lower and upper middle class respectively.[36] The study noticed the proliferation of what it called mental labour, which included writers, doctors, artists, lawyers and journalists among others. However, the phenomenal expansion of the lower middle-class category of government employees from 1950–1 to 1963–4 far outpaced the growth of the middle-class category.[37]

Partition typically transformed the status of the lower middle class into the middle class. In particular, refugees got allotments, official help in business openings for them, and recruitment to jobs in the government and the tertiary sector such as banking and insurance in the general vacuum created by the exodus of the Hindu and Sikh educated and professional middle class. Indicators of the status of the middle class included banking, insurance, motor vehicle registration, radio and telephone lines and electricity bills, as well as the pattern of consumption of cosmetics, clothing and sewing machines, among others. As cities expanded, so did the middle class. It filled new jobs and businesses, owned property in the rapidly developing residential and industrial areas and constituted the professional elite. From the 1950s to the 1990s, the total population of Pakistan increased by 236 per cent while the rate of urbanization was 49.5 per cent. This resulted in the emergence of two megacities, Karachi and Lahore, along with six cities of one million or more population.[38] The study focused on the emergence, maturation and, in some sense, domination of the middle class over the way the policy framework of the new country and the future vision of the nation were shaped.

Defining the political character of the middle class obviously brings in the question of its numerical strength, financial status and ideological orientation. According to one generous estimate, 60 per cent of people belonged to the middle class.[39] Financially speaking, the middle class's spending increased from $71 billion in 2001 to $120 billion in 2011, whereas its share in investment stood at $523 billion.[40]

Rapid urbanization and burgeoning restaurants, bakeries, and the growth in the number of internet users, are proof of the middle class's growing influence.[41] The middle class supported the anti-corruption agenda of each military ruler directly after his takeover. During the 2013 and 2018 elections, quite a few from this class voted for the PTI in pursuance of its anti-corruption rhetoric.[42]

The ingredients of the middle class's worldview carry great explanatory value for understanding the institutional and attitudinal perspectives of what is the informal, amorphous, opaque, indeterminate and nebulous but, in an ultimate sense, ruling class of Pakistan. This argument is different from the generally accepted definitions of the 'ruling class' or even 'class'. It does not, for example, compare or contrast it with another class with reference to the classical Marxist model of relations of production based on the two pairs of opposite classes of landlords and peasants, bourgeoisie and proletariat.[43] My points of reference include Muslim middle-class attitudes to religion, custom, values, social power, economic vision and Islamic civilization in general.

In Britain, the emergence of the middle class – gauged by individuals and families, morals and manners, and economic and political views – has been traced typically to the late eighteenth century. The 1832 Reform Bill, which opened the door to the middle class for entry into the 'political nation', lent periodicity to this phenomenon by locating it in the preceding half century. Some confused the middle class with industrial entrepreneurs. Others attributed middle-class ideals to the Victorian 'age of equipoise'. Some thought that the middle class failed to be 'epitomized in its ultimate gentrification'.[44] As utilitarians addressed the 'public', their ideas travelled to India in the early nineteenth century and transformed the country from a Persian-based to an English-based state within decades, engendered reformism as the hallmark of the new literati and, over time, created a proto-middle class.

The British middle class spoke a political language that mixed the relatively incompatible idioms of 'classical republicanism', 'medieval scholasticism' and 'natural jurisprudence'.[45] It had learned the art of transforming the relative indeterminacy and complexity of an explanatory theorem into a cogent statement of the link between cause and effect.[46] Indeed, the colonial state in India itself drew heavily on the British middle class, which founded an administrative state par excellence. Nearly 85 per cent of British officers in India belonged to the middle class, rooted in the public school tradition.[47] They had a distinct way of looking at India: as 'guardian bureaucrats' who knew where the public interest lay, certainly not in the aggregate public will.[48] In the post-1857 period, when the wars between British colonialists and Indians had been won and lost respectively, the local middle class – with Muslims as a poor second – started to become visible through the modern educational and professional institutions. By the late nineteenth century, a sizeable, elitist, revivalist and ambitious middle class made its presence felt as intelligentsia, lawyers, businessmen, philanthropists and writers. The social make-up of the elite that took over the state from the colonial rulers in the two dominions after partition has not yet found a significant place in academic research.

The British took power from one class – the Ashraf, the landed aristocracy – and handed over the responsibility for managing the state to another class: the middle class. In Pakistan, while the Muslim League inherited the legal and legitimate authority, the middle class was responsible for policy formulation and power distribution through the bureaucracy. Jinnah, the epitome of the new Muslim middle class, was in constant liaison with governors and secretaries from provinces, who prepared dossiers about politicians for him as governor–general.[49] If the Muslim League was led by the landed elite, the Congress was a 'middle-class' party inasmuch as its high command upheld a reformist agenda, especially about land reform which was anathema to the landed elite, especially the Muslim Ashraf.[50] In other words, the Indian middle class was represented in the party system as well as through the parliamentary framework.

In Pakistan, the middle class found its institutional expression essentially in the bureaucracy and, increasingly, in the officer cadre of the army as its recruitment area gradually shifted from the rural to the urban lower middle-class section of the population from 1965 onwards.[51] The migrant middle class had an edge over its local compatriot, by both higher education and initially by seniority of positions.[52] This lent a certain all-India character to the middle class, which was able to put the political class on the defensive in terms of the latter's constituency-bound local power base that was considered fit only for patronage not policy. The middle class and the political class belonged to two different moral universes, one pan-Indian in social origins and led by migrants, and the other 'local'. In S. J. Burki's view, the 'outsiders' had an edge over the 'insiders' in terms of talent, expertise, and vision of public service.[53] The meritorious middle class cast aspersions on the educationally and professionally less accomplished political class, which mainly comprised the tribal and landed elite. The 1958 military coup indeed represented the vision and aspirations of the middle class reflected through General Ayub's agenda of modernization and globalization as opposed to politicians' perceived traditionalism and localism.

Genesis of the Middle Class

The origins of the middle class in Pakistan can be traced in the process of the transition from the pre-colonial to the colonial and postcolonial phases of history. In this context, I want to focus on three dimensions of the transformation of public commitments: (1) from region to religion; (2) from *harem* to household; and (3) from a sense of private money to a sense of public money. While the other classes were similarly influenced by this process to a varying degree, the middle class is the most direct legatee of British colonialism in terms of social, cultural and behavioural patterns.

First, in the context of the transition from region to religion, people's commitment to laying down one's life for one of the scores of local 'sovereign' states belies the generally held thesis of the Hindu–Muslim conflict as the very stuff of Indian history. Aurangzeb's forces comprised both Muslims and non-Muslims, who fought the Muslim successor states of the Bahmani Sultanate in south India for a quarter of a century. The latter also had their armed forces, which included Hindus and Muslims. These states, which ruled before the importation of the concept of nationalism from the West under the colonial impact, relied on their subjects who generally identified themselves with the ruling dynasty rather than its religious denomination.[54] This pattern continued to operate in pre-annexation UP, Punjab, Sindh and Maharashtra, as well as the non-annexed state of Hyderabad Deccan and scores of other princely states. The quintessential source of identity for the purposes of conflict and war was territory. The local population, which belonged to different faiths, fought for Tipu Sultan, Bahadur

Shah Zafar, Rani of Jhansi, Maharaja Ranjit Singh, Wajid Ali Shah and dozens of other rulers. In contrast, extreme brutality was exercised on co-religionists belonging to different political states in India. The story of the violence of Shujauddaula of Awadh against Rohilas of Rohilkhand included expropriation of people from landed and urban property, driving them to beggary, burning their villages, murdering them and then throwing the dead bodies out to be devoured by vultures, and the killing of children suckling at their mothers' breasts. Muslim conquerors from Awadh perpetrated extreme cruelty on the Muslim rulers and multi-faith masses of the conquered Rohilkhand.[55] The conflict per se was not between Hindus and Muslims, as writers of school textbooks in Pakistan would like us to believe, but between dynastic rulers. The ideology of nationalism itself emerged as an importation from the West in late colonialism.[56]

Margrit Pernau has provided an insightful account of the transition from Ashraf to middle class in the framework of Delhi College. In pre-colonial Muslim society, the two categories of Ashraf (belonging to non-Indian origins) and Ajlaf (Indians converted to Islam) were often fluid. Ajlaf could become Ashraf within a few generations through the administrative hierarchy, marriage and piety.[57] The Ashraf culture was powerful enough to compel the newly dominant early generations of the British elite from the late eighteenth and early nineteenth century to follow it in their private life. These 'White Mughals' lived in large mansions divided into the male and female (*zenana*) quarters, kept Indian *bibis* who ran their households, produced children who were raised by *aiyas* (governesses) as Anglo-Indians, and travelled in cavalcades in the style of Indian princes with elephants, horse-carriages and concubines.[58] Ashraf status, however, was rooted in the era that began to fade in the early nineteenth century when the utilitarian ideas of social reform impacted the colonial philosophy and created a new public sphere carved out by merit rather than genealogy. Power shifted from the individual to the office and to the officeholder under the new 'liberal' framework of governance.[59] The emergence of newspapers — in Persian, Urdu and later in English — created a public sphere that started to dismantle the mental, cultural and political boundaries of the locality. For Muslims, the print media produced pan-Indian causes that served as sources of a rebellious spirit that was couched in the Islamic cult, as in the case of the murder of one William Fraser whose killer was declared a martyr.[60] Two centuries later, the 'martyrdom' of various Islamic warriors pursuing religious and sectarian causes reflected the same clash between the modern legal state and the traditional mindset of Muslim society.

At the other end, British ideas of 'universal values' gradually transcended the primordial commitments of the students of Delhi College in what can be called the proto-civil society of the mid-nineteenth century India. Emergent translation societies sought to transmit European knowledge into Indian languages. In all this, Delhi College cultivated a sense of community among its graduates, who were increasingly public spirited in their approach to Indian Muslim causes.[61] What has been criticized as communalism with reference to the project of Pakistan was indeed the new sense of community rather than faith itself.[62] The Muslim middle class took the first step to community formation and the second step to nation formation. In the sphere of knowledge, the banning of references to mythological figures and events became the touchstone of scientific thinking, as happened in the case of Sir Sayed's revised 'secular' edition of the book *Asar ul Sanadid*.[63]

After 1857, the emergent public space was increasingly occupied by cultural and identity-based activities, such as religious rallies or enactment of faith-based carnivals.[64] Once dynastic and regional identities lost significance, the new legal regime, railroad network, and print media produced a social and cultural space that allowed cross-country activist groups and organizations. These included religious movements such as Arya Samaj among Hindus and a flurry of Muslim and Sikh revivalist movements. The last quarter of the nineteenth century was the age of religion. Horizontal mobility spread the anti-colonial movement throughout India, including the *qasbas* (townships), which still maintained a hierarchical pattern of communal living, with Muslim Ashraf typically in a leading social and cultural position long after annexation with British India.[65] The Khilafat movement (1919) typically brought the Muslim masses onto the street, mobilized by the new religious idiom. The macro-level narrative of denominational identities moved down to the locality and created a faith-based politics of difference among the communities. An Islamic reformist agenda became the hallmark of the emergent Muslim middle class as representative of a community that operated through the press, petitions, political authorities and street demonstrations.[66]

Post-1857 India led to a battle of profiles whereby the British emerged as the supporters of a rational, humane and progressive force while the local dynasties represented extravagance, lack of discipline, intemperance, cruelty and despotism.[67] Punjabi traders, as the first non-Ashraf Muslim elite in and around Delhi, took a keen interest in donor activity and in the management of schools and mosques, and thus set a pattern for the middle-class reformist agenda.[68] The new planning mind applied to management of resources by way of time and money, for which family and school provided the essential input.[69] The Aligarh movement cultivated an identity on the basis of Muslim community that prepared its members to penetrate the available career space in the colonial state system.[70] From the late nineteenth to the mid-twentieth century, the new educated elite of Aligarh University represented the quintessential middle class that upheld the cause of Muslim renaissance. Commitment to religion finally overtook loyalty to region and dynasty.

Turning now to the second dimension of the transformation of public commitments, the middle class was shaped by a journey from the harem to the household as the pivot of its social life in the post-1857 period. The discreet image of courtesans, which provided the cultural and literary symbols of the nobility's taste and manners, was progressively replaced by an agenda of reform about women in the household who needed to be educated, especially for studying the Holy Scriptures.[71] The new reformist literature dealt with the household, distinguishing between good behaviour and bad behaviour, especially among female characters such as in Deputy Nazir Ahmed's novel *Tauba-Tun-Nasooh*.[72] The reformist movement in Urdu literature, identified with Hali, Deputy Nazir Ahmed and Zakaullah, struggled against the alleged libertarianism in Urdu poetry, as in *Mathnavi Zehr Ishq*.[73] For men, the journey from Ashraf to middle class reflected a shift from a culture of harem to a culture of household, whereby they were no longer supposed 'to consort with maids, and certainly not with the Hindu women of the lower classes, let alone with dancers and musicians'.[74] History is replete with the life of Nawabs of Lucknow. Shuja-ud-Daula's cavalcade typically included several concubines who

163

accompanied him during travel precisely for keeping him in good humour while he was travelling for long or short journeys.[75]

The journey from harem to household was the hallmark of the emergence of the middle class in British India. Nazir Ahmed wrote novels that focused on good household norms, husbands avoiding relations with women other than their wives, and educating household women so that they could read the Qur'an and other classical Islamic literature. Maulana Ashraf Ali Thanvi's magnum opus, *Bahishti Zewar*, became the most popular didactic, moralizing and hortative book for Muslim women in late colonialism.[76] After hundreds of years of harem life, men in high positions who were given to a hedonistic life style were now being persuaded to live a pious life, with its epicentre in the household and a daily routine couched in a conservative set of values. Axiology moved to the center of things, with instructions about what was valuable and desirable in life. The household emerged as a breeder of conscience, decency, and integrity for the new urban educated middle class. The new influence travelled gradually from the urban to the rural sector and from the middle to the lower classes, with a declining trend in qualitative terms.

The third major change occurred in the way the middle class handled money matters. The new values included thrift, philanthropy, hard work, earning for living and achievement status, with education operating as the open sesame.[77] Frugality, spending within the means of salary-based jobs that limited the imagination and style of people to resource-bound patterns of behaviour, and a commitment to financial security for one's future, emerged as new values. In Mirza Ruswa's novel, *Amrao Jan Ada*, the protagonist courtesan observes that the days of reckless spending that often resulted in the destitution of the landed aristocracy were gone, while under the British suzerainty people were held accountable for all money matters. A new distinction between public and private money emerged that rendered mixing the two roles as corruption.[78] In other words, the 'bourgeois' sense of money began to dominate the 'feudal' sense of money.[79]

However, these norms were essentially transmitted to those who came into regular contact with the colonial state one way or the other, for example, those living in cosmopolitan centres, the educated and professional elements, the Indian component of the bureaucracy, and the intelligentsia in general. Society at large took much longer to embrace these values and did so to a lesser extent. The process of indigenization of the state empowered the legislatures emergent from the days of diarchy enshrined in the 1919 Montagu–Chelmsford Reforms onwards and expanded the franchise that made legislators the elected representatives of the public at large.[80] An embryonic political class emerged on the scene. At the other end, there was an extension of constitutional protection to the civilian bureaucracy as well as provision of its operational autonomy. The bureaucracy had long represented the colonial state in its pristine form, as an institutional set-up accountable only to a remote parliament in London, both formally and symbolically. The two sides – the political class, and the middle class with officialdom as its base – eventually emerged as the two power centres in Pakistan.

Middle Class: Progress, Piety and Property

Markus Daechsel mentions how after partition 'the middle-class was progress personified'.[81] It was given the credit for the national struggle for independence and considered a guarantor of modernization in future.[82] He finds the political attitude of the self-expression of the middle-class as 'anti-societal form of politics' that marks a break from the interest-based politics of the political class proper.[83] He even finds the proponents of this self expressionism 'fascism's fellow travellers'.[84] In S. J. Burki's view, the middle class is inherently progressive. Of course, the middle class has been the harbinger of development through bureaucratic planning and the implementation of the growth agenda at the macro level. Burki also maintains that this class has a significant presence in the Pakistani diaspora, which is 'more modern and secular than the native populations from which they are drawn'.[85] This argument, however, needs further exploration. Various studies point to the de-culturation of expatriate Pakistanis and their enhanced Islamic identity as 'aggrieved' Muslims in the West.[86] Also, in Burki's view Bhutto was supported by the middle class.[87] He seems to argue that there must be a conjunction between a 'progressive' leader and what he considers an inherently progressive middle class. However, the available research testifies to the fact that the middle class was typically, if not in every case, opposed to Bhutto's populist movement in the 1970s, and was not its constituency by any stretch of imagination.[88]

Shahid Kardar has argued that the middle class grew faster than the population as a whole, especially in central and northern Punjab. In his view, the income/consumption/asset trio defines what is indeed a 'class of seekers and strivers'.[89] However, his idea that the middle class is a bedrock of democracy seems to be a borrowing from modernization theory. This is indeed symptomatic of the fact that the middle class controls the narrative through the print and electronic media, manages social media and education, builds its own image as a driver of change and liberalism, and espouses the agenda to get rid of political dynasties and eliminate corruption.[90] It has a mono-causal approach to the national crisis focused on corruption, and a reductionist view of the solution in the form of an honest leader.[91]

Ammara Maqsood argues that middle-class subjectivity in Pakistan is shaped by a politics of both modernity and piety.[92] The idea that the middle class is inherently progressive has led certain analysts to see it as a transformative force. For example, Vali Nasr argued for the emergence of a powerful middle class in the Middle East that would change not only the configuration of the powers ruling that region but also its profile as an open and eventually democratic part of the globe.[93] His argument is based on imagining the ascendancy of the middle class and its progressive role in opening the relatively authoritarian and closed political systems of the Middle East. This is Alice in Wonderland. In Nasr's view, the middle class in Pakistan is a symbol of stability, and is indeed a 'pillar of democracy', a proposition that is tantamount to turning history upside down.[94] He makes claims that the business-minded middle class in the Middle East is the 'key' to winning the cold war against Iran and that future battles will be fought over business and capitalism, not religion.[95]

Similarly, in Adnan Rafiq's formulation, the new contestation in Pakistan is between the military, the civilian elite and the emergent middle class.[96] This argument is somewhat polemical. It lacks both an institutional and class analysis and a clear delineation of distinct spheres of action of otherwise grossly overlapping social categories. Rafiq makes an unsubstantive claim that the middle class was against both 'traditional political parties and the military rule'.[97] Rafiq's following observations fall in the same category. For example, urban middle-class youth is becoming interested in politics. The future of democracy would depend on the state's ability to render services and power to this class. The landed elite and military have always shared power in Pakistan. Politics today focuses on 'service delivery' whereby political parties compete to deliver services to their constituents. Youth hates dynastic rule and VIP culture. The middle-class ambition for power is the 'antithesis' of authoritarianism.[98] These observations are based on a highly skewed understanding of the middle class in Pakistan. Landlords are clients of the military rulers, often grouped together in a King's party in parliament. Political parties compete for power to deliver patronage to their clients, which hardly makes delivery of service a real issue for them. The middle class has been a potential constituency of the army's rule. The twin agendas of nation-building and state-building championed by this class led to political and constitutional moves such as One Unit.[99]

Student politics was at its peak during the 1960s and 1970s. It carried ideological orientations of the left and the right, and showed tremendous organizational potential.[100] Student politics steadily declined after Zia banned student organizations. Study of the political role of youth is typically an extension of the analysis of the middle class. No youth surveys point to an increasing interest of young people in politics. Youth activism has been limited to mobilization for the vote. After the 2018 elections, no youth wing within the PTI, nor any other youth organization in civil society, became part of the institutional framework of the state or non-state sectors. Nor did an agenda of demands by youth become part of the national debate or a sustained political activity. Nor indeed did the youth pursue national and international causes such as environment, water, energy, poverty, and gender, barring a few pockets of activism in educational and professional institutions.[101] Even more than the politics of the middle class, the politics of youth is misunderstood as a progressive force, one capable of changing the destiny of the nation.

Of course, youth has been the focus of political attention in the populist movements of Z. A. Bhutto in the 1970s and Imran Khan from 2011 onwards. The mystique of youth is commensurate with the mystique of populism in terms of an undefined, unbounded and uncrystallized framework of thought and action. The youth wing of Imran Khan's party (Insaf Students Organization) had a tremendous input into mass mobilization. Indeed, Punjab's chief minister, Shahbaz Sharif (2008–18), took very seriously Imran Khan's relentless effort to win over the youth of the country, and distributed thousands of laptops to college and university students to keep their sympathies with his own party, PML-N. However, the youth of the country generally ended up as a passive target of paternalism on the part of the PPP, PTI and PML-N leadership. It hardly contributed to the policy debate within or outside a party of its choice. Casting the ballot was most typically the last 'political' act in any activist phase of youth politics.

Available scholarship generally uses the same brush for addressing, defining, and projecting the demands of youth from different sectors, genders and classes. Not surprisingly, most of the field research tends to focus on 'students', which creates a bias in favour of the urban-based middle class, and even gives a false image of female social ascendancy in the context of co-education at university level. Given these constraints, the findings of Marie Lall and Tania Saeed about the political views of youth generally conform to the overall middle-class worldview, couched in an enhanced sense of remoteness from the way the state operates and from the meaning of democracy as public representation. This study makes significant observations about the political attitudes of youth. For example, the state starts to become visible only when the military takes action by way of disaster management or otherwise. The state means neglect, especially in terms of providing security. Politics is another name for corruption and moral degeneration; democracy is not suitable for Pakistan because people are uneducated. Democracy is dysfunctional whereas the army is functional.[102] Not surprisingly, young people become 'either apolitical or antipolitical'.[103]

The pendulum of political initiative in Pakistan has been shifting between the state elite as representative of the middle class and the political class proper. The holding of general elections under the 1956 Constitution led to a new battle between the state elite and the political elite, one elite seeking to avoid the polls by constantly postponing the elections, the other demanding they be held as soon as possible. Under Ayub, the King's party, Pakistan Muslim League (Convention), emerged as a broker between the state elite and the political elite, as did the subsequent King's parties, PML under Zia (1986–8) and Pakistan Muslim League Quaid-i-Azam (PML-Q) under Musharraf (2002–7). The Bhutto government (1971–7) represented the only period when a modicum of civilian supremacy operated and the political elite snatched the initiative from the state elite in the aftermath of military defeat in East Pakistan. Bhutto's movement sharpened the divide between the state elite and the political elite, even as he tried to put the genie back in the bottle in the latter part of his rule. Under Bhutto, bureaucracy took a severe beating. The 1972 civil service reforms took away constitutional protection of the tenure of, and much of the lustre and privilege attached to, the bureaucracy.[104]

Under Zia's martial law (1977–85), the pendulum swung back to the state elite. That was followed by the initiative of the political elite in the 1983 MRD movement, which led to Zia's announcement of the 12 August to hold elections after two years. Zia started to play politics: the 1984 presidential referendum, the February 1985 non-party elections, the March 1985 Revival of the Constitution Order (RCO), and the 1985 8th Constitutional Amendment. Zia's dissolution of the National Assembly under Article 58(2)(b) and dismissal of Prime Minister Junejo on 29 May 1988 seemed to shift the initiative back to the army. However, after Zia died in an air crash, the Supreme Court allowed political parties to participate in what was scheduled as a non-party election. And yet the gain for the political elite was limited.

Article 58(2)(b) took away three more civilian governments of Benazir Bhutto (1990), Nawaz Sharif (1993) and again Benazir Bhutto (1996). Nawaz Sharif passed the 13th Amendment in April 1997 to do away with the killer clause.[105] For each dissolution of the National Assembly, the Chief of Army Staff would provide the 'political will' to dismiss the civilian government, while the president would act as a legal instrument for that purpose. Under the 'civilian' interregnum (1988–99), under Musharraf (1999–2008) and later under the PPP (2008–13), PML-N (2013–18) and PTI (2018–) governments, civil bureaucracy gradually regained its powers through the relatively invisible office 'file'. The two PML-N governments in Punjab (2008–18) were specially known to follow the bureaucrats' diktat about financial and administrative matters.[106] Given that the bureaucrats were obliged to withdraw from an overt role in public, the term 'establishment' was increasingly reserved for the army. This term was frequently used in the context of the battle of nerves between Prime Minister Nawaz Sharif and General Raheel Shareef before the latter's retirement in November 2016. During the tempestuous days of political turmoil in the wake of the Panama Leaks case proceedings against Nawaz Sharif in 2016–18, it was the military establishment that was generally considered responsible for his removal, even as it was the Supreme Court that formally dismissed him.

A major determinant of the establishment's power and thinking is the middle class. While the middle class is influential behind the scenes, in the form of nameless and faceless state functionaries in a collective sense, the political class is symbolized by public figures individually known as party leaders, who dabble in mass mobilization through electoral activity. We have already mentioned the genealogy of the middle class from areas where Muslims had acquired higher education and got jobs. UP was at the top in this respect, followed by Muslims from the presidencies of Bombay and Bengal. This middle class was relatively 'liberal' but not secular. The Muslim middle class had emerged from three routes: the impoverished siblings of the landed elite who made inroads into services and professions; the business community from western India that wanted to break the perceived shackles of the powerful Hindu business class; and enterprising students from small towns, backward districts and even the rural sector, who excelled in education and moved into jobs. Together they served as a group of Muslim revivalists and revanchists spread all over India. Since the middle class was unconstrained by locality as its power base, it upheld an idealized 'national interest' as opposed to the 'public interest' upheld by the political class. The middle class carried an all-Indian perspective of Muslim separatism and a supra-territorial vision of the Muslim homeland. The leading ideas of Pakistan are middle-class ideas. These include the need for unity against provincialism; elimination of corruption; religion as the raison d'être of the state; Urdu as the national language; the perceived Indian hegemony; Kashmir as the lifeline of Pakistan; pervasive anti-Westernism; and an irresistible conspiracy theory.

It is interesting to peep into the mind of the middle class. This class has enjoyed mediated communication led by the English press with its limited circulation, as opposed to the Urdu press that has had a mass circulation reaching out to millions. Not surprisingly, the middle class lived in a world of its own that was different from the world of the 'silent majority'. It cherished merit, hierarchy, discipline, unity of action and thought, deification of the state and an agenda of economic development through technology. It assumed a paternalistic attitude towards the 'ignorant' but 'innocent' masses, who needed to be guided to modernity. It understood democracy as a combination of palace intrigues, factional strife, party defections, election rigging, vote-buying, abduction or killing of political opponents, nepotism and rampant corruption. The middle class is committed to modernity sans democracy. Over time, corruption has become a middle-class issue par excellence. It provides a reason to detest politicians and indeed democracy itself. Each military government embarked on a vehement process of accountability of politicians for their alleged corruption. Imran Khan eminently represented the middle class ethos of hatred against the West and dynastic politics at home.[107]

However, the corruption–accountability nexus lacked potential for ideological mobilization of the people for whom 'corruption' was the system itself. It is in this context that Zia's Islamization programme had a tremendous impact on the middle class in terms of popularizing a divine source of legitimacy. This class is typically characterized by a deficit of liberalism, urbanity and cosmopolitanism, barring a small but significant section of the 'progressive' intelligentsia. Insularity, conspiracy, and ideological orientation define the dominant perspective of the middle class. It wants to wean away Hindu influences from society by rendering certain wedding ceremonies and the Basant festival un-Islamic. However, it has also adapted to the modern habit of celebrating birthday parties, Valentine's Day, Mother's Day, Father's Day, even Halloween in some 'modern' enclaves. It is fond of watching Indian films on Netflix and YouTube, along with enjoying print media coverage of the life and times of contemporary Indian actors and actresses, ranging from Shahrukh Khan and Amir Khan to Madhuri Dixit and Karina Kapoor, among others. Hating America and seeking admission for higher studies and a career in the USA do not pose a contradiction in terms for university students. The middle-class agenda in Pakistan, much like in India, seeks rational and conscientious politics.[108] A sustained disillusionment with democracy in Pakistan can be located to platforms for making and expressing public opinion controlled by the middle class, such as educational institutions and media forums. The middle class inherited the official colonial line that elections were not the right solution for India. In Lord Salisbury's words, as quoted by Myron Weiner, 'representative government was not an Eastern idea', due to the multiple 'social cleavages' that would make it impossible to run a representative electoral system.[109]

In Pakistan, the middle class finds elections a challenge to the status quo. As Fred Heyward points out, the state elite is often against mass participation because it could come at the cost of its control.[110] Yadav seems to be writing more about Pakistan than India, when he says: 'Hidden behind the ideological mask of I-love-democracy-but-hate-politics and often articulated in the form of a middle class utopia of sanitized politics, it points to a deep fear of politics, the fear of the masses taking over and running it any way they like.'[111] This perspective 'is not unrelated to the middle class fantasy of being the guardian'.[112] It wants to see the rational self-undergirding of the state machinery, while it faces the real fear of power being chipped away from it.[113] As Myron Weiner argues, the middle class thinks of the state as an arbiter that serves the demands of a certain ethnic group so that it can expand its own middle class.[114] Thus, Punjabization of the state in Pakistan can be analysed in the context of a rapid rise of the middle class in Punjab. Overall, the middle class is reluctant to join political parties and is not even keen to cast its vote. In the light of the continuing struggle between the 'establishment' and politicians, Barlas concludes that no one class has been able to establish its hegemony.[115]

The Political Class – I: Party Politics

The current and next sections deal with the political class as the second power centre in Pakistan in the context of party politics and electoral politics, respectively. Under late colonialism, education, the media, the railroad network and other public utilities spread political awakening all over India. The new legislators after the 1919 Montagu–Chelmsford reforms typically belonged to the landed elite, which was part of the 'collaborative mechanism' of colonial rule.[116] This elite was the bedrock of British imperialism in India, be it through the 1900 Land Alienation Act,[117] the Sandeman System,[118] the opening of public schools such as Aitchison College in Lahore, direct nomination to positions in service cadres, or the establishment of camaraderie between the district bureaucracy and the landed and tribal elite. British colonialists were able to establish a system of collaboration with the local elite to rule conflict-ridden polymorphic societies such as India. This system was based on exchange of patronage with help in preserving the status quo, as opposed to the newly educated elite demanding an ever increasing share in the state administration along with policy-making power. The British policy of containing the influence of the middle class by relying on the landed elite lost its utility after the latter formed governments in the provinces after the 1937 and 1946 elections. For decades after independence, the intelligentsia criticized the land-lord-cum-legislators for having collaborated with the colonial masters in the past. At one end, the civil bureaucracy and military emerged as permanent insiders of the 'modern' state, and thus as guardians of its institutional ethos. At the other end, the political class represented the vast rural hinterland studded with devotional sites and social structures based on ethnicity, caste, sub-caste, sect, sub-sect, tribe and sub-tribe. Politicians found democracy the only game in town where they could utilize their political resource in the form of a mass mandate to move inside the state. Not surprisingly, the state elite inside discounted this resource and shunned democracy. This led to a persistent tug of war between the two classes.

The Party System

In Pakistan, like elsewhere, the political class operates through a party system. We find the concept of the party system helpful in delineating the types and phases of the party-based conflict in the country. Any talk of party system would start with Sartori's typology of effective parties, which included a variety of models ranging from one-party and two-party systems to hegemonic and predominant party systems.[119] At the heart of this approach lies the number of contenders for power in the form of effective parties and their experience with fragmentation and coalition-making.[120] It has been argued that Canada has four party systems since:

(1) there were two larger parties, the Liberals and Conservatives, up to the First World War;

(2) there were protest parties with their regionalist agendas, such as the Co-operative Commonwealth Federation, up to the 1950s;

(3) there was a broad two-way contest that led to a three-way fight after the emergence of the New Democratic Party that

highlighted the leadership factor and a Keynesian tilt towards public responsibility away from the pure market dynamics; and

(4) there was a move back to capitalism as the dominant ideology, along with social welfarism and the contest among titans.[121]

Modi's victory in the 2014 and 2019 elections has been termed as India's fourth party system.[122] The first party system (1952–67) was a referendum for the catch-all party, the Congress. The second party system (1967–89) was characterized by regionalization of politics when the Congress lost its monopoly over state-level politics. The third party system (1989–2014) was based on coalition politics. Three intervening variables – *mandal*, *mandir* and *mandi* – led to a realignment of forces. The Mandal Commission provided reservations for Other Backward Classes (OBCs) and expanded political participation downwards in caste terms. The 1992 Babri Masjid-Ram Janambhoomi riots brought forth the Bharatiya Janata Party (BJP) to the national platform. The 1991 liberalization of the economy opened the doors for the national bourgeoisie to the global market. As a result, the third party system expanded competitiveness with low victory margins, and rendered the initiative to state-level parties. The fourth party system (2014 onwards) drew votes for the BJP from all castes and classes, re-elected 67 per cent of incumbent legislators, and increased vote margins for the winner to 19.3 per cent in 2019.[123] Indeed, elections became a referendum for or against Modi, and the BJP became a 'system-defining' party.[124]

In Pakistan, no elaborate attempt has been made to draw the features of one or more of the party systems, even as scholarly work on individual parties, their role at the district and constituency level and their organizational and ideological orientations have been part of the political analysis. In several ways, the task of delineating the party system in Pakistan has been complicated by the establishment's intrusive role. The latter cut parties off from people by declaring them defunct for years. It subjected political leaders to summary dismissal from politics under charges of corruption under an Elected Bodies Disqualification Order (EBDO), through individual cases against them under a Public Offices Disqualification Order (PODO) or via the Public and Representative Office Disqualification Act (PRODA), and under the National Accountability Bureau (NAB) from Musharraf

(1999–2008) onwards, especially under Imran Khan (2018–). It induced mass-scale defections in parties before and after elections to bring the favourite parties to power through fraudulent elections. It created Islamic parties that fought elections from an extremely narrow base, undermined the electoral chances of candidates from larger parties, thus turning winners into losers and losers into winners. The establishment sought to impose its preferred leadership on the nation through elections, as opposed to the genuine representatives of people. That led to support for some candidates and opposition to other candidates, groups, and parties from behind the scenes. During the 2018 elections, Imran Khan was touted as the establishment's favourite in the national and world media. The military establishment was credited for creating PML (Convention) in 1963, the National People's Party (NPP) in 1980, MQM in 1984, SSP in 1985, PML (Junejo) in 1986, Islami Jamhoori Itehad (IJI) in 1988, Jamiat Ulema Islam-Samiulhaq (JUI-S) in 1988, MQM-Haqiqi in 1992, PML-N in 1993, MMA in 2002, PML-Q in 2002, PPP-forward bloc led by Faisal Saleh Hayat in 2003, Defence of Pakistan Council in 2011, Pak Sarzameen Party (PSP) in 2016, Balochistan Awami Party (BAP) in 2017 and TLP in 2018. The establishment sponsored political leaders such as Ilahi Bux Soomro, Junejo, Arbab Rahim, Liaqat Jatoi, Nawaz Sharif, Shujaat Hussain, Pervaiz Illahi, Imran Khan, Mustafa Kamal, Maulana Samiul Haq, and a host of others. The result is that, often, the 'elected' representatives represented the establishment rather than society. Multiplication of parties, often at the instance of the establishment, has increasingly made elected assemblies unrepresentative of the public by lowering the number of winners' votes.

However, these problematic features of party politics notwithstanding, we can outline some stable trends of the election campaigns: leader-domination, large public meetings, hollow and meaningless party manifestoes, the disconnect between the party leaders and workers, and a readiness to play ball with the extra-parliamentary forces. The lack of autonomy of the party system in Pakistan provided a running theme in a recent volume of contributions on the subject.[125] We can define the party system of Pakistan in a longitudinal context, defined by the location of parties along a stable dimension of structural presence with reference to the state elite. The 'organizational' approach to political parties signifies the institutional 'design' and its application to practical politics.[126] Elsewhere, I have discussed the 'operational' role of political parties in terms of the way the leadership maintains a certain level of equilibrium between those who are often disgruntled, at the bottom, and the powerful and ambitious elite at the top enjoying a near monopoly over the political initiative.[127]

The decisions of political parties are guided by two kinds of the political strategy: 'mobilizing strategy' and 'chasing strategy'. The former focuses on policies, core voters and ideological heritage, while the latter focuses on means rather than ends and form rather than content, and thus aims to increase the party's appeal within the mould of status quo orientation.[128] The PPP and the Awami League in 1970 fully employed a mobilizing strategy. The PTI in 2013 and 2018 reflected the mobilizing strategy for propaganda but the chasing strategy for keeping the status quo.

The general typology of political parties in Pakistan comprises three broad categories:

(1) The PML-N, PPP and PTI are mainstream parties.
(2) The Awami National Party (ANP), Balochistan National Party Mengal (BNP-M), MQMs, Jamhoori Wattan Party (JWP) and Jeay Sindh Qaumi Movement (JSQM-A) are ethnic parties.
(3) The JI, Jamiat Ulema Islam Fazlur Rehman (JUI-F), Tehreek Jafria (TJ), along with militant outfits including SSP, Lashkar-e-Jhangvi (LJ), TTP, JuD and Lashkar-e-Taiba (LeT) are Islamic parties.[129]

The first group of parties is motivated by the prospects of government formation in Islamabad and one or more of the provincial capitals. The second group can aspire to join a coalition government as junior partners at one or both levels. The third group is important for its votes more than its seats because it could operate in tipping the balance in favour of certain candidates from the first or second group. The rule of an alliance of Islamic parties MMA in Peshawar (2002–7) remains an exception to the rule.

While this typology carries a great heuristic value, we need to explore the 'party system' that undergirds the functioning of these parties in terms of lending a meaning to them as actors on the political stage along a reasonable stretch of time. It is argued that the party system of Pakistan can be understood as an operational network of various sets of political parties that function along parallel lines, often colluding and colliding amongst themselves. These parties have played an identifiable role over time that helps give them a specific place in the overall paradigm of the party system. I shall argue that the party system in Pakistan comprises three categories of parties. First, there is the ever present, second-fiddle umbrella party, Muslim League, often divided into factions, bearing the initials of their leader's names, ready for co-option by the establishment, and sinking or floating in different periods. Second, there are other parliamentary parties – a dozen or so – imbued with ideology, identity, mission for change, or keeping the memory of a patriarch alive, such as Ghaffar Khan. Third, there are non-parliamentary parties, often floated by the establishment, carrying appeal among the bazaar classes, the sectarian groups, and the smaller factions of the big party factions.

Various factions belonging to the Muslim League for seven decades represent the first category of the system that seeks out power through the establishment, or that is sought by the latter as a patchwork of electables or legislators to serve as the King's party. In British India, the All-India Muslim League had no role for ideologues for three decades after the introduction of separate electorates in 1909 that ensured the 'victory' of Muslim notables. Their electoral constituencies consisted of vast areas of influence based on large landholdings and intra-elite packages of support. The electorate was a small fraction of the population that did not move beyond 15 per cent until the end of colonial rule. This electoral framework eschewed the need for supra-local input in the form of organizational activity or ideological mobilization. However, the 1932 Communal Award and the 1935 India Act were followed by the vehement pursuit of an ideological mission for establishing a Muslim homeland by a legion of committed workers from within and outside the Muslim League. After partition, the vast urban-based cadre of ideologues of this party atrophied, and the Muslim League and its breakaway factions were reduced to intellectually barren organizations. For a quarter of a century, this archetypical mainstream political party in Pakistan operated either with an ongoing tussle between its weak ideological and strong electoral wings or without ideologues altogether. It represented the classic category of 'catch-all parties' that managed to get votes from different social groups.[130]

Since no elections were held at the national level on the basis of adult franchise for a quarter of a century, no comprehensive exercise was undertaken by the PML leadership to establish a cadre of political intelligentsia to reach out to the masses. Under Ayub, the revival of political parties in 1963 was led by 'ministerialists', i.e. those ministers who carried political affiliations, whereby politicians from the Muslim League and the Republican Party, who had been subjected to EBDO, struggled to ride the tide.[131] Since the presidential and parliamentary elections in 1965 were held indirectly, i.e, by the electoral college of Basic Democrats and not on the basis of adult franchise, there was no need and no role for mass contact and thus for party cadres.[132]

After the Bhutto interregnum (1971–7), followed by Zia's martial law (1977–85), the Muslim League again appeared on the surface as part of what was virtually a two-party system (1986–99 and 2002–18). This party included the landed elite from various districts of Punjab along with Sufi *pirs*, lesser *biradaris*, and the middle-class commercial and professional elements. It has continued to retain a few blocks of solid support in Sindh, KP and Balochistan for generations. From 1993, when Nawaz Sharif was sacked as prime minister by President Ishaq, the former outgrew the military's support and established an 'independent' vote bank for the elections.

The Muslim League has all along enjoyed a high level of legitimacy as the creator of Pakistan. The extra-parliamentary forces continued to create factions out of the party, which served as a pool of willing partners in the game of numbers on the floor of elected assemblies. The low organizational level of the Muslim League has attracted the attention of scholars, who hold it as the key failure of democracy in Pakistan.[133] The recalcitrant elements were bullied into acquiescence. As early as 1948, the Sindh supplies minister was subjected to the ordeal of a gruesome 'interview with the premier' after he had alluded to the standing committee of the Sindh Assembly Muslim League as the premier's yes men and made a defiant posture.[134] In 1956, as it was cynically expressed, a large number of members of the Constituent Assembly slept as Muslim Leaguers and next morning woke up as Republicans.

The establishment, led by the bureaucracy at that time and the army after 1958, exercised an enormous capacity and finesse in creating factions, sometimes comprising a majority of the Muslim League's erstwhile legislators, as happened after the passage of the 1956 Constitution and again during the 2002 elections. Similarly, 18 members of the Balochistan Assembly from the PML-N abandoned their party in 2017 and formed a coalition government with the opposition. These mass defections were brought about, respectively, by President (General) Iskandar Mirza, President (General) Musharraf and, allegedly, the Inter-Services Intelligence (ISI) respectively. When the PML-N formed the government in Lahore after the 2008 elections, and later in both Islamabad and Lahore after the 2013 elections, its leader Nawaz Sharif accommodated yesterday's turncoats back into the party. In other words, the Muslim League's electables and legislators trafficked between the civilian-led and military-led factions with great ease. Therefore, we can argue that this party is the symbol of the status quo in terms of representing the dynastic families from the districts.

At least part of this arrangement can be compared with the 'Congress system' in India under Nehru, where an aggregate of elite groups across the country served as the support base for the ruling party beyond the secular ideology of the state and the party's reformist agenda.[135] Various factions of the PML that joined successive governments (1947–58) or served as a King's party under Generals Ayub, Zia and Musharraf, or even a party-in-office under Nawaz Sharif (1990–3, 1997–9, 2013–17), constituted what can be termed a 'subsidiary' Muslim League system. After Nawaz Sharif outgrew the hold of the establishment in 1993, the latter started to look for an alternative leadership. Imran Khan founded his party, PTI, in 1996, allegedly under the auspices of the establishment. Musharraf banked on the Choudhary brothers from Gujrat – Shujaat Hussain and Pervez Elahi – who led the ruling faction PML-Q. However, they complained to Musharraf about the efforts of the ISI chief, General Shuja Pasha, to persuade electables from their faction to join Imran Khan's PTI. During the vacuum, Nawaz Sharif's leadership-role-in-reserve remained unscathed as a civilian counterpart to Musharraf after nearly a decade of exile in Saudi Arabia. In a political system beset with successive military coups, dynastic politics added to the weak institutionalization of political parties.[136]

The PML's organizational fluidity kept the boundaries of the party porous, which kept it as a fallback option for all kinds of political careerists. The party has typically shunned ideology. As a club of locally respectable and electable persons, the party's real concern is to acquire potential access to the state's administrative resources for articulation of the interests of their own members and their cohorts and constituents. As Zia's legatee, the party tried to keep the Islamic agenda alive. Nawaz Sharif generally took a middle-of-the-road position in religious matters, which was more in line with establishment thinking in the pre-Zia and post-Zia periods. The party has no bureaucracy, no ideologues and, most importantly, no army of workers. It has a heavy belly but slender legs to stand on insofar as it has dynastic presence at the top but no street power at the bottom. It is not a movement party per se. Far smaller parties than the PML-N, such as the MQM, were able to mobilize hundreds of thousands of people to demonstrate on the road. Only once in 2009, when the PML-N government in Punjab was dismissed due to a technicality,[137] in the midst of a larger controversy about the issue of the restoration of Justice Iftikhar Choudhary as chief justice, did Nawaz Sharif launch his march from Lahore to Islamabad for the 'noble' purpose of judicial independence. He stopped short of moving beyond Gujranwala because of President Zardari's acquiescence to his demand.

The establishment's search for alternative leadership was rooted in an agenda to defeat the mass mandate of the PML-N's leader. After it failed to stop Nawaz Sharif from getting elected for a third time in 2013, it propped up Imran Khan in a bid to create a 'shadow' Muslim League in the form of the PTI and bring as many electables to his side as possible in 2018. While the PML-N was able to win a substantial number of seats in Punjab for both the National and Punjab assemblies, the die was cast in favour of the PTI. Three years into Imran Khan's government (2018–21), which moved from crisis to crisis, there were rumours of Shehbaz Sharif being in contact with the establishment for a reappraisal of his party's position by the latter, and possible withdrawal of corruption cases pursued by the NAB against the party leadership, or even an amendment to the NAB's legal authority.[138] The profile of the PML-N has been characterized by its dynastic leadership, its vast baggage of corruption charges, weak organizational structure and vulnerability to factionalism, which is often induced by the establishment – for example, before the 2002 elections by floating the PML-Q and again prior to the 2018 elections by creating a breakaway faction in south Punjab.

The second major segment of the party system relates to the leaders and cadres who develop an organization imbued with a mission, an ideology, and a policy orientation towards reform. The leadership plays a dual role. First, it puts together a coalition of co-travellers in the context of making alliances. These could be factional groups operating through different party platforms, like-minded ethnic entrepreneurs, or fellow enthusiasts seeking to reform the 'system'. A group of potential winners in the parliamentary elections most typically has a support base in the form of committed voters, such as tenants and peasants, *biradari* networks operating along horizontal lines, an urban enclave of ideological cadres and social influentials, or a solid ethnic or tribal following. The first rule of thumb is: no electables, no party as an election entity.

Secondly, the leadership seeks to develop a mass appeal. This needs much more than a group of electoral heavyweights: only those parties that are committed to a certain ideological framework can deliver in terms of generalizing, popularizing, and synthesizing the party message for the public.[139] This framework can be a 'socialist' agenda, as in the case of PPP; an ethnic cause, as in the case of MQM, the ANP, the Pakhtunkhwa Milli Awami Party (PKMAP), the National Party (NP), the BNP-M, the Sindh United Party (SUP); or a transformative agenda, as in the case of the PTI. They have to create, establish and maintain a supra-individual entity, a political party that will have a life of its own beyond the leader and the so-called 'winning coalition'.[140] The party is required to be something larger than its constituent parts, along with a vision of the future that must transcend the present. This brings in the ideological and organizational role for party cadres. They established new parties – for example, the PPP (1967), the MQM (1984) and the PTI (1996) – whereby the leftists, Mohajir nationalists and the 'system' reformists pursued their respective agendas. Between the two kinds of contentious politics – 'contained contention' and 'transgressive contention' – a representational party such as the PML-N would usually opt for the former while a mobilizational party such as the PPP, remotely followed by the PTI, was most likely to opt for transgressing the charted path.[141]

After the initial years of consolidating the party's structure in terms of opening branches at the district and sub-district levels and crystallizing the message for the public, the electoral dynamics would take over. The leader looks for electables, often from within the available pool of local influentials. A war of attrition sets in. The ideologues struggle to keep the original 'message' alive and maintain their role as mobilizers of the voting public. But the party leader cannot wait endlessly to convert voters to his cause. He must enlist the support of potential 'winners' to his side from outside the party. The ideologue represents change, the electable represents the status quo. The leader, Z. A. Bhutto or Imran Khan, must keep the balance between the two, most often by bringing the winners on board while seeking to appease the cadres and, in the process, alienating quite a few of them. The PPP in the 1970s and the PTI from 2011 to 2018 represented a consistent pattern of infighting between the two sides on the issue of intra-party elections, allocation of party tickets for general elections, and the alleged corruption of public office holders.[142] Maulana Maududi had an early fight with the JI's ideological wing led by Amin Ahsen Islahi, who led his faction out of the party to form his own group.[143] A leading party worker, Mohammad Sarwar, who acted as a 'conscientious objector' and therefore as a constant source of irritation, also became a thorn in the side of Maulana's leadership.

The third segment of the party system outnumbers political parties from other categories by a huge margin. These are often called mushroom parties, miniscule parties, riff-raff parties or one-man parties. These parties often 'stake out turf' by fielding themselves in elections without really aiming at coming to power.[144] They relate to the residuary part of the election machinery as niche parties, miniscule parties, fringe parties, aperture and nook parties, correspondingly defined in terms of their small size, paucity of relevance for the party system as a whole, and narrow opening into the larger political space. Never a contender for power per se, these parties were nevertheless manipulated into the game of power whenever there was a role for them, most often at the behest of the establishment.

Party Dynamics

Divisions and sub-divisions in the political community are reflected through the personal cliques and factions that contribute to the increasing number of parties as players on the political stage. Conversely, parties formed new coalitions based on a shared interest to have access to state patronage irrespective of divergent ideological or policy orientations. On 9 September 1956, six parties – Sindh Awami Mahaz (SAM), Sindh Hari Committee (SHC), Ustman Gul (UG), Wrore Pakhtoon (WP), APP and Khudai Khidmatgar (KK) – merged to form a new party, the Pakistan National Party (PNP) with an agenda to dissolve One Unit. The PNP represented ethnic leaders from the erstwhile smaller provinces of West Pakistan and progressive elements from the whole province. The initiative anticipated early elections after the passage of the 1956 Constitution. This paved the way for the emergence of the NAP in 1957, which in turn attracted many from the Democratic Youth League (DYL), Ganatantra Dal (GD), PNP and the Awami League (AL).[145] Similarly, the PPP joined hands with its nemesis, PML-Q (2012–13), the PTI with JI in Peshawar (2013–18), the PML-N with MQM in Islamabad and Karachi (1990–2), and the PPP with MQM umpteen times in Islamabad and Karachi from 1988 onwards. Low significance of policy meant hollowness of the whole exercise in preparing and disseminating election manifestos. Often these were interminable and high-sounding wish lists that had no relevance for the resource base of the economy and the polity. The party membership was a bottomless pit where locally active citizens felt lost in the maze of the party hierarchy, in a disconnect with the leader at the top.

With no annual party conventions, members had absolutely no way of putting forward their demands for policy considerations. The NAP was a typical 'outsider' party that put together the local ethnic leaderships and intellectual cadres from KP, East Pakistan, Sindh and Balochistan.[146] The leftist party intelligentsia, which considerably thinned down after the proscription of the Communist Party in 1954, joined the NAP in significant numbers, many of them Mohajirs and Punjabis. The ethnic elite from other provinces, and the left in general, found their demon in the establishment, which represented the all-powerful central government, the civil bureaucracy and the army. In the 1970 elections, the ethnos and leftists took to separate ways largely because East Pakistan, Sindh, KP and Balochistan struggled with their identity politics while Punjab was radicalized along class lines. After Bhutto, part of the PPP's left wing was gradually absorbed into the mainstream political stratum, while several activists, trade unionists and hard-core ideologues were left in the lurch and were progressively alienated.

Apart from MQM in Sindh and ANP in KP, a plethora of ethnic parties from Balochistan represented 'tribal family politics', which passed through numerous internal splits and horizontal mergers.[147] The MQM, an ethnic party of the Urdu-speaking community in urban Sindh, missed out on both geography and history. Sacrifice of life and property in the process of migration after partition provided a transcendental frame for the movement, and thus operated as political agency.[148] Over three generations, migrants from upcountry and interior Sindh and south Punjab dramatically changed the demography of Karachi. The MQM struggled to stop the influx of internally displaced persons (IDPs) after the 2009 operations in the Federally Administered Tribal Area (FATA) and Swat. It sought to put an end to the quota system that favoured Sindhis. Its electoral behaviour was always criticized for coercion, registration of bogus votes, and the large-scale rigging of elections. In 2016, the establishment floated a new party, the Pak Sarzameen Party (PSP) led by Mustafa Kamal, the ex-mayor of Karachi from the MQM. Following the 'treasonable' speech of Altaf Hussain on 22 August 2016, and the subsequent attack by protestors on two TV stations, a crackdown from the security agencies followed whereby the party effectively abandoned its leader. Senior party leader Farooq Sattar took over, forming MQM-Pakistan.[149] Before and after the 2018 elections, the party split further into two factions led by Farooq Sattar and Khalid Maqbool Siddiqui. The courts' decision about leadership in favour of the latter sealed the fate of institutional autonomy. At one-quarter of the population of Sindh as a whole, Mohajirs' political ascendancy in that province was not possible in electoral terms. Being a dominant minority in Sindh, the only hope for Mohajirs to get a foothold in the political set-up was through an autonomous local government system in urban centres, where it had a fast-shrinking majority. As a minority party, the MQM had no other option other than joining the coalition governments with the PPP, PML-N, PML-Q and PTI in Islamabad. Sindhi nationalists all along looked at the MQM as a Trojan Horse. The MQM overreached itself in terms of unbridled periodical violence vis-à-vis the establishment, and perished.

Each party has had its own mechanism for managing ideologues. The mainstream parties provided space for cadres in the form of party tickets for elections to the provincial assemblies, while the electables reserved most of the plum seats of the National Assembly for themselves. Another outlet for the intelligentsia was the Senate, where those with no mass constituency could be accommodated in recognition of their long party careers for elections under the proportional representation system. Women MNAs, MPAs and senators get nomination from amongst the extended families of politicians, especially from the provincial capital cities. They represent a far less substantive part of the party structure than the typical party workers and cadres, despite outperforming their male counterparts on the floor of the elected assemblies.[150] Women legislators, elected typically by male legislators, and non-Muslim legislators elected by Muslim legislators, have created a relatively inelastic patronage structure at the disposal of the party leadership over the years. It has been argued that successive elections would expand the influence of the non-elite as the allocation of resources casts a wider net, such as in India. However, a study of the electoral heavyweights in Sargodha district in Pakistan clearly brings out a pattern of reinforcement of their power and privilege after a series of electoral victories.[151] The inexorable march of the party leaders – with Imran Khan as a glaring example in 2018 – towards winning over to their own side the potential winners from other parties, remained a constant feature of the party system.

The case of Islamic parties defines the role of religion in the statecraft. They started as street agitators and as a religious lobby. The organizational weakness of the major political parties gradually provided space to Islamists, whose vote could tip the balance in favour of one or other 'electable' in the constituency. However, the denominational parties failed to win elections in numbers, due to their lack of capacity to provide patronage as compared with the political elite. But they shaped the public discourse that defined an enduring, interpretative community.[152]

The JI is generally understood to be a well-organized party that holds elections for leadership positions and represents Islamic ideology, national and international networking, vigilante culture and a permanent anti-Indian, anti-American, and anti-Zionist ideological orientation. The party has made no secret of its affinity for the slain Al-Qaeda leader, Osama bin Laden.[153] The JI is a 'vanguard' party of virtuosos committed to heralding the movement toward an Islamic revolution from the top, presuming that it would have a trickle-down effect.[154] A former JI Amir, Syed Munawwar Hasan, had asked the 'liberals' to register themselves as minorities.[155] During its partnership with the PTI government in KP (2013–18), Munawwar Hasan had refused to acknowledge the sacrifices of armed forces personnel fighting against the Taliban.[156] Following the 2014 Army Public School (APS) attack and the establishment of military courts, the new JI chief, Sirajul Haq, demanded the establishment of Sharia courts to tackle terrorism.[157] The JI has condemned madrassah reforms as an exercise in appeasement of the USA and the West.[158] The conventional diplomatic wisdom has it that the JI was Zia's constituency or its political wing, even as publicly it maintained its distance; that Zia may have been embarrassed by some of the JI's 'teachings'; and that the JI could probably drop Zia anytime.[159] By the early twenty-first century, the JI lost its relevance for the establishment, which had instead opted for jihadi parties.[160] The JUI represents tribal Islam of the Pakhtun variety and a mosque and madrassah network. It has been a strident Deobandi sectarian party close to the Taliban in terms of ideological moorings and organizational links, and a vocal advocate for establishing Sharia law in the country.[161] It mediated between the Taliban and the government in the signing of peace deals in FATA in 2009.[162] While the Taliban perpetrated violence against the 'liberal' parties, MQM, ANP and PPP, during the 2013 election campaign, the JUI-F leader, Maulana Fazlur Rehman, refused to criticize religious militancy even though he was himself twice a victim of suicide attacks.[163] The party has remained a staunch opponent of madrassah reforms in the country.[164]

The JUI-F again mediated in the talks between the Taliban and the government in 2014 and criticized the latter for intentionally aborting negotiations in order to launch a military operation.[165] The JUI has been part of various alliances – the Democratic Action Committee (DAC) (1968–9), the United Democratic Front (UDF) (1973), the Pakistan National Alliance (PNA) (1977) and the Pakistan Democratic Movement (PDM) (2020–1). It has entered into political coalitions with socialist, 'secular' and ethnic parties. It was a signatory to the 1973 Constitution even though, in its view, it did not come up to its Islamic aspirations. Pirzada argued that divergence between theory and practice led the party to borrow freely from conflicting philosophies and incorporate them into its Islamic programme.[166] However, that may not be true. When Musharraf introduced the requirement of graduation as the minimum qualification for election candidates in 2002, he accommodated the MMA (mainly JUI-F candidates in KP) by elevating madrassah degrees to the equivalent of university degrees. In general, the annual congregations of religio-political groups performed several functions, including an opportunity for social networking and solidarity among participants for spreading their religious and political messages, for reflecting their size and support base, narrating success stories of jihad such as in the case of LeT, and promoting the concept of the Muslim *umma*.[167]

The Bhutto legacy has survived at the national level after half a century, though its electoral expression nosedived outside Sindh after the resurgence of the PML under Zia as the new King's party in 1986. Two decades later, the emergence of a new populist party PTI ate into the PPP's vote in Punjab in 2013 and 2018. After Bhutto, the PPP formed governments three times in Islamabad (1988–90, 1993–6, and 2008–13), along with its ruling dispensations in Karachi where it continued to be in office even under the PML-N (2013–18) and PTI (2018–) governments in Islamabad. After getting Bhutto out of the way in 1979, Zia banned all political activities that could stir up any political controversy, for example, by issuing political statements or hoisting the party flags. Still, the press carried reports of the detained leaders who continued to keep their followers firmly behind them. The threat of the PPP's street power seemed to recede gradually. By 1982, there had been no substantial threat to the Zia regime because the alliance of opposition parties, the MRD, was hardly a cohesive entity. The establishment was determined to outclass them in their capacity to challenge the regime.[168] Socialists such as Meraj Muhammad Khan and Fateyab Ali Khan declared that they had no choice but to join the MRD in the absence of a 'progressive' alternative. Such ambivalence rendered the movement a mere 'alliance of convenience'.[169] Begum Nusrat Bhutto and Farooq Leghari assured the diplomats that the PPP was not anti-Western, that it was like the Social Democrats and that it shared the West's concern about an expansionist Soviet Union.[170] The 1983 MRD movement, which represented a delayed reaction to Bhutto's hanging in 1979, was marked by Gandhian style 'courting arrests' for breaking martial law regulations by addressing public meetings.[171] This has been the only mass agitation against a martial law government in the country's history. While its agitational potential was highly visible in the sense of facing the most ruthless government in Pakistan, in the end it diminished the aura of the PPP as a party of *jialas*, the mobilized party workers. Later in the year, when the MRD central committee decided to boycott the 1983 local bodies' elections — the Tehrik Istiqlal (TI) and certain other parties complying with it — the PPP decided to participate in the 'dubious' company of the PML (Pagara group) and the JI.[172] Later, the PPP and other parties of the MRD were not able to convince people that the 1985 non-party elections were only held to provide 'respectability and legitimacy to martial law' in an attempt to boycott the elections.[173] One could argue that the citizen is quintessentially a voter who would jump at any opportunity to cast a ballot, because otherwise the state system is inaccessible. The state elite found in the vote a catharsis for the people. Zia considered elections a 'bitter pill' that had to be taken at one time or another, while ensuring that 'the direction we have taken is not upset unnecessarily'.[174]

The ANP has been a self-confessed 'secular' party, for which it has often become a target of Islamic militants. Between 2008 and 2013, as the party-in-government, it lost 800 leaders and workers to TTP attacks.[175] Islamic militants targeted areas where people voted 'secularists' into office.[176] Not surprisingly, the latter were reliant on the support of the violence-hit communities which would have powerful electoral incentives to quell attacks.[177] The party was almost wiped out in the 2013 polls after having their party activities suspended due to the Taliban's attacks.[178] The party had openly supported the army's Zarb-e-Azb operation in KP against the Taliban.[179] It remained a staunch opponent of the Kalabagh dam.[180] At the other end, the BNP-M and PKMAP demonstrated a liberal and progressive perspective on issues of de-conflation between religion and politics, devolution of power to the federating units, and adoption of democratic means to achieve political goals.[181] The PKMAP, led by Mehmood Khan Achakzai, remained critical of military operations in FATA and the latter's merger with KP in 2017, and questioned the Islamists' support for the Afghan mujahideen and the Taliban.[182]

The media gave prominence to political leaders according to their newsworthiness in terms of their flamboyant style or harsh criticism of the 'system' as a whole or targeting specific political rivals, thus raising the entertainment value of the news channels. Imran Khan was a great beneficiary of the media's choices in this regard during and after the 2007 anti-Musharraf lawyers' movement and again from his marathon public meetings from October 2011 onwards. He was clearly a product of the media during the 1997 general elections that suddenly built his profile as a third option after Benazir Bhutto and Nawaz Sharif, even as his party ended up winning only one seat in the 2002 general elections. Overall, smaller parties gained while the larger parties lost by way of coverage on the TV screen. The former typically challenged the status quo and provided alternative options in the realm of political narrative and leadership profile, and thus created space for themselves. The PTI was virtually a one-man party from 1996 to 2011. It was generally dismissed as a product of the intelligence agencies. But Imran's rhetoric gave public expression to the deep concerns of a large section of the educated middle class. Although the party had its own Chief Election Commissioner, a published manifesto and a youth wing, it lacked the trappings of a typical political party in terms of a viable and stable hierarchical structure, ideological and policy orientation of cadres and workers, and networks of influential locals as potential winners. Prior to the 2018 general elections, several electables from the PML-N, PPP, JI, JUI-F, MQM and other parties defected, allegedly pushed by the intelligence agencies. Imran Khan was criticized for his incessant rhetoric of change, which, however, lacked any policy vision.[183] In this process, the party transformed itself from a bottoms-up party showing defiance against political dynasties to a top-down party through a lateral entry of potential winners who finally marginalized the ideological cadre. The leadership soon abandoned the agenda for inner party democracy. The penchant for institutionalization gave way to a cult of personality.

Patterns of Leadership

Since policy has gradually eroded as a hallmark of the agenda of political parties on the left and right of the political spectrum ever since the PPP's first stint in government (1971–7), the leadership factor has emerged as the dominant identity marker in this regard. The course of action of a political party is typically underscored by the personal input at the top. In other words, strategic preferences are crystallized outside parliament rather than inside it.[184] Z. A. Bhutto emerged as a party leader through a mass movement. Benazir Bhutto inherited her father's charisma. Asif Zardari became the custodian of Benazir's political heritage. Altaf Hussain symbolized Mohajir destiny at the top of the MQM. Asfandyar Wali Khan relied upon the reputation and charisma of his grandfather, which had diluted after two generations. Thus, we find a party identification model fully operational in Pakistan whereby the party is most typically known by its leader.[185] The same applied to Imran Khan (2018–) and his symbiotic relationship with his party, the PTI, which had no semblance of an organizational entity. This party had no 'policy-based' profile except that it claimed to be the janitor that would clean the dirty stables of politics. In the absence of any organizational policy, it was the populist appeal of Imran Khan as a leader that kept the party going.

Factionalism, opportunism and shifting loyalties of politicians often made the headlines. Diplomats often communicated public opinion back home, which was critical of the political class. For instance, the ministers of the Republican Party government in West Pakistan in the 1950s were described either as personal enemies of Daultana, as supporters of Gurmani, or as self-seekers; in many cases all three descriptions applied.[186] Ministers of the West Pakistan government in early 1958 were described in negative terms: Mamdot as less than honest; Dasti with corruption charges hanging over him 'probably fully justified'; Syed Hasan Mahmood 'almost a byword for corruption'; and Rizvi 'a timeserver'.[187] Mamdot was totally inept and silent and in the assembly Khizr Hayat once called him the dumb wrestler, much to everyone's joy. Daultana was the most able, but he was inexperienced, a bit of a dreamer and had leanings to the left. Shaukat Hayat was young and inexperienced. Kamal Ali was a man of very ordinary ability and was not above suspicion. This team as League leaders never enjoyed the confidence of the people in Punjab, and Mamdot was only kept going by Jinnah's support.[188]

Leadership is the most important single factor in the structural domain of political parties. As founding chairpersons (Altaf Hussain, Nawaz Sharif, Imran Khan) or as the offspring of the founder (Asfandyar Wali Khan, Akhtar Mengal) or as dynastic descendants (Bilawal Bhutto), leaders carry a superordinate position in their respective parties. They meet the public's need for party identification in the absence of clear ideological or policy orientations. The transition from inheriting the mantle of leadership to becoming the leader unto oneself is far from smooth. Benazir cornered the 'old guard' comprising the infamous 'uncles' – Jatoi, Mumtaz Bhutto, Hafeez Pirzada, Ghulam Mustafa Khar, among others. One is reminded of the way Indira Gandhi got rid of the Congress bosses led by Kamraj in 1969.

In Pakistan, inter-generational transition of political careers has found an important place in the scholarly analyses. However, this is more of a myth than a reality. One is struck by the absence of a linear relationship between successive generations of political leaders. Nobody seems to have survived as a leader from among the top-ranking political leadership from the first generation, including Liaqat Ali Khan, Nazimuddin, Shaukat Hayat, Iftikhar Mamdot, Mumtaz Daultana, Feroz Khan Noon, Sardar Nishtar, G. M. Syed, Qayyum Khan, Suhrawardy, Abdullah Haroon and others. Similarly, religious leaders such as Shabbir Ahmed Usmani, Suleman Nadvi, Abul Ala Maududi, Shah Ahmed Noorani, Maulana Sialvi, Maulana Hazarvi, and Maulana Abdussattar Niazi left no 'dynastic' heirs. Only Maulana Fazlur Rehman of JUI-F represents the generational transition. Asif Zardari represented lateral transition instead. The two cases of transition from Wali Khan to Asfandyar Wali and from Asif Zardari to Bilawal Bhutto represented a long period of apprenticeship under the patronage, training, and guidance of the paterfamilias. During this period, however, party fortunes went down in both cases. The question of dynastic rule in the Sharif family was something of an enigma. The younger brother, Shahbaz Sharif, was a kind of heir apparent from 1990 onwards for three decades. After the ouster of Nawaz Sharif as prime minister in July 2017 when Nawaz's daughter Maryam hit the street with her father to protest against the Supreme Court's verdict, a tussle ensued between the lady and her uncle Shahbaz Sharif for the party leadership.

In the PPP, Fatima Bhutto lost out as a daughter of Murtaza Bhutto – the slain brother of Benazir. In India, Maneka Gandhi similarly lost out to Sonia Gandhi, after her husband Sanjay Gandhi died in an accident. In both cases, a direct connection with the dynastic leadership overruled an indirect connection through siblings. One can find an example of delayed charisma in the case of Ms Fatima Jinnah's presidential candidature against Ayub in 1965. She was able to mount huge pressure on the military president and probably would have won in a direct election. One is reminded of such a case when Napoleon III won elections in France in 1853 drawing on his inheritance of the charisma of his grandfather, Napoleon Bonaparte, after a gap of three decades.

A major source of transition has been the army's commitment to getting rid of the current generation of political leaders and replacing it with 'fresh blood' that often belonged to the former's kith and kin or their direct descendants. Ayub's government (1958–69) virtually wiped out the whole post-independence generation of leaders from Sohrawardy to Daultana, from Ghaffar Khan and G.M. Syed to Samad Achakzai. In 1970, a new generation emerged, including Z. A. Bhutto, Mujibur Rehman, Wali Khan, Asghar Khan, Ghaus Bux Bizenjo, Ataullah Mengal and Khair Bux Marri. Zia's martial law put an end to the second generation of political leaders. After Zia, the mantle of leadership fell to the third generation, comprising Benazir Bhutto, Nawaz Sharif, Asfandyar Wali, Mahmood Achakzai, Qazi Hussain Ahmed and Junejo among others. However, Musharraf did not succeed when he aimed to bring 'new faces' into the system in 2002. Only 18 per cent were running their first election and 33 out of the 119 MNAs had more than thirty years of experience behind them. As we have seen, Musharraf set a minimum educational requirement of graduation for holding public office.[189] This affected 25 per cent of the MNAs and 22 per cent of the Senators. In the case of the PML-N alone, 53 MNAs and 8 Senators did not qualify. It was a way for Musharraf to cut down his political enemies.[190]

Political leadership at the top and at the constituency level is a function of property holding. MNAs in 2004 also held high social and economic standing and their average assets were Rs 17,289 million.[191] It is imperative for the political class to participate in elections to keep, consolidate and enhance its power. Election as a non-combatant form of projection of social power through electoral mobilization is the only game in the town. Access to the state's authority is keenly sought by client-voters in the case of elections for the national or provincial assemblies. This fact engenders the issue of inheritance of a political role across generations. Where property does not play a significant role, and therefore territorial constituency is rendered irrelevant, succession has no meaning. For example, the ulema occupied a high status essentially through their written work, and their organizational network of ties with sectarian followers or madrassah chains. Far from territorial representation, it was piety, religious hierarchy, and the on-again/off-again status of a client of the army such as under Zia and Musharraf that put the leading Islamic figures in high places. Otherwise, one does not find 'religious families' across generations. In the case of the 'left', socialist workers and ideologues most often operated through syndicates of like-minded intellectuals, trade unions and peasant associations, with no territorially defined constituencies and thus no penchant for electoral politics. Under these circumstances, inheritance of political leadership has simply been untenable on the left.

There has been a diminishing trend in the domination of landlord–politicians in the legislatures of Pakistan.[192] A major transition was reflected through Nawaz Sharif's assent to power in Punjab from the mid-1980s onwards. As a scion of an industrialist family, he represented a shift in the party leadership from the rural to the urban sector. This shift potentially transformed the party dynamics away from a 'land-to-rule model'.[193] The new bid for power drew on the big business enterprise. The political class expanded beyond the landed and tribal elite to the business community and the professional middle class. His ancestral land-base in Nawabshah notwithstanding, Asif Zardari was also not a typical landlord politician. His property interests severally operated in the urban sector even as the family's landholdings remained part of the larger framework of his status. The urban credentials of the PTI's Imran Khan and the MQM's Altaf Hussain remained undisputed. In other words, the leadership of the top four parliamentary parties – the PML-N, PPP, PTI and various MQM factions – did not fit the classical mould of landlord–politician. However, the secondary leaderships of these parties, excepting the MQM, and the top leadership of the smaller parties, including the ANP, BNP-M, PKMAP, JWP and JUI-F, often belonged to the traditional elite comprising the landlord stratum, tribal elite and ulema.

Political leadership in general has displayed social conservatism commensurate with the nature of its electoral constituency. Peasant and tribal society, as well as its recently urbanized segment, has practised varying degrees of cultural oppression in the form of honour killings and other anti-women attributes. The political class comprising public representatives, has been under pressure from these customary laws, in practice on the margins of the prevalent legal system, often splashed through the media due to their perceived brutality.[194]

At the other end, the monopoly of the modern state sector over financial, administrative, ideological and educational resources meant that the political elite could only deliver on patronage not on policy, which remained the preserve of the state elite. As MNAs and MPAs, politicians facilitate dispensation of justice at the district level and mediate between their constituents and the bureaucracy to unblock administrative bottlenecks. In this sense, the political elite is the biggest stakeholder in electoral democracy. Ironically, Maya Chadda has described the landed and tribal elite as anti-democratic.[195] But the widely researched framework of 'patronage politics' points to the need for politicians to have access to the state machinery at the district and provincial levels. This need to have a foot inside the political system to act as a broker between the state and citizen is so acute that politicians would be willing to join hands with a military president before or after elections as part of the King's party. Similarly, under civilian governments the opposition MNAs and MPAs often joined the ruling party under pressure from their voters, who needed access to district courts and provincial secretariats to redress their grievances.

Elsewhere, I have analysed the operation of political parties within the grey area between martial law and democracy that brings out the limited scope of their role.[196] Bhutto remains the only example of a leadership that emerged from a popular movement against the establishment. As a minister, he was the second most important person under the Ayub regime. The general impression was that he was dismissed under US pressure after the Consortium crisis of 1965, and also due to his rigidity towards India and romance with Soekarno's Indonesia. Bhutto's departure was highly regretted by the press. In Pakistan, a coup became almost a default option, simply because Bhutto had resigned with great pomp and show.[197] Bhutto and his pro-Chinese policies provoked British diplomats into describing him as 'untrustworthy' and 'a self-seeking intriguer'.[198] During the 1970 elections, the Bhutto's party PPP developed a strong base in urban Punjab due to its class-based agenda, with a special appeal for industrial labour and youth. Similarly, Bhutto's popularity in rural Punjab represented a sharp break from the traditional pattern whereby the landed elite generally managed to win seats. Bhutto's promise of land reforms couched in the message of giving land to the landless and improving the share of the sharecroppers had a magical effect all around. Similarly, students saw in him the messiah who would guide them to the Promised Land. However, the party faced a tough fight in Karachi where the right-wing ulema parties such as the JUP and JI fared far better.

The 1970 elections divided Sindh. Mohajirs had the image of being a privileged community who were obviously committed to preserving their position in the face of the 'nativist' upsurge. Sindhis had the profile of being underprivileged. The PPP, with its Sindhi leader, was understood to be a Sindhi party in Sindh that was destined to upset the status quo if elected to power. The Mohajirs' worst fears came true as the election results were announced. 'Victorian Pakistan' was threatened by the rise of the Bhutto phenomenon; politics after Bhutto depended on how his successors handled these new forces released by him.[199] As diplomats in Islamabad would report, 'Mr Bhutto, however arrogant and paternalistic in practice his own political style may have been', nonetheless did try to harness mass support after he had brought about the highest level of political awareness in the country's history.[200] During his years in power (1971–7), Bhutto was in firm control of 'the levers of administrative and political power' and faced only a 'weak, divided and seemingly impotent opposition'.[201] Bhutto's belief in the strategic role of the army led him to military operations in Balochistan, whereby he unwittingly invited eight long years of Zia's martial law.[202] Hatred between Bhutto and Asghar Khan was legendary. The former 'won' the controversial 1977 elections in West Pakistan. The latter won only one seat in the National Assembly and was never able to move back into parliamentary politics after Zia's coup. Asghar Khan openly denied that there had been any agreement between the PPP and PNA in July 1977.[203]

Factionalism and Patronage Politics

Local party organizations typically, if not in every case, lacked autonomy in financial matters and candidate selection. The bottom tier generally did not feed the upper tier nor contribute to decision-making, with the possible exception of the MQM under Altaf Hussain. Again, except for the MQM, the high organizational potential of political parties such as the JI and ANP did not have a significant impact on their vote bank. For example, the JI was never an electoral party of any significance in terms of government formation, except for the manoeuvred elections of 2002. Similarly, the MQM increasingly became the most controversial party in the country because of allegations of murder and extortion against party workers and leaders, including Altaf Hussain.

Compared to the JI and MQM, the three mainstream parties – PPP, PML-N and PTI – have had a lax organizational structure, characterized by a charismatic leader, absence of meaningful party elections, and a low level of party discipline that has made them dependent on electables. The PPP and the PML-N, however, along with their breakaway factions have been able to get 70 per cent of the vote over past decades to form their governments in the centre.[204] In 2012, the PML-N workers' conventions, which were organized to elect the provincial chiefs of the party, ended in chaos in the provinces other than Punjab. The party faced internal revolt from various factions that refused to endorse the elected candidates.[205] Similarly, Z. A. Bhutto had discounted the need to organize his party, dispensed with the ideological cadres and gradually embraced the 'deep state' by relying on bureaucracy and other state institutions.[206]

Political parties generally operated in accordance with the Iron Law of Oligarchy.[207] The intra-party elections, whenever they were conducted, were only a formality. The already weak inner party democracy further eroded in 2017 when those parties that had boldly experimented with 'genuine' party elections succumbed to the prevailing norm of polls for the sake of fulfilling a legal formality.[208] The 'election' of the second-tier leadership has most often been directed by the party high command; in addition, the party office holders have often been public office holders as well, which has meant a loss of oversight of the government by the party leadership.

Party factions can be created by an external factor such as 'cohesive primordial or interest groups', which may 'colonize a party'.[209] A party faction adopts a 'two-track policy' of identifying with the leader at the top and outmanoeuvring the rival faction at the local level.[210] As in Mexico, there are clear 'party switching incentives' for the candidates from the perceived losing parties.[211] In the 2018 elections in Pakistan, the loyalties of politicians from several parties switched as the establishment and the media gave clear signs of the PTI party being the favourite.

The power of local groups depends on the power of the leader/patron. The mainstream parties, the PML-N, PPP and PTI, clearly represented this case. Only cadre parties such as the MQM and JI, which were organizationally strong, disallowed the middlemen in the hierarchy. Political parties made alliances in order to overcome their weakness.[212] Networking, not organization, is the hallmark of a typical political party in Pakistan. Personality-based party differences often led to factions or patronage clusters within political parties. On some occasions, a mass exodus of party members took place, which brought about regime change through a King's party.

The fragmentation of the political community, especially from 1988 onwards, ensured that no party was able to dominate the government at the federal and provincial levels in the absence of coalition support. After the 2018 elections, the federal, Punjab and Balochistan governments were coalition-based. Even 'independent' candidates eventually need to align to a political party to seek political patronage. It happened in the 2020 elections in Gilgit-Baltistan where the PTI formed the government after co-opting independents. Electoral alliances belong to two categories: the inclusionary model, i.e. the joint fielding of candidates under the same symbol, for example, the MMA in 2002 and again in 2018; and the exclusionary model, i.e. seat adjustment among parties, whereby they do not field candidates against their 'allies' in certain constituencies.[213]

Parties and politicians display a decreasing trend of using the ideological narrative to appeal to their voters. Endemic poverty and governmental dysfunction make free, reasoned and responsible judgement irrelevant.[214] In South Asian politics, 'patronage' is an imperfect gloss over a widespread moral discourse that helps citizens escape the gridlock of liberal political heuristics and disables them from seeing through the local combatants' normative rhetoric. Patrons are wealthy, politically influential and socially privileged. They control what others need or want, making their clients at best dependent and at worst oppressed.[215] At one level, patrons' relations with their followers are legitimized by reciprocity – and the 'equality' it implies – suggesting that patrons and clients occupy a shared moral world. At another level, inequality lies at the very heart of patronage: the patron's authority depends on access to status and power which transcends that of his followers.[216] In the midst of unequal reciprocity and political deal-making, the 'free agency' of voters – formalized as free choice – has been magnetically drawn to the efficacious and community-minded patrons.[217] The law, which was meant to protect the principle of voters' free choice, actually highlighted and sustained patronage as the foundation of democracy.[218] Politicians operating within 'political society' circumvent and even break the law, sometimes to appease their constituents, making what they consider the rigid and unresponsive legal structures of the postcolonial states more amenable to ordinary people's needs. Shandana Mohmand locates the process of shift from domination of the landed elites to intermediation on way to developing a model of political engagement in a village in Punjab.[219] In the perspective of the two types of colonization in Punjab represented by proprietary and crown villages, she traces the patterns of inequality and its management by the landed elites through bargaining.[220]

The social costs of patron–client relations outweigh their benefits because clientelist exchanges are ultimately beneficial to the political elite. Patronage undermines universal public service provision.[221] The de facto privatization of governmental services via patronage bonds reproduces both clan-based and class-based patterns of dominance and, in the process, prevents the expansion of rights of citizenship to the rural poor. Patronage denies agency to the voters. It follows the colonial wisdom: those who cannot represent themselves must be represented by others. Thus, patronage prevents class-in-itself from becoming a class-for-itself via mobilization along issues and policies. The 'subalterns' align themselves vertically to powerful patrons in search of specific benefits instead of making horizontal alliances for a longer-term agenda for change.[222]

Understanding the priorities of the establishment is key to the way that political parties define their election strategies, such as making alliances, shaping the agenda, and focusing on electables rather than voters. Elections operate within the framework of an 'establishmentarian democracy'.[223] We shall discuss this concept in the next chapter, where we define the nature and character of the democratic set-up in Pakistan. In 2009, parliament had decided to conduct peace negotiations with the Taliban in KP but the army went ahead with an operation anyway, neglecting the decision of public representatives.[224] Various sections of the political class generally operated as clients of the army. In the 2002 elections, a 'religio-political alliance' MMA managed to outperform the PPP and the ANP in KP due to the establishment's critical input.[225]

In August 2019, Prime Minister Imran Khan issued a notification for awarding an extension to COAS General Bajwa, who was set to retire on 28 November. Two days before that, the Supreme Court suspended the notification due to a purported legal vacuum and gave 6 months to the government to rectify the situation in the form of legislation by parliament. The court challenged the official reliance on Article 243 of the constitution and Regulation 255 of the Army Regulations (Rules). It referred to three points which the government needed to consider: the law dealing with extension and its duration; the adoption of proper procedure; and the grounds for extension.[226] Later, the chief justice observed that the bench was labelled an Indian agent and a CIA agent in the social media, simply because it had examined the Army Act. Conversely, the attorney general told him that India had taken advantage of the court's arguments. Subsequently, the government and the opposition joined hands to pass the bill for COAS's extension. The social media lambasted the opposition, especially the PML-N and PPP, for meekly bowing down to the establishment.[227]

The new mainstream 'client' party, the PTI, was visibly supported by the establishment in the 2018 elections through a firm middle-class support base, an obliging judiciary, and control over media. The establishment's preference for client parties contributed enormously to a weak and vulnerable party system in Pakistan.

Political Class — II: Electoral Politics

'Electoral governance' is supposed to have an 'enabling function' that gives credibility to the process of administration, supervises the system by bringing in accountability for performance, and communicates the mechanism to citizens effectively.[228] Elections bring the potential rulers and the ruled into contact with each other, at least for a limited time and purpose. In Pakistan, the electoral dynamics were controversial from the beginning. The Hindu minority opposed the recommendation of the 1952 Report of the Basic Principles Committee for separate electorates. They objected to

Islam becoming interwoven with the constitution.[229] The Joint Electorates Bill was passed by the West Pakistan Assembly in 1957 in the teeth of opposition from the Muslim League, supported by the AL and PNP led by G. M. Syed along with some republicans who were unsure. The average citizen, however, was not much concerned.[230] After the 1956 Constitution was abrogated, the theory and practice of elections was managed by two military rulers: Ayub and Yahya (1958–70). In the official view, the 1959 Basic Democracies elections, based on a two-tier system, were meant to bring forward leaders from the middle strata, bypassing the landed elite. But it turned out to be a vassal system that would serve the superstructure of an indirectly elected system of governance.[231] As per the 1963 Franchise Commission, there were three requirements that an electoral system had to fulfil: a stable government that worked for national unity; a powerful executive branch which ensured fair and efficient distribution of resources; and a government that was representative of the public voice.[232] In this report, policy was inextricably mixed with ambition: the electoral system and national unity seemed to have a symbiotic relationship; a strong executive was supposed to deliver a fair distribution of resources; and an 'elected' government was considered to be representative of the public will. The justifications of the Franchise Commission for its recommendations smacked of naivety and a high level of subjectivity in preparing its agenda.

More than half a century later, it was more of the same. Fair allocation of resources in the 2018 elections remained elusive both as agenda and policy. The elected government of the PTI was hardly considered representative of public opinion in the wake of a wide perception of pre-poll and polling-day rigging at the hands of the establishment. Much as in India, the way representation works has been disturbed by the dissociation of electoral mandate from policy.[233] Furthermore, the 2018 election in Pakistan was a glaring example of a clash of interests between (legal–institutional) 'structure' and (supra-parliamentary) 'agency'. The laws and procedures of the Election Commission were most advanced in Pakistan's history in 2018 after several reform efforts. However, these elections were publicly called the dirtiest elections ever.[234] The problem lay elsewhere, not in the domain of reforms.

Elections: The Design and the Practice

In a way, the 1970 elections ended an era of perceived inequalities and injustices. This time, a largely illiterate public was mobilized with the message that they were poor because others were rich.[235] Class politics did not surface again at that scale in the following half century. Indeed, class dynamics eroded both in electoral terms and as part of the public imagination. The absence of a public committed to service delivery has rendered formulation and implementation of policy redundant. This has reduced parties into election entities per se and party manifestos into barren wish lists.[236] As for the electoral system, votes are more a result of social and political influence than the outcome of electoral laws.[237]

Even if all factors in a political system, from the Election Commission to election laws, are 'democratic' in nature, the entire system may still not be democratic if actual power lies in non-elected hands. These are, then, 'mimic democracies'.[238] Since the leadership prefers electables over party loyalists for issuing party tickets, the election campaign is candidate-orientated rather than citizen-orientated. In other words, the leadership is not fully aligned with the public at the local level in term of the latter's demands. Electables are privileged over party workers because they wield influence in the constituency, and they are selected by the party leadership at the top.[239]

While the law sought to make party affairs transparent and democratic through intra-party elections, the top-down character of the flow of authority within parties massively inhibited their organizational growth. The bottom tier hardly contributed to the policy and strategy of the upper tier, be it about ideological profile or the issuance of party tickets or the election of office holders. The provision for party elections has been flaunted in public in the form of essentially uncontested although formally contested polls. In the absence of a system of public funding, parties drew on the financial input of their wealthier members for the organizational work.[240] Individual candidates bore the brunt of their own election expenses.[241]

One can analyse three basic dimensions of electoral politics in Pakistan. First, following the Mosaic myth, the party leader claims to lead the nation to 'the promised land'. Millions of people have believed passionately in the message of leaders ranging from Z. A. Bhutto to

Imran Khan. Second, there is always a villain, such as a non-delivering corrupt system, rulers such as Ayub Khan, Nawaz Sharif, Asif Zardari, elite groups such as the army, civil bureaucracy, the landed elite, the industrial elite and ulema, the ruling dynasties such as the Bhuttos and Sharifs, and the USA as the 'other' in reserve. Third, the organizers and ideologues of the party, usually from the middle and lower middle classes, bear the responsibility to formulate the party's narrative and organize rallies and public meetings. They firmly believe in their leaders' sagacity, moral uprightness, and capacity to deliver and win over what they consider the wily, deceitful, and corrupt rulers. However, they often become the first casualty after an electoral victory. The process of government formation tends to push them into the dustbin of history. The relative stridency of the PTI in the 2013 elections, which failed to deliver, pushed the party leadership to the use of hard-hitting, hostile, and often obscene language for five years up to the 2018 elections and beyond. Three decades ago, the MQM under the leadership of Altaf Hussain adopted slander, violent speech and street violence as the way to achieve a breakthrough into the political system.

According to Duverger, the structure of elections has both mechanical and psychological effects. The mechanical effect has to do with the number of seats, while the psychological effect deals with the strategies of both voters and parties.[242] Often, the psychological effect constitutes the substance of the election study proper, because that involves balancing choices defined and offered by family ties, traditional bonds, current issues, the reputation of candidates and party profiles. In other words, the social context of electoral politics impinges on the voting behaviour of people far more than the rules and regulations. An essential part of a functioning democracy means that 'losers are not punished by the winners', because democracy is a way of governance and a framework, not an alignment of forces with certain objectives.[243] But this is precisely the problem with democracy in Pakistan. For example, Zia's pursuit of 'positive results' pre-ordained the establishment's indulgence in the way elections were held, contestants acquired a public profile, and the judiciary injected a supra-political authority conceived in constitutional and moral terms. Interestingly, a large part of the body of law covering political parties (electoral laws, campaign laws, party finance laws and laws for the election of party office holders) was instituted by the military-led governments of Ayub, Zia and Musharraf. The Election Commission of Pakistan (ECP) has been rendered grossly controversial. Following the 2013 polls the PTI launched street agitation against the ECP for misconducting the polls.[244] The ECP again came under severe criticism from the PML-N, PPP and other parties following the 2018 elections, about issues pertaining to rigging on polling day.[245] Somewhat on the pattern of Duverger's Law,[246] the FPTP virtually produced a bipolar party system led by the PML-N and the PPP for more than a quarter of a century (1988–2018). In a single-member plurality system, the dominant party overpowers the smaller parties. This winner-takes-all syndrome makes it hard to execute power-sharing or to promote a balanced legislature.[247]

The FPTP system operates in favour of the larger parties, which win a greater number of seats than their percentage of votes. In the 2013 elections, the PML-N received 32.77 per cent of the total votes and formed the government in the centre, carrying 126 of the 272 contested seats.[248] Similarly, the PTI received 31.82 per cent of the popular vote in the 2018 general elections and got 116 seats.[249] This system also divides the vote, sometimes to a ridiculously low level that enables an election victory with a very low margin. For example, the speaker of the Balochistan Assembly, Abdul Quddus Bizenjo, was elected chief minister of the province after having won a provincial assembly seat in 2013 with just 544 votes out of 57,666 registered votes, a result that was widely criticized as unrepresentative and thus undemocratic.[250]

The fact that elections increasingly operated at the level of the candidate rather than the citizen led to an electoral de-alignment in the form of a growing gap between voters and political parties. The 'cleavage de-alignment' pointed to people dismissing their links with political parties in different 'social locations', while 'partisan de-alignment' addressed decreasing party membership in general.[251] This phenomenon is rooted in the shifting loyalties of politicians and in cynicism about zero prospects of a change in policy. In Imran Khan's case, it was his profile as leader rather than his hodge-podge party that attracted voters in 2018. The MQM, however, represented the opposite model of syncretization between the leader and voters through a disciplined cadre of party workers. Altaf Hussain's demagogic leadership kept the party together for a generation. But in 2018, when the party was in total disarray, many Mohajirs reverted to pre-MQM mainstream politics by voting for the PTI while others stuck to the shrunken MQM factions.

In KP, while the local PTI government (2013–18) was affected by controversy due to corruption scandals, the messianic appeal of Imran Khan remained unscathed for the next elections. In Balochistan, ethnic de-alignment in general, and the passing of the older generation of tribal leadership in particular, opened up the field for 'independents', the new Balochistan Awami Party (BAP), and the Islamic alliance MMA, all three beholden to the establishment. The PTI won seats from the military recruitment area of northern Punjab and from the incipient Seraiki movement in southern Punjab. The Islamic vote of the TLP variety made inroads into the PML-N's vote in central Punjab, surreptitiously at the instance of the establishment.

A study of the 1990 elections has shown that the ties of the *biradari* system were stronger than political parties. When candidates failed to secure a party ticket and ran as independents, they often took the *biradari* vote with them.[252] Subsequent elections for three decades have moved between these two poles. It has been argued that there is a difference between choice and preference, and the act of voting turns it into a boundary-producing phenomenon because one party is chosen while all others are not.[253] The role of the ballot in creating partisanship within a community needs to be researched in the context of Pakistan. In the US context, we find a dichotomy between 'attitude consistency', whereby voters stick to a position, and 'issue voting', where the issue comes first and the party comes second. In Pakistan, the class-based issue topped voter preference in Punjab in the 1970 election, while the issue of corruption brought some dividends for the PTI in 2018. Otherwise, 'attitude' via party affiliation has been the norm: the vote will go to the candidate whose affiliation is supported.[254]

One can look at two kinds of effects on voters: priming effects, which cause a shift in the support of the candidates, and lagged effects, which develop gradually over a long period of time. In the case of Pakistan, the PTI symbolized priming effects in the 2013 and 2018 elections, while the PML-N, PPP, ANP, JUI and various other parties experienced lagged effects from the past. An adversarial rather than consensus orientation about issues and policies underscored the discussion on TV shows. This helped Imran Khan pick up on confrontation on several dimensions of bad governance. The PTI, with its express appeal to the youth, capitalized on the social media in 2013 and 2018, while the PPP and PML-N's use of social media remained limited. Indeed, the PML-N suffered under the gaze of the media because the TV channels' coverage of the Panama Leaks case was blatantly partisan prior to the elections. The newscasters and discussants treated the accused as if they had already been convicted and found guilty, and thus shaped a negative profile of the Sharifs under trial. There was partial censorship of the PML-N and MQM during the campaign for the 2018 elections.[255]

Outside mainstream electoral activity, there was a continuing source of irritation for the PTI in the form of a foreign funding case that seemed to linger on endlessly. The major stakeholders – PTI, PML-N, PPP, ECP, the higher courts and, indirectly, the establishment as an alleged supporter of Imran Khan – were involved on opposite sides: either seeking an early verdict or prolonging the proceedings ad nauseum. This foreign funding case was an albatross around the neck of Imran Khan for years before and after he became prime minister. Procedurally, this grim episode involved a challenge to the jurisdiction of various institutions, among them the ECP, the Supreme Court and at least more than one high court. Substantively, the proceedings of the case pointed to a systemic meltdown inasmuch as the law served as a public arena for a hardcore political conflict. A dissident member of the PTI filed a case with the ECP in November 2014 that the party had collected approximately $3 billion from 'illegal foreign funds'. These funds were collected through 'illegal *hundi* channels' from the Middle East going into the accounts of PTI employees. Also, these funds were not declared for the party's annual audit reports, which were submitted to the ECP.[256] After the ECP's objection concerning the failure to disclose the details about the party funds, the PTI challenged the ECP's jurisdiction in Islamabad High Court (IHC) which, however, remanded the case back to the ECP. A member of the ECP accused the PTI of using delaying tactics. The PTI filed a case in the IHC for suspension of the scrutiny of its accounts. Subsequently, the IHC rejected the PTI's plea regarding the *locus standi* of its dissident member, Akbar S. Babar.[257] Later, the PTI applied for secrecy in the scrutiny of its case.[258]

The ECP objected to representation of the PTI by the deputy attorney general. It maintained that he 'should rather protect the state and not the party which are two completely different entities', and that 'the learned council should have preferred the state over the interests of the party'.[259] However, in the PTI leader's opinion, the ECP was 'neither a court nor a tribunal' where only lawyers could speak.[260] The petitioner, Babar, made a fresh application in which he mentioned the PTI's delaying tactics including applications, adjournments and court petitions, while the scrutiny committee had met 42 times and issued 16 orders.[261] Following the PTI's demand that the accounts of the other mainstream parties should also be scrutinized, the ECP duly obliged. However, it was feared all along that a negative court verdict would pull the rug from under the feet of the PTI through disqualification of its legislators and office holders. This was a potential Watergate of Imran Khan. The PDM marched to the ECP building in January 2021 to demand a verdict of the 7-year-old case.

The 2018 Elections

A series of manipulations, interventions, and acts of harassment of electoral candidates gave the 2018 polls the profile of an engineered election. There was a lack of a level-playing field for the political parties in the 2018 general elections, whereby the judiciary and the NAB were seen as putting pressure on the PML-N.[262] There were two running themes: (1) the humiliation and removal of Nawaz Sharif from the political scene, which made some of his party men look for an alternative; and (2) the unmistakable impression that Imran Khan was the establishment's favourite candidate for prime ministership and was thus destined to win.

In Punjab, relative satisfaction with the public service delivery of the Sharif administration in the areas of education, healthcare, transport and electricity was partially countered by the dissatisfaction of the voters due to allegations of corruption. A survey found that 81 per cent of respondents in Punjab who intended to vote for the PML-N considered the party honest whereas 66 per cent of those who intended to vote for the PTI considered the PML-N dishonest.[263]

Citizens were subjected to the media operating as a shopping mall for party profiles. They were on the receiving end of a technological product: the 'iconography'. Their opinions were shaped through the framing of debates in various talk-shows in and around the issue of the 'proven' corruption of Nawaz Sharif, and the 'infallible' Imran Khan. Intimidating calls to media outlets, hindrance in broadcasting and printing news, and harassment of journalists became the order of the day. Since Article 19 provides freedom of expression subject to 'any reasonable restrictions imposed by law', there were excessive content limitations citing security as well as religious and moral concerns.[264]

The PML-N was featured most on television, but two-thirds of its coverage was negative, relating to recent court cases about corruption.[265] There was a 'systematic effort to undermine the former ruling party through cases of corruption, contempt of court and terrorism against its leaders and candidates'.[266] Several media outlets were asked to censor 'anti-judiciary' talk. The concerns of the PML-N, the PPP, the ANP and other party leaders about the establishment's intrusiveness were not aired. The public's access to a full political narrative was barred to prevent any challenges to the state institutions. A Lahore High Court judgment upholding the ban on 'anti-judiciary speeches', based on Articles 19 and 68 of the constitution, was often quoted by media outlets in this regard.[267]

When *Dawn* published an interview with Nawaz Sharif in May 2018, distribution of the newspaper was barred from the cantonment areas and defence colonies in various cities.[268] International opinion was critical of the way that politicians from other parties were persuaded to join the PTI, the media was pressed into giving positive coverage to the PTI, PML-N workers were rounded up, detained and otherwise harassed, and attempts were made to disqualify PML-N election candidates.[269] Senators Raza Rabbani and Farhatullah Babar expressed their reservations about men in uniform being provided with magisterial powers for their duties in and around the polling stations.[270] The election observers were kept off-limits and their accreditation was grossly delayed. Ironically, for Imran Khan this was not an embarrassing moment: he claimed that the country's 'umpires' would step back if he were not elected. But Mr Khan's promised 'New Pakistan' started to look rather like the old one.[271]

It was the judges' election par excellence, a mirror image of the 2013 elections. The ECP comprised five members, four of whom belonged to the judiciary. The returning officers (ROs) were members of the lower courts and were responsible for receiving, scrutinizing, accepting, or rejecting nomination papers. Any appeals against the

RO's decisions could be filed, again in the higher courts. Before the elections, Imran Khan approached the Supreme Court to render null and void Articles 9, 10 and 203 of the 2017 Election Reforms Act passed by parliament, that provided constitutional cover for Nawaz Sharif's bid for continuing as party leader after his disqualification in the Panama Leaks case. The PTI, which had a small minority of 35 members out of 342 members, managed to get a law that had been earlier passed by the majority overturned through the judiciary. From the 2017 controversial verdict in the Panama Leaks case onwards, the PML-N leadership was able to take the judiciary to task for issuing statements in defence of the verdict, which was understood to be contrary to general practice.

Islamist parties and alliances ranging from the TLP and Ahl Sunnat Wal Jamaat (ASWJ) to MMA fielded hundreds of candidates throughout Pakistan. The establishment allegedly favoured the mainstreaming of the jihadi parties and extremist elements and revived the MMA with the idea of cutting into the PML-N's vote bank.[272] The emergence of 925 extremist-linked political party candidates in the ECP's final list of candidates was an alarming figure, undermining the genuineness of its nomination process.[273] Similarly, in 2018 the failure of the results transmission system (RTS) was allegedly a result of not pre-testing it. Thus, presiding officers (POs) manually transmitted the results to the ROs in several constituencies marred by undue delays. In this way, the ECP failed to ensure that the results were not tampered with. The Pakistan Institute of Legislative Development and Transparency (PILDAT) had already warned about the usage of the RTS system, citing the case of Kenya's general elections where a similar system had failed, which led to the election being declared null and void by the Kenyan Supreme Court.[274]

In addition, the POs did not have an adequate number of copies of Form 45, which is a statement of the count, the accepted and rejected ballot papers, and the male and female voters in mixed polling stations. This led to several results being transferred to blank paper, leaving ample room for vote tampering.[275] Since Form 45 was received late by the ROs due to the failure of the RTS, and in insufficient quantity, the processing of results through the results management system (RMS) was delayed. All this resulted in the ECP taking around forty-eight hours to announce 99 per cent of the results.[276] There was a horrendous increase in the number of rejected ballots, a staggering 11.7 per cent increase upon the previous election, with Islamabad's excluded ballots being double those in 2013.[277] Despite a legal requirement for ROs to examine the rejected ballots, the judicial commission that had enquired into the 2013 elections noted that such was not the case. In the 2018 elections, 1.67 million ballots were thus excluded from the counting process. Most significantly, the margin of victory was less than the number of rejected ballots in 169 national and provincial constituencies. Obviously, the lack of review by the ROs significantly impacted the results in favour of the declared winning party, the PTI.[278]

The only silver lining was female participation in the elections. The ECP led a women voter and national identity card campaign, which resulted in the addition of 4.3 million registered women voters between October 2017 and May 2018.[279] Female voter turnout in the 2018 elections improved significantly upon the last elections. In the Upper Dir District and North Waziristan, women voted for the first time.[280] In Upper Dir, more than 38 per cent of registered women participated in polling, compared to only one woman who came out to cast her vote in 2013.[281] In NA 221 Tharparkar-I, women set a record as 72.83 per cent of registered female voters cast their votes.[282] Indeed, female turnout was more than 70 per cent in five national and provincial constituencies of Tharparkar. Female turnout remained higher than male turnout in these constituencies, and their overall voter turnout was the highest across the country.[283] In the constituencies where the female voter turnout was less than 10 per cent of the polled votes, such as in NA-10 (Shangla) and NA-48 (North Waziristan), a re-election was announced.[284]

The political class is remarkably resilient in terms of maintaining its presence in the political system as legislators. Some candidates fought elections umpteen times, for example, Choudhry Nisar Ali for the ninth time and Sheikh Rashid for the eighth time. Of the National Assembly seats in Punjab, 53.4 per cent were held by 'dynastic' politicians in 2008. Dynastic leadership remained a permanent feature of the elections.[285] In Punjab, more than 80 per cent of candidates who had won in 2013 were in the hunt for another stint at the national or provincial level in 2018. This figure is only slightly lower for other provinces.[286] A *Herald* study put the figure for dynastic holders of office across Pakistan at around 45 per cent.[287] The 2018 elections presented the highest number of registered voters aged 18–35, comprising 44 per cent of total voters. It was claimed that this section of the population – the 'youth bulge'[288] – could be either good for democracy, or bad for it if not equipped with the required knowledge and options.[289] This is as misleading as it is blunt. As discussed earlier in this chapter, youth is a given reality in Pakistan, whose political attitudes cannot be judged according to certain hypothetical conditions such as 'the required knowledge' and 'options'. There was no distinct pattern of young voters.

The post-2018 by-polls in the National Assembly constituency of Daska in Punjab on 19 February 2021 were marred by gunfire, murder, harassment, and the disappearance of the POs of 20 polling stations at the end of the polling day. POs reported back to duty in the early hours of the morning along with ballot boxes filled with fake ballot papers. The social media blasted the PTI government for abducting the POs. The ECP declared the elections null and void as per Article 218 (3) of the constitution read with Section 9 (1) of the Elections Act 2017 and ordered re-election on 18 March (later postponed to 10 April). The ECP suspended Sialkot's Deputy Commissioner and District Police Officer and recommended the transfer of the Gujranwala divisional commissioner. The Chief Secretary of Punjab, who did not attend any of the ECP's calls at midnight after the first call, was summoned for ignoring his duties. [290] After the Supreme Court confirmed the date for re-election, the by-polls were held 'fairly'. No punitive action was taken by the ECP, the Supreme Court or the PTI government against the POs who had disappeared with the ballot boxes in the fog of night.

How does a party behave in office? The post-2018 government has been quintessentially inept and inefficient in its economic performance. The GDP per capita declined from \$1,566 to \$1,360 and the GDP from \$315 billion to \$278 billion (2018–19). Economic growth decreased from 4.7 per cent to 1 per cent, and investment from 15.8 per cent to minus 12.8 per cent. Inflation jumped from 3.2 per cent to 12.7 per cent and the exchange rate from 104.9 Rupees per US dollar to 150.4 (2016–19).[291] In Akbar Zaidi's estimate, the PTI government was delayed by ten months in reaching an agreement with the IMF, which worsened the situation on the ground and pushed the IMF to take a hard line.[292] Negative economic indicators peaked under Imran Khan's government: these included inflation at 14.5 per cent, i.e. the highest for a decade, food inflation at 25 per cent and a forecast for economic growth at 1.2 per cent. Akbar Zaidi woefully wished if only 'the PTI government had been on the "same page" as the dispossessed and working people' instead of claiming to be on the same page with the establishment.[293] As per Transparency International's Corruption Perception Index, Pakistan slipped a wee bit down the ladder of corruption from its position at 120 to 124.[294]

At the end of this section, I venture into drawing a longitudinal picture of the election pattern in Pakistan. As Table 3.1 shows, there is a consistently strong role of parties and leaders throughout history. As per the party identification model, the leader party is the prototype of election entities. Similarly, policy remained irrelevant for elections despite the elaborate party manifestos and promises made from the stage of public meetings. Only the PPP's election campaign in 1970 and 1977 scored high in the field of policy as a credible and substantive framework of reforms. Elections have been relatively non-ideological across the board, except for the 1946 elections underscored by the one-point agenda of partition, the 1970 and 1977 elections defined by socialism – more in the former case and less in the latter case – and the 2002 elections underlined by the Islamic agenda of the MMA, though confined to KP only. Class dynamics has never played a decisive role except the two elections in the 1970s as part of the Bhuttoist wave. Ethnicity dominated the vote pattern in the 1970 elections in East Pakistan, Sindh, KP and Balochistan. In other elections, this factor has been operative mainly in Sindh, where Sindhi and Mohajir nationalisms battled for political space from the 1980s onwards. Ethnic politics in Balochistan fractured along tribal lines subsequent to the 1970 elections, while the new middle-class nationalists chose to move along 'pragmatic' lines as part of both the government and the opposition. The arch-Pakhtun nationalist party ANP (previously NAP) never regained its level of popularity and mass appeal after 1970.

Table 3.1 testifies to the fact that the 'low' category points to the prevalence of a political attitude limited to one of the smaller provinces or a residual factor continuing from the previous elections. Socialism was at the top of the ideological battle only in 1970. Ethnicity has gradually lost ground as a political factor except in urban and rural Sindh.

Table 3.1 Elections: Patterns of leadership, alignment and commitment

Year	Party	Leadership	Ideology	Class	Ethnicity	Policy
1946	High	High	High	—	—	—
1965	High	High	Low	—	—	—
1970	High	High	High	High	High	High
1977	High	High	Low	High	Low	High
1985	—	—	—	—	—	—
1988	High	High	—	—	Low	—
1990	High	High	—	—	Low	—
1993	High	High	—	—	Low	—
1997	High	High	—	—	Low	—
2002	High	High	Low	—	Low	—
2008	High	High	—	—	Low	—
2013	High	High	—	—	Low	—
2018	High	High	—	—	Low	—

The right to vote for the expatriate Pakistani community has often surfaced in the national discourse. More than half the estimated 9 million expatriates belonged to the Gulf, of whom half resided in Saudi Arabia. The $20 billion annual remittances (on average) staved off the crisis of payments in the years 2019–21. The PTI government facilitated the transfer of money from abroad through the Roshan Digital Account and Naya Pakistan Certificates.[295] Imran Khan was the most popular leader among expatriates.

There is a provision for the right of expatriates to vote under some circumstances in some countries. But overall, this right has not been exercised in a meaningful way. In the context of Pakistan, there are two broad schools of thought. One focuses on the expatriates' remittances back home, and their passionate nationalism from a distance. The other school finds it superfluous, even risky in the presence of pockets of Islamic extremists and ethnonationalists among expatriates. The former points to distant nationalism, the latter to the gap of information. The party funding case against the PTI, which lingered on for several years from 2014 onwards, related to funds raised by Imran Khan from amongst expatriates, especially in the USA. As we have seen, the case included the matter of the personal accounts of the lower staff of the PTI, who got hefty amounts of money transferred from the Gulf. The most contentious issues were the clandestine means of transfer of the money from abroad and the lack of accountability for that money once it reached the shores of Pakistan. Given Imran Khan's popularity overseas and the funding received from abroad, the PTI government was keen to define a meaningful role for the expatriates who had wholeheartedly supported its agenda to 'cleanse' society of all its ills. The government built a mini cult of expatriates as super-patriotic Pakistanis. It frequently took up the matter of developing a mechanism for giving them voting rights, hoping to bag a majority of expatriates' votes in future elections. In 2021, the PTI government passed a bill that provided for the right to vote for Pakistani expatriates. The PTI had a stable constituency among the expatriate community. At the other end, there are skeptics who find the whole move as a leap in the dark. The state in Pakistan, which has been constantly engaged in intelligence activity about its own citizens, would be obliged to open its doors to those whose educational, cultural, religious and political attitudes would be at best unknown. In the past, the MQM had demanded the right to vote for Mohajir expatriates. The expatriate community included those who fled persecution at the hands of the successive governments of Ayub, Bhutto and Zia, among them leftists of various persuasions, NAP activists and PPP workers and cadres in their thousands, respectively.

According to the second school of thought, parliamentary democracy defines the process of representing territorial constituencies essentially within the framework of a locality. Overseas Pakistanis in their hearts and minds upheld the cause of Pakistan and all-Pakistanism but not an electoral constituency in the real sense. It was argued that their vote would be a negation of constituency politics per se. Periodical elections ensure that candidates preside over the shifting sands of mass mandate as per their performance after elections by way of constituency service. Between the elections, voters can stay either neutral or, more typically, turn for or against the incumbents. Periodicity is the key to electoral democracy. Expatriates, however, typically visit Pakistan and interact with the local population after long spans of time. Their input by way of changing public opinion, or being shaped by it, is hardly relevant for the body politic of the country.

The cultural, ideological and educational socialization of people across tribe, caste, ethnicity and the nation contributes fervently to issue formation in Pakistan. Expatriates, by contrast, are far better aware of issues that affect them in the context of their own daily life: for example, those in the USA or UK or other Western countries are constantly obliged to deal with issues of race, culture, and religion, especially in the case of youth.[296] Only a minority of young men and women were assimilated into the mainstream culture. A decidedly large majority developed negative sentiments about the white Christian majority in terms of their attitudes to sex, gambling, dress code, secularism, human rights, women's rights and the crime and punishment regime as well as foreign policy issues about the Middle East. They faced Islamophobia at home and, in a few cases of radicalization, opted for terrorist attacks and even going to the Middle East to join ISIS to wage jihad. These sentiments were transferred into aggressive political attitudes and worldviews. As voters in Pakistan, they would behave accordingly, i.e. not in consonance with the people in general.

Some even suggested that expatriates should be allowed to contest elections. They included Pakistanis who were citizens of another country, or had dual nationality, or had residential rights in a foreign country. They lacked credentials as representatives of people with a history of social and political work. Indeed, the Constituent Assembly of Pakistan had passed a resolution in 1948 to debar non-residents from becoming its members. The PTI government (2018–) appointed several people as advisors and special assistants to the prime minister, including some people with dual nationality and some others enjoying rights of permanent residence abroad. This created controversy both within and outside the federal cabinet.[297]

Conclusion

This chapter has sought to focus on the two power centres – the middle class and the political class – as the source of influence, privilege and inspiration for combatants engaged in competition to rule the country. I have taken a sociological approach to delineating the wellsprings of power as embedded in social, cultural and ideological pursuits. I have traced the origin and development of the attitudes and norms of the burgeoning middle class in the past two centuries through modernization, professionalization, self-reproductive meritocracy, public morality and status quo-orientation. The middle class is socially progressive, politically conservative. Youth is often studied as part of the middle class, especially through student surveys in cosmopolitan cities. However, youth is an amorphous category that cuts across sector, class and gender. Youth remains a grossly under-researched area per se.

The middle class is a stable constituency for military rule, or at least for a watered-down version of establishmentarian democracy. I have highlighted two leading projects of Islam and nationalism grounded in broad civilizational aspirations. The middle class has developed a globality of its own characterized by a world-of-Islam perspective. With urbanization, vertical mobility, and remittances from abroad, the internal dynamics of the middle class have been changing, especially in terms of taking up modern behavioural patterns at one end and performing religious and cultural rituals at the other.

While drawing on Sartori's theory of the party system, I outlined the political class in the context of both organizational terms as political parties and operational terms as election entities. I discussed the first and somewhat 'permanent' part of the party system as the catch-all, elite-based power-accumulating national party Muslim League that had delivered independence. The second domain of the party system related to the ideologically motivated, agenda carrying, system-reformist and relatively articulate section of the population that provided, organized, planned, and projected the party profile, often accompanied by internal contradictions. They took up populist causes that generated splits between the electoral heavyweights and ideologues. The third part of the Pakistan's party system was residual in nature. Never a contender for power per se, these parties were manipulated into the power game whenever there was a role for them, most often at the behest of the establishment. These parties have been up for bidding as an instrument of negative voting that can cost the leading party a few thousands of winning votes. The establishment kept some of them in reserve for tipping the balance in favour of one or the other candidate and the party.

Electoral politics remains the be-all and end-all of the political class. One can trace the origin of this class to the local government elections in the late nineteenth century. Carefully nurtured as colonial collaborators after 1857, the landed elite was incrementally accommodated in the expanding legislative system, while the district emerged as the state-in-the-field to articulate its interests and facilitate electoral management in its favour. From the beginning, policy evaded the mass mandate. An elaborate exercise in election manipulation became part of the establishment's pursuit of 'positive results'. There is a long history of gross interference of extra-parliamentary forces to shape the election results. The more the ECP tried to reform the machinery for conducting free and fair elections – especially from 2008 onwards largely due to donor funding from the United States Agency for International Development (USAID), the Department for International Development (DFID), and the Institute for Democracy and Electoral Assistance (IDEA) among others – the more ineffectual was its input. I have discussed how the huge distance between design and practice in the electoral arena reflected the gap between the power dynamics shaped by the establishment and the formal agency of elections – the political class.

4

AN ESTABLISHMENTARIAN DEMOCRACY

Introduction

The issue of democracy has been a major source of political conflict in Pakistan. The current system of governance in the country, along with other countries that are usually defined by electoral authoritarianism, has been analysed in terms of a tutelary illiberal hybrid regime.[1] This means that the system is democratic in form but not in substance. I plan to analyse this phenomenon in three ways.

First, I compare India and Pakistan as the two successor states of British India going their separate ways, and I look for reasons behind this divergence. In this context, I shall locate the uneven pattern of constitutional politics that created incessant political crises in Pakistan. I argue that Pakistan is an establishmentarian democracy, which is somewhat different from other South Asian countries even though they shared the British Indian legacy of rule of the state elite. In India, the establishment – by way of the Indian Civil Service (ICS) transformed into the Indian Administrative Service (IAS) – was a continuous and stable institution that was even stronger in power and privilege in some ways than its counterpart in Pakistan. In Sri Lanka, the rise of the army during the war against the Tamils threatened to shift the political initiative away from the political elite, but a generous allocation of resources to men in uniform by way of jobs and businesses contained

217

Bonapartism.[2] The 2020 presidential and parliamentary elections transformed the Rajapakse brothers – as president and prime minister – into a dynasty, and consolidated the politicians' hold on power. In Bangladesh, the two military governments of General Ziaur Rehman and General Irshad carried out a democratic experiment by founding parties and fighting elections, but they could not establish 'indirect' rule of the establishment through electoral democracy. Sheikh Hasina's three successive terms as prime minister (2009–) confirmed the politicians' hold over the state's authority.[3] I first deal with the question of how Pakistan developed a peculiar form of democracy, different from India. Secondly, I shall focus on the militarization of politics that hampered the growth of democracy in absolute terms. This model points to the hold of the 'deep state' over politics and policy. Thirdly, I shall focus on judicialization of politics. I analyse the institutional, constitutional, and populist patterns of behaviour of the judiciary, and attempt to outline its role in putting in place an establishmentarian democracy.

A (mal-)Functioning Democracy

In this section, I want to draw a profile of democracy in Pakistan through a comparison with India. I also attempt a critique of the prevalent orthodoxy of 'hybrid regime' in favour of my argument for an establishmentarian democracy. I shall also discuss the gap between the 'design' and 'practice' of democracy in the country, which has persistently shaped the contours of the political conflict.

Democracy in India and Pakistan: Divergent Paths

Analysis of democracy in Pakistan has typically revolved around the following question for almost two generations: why was India a democracy and Pakistan not so?[4] Most often, the country was described as a military state or an authoritarian state per se.[5] While observations about this dichotomy abound in books and articles in general, some studies have specifically focused on the divergent paths taken by the two countries after partition. Tudor, Jaffrelot, Chadda and others highlighted the role of the Congress in India that upheld a programmatic

218

and social reformist ideology, along with an institutional level that was much higher than in the case of the Muslim League in Pakistan.[6]

Tudor refers to Diamond and Gunther's model of ideal-type parties along a spectrum of elite-based thin organizations at one end and mass-based thick organizations at the other.[7] In her scheme of things, the former is the prototype of a postcolonial state. She finds an additional strength of the Congress in the 'distributive coherence of its core alliance'.[8] As opposed to the Congress high command that represented collective leadership, the Muslim League had only 'the sole spokesperson', who was not privileged to have a team of party stalwarts – the second-rank leadership – that would have served as the principle of continuity after him.[9] 'The primacy of political parties' in India and not in Pakistan made all the difference between the two countries in the context of 'regime stability'.[10]

Tudor's other observations about the lack of democracy are, however, questionable. In her view, the landed aristocracy at the top of the Muslim League was anti-democratic per se because of its need to safeguard its class interests from encroachments by other groups. This is tantamount to not acknowledging the fact that the state in British India, along with its postcolonial version, was a bureaucracy, and the only way the landed and tribal elite could enter this state before and after partition was through elections. Tudor's claim that the Pakistan movement created an alliance between 'a landed aristocracy and a peasant movement'[11] is not supported by evidence. Poor Muslim peasants of East Bengal were mobilized in the name of Islam against the Hindu landed elite. But their absolute majority belonged to the 85 per cent non-enfranchised public and was therefore irrelevant in the final count of votes. Their alliance with the remote landed aristocracy of the UP, and further away with Punjab and Sindh, is inconceivable. No research is available to show that these two classes from distant regions had been put into contact, much less into a contract for an alliance. A similar claim that political power after partition was in the hands of elites from the provinces of Sindh and Punjab and not in the hands of civilian bureaucracy[12] is not sustainable. It was exactly the bureaucratic elite that ruled the country by bypassing parliament for the first decade and even later under General Ayub (1958–69).[13]

One cannot presuppose the existence of a compact entity of British India whose inheritors should therefore have behaved in the same way. The Muslim minority provinces, with their epicentre in the UP, represented the 'centre' of first the Mughal and later the British Indian empires, while Pakistan inherited the 'periphery', which was politically and economically underdeveloped.[14] Direct bureaucratic rule, rather than representative bodies at the district and higher levels as platforms for political participation, was the norm in Punjab as elsewhere in this 'periphery', which occupied a far larger space in relative terms in Pakistan than in India.[15]

Secondly, and most crucially, India after 1947 was ruled by those who represented the 'natural leadership' of the territory of the new state. Pakistan, however, was dominated by migrants from India who had conceived and operationalized the Pakistan project and now ruled the new country. They generally represented the relatively more modern stratum of the society compared to their compatriots in their new 'peripheral' homeland. Many of them had lost their electoral constituency in India. In Pakistan, they soon learnt the message: hold elections and it is your political death. In this situation, power drifted to the higher bureaucracy that was itself dominated by migrants from both Mohajir and Punjabi stock.[16] Some of these bureaucrats later occupied high public office, among them Prime Minister Chaudhary Mohammad Ali, Governor General Ghulam Mohammad and President Iskandar Mirza. Elections in a migrant state were inherently dysfunctional as far as the security of elite positions was concerned. In other words, it was structural discontinuity in Pakistan, as compared to structural continuity in India, that sealed the fate of the democratic agenda in the former's case. Thirdly, Punjab emerged as the power base of the new country with a narrow numerical base of 38 per cent of the population. In Jaffrelot's formulation, it faced the challenge of the 'law of numbers', which favoured the demographic preponderance of East Bengal at 55 per cent.[17]

In this context, one needs to bring in the critical role of the system of separate electorates – not regarding its purported role in Muslim separatism as brought out by historians[18] but as a mode of electoral politics for the Muslim community in British India. One the one hand, the Congress fought elections on general seats and was exposed to constituency politics, the intricate social networking involving caste and class, and a viable framework of electoral campaigns bounded by territory and local identity markers. On the other hand, Muslim candidates campaigned across large areas sometimes spanning several districts, making community-based rather than constituency-based promises, not for 'serving' them but for 'delivering' their wards from the impending disaster of the perceived Hindu Rashtra. The Muslim League was not only shielded from mass politics in an ultimate sense, it was also not exposed to the workings of the state system in an official capacity. For example, the Congress formed governments exclusively in eight provinces after the 1946 elections: therefore, it became fully entrenched in the legal–institutional framework of the state. However, the Muslim League was nowhere exclusively in government. It never ruled Punjab – the future power base of Pakistan – until after partition. KP (then NWFP) was ruled by the Khudai Khidmatgars (KK)–Congress government. In Bengal and Sindh, the ruling dispensations comprised shifting coalitions among the Muslim League, and lesser parties and groups. Additionally, India experienced continuity of political initiative in the hands of the Congress after the 1946 elections in the centre and provinces. The Muslim League high command, however, smashed the ruling coalition in Punjab, led by the Unionists, through street agitation shortly before partition. It dismissed Dr Khan's Congressite government in KP within a week of partition. It installed its henchman, Nazimuddin, in Bengal as chief minister after replacing Suhrawardy. It dismissed Ayub Khuhro's government in Sindh in 1948. The same year, it coerced Khan of Kalat to annex Balochistan with Pakistan. Thus, the story of Pakistan began with a migrant state most typically presiding over the dismissal of 'locally' elected governments in the provinces. One can borrow the title of Rajni Kothari's book, *State against Democracy*[19] – ironically about India, although in a different context altogether – to describe the inauspicious beginning of the state in Pakistan.

New coalitions were cobbled together in various elected assemblies of Punjab, KP, Sindh and East Bengal. New chief ministers were installed who later won the vote of confidence on the floor, and new rules of the game were formed that rendered the power of overseeing the performance of chief ministers into the hands of governors.[20] Yogendra Yadav has talked of Indians having 'creolized' the concept of democracy by lending it a peculiar Indian character.[21] Politics in Pakistan, which drew on the mass mandate as the ultimate source of legitimacy, was also 'creolized' – of course with a different trajectory

– whereby a bifocal authority system prevailed for more than seven decades. The major difference continued to be the principle of civilian supremacy over the armed forces, keenly preserved in India and most typically violated in Pakistan.

Civilian bureaucracy was not a major part of the nationalist movement of the Congress, as opposed to the case with the Pakistan movement.[22] Hamza Alavi highlighted the role of the salariat in the making of Pakistan, even though it was the Muslim League that was formally at the helm of affairs.[23] Ayesha Jalal has criticized Marxists for not being able to solve the puzzle of India and Pakistan going their separate ways of democracy and military rule despite their shared colonial legacy.[24] At least in Alavi's case this criticism does not hold, because his argument focused on the deterministic power of the state apparatus whatever the regime type may be – democracy or otherwise – and he did not exclude India from his argument. In that sense, Jalal's own position about 'structural authoritarianism in India', along with 'formal democracy' as compared to democracy's 'apparent failure' in Pakistan, approximates Alavi's formulation of the postcolonial state.[25] She sees 'India's paradoxical achievement of a democratic authoritarianism' as an expression of failure to square its assertion of monolithic sovereignty with a politics of exclusion.[26]

Jalal criticizes the concept of a dichotomy between democracy and authoritarianism as applied to India and Pakistan. In her view, the two categories are overlapping, and the patterns of dominance and resistance are expressed through the interaction of state structures and political processes.[27] As opposed to this, Tudor, Jaffrelot and Oldenburg among others have expressed reservations about Jalal's model, seeing in it de-acknowledgement of a continuous democratic polity in India as opposed to the military-dominated state in Pakistan. Both Jaffrelot and Oldenburg argue that a strong political society supported by networks of institutions and patterns of leadership contributed to democracy in India, while a weak political society cost Pakistan in this pursuit.[28] Jaffrelot also mentions caste-based civil society as a stabilizing factor for India's political society.[29]

In India's case, controversy revolves essentially around the question of the consolidation of democracy in the face of the relative erosion of institutions and the personalization of politics.[30] Here, the key variable for transition to democracy, as per elite bargain theorists, was the context of the nation-building project whereby the leadership was obliged to expand the scope for consent among the regions and communities constituting society.[31] Meanwhile, Pakistan developed a forum for devising policy and exercising power in the form of a Committee of the Cabinet. It comprised the bureaucratic elite, parallel to the formal, constitutional and parliamentary government that represented a majority on the floor of the parliament. Not surprisingly, the all-powerful Secretary General Choudhary Mohammad Ali acted as a virtual prime minister.[32] Indeed, Imran Ali pointed to the 'entrenchment' of the state bureaucracy during the process of colonization of irrigated lands in Punjab for several decades preceding partition, by way of allocation of land, distribution of water, management of canals and collection of revenue.[33] The landed elite of Pakistan, which thrived on the colonized lands of Punjab, was typically beholden to civil bureaucracy for its privileges from colonial times.[34] District emerged as the foundation of an informal lateral contract between the state-in-the-field and the landed elite as the grand principle of political stability. Over time, the district encapsulated electoral politics whereby the local dynastic families managed to win elections in succession. In other words, the bureaucratic stranglehold shaped politics from top to bottom.[35]

Two additional factors relating to migration undermined democracy. First, migrants amounted to 20 per cent of the population in post-1971 Pakistan, as opposed to migrants in India at 1 per cent, i.e. twenty times more than in the latter's case. For refugees, the foremost issue related to their rehabilitation, whereby the agenda of democracy was pushed into a secondary position. Second, the parts of the two partitioned provinces of Bengal and Punjab that fell to Pakistan – with all the associated misery, violence, hatred, communal riots, arson and rape – accounted for 82 per cent of the country's population in 1951.[36] The Indian parts of the two partitioned provinces constituted a mere fraction of India's population, with a far less negative impact on the vast regions of north, west and south India. In this way, discontinuity in the life-pattern and administrative machinery took Pakistan away from the model of parliamentary democracy that was shaping up in late colonialism.

Towards a Model of Establishmentarian Democracy

My argument is that the conventional wisdom about tutelary illiberal hybrid regimes such as Pakistan needs some refurbishment and conceptual stretching.[37] The purpose is to bring out the hidden and not-so-hidden role of the state elite in shaping the contours of the electoral contest that put the political elite in office. As opposed to the general perception about the adoption of 'illiberal' ways and means by incumbent governments for the purpose of self-perpetuation, I argue that it is the permanent repository of the state authority – the establishment – that seeks to put governments in and out of office through elections, often successfully. There is an increasing perception among state managers that 'democracy' is the only game in the town. Therefore, the establishment is obliged to follow what it thinks are the new global rules of game, which are becoming less tolerant of military rule.

While incumbent civilian governments traditionally indulged in election rigging, the establishment's manipulation of elections has become the dominant pattern in this regard. Of course, there are examples when it has failed to achieve its goals. This happened in the 1970 elections under General Yahya, in the 1988 elections after General Zia's death in an air crash, and in the 2008 elections when the sympathy vote for Benazir Bhutto after her assassination on 27 December 2007 overtook the establishment's elaborate plans to rig elections in favour of General Musharraf's King's party PML-Q. For the clue to electoral dynamics we need to look beyond the input of the formal 'agency', i.e. political parties that compete amongst themselves as contenders for power. My argument is that it is in the extra-systemic input that one should look for the hybrid character of the regime that seeks to mimic democracy.

For nearly two decades, scholars have found the concept of hybridity useful to explain the lack of substance in the democratic claims of regimes collectively put under the umbrella of the 'third wave of democracy'.[38] They studied countries that experienced transition to democracy from communism (Russia), dynastic rule (Nepal) and military rule (Argentina, Brazil).[39] By all accounts, hybridity has a lumpy effect in terms of its application to different regimes belonging to different countries from different continents. The idea that hybrid regimes were different from bona fide democratic regimes is a great leap forward in the direction of conceptualizing the other, less democratic political systems. But hybridity is obviously found in the generally and typically missing part, i.e. in the half of the glass that is empty and not in the half of the glass that is full. One needs to analyse the players around the chessboard of politics for an understanding of the 'pragmatic rules' that go beyond the institutional design. For example, courts operate in support of moves from outside the electoral contest among political parties.

Hybridity's explanatory value is grossly compounded by its evaluation of different countries that do not qualify as democratic or 'free' countries according to the Freedom House index.[40] This index categorizes, rather than analyses, hybrid regimes, far from locating the sources of their hybridity, as well as the prospects, direction and potential of change in the nature and quantum of hybridity. Obviously, the term hybrid does not delineate the distinct nature and character of political systems lumped together in this group. Most of these countries are postcolonial societies, ranging from the Philippines, Malaysia, Sri Lanka, Algeria, Nigeria and Kenya to Brazil and Argentina. But this group also includes Turkey and Russia – legatees of the Ottoman and Russian Empires respectively – and Nepal, Thailand and Afghanistan, as buffer states from the colonial era. Furthermore, the colonial model itself was divided between the areas under direct and indirect rule, most of British India belonging to the first category and most of the African colonies belonging to the second. This fact was responsible for creating the issue of integrating modern and traditional ruling set-ups within postcolonial states such as India and Pakistan, leading to enhanced nationalist fervour in pursuit of unity and thus to a tightening of the noose around groups and communities supporting sub-national identities.

The colonial state was a bureaucracy par excellence cushioned by the military as the security apparatus. In British India, as with Pakistan's colonial legacy, the modern state controlled and regulated the rule of law.[41] Transition from colonial to postcolonial state changed the relationship between the state apparatus and the emergent political class that wanted to control it. The clue to the precise nature of this relationship, given the level and scope of the institutional imbalance between the two sides, adversely affected the constitutional framework, the party system, and electoral politics.

The present study argues that elections have been influenced by the state elite – the establishment – far more in Pakistan than has been the case with its South Asian neighbours, India, Sri Lanka and Bangladesh, which otherwise shared the same colonial experience. Pakistan is closest to India in sharing not only the institutional/constitutional conundrum ruling the country but also a voting behaviour drawing on caste/*biradari* association, tribal affinity, ethnic bondage, patron–client relations and ties with the village community. Indeed, the Pakistani voter is far closer to the Indian voter than to the voter in any other 'Muslim' country in terms of primordial commitments, role of party factions and dynastic leadership. The same applies to the populism of the left and right, represented respectively by Indira Gandhi and Z. A. Bhutto in the 1970s and Modi (2014, 2019) and Imran Khan (2018–). Still, India and Pakistan produced two separate patterns of electoral behaviour, even as they shared the phenomena of multiple political parties leading to multiple contests in electoral constituencies and a general acceptance of mass mandate as the constitutional source of legitimacy. In both countries, religion has played an increasingly significant role in politics, although in different ways and leading to entirely different outcomes. This needs an explanation in terms of the game-changing role of the input from players other than the formal election entities.

I argue that the establishment was able to shape 'democracy' in Pakistan for a variety of reasons. For example, people do not vote for Islamic parties in Pakistan in significant numbers. Their average vote is around 5 per cent, which rose to 11 per cent in 2002, an exception as a spillover effect of the US bombing in Afghanistan after 9/11 and General Musharraf's skilful manipulation of the religious vote for the purpose of keeping himself in power. A relatively high number of the Islamic votes – around 10 per cent in the 2018 elections – was again due to the establishment's patronage of Islamic parties and alliances such as TLP and MMA. In India, the religious vote increased substantially during the quarter of a century after the destruction of Babri Mosque in 1992. The question arises as to why religion made inroads into mainstream politics in India, which had a secular constitution, while there was only a meagre chance of a government of Islamic parties being voted into office in Pakistan, where Islam was the official religion. Given a generally similar level of religiosity among Hindus, Muslims,

Sikhs, Christians, Buddhists, and other denominational communities in South Asian countries, one needs to explore the different role of religion in the politics of India and Pakistan.

The civilizational and territorial dimensions of Hindutva have been frequently highlighted in a social and cultural milieu that was deeply influenced by a secular ideology, a liberal Westernized elite and the pluralist fabric of society.[42] A significant part of it related to Hindu political ascendency on the ashes of a perceived 'wounded civilization'.[43] Pakistan, on the other hand, as an elite project par excellence had its source of inspiration in the legacy of Muslim India along with its imperial history. Here, religion drew the outermost boundary of the envisioned state of Pakistan, essentially to distinguish it from the anthropomorphic understanding of its 'Hindu counterpart'.[44]

The ascendancy of Hindu nationalism in India over the half century after partition through electoral democracy converted the latent religiosity of the masses into votes at the hands of the upper castes. This can be contrasted with the state-forming role of religion in Pakistan, where the elite was firmly ensconced in positions of strength from outside the electoral framework of politics. Religion's bottom-up movement in India and its top-down movement in Pakistan represent two models of populist religion and manipulative religion, respectively. Political conflict in Pakistan was rooted in competition between the two power centres expressed through the state elite and the political elite. The former resorted to the creation of a divine source of legitimacy, most prominently by Zia's military government, to counter the constitutional source of legitimacy. Religion in Pakistan served the interest of the state elite, while religion in India served the interest of the political elite.

'Establishment' has become a household word in Pakistan. Politicians talk daily on the TV screen about the establishment as the 'third force', i.e. after counting the government and opposition as the two visible political forces operating within the parliamentary set-up. During the 2018 elections, Nawaz Sharif declared that he was actually fighting 'aliens', by which he meant the (military) establishment that was believed to be supporting an array of political parties ranging from Imran Khan's PTI to the Islamic extremist party TLP. Prime Minister Shahid Khaqan Abbasi (2017–18) also referred to 'people from space' who were streamlining the elections.[45]

The army as 'establishment' carried the meaning of a force that was way beyond the democratic calculus of a majority-based, power-wielding civilian authority supposed to be accountable to public representatives. In this sense, the establishment is more than a mere 'agency', i.e. more than a security apparatus along with its institutional ethos. In reality, this points to an army-led structure of power and policy that incorporated a relatively invisible bureaucracy as a co-ordinate body and an intellectual group that conjured up an ideological defence of the establishment's manoeuvres with reference to the perceived Indian or American conspiracies. This showed fierce determination to root out all challenges to the master narrative, represented by the lesser discourses emanating from 'liberal' or ethnic activists.

We need to explore what is the establishment, what is its agenda, why it would allow 'democracy' to remain in place, and what is its final product as the ruling mechanism in Pakistan. It has been argued that the 'establishment' is a small segment of the population that holds the key to the system. It operates behind the scenes. It redirects the anger of the people towards carefully selected scapegoats, both internal and external, to deflect attention from gross income inequalities.[46] It consciously shapes the national debate around certain issues that would otherwise be simply ignored, and thus deflects public attention from the core issues at any given time.[47] It is bound together by unaccountable powers, often by bending the law. It is an organic, dynamic system based on shared economic interests and mentalities. It is a pejorative term that provokes negative feelings in the public and thus leads to conspiracy theories.[48] It seeks to 'manage' democracy by operating as a firewall that would keep it safe from unbridled mass mobilization in the name of democracy. It is a 'shape-shifter' whereby it has the ability to adopt both policy and profile according to the pressures from below and across the political system.[49] It is a plutocracy that finds its nemesis in democracy, i.e. when the latter is not 'managed' well and becomes a threat to real stakeholders. The establishment relies on the media to give vent to people's anger in the direction of certain issues and personalities. In today's age of electronic media, the impact of this direct and forceful way of communication cannot be overstated. In the end, the establishment is the guarantor of the status quo.[50] It has a profile of triumphalism.[51] It has its 'outriders' all around:[52]

228

spin-doctors, think tanks, centres of higher education, popular press, and others.[53]

The establishment, as a representative of the middle class, is the leading power centre in Pakistan. The second power centre, which operates generally on parallel but often conflictual lines, draws heavily on constitutional sources of legitimacy, especially the mass mandate. This shows that the 'establishment' does not have all its eggs in one basket. If the army had the political initiative totally in its hands, then military presidents Ayub, Zia and Musharraf would not have faced nationwide agitation in 1968–9, 1983 and 2007–8 respectively, whereby two of them had to quit and the third barely survived in office through the brutal use of force against the 1983 MRD movement.

While the constitutional tradition has been too weak to stop military takeovers, it has been too strong to allow generals to rule in their own name for a long stretch of time. Military rulers have declared straight after taking over that the country would be ruled according to the constitution, which had been abrogated or suspended a few hours earlier. While parliament and political parties were rendered defunct, most of the constitutional provisions remained intact and lent meaning to the operational dynamics of the state institutions, ranging from civil bureaucracy, higher judiciary and district courts to training academies and financial bureaus. The Bonapartist generals formally and symbolically sought legitimacy through black letter law.

It is interesting to see one-dimensional views about individual generals' personalities at the cost of an institutional analysis. For example, in British diplomat Sir Cyril Pickard's view, Yahya believed that the *khaki*'s 'job was to hold the ring, and to let people decide their future… thus willingly handing over power to the representatives of the people'.[54] This is horrendously misleading because Yahya had lost the game after the 1970 elections and would have spared the nation a bloody civil war if he had 'willingly' handed over power to public representatives.

By 2021, the army had been directly in control for seventeen out of the seventy-four years of post-independence Pakistan. It typically felt obliged to put together a façade of constitutional government through elections. When the army was not ruling directly, the civilian dispensation tended to carve out a space for itself in the system, sometimes beyond the tolerance level of the establishment, which dissolved assemblies and dismissed governments. From 2002 onwards, Pakistan has been administered under civilian set-ups, first under Musharraf as military president and later under President Zardari, Prime Minister Nawaz Sharif and Prime Minister Imran Khan. Zardari (2008–13) was able to fight for his survival under extreme pressure from the army, which reached a crescendo during the Memogate scandal in 2011. Table 4.1 shows this recurring pattern of establishmentarian democracy through various phases of Pakistan's history.

Table 4.1 Establishmentarian democracy in Pakistan, 1947–2021

Direct military rule	17 years	1958–62 Ayub; 1969–71 Yahya; 1977–85 Zia; 1999–2002 Musharraf
Civilian supremacy	6 years	1971–7 Z. A. Bhutto
Establishmentarian democracy	*51 years*	
Elected governments in a bureaucratic polity	11 years	1947–58; from Liaqat Ali Khan to Feroz Khan Noon
Elected governments under military presidents: 'King's party' model	16 years	1962–9 Ayub; 1985–8 Zia; 2002–8 Musharraf
Elected governments under civilian presidents: 'Rule of troika' model	11 years	1988–90 Benazir Bhutto; 1990–3 Nawaz Sharif; 1993–6 Benazir Bhutto; (caretaker government 1996–7); 1997–9 Nawaz Sharif
Elected governments constantly facing military contention	10 years	2008–13 Zardari/Gilani–Pervez Ashraf; 2013–18 Nawaz Sharif–Shahid Khaqan Abbasi
Elected government on the same page with military	3 years	2018– Imran Khan

The establishment brought about a generational transition of political leadership three times after military takeovers by Ayub, Yahya and Zia. Presidents Zia, Ishaq and Leghari dissolved the National Assembly and thus dismissed the 'recalcitrant' elected governments four times under Article 58(2)(b), in 1988, 1990, 1993, and 1996. The Supreme Court disqualified two prime ministers:

Yusuf Raza Gilani (2012) and Nawaz Sharif (2017). Musharraf arbitrarily changed the rules of the game for election candidates, for example, by excluding non-graduates and including diploma-holders from madrassahs who were anointed as graduates (2002). The media let the word go round about the establishment's favourite horses, so that voters should know who was going to be the winner. Military rulers arranged for the sharing of power with the King's party under a system of diarchy.[55] The principle of 'His Majesty's Loyal Opposition' reigned supreme. The leader of the opposition in the National Assembly under Ayub Khan was his own brother, Sardar Bahadur Khan (1962–4). Musharraf appointed a person of his own choosing – JUI-F chief, Maulana Fazlur Rehman – as leader of the opposition (2004–7) without the support of a majority of the opposition. Indeed, the JUI-F and the King's party PML-Q were coalition partners in Balochistan. The Musharraf government encouraged its ally MQM to carry out a violent demonstration of mass power in Karachi against the visit of suspended chief justice, Iftikhar Choudhary, on 12 May 2007 to address the bar association and attend the Sindh High Court anniversary salvation. The military president's personal vendetta against the Chief Justice was played out on the streets of the metropolis, taking fifty-seven lives and injuring more than a hundred people. In 2014, the establishment allegedly facilitated Imran Khan's sit-in against the Nawaz Sharif government. In 2017, the Faizabad sit-in against Prime Minister Shahid Khaqan Abbasi's government led by a cleric, Maulana Khadim Rizvi, came to an end through an agreement signed by a major-general.[56]

Moving Away from Institutional Design

Can the successive constitutional breakdowns, electoral malprac-tices, diarchal pattern of rule under civilian and military dispensa-tions, and the final authority lying outside the elected representatives, allow Pakistan to be considered a serious candidate for democracy? Two other countries that may be said to have a similar claim are Turkey and Malaysia. Turkey seems to have moved to 'democracy' in a substantive way, even as the coup attempt against Tyap Erdogan on 15 July 2016 shook the country out of its complacency. While Erdogan survived and regained control of state authority, his power has yet to be institutionalized in terms of civilian supremacy over the armed forces, both in theory and practice. His intolerance towards the political opposition and the media pointed to a constant move to outgrow the framework of democratic politics beyond the mere fact of electoral victory. By contrast, Malaysia has never had a military coup. However, its colonial heritage of indirect rule, like elsewhere, meant the underdevelopment of modern statehood in terms of fundamental rights of citizens, freedom of expression and effective institutional safeguards against oppression. Table 4.2 shows where we can place Pakistan along the spectrum of democracy.

In 1981, General Tajammul Hussain attempted to bring about a 'genuine' Islamic revolution as opposed to what he and his colleagues imagined as the fake Islamization of Zia.[57] Only two years previously, Islamists had tried unsuccessfully to bring about a similar Islamic revolution in Saudi Arabia by capturing the holiest shrine of Muslims in Makkah. In 1995, more than fifty senior and middle-ranking army officers led by 'shadow warrior' General Zaheerul Islam Abbasi tried to replace the ruling dispensation under Benazir Bhutto by the rule of Sharia under Operation Khilafa.[58] They were charged under the Pakistan Army Act Section 55, 59 with Section 121-A and Section 31-D of the Pakistan Penal Code, respectively. In the following paragraphs, we deal with the military question by tracing the way in which the political system was steered away from the original 'design' of democracy.

Militarization of Politics

The general understanding in Pakistan is that there is an 'Army Party' on one side and, on the other side, the 'people', who are represented by all other parties.[59] Establishmentarian democracy operated essentially in an arena carved out of two contradictory factors. First, the institutional design of the state drew on the constitutional source of legitimacy based on mass mandate as a legacy of British India. Second, the existential problem of the security of the new state in the context of perceived Indian bellicosity, tended to overrule constitutionalism, the rule of public representatives, and human rights. On the one hand, the 'design' of democracy was inextricably linked to the constitutional state. This remained a fundamental part of the army's institutional calculations that drew its own legitimacy from the constitution. On the other hand, the army at the heart of the security

AN ESTABLISHMENTARIAN DEMOCRACY

Table 4.2 Democracy in Pakistan: Grey Area between Design and Practice

Prime minister Liaqat Ali	• Virtual prime minister Choudhary Mohammad Ali (Secretary General of Pakistan) 1947-51
Federalism at stake	• Dismissal of provincial governments (9 times in the 11 years 1947-58); 1973 and 1988 (Balochistan); 1992 (Sindh); • 'Constitutional terrorism'
Gaps in the state's authority	• Failed coup attempts: 1951 (Rawalpindi Conspiracy Case), 1974 (Air Force officers); 1981 (Gen. Tajammul Hussain); 1995 (Gen. Zaheerul Islam) • Military operations: Balochistan 1948, 1958, 1963, 1973-77, 2006…; East Pakistan 1971; Sindh 1983, 1992-94/5; Swat, FATA, South Waziristan 2009, North Waziristan 2014
The elected accountable to the non-elected (governors, military governments, courts)	• Governors reporting on elected governments in the provinces from the first decade onwards • 'First accountability, then elections': Zia's prognosis for successive postponement of elections from 1977 to1985 • Guilty verdict of Benazir's corruption trial 1996-97 (a week before elections), pushing her voters away from the polls • Guilty verdict of Nawaz Sharif corruption trial 2017 (20 days before elections) with a negative impact on his voters
A non-sovereign parliament	• Low on law making • Low on accountability of the executive to parliament (no-show ministers Nawaz Sharif, Imran Khan) • Parliament renamed and dwarfed as Majlis Shura (Advisory Council) via the 1985 8th Amendment • President's power to dissolve the National Assembly: Article 58 (2) (b) in the 8th and 17th Amendments • Rule by presidential ordinances
Decline of the constitutional state	• Members of parliament: gross decline of exposure to and training in the constitutional law • Constitutional breakdowns: 1958, 1969, 1977, 1999, 2007
Divine source of legitimacy	• From constitution to religion as the ideational sanction of the state from the 1980s onwards
De-ideo-lo-gization of vote politics	• Decline of socialism after the 1970s; religion not a typical vote catching device despite Zia's efforts • Status quo orientation under Zardari-Nawaz Sharif-Imran Khan

apparatus operated according to what C. Wright Mills called 'military metaphysics', which pointed to 'a military definition of reality'.[60] That made all the difference. The political leadership, the 'progressive' intelligentsia and ethnic elites from provinces other than Punjab – the core area of army recruitment – did not share the intense level of belligerency towards India for most of the post-independence period.[61] Securitization of the national vision became the hotly pursued agenda of the army both inside and outside the framework of direct military rule.

Not surprisingly, civil–military conflict has been the master conflict in Pakistan, along with its attendant problems for democracy, which was relegated to a secondary position. The argument relied on the commonsense view that you first needed to secure the state and only then plan whatever kind of political system you wish to have. In this way, the doctrine of state necessity became the handmaiden of the judiciary in justifying a military takeover. In the wider context, the army cultivated a spirit of deification of the state in the public at large in its pursuit of the 'national project' through a cult of unity.

'Military Metaphysics'

While talking of post-war America, C. Wright Mills wrote:

> No area of decision has been more influenced by the warlords and by their military metaphysics than that of foreign policy.... Once war was considered the business of soldiers, [and] international relations the concern of diplomats. But now that war has become seemingly total and seemingly permanent, the free sport of kings has become the forced and internecine business of people, and diplomatic codes of honor between nations have collapsed. Peace is no longer serious; only war is serious. Every man and every nation is either friend or foe, and the idea of enmity becomes mechanical, massive, and without genuine passion. When virtually all negotiation aimed at peaceful agreement is likely to be seen as 'appeasement,' if not treason, the active role of the diplomat becomes meaningless; for diplomacy becomes merely a prelude to war or an interlude between wars, and in such a context the diplomat is replaced by the warlord.[62]

AN ESTABLISHMENTARIAN DEMOCRACY

The words of C. Wright Mills serve to highlight some fundamental characteristics of the way the army has handled various issues relating to the functioning of democracy in Pakistan. The army is not a Leviathan in the Hobbesian sense, carrying ultimate and unaccountable authority, nor a hegemon in the domestic context nor indeed a mere security apparatus. However, it is well known that the army in Pakistan has taken over the function of shaping and conducting foreign policy. It has made war into a seemingly permanent national pursuit that has morphed into a philosophy of the state. It has made war a business of people through national mobilization and incessant glorification of martyrdom. It has attached a value to war, which is superior to peace. The activities of forums such as the Pakistan–India Peoples' Forum for Peace and Democracy (PIPFPD), the South Asian Free Media Association (SAFMA) and the Pakistan Peace Coalition were bound to raise the eyebrows of the establishment. Any initiatives for peace such as Aman ki Asha (Hope for Peace) taken by the two media houses, the Jang Group (*The News*) from Pakistan and *The Times of India* from across the border, were rendered suspect. Similarly negotiations for peace with India are considered akin to appeasement, sell-off, even treason such as in the case of an informal meeting between Modi and Nawaz Sharif in 2015 in Lahore. Military metaphysics is rooted in the post-recruitment socialization of men in uniform. The civil–military conflict mutated into other conflicts relating to an enhanced consciousness about allocation of financial resources, technological advancement for the purposes of warfare, control over media and manipulation of education. There was a controversy about the 18th Amendment as a federalist arrangement for sharing power between the centre and the provinces. This conflict led to the quest for a supra-constitutional source of legitimacy in religion under various military governments. 'Military metaphysics' sought to displace the prevalent cultural, political, and intellectual narratives of various sections of society on the way to providing its own version of the national imaginary.

Table 4.3 'Military Metaphysics' in Pakistan

High institutional level	• Hierarchy; discipline; accountability; integrity; merit-based recruitment and promotion
Self-image based on high moral ground	• Military officers' autobiographical writings: claiming truth, objectivity, dispassionate account of persons and events
Characteristics of the political class	• Corruption, nepotism, parochialism, favouritism, opportunism, sectarianism, inefficiency • No commitment to national interest; inability to see the Indian chicanery
Construction of Hindu demon	• Hindus responsible for Partition out of ambition to suppress Muslims and rule over India • Hindus responsible for break-up of Pakistan in 1971 through their intellectual domination over East Pakistan
Who failed whom?	• Liberals and secularists failed the nation after Partition by neglecting Islam • Political leadership failed the military leadership in 1971 • The high command of army failed young officers in 1971
Cult of soldier	• 'Execute your order'; 'do your duty'; junior not subordinate; vocation not career; pride in genealogy ('fourth generation of military service')
Cult of martyrdom	• 'Dying to serve': the sacrifice syndrome
Cult of war	• Islam vs the West • Unstable region: India (Kashmir dispute); Iran (post-revolutionary Shia state); Afghanistan (Russian, American, Indian influence)
Cult of unity	• For One-Unit (1955-1970), putting an end to federalism in (W) Pakistan • Against the 2010 18th Amendment (rendered akin to Mujibur Rehman's Six Points)
Guardians of ideological frontiers	• Indo-Pakistan conflict: a mini-clash of civilizations • The world-of-Islam perspective • Army-nation-Islam symbiosis

As Table 4.3 shows, the grand feature of the army's institutional life is the *esprit de corps*. The transition from the middle and lower-middle class to a lofty pyramid of power is essentially transformative in nature since it gives young officers a sense of purpose, faith in the national destiny, the high moral ground and a collective identity that transcends hierarchy. The officer cadre experienced social and cultural aloofness from society at large by way of living in cantonments, socializing within the community, and defining themselves in terms of the 'other' – the civilians. Here, the civilians were often symbolized by the political class, which was considered corrupt and selfish and given over to caste, tribal and ethnic interests and identities at the cost of the national interest. What the army has found thoroughly devious about politicians has been their lack of understanding about the 'true' nature of India, the devil next door. In the army's view, Hindus showed hostility, lack of generosity, a sense of revenge for centuries of Muslim rule over India and no accommodation for the Muslim demands that finally led to partition. The post-1971 military mind believed that it was Hindu influence in the universities and intellectual circles of East Pakistan that inspired Bengali nationalism.[63] It held the political leadership more than the military command structure responsible for the defeat.[64]

Military metaphysics has persistently and incrementally cultivated various cults. The cult of soldier carried a commitment to do or die in the line of duty, often supported by a family legacy of serving the army for generations.[65] The cult of martyrdom beset the private pain of the family in the collective pride of the army and the nation.[66] The cult of war has been rooted in the accumulated anger over a sense of estrangement from neighbours such as India, Iran and Afghanistan and the West in general. The cult of unity sought to override national diversity in terms of ethnicity, language, culture and custom by opposing the federalist arrangement for the division of powers.[67] All this produced a mission-mantled army that felt obliged to guide the nation to its destiny.

A recurrent theme in the military officers' discourse related to the absolute necessity to help Kashmiris in moral and material terms.[68] General Sher Ali would have liked to prevent Bengalis' racial identity from challenging Pakistani national identity before it became too late by 1971. He chided the 'poor' Bengali voters, who should have been more careful in selecting their leaders, and bemoaned the fact that the army was humiliated, which robbed it of its supreme role 'above politics'.[69] In General Hakim Arshad's view, the people did not adhere to Islamic values and thus national unity was 'foredoomed'.[70] It was regretted that belief in Pakistan being the 'finest expression of nationhood' was broken throughout the period of crisis.[71] After a decade of the Bhuttoist legacy that dominated politics in Pakistan, General Arif was confident that communism and atheism were not suitable for a religion-loving people.[72] Siddiq Salik stressed the need for building the partition sentiment into a military force.[73] Jinnah's aide-de-camp, Ata Rabbani, blamed the Congress for 'the bigotry, rigidity and cupidity' that made Pakistan possible in the first place.[74] He reiterated the accusation that the British had discriminated against the Muslim middle class and pushed it to poverty.[75] As a reflection of the sentimental images in the collective memory of the new nation, he envisioned Jinnah on horseback in an imaginary fourth battle of Panipat after the three preceding battles.[76]

In General Musharraf's view, elected individuals were vulnerable to corruption per se, which could lead to a military takeover.[77] He also used the idiom of politicians dragging army chiefs into politics.[78] This was repeated by the Chief of Army Staff, General Bajwa, reacting to Nawaz Sharif's diatribe against him through the social media in October 2020 during the PDM's public meetings. Similarly, monopoly over truth remained a source of pride for military officers.[79] There is a clear 'project-mindedness' that steers the strategy and action of military officers, which in turn leads to analysis of right or wrong policies underscored by the need for quick results.[80] Hatred for India and the Congressite leadership constantly underlined the military discourse. Most intriguingly, General Wajahat Hussain believed that Gandhi's non-violence provoked violence and cost a million lives in the greatest bloodbath in history.[81] There is an occasional reference to public resentment against the army after defeat in East Pakistan and the way it was controlled.[82] Also, there was a feeling that Yahya and his 'courtiers' exploited the people in the name of ideology.[83]

In fact, it has been argued that there is 'a separate military public' with its own network of defence clubs, schools, social activities and symbols.[84] Military officers' autobiographies testify to their views about the self and the world. As discussed by Uebersax with reference to Bourdieu's cultural reproduction framework, autobiographies represent the discourse of social agents who act 'disinterested' and seek to accumulate symbolic capital for themselves.[85] In Christine Fair's view, military is an 'epistemic community' in the context of producing a discourse of its own.[86] There is a tendency to use the term 'class' for the military officer's cadre. However, as Aqil Shah argued, institutions have, unlike the classes or class factions that these drew on, their own agendas and interests, in pursuit of which they often employ non-coercive methods.[87] In Maria Rashid's formulation, the military in Pakistan uses affect as a technology of rule by employing empathy to regulate and channel the pain of military deaths into pride in the nation.[88] Her study of the annual martyrs' day on 30 April from 2010 onwards focuses on the state's management of grief in the perspective of what Katharine Verdey considers the 'strong affective dimension of dead-body politics'.[89] This annual event focuses on the theme of the symbiosis between the military and the nation woven into the tragedy that is martyrdom over and above ordinary grief.[90] The use of religious idiom for matters of life and death, such as military action in the line of fire, has always been a significant part of military socialization.[91]

There is an interesting study of the autobiographies of military officers which amply brings out the military metaphysics in Pakistan.[92] General Chishti criticized that truth is often the casualty in scholarship, which he sought to correct.[93] Admiral Sirohey's autobiography upholds the same cause of telling the 'truth', giving an 'objective' account of the facts.[94] He lambasts politicians for corruption, nepotism and sectarian hatred. General Sher Ali was another supporter of the cause of truth, as was General Shahid Hamid, a promoter of a 'dispassionate and objective account of men and matters'.[95] General Fazl Muqeem believed that the Muslim soldier was too simple and trusting and did not believe that Hindus would refuse to share power with Muslims. General Shahid Hamid also held Hindus responsible for partition because of their arrogance.[96] In his view, after 1857 Hindus got support from the British even as they maligned them.[97] In General Akber Khan's view, Kashmir was lost because of the military high command and the government, which first supported the tribal raiders and then got cold feet. General Sher Ali highlighted religious identity over and above 'older racial identities'.[98] General Musa went further and considered the creation of Pakistan itself a 'divine act'.[99]

However, a minority among generals, such as General Gul Hasan, believed that Jinnah favoured a secular state. In his view, Pakistan was destroyed by politicians – 'inveterate, opportunists and chronic freebooters'.[100] Conversely, General Tajammul Hussain Malik sees the project of the Islamic state as being highjacked by what he called the British generation of military officers: 'Anyone who talked about religion was considered to be a backward type and sometimes even ridiculed in public.'[101] In General Wajahat Hussain's view, the military's entry into politics led to 'sycophancy, unlimited power, authoritarianism and the acquisition of perks and privileges'.[102]

For the generation that fought the 1971 war, 'the best relief was provided by religion'.[103] Defeat in the 1971 war was put squarely on the shoulders of Hindus and intellectuals in Bengal – both overlapping categories. Admiral Sirohey bemoaned that a lack of religiosity led to defeat in 1971 because '99 percent of the Pakistani population was unaware of the teachings of the Quran'.[104] One military officer who later led a failed coup attempt against Zia, held the senior military generals responsible for the defeat. He claimed that they 'did not like the smell of gun powder' and wanted to continue with their 'dinner and drinking parties'.[105] The man who surrendered in 1971, General Niazi, upheld the conspiracy theory and blamed the high command, which 'wanted me to be defeated in the first encounter with the Indian army'.[106] He claimed that 'like Nero they played while Dhaka burned'.[107] Another soldier's narrative sees Indian conspiracy behind it all through indoctrination. An officer of the air force considers that the nation's defence plan 'played on sand model'.[108] Interestingly, he repeatedly blames the 'Punjabi cabal' for the 1971 tragedy. Self-description as a soldier is usually the result of post-recruitment training – more so if one belongs to a military family – with a commitment to do one's duty.[109] Soldiership is simply about obeying the order, considering military service a vocation not a career, and being junior but not subordinate.

In Pakistan, control over the nuclear command and control system, and the policy framework covering conflicts across the border with Afghanistan and India, remained the military's 'reserved domains' for decades during the second phase of democratization symbolized by Benazir Bhutto's assumption of office in 1988.[110] The curriculum of the Pakistan Military Academy (PMA), the Staff College at Quetta, and the National Defence University (NDU) in Islamabad provides a lens through which an officer develops views on domestic and foreign politics.[111] In Aqil Shah's view, the officer corps of the Pakistan army is trained at NDU through a 'dominant organisational narrative' that highlights the institution's key role as defender of internal and external security.[112] It has been argued that a typical Third World country undergoes tremendous institutional pressures in the process of state-making at home. Combined with the fact that it does not control the international environment in which it operates, it finally creates an acute security predicament.[113] This situation can lead to even further securitization of the national vision if global powers subordinate the regional security dynamics to their own strategic framework, such as through proxy wars or troop deployment in the region.[114].

The military's 'reserved domains' remained operative under civilian set-ups and sometimes even expanded, such as under Imran Khan (2018–). It has been suggested that Pakistan carried forward the 'gun and hat' mode of government after the colonial period.[115] The decade of the 1970s led to a surge in securitization of the national vision after the debacle of Dhaka in 1971, the Indian nuclear test explosion in 1974, the Iranian revolution in 1978 that sparked off the Shia–Sunni conflict in Pakistan, and the 1979 Soviet incursion into Afghanistan.

Retired military men have been active by other means. More than 60 per cent of corps commanders worked for the government after retirement. Being highly professional in some respects, they could be very unprofessional in other contexts. In Pakistan's situation of 'military ruling without governing', Staniland et al. focus on the careers of individual officers: 50 per cent from Punjab, 21 per cent from KP, 3 per cent each from Sindh and Azad Kashmir and 2 per cent from Balochistan.[116] Apart from plum jobs as ambassadors or as general managers of what Ayesha Siddiqa calls 'Military Inc.', retired generals occupy positions ranging from defence secretary to heads of NGOs, schools and private security companies.[117]

The Pakistan army has had two incarnations. One was committed to the preservation of its profile as the most honest, non-controversial and paternalistic institution as well as the most elevated and reified expression of the national interest and identity. The idea was that its majestic seclusion from public life was a source of strength that made it a sublime icon of national pride over and above the partisan attitudes of people. It was argued that, in the words of Roedad Khan, any direct 'contact with army would disillusion the people and destroy the charisma, a resource that had to be cherished and conserved for it was invaluable in time of crisis'.[118] This would guarantee 'the perpetuation and safeguarding of the power of the army'.[119] Ayub and Yahya amply belonged to this school of thought.[120]

The army's second incarnation can be defined as a strident march into the political, religious, ideological, and socio-cultural domains of public life. Zia was the epitome of this mode of action and thought. After him, there was no going back to the idyllic world of sublime disengagement from the mundane life of politics. The new pattern of civil–military relations was based on mutual distrust and suspicion, especially during the rule of troika (1988–99). Chief of the Army Staff General Jehangir Karamat delivered a controversial speech in the Naval College Lahore in 1998 where he criticized the ruling dispensation of Nawaz Sharif for bad governance and proposed the setting up of the National Security Council (NSC) to oversee the governance. Nawaz Sharif had all along suspected that General Karamat had a role in the former's showdown with Chief Justice Sajjad Ali Shah and President Leghari in December 1997. General Karamat's act of submitting his resignation to his 'civilian' superior after the speech upbraided the higher echelons of army, who ridiculed him for being gutless. They vowed to take over whenever next a civilian government would try to sack a chief of the army staff. This is exactly what happened on 12 October 1999 when Nawaz Sharif sacked General Musharraf. Within hours, his own government was toppled. At other times, the army considered it wise to step back whenever the cost was high. When the coalition government of the PPP and PML-N made their move to impeach President Musharraf in 2008, the army leadership was averse to the idea of its former chief being impeached by the 'civilians'. It prevented a precedent being set and staved off the crisis through Musharraf's resignation.[121] After a bit of aquaplaning, the person at the wheel, COAS General Kiyani, managed to drive back to the middle of the road.

A Tug of War between the Two Power Centres

Cohen argues that Pakistan could have been a lot stronger had it not been 'hijacked' by its quest to develop a strong conventional and military capability 'in the service of balancing out a more powerful and seemingly implacable India'.[122] According to him, just like the military, there were radicals who found fertile ground in the rampant social discontent to develop a 'lust of power' like the Bolsheviks.[123] Cohen claims that 'the army's way has been Pakistan's way'.[124] He sees the post-Zia rule as characterized by 'irregular or covert warfare'.[125]

Generals in Pakistan who swear by the constitution face the issue of legitimacy after a coup. That prevents military regimes from holding power too long in the context of the non-availability of alternatives.[126] Since the state in Pakistan has a presumably high potential for defining and sanctioning the exercise of legal authority, it is the 'constitutional' approach of the Pakistan army to the business of the state that distinguished it from its counterparts in Latin America. The first speech of all four coup-makers after takeover was symptomatic of the vision and strategy of the army. Most typically, they declared that the country was going downhill, condemned civilians, felt obliged to topple the government, lionized the army, and described the coup as something unpleasant but necessary.[127]

However, constitutionalism has been grossly underscored by securitization of the national vision by the army, both in power and out of power, defined by the 'India syndrome'.[128] In Ayesha Siddiqa's view, threat perceptions vis-à-vis India produced two major schools of thought among the elite: one conservative, which looked at India as a potentially hegemonic power in the region; and the other ultra-conservative, which saw India seeking to destroy Pakistan at the first opportunity.[129] After Bangladesh, the army's recruitment pattern changed in class and regional terms in the 1970s.[130] That brought in hawkish elements who would typically like to set things right in all spheres of public activity, nab corrupt politicians and uphold a right-wing reformist agenda as well as embrace Islamic ideology as the ultimate ideational sanction of the state. Pakistan's 'revisionist' nationalism has been at the root of the domestic supremacy of an army which faced the conflict in the region.[131]

The power of the military is reflected through the legacy of Bonapartist intervention in terms of the scope and extent of constitutional engineering, the presence of military personnel in the civilian sector, and the military's economic and business interests.[132] In Ahmed Rashid's view, Pakistan's use of Islamic militants in addition to diplomacy and trade to pursue its defence and foreign policies even after 9/11 antagonized its neighbours and 'isolated' it.[133] Charles Kennedy has given an interesting checklist of measures which the coup-makers in Pakistan felt obliged to implement after taking over. These would typically 'avoid legal chaos', 'make things legal in the short term', 'reinvent local government', 'intimidate the civil bureaucracy and the superior judiciary' and 'rewrite the Constitution'.[134] Each time a new Bonaparte launched a coup, he faced the issue of' 'constitutionalizing' his action.

In the context of electoral democracy, the army's political vision focused on the leadership factor not the participation factor. An executive president was considered ideal for leading the nation. A military government focused on the local bodies' elections at the district and sub-district levels, where no transfer of power was envisioned. The system was meant to de-politicize society, thereby seeking to revive the classical British colonial model of a top-down flow of patronage to the district outside the domain of the political class represented in the national and provincial legislatures. The idea was to disenfranchise the masses and deny them direct input into the business of the state. At the same time, the local bodies' elections served the function of providing a source of legitimacy at the grassroots level where people craved to exercise their vote in the ballot.[135]

Veena Kukreja argues that military takeovers in Pakistan were a result of 'reactive militarism' within the domestic context and not 'designed militarism' such as against a foreign threat.[136] For example, Ayub forestalled the looming elections scheduled for February 1959. Yahya sought to control the street demonstrations in 1969, as did Zia in 1977. Musharraf reacted to his dismissal as COAS by Nawaz Sharif in 1999. In the context of establishing stable civil–military relations, the transition process is key to restructuring the ruling set-up. Three concepts cover this relationship: the 'garbage can model', which disposes of the unnecessary burden; the 'path dependent political process', which ensures continuity in change; and the organizational environment, which keeps the institutional balance intact.[137] Pakistan has been ruled by 'military metaphysics', as described by Wright Mills, i.e. a habit of thought which categorized political issues as military concerns and considered the army the only institution that could resolve them. Political parties have been prone to becoming 'establishment machinations' to sell their support for certain returns.[138] Ironically, Zia's attitude toward Sindh was revealing insofar as he mistook silence as acquiescence after Bhutto's execution. Indeed, he believed that the people of Sindh wanted martial law for another six years. But the violence, including robberies and kidnappings, in Sindh kept the law enforcement agencies heavily engaged.[139]

Nawaz Sharif attempted to shift from the 'troika' model of government by sacking COAS General Jehangir Karamat in 1998 and dismissing Musharraf as COAS in 1999 before the coup.[140] Hasan Askari described the military's expanding corporate interests as colonization of civilian institutions.[141] From the transition from civil to military rule in 1999 to the transition in the reverse direction in 2008, history came full circle: from men in uniform taking over high positions in the state apparatus to vacating them for their civilian counterparts. The new Chief of the Army Staff, General Kayani, felt that the profile of the army had suffered during the year-long public protests against Musharraf, and announced withdrawal of 300 serving military officers, including a 3-star general and several major-generals from their civilian positions.

There were two poles of power in the government for several months after the February 2008 elections, one led by the PPP's PM Gilani and the other led by President Musharraf, who still carried the power to dissolve the National Assembly under Article 58(2)(b). From 2013, Musharraf's trial for treason for declaring a state of emergency on 3 November 2007 became a three-way conflict between the army, the judiciary and the civilian governments. COAS General Raheel Sharif 'saved' Musharraf from appearing in court for his trial and arranged for his exit from the country. The military leadership was not ready to countenance a profile of civilian supremacy, even by default. The issue of the insertion of the provision for democracy in the 2009 Kerry–Lugar–Berman Bill for aid to Pakistan set the civilian and military leaderships against each other. The army termed the bill an insult, while the PPP government described it as a big success.[142] Presidential spokesperson Farhatullah Babar perceived the military's reaction as crossing the red line.[143] The crisis was dissipated after the US Congress attached an explanatory statement stressing that Washington did not want to micromanage Pakistan, nor did it want to impugn its sovereignty.[144] The bill was finally approved by the federal cabinet after accepting the explanatory annexure.[145] In the regional context, the military establishment disapproved Zardari's diplomatic ambitions to establish peace with India.

The Abbottabad Operation, in which Al-Qaeda leader Osama bin Laden was killed by the US elite force SEALS, exposed the deficit of trust and communication among and between the civil and military wings of the state and the USA.[146] While PM Gilani termed the event a result of intelligence sharing,[147] the USA claimed that Islamabad was only informed after US forces had left Pakistan's airspace.[148] Pakistan was considered either an accomplice in keeping Osama in Abbottabad or incompetent. Subsequently, the top military officials of Pakistan admitted intelligence failure.[149] Musharraf pointed to the possibility that lower-level rogue members of ISI (Inter-Services Intelligence) might have known about Osama's location.[150] A five-member commission, formed to investigate the incident, asked the country's civil and military leadership to apologize to the nation for their 'collective failure'.[151] While the USA later said that Pakistan did not know about Osama's presence,[152] Wikileaks claimed that twelve ISI officials knew that Osama was in Pakistan.[153] The ex-ISI chief, General Asad Durrani, also suggested that the country's intelligence services had most likely sheltered Osama.[154]

Closely following the Abbottabad Operation, the 2011 Memogate scandal fully exposed the civil–military imbalance in the power structure.[155] The PPP government was embroiled in a tussle with the army as well as the judiciary.[156] The sacked Pakistan ambassador in Washington, Husain Haqqani, had long been on the army's radar due to his anti-establishment views.[157] During the Memogate proceedings in the Supreme Court, the government conceded that it had no operational control over the armed forces or ISI.[158] During the 2014 PTI protest, the opposition parties, PPP, ANP, JI and others, rallied behind the government to thwart any extra-constitutional intervention.[159] An ISPR (Inter-Services Public Relations) release later stated that the chief of the army staff was asked by the government to act as facilitator.[160] ISPR denied having any links with the protesting leaders, Imran Khan and Tahirul Qadri, in order to quell the general impression to that effect.[161] When COAS General Raheel Sharif was allotted 90 acres of land estimated to be worth Rs 1.5 billion by way of a pension after his retirement in 2017, ISPR defended the move as following 'constitutional provision'.[162] Lodhi points to the general opinion that it was difficult to see agitational movements with no support from the establishment.[163] In his view, each party has some members who can and do communicate with GHQ.[164]

Punjabi society continues to have a positive disposition towards the military, and there is an absence of the robust alternative political discourse that could one day make the military less of a reality in the country's power politics. Without a potent combination of electoral democracy and political liberalism, democracy is likely to remain weak.[165] Instead of reporting bare facts and letting people draw their own conclusions, the media managers, assisted by a string of 'defence experts', have burnished the traditional narrative of national insecurity with a sense of apocalypse. Terrorist attacks, even when claimed by the Pakistani Taliban, were ritually blamed on American private security agencies.[166] For its part, the establishment played a vital role in helping certain stakeholders climb the ladder to the elite circles, which made it an intrinsic part of the elite formation process.[167] Kiessling quotes Director General ISI General Hamid Gul: 'the Foreign Office has to convert but not to design the country's foreign policy'.[168] According to Hasan Abbas, Osama bin Laden secretly met Punjab's chief minister, Nawaz Sharif, through a former ISI official in 1989, and offered him financial support to topple Benazir Bhutto from power.[169] This despite the fact that ISI and Osama bin Laden were not formally working together, as Pakistan was too dependent upon Saudi financial grants and subsidised oil to work hand-in-glove with someone publicly challenging the House of Saud.[170] Husain Haqqani claims that the attempt to counter terrorism was frustrated by an informal alliance between Islamists and the garrison.[171]

ISI's involvement in domestic affairs drew not only on the military's felt need to be constantly updated with politics, to exercise influence and outperform the civilian intelligence carried out by the Intelligence Bureau (IB), but also on the absence of a real external security threat.[172] The NSC under Musharraf, and for a short time under Zia, had provided a supervisory role to the services chiefs in the government. Even when the NSC was no more, the military's influence was hard to roll back because of the 'informal blocs' of opinion and their supporters.[173] Journalist Hamid Mir survived an assassination attempt in 2014, which his brother blamed on ISI. After the Geo TV channel repeated the allegation for several hours, ISI managed to get Geo TV's transmission licence revoked. Similarly, the Dawn Leaks scandal related to a confidential meeting between the Nawaz Sharif government and army personnel in which the former complained about growing international isolation because of the latter's alleged protection of Islamic militants. The military side agreed not to interfere if law enforcement agencies would act against the militant groups.

The government also showed its interest in investigating the Pathankot incident as well as the stalled investigations into the Mumbai attacks.[174] The publication of the news by Cyril Almeida next day in *Dawn* led to a severe reaction from the army that obliged the government to deny forcefully that it had leaked the news.[175] The government sacked its information minister for what was considered a lapse on his part.[176] A subsequent enquiry committee refuted speculation that the news was planted by the civilian government. This was publicly 'rejected' by the army, as announced by the DG ISPR.[177] In subsequent behind-the-scenes manoeuvring between the two sides, the army formally withdrew the tweet, but the damage was done.[178]

A former US ambassador to Pakistan, Cameron Munter, maintained that ISPR and religious parties were involved in fanning public anger against the drone strikes, which were an integral part of US policy in Afghanistan.[179] Lawyer and activist, Asma Jahangir, demanded that the Supreme Court monitor ISPR.[180] At the same time, speculation about the involvement of intelligence agencies in cases of enforced disappearance continued to surface. In 2016, there were at least 1,400 unresolved cases of enforced disappearance in Pakistan, as per the International Commission of Jurists (ICJ). Several activists working on human rights and social and development issues had disappeared.[181] Bereaved families found no respite through the legal process due to the resistance of the police and the constant postponement of the cases in the courts. Some of the victims were quietly handed over to the Rangers for a 90-day remand. Often the families of the missing persons and returnees were afraid of exercising the option of pursuing a legal remedy.[182] With Pakistan being a signatory to the UN International Convention for the Protection of All Persons from Enforced Disappearance, adopted in December 2006, the 'official' stance regarding this issue tended to override the issue of human rights ostensibly to ensure national security.[183] When Musharraf declared a state of emergency in 2007, he pointed to the Supreme Court's interference in the operations related to the war on terror, by which he allegedly meant the issue of the disappearances.[184]

The clash of institutions was never ending. The Pakistan Ex-servicemen Association (PESA) remained a vocal critic of the civilian authorities on issues relating to elections, the quantum of Rangers' powers in Karachi, and Musharraf's treason trial.[185] In Hamid Khan's view, the military often played a part in appointing judges — for example, in the case of Justice Iftikhar Hussain Chaudhry as chief justice of Lahore High Court. He claims that it led to the removal of 'honest' judges from office and their replacement with those who would oblige.[186]

A lot has been written on the army's cultivation of Islamists as lobbyists, electoral entities, and non-state militant actors. This has become an almost permanent feature of politics in the country for half a century. The logic of the garrison–mullah alliance (Table 4.4) did not deter the army from carrying out operations against 'Islamic terrorists' or mainstream Islamists for showing their support for the Taliban. In this context, a major showdown between the Musharraf government and the pro-Taliban activists of the Red Mosque in Islamabad shook the capital in 2007.[187] The JI chief drew strong ire from the army when he called the slain TTP leader, Hakeemullah Mehsud, a martyr, while not acknowledging the martyrdom of military personnel.[188] Some found that the security establishment's policy vis-à-vis LeT amounted to appeasement inasmuch as the group still provided much-needed leverage against India.[189] State sponsorship of the Deobandi ulema for strategic purposes also upset the sectarian balance in what was a predominantly Barelvi country. In addition to helping the Taliban resettle in FATA, the alleged 'rogue' ISI operatives built a command-and-control structure for them in Balochistan from where they launched attacks on American and NATO forces in southern Afghanistan.[190]

It is clear that the military establishment has shaped the contours of democracy in Pakistan in a substantive way. 'Military metaphysics' is a self-propelling mode of imagination that securitizes the national vision and seeks to manufacture electoral politics accordingly. The thinking of the top military officers was heavily influenced by ideology, morality, sense of mission and boundless confidence in delivering the nation to the promised land. A war of attrition between the civil and military wings of the state comprehensively defined politics under a series of 'democratic dispensations'. In this context, the military–mullah alliance emerged as a bulwark against the perceived challenge of mainstream, ethnic and sectarian parties and groups. The establishment stood clearly against the participatory dimension of democracy in terms of both input as mass mandate and output as policy.

Table 4.4 The garrison–mullah alliance

Definition	Character	Policy/Law	Consequences
• Pre-Alliance Period 1947–70	• Rawalpindi Conspiracy Case 1951 • Crackdown on Islamists (the Ahrars, the JI) for anti-Ahmadi agitation1953; local martial law in Lahore	• The repugnancy clause in the 1956 and 1962 Constitutions • Dropping 'Islamic' from the name of the country 1962 (later revived) • Family Planning Programme (vs Islamists' opposition) • Dr Abdus Salam (later Nobel Laureate) appointed Ayub's Advisor for Science	• Objectives Resolution 1949 • 1953 anti-Ahmadiya agitation forcibly contained • 1954 Munir Report critical of ulema (showing no consensus about who is a Muslim) • Modernists win the initiative for constitution-making
• Co-optation of Islamic elements: 1970–2021	• 1970: Army's support for Islamic parties against Bengali nationalism and Bhutto's 'leftist' movement • 2012 Asghar Khan Case: conviction of former COAS Gen. Beg and ISI Chief Gen. Durrani (for funding the IJI in the 1990 elections) • Supporting or creating new Islamic parties: chipping away the winning margins of the potential government-forming parties, 1970 (JI, JUI, JUP), 1993 (JI), 2013 (Taliban's attack on 'liberal' parties PPP, MQM and ANP), 2018 (TLP)	• Attempting election rigging for Islamic parties against AL (1970) and PPP (1970, 1988, 2008) without success • Election rigging 1990 (IJI), 2002 (MMA) • Supporting Islamic parties (JUI-F) against Pakhtun and Baloch nationalists	• 1970: Mainstreaming Islamic parties – I (from lobbyists to 18 Islamic MNAs 1970) • 2002 Mainstreaming Islamic parties – II • A strong contingent of MMA's MNAs and a majority of MPAs in KP Assembly in the 2002 elections • Formation of the MMA government in KP; (first and last 'Islamic government' at a provincial or national level up until 2021)

• Co-optation of Islamic militants	• 1971: Co-optation of militant non-state actors in East Pakistan (Al-Badr, Al-Shams) • 1980–90: Creating mujahideen against the Red Army in Afghanistan • Jihadi industry: LeT, Jash Muhammad (JM); Hizbul Mujahideen (HM) (the IHK insurgency in 1989–2003) • 1980s: Support for the sectarian militant party SSP against Iran-backed TNFJ (Tehrik Nifaz Fiqh Jafaria)	• 1992: Picking up the Taliban • ISI Chief Gen. Hameed Gul: self-proclaimed godfather of the Taliban • 2000s: Good Taliban (against Kabul) vs bad Taliban (against Islamabad) • 2009 military operation in Swat; 2014 operation in North Waziristan after the Taliban attack on APS • 13 agreements with Taliban • The alleged establishment of the Quetta Shoora (Taliban) • Trump's 2019 allegations about Pakistan's double dealing in the war against terror 2019 • Pakistan's facilitation of the US–Taliban agreement in Doha 2020 • 2021: Post-US withdrawal Taliban's rule over Kabul, speculation civil war under the new dispensation	• 2001–20: Long haul against Pakistan's international profile as a terrorist (producing and exporting) country; diplomatic isolation • 2002: Close brush with war with India after a terrorist attack on the parliament in Delhi • Anti-Americanism post-9/11 (wars: 2001 Afghanistan; 2003 Iraq; drone attacks on Taliban strongholds in Pakistan; 2011 Abbottabad Operation; 2011 US 'friendly' fire on Silala checkpost (suspension of NATO's military supplies to Afghanistan) • 'Yankee don't go home from Afghanistan' 1989 (leaving us in the lurch) vs 'Yankee go home' (leave Afghanistan) 2017–21 • 2018: Mainstreaming Islamic militants – III

While the scholarly research generally finds the establishment responsible for the downslide in democracy, it is not uncommon to see the opposite view that puts the military in a 'neutral' position vis-à-vis politicians and even credits it for showing deference to civilian leaders. The following observations represent this view. The military has moved 'from hegemony to co-equals'. General Kiyani's extension as COAS for three years in 2010 showed 'an improved level of trust' between the two sides because this established the principle of 'supremacy of civilian leadership'. COAS General Bajwa's appearance in the Senate in December 2017 meant that 'the military considered the parliament supreme'. The prime minister 'was decisive in selecting the army chief' but he had little to no homework in 'subordinating the military to civilian supremacy'.[191] After the 2013 elections, Nawaz Sharif set about 'securing the subordination of the military'. COAS General Raheel Sharif showed 'surprising inactivity' during Imran Khan's sit-in in Islamabad. The current generation of army leadership appears to be 'showing greater forbearance towards political leadership'. The military won 'global recognition and legitimacy' for showing support for democracy and 'determination to destroy terrorist networks'.[192]

Judicialization of Politics

Many consider the judiciary a factor in the underdevelopment of democracy in Pakistan ever since the 1954 Tamizuddin case. The judiciary has exercised political initiative by keeping law as the essential idiom of political conflict through court cases. I shall argue that it has gravitated towards a position of putting the constitution as an entity over and above parliament, thus appropriating the ultimate source of legitimacy through interpretation at the cost of the political class.[193] I shall focus on judicial activism spread over the first quarter of the twenty-first century. Confrontation between the executive and the judiciary reached two high points under chief justices Iftikhar Chaudhry (2005–7, 2009–13) and Saqib Nisar (2016–19). Sometimes it led to speculation about the imminent collapse of the democratic system, given the history of military takeover in the context of a power vacuum. The use of judicial review, whereby the court exercised the power of interpreting the constitution with impunity, was widely criticized as an attempt to encroach on the territory of the legislature through case law. At the institutional level, the court sought to exercise the power of veto over the appointment of judges and thus deny the right of oversight to parliament in this regard. The court's pursuit of litigation through frequent *suo motu* notices taken in a populist mode of action led to brinkmanship on the part of the executive and the judiciary. However, despite this power play the court's operations generally fell into the category of modus operandi, in pursuit of some middle ground as a solution to a seemingly intractable conflict instead of taking the fight to the finish.[194] For example, under the restored Chief Justice Chaudhry the Supreme Court in 2009 condoned the holding of the 2008 election, forfeited the move to hold President Musharraf accountable for violating the constitution by declaring a state of emergency, and validated the election of the PPP-led government.[195]

I want to analyse the operational dynamics of the judiciary in its mode of interaction with the political executive in contemporary Pakistan, especially under the post-Musharraf democratic dispensations from 2008 onwards. The higher courts were credited for their newly gained independence by a large section of the people. The main vehicle for this 'independent' judiciary, the Supreme Court, assumed a populist role in the context of its pursuit of the 'big fish' in its accountability drive. In this process, the court ran into controversy over the issue of stepping into the domain of the executive. Both sides projected rival interpretations of the constitution relating to institutional powers and responsibilities. My argument dwells on the judiciary's role in judicial review, the Supreme Court's constitutional engineering by default, and populism as demonstrated through the court's penchant for public interest litigation underscored by the cult of Chief Justice Choudhry.

The War of Attrition between the Judiciary and the Executive

Sweet points to three aspects of the judicial process: 'normative structure, dyadic contraction and triadic dispute resolution', respectively pointing to the institutional ethos, the positioning of litigants, and supra-conflict judgement.[196] This is how political life is judicialized – by way of first interpreting rules, then admitting the cases or otherwise, and finally bearing the seeds of consequentialism that can involve regime change. In functional terms, the courts can act as 'bridges' between the state and the polity while dealing with constitutional provisions and institutional powers. However, in structural terms, courts could in fact end up representing the 'state's distance from the political society' in their capacity as part of the institutional apparatus of the state.[197] In recent decades, the judiciary in both India and Pakistan has taken the position that the constitution is above parliament, as opposed to parliament's position that it is the creator of the constitution itself.

In the context of a clash of institutions, two models have emerged from recent decades. First, assemblies have been dissolved ostensibly due to cooperation between the army and the judiciary (1988, 1990, 1993 and 1996). Second, the person-specific charges of contempt of court and corruption have led to the dismissal of prime ministers Gilani and Nawaz Sharif (2012, 2017 respectively). The traditional pattern of courts demanding 'separation of powers' has effectively been replaced with parliament demanding separation of powers as a security mechanism against judicial activism. The March 2007 suspension of Chief Justice Iftikhar Chaudhry, followed by the dismissal of scores of judges from the higher courts under the state of emergency declared on 3 November 2007, turned judges into martyrs for the cause of the independence of the judiciary. The restoration of the judges in March 2009 after a vehement and prolonged movement by lawyers supported by the media, civil society and political leadership, transformed them into heroes. However, the subsequent issuance of high-profile court decisions over the next few years constantly put the PPP-led government in Islamabad (2008–13) in the dock and produced wild predictions of the latter's imminent downfall. The issue of the independence of judiciary thus became intertwined with the question of whether a strident Supreme Court would hasten the end of the current experiment with democracy. There were powerful elements – including the business community, the professional middle class, the bureaucracy and technocrats as well as their supporters in the media and civil society – who consistently upheld the cause of the independence of the judiciary. They focused on the specific agenda of holding President Zardari and his party accountable for corruption and bad governance.[198] It was speculated that the conflict between the executive and the judiciary would push the government out of office through legal action by the Supreme Court.

How ought one to define the independence of the judiciary? Joel Verner attempted to draw a typology of courts by placing them along an independent–dependent continuum: independent-activist; attenuated-activist; stable–reactive; reactive–compliant; minimalist; and personalist.[199] This typology, however, is sensitive mainly to the relatively stable executive–judiciary relations in individual countries rather than to longer-term political transformation that could change the quantum of the executive's control over the judiciary from one model to another. For example, the Supreme Court in Pakistan approximated the independent-activist model in 2009–13. However, it had no reasonable prospect of staying in that category in the event of regime change. In that respect, the attenuated-activist model was more applicable to the country because the independence of the judiciary was relative to the nature of the regime. Similarly, by way of the stable–reactive model, the Supreme Court could not be considered stable in view of the spasmodic nature of its activism, as in the cases against Nawaz Sharif, Imran Khan and Jahangir Tareen in 2017. It was also not reactive because of its on-again/off-again activism in a voluntary mode of action, often in response to media coverage of those who were considered to be on the wrong side of justice. Again, it was typically compliant under General Musharraf but not reactive. It was not minimalist in the sense of a negligible triadic role in dyadic conflicts among and between state agencies and citizens. Nor was the court 'personalist' by way of total subjection to the will of a strongman except in the period immediately following the military's takeover under Zia (1977) and Musharraf (1999), and later after the imposition of a state of emergency by the latter in 2007.

The Bhutto trial (1977–9) evinced two contradictory interpretations from British diplomats in Islamabad. One was that the 'British legacy of an independent judiciary remains strong in Pakistan'.[200] The other was that 'the four Punjabi judges found guilt firmly proven, while the three non-Punjabis ruled equally firmly for acquittal on the grounds that the testimony of the main prosecution witnesses was unnatural, improbable and untrue'.[201] One focused on the legal procedure, the other looked at the purported ethnic bias.

Courts usually give the polity a vocabulary 'with which to speak when the political language has neither been accurate or reliable'.[202] In Pakistan, the language of policy gave way to the language of law. This meant that the policy-seeking electorate was left high and dry in the face of a compliance-seeking judiciary which was formally extraneous to the political context altogether. In the process of adjudicating the dissolution of the National Assembly in 1988, 1990, 1993 and 1996, the 'integrity of the courts' was compromised because of the fact that 'deciding the merits of the respective dissolutions is inherently political'.[203] When the Supreme Court of the UK rejected Prime Minister Boris Johnson's suspension of parliament for one month by consensus in 2019, it was similarly charged with giving a political decision.[204] In the context of the Bush election in the USA in 2002, Nicholson and Howard distinguish between 'specific support', expressed through the court's 'confidence in office holders', and 'diffuse support', which had to do with 'institutional legitimacy'.[205] Alternatively, in Nawaz Sharif's case in 2017, the Supreme Court had scant trust in the public office holders of his government not least because of the attitudinal difference between the two power centres, as discussed in Chapter 3. Did the court display middle-class prejudice against the political class?

In theory, the independence of the courts unfolds itself through the role of a neutral third, which has no interest in litigants or in the outcome of a case. This calls for insularity from social and political forces seeking to use the court as an instrument for pursuit of their agenda. But in Pakistan various exogenous factors influenced the procedural and substantive aspects of the judicature. A judge in a lower court was obliged to issue a verdict in favour of the crowd outside the court which demanded a verdict of its choice, in the face of a genuine fear for his life.[206] In other words, one also needs to identify social and political obstacles on the way to the independence of the courts rather than simply rely on the legal and constitutional provisions. The test for independence lies in the ability of the courts 'to regulate the legality of state behaviour'.[207] That, in turn, depends on the stability of the justice system, from the input in the form of the appointment of judges to the output such as the court verdicts.

A major controversy in Pakistan after 2009 related to the issue of those judges who were appointed by President Musharraf under the state of emergency promulgated in November 2007, despite the court order issued within hours of its announcement that rendered it unconstitutional. In this situation, we can understand judicial independence in the context of 'regime relativity'.[208] Article 63 effectively replaced Article 58(2)(b) as an instrument to dismiss public office holders instead of dissolving the National Assembly itself. In 2017, Chief Justice Saqib Nisar gave judgment that any person who suffered from lack of qualification under Article 62 or disqualification under Article 63 of the constitution was debarred from holding the position of 'party head'. That person was also prohibited from exercising any powers provided under Article 63-A of the constitution, or in any other capacity under any law, rule, regulation, statute, instrument or document of any political party.[209]

Earlier, while dismissing an appeal seeking Nawaz Sharif's disqualification in 2015, Justice Khosa opined that many provisions of Article 62 were not amenable to 'legally enforceable standards'. Referring to Article 62(1)(f), he wrote: 'it is proverbial that Devil himself knoweth not the intention of man. So, why to have such requirements in the law, nay, the constitution, which cannot even be defined, not to talk of proof'.[210] In other words, the jurisprudence on the applicability of Articles 62 and 63 of the constitution was still underdeveloped and remained controversial.[211] Chief Justice Nisar, while disqualifying Nawaz Sharif for life in the 2018 verdict, remarked that the public deserved 'leaders of good character'.[212] It has been argued that Article 184(3) of the constitution was being used in conjunction with 'morality' clauses, i.e. Articles 62 and 63, to serve the ulterior motive of operationalizing fundamental rights in contravention of the rights of association.[213]

Judicial Review

Hussain has discussed the origin and genealogy of judicial review in the doctrine of *ultra vires* to assess the legality of legislative or administrative actions, and in Lord Coke's assertion of the Common Law to render void an act of parliament if it was against the common right and reason.[214] In Pakistan, the Federal Court rendered void the governor general's Emergency Powers Ordinance in 1955 through which he had extended his powers. Justice Munir took the 'necessity' view, while Justice Cornelius took the legal view – considering law as law without looking into the operational aspects.[215] The fact that the judges extended legitimacy to abrogation or suspension of the constitution to which they had sworn, and, through a Provisional Constitutional Order (PCO), acquiesced to swear on martial law or its legal equivalent instead of the constitution, created a dilemma of jurisdiction.[216] The judicial review moved away from this position, whereby the court would not take up a *pro bono publico*. Instead, it picked up a case of public importance affecting the marginalized and dispossessed groups as per Article 184(3), thus largely bypassing the *locus standi*.[217] This opened the floodgates for *suo motu* cases in pursuit of public interest litigation.

A major consideration was the court's indulgence in tackling political cases, by implication crossing the principle of separation of powers. For example, in the 2010 Memogate case, instead of the merit of *certiorari*, the Supreme Court under Chaudhry linked a foreign policy issue with the fundamental rights of citizens.[218] The court set aside the 'political question' doctrine, meaning that it took up the cases dealing with politics with impunity. Thus, the judiciary, despite its legal sophistry and commitment to the trichotomy of the ruling set-up, placed the political class in jeopardy. Was it a case of the state elite going after the political elite through the judiciary's involvement of the military institutions such as ISI (Inter-Services Intelligence) and MI (Military Intelligence) in the deliberations of the JIT investigating Nawaz Sharif in 2017–18?

In the 1990s, several elected governments faced intervention from extra-parliamentary forces in the middle of their tenure. The eleven years of the 'rule of troika' (1988–99) comprised chief of the army staff, president and prime minister in that order, a fact that put parliament at a discount. The new troika following the reinstatement of Chief Justice Iftikhar Chaudhry in 2009 comprised the chief of the army staff, President Asif Zardari, and the chief justice (2009–13). Indeed, Punjab's chief minister, Shehbaz Sharif, publicly demanded that the army and judiciary be brought in to settle the intractable issues of governance.[219]

The history of a symbiosis between the judiciary and other unelected institutions – including the civil bureaucracy and the army – against the elected institutions, dates back to the 1954 Tamizuddin case and the 1958 Dosso case, in which the apex court legitimized a bureaucratic coup and a military coup respectively.[220] In 2009–11, various sections of civil society and the legal fraternity were alienated by the Supreme Court's decisions, which de-recognized the oversight of the executive's functions of the appointment, promotion and transfer of bureaucrats and judges. A clash of institutions seemed imminent. The bar and the bench gradually drifted apart.

Given a long history of the vulnerability of the political system to Bonapartist generals, underscored by a series of court decisions in support of military coups, tension between the executive and the judiciary represented a challenge to democracy. Justice Choudhry was able to transform the issue of his suspension in 2007 into a political crisis by taking the matter to the bar association and thus mobilizing public pressure in his favour.[221] Much as Justice Chaudhry wanted Musharraf to be held accountable according to the constitution, and those PCO judges who had taken the oath in violation of the constitution to be brought to justice, the court's adherence to modus operandi remained the method of not taking the matter to the finish since neither judiciary nor the political executive wanted their hands to be soiled.[222]

The issue of the independence of the judiciary that had been part of the political lexicon of Pakistan for six decades was triumphantly revisited in 2009. However, the profile of independence was crystallized in a personal rather than institutional framework, as symbolized by Justice Chaudhry, along with the legal and political implications of a number of random spurts of justice through a series of court decisions. The Supreme Court clearly showed its commitment to security of tenure for the higher judiciary and registered its disapproval of such positions as additional judges, acting judges, and ad hoc judges.[223] On parallel lines, the Indian judiciary had graduated from a merely consultative position to power of veto for the chief justice over the appointment of judges, as it moved from the First Judges Case to the Second and Third Judges Cases.[224] However, the issue of the need for the external scrutiny of judges for their appointment and accountability by an agency outside the court remained unresolved in both India and Pakistan.

The quest for independence was 'externalized' insofar as the Supreme Court of Pakistan judged its functional and structural autonomy in relation to the executive – tied with the 'political' issue of the right of the courts to assert their free will – rather than to the 'professional' issue of the dispensation of justice. Musharraf's referendum in 2002 was challenged before the Supreme Court but the case was declared 'premature' and was struck down.[225] After Musharraf forced the sitting judges to take a fresh oath under PCO in 2000, there followed a saga of arbitrary appointments, transfers and promotions of judges with the express purpose of strengthening the hands of the military regime. Musharraf faced the issue of dealing with an increasingly 'independent' Chief Justice Chaudhry, who began to show a new keenness towards the issue of 'forced disappearances', which was not welcomed by the ruling dispensation.[226] After declaring a state of emergency in November 2007, Musharraf appointed a new Chief Justice Dogar along with other judges who took oath under PCO, the second time under his rule. When Chaudhry was restored as chief justice in 2009, he invalidated the PCO-II oath, and dismissed seven out of the seventeen judges of the Supreme Court. Regime relativity defined court action both under and after Musharraf.

To understand the role of the Supreme Court as a referee in constitutional matters, we need to be aware of the existence of two power centres in Pakistan, represented by the state elite and the political elite. The apex court had relied on the doctrine of state necessity to legitimize the dissolution of assemblies from the 1954 Tamizuddin case to the 1977 Begum Nusrat Bhutto case.[227] 'Statism' emerged as the dominant judicial perspective on constitutional matters. Later, 'constitutionalism' became the new orthodoxy for the judiciary.[228] Courts sat in judgment over acts of dissolution of elected assemblies that reflected their impugned power of interpretation of black letter law. As Osama Siddique has argued, judges referred to certain legal provisions with a measure of manipulation so as to put their seal of approval on the new post-dissolution political order. This required some stretch of the imagination, which created a lasting controversy in legal and political circles. The courts declared certain laws unconstitutional, often disregarding the opinion of the political leadership.

In the 1997 Mahmood Khan Achakzai case about Article 58(2)(b), which empowered the president to dissolve the National Assembly, and which was allegedly abused four times within a decade, the Supreme Court confirmed the amendment as a valid part of the constitution. It put the responsibility for not amending that amendment on parliament itself, which, in its view, acquiesced to its ratification by implication through its inaction.[229] However, the court took a different view of the National Reconciliation Ordinance (NRO). The NRO was issued after a deal between Musharraf and the PPP chairperson, Benazir Bhutto, mediated by Washington to help build popular support for the military ruler and to facilitate the participation of the PPP and other parties in the political process. In 2009 the Supreme Court itself asked the PPP-led government to pass the 2006 NRO as an act of parliament.[230] The government failed to oblige due to the last-minute defection of the PPP's coalition partner, MQM. On 16 December 2009, the Supreme Court rendered the NRO null and void.[231] Deletion of the NRO from the statute book put President Zardari in the dock. Various court cases against him, pursued by the Nawaz Sharif and Musharraf governments for nearly two decades, now stood revived.[232]

The judiciary had a clear advantage over the executive in terms of its professed right and duty to interpret the constitution and the obligation of the executive to implement its verdict. This aspect of the constitutional state in Pakistan has typically been ignored by commentators on the country's law and politics. The profile of Pakistan as a military state has generally undermined analysis of the intricate legal balance between the executive and judiciary. As Siddique has argued, provisions such as Article 58(2)(b), as typically validated by the Supreme Court, were even more destructive of the democratic ethos than martial law.[233]

Constitutional measures created controversy about the way in which institutions exercised power. In April 2010, the passage of the 18th Amendment caused a severe reaction in certain sections of the judiciary, that deemed it to be in violation of the basic structure of the constitution. At issue was the composition of the Judicial Commission as well as the locus of the final authority for the approval or disapproval of the appointment of judges and the jurisdiction of the Supreme Court over the matter of striking down a constitutional amendment.[234] The proceedings of court cases against the 18th Amendment frequently referred to Indian cases relating to the basic structure of the constitution. In 1967, in the case of *I.C. Golaknath* vs *State of Punjab*, the Supreme Court of India had maintained that parliament could not abrogate fundamental rights.[235] Later, the 1973 Kesavanada Bharati case laid down a new doctrine whereby parliament could not alter the basic structure of the constitution.[236] Analysis of this structure generally evaded a generation of scholars after that, except that the issue revolved around fundamental rights.[237]

Legal opinion in Pakistan was divided on this issue. One side followed the Indian model and argued vehemently that the Supreme Court had similarly posited a doctrine of the basic structure of the constitution as comprising federalism, parliamentary democracy, Islamic provisions and the independence of the judiciary, as per the 1997 Mahmood Khan Achakzai case and the 2000 Zafar Ali Shah case.[238] The courts in Pakistan have not generally countenanced their own jurisdictional ouster as per Article 239(5) and (6).[239] The other side argued that the superior courts had, for thirty-five years, typically shied away from exercising jurisdiction over striking down constitutional amendments.[240] In various cases, the courts noted the Kesavananda Bharati verdict but bypassed it.[241] In the Achakzai Case, Chief Justice Sajjad Ali Shah acknowledged the existence of certain 'basic features' of the Pakistan Constitution. However, the Supreme Court later maintained that it was not its job to enforce these basic features.[242] This debate revolved around constitutionalism as the defining variable for the courts' interpretive mode of operation. In this way, the Supreme Court's periodical assertion of power and responsibility for bestowing or denying legitimacy to an incumbent government became a great political resource inasmuch as it could override the mass mandate as a constitutional source of legitimacy.

In India, Prime Minister Nehru's complaint against the judiciary for having 'purloined' the constitution pointed to the Supreme Court's formidable potential to assume the high moral ground and by default to raise its own institutional capacities. Judicial power operated at the cost of constitutional politics, not least through the court decisions about how judges would be appointed.[243] In Pakistan, the PPP felt that it had suffered at the hands of the judiciary in a series of cases ranging from Bhutto's hanging in 1979 to the dismissal of the Benazir government in 1990. Under her second government (1993–6), Benazir packed the courts with her nominees, which triggered the judiciary's move towards independence in the famous Al-Jihad Trust case in 1996. This case got its impetus from the 'controversial appointments' that shook the superior courts out of complacency.[244]

The judiciary operates as a triadic entity that jealously guards its own institutional efficacy as well as legal and moral legitimacy in the process of dispensation of justice in dyadic conflicts.[245] A court verdict indirectly contributes to rule-making, which is actually a function of the legislature. It is obvious that the parliamentary leadership would seek to constrain this power of reconstructing the legal edifice through case law, and keep this function for itself.[246] This conundrum entails a clash between institutions in the context of the exercise of state power, whereby the courts' functioning tended to make constitutionalism a matter of institutional design rather than social consensus.[247] Judicial activism drew on not only the courts' enactment of the relevant constitutional provisions but also the executive's much touted inefficiency and bad governance. Research on the political and judicial history of Pakistan carried multiple examples of arbitrary appointment, transfer, promotion, and suspension of judges, and asking some of them to take the oath under PCO after a military coup, while excluding others from taking the oath. The former Supreme Court judge, Fakruddin G. Ebrahim, refused to become part of the committee formed by the PPP and PML-N for deciding the cases of judges inducted after the state of emergency on 3 November 2007. He argued that the committee was interested more in retention of the PCO judges than in reinstatement of the deposed judges.[248] The 1996 Al-Jihad Trust case about the judges' appointment made consultation with the chief justice mandatory by requiring it to be effective, meaningful and purposive, thus not leaving any room for arbitrariness.[249] This forced the government to accept the opinion of chief justices of the Supreme Court and high courts for the appointment of judges.

In February 2010, the Supreme Court took *suo motu* notice of a presidential order regarding the appointment of Chief Justice Lahore High Court Khawaja Sharif as a Supreme Court judge and Justice Saqib Nisar as acting chief justice of Lahore High Court and suspended it within hours. The Supreme Court found the notification to be in violation of Articles 177 and 260, whereby the president was bound to accept its recommendations in this regard. Conversely, when the newly formed Judicial Commission extended the tenure of six additional judges of the Lahore and Sindh high courts, there was an adverse reaction in the lawyers' community and in the media. Both found the extension to be contradictory to the spirit of the judgment given in the Al-Jihad Trust case against appointing judges to temporary positions.

In March 2011, the parliamentary committee refused to grant extension to certain judges in view of the adverse remarks of the respective chief justices of the Sindh and Lahore high courts. However, the Supreme Court rejected it and ordered issuance of appointment notifications to the judges. The president of the Supreme Court Bar Association, Asma Jahangir, criticized the court's judgment for thus undermining parliament and allowing unscrupulous persons to manipulate their way onto the bench.[250] In fact, she lamented the fact that the Supreme Court had colluded with a petitioner who had sought to promote the interests of a few sub-standard candidates for appointment.[251] The parliamentary committee filed a review petition in the Supreme Court, which was rejected. President Zardari was thus obliged to administer the oath to the Supreme Court nominees. The whole saga amounted to the virtual annulment of the 2010 19th Amendment. While critics postulated that the court was thus seeking 'secession' rather than independence, others argued that the court had not challenged the supremacy of parliament but only reviewed an executive action.[252] However, since the parliamentary committee represented an equal number of members from the treasury and opposition benches, it could hardly be considered a part of the executive. Clearly, the judiciary had resolved that the way to independence lay in total control over the process of the appointment of judges.

Judicial Populism

How did Chief Justice Choudhry and his Supreme Court reach the exalted position of legislating over the style and substance of governance and winning the hearts and minds of people in the first place? The new icon of the independent judiciary addressed several issues of common interest, ranging from corruption at the highest level to the pricing of sugar and petroleum, i.e. issues that put the common man's life in dire straits. Just as the judiciary in India emerged stronger out of the 1975–7 state of emergency, the lawyers' movement against Musharraf produced a triumphant Supreme Court in Pakistan in 2009. Supreme Court Judge Javed Iqbal claimed that the judiciary had indeed heralded the current era of democracy.[253]

The new 'independent' judiciary had a penchant for *suo motu* notices. The Supreme Court's finding that there was no justification for the imposition of a carbon surcharge on petrol referred to the mention of social justice in the preamble of the constitution, with the implication that this provision was justiceable.[254] The *suo motu* actions won the title of 'people's judiciary' for the Supreme Court.[255] The Supreme Court blocked a controversial sale of 240 acres of land in Karachi. It asked Haris Steel to repay a loan worth Rs 9 billion to the Bank of Punjab. It took *suo motu* notices of the increase in the price of sugar, mega-corruption in Pakistan Steel Mills worth Rs 22 billion, and the cutting down of trees because of the extension of a canal road in Lahore. It took notice of illegal allotment of land by the Federal Government Housing Foundation, the alleged embezzlement of Rs 7 billion by the Pakistan Cricket Board, and electricity misuse by Musharraf and other residents of a wealthy area, Chak Shehzad near Islamabad.[256]

There followed a series of appointments on the crucial position of the chairman of the NAB after the resignation of successive incumbents of the job in the midst of cross-pressures from the Supreme Court and the government. Meanwhile, the general public had internalized the whole saga of corruption cases as amplified through the media for nearly two decades. They wanted the new 'independent' judiciary to finally deliver on that issue. The middle class, which showed a disdain for electoral politics in general and for the PPP in particular, eagerly awaited punishment of President Zardari for corruption through impeachment or otherwise. Chief Justice Choudhry massively impressed the people as a saviour. He created a myth of citizens' sovereignty, claimed moral uprightness for himself as opposed to the corrupt class of politicians, and cultivated a patriarchal image of the judiciary as guardian of the interests of the downtrodden people.[257]

Public interest litigation became the legal mechanism for the Supreme Court's populist stance. However, the lower courts continued to suffer through the small number of judges at the district level, their lack of professional skills and their rampant corruption combined with procedural delays. The malaise of a malfunctioning lower judiciary has been underscored by non-delegation of the powers of judicature from the *suo motu* savvy judges of the higher courts to the district and session courts.[258] The low conviction rate of around 5–10 per cent made the justice system of Pakistan most unenviable and depressing. In November 2016, the federal government tabled the 24th Amendment in parliament, which proposed changes in Article 184 to give the right of appeal to an aggrieved party against a judgment of the apex court in *suo motu* cases, in line with the principle of the fundamental rights of citizens.[259] However, the bill never moved further. During the tenure of Chief Justice Iftikhar Chaudhry, more than 450 constitutional petitions were entertained under Article 184(3) and hundreds of *suo motu* notices were taken.

The higher judiciary gained more out of the executive's loss – by way of the latter's lack of good governance – than out of the courts' own performance. The most typical reaction of the executive was to publicly commit itself to implementation of the Supreme Court's decisions and then rely on delaying tactics or on misinterpretation of the Supreme Court's verdict. The PPP government thwarted the pressure to open the corruption cases against President Zardari in the Swiss courts after the National Reconciliation Ordinance was rendered null and void in 2009. Another strategy was to file a review petition in the Supreme Court, as in the case of the latter's rejection of the decision of the parliamentary committee concerning the non-extension of additional judges in the Lahore and Sindh high courts. The government was obliged to implement the Supreme Court's judgment in the absence of all other options. On 20 April 2010, the Supreme Court cancelled the government's notification for the promotion of 53 officers into Grade 22 because they had superseded 173 officers who were senior to them. The government was obliged to withdraw the notice. There was a public outcry that the Supreme Court was operating as a court of appeal over the exercise of authority by a lawful organ of the state.

At one level, the Chaudhry Court was lauded for upholding the constitutional perspective, serving people through public interest litigation, the rule of law, accountability for corruption, and indeed representing a new dawn.[260] At another level, the government was able to establish links in the legal community where sentiments against the Supreme Court and certain high court chief justices had been building up for some time. The election of Asma Jahangir as president of the Supreme Court Bar Association for 2010–11 signalled a weakening of the constituency of the bench in the bar because she belonged to the anti-Choudhry group of lawyers.

All along, the government continued to respond 'politically' to the judicial challenge by keeping itself visible on certain channels of the electronic media. The PPP government mobilized street protests in Sindh against the Supreme Court's judgment dismissing Justice Deedar Hussain Shah as chairman of the NAB in March 2011. Subsequently, the two organizers of the province-wide strike were summoned by the Supreme Court to explain their conduct as an alleged contempt of court. They were accompanied by a large number of legislators of the Sindh Assembly as a symbol of their political constituency. The court baulked in the face of a show of public support on the part of the PPP. Later, one of the two persons was appointed minister of information in the Sindh government. Similarly, when a section of the press published the news that the government was considering cancellation of the prime minister's initial order of reinstatement of Chief Justice Choudhry and other judges in the Supreme Court issued on 16 March 2009, the Supreme Court asked for a written assurance from the prime minister that no such action was under consideration. The prime minister would not provide that, and the Supreme Court felt obliged to look the other way. All along, the two sides exercised brinkmanship. The Supreme Court felt obliged to tackle the wider issues of governance in order to alleviate people's grievances, while it was unaccountable for its own actions to any institution, group or community except, in hypothetical and abstract terms, to citizens at large.

Choudhry's immediate successors, Justice Jilani and Justice Nasirul Mulk, adopted a policy of judicial restraint and took very few *suo motu* notices. However, during Chief Justice Nisar's term (2016–19) 294 constitutional petitions filed directly in the apex court were pending as of September 2018, while decisions on 177 human rights cases and 59 *suo motu* matters were still awaited.[261] The court's incessant employment of *suo motu* powers and Chief Justice Nisar's visits to hospitals and medical colleges, and projects such as the funding of the Diamer–Bhasha dam construction, were meant to advertise successive governments' failures in a populist mode of action. Chief Justice Saqib Nisar was prone to exercising the powers relating to Article 184(3) and expanded its scope to an unprecedented level.

There was public outcry over an alleged balancing act of the two Supreme Court benches in terms of giving controversial judgments.

Chief Justice Nisar stressed that it was a mere coincidence that the decision to reopen the Hudaibiya Paper Mills of the Sharif family was delivered on the same day as the verdicts on Imran Khan's acquittal and Jahangir Tareen's disqualification.[262] He swore that he had no political agenda.[263] His use of traditional metaphors, such as referring to the role of the Supreme Court as akin to the wise old man of the village Baba Rehmate, to induce the element of affect into his public visibility, smacked of folkloric wisdom.

Nisar's populism about the court's leadership relied on the mission to establish 'good governance' by focusing on eliminating corruption. He publicly snubbed an additional district and sessions judge in Larkana in an ongoing court hearing when the latter was seen using his cell phone.[264] The Islamabad High Court declared that the chief justice was well within his rights to annul any verdicts of the lower courts deemed inappropriate but that he lacked authority to insult his juniors in an open court.[265] The Karachi Bar Association condemned the humiliation of judicial officers on live television.

Nisar took a *suo motu* notice of the exorbitant fees of private hospitals and summoned their owners and shareholders. Similarly, notices were issued to the Doctors Hospital, Surgimed Hospital, Omar Hospital, Hameed Latif Hospital, Mid City Hospital, National Hospital, Farooq Hospital and Al-Raazi Hospital in Lahore. He ordered that private hospitals would be slapped with Rs 10,000 fine to be deposited in the 'Dam fund' for each vehicle found parked outside their parking areas.[266]

During the hearing of the matter of Justice Amir Raza's resignation from the Board of Punjab Healthcare Commission, Nisar insulted the veteran journalist Hussain Naqi in open court, while dissolving the board itself. When Mr Naqi tried to defend his position, he was warned of contempt and was removed from the court. He added insult to injury by asking: 'What kind of people have you appointed as Board members?'[267] Just as in the case of Nisar's populist predecessor, Iftikhar Chaudhry, dispensation of justice took a secondary role. The Women's Action Forum (WAF) filed a reference against the chief justice before the Supreme Judicial Council (SJC) alleging: 'He has failed to keep his office free of controversy or to discharge the mountainous heaps of pending cases that plague the judiciary and prevent it from serving as an efficacious provider of justice and due process to the citizens.'[268]

Contempt of court has loomed like a sword over the court's critics ever since the Nehal Hashmi Case.[269]

In a quixotic move, Chief Justice Nisar evoked the Supreme Court's jurisdiction under Article 184 (3) in conjunction with Article 9 (Right to life) to start the project of raising funds for the Diamer–Bhasha and Mohmand dams. He claimed that the right to life is a fundamental right and there could not be existence of life without water. Building water reservoirs was thus not a question of quality of life but of the existence of life itself.[270] In what was generally considered a grotesque move, he warned his critics that they could be tried under Article 6 of the constitution for high treason.[271]

During the Panama Leaks case, the constitution of the Joint Investigation Team (JIT) investigating Nawaz Sharif's assets was mired in controversy because of the inclusion of two members of the military's intelligence agencies. The civil-military crisis clearly overlapped with the executive-judicial tension.[272] In September 2018, the Islamabad High Court suspended the Sharif family's imprisonment terms. Justice Athar Minallah remarked that the NAB could not successfully bring evidence of Nawaz Sharif's ownership of the Avenfield property.[273] This decision was upheld by the Supreme Court in January 2019. Ironically, two years later the high court in London issued the judgment in January 2021 that the property rightfully belonged to the Sharifs.

At home, the inclusion of the two judges who had voted for disqualification of Prime Minister Sharif in the bench formed before the 28 July 2017 judgment was considered to be against the spirit of justice. After expanding the bench from three to five members, only one judge (instead of two) could have produced a majority of three, with two judges already carrying their negative vote.[274] Advocate Khawaja Haris, appearing on behalf of the Sharifs, argued that the two judges who had written dissenting notes against the latter in the 20 April 2017 judgment should not have signed the verdict issued by the five-member bench on 28 July.[275] To this, Justice Khosa replied that the bench members only disagreed over the formation of the JIT, not the disqualification of the incumbent.[276] In public view, arbitrariness penetrated deep into the judicature. For example, General Musharraf was allowed to go abroad in the midst of his trial after the Sindh High Court removed his name from the Exit Control List (ECL). The American contractor, Raymond Davis, who had killed two Pakistani citizens who had allegedly chased his car on a busy road in Lahore, was allowed to leave the country after a court held that the payment of blood money to the victims' families entitled him to his acquittal.[277]

The media considered the judiciary to be more often than not bound by the establishment's will and ethos.[278] After the NRO was declared null and void in 2009, out of more than 8,000 persons accused of corruption, the Supreme Court mainly, if not exclusively, referred Zardari's cases of corruption to the NAB, which dealt with the Swiss scam.[279] Similarly, the Panama Leaks case revealed more than 400 names of Pakistanis who had off-shore companies, including Imran Khan, but only the cases of Nawaz Sharif and his family were hotly pursued. Selective justice became the hallmark of the two chief justices, Iftikhar Chaudhry and Saqib Nisar. The former focused on Zardari and the latter on Nawaz Sharif. The Nawaz Sharif case was a media trial by default because the Supreme Court of Pakistan had let public comments be aired within its precincts outside the courtroom. Both parties would come out to argue their case on the dais placed for that purpose. This pointed to the idea of shaping public opinion prior to announcement of the verdict. The articulate section of the public had already decided that Nawaz was corrupt and that he must go.[280]

From 2008 onwards, an implicit clash of institutions in the context of relations between the executive and judiciary over the issue of interpreting the constitution had provided the overall legal context for the battle of wills between the two wings of state. The virtual stalemate cost both parties in the conflict. The inability of the PPP-led coalition government to take effective political and administrative action in the face of a strident judiciary grossly discredited it and undermined its potential to take the initiative in various fields of public policy. On the other hand, the judiciary's constituency in the lawyers' community felt grossly alienated. Chief Justice Chaudhry faced severe criticism because the decline in the power of representative institutions created fears of another bout of Bonapartism.

While the law served political ends, politics underscored the legal imagination of contenders for power. The Supreme Court's operational dynamics relied on some key variables of indeterminate quality, such as the personal aura of Chief Justice Chaudhry. This amounted to shielding judges from scrutiny at the hands of a public agency at the entry point for appointment and from accountability at the delivery end for issuing verdicts.

Judicial activism in India was understood to be selective about certain issues: religion in the context of Hindutva decisions, Muslim personal law, women's rights such as reservation of seats in *panchayats*, and affirmative action policies relating to Other Backward Classes. However, issues relating to communal violence, with the possible connivance of state institutions, or to civil liberties impinging on preventive detention, evaded the watchful eye of the Supreme Court.[281]

In Pakistan, the Supreme Court's deliberations typically evaded a rights-based discourse. Instead, it followed the 'political' approach of selecting certain issues and neglecting certain others. The latter included the case involving the role of ISI in allocating money to the IJI during the 1990 elections.[282] Former COAS General Mirza Aslam Beg confessed that he received a donation of Rs 140 million from Yunus Habib of Mehran Bank, of which Rs 60 million were spent on the 1990 elections while the remaining Rs 80 million were deposited in the special funds of ISI.[283] In the Asghar Khan case, the Supreme Court directed the federal government in its detailed verdict to take necessary action under the constitution against General (retd) Aslam Beg and ISI chief, Lieutenant-General (retd) Asad Durrani, for their role in facilitating the IJI's success in the 1990 elections.[284] The fact that the Asghar Khan case took altogether twenty-two years to come to a verdict shows the prudence of the judiciary vis-à-vis the establishment.[285]

On 16 December 2019, the military establishment had its darkest day in the judicial history of Pakistan when a special court led by the Peshawar High Court Chief Justice Waqar Ahmed Seth sentenced ex-President General Musharraf to death for committing high treason by declaring a state of emergency on 3 November 2007 in violation of the constitution. The court observed that the accused had 'stubbornly strived ever since the commencement of this trial, to delay, retract and in fact evade it'.[286] It observed that the accused 'deserves exemplary punishment'.[287] It also maintained that 'all involved (if any) in facilitation of the escape of the fugitive accused may also be brought in the net of due course of law'.[288] Musharraf had earlier said on TV that it was COAS General Raheel Sharif (2013–16) who had facilitated his escape to Dubai. Most controversially, para. 66 of the verdict, which was written by Justice Waqar Seth, asked the law enforcement agencies to apprehend the accused; 'if found dead, his corpse should be dragged to the D-Chowk, Islamabad, Pakistan and be hanged for 3 days'.[289]

This dimension of the verdict elicited strong criticism from 'liberal' sections of the legal fraternity and intelligentsia, apart from the fact that there was no provision in the constitution for hanging a corpse, nor the public hanging of a convict. There was a public outcry that this part of the verdict was medieval and brutal. ISPR reported the pain and anguish felt by the rank and file of the armed forces, and criticized the verdict of the special court for 'concluding the trial in haste'.[290] The whole episode jolted the establishment out of complacency right at a time when it felt confident that, with Imran Khan as its proxy, and the 'dissident' judges, including Justice Faez Isa and Justice Shaukat Siddiqui against whom references had been filed in the SJC 'restrained', it had the political initiative in its own hands.

Typically, the phenomenon of inordinate delay of justice, which created a large increase in pending cases in courts at various levels, had led to suggestions for intra-institutional reforms such as increasing the number, and enhancing the quality, of judges along with their staff, making available the latest technology and increasing the number of courts.[291] The institutional reform of the judiciary itself compared poorly with the courts' function of overseeing the executive's performance. In the conference on implementation of the 2009 National Judicial Policy, the Supreme Court registrar, Faqir Hussain, revealed that there were 1.5 million cases pending before the courts, 19,000 of which were pending before the Supreme Court and the high courts.[292] This number increased to 1.8 million by early 2018 under Chief Justice Saqib Nisar, out of which nearly 39,000 cases were pending before the Supreme Court alone.[293] There were thousands of petitions in the higher courts seeking *suo motu* action on public grievances under the two populist chief justices, Choudhry and Nisar. New cases were filed at all levels – 2,643,182 in one year alone (2009–10) – along with a backlog of 1,296,866 cases, while the human rights cell of the Supreme Court daily received more than 200 complaints.[294] Various judicial steps, such as dismissing 110 judges of the higher courts in one go in 2009, as well as the delay in the case against Musharraf for declaring Emergency on 3 November 2007, under Article 6 of the constitution, was widely understood in the context of consolidation of democracy in the country.[295]

The court was preoccupied with expanding the 'external' frontiers of the court system but failed to formulate and implement the 'internal' agenda to rid the courts of procedural bottlenecks and legal black holes in the process of dispensing justice. The transformative potential of the phase of judicial activism remained limited because of the courts' retroactive rather than prospective attitude. The Supreme Court under Justice Hamood-ur-Rehman had similarly fought the last dictator, Yahya, in the famous 1972 Asma Jilani case. However, that did not stop General Zia from taking over in 1977.

More than merely superseding the legislature, the court further befuddled 'the uncertain constitutional resilience' in Pakistan.[296] All along, the Supreme Court faced a moral dilemma in the context of dealing with the judges belonging to the erstwhile military regime, in view of the fact that Chief Justice Choudhry, an icon of justice, had himself taken the oath under Musharraf's PCO in 2000. He, along with fellow judges, passed judgments in favour of Musharraf, by validating his coup, his presidential referendum in 2002 and the 2003 17th Amendment, as well as his retention of the two offices of president and COAS in 2005. After their restoration, the PCO-I judges pushed the PCO-II judges out of the court. The independence of the judiciary thus emerged as a matter of when, rather than why, the judges typically accepted the generals' pressure to take oath on their legal frameworks.

As mentioned earlier, the higher judiciary functions in the framework of modus operandi. In Reema Omer's words: 'As is often the case with such sweeping judgments, the analysis is very powerful but the directions lack teeth… What is hate speech? What are unreasonable restrictions? We get restatement of the law – not much clarity.'[297] The Supreme Court used calculably soft words for asking various institutions in the security sector not to exceed their respective mandates,[298] as well as for dissuading these institutions 'from engaging in any kind of political activity, which includes supporting a political party, faction or individual'.[299] Occasionally, the Supreme Court highlighted the role of the armed forces in civilian matters, such as in the 2017 Faizabad sit-in judgment. Justice Qazi Faez Isa opined:

> Pursuant to the judgment in Air Marshal Asghar Khan's case, the involvement of ISI and of the members of the Armed Forces in politics, media and other 'unlawful activities' should have stopped. Instead, when TLP's *dharna* participants received cash handouts from men in uniform, the perception of their involvement gained traction. The Director General of the Inter-Services Public Relations ('ISPR') has also taken to commenting on political matters: 'history will prove the 2018 general elections were transparent'....[300]

Justice Isa also referred to the 12 May 2007 incident, when unarmed citizens were shot and killed on the eve of Chief Justice Chaudhry's arrival in Karachi.[301] This was indeed very rare on the part of the judiciary to take such a stance which was against the general strategy of modus operandi adopted by the courts. For our purposes, the reaction that followed can be explained with reference to our model of establishmentarian democracy that prevailed in Pakistan for a long time.

Soon after this judgment a resolution was filed against Qazi Faez Isa by a few members of the Punjab Bar Council, much to the legal fraternity's embarrassment. The resolution demanded his removal from the Supreme Court because they believed Justice Isa made the aforementioned claims without any evidence and weakened the country's position by supporting the Indian narrative.[302] Although this resolution was rejected by the Pakistan Bar Council, the judgment delivered by Justice Isa was targeted via several review petitions filed by the PTI, Ministry of Defence, IB, ECP, Railways Minister Sheikh Rashid, the Pakistan Electronic Media Regulatory Authority (PEMRA), Ejaz-ul-Haq and the MQM.[303] Later, references were filed against Justices Isa and Karim Khan Agha under Article 209 of the constitution by the prime minister's special assistant for accountability Shehzad Akbar and his Asset Recovery Unit (ARU). A spokesperson for the law ministry said: 'The (law) ministry on its own has no mechanism to look into the assets of any judge and therefore is bound to process complaints it receives from the ARU and the Federal Board of Revenue (FBR) in the best interest of the country.'[304]

In the aftermath of the issuance of a presidential reference against him, Justice Isa wrote a letter to the president to disclose the reference filed against him, stating that 'selective leaks amount to character assassination, jeopardise my right to due process and fair trial and undermine the institution of the judiciary'.[305] The SJC issued two show-cause notices to Justice Isa, one in connection with properties in the UK in the names of Qazi's wife and their children and the other about writing a letter to the president.[306] While he was acquitted of the allegations under trial, the case of his wife's foreign property was referred to the FBR, which was resented by public opinion in general. The case against Justice Qazi Isa continued to remain in the public eye in 2021. While he was acquitted of the allegations referred to in the presidential reference, the court asked the FBR to start an enquiry into his wife's foreign assets. Justice Isa himself sought to fight his case in the courts, where he was critical of the conduct of his fellow judges and asked for a public hearing of his case. That divided the bench along pro- and anti-Isa judges.

We can observe that the courts' operations in an activist mode carried the potential to discredit civilian governments that operated within the framework of a military-dominated power structure, with scant resources at its disposal to survive in office for long or to safeguard the system from breakdown. At the same time, I have argued that the Supreme Court remained, except in two populist phases, typically wedded to the idea of restraint. It expressed high principles of accountability and demands of justice in court proceedings but gave the final judgments based on a balancing act, thus sometimes letting the government off the hook at critical moments and withdrawing at a point at which it would have undermined the prevalent set-up. The court's behaviour approximated the pattern of modus vivendi as practised in India rather than an exercise in straightjacketing the incumbent government altogether.[307]

Conclusion

This chapter picked up on the eternal question: Why did India become a democracy while Pakistan did not? My argument has rested on the observation that the areas that fell to Pakistan were relatively more administratively ruled than those in the presidencies of Bengal, Bombay and Madras on average. Also, the emergence of a migrant state contributed to discounting the mass mandate as a source of legitimacy because the leadership had already lost its constituency in India and thus had no chance of winning a sizeable number of seats in the new country. Pakistan displayed a mono-ethnic tendency whereby Punjab became the power base of Pakistan as a military recruitment area, and the fallout region of UP in cultural and linguistic terms. Muslims in British India had experienced identity-based politics under separate electorates that cut them off from constituency-based politics. Before and after parti-tion, the Muslim League high command brought down governments in Punjab, KP, East Bengal and Balochistan and undermined provincial lead-erships in general. Ayesha Jalal turned the whole binary of describing Indian democracy and Pakistani authoritarianism on its head by focusing on authoritarianism in both countries, managed well in India but not in Pakistan. However, the consensus remains that the two countries devel-oped along different paths.

In this chapter, I have developed the model of an establishmentarian democracy in Pakistan. The establishment expanded its electoral operations to almost all stages, ranging from the filing of applications for candidates for the polls to the issuance of election results. The establishment supported some electables, 'informally' fielded candidates in certain constituencies, dissuaded others from contesting them, shifted the loyalties of candidates to parties or alliances other than their own, and meanwhile let the word go round about the winning horse. All this led to consolidation of the grey area between the design and practice of electoral democracy in Pakistan. In this process, parliament lost its fiat along with its sovereignty in favour of an establishmentarian democracy.

I have elaborated on 'military metaphysics' to analyse the institutional ethos characterized by the military's thought-patterns and ideological commitments, largely based on autobiographical notes and military studies proper. The tug of war between the civil and military wings of the state peaked under the PPP and PML-N governments (2008–18). I mentioned a series of events, court verdicts and public statements that shaped the contours of the conflict between them. The two sides lived with mutual suspicion, which applied even to the PTI government (2018–), allegedly the establishment's own handiwork. The army's cultivation of Islamists of a large variety in different capacities injected a potentially destabilizing element into the politics of Pakistan. Islamists served the establishment's purpose of opposing mainstream parties in elections and of mobilizing people in pursuit of ideological, programmatic and divinely ordained aims and objectives at the cost of hard-core economic and class-based issues.

Apart from the military establishment, along with its religious cohorts, the judiciary can be considered a force apart. The forte of the army is power and policy. The forte of the judiciary is moral high ground. It moved from the 'statist' position of transcending the constraints of law by upholding the ideology of nationalism, to holding the constitution above parliament. The judicial review has on balance pushed the political class away from taking its rightful place at the top. The combined effect of the influence of the army and the judiciary has been negative for democracy. Courts lent a vocabulary to the political conflict that has kept black letter law at the centre of the discourse, although procedurally the whole debate became an exercise in endless litigation. The institutional dynamics of the military and the judiciary effectively puts them over and above the aggregate will of the people as expressed through the mass mandate. Public interest litigation gave legal, moral and, in the end, political power into the hands of the higher courts, that often led to regime change. A serious jurisdictional crisis arose in the body politic of Pakistan that violated the much-cherished principle of the separation of powers. I have argued that the executive's loss by way of governance remained the jurisdictional gain of the higher courts. Populist judges saw a constituency beyond courts in the public at large, which eagerly awaited a verdict against politicians. I have discussed that Pakistan is an establishmentarian democracy due to the increasingly non-substantive role of parliament. In this context, political parties comprehensively lost initiative as 'agency'.

5

CONSTITUTIONAL DYNAMICS

Introduction

There is a running theme in this book – that law is politics. At one end, constitutionalism shaped politics in the context of parliamentarism, federalism, adult franchise, bicameralism and the rule of public representatives among a host of other provisions relating to public life. At the other end, constitutionalism has experienced formidable challenges from various contenders for power who sought to re-shape it according to their own interests and ideologies.[1] Ideally, the constitution provides a framework of laws and institutions that operates as a mechanism for the resolution of actual or potential conflicts. My argument is that the potential for law to perform the function of conflict resolution has been constrained by various institutional, ideological and political developments that often served opposite ends.

In Pakistan, the juridical problem of power has often drawn on political competition which then got embroiled in the legal net. I address this issue in the context of the long-drawn struggle of parliament for sovereignty, which involved a legal battle with extra-parliamentary forces initially led by civil bureaucracy and later by the army. In this process, the higher courts were given the unenviable role of adjudicating the issue of parliamentary sovereignty from a weak and increasingly vulnerable position vis-à-vis other state apparatuses. The

279

higher courts generally upheld the executive's position as being above parliament. In this process, the doctrine of state necessity and the tacit acceptance of the military's pursuit of constitutional engineering often led to a diarchic arrangement for sharing power, such as in the form of 'presidentializing' the parliamentary system.[2]

Constitutionalism in Pakistan cannot be grasped fully unless the policies and actions of the major players such as the army, Islamic groups, mainstream political parties and ethnic forces are analysed as proponents of different legal and institutional perspectives. Pakistan has been passing through a longer-term, low-intensity constitutional crisis that has underscored the civil–military, religio-sectarian and ethno-nationalist conflicts. The power dynamics has operated through legislation on the floor of elected assemblies, through case law in terms of the courts' law-making potential, through street demonstrations and through the relatively amorphous 'Islamic establishment'.

I discuss constitutionalism in Pakistan in the context of three broad areas of power struggle: parliamentary sovereignty, federalism and Islamism. Firstly, constitutionally speaking, parliament was at the centre of things. There were two principles in the early days of partition: that the cabinet be constituted of members of the constituent assembly; and that the assembly could only be dissolved through its own action. The concept of 'legal-constitutional design', which is independent of politics, remained the dominant perspective in normative terms.[3] Constitutional engineering under military governments undermined the parliamentary system, and weakened the federal project. An increasingly intense ideological socialization led to circumvention of the process of the legal socialization of people, hampered the project of citizen formation, and lowered the potential for meaningful societal input into the process of constitutional development.

Secondly, the institutional framework of federalism was critiqued by ethno-regional forces against the backdrop of the perceived Punjabization of the state. In this context, provincial autonomy provided the basis for re-charting the constitutional framework in the form of the 2010 18th Amendment. While this amendment empowered the majority communities in the four provinces by accommodating their ethnic identities, it also created a demand for the creation of new provinces from minority communities within those provinces. In the presence of constitutional bottlenecks on the way to creating new provinces to accommodate the sub-provincial groups, smaller ethnic communities remained unrepresented in the state.

Thirdly, the politics of Islam led to incremental growth in the religious content of legal and constitutional provisions from the 1949 Objectives Resolution onwards. The constitutional rules of the game for resolution of contentious issues brought in new pressures for Islamization. After the military government of General Zia (1977–85), a spate of judicial cases in the 1990s together with political parties belonging to the Islamic right pushed the agenda of Islamization of laws. I shall argue that this situation has created a religious sub-system in the framework of 'unstable constitutionalism' in Pakistan.[4]

Parliamentary Sovereignty

Apart from being an institution assigned the task of law-making, parliament provides the forum for deliberations on issues and positions beyond the domain of policy. Individual members of parliament have had bonded relations with their respective constituents by way of patronage that has included out-of-term favours, expediting the system, meeting pork-barrel demands and helping the helpless.[5] In theory, parliament represented meta-governance in the sense of a moral universe, in this case defined by territorial, cultural and linguistic representation. Parliament represented its purported but largely non-existent sovereignty. Structurally speaking, parliament has been defunct under military rulers for seventeen years (1958–62, 1969–71, 1977–85 and 1999–2002). It was subjected to the operations of the killer clause Article 58 (2)(b) for nineteen years (1985–97, 2003–10). The representative character of the National Assembly has been low. Firstly, it includes the FPTP system of elections, which transforms small vote margins into big seat margins, often in the case of larger parties.[6] Secondly, multiple candidature for a single constituency, in some cases ten or more candidates fighting elections for one seat, brought down the winner's vote to less than one-third, one-quarter or sometimes an even lower proportion of the total polled votes. In the 2018 elections, the winners got as few votes as 18, 19, 20, 21, 21.3, 22, 22.9, 23.4, 24 and 24.05 per cent of the polled votes. Only 48 out of 271 contenders, a mere 17.71 per cent of winners, got more than 50 per cent of the polled votes. In the past the establishment's input by way of managing the elections often manufactured a majority in the house. Furthermore, it pushed for legislation – for example, for the creation of military courts – and brought elected assemblies to an early end through 'constitutional' or supra-constitutional methods.

Parliamentarism in Pakistan has suffered from arbitrary legislation over its head through presidential ordinances issued under Article 89 of the constitution. In Bilal Mehboob's reckoning, successive governments in Pakistan issued 1,774 ordinances from 1973 to 2019. These included 680 ordinances issued by presidents Zia and Musharraf, 954 ordinances by 16 civilian governments and 140 ordinances by 10 caretaker governments.[7] The PTI government (2018–) alone promulgated 51 ordinances in the first two-and-a-half years of its tenure, which amounted to 55 per cent of all legislation at the federal level. Indeed, in 2019 the PTI government passed 33 laws out of which 27 were ordinances, a rare feat of negative performance by an elected government even by Pakistani standards. It issued 8 ordinances in a single day: 31 October 2019.[8]

From the beginning, the issue of parliamentary sovereignty became the apple of discord between the elected and un-elected institutions of state. The 1996 Al-Jihad Trust case served as a watershed in the march towards judicial autonomy in the context of the appointment of judges. The way the 19th Amendment tilted the balance in favour of the judiciary at the expense of parliament can be taken as an example of an implicit clash of institutions, especially as the Supreme Court later sent home prime ministers Gilani (2012) and Nawaz Sharif (2017), while they had the support of the majority on the floor of the National Assembly.

The constitutional source of legitimacy in terms of mass mandate has been the greatest political resource for parliament. Discussion of electoral politics in Chapter 3 provided us with the clue to territorial constituency politics, local power dynamics, and the ways and means of subverting the free and fair character of elections at the hands of both military and civilian rulers. Following Migdal, we look at the state as one of the contenders for power, which clearly reflected the fact that all eggs were not in one basket.[9] The 'establishment' clearly lost out in the elections in 1970, in 1988 and in 2008, when its game plan flopped and its protégés did not make it to the top in the end.

While dealing with the conflict, co-habitation and collision between the political elite and the establishment, we will take up the corruption–accountability nexus as an instrument in the hands of successive military regimes to gain legitimacy by de-legitimizing the previous civilian governments led by, for example, Iskander Mirza (1958), Z. A. Bhutto (1977), Junejo (1988), Benazir Bhutto (1990), Nawaz Sharif (1993) and again Benazir Bhutto (1996). In the contemporary framework of politics, where media has had an extremely powerful role in exposing corruption scandals, incumbent governments were daily taken to task for bad governance.

Pakistan can be located on the constitutional matrix of the contemporary world as a typical postcolonial state immersed in its European heritage of legal philosophy. It is necessary to investigate the meaning of constitutionalism in the context of the power struggle on the ground. Even after seven-and-a-half decades, the broad contours of the nation's constitutional edifice are still being shaped, and the future remains uncertain in this regard. Pakistan reflects an inherent contradiction between 'external' and 'internal' sources of jurisprudence, represented by the colonial legacy on the one hand and the local, historical and traditional – in sum 'national' – wellsprings of legal norms and practices on the other. Similarly, there is a difference in the focus of the political discourse between individual citizens on the one hand and the community defined in ethnic, religious or sectarian terms on the other. Pakistan experienced a transition from a rights-based discourse, which addressed the issues of equal protection under the law, to an identity-based projection of legal and political agendas. My aim is to discuss the unfinished task of constitution-making in Pakistan in a way that reflects the incompatible pressures and strategies of multiple actors on the political stage.

Constitutionalism in Pakistan has operated as both an independent and a dependent variable vis-à-vis the power dynamics. As an independent variable, it provided the foundational structure of the new state in the form of the 1935 India Act, as amended by the 1947 Independence of India Act. The internally differentiated legal–institutional matrix of the Act meant that all meaningful power would be exercised by public office holders and the administrative hierarchy. The sanctity of law had been cultivated as a source of instruction for rules of public behaviour for a hundred years after the British annexation of northwest India by the middle of the nineteenth century. Muslim nationalism in pursuit of Pakistan represented an ideological input into what was a purportedly 'secular' ruling set-up of British India.

The separatist project of carving a state out of India, which was a 2,000-year-old continuous civilizational entity, was a task of gigantic proportions. It involved the issue of defining Pakistan, mobilizing a vast number of people in pursuit of the cause for a Muslim homeland – in millions of cases, away from their homes and hearths – and negotiating accordingly with the British government. Compared to this 'seceding' state, India operated as a successor state, with its political centre continuing to be located at Delhi and its institutional apparatus remaining largely intact. Indian nationalism was defined more by default – with reference to territory, history, tradition and (most recently) administrative unity under the British – than by design, as in the case of Pakistan.

Partition did not end in 1947. The artefacts of Indian civilization, such as languages, literatures, arts, music and dance at one end and ethnic, caste, sub-caste, tribal and sub-tribal loyalties at the other, continued to operate through social, cultural and political practices in Pakistan. Not surprisingly, the state managers embarked on a long journey of cultural partitioning through Islamization, which brought about significant changes in the constitutional framework. The new ideologically orientated innovations were superimposed on a relatively cohesive legal framework, thereby adding multiple rights and policy directives that cut across each other.

The power-wielding bureaucratic apparatus first ruled the country under the constitutional 'cover' for a decade but then gradually lost the initiative to the army at the top of the state's decision-making forums. The army leadership, in turn, took up an ambitious project of constitutional engineering through the 1962 Constitution, the 1985 8th Amendment, and the 2003 17th Amendment. These constitutional initiatives essentially centralized power in the hands of the federal government at the cost of provinces, and presidentialized the form of government directly in 1962 and indirectly in the latter cases. Correspondingly, the elected political leadership passed the 1973 Constitution, the 1997 13th Amendment, and the 2010 18th Amendment in an effort to restore parliamentarism. However, some constitutional innovations of the military ruler Zia relating to Islam remained on the statute book, thwarting all attempts of civilian rulers to bring about even procedural changes. Similarly, Musharraf felt confident that no parliament could overturn the twenty-nine amendments made by him.[10] Although the army abrogated or suspended the constitution several times and sought to change it to suit its preferred model of government, each time it had to deal with the judiciary for validation of its takeover. That rendered the role of the higher courts controversial inasmuch as they often earned the opprobrium of the political class for bestowing legitimacy on Bonapartist generals.

While the 1985 8th Amendment bestowed the power of amendment to parliament, the Supreme Court held in 1997 that such power could not be unlimited.[11] Justice Jawwad Khawaja similarly attacked the concept of parliamentary sovereignty, relying on a House of Lords judgment and concluded that such a system was 'losing currency even inside Britain where it originated'.[12] The 2015 21st Amendment to the constitution established military courts for two years, which brought the army to the forefront. The sunset clause in the amendment did not carry much significance, given the extension provided to the military courts through the 23rd Amendment two years later.[13]

Parliamentarism: Fact and Fiction

How to measure the operational effectiveness and institutional autonomy of parliament in Pakistan? One way is to examine the manner in which emerging jurisprudential thinking and practice attributed a superior position to both the state and the constitution over and above parliament. I argue that the legal philosophy of the new country purportedly stood on these two pillars.

Typically the odds were heavily weighed against parliament throughout the post-independence period. I have noted how the establishment shaped legislation while lobbying from outside parliament – for example, creating military courts to deal with cases of terrorism. This points to the need to go beyond the written word of law to understand the dynamics of power. It is generally argued that a constitution is the embodiment of the way the state seeks to resolve conflicts and that it constitutes the relations of power in society.[14] However, this view is not amenable to straightforward application to the postcolonial world. The rule of law in British India was exercised by a colonial government that was only remotely 'covered' by Acts of Parliament in London. Colonial government was a bureaucracy par excellence.[15] The exercise of power by the civil bureaucracy cushioned by the army did not necessarily correspond to the constitution's formal provisions.[16] Indeed, the constitutional source of legitimacy in the form of the rule of public representatives emerged in a real sense only on the eve of independence. This came at the end of a long process of transition from semi-representative to representative to semi-responsible to fully responsible governments corresponding to the establishment of limited self-rule at various levels.

Constitutionally speaking, state formation in Pakistan passed through two processes: the 1946 elections for provincial assemblies that in turn elected the constituent assembly, and the transfer of sovereign power to that assembly, legally and formally. It was taken for granted that this constitutional process would shape the contours of the emerging framework of the ruling set-up in the new dominion of Pakistan along the lines of the parliamentary form of government. However, the parallel and initially stronger structure of bureaucratic power operated with relative impunity, thereby leaving an indelible imprint on the way constitutionalism was conceived and operationalized in later years.

The state in Pakistan often opted for reform, suspension, abrogation or reformulation of the constitution according to the priorities of the changing dynamics of the ruling dispensations. India is an exception that proves the rule that postcoloniality typically puts the newly founded state above the constitution. Deification of the state in the Third World has been ascribed to the ruling elite's fear of the existential threat to its security.[17] The idea is that, ultimately, law is dispensable whereas the state is not. As discussed later in this chapter, the verdicts in court cases dealing with the dissolution of elected assemblies at the hands of the bureaucratic, political, and military rulers often relied on the doctrine of state necessity, which justified violation of the constitution ostensibly for a short time and for limited purposes. I want to argue that the jurisprudential upgrading of the state above the constitution in this context, combined with contradictions between British Common Law and Islamic provisions, was bound to dilute the binding character of black letter law in the emerging statecraft in Pakistan. After all, constitutions are inert on their own unless they are operationalized by those at the helm of affairs in their specific ways.[18]

286

The Indian Constitution has been described as a 'seamless web' with contradictory strands such as democracy and social revolution, as well as national integration through secularism and the preservation of the identity-based, minority–majority conundrum of public policy.[19] In Pakistan, the web was characterized even more strongly by contradictory strands as the emerging religious/constitutional provisions undercut various other provisions concerning equality between religious communities and genders. It is not surprising that an endless process of interpretation and counter interpretation of the constitution characterizes the legal history of Pakistan. This phenomenon defined the debate between the ritualistic and civilizational approaches to Islam based on the rule of Sharia and Muslim identity respectively. At the institutional level, this debate served to define the conflict between the judiciary and the executive. For years, the executive had an upper hand because it controlled the judiciary through its power of the appointment and transfer of judges of the higher courts. However, the Supreme Court's verdict in the Al-Jihad Trust case in 1996 guaranteed institutional autonomy for the judiciary.

Under Chief Justice Sajjad Ali Shah (1993–7) and Chief Justice Iftikhar Chaudhry (2005–7, 2009–13), the judiciary rebounded with renewed vigour. The 2010 18th and 19th Amendments, which streamlined the appointment of judges by the Judicial Commission of Pakistan (JCP), virtually rendered the role of the parliamentary committee redundant. This tension remained unsettled as the Chaudhry court, which had achieved pre-eminence on the issue of the independence of the judiciary in 2007, succumbed to deep controversy in 2011–12.[20] The Chaudhry court was criticized for issuing too many *suo motu* notices, for harassment of the bureaucracy, for dismissing Prime Minister Gilani in 2012, and for taking only half-measures in the Asghar Khan case relating to allocation of election funds to the PML-N leader Nawaz Sharif among others in the 1990 elections against the PPP.

The story of constitutionalism in Pakistan in more than seven decades is one of a struggle between the political elite and the state elite to make the written law conform to their own respective preferences and priorities. The central issue of this conflict revolved around the question of parliamentary sovereignty. As a visible symbol of a shift in power to the constituent assembly, Section 8 (C) of the

1947 Independence of India Act sought to eliminate the extraordinary powers of the governor general provided under the 1935 India Act. However, unlike in India, the governor general continued to be the chief executive in Pakistan. The difference between the two countries in this matter can be partially attributed to the fact that the father of the nation, Jinnah, became governor general. He enjoyed all the meaningful power of that office. Across the border, Nehru's charisma as prime minister empowered parliament whereas Governor General Mountbatten was merely a symbol of a dying imperialism rather than of an ascendant independent statehood.

The governor general in Pakistan had the power of key appointments, ranging from cabinet ministers, governors, law officers and higher court judges to supreme military positions. Indeed, the *Report of the Basic Principles Committee* of 1952 recommended that cabinet ministers and other public office holders should hold office in the pleasure of the governor general. In 1954, the constituent assembly amended Sections 9, 10, 10-A and 10-B of the 1947 Act to eliminate the governor general's power to dismiss the Council of Ministers. This so-called 'constitutional coup' turned out to be costly because it was countered by a 'civilian coup' in the form of the dissolution of the constituent assembly itself by Governor General Ghulam Mohammad.

Partially complying with the federal court's verdict in the 1955 Special Reference case (discussed later in this chapter), the governor general called for a constituent convention to be held on 10 May 1955 in order to validate the Emergency Powers Ordinance No. 9 issued by him under the 1935 India Act (Section 42). However, the court disapproved of the idea of a constituent convention and ordered him to have the constituent assembly re-elected under Section 8 of the act. The second constituent assembly thus elected passed the 1956 Constitution, which provided a significant role for the president, mainly as a compromise between the proponents of parliamentary sovereignty and the defenders of 'the establishment'. The real power remained in the hands of the bureaucrat Governor General Ghulam Mohammad and Governor General and President Iskandar Mirza, who together dismissed six prime ministers.

Conflict between the head of state and the head of government cast a shadow on the country's politics. At the same time, it became clear that it was constitutionalism that defined the state because bureaucrats could not rule in their own name, a fact that guaranteed a space for parliament even though its sovereignty was circumscribed. The 1962 Constitution took the matter of presidential domination of state authority still further, whereby the president shared the legislative authority at the highest level with the National Assembly (Article 19).[21] The president had emergency powers to dissolve the National Assembly, a provision that led to re-enactment of similar legislation in the following years at the hands of successive military presidents. Parliamentary sovereignty was rendered into a figment of politicians' imagination. The provision for impeachment of the president was tantamount to harassment of legislators. If the sponsors of an impeachment resolution failed to win a simple majority of the National Assembly, they would be removed as members of the house.

The 1962 Constitution divested parliament not only of its output function by way of legislation in this way but also of the input function of mass polls in the absence of an adult franchise to elect the parliament. Ayub devised an ingenious method of election by means of an electoral college consisting of local councillors at the union level, the Basic Democrats, who then voted for the national and provincial assemblies and the president (Article 165). In this way, neither parliament nor the president was directly representative of the initial voters.[22] The 1968–9 anti-Ayub movement that toppled the government finally buried the presidential form of government. However, its adherents from outside the political class have continued to support it to this day, and the subsequent militant rulers, Zia and Musharraf, subordinated parliament to the president within the juridical framework of parliamentary democracy.

The 1973 Constitution restored parliamentarism in post-Bangladesh Pakistan, whereby the prime minister became a powerful chief executive. The president was a ceremonial head of state, with no influence over legislation or the selection of prime minister. He had to abide by the prime minister's advice in all matters. Provisions such as naming a successor in a no-confidence move against the prime minister purportedly aimed at creating political stability. Critics of Z. A. Bhutto perceived the provisions giving the prime minister such prominence as a model of self-serving parliamentary sovereignty. The constitution was altered substantially by the 1985 8th Amendment and the 2003 17th Amendment, along with incorporation of several ordinances issued by the military governments of General Zia (1977–85) and General Musharraf (1999–2002) respectively. Unlike the 1956 and 1962 Constitutions, which were abrogated, the 1973 Constitution was only suspended by the coup makers in 1977 and 1999. This happened ostensibly because of Article 6, which heavily sanctioned abrogation of the constitution as treason. Also, there was the fear that without the 1973 Constitution – the only consensus-based constitution in the history of Pakistan – a real feat of performance by public representatives, the nation might never again achieve agreement on any constitutional formula. After the 1985 elections were held on the way to civilianization of Zia's military regime, the project of keeping political power and policy initiatives outside parliament was euphemistically couched in discourse about restoring the balance of power between the president and the prime minister.[23]

The 8th Amendment, passed on 30 December 1985 before the lifting of martial law and largely based on the Revival of the Constitution Order issued earlier by Zia in March that year, provided for presidential power to dissolve the National Assembly by introducing Article 58(2)(b). The president could now 'dissolve the National Assembly in his discretion' after a vote of no confidence against the prime minister was passed or if a situation arose whereby the 'government of the federation cannot be carried on in accordance with the provisions of the Constitution'. It also provided that the validity of anything done by the president at his discretion would not be called into question on any grounds whatsoever. The president could appoint a prime minister at his discretion for the next five years. Article 90(2) prevented parliament 'from conferring by law functions on authorities other than the President' and thus tied the hands of the national legislature in the matter of redistributing state authority either horizontally or vertically.

The most far-reaching and substantive aspect of the 8th Amendment related to the indemnification clause (Article 270-A), whereby all orders, ordinances and martial-law regulations, as well as the presidential referendum of 19 December 1984, were validated as part of the statute book. Parliament was deemed to have passed all these laws spread over eight years of martial law. Ingeniously, parliament was renamed *Mailis-e-Shoora* (Advisory Council). The new nomenclature transformed its role from a law-making body to a mere advisory body that had typically served the Amir in early Islamic history. The 8th

Amendment transformed the state into a semi-presidential system and dwarfed parliament to a secondary role in the authority structure.

Article 58(2)(b) of the 8th Amendment played havoc with the nation because, in less than a decade, four elected governments were dismissed consequent upon dissolution of the National Assembly at the hands of presidents Zia (1988), Ishaq (1990, 1993) and Leghari (1996).[24] Soon after the election of Nawaz Sharif as prime minister in 1997, parliament passed the 13th Amendment, which deleted Article 58(2)(b) and its counterpart for the provinces, Article 112(2)(b). The Nawaz Sharif government was toppled in 1999 and the 2002 elections were held, and President Musharraf got the 17th Amendment passed by parliament in 2003, which restored Article 58(2)(b). The new civilian government of the PPP, elected in 2008, initiated a comprehensive process of constitutional reform that once again deleted Article 58(2)(b) in an effort to restore parliamentary sovereignty through the 2010 18th Amendment. The president was once again denied the power of a chief executive. He was supposed to act on the binding advice of the prime minister for appointment of armed services chiefs and higher court judges, even as the power of judicial appointments now shifted to the Judicial Commission.

The configuration of the power elite ruling the country after the 2013 elections was based on a consensus on the issue of parliamentary sovereignty. However, under Imran Khan (2018–), parliament lost its credibility for two reasons. First, the impression of rigging of the 2018 elections was endorsed by the national and international media along with the opposition. Under these circumstances the National Assembly and the leader of the house were considered 'selected' rather than 'elected'. Second, the 'establishment' carried the image of a king-maker as the source of the PTI government's power and privilege even while Article 58(2)(b) was no longer on the statue book.

Newberg has argued that Pakistan had been characterized by incomplete constitution-making that, in turn, put the burden of interpretation of the constitution on various institutions, including the bureaucracy and the army; in this way the courts along with lawyers reconstituted the state in legal terms.[25] This reconstruction essentially reflected the de facto situation of power dynamics on the ground rather than the de jure situation couched in the provisions of the constitution. It acknowledged the perceived superior authority of civil or military executives as compared to parliament, and thus underscored the rule of the state elite without societal input.[26] The issue was far from clear, however, because individual judges continued to vacillate between the two positions of upholding the executive and legislative pre-eminence.

For our purposes, parliamentary sovereignty is understood as a symbol of the supremacy of the law-making body both operationally in the form of an unhindered process of legislation and structurally by way of safely completing its tenure, managing its own agenda and following its own rules of game. The clearest example of not upholding the former was the supra-parliamentary pressure to pass the 2015 21st Amendment that led to the creation of military courts.

Structurally speaking, there is a long series of dissolutions of the national legislature. In the first major case of dissolution of the constituent assembly in 1954, the Chief Court of Sindh refused to entertain the official argument that Section 223-A of the 1935 India Act did not receive the governor general's assent per Section 6(3) of the 1947 Independence of India Act, and was therefore not law. The federal court reversed the decision and agreed with the government's view that the governor general's assent was necessary for making Section 223-A a proper law, thereby rendering 46 Acts invalid and creating a huge constitutional vacuum.[27] When the governor general issued Emergency Powers Ordinance No. 9 to give his assent retrospectively to these acts, the ordinance was invalidated.[28] Later, he filed a Reference in the federal court to extricate himself from the legal mess. In view of the negative consequences of the legal void, the court justified the dissolution of the constituent assembly based on 'the common law [of] civil or state necessity'. But it denied the right to 'give' the constitution to the governor general because that was the prerogative of the constituent assembly. The judiciary emerged as the custodian of the constitutionality of the political system at this stage, a role that it persistently – although often controversially – played for several decades after 1954.

Interestingly, governments all along deferred to the judiciary in an ultimate sense, despite the judiciary's critical and at times condemnatory attitude towards the political leadership. This attitude can be attributed to an 'insider' perception about the higher courts as part of the state apparatus that consisted of selected (not elected) judicial officers. Indeed, some senior judges initially belonged to the prestigious Indian Civil Service itself. The courts in turn bestowed legitimacy on the state, which enormously benefited from this 'judicial largesse'.[29]

In the famous 1958 Dosso case, concerning the first military coup, the Supreme Court observed that the new Laws (Continuance in Force) Order was 'a law-creating organ', with reference to Kelsen's theory of legitimation of a successful revolution through its own volition.[30] By default, judicial thinking has taken long strides towards declaring the rule of black letter law in supersession of the rule of public representatives as a source of legitimacy. This applied to both the 'necessity' approach in 1955 and the revolutionary self-legitimation approach in 1958. When the Supreme Court declared the 1969 coup an act of usurpation in the 1972 Asma Jilani case, Z. A. Bhutto's civilian government was already in place, and the reality on the ground was no longer in favour of the coup maker. Curiously, the court also criticized legitimation of the 1958 coup based on Kelsen's theory. In its opinion, this theory was not universally accepted as either a source of modem jurisprudence or as an extension of the recognition of state sovereignty in international law to the legitimacy of a regime at home; the latter could take place only through the municipal laws of the state under consideration.[31]

In the 1977 Begum Nusrat Bhutto case, the verdict took a position that was midway between that of the 1958 Dosso case – self-legitimation of a successful coup – and the 1972 Asma Jilani case – coup as an act of usurpation. The case focused on acknowledgment of the tenacity and legitimacy of the new legal order – the new *grundnorm* as a meta-legal fact – and usurpation of constitutional authority by extra-constitutional means, respectively. The Supreme Court harkened back to the 1955 Special Reference Case and justified Zia's martial law as a constitutional deviation following the doctrine of necessity. As Wolf-Phillips paraphrased, Pakistan moved along several jurisprudential positions: 'the safety of the state is the supreme law' (1955); 'nothing succeeds like success' (1958); 'usurpers, beware' (1972); and 'constitutional deviation dictated by necessity' (1977).[32]

Clash of Institutions

Dissolution of the National Assembly by the president in 1988, 1990, 1993 and 1996 elicited court verdicts that generally confirmed the need to resort to a fresh mandate under Article 58(2)(b). Judicial review became an instrument of regime change through elections: from Junejo to Benazir Bhutto (1988), to Nawaz Sharif (1990), again to Benazir Bhutto (1993), and again to Nawaz Sharif (1997). The Supreme Court's judgment in the 2000 Zafar Ali Shah case validated Musharraf's coup in 1999 on the basis of state necessity in line with the 1955, 1977, 1988, 1990, and 1997 cases, following the principle of *salus populi suprema lex*.[33] In a spirit of a clear extra-constitutional mode of thinking, the Supreme Court gave Musharraf powers to amend the constitution, similar to Zia in the 1977 Begum Nusrat Bhutto case. Indeed, Musharraf was deemed to be holding a constitutional office.[34]

In recent years, Pakistan has experienced a strong current of judicialization of politics running through public interest litigation. Chief Justice Iftikhar Chaudhry essentially drew on his immense mass popularity. In that capacity, he was able to override parliament's role as a sovereign body in the debate about the basic structure of the constitution, which largely reflected the Indian debate on this issue from the 1973 Kesavananda Bharati case onwards. The potential of this controversy to discredit the concept of parliamentary sovereignty was real, especially as the court upheld the supremacy of the constitution. In this way, constitutionalism emerged as the moral preserve of the judiciary over and above parliament and thus became a default function of the prevalent institutional design. When a short order of the Supreme Court of Pakistan disqualified Prime Minister Gilani from holding office on 19 June 2012, it made parliament a 'lame-duck' institution.

The cause of parliamentary sovereignty that previously suffered at the hands of, first, the bureaucrat–politicians and then the Bonapartist generals, now faced a strident judiciary that was widely criticized for encroaching on the domain of the executive and the legislature. Gilani was held responsible for contempt of court for not writing the letter to the Swiss court for investigation of President Asif Ali Zardari. However, the revived corruption case against Zardari was most visibly heard by the Supreme Court under, Iftikhar Chaudhry. On 26 April 2012, the court sentenced Gilani to internment till he left the courtroom a minute or so afterwards. But this led to wild speculation about the real consequences of this verdict. The PML-N and the PTI held protests against his continuation in office inside and outside parliament respectively. Subsequently, the speaker of the National Assembly gave her ruling in favour of Gilani's continuation as prime minister. This led to fresh litigation in the Supreme Court, which finally overruled the speaker's ruling on 19 June 2012. This was widely interpreted as a clash of institutions, between the judiciary and parliament. Only a few weeks earlier, one property tycoon, Malik Riaz, had levelled serious allegations against the chief justice's son, Arsalan Chaudhry, for accepting Rs 340 million from him as bribe to get court cases fixed through his father. Critics of the chief justice led a whispering campaign which suggested that his disqualification verdict against Gilani was a reaction to the charges levelled against his son.

Disqualification of Gilani was termed a judicial coup by the international media. At home, this led to speculation about the formation of a caretaker government for holding elections that could ostensibly tackle corruption before going to the polls. This had happened in Bangladesh in 2009 when a caretaker government, supported by the army from behind the scenes, postponed elections and initiated a process of accountability for corruption. The general impression was that democracy had been weakened by the use of a legal instrument for the removal of the prime minister, who enjoyed the majority's support on the floor of parliament.

The National Assembly emerged as a fractured institution at the hands of extra-parliamentary forces, earlier the army and now the judiciary. The treasury and opposition benches often resorted to brinkmanship, even as they were conscious of the risk of losing out to the non-parliamentary forces. The level of bellicosity between the PPP-led government and the PML-N opposition under President Zardari reflected the past hostility between the two parties in the 1990s. The degeneration of relations between parliament and the Supreme Court in 2012 pointed to the possibility of another cycle of collapse of civilian rule, leading to an overt or covert role for the army. As for the dismissal of Prime Minister Gilani, critics found in it a case of short-circuiting the disqualification procedure as provided by the constitution, which required routing the matter through the chief election commissioner. The government accepted the verdict with reservations about a non-political institution bringing about a political change at the top. Meanwhile, the Supreme Court was criticized for legislation through case law. The 18th Amendment, which provided for a parliamentary committee and a judicial commission for the appointment of judges, led to a backlash from the Supreme Court against the parliament's oversight function.

The Chaudhry court in Pakistan made it clear, if not in letter then certainly in spirit, that the interpreters of the constitution were above the makers of the constitution. In the case of the NRO, Gilani had taken the plea that the president enjoyed immunity under Article 248 of the constitution and that was why he had not written the letter to the Swiss court. The Supreme Court refused to accept this argument.

Meanwhile, the Memogate case further muddied the waters in 2011. Nawaz Sharif filed a case for investigation into a memo, self-confessedly written by one Pakistani American, Mansoor Ijaz, and allegedly dictated by Pakistan's ambassador in Washington at the behest of President Zardari. In this memo, President Zardari allegedly sought help from the US military in the wake of the perceived Bonapartist moves of the Pakistan army after the Abbottabad operation that killed Osama bin Laden on 2 May 2011. The Supreme Court established a commission of enquiry to which COAS General Ashfaq Parvez Kayani and ISI chief General Ahmed Shuja Pasha submitted their affidavits confirming the existence of the memo. Prime Minister Gilani retaliated by calling the submission of affidavits illegal and unconstitutional, and sacked the defence secretary for processing these affidavits without consulting his superiors. This led to the lowest point in civil–military relations under a civilian dispensation, with the possible exception of the post-Kargil phase of politics in 1999 when Prime Minister Nawaz Sharif and COAS General Musharraf displayed complete distrust for each other in public.[35] While the two sides managed to draw back from the precipice in the following weeks, the judiciary continued to push the Memogate investigation to its logical end for some time.

The trust deficit between the government and the judiciary further deepened as the Supreme Court twice summoned the prime minister to NRO hearings. Indeed, the whole process of litigation on the issue of the NRO resonated throughout civil society, which lent tacit strength to the Supreme Court in the context of the 'corruption–accountability nexus'. While the court trial passed through high and low phases vis-à-vis an increasingly beleaguered government, the media trial of the president and the prime minister on the issue of corruption carried on in full swing. The party representatives tried vociferously to defend their respective leaders on a host of issues relating to their constituencies, policy frameworks and alleged corrupt practices. In this way, the 'formal' political actors were engaged in a losing battle to safeguard their public profile, while the 'informal' but far more powerful players – the army and the judiciary – typically if not always remained safe from trial by the media. This was at least partly due to the legal bar against placing these two institutions in disrepute. Thus, the media attack led to a further loss of balance in the already skewed relations between the establishment on the one hand and parliament on the other. The protagonists of parliamentary democracy were clearly caught on the wrong foot.

While the court trial and media trial put the political class, especially the PPP, in the dock, there soon followed on the heels of the Malik Riaz–Arsalan Chaudhry case a new wave of what can be termed 'bar trial'. A large majority of lawyers stood in solidarity with the chief justice against what they considered a vilification campaign against him. They barred the critics of Iftikhar Chaudhry from entering the premises of the bar, including Asma Jahangir and Yaseen Azad, the two former presidents of the Supreme Court Bar Association. This bar-from-the-Bar approach put those lawyers who would consider taking up the case of Malik Riaz against Arslan Chaudhry at risk. This approach virtually barred the way to justice in terms of pre-judging the case and the guilt of the parties.

The post-19 June relations between the bar and the bench harmed relations between the executive and judiciary tremendously. The drama of the perceived conflict between these institutions can be viewed against the template of separation of powers. In this context, the judiciary's operational dynamics sometimes ended up simultaneously taking on the two intertwined institutions of the executive and the legislature. Not surprisingly, the two reacted together to what was understood by them as judicial overreach. The speaker of the National Assembly had given a clear ruling against the disqualification of Prime Minister Gilani, but to no avail. In the subsequent vote of confidence on the floor, Gilani's successor, Raja Pervaiz Ashraf, got 211 votes as opposed to the opposition candidate's 89 votes out of the 300 polled votes. The PPP's co-chairman, President Zardari, continued to be a bastion of power for the government. It is hard to imagine a PPP-led coalition surviving the court verdict otherwise. Soon, however, Lahore High

Court debarred Zardari from performing the two roles of President of Pakistan and co-chairman of his party. Later, in the Panama Leaks case, the Supreme Court's jurisdiction was invoked under Article 184(3) of the constitution, which led to disqualification of Prime Minister Nawaz Sharif under Articles 62(1)(f) and 63(2) of the constitution as well as the 1999 National Accountability Ordinance. The court's ultimate reasoning was based on the acquisition of assets beyond means by the Sharif family and its refusal to show on record how the said assets were acquired. As per Justice Asif Saeed Khosa, when Prime Minister Sharif was instructed to show the record of several of such assets, he simply stated that 'no such record existed'.[36] Hence, he was declared to be neither '*Sadiq*' (honest) nor '*Ameen*' (upright).

One can argue that constitutionalism in Pakistan reflects, more than the power structure of society does, the development of a body of laws as well as an apparatus for the exercise of these laws that puts in place a somewhat autonomous institutional framework outside parliament.[37] Whereas military presidents took away parliamentary sovereignty whenever they moved to civilianize their regimes (1962, 1985 and 2003), civilian governments restored parliamentary sovereignty in 1973, 1997 and 2010 respectively. The judiciary's intervention arose because of the conflict between the supporters of parliament and extra-parliamentary forces. By and large, if not in every case, the judiciary shared the perspective of the state elite, as opposed to the political elite, by upholding 'constitutionalism' over and above 'parliamentarism' in the sense of the unconstrained rule of public representatives. Whenever this instrument of supra-parliamentary control was not available to the state elite, the military took over directly. The judiciary upheld 'statism' over constitutionalism by frequently approving dissolution of the National Assembly as an act of state necessity. However, the courts preserved the idea of the constitutionality of the state for legitimacy purposes. This fact was brought out at times by the minority opinion in court verdicts such as in 1954, 1955, 1990 and 1993. At other times, the Supreme Court restored the prime minister (1993), because he was accountable to the National Assembly and not to the president.

The power dynamics of the country, as reflected through both the personal and institutional roles of judges, clearly defined the expanded parameters of the currently operative jurisprudential thinking. Ultimately, the Supreme Court's award of the power of amendment in the constitution to two military dictators, General Zia and General Musharraf, was tantamount to de-acknowledging the role of parliament as an institution that enjoyed exclusive authority over law-making at the federal level. It is here that the subservience of the judiciary to the diktat of a military ruler reached its nadir and parliamentarism was pushed down the hill.

Federalism and Provincial Autonomy

Federalism in the new states has been strongly considered a recipe for the disintegration of the nation by the state managers, but wholesomely supported by those at the wrong end of the equation who conceived the country as a multi-nation rather than a nation-state. In comparative terms, federalism has been understood as the way to promote choice, foster participation, facilitate competition and ward off a national Leviathan.[38] The conflict between federalists and nationalists has been traced to arguments that allow that 'means bleed into ends'.[39] It has been argued that provincial autonomy and national power have been wrongly treated as ends whereas these should be treated as means to the end of 'intrastatutory federalism' or 'cooperative federalism' based on 'integrated regulatory structure'.[40] Katharine Adeney's comparative study of federalism in India and Pakistan brings out the distinct features of the two systems that contributed to different outcomes. She mentions the Muslim League's consociational appeal to federalism in British India, which reflected a community-based approach because of the dispersal of Muslims all around.[41] Not surprisingly, federalism in Pakistan has been territorially agnostic. The federating units could not be acknowledged as bearers of ethnic identity. The state remained inimical to the idea of reorganizing provinces on a linguistic basis.

One can bring in an extra-constitutional, even foreign, input as a factor in creating a dysfunctional impact on the federal arrangement for the distribution of resources. Boni and Adeney pointed to a disconnect between the decentralizing nature of the 18th Amendment, as opposed to the centralizing pressures of the China–Pakistan Economic Corridor (CPEC), whereby China favoured dealing with Pakistan as one unit. Indeed, the authors claim that China pressed for reversion of the 18th Amendment itself.[42] While Islamabad dealt with the infrastructural projects directly, with an alleged bias in favour of the so-called Western route that passed through Punjab and Sindh, both KP and Balochistan demanded activation of the Eastern route for establishing the communications network. Some even called the CPEC the China–Punjab Economic Corridor. Not surprisingly, KP and Balochistan asked for control of the project to be transferred to the Council of Common Interests (CCI), where chief ministers of all provinces were represented.[43]

Two factors were responsible for keeping the federation in Pakistan in flux. First, ethnic communities overlapped the provincial boundaries. Second, the cult of unity underscored the non-acceptance of the idea of reorganizing provinces on a linguistic basis. This kept the constitutional bottleneck intact, barring the way to re-defining and re-shaping the provinces. As opposed to the Indian model of asymmetrical federalism, which aimed at avoiding the anomaly of smaller states overriding the larger states, Pakistan's model of symmetrical federalism was not sensitive to the geographical size, demographic strength and resource base of the federating units.

The evolving constitutional thinking among the opposition's ranks under Musharraf served as steps to the passage of the 18th Amendment in 2010. The 2006 Charter of Democracy signed by Nawaz Sharif and Benazir Bhutto in London broadly shaped the agenda in this context. The 18th Amendment included various demands of the Charter, such as doing away with Article 58(2)(b), abolishing the Concurrent List, giving representation to minorities in the Senate, and appointing judges through a judicial commission. The demand for integrating FATA with KP was accepted only a decade later. Instructively, demand for the accountability of ISI, Military Intelligence (MI) and other security agencies was neither pressed for nor publicly aired after the formation of the PPP/PML-N coalition government in 2008. Apart from the Charter, the 2009 7th NFC (National Finance Commission) Award was a major milestone in the march towards federalism.[44]

Was the federal government adversely affected by the 18th Amendment after transferring forty legislative subjects to the provinces? Islamabad continued to preside over a centralist bureaucracy operating in the provinces, along with enjoying a lion's share in the revenue-raising power that still lay in the hands of the centre. Indeed, the federal government lost out not vertically, i.e. vis-à-vis the provinces, but horizontally, i.e. vis-à-vis the two state apparatuses and the judiciary. The army was not cognizant of what it considered dissipation of state authority in the form of the 18th Amendment. As opposed to the perceived diminution of the federal government's fiscal and administrative prowess, the army's power, prestige, and financial muscle remained untouched. The civil bureaucracy allegedly rendered the whole devolutionary framework rudderless by duplicating departments and delaying the transfer of funds to the provinces. The decline in federal–province relations in the context of Sindh marked the PTI government (2018–). When COVID-19 broke out, Sindh took prompt action to impose lockdown on the affected areas, while the federal government was relaxed about it elsewhere. The debate became a PPP versus PTI contest that extended beyond the implementation of health policy.[45] Another issue related to sales tax collection rights on services as per the 2009 NFC Award. Karachi publicly complained when Islamabad conceded to the IMF that the tax had increased the cost of doing business and alienated the commercial elite, and hinted at eventually moving to a single tax collection agency.[46] Similarly, the anomaly of the centralist bureaucracy working in the provinces often created tension. The Sindh minister, Nasir Hussain Shah, accused the federal government of transferring capable police officers away from the province, which could lead to a deterioration in law and order.[47]

While parliamentarism privileges citizens as political participants in the context of their use of the ballot as agents of government formation, federalism protects and enhances an equitable distribution of powers at the sub-national level, especially based on identity politics in ethnically plural societies. Providing territorial autonomy can be a vehicle for what Tully calls 'citizenization'. In his view, the four relevant indicators for citizenization are: the absence of violence or terrorism by either the state or the minority; ethnic politics being a matter of ballots not bullets; sub-state governments not having any prerogative to curtail individual freedom in the name of cultural purity; and neither minority nor a majority having any kind of preponderance over the other, including equality in both cultural and economic terms.[48] A major problem for constitution-making in Pakistan has been the issue of devising a mechanism for power distribution between the centre and the federating units. Whereas the 1935 India Act was federal in nature, there was enough room to manoeuvre in the 1947 Independence of India Act for centralizing power in the capital of the new state.

Institutional pluralism provided the undercurrent of federal thinking in Pakistan, much as in India, whereby ethnically defined provinces represented historical entities and identities.

Federalism at Bay

Partition created two demographic anomalies in Pakistan. First, East Bengal became the largest province at 55 per cent of the population, larger than the population of all the other provinces put together. Second, Punjab emerged as the largest province of (West) Pakistan with 38 per cent of the population, larger than that of all the other provinces of that wing combined. East Bengal's demographic preponderance shaped the political attitudes of Punjab. The latter presided over the formation of One Unit, comprising the whole of West Pakistan, which provided the foundation for both the 1956 and 1962 Constitutions. After Bangladesh, the logic of numbers favoured Punjab because electoral democracy no longer threatened its preponderant representation in the power structure.

From the very beginning, the Bengali Muslim Leaguers were inspired by the idea of creating 'purba Pakistan' (eastern Pakistan) as an independent state consisting of Bengal and Assam. Abul Hashim had already warned about the dangers of a united Pakistan, which could result in the imposition of an alien culture and bureaucracy.[49] In the end, within months of partition the Urdu daily, *Nawa-i-Waqt*, asked for integration of all West Pakistan provinces 'in the supreme national interest'.[50] In 1954, lawyers from Peshawar put forward the demand for merging the West Pakistan provinces to save the country from being 'rocked by the hurricanes of provincialism'.[51] It took nine years for Pakistan to make the first constitution in an effort to create an ethnic balance of sorts. The first major move towards developing the foundation of a federal constitution was the destruction of federalism itself at the level of West Pakistan, where the four provinces and several princely states were merged into one mega-province called One Unit. The 1956 and 1962 Constitutions were based on the principle of parity between East and West Pakistan. The National Assembly was to be elected on the basis of an equal number of legislators from the two wings: 75 and 150 each in the 1956 and 1962 Constitutions respectively.

Alfred Stepan distinguishes between coming-together federalism, in which various entities give up part of their sovereignty to achieve shared economic and political goals, and holding-together federalism, which can be heavily coercive through the centralizing power of the state.[52] Pakistan clearly falls into the second category. Here, the federalist project has followed a top-down approach, whereby the federating units other than Punjab have been clamouring for justice and equity. There is a big chasm between the state at the top and the citizen at the bottom in terms of sharing the ends and means of governance. Pakistan comes close to prefectural federalism, such as in India where the federation has stultified provincial autonomy and often dismisses provincial governments.[53] However, distribution of funds to the provinces in India is based essentially on their revenue and not the size of the population, which is the practice in Pakistan.[54] A lot depends on the political reality beyond the mere institutional design. For example, in India, as Arora argues, the split created by the move away from single-party dominance for a quarter of a century was 'smoothed' through the help of 'executive federalism'.[55]

The national project in Pakistan faced the challenge of integrating the constituent parts of the new country. There was neither a compact historical identity nor a continuing political entity from the past. Demands based on ethnicity were considered dangerous for national unity. One Unit was formed in the name of the 'indivisible unity of our people', 'their essential oneness' to fight provincialism.[56] The 'steam-roller' of One Unit,[57] and the centralization of power in the federal capital, led to a backlash in the form of ethnic nationalism of the Pakhtuns, Bengalis, Sindhis and the Baloch. The 2018 SDPI–*Herald* survey revealed that the people of the four provinces – ranging from 19 per cent in Punjab to 67 per cent in Balochistan and Sindh – believed that there was an unequal distribution of resources, and that cities such as Hyderabad, Karachi and the region of northern Punjab received an unfairly high share.[58] At the other end, the official quarters feared that the net effect of a federation with powerful provinces would create centrifugal tendencies that would empower the provincial elite and not the people at large.

Following the agenda of de-federalizing the state machinery after partition, the centre gradually expanded constitutional powers under Section 102 to include declaring a state of emergency in a province, and then legislating for it. Tax revenues meant for the provinces, especially income tax and sales tax, were appropriated by the centre after 1947. In Pakistan, sales tax was a provincial source of revenue until 1951 when it was 'temporarily' handed to the centre in the wake of 'abnormal conditions' created by the large influx of refugees and additional defence requirements. But this change has still not been undone even after the dissipation of the 'abnormal conditions' long ago.[59]

The centre was further empowered to impose certain duties and responsibilities on the provinces (Sections 122, 124–2). Section 126 extended the powers of the centre to direct the executive authority of a province in certain matters of economic importance. Section 92-A gave the centre the power to impose the governor's rule over a province. These powers were exercised most controversially nine times in eleven years (1947–58). When the names of civil servants who would occupy senior posts were announced on 4 April 1970, Ejaz Naik was appointed as chief secretary of KP even as his knowledge of the province was 'virtually nil'.[60] Indeed, none of the new inspectors general of the police or home secretaries was a native of the province of his appointment. One view was that the purpose of this exercise was the impartial supervision of law and order instead of 'depth of knowledge' about the region. Intriguingly, all four chief secretaries were Punjabis.[61] The federation's powers had been underscored by a centralist bureaucracy after the establishment of a unified system of Central Superior Services in 1948, which eliminated the system of provincial cadres used in the Indian Civil Service (ICS). This left little space for the provinces to manoeuvre.

An interesting case was the battle for Karachi. The governor of Sindh threatened to resign in protest against the central government's proposal to move the capital of Sindh from Karachi to Hyderabad. The dismissal of a recalcitrant Ayub Khuhro as chief minister of Sindh in turn led to mounting pressure on the provincial government to accommodate incoming refugees.[62] Later, potential opposition from Sindh against Chief Minister Pirzada Abdus Sattar cost him his government in 1954 as the centre's project of One Unit took off. His replacement, Ayub Khuhro, duly obliged the federal government in this matter.[63] The only opposition to the One Unit scheme in Sindh came from G. M. Syed's group.[64] The news from Balochistan was that the Khan of Kalat had lowered the Pakistani flag and repudiated the initial accession of his state to Pakistan in 1948.[65] The political situation in Balochistan was again tense when almost 400 people were allegedly killed in a military operation launched in the Chamalang region.[66]

Centralization of power in the first decade after partition led to a pattern of resistance from various provinces that eventually contributed to the formation in 1957 of the archetypical provincialist party, NAP, from the 'left' of the political spectrum. As opposed to the vision of the ruling elite for an administrative, territorial and symmetrical federalism, provincial leaderships pursued the ideal of an ethnic federalism whereby their historical, traditional, and linguistic identities would define the basis of a shared statehood. As the movement to undo One Unit gained momentum after the passage of a resolution to that effect by the new West Pakistan Assembly in 1957, President Iskandar Mirza and Commander-in-Chief General Ayub clamped down on the system in 1958. For at least another decade, they sealed the fate of the agenda of restoring the four provinces.

An alternative constitutional framework based on the 1940 Lahore Resolution began to appeal to restive elements in the erstwhile minority provinces of West Pakistan, i.e. Sindh, KP and Balochistan.[67] The clue to this parallelism lies in the twin message of the Lahore Resolution – now popularly known as the Pakistan Resolution – as reflected through the interplay of the 'separatist' and 'federalist' patterns of thinking. The largely forgotten dimension of the 1940 Lahore Resolution relates to its federalist provisions for maximum provincial autonomy. This dimension was rooted in two developments in British India.[68] First, province emerged at the heart of British constitutional thinking as reflected in the provisions for provincial autonomy within the emerging federal scheme for India. Second, while the prospects of a Hindu-dominated federation looked imminent and therefore daunting, the Muslim League's political thinking gravitated towards a loose federation that would safeguard autonomy for the Muslim-majority provinces. The Lahore Resolution demanded that the Muslim-majority provinces of northwest and northeast India 'should be grouped to constitute Independent States in which the constituent units shall be autonomous and sovereign'.[69]

The Lahore Resolution raised more questions than answers. Would there be one or more groupings? What was the meaning of independent sovereign units? How many states were visualized for Muslims? The current imperial thinking a decade before partition feared losing the political initiative to the centre and instead took up the question of provinces joining or opting out of a dominion at their choice. It thus shifted the current federalist thinking in the direction of what was, until recently, an amorphous constitutional entity of provinces.[70] During the following years, the Muslim League leadership moved from a federalist to a 'separatist' mode of thinking that put the issue of provincial autonomy on hold. Accordingly, the 1946 resolution passed by the All-India Muslim League's legislators conference asked for an independent Pakistan. Since partition, the 'separatist' message of the 1940 Lahore Resolution is celebrated each year on 23 March as the constitutional foundation of the state, while the 'federalist' message is considered anathema by the mainstream political thinking. The United Front in East Bengal presented a 21-point agenda for elections for the provincial assembly in 1954 and demanded a federation on the basis of the 1940 Lahore Resolution. While referring to that resolution, it was claimed that 'religion and culture are not the same thing, religion transgresses the geographical boundary but *tammadun* (culture) cannot go beyond the geographical boundary'.[71]

In 1966, the Awami League leader from East Pakistan, Sheikh Mujibur Rehman, presented his Six Points formula for re-shaping the federation. He called the 1940 Lahore Resolution the Magna Carta for contemporary Pakistan because of its autonomist provisions. He pleaded for a two-subject centre largely drawing on the three-subject centre envisaged by the 1940 Lahore Resolution. He also demanded two separate reserve banks for the two wings, based on a two-economy thesis, transfer of taxation and revenue collection from the centre to the provinces, the right of provinces to establish direct trade relations with other countries, and the creation of paramilitary forces for East Pakistan.[72] After winning the 1970 elections, Mujibur Rehman negotiated with President Yahya on the basis of his Six Points. The breakdown in negotiations led to civil war and the emergence of Bangladesh in 1971.

The Federal Project

The 1973 Constitution can be considered the first 'genuine' federalization project, not least because the shadow of Bengali separatism loomed large in the thinking of the new state managers. In Vali Nasr's view, the province of Sindh represented 'politics in a non-institution-alized state'.[73] It had been seething with negativity towards the centre for two decades on such issues as the migration and settlement of millions of refugees from India after partition, the separation of Karachi from Sindh and the merger of Sindh in One Unit. Balochistan had passed through various phases of ethno-nationalist agitation against the centre on issues such as annexation with Pakistan allegedly by coercion,[74] the persistent demand for provincial autonomy, and successive military operations.[75] The new federalist arrangement sought to constrain Punjab as the majority province through bicameralism, whereby each of the three minority provinces would have representation in the Senate equal to Punjab. The *demos*-controlling role of the upper chamber was an innovation.[76] However, the Senate's lack of control over financial bills reduced its policy scope. The system of proportional representation for electing the Senate through an electoral college composed mainly of the MPAs further diluted its representative character as compared to the directly elected National Assembly. That turned the former into a mere extension of the latter. Instead of enhancing the quality of representation of smaller provinces in the state, the Senate sank into an effete institution and sometimes became a pawn in the hands of the president in his conflict with the majority-wielding prime minister belonging to the National Assembly.[77]

Ideally, democratic federalism reduces conflict to 'manageable proportions' whereby extreme demands are diluted. This leads to the 'development of a national consciousness' among people who otherwise carry a 'weak national identity'.[78] The idea of federalism potentially seeks to stabilize the system by providing space for those regions, communities and groups that are under-represented in the state. However, the 1973 Constitution provided for only two lists of subjects, federal and concurrent, with no provincial list except those subjects not covered by the two lists that would fall into the residual category controlled by the provinces. Conversely, fiscal federalism started to take off. The Council of Common Interests (CCI), created pursuant to Article 153, emerged as a mechanism for the resolution of conflicts among and between the provinces and the centre. Similarly, Article 160(1) provided for the National Finance Commission (NFC) as a mechanism for resource transfer from the centre, which raised 90 per cent of the national revenue, to the provinces which raised as little as 8–9 per cent. The 1996 NFC Award comprehensively raised the provincial share of the divisible pool of revenue from 28 per cent to 45 per cent. The 2009 NFC Award took the provincial share from 47.5 to 56 per cent of the pool for the current year and to 57.5 per cent for the following years. Among the provinces, it brought the share of Punjab down to 51.74 per cent and doubled the share of Balochistan to 9.09 per cent.[79] In this way, both the vertical and horizontal redistribution of resources strengthened fiscal federalism before and after the turn of the twenty-first century.

In a parallel situation, the Sarkaria Commission in India observed that the 'reliance of state governments on the central government had diminished through the impact of economic liberalization policies, thereby shifting debates on federalism from "inter-governmental cooperation" to "inter-jurisdictional competition"'.[80] In Pakistan, the NFC Awards, along with the operative clauses of the 18th Amendment, initiated a similar controversy about jurisdiction that re-emerged with full vigour in 2020–21.

The federal arrangement that emerged in the 1970s in many ways exacerbated inter-ethnic tensions. Political negotiations now took place along ethnic lines, which resulted in a further 'entrenchment of traditionally conspicuous ethnic identities' and elevated the position of certain ethnic groups in comparison with others. In Maryam Khan's formulation, the ethnic conflict in the 1980s represented the 'minorities-within-minorities phenomenon', pointing to the position of a Mohajir minority within the minority province of Sindh.[81] The construction of a separate Mohajir identity in the 1970s was not the result of economic deprivation as much as the anticipation of a 'loss of political and economic dominance' that the new federalist arrangement threatened.[82] Being a community undefined by territory, the incipient Mohajir nationalism at that stage folded back from the all-Pakistan narrative to an ethnic idiom relating to Sindh, even if not to Sindh's precarious position in the federation.

In 1985, Sindhi politicians and intelligentsia-in-exile, combined with Baloch and Pakhtun politicians within and outside Pakistan, founded the Sindhi Baloch Pashtun Front (SBPF). The SBPF invoked the 1940 Lahore Resolution to demand autonomy and sovereignty for the constituent units of Pakistan. It claimed that the Muslim League had confirmed the right of provinces to opt out of their designated zones in its correspondence with the cabinet mission in 1946. It interpreted the 1940 Lahore Resolution essentially as a confederal formula based on the equality of all four nationalities and their voluntary association with the union, which would control only four subjects. Holding a diametrically opposed position, Zia offered to divide the country into 53 small provinces and thus to eliminate language as a source of identity in pursuit of his idea of national integration.[83]

The 2010 18th Amendment represented a breakthrough in the constitutional edifice of the country. Earlier, the two leaders in exile, Benazir Bhutto and Nawaz Sharif, had signed the Charter of Democracy in London in 2006. The charter demanded a 'cooperative federation with no discrimination against federating units, the decentralization and devolution of power [and] maximum provincial autonomy'. It also demanded that the Concurrent List be abolished.[84] Under President Zardari (2008–13), the formation of the Parliamentary Committee for Constitutional Reforms (PCCR) in 2008 reflected a credible representation of ethnic parties from the smaller provinces. Both the composition and thinking of the PCCR, with its overwhelming anti-Punjab and anti-centre sentiment, promised to expand the frontiers of ethnic space in law through the 2010 18th Amendment within the framework of devolutionary federalism. The Concurrent List of subjects was deleted from the constitution. Out of forty-seven subjects, forty were transferred to the provinces. The amendment provided for the right of prior consultation on hydroelectric projects by the centre; raising loans at home and abroad; joint ownership of mineral wealth with Islamabad; and issuing guarantees on the provincial consolidated fund.[85]

In Burki's view, the 18th Amendment was unlikely to increase efficiency. As capital moved across national frontiers, various federating units would start to compete with one another for scarce capital flows. In this, Sindh would try to outbid other provinces in attracting real estate investments from the Middle East.[86] Nishtar argued that the National Health Policy that was institutionalized with the help of various donors could not be replicated in the provinces because the federal departments carried a clear mission for the whole country whereas institutions at lower levels only had the 'health service delivery mandate'.[87]

Among 102 articles of the constitution amended by the 18th Amendment, many related to parliamentary sovereignty. The president could now issue only one ordinance at a time when the National Assembly or the Senate was not in session. This measure was expected to restrain the executive on whose advice the president issued an ordinance.[88] It is significant that the Sixth Schedule, which required prior consent of the president for amendment in thirty-five laws, was deleted, thereby removing constraints on parliament's law-making authority. Similarly, the Seventh Schedule was also deleted, which included eight laws that could be amended only through a procedure prescribed for a constitutional amendment that required a two-thirds majority vote of parliament.

On the one hand, parliament's pursuit of accumulation of power relied – obviously and most naturally – on changes in the law. On the other hand, the task of implementing legal provisions remained in the hands of a civil bureaucracy that was recruited, trained, posted, transferred and promoted by the federal government. The bureaucracy ultimately operated in the pleasure of the federal government, even when it was placed in the service of a provincial government. The progress of the country towards devolution of power as per the 18th Amendment has been slow and only partially implemented. The centralists led by the state elite, the commercial and professional middle classes as well as Islamists, have continued to look at the amendment in negative terms as a recipe for disintegration of the nation.

Whereas the federal government has been far from keen in devolving power to the provinces – the stronghold of the political class – the latter, in turn, are uninterested in further devolution of power to the district level. Successive military governments sought to bypass the province and empower local government institutions with the express purpose of undermining the constituency-level party workers and cadres of political parties. In theory, decentralization leads to closer interaction with the people and to more consensus and better services. In reality, de-centralization gives way to 'elite capture' at the lower levels.[89] General Musharraf's 2001 Devolution Plan aimed to create an apolitical local leadership as a rival to the political class in the name of providing government at the doorstep. The donor community flocked to help him in his endeavour. After each transition from military to civilian rule (1971, 1988 and 2008) the newly elected provincial governments pushed the agenda for keeping local bodies elections lower in the hierarchy of issues than commanded by the erstwhile military governments.

The 18th Amendment provided for provincial governments to enact local government laws for the devolution of power to the district and lower levels and to hold local bodies elections (Article 140-A). After the 2013 elections, several parties which were signatories of the PCCR report preparatory to the 18th Amendment now occupied government office in the centre and the provinces: the PPP in Karachi; the PML-N in Islamabad and Lahore; and the Pakhtunkhwa Milli Awami Party (PkMAP), the National Party (NP) and the Balochistan National Party (BNP) in Quetta. In view of their obvious lack of enthusiasm for local government, the Supreme Court asked the latter to hold local bodies elections by 5 September 2013. Several issues emerged as impediments on the way to elections, including the short time for passing the requisite laws, the re-demarcation of electoral constituencies, and the arrangements for the printing of millions of ballot papers. The Election Commission of Pakistan (ECP) agreed with the stance of political parties that there was too little time for holding elections. The local elections in Balochistan were held on 7 December 2013 but were postponed elsewhere until January 2014 and even later. Ultimately, the whole process for holding elections in all four provinces took more than two years, and another year to put the elected members of district and union councils formally in office.

A parallel concern was whether local elections should be held on a party basis. This was an old controversy. Elections at the local level had always been held on a non-party basis. The Sindh government announced party-based elections, hoping that the dichotomy between the two leading ethnic communities of Mohajirs and Sindhis would ensure that its Sindhi-speaking constituency would return the PPP candidates in large numbers. Similarly, the MQM bagged Mohajir voters in a quintessentially ethnic commitment.

The agenda for non-party elections in Punjab was challenged in the Lahore High Court, which ruled in favour of party-based elections. Local bodies elections in KP organized by the PTI government in Peshawar were extensively rigged.[90] That led to a nationwide furore against the elections. Even Imran Khan's coalition partner JI in KP publicly condemned the electoral malpractices in the province. While he was visibly embarrassed, Imran Khan offered to hold local bodies elections in the province again.

The moot point is that, under a civilian set-up, local government was grossly discounted. All four provincial assemblies passed laws for their respective local bodies. However, these laws bypassed the issue of the devolution of effective power to the district and sub-district levels, which was previously exercised as per the Devolution Plan of 2001. In 2020, when Imran Khan's government picked up on the issue of revising the 18th Amendment, he declared that provincial governments had not devolved power downwards to the district level. However, it was only a matter of the passing of the new legislation about local government by provincial assemblies, three of which (Punjab, KP and Balochistan) were ruled by coalition governments, including Imran Khan's own party, the PTI.

In 2019, the PTI government in Punjab disbanded local bodies in one go. At the end of a two-year long process of litigation on that issue, the Supreme Court finally restored local bodies in 2021. However, the PTI government resorted to dilly-dallying tactics on this issue. The dynamics of politics in smaller provinces that had pushed for the 18th Amendment was constrained by the country's power structure enshrined in the state apparatus that was dominated by the arch-centralist province of Punjab. As soon as the first democratic transition took place after the 2013 elections, the PML-N government formed a committee to review the 18th Amendment, for removing 'anomalies'. This elicited criticism, including from PPP senator Raza Rabbani, who as chairperson of the PCCR had authored the 18th Amendment. Given that legal implementation and devolution of powers had to a great extent taken place, the provinces feared reversion.[91] Islamabad exerted its influence through the process of implementation of the 18th Amendment by halting the transfer of certain departments from the centre to the provinces and by dividing others, creating new divisions, and committees, and then keeping them in the hands of the centre, as well as generally delaying the entire process.

There was a spurt in demand for the creation of new provinces because the 18th Amendment lent power, privilege, influence and identity to the majority communities of Sindhis in Sindh, Punjabis in Punjab, Pakhtuns in KP, and the Baloch in Balochistan. This was instrumental in creating a backlash among the minority communities in these provinces, i.e. Mohajirs in Sindh, Siraiki-speaking people in Punjab, Hindko-speaking people of Hazara in KP and Pakhtuns in Balochistan.[92] The creation of new provinces remained problematic because the constitution required a two-thirds majority vote in the National Assembly as well as in the concerned provincial assembly. Furthermore, this was an issue submerged in the larger currents of macro-politics.

The fear of a severe reaction from Sindhi nationalists against any prospects of a division of their province kept the MQM and its factions from publicly and consistently pressing for it. People in the Siraiki region have been divided between the Bahawalpur-centred and Multan-centred movements, and between Siraiki speakers originally belonging to the area and Punjabi settlers who came in the wake of the opening up of irrigation canals in the early twentieth century. The Hazara region in KP has been too small an entity to merit the status of a fully fledged province and has often been dismissed as a mere district-and-half by the Pakhtuns. The Pakhtuns in Balochistan who are dominant in Quetta, as well as along the border with Iran and Afghanistan and the upper coastline have not been keen to demand a separate province. Only the PKMAP and NP wanted FATA to be renamed Pakhtunkhwa Central and the Pakhtun areas of Balochistan to be a separate province called Pakhtunkhwa Southern, apart from KP as Pakhtunkhwa proper.[93]

The majority-constraining federalist arrangement represented by the 1973 Constitution, with additional input from the 2010 18th Amendment, remains problematic in view of the powerful centralist framework of the bureaucracy and the army. This provides a clue to support for presidential rule as a symbol of unity, as envisaged by extra-parliamentary forces led by the army. Intriguingly, during his address to the Senate in December 2017, COAS General Qamar Javed Bajwa said that the presidential system was a recipe for national disintegration and that parliamentarism, especially in its federalist incarnation, was an expression of institutional pluralism. The federalist agenda has survived the struggle of ethno-regional forces. The latter often point to the 1940 Lahore Resolution that had promised autonomous federating units in future Pakistan. Bicameralism has gained strength in view of the empowerment of the Senate by the 18th Amendment, but this amendment ultimately fell short of safeguarding the interests of smaller provinces inasmuch as no shift in the power balance took place on the ground. The National Assembly remained sensitive to the demographic preponderance of the majority province of Punjab. The differential in the policy scope of the two houses of parliament meant that the Senate remained weak and non-effective. The 18th Amendment was considered to be the latest expression of the legal and institutional demands of the federalist forces, which consistently sought to attain maximum provincial autonomy.

The issue of expanding the federation by creating new provinces was put on hold in the face of formidable constitutional bottlenecks, underscored by the proclivity of mainstream and leading ethnic parties to maintain the status quo in this regard. The reluctance on the part of provincial governments to empower local governments under Article 140-A of the constitution was fairly obvious and by no means a positive step towards strengthening federalism at its roots.[94]

At the other end, centralist forces were keen to dismantle the federal edifice erected by the 18th Amendment, wholly or partially. In 2019, the chief of the army staff spoke out against the 18th Amendment as being a 'problem bigger than the Six Points of Sheikh Mujibur Rehman'.[95] Back in 2015, Ishaq Dar had called the spending on security and repatriation of IDPs an 'extraordinary expenditure' and claimed that the NFC Award restrained the government's fiscal resources.[96] It was argued that the provision of the 18th Amendment — that a province's share in an NFC Award cannot be lower than that in the previous award — could intensify conflict between the centre and the provinces in future negotiations for revenue distribution.[97]

Indeed, the immediate negative reaction to the passing of the 18th Amendment came from the judiciary. The Supreme Court referred what it considered the controversial provisions of the amendment relating to the appointment of judges back to the PCCR for review. The court demanded that the forum for the appointment of judges should have a majority of judges. The PCCR duly obliged. Accordingly, it took up the issue and deliberated on the 19th Amendment, which was later passed by parliament and signed by the president on 1 January 2011. The federalist provisions of the 18th Amendment remained intact.

The process of the transfer of ministries from federal to provincial capitals started in the last quarter of 2010. There was a lot of confusion about the continuation of federal departments even after the new divisions in provinces were established, thus creating duality of purpose and wastage of national resources. Ethno-nationalist elements from Balochistan and Sindh remained acutely sceptical about the sincerity of purpose behind the move. The impression of the dominance of the province of Punjab over the federation was by no means diminished in the absence of a qualitative expansion of the recruitment base of the two state apparatuses and a change in their upper echelons. Sceptics did not see a comprehensive change of policy on the political horizon pursuant upon the provisions and commitments of the 2009 Balochistan initiative, the 2009 NFC Award and the 2010 18ᵗʰ Amendment.

While no new provinces have been created, two developments in this regard need to be mentioned. First, the merger of FATA with KP in 2018 has the potential for changing the allocation of seats in the National Assembly and adversely affecting the demographic preponderance of Punjab. Second, demand for the status of province for Gilgit-Baltistan (GB) reached new heights after the Indian government under Modi scrapped Article 370 of the Indian Constitution and eliminated the autonomous position of the state of Jammu and Kashmir in 2019. The merger of FATA with KP, and thus with Pakistan, legally and administratively, elicited a negative response from the JUI-F and other Islamic elements on the one hand and local Maliks represented through the FATA Grand Alliance on the other. There were concerns about whether the transition would be smooth and whether there would be any violent resistance. It was expected that control over the judicature would move from society – for example, the *jirga* system – to the district and higher courts controlled by the state. The constitution would be the new legal mechanism for rule over FATA. It was expected that police would replace *khasadars* and the *levies*. However, it was feared that these measures would create a sense of insecurity among people regarding their traditional attachments with tribal norms and practices and their sense of autonomy. Institutionally speaking, agency councils comprising Maliks and the political agents (PA) would be replaced by elected legislatures in Peshawar and Islamabad at one end and by the administrative machinery comprising members of the centralist bureaucracy at the other. Intriguingly, the FATA MNAs who had no jurisdiction over FATA before merger stood to gain ground in the locality through the system of patronage that was operative elsewhere in Pakistan.

Electoral politics moved into the erstwhile FATA from 1996 onwards, when adult franchise was introduced. Political parties were allowed to participate in elections as per the 2011 Political Parties Act. However, while electoral politics had been introduced in the area, there was little input from the party dynamics of KP or the mainstream politics of Pakistan. The scope of the 2018 elections was not extended to FATA even after its merger. But the next elections at the national and provincial levels were expected to bring in the political parties operating outside FATA. The three mainstream parties – PTI, PML-N and PPP – were expected to give an 'integrationist', all-Pakistan, developmental and nationalist message. In this way, local upwardly mobile 'middle class' political activists would seek identification with the 'state' through voting for one of the mainstream parties.

Among the Pakhtun nationalist parties, the old guard ANP and the new FATA-based Pashtun Tahaffuz Movement (PTM) would compete for space in identity politics. Islamic parties led by the JUI-F showed tremendous resilience in the face of the encroachment of the modern state system into FATA. Previously, the merger of the princely state of Swat in 1969 had led to gradual alienation of local people with the 'alien' rule of Islamabad. Within a generation there emerged a vociferous campaign for Tehrik Nifaz Shariat Mohammadi (TNSM) under the leadership of Sufi Mohammad. Nostalgia for the *ancien régime* had taken the form of a religious movement for Islamization. Both Prime Minister Nawaz Sharif and President Zardari issued new constitutional packages for a legal and judicial system for Malakand division. Would the experience of FATA be similar – in the form of an Islamic backlash to the imposition of an English-based state system, maybe after two decades?

Of course, no two situations couched in different circumstances and different periods of time could necessarily produce the same result. For one thing, FATA had become part of the larger Pakhtun entity, KP. It would lose autonomy in the matter of the party nomination of candidates for national and provincial assemblies. That could lead to a generational transition in the leadership. It was an open question whether the PTM, with its young leadership and an agenda of rehabilitation of DPIs, would be able to compete with the larger parties based in KP. With the additional seats of the KP Assembly, the quota of seats for the National Assembly would also increase. This would influence the Senate elections in 2024, when the legislatures at the national and provincial levels would serve as the electorate for the Senate seats. The transition had the potential for conflict in various forms. For example, there would be a perception about the 'colonial' rule of Islamabad. The DPIs' rehabilitation could continue to be an unsettling issue. Would the provinces' less-than-positive response to the official demand for keeping 3 per cent of the divisible pool aside for development of FATA be problematic for the newly expanded federation? The Pakhtun internal diaspora in Karachi and the external diaspora in the Gulf and beyond could be a factor in expanding the federalization agenda after the US withdrawal from Kabul.

The potential for Gilgit-Baltistan (GB) becoming a separate province has far greater significance for the federation of Pakistan.[98] In this context, one needs to take into account three factors. First, there is a legal dispute about Kashmir, and GB is involved as part of the dispute between India and Pakistan, especially for the purpose of fighting Pakistan's case in the international forums. Second, GB would be the only Shia-dominant province in an otherwise Sunni-dominant country. This factor has all along been part of the calculation of state managers. Third, efforts have been afoot to change the demographic composition of GB by facilitating the immigration and settlement of Sunni groups of both Pakhtun and Punjabi extraction.[99]

Islamization of Laws

The colonial legacy of British common law, combined with the new ideological force of Islamic jurisprudence, charted the new constitutional path in Pakistan. The independence generation of the relatively liberal and cosmopolitan Muslim League leadership gave way to increasingly religious and conservative generations in ideological terms. Rubina Saigol has argued that the Islamic project in colonial times focused on preserving what was traditional and sacred. It sought to protect women against the stranger in an elaborate physical sense. She refers to Maulana Ashraf Ali Thanvi's book, *Bahishti Zevar* (Jewellery for Paradise), that commands that the hair of a woman's head left in the comb as well as the nails – when cut off – should be placed safely away from the stranger's eyes.[100] As opposed to Maududi's ideas about the requirement of the use of veil for women being devised by the Qur'an, others believed that the custom of purdah was borrowed from the pre-Islamic period and that seclusion of women was not warranted.[101] The original aim to prohibit drinking in public places after 1 April 1948 ended in complete prohibition, although 'not a single Minister favoured it'.[102]

The founding fathers, who actually grew up in the secular legal environment of both England and British India, cautiously – even reluctantly – put in place the Islamic principles of state policy from the 1949 Objectives Resolution onwards. This paved the way to defining the potential and scope of the subsequent constitution-making initiatives. The later generations did not share the quantum or direction of legal socialization with their predecessors. Instead, they drew largely on the nationalist framework of thought that embraced an all-encompassing Islamism couched in the perceived requirements of state-building. They felt obliged to recast the major constitutional ideas, norms and the related institutional patterns that had come to British India for two hundred years, into the mould of an Islamic state.

The British legacy covered three main areas of legal and institutional activity. First, the political economy of colonialism required political stability as well as protection of property and contractual security sanctioned by the courts to create wealth that was conceived as production in the framework of a broad utilitarian philosophy. In other words, the colonial state put in place a legal framework that would guarantee the operation of private enterprise in India. Second, the British introduced a uniform codified law that led to a transition from the use of force to the rule of legitimate authority and from the concept of the inchoate masses to a 'public' infused with rights to legal protection. While ultimately the law served as an instrument of self-legitimation for the state, the new state in turn created potentially rights-bearing citizens who were destined to claim ownership of the country after independence. Third, the new administrative hierarchy was characterized by structural differentiation, a rational–legal organizational ethos, and government by policy rather than by patronage.[103] Thus, the modern state apparatus was ensconced in a position from where it could self-consciously direct public life and implement public policy in a relatively unhindered way.

European principles had taken deep roots in the alien land of British India during the colonial period. However, after independence the flow of these principles was gradually cut off from its classical and contemporary sources in European legal philosophy and the substantive as well as operational behaviour of the European courts. The nation now faced the task of constitutional progress toward the coveted goal of re-shaping laws and institutions on the basis of Islamic jurisprudence. Several leading thinkers, ranging from orthodox and conservative religious scholars to modernists of various degrees, offered their theses about constitutionalizing Islam, now that the Muslims of British India had a country of their own. Continuation of the colonial legacy of laws and institutions was considered the abject negation of the very idea of independence.

In opposition to this, state managers typically adopted a strategy of defence against the perceived religious encroachment upon the British constitutional legacy. They often devised ways and means of deflecting the pressure of Islamists by accommodating their demands in letter if not in spirit and through legal symbolism if not through administrative implementation of laws. The Zia regime supported madrassahs so that their graduates could serve in the bureaucracy, 'relevant to the needs of the changing society and economy', thus leading to the emergence of the 'new Islamic bureaucracy'.[104] The JI members became part of the civil administration as 'trusted technocrats' or higher bureaucrats.[105]

The process of the Islamization of laws was a direct result of ideological input into the body politic that was fundamentally extraneous to the tradition of constitutional law in British India. As the declared foundation of the new state, religion impinged forcefully on the first major expression of intent for the formulation of the constitution in the form of the 1949 Objectives Resolution. It was declared that 'sovereignty over the entire universe belongs to God Almighty alone' and that 'He has delegated authority to the state of Pakistan for the sovereignty being exercised within the limits prescribed by Him'.

Over time, the 1949 Objectives Resolution created an ideological framework of its own, distinct from the current constitutional edifice. Callard has argued that A. K. Brohi found the Objectives Resolution as simply 'grounded on a proper metaphysical insight in the ultimate source of law', the 'spirit of the constitution' but not its contents.[106] In Inamur Rehman's view, Brohi turned the debate away from 'vague generalities' toward the 'hard realities of conflicts' inherent in any discussion of the Islamic state.[107] Actually, the reverse is true. The ulema had a clearer vision of reviving the holy book as the source of Islamic law. It was the modernist elite that shrouded the debate in a philosophical mode of argument with the purpose of defending the modern institutional–constitutional conundrum of the state by 'outsourcing' it to the realm of Islamic metaphysics. The 'universal' import of the Islamic message transcended the contours of state-specific constitutionalism that was typical of the contemporary world.[108]

It is easy, however, to overstate the influence of Islam on the body politic at this early stage, even as the Objectives Resolution followed by the 1952 Basic Principles Committee (BPC) report and the emergent Islamic institutions pointed in that direction. Diplomatic observers expected that the commitment to Islam in the BPC report would be diluted in the forthcoming constitution, which would have brought the hitherto estranged Hindus back into the mainstream at the moment of constitution-making.[109] However, that was not to be: Pakistan emerged as a constitutional state in retreat in the context of the ideological input into the colonial 'secular' framework of authority. Although the main body of the constitution's text remained intact and operated as a reference point for litigation, it now had to contend with an elaborate religious system of rules and regulations. This fact obligated several scholars to use the term 'political Islam' to describe the conflation between religion and politics, because the state was now obligated to implement Islamic laws thus conceived and promulgated.[110] Zia's Islamization project started through the judiciary, comprising three dimensions: the call for speedier justice; revision of the law in the light of Qur'anic injunctions; and dependence on martial law for implementation of the new legal code.[111] Zia did not want to find himself in a clash with the judiciary. He thought that after the army, the judiciary was the second 'great institution'.[112] The state was now obliged to draw legitimacy from what could eventually turn out to be its greatest rival for commanding the allegiance of the general public, i.e. the classical Islamic provisions that gradually penetrated the judicial and jurisdictional space in public life.

Neither scholarly research nor public opinion in general would have described Pakistan in 2021 as an Islamic state as per the vision of the three generations of the religious lobby. Does the use of Islamic metaphor in politics show the limits of the modern political discourses?[113] While the Islamic Research Bureau had started to operate under the leadership of Maulana Shabbir Ahmad Usmani, it was doubtful whether a Sharia constitution would be promulgated.[114] Pakistan's desire for an Islamic state was expected to entail 'no great surrender' to the ulema.[115] From the middle of the twentieth century to the first quarter of the twenty-first century, every small excitement in the direction of Islamization was described as the arrival of the promised land. Zardari's promulgation of Nizam-e-Adl in Mohmand Agency in 2009 was greeted in that spirit.[116] Indeed, conflation between religion and politics led to tension between democracy as mass mandate and constitutionalism as black letter law as two sources of legitimacy that stood as separate entities carrying the potential for a clash of institutions. The transcendental vision incrementally superseded popular sovereignty as defined in terms of ideology.

The examples of Turkey and Iran illustrate the role of 'guardians' as the non-elected and institutionally non-accountable forums operating from outside the elected parliament to protect the constitution's basic features. This role is operationalized through the ideological goals enshrined in the preambles of the two constitutions – Islam in Iran and secularism in Turkey – and the instrumentality of courts to translate these goals into constraints over what is considered unbridled legislation. In Iran, individual piety acts as a factor in the accountability of the rulers to the person of *faqih* (Imam Khamenei) and the institution of the Guardian Council.[117] At the other end, the Turkish model holds that the state should co-opt religion. In recent decades, it has considered religion as an instrument to be used against class-based or ethno-nationalist forces threatening political stability.[118] The experience of Pakistan can be placed in the middle of these models of 'dual sovereignty'. It is based on a dichotomy between an amorphous and extra-constitutional entity outside parliament in the form of the religious lobby and the properly institutionalized forum of parliament.

From the beginning, the political leadership of Pakistan claimed Islam to be the raison d'être of the state by a show of intent and by transforming this intent into specific constitutional provisions. There followed a series of attempts at resistance to Islamic legislation and its implementation, often involving litigation. Some scholars, for example Louis Hayes, argued that since Islamic Law was the work of purists, legal authority was private and personal, even though the ultimate sanction drew upon precedent traced to the Qur'an.[119] Keith

Callard noted the prevalent dichotomy between the modernist players on the political stage and Islamists such as the JI. The former came from Cambridge and the Inns of Court, not Deoband. In his view, they ran 'a secular campaign to create a state based on a religion', thereby using constitutional methods. The case for Pakistan was derived from the liberal nationalism of the day, 'not the law books of Islam', whereby a small group of Westernized leaders, civil servants, judiciary and military had allowed their Islamic fervour to be 'overlaid by the institutional approach produced by secular education and training'. Similarly, there was incongruity between talking of the Islamic system and thinking of the Western system in the same breath.[120]

While responding to the question of whether Islamists can be democrats, it was argued that greater democratization would help serve the Islamist movement's organizational goals.[121] While looking at the phenomenon from a broad perspective, the voices in favour of a separation between politics and religion grew weaker over time. The 1949 Objectives Resolution led to questions about several issues. Where does the locus of sovereignty lie – with God, people, parliament or the state?[122] Which principles of state policy were outlined for enabling Muslims to live according to Sharia? What was the actual mode of delegation of divine authority to the state, which was closely identified with its founder Jinnah? In Fazlur Rehman's words, the 1956 Constitution and subsequent constitutions represented an 'Islamic fetish' in the form of a mechanical application of the Islamic idiom.[123] Not surprisingly, Article 25(2), the enabling clause of the constitution from outside the 1949 Objectives Resolution, remained unenforceable as a directive of state policy.

Beyond the constitution's text, court cases and parliamentary legislation, the cumulative effect of the demand for removing un-Islamic laws from the statute book and establishing laws on the basis of Sharia set the stage for an ever-expanding agenda for the Islamization of laws. Martin Lau argues that 'non-democratically elected governments' inject Islamization into the constitution that derails the system from within.[124] In his view, many of the Islamic provisions were added to Pakistani law unconstitutionally, and then got protected by the constitution with which its principles clashed in many ways.[125] From a 'matter of conscience' for the Muslim League leadership on the eve of independence, Islam emerged as a matter of public policy.[126] The 'repugnancy clause' (Article 198(1)) of the 1956 Constitution, which forbade enactment of un-Islamic laws, was deemed a victory of the modernists over the ulema ostensibly because the former did not agree to the latter's demand to draw the constitution entirely on the basis of Sharia.[127] Instead, the whole issue boiled down to eliminating the un-Islamic provisions from law. The interregnum of the 1962 Constitution maintained the status quo in religious matters, except for deviation from the name Islamic Republic of Pakistan to Republic of Pakistan and then back again.

From 1956 to 1973, Islamic discourse took long strides forward, especially during the 1970 elections when the Yahya government sponsored Islamic parties and groups against the 'socialist' and Bengali nationalist movements in West and East Pakistan, respectively. Ironically, the ruling party, the Muslim League, was able to withstand the pressure of the ulema to Islamize laws in the 1950s because it enjoyed a high legitimate position as the creator of Pakistan. The PPP government (1971–7), however, operated from a numerically strong but politically vulnerable position as an 'outsider' in the face of opposition from powerful forces, such as the army, the bureaucracy, the landed elite, the business community, and the ulema.[128] It is not surprising that Z. A. Bhutto accommodated heavily on constitutionalizing religion in the interest of developing a consensus, and thus conceded to Islamists in this field. Farzana Shaikh traces 'the formative weakness' of the Pakistani state to the 'paradoxical evolution' on the basis of 'cultural nationalism'.[129] In the following decades, almost every institution was ascribed some kind of Islamic sanction. It was not uncommon to see chapter titles such as 'Islam and Local Self-Government' in books dealing with local bodies along with their colonial antecedents.[130]

The concept of repugnance to Islam provided a major undercurrent of Islamic jurisprudence in the country. Article 198(1) of the 1956 Constitution provided that repugnance to injunctions of Islam – the word Sharia was avoided – was to be interpreted by the relevant Muslim sects for legislation purposes. Interestingly, the constitution mentions delegation of authority to people – but not specifically to Muslims – at this early stage of constitutionalism.[131] The 1956 Constitution had sought and established compromise rather than consensus that would have made it mandatory to accommodate the dissident Islamist voices on the floor of the parliament. The idea was that Islam was a matter of policy rather than law for parliament.[132] The 1962 Constitution reiterated the principle of repugnancy (Article 1). It also took the first step toward institutionalizing Islamic influence by establishing the Advisory Council of Islamic Ideology (A-CII) (Article 6(1), the first of a series of state institutions to provide advice on Islamic interpretation of the legislative agenda. These institutions gradually took on a life of their own, often producing edicts that challenged the existing law. While Article 198 of the 1956 Constitution for the establishment of the rule of the Qur'an and Sunna was enforceable there was no comparable provision in the 1962 Constitution. This again showed that Islamization of laws inside and outside parliament did not move along a linear path. Instead, the process was characterized by a 'tug-of-war' between modernists and traditionalists that has remained inconclusive up to this day, even as both substantive and procedural laws have been incrementally Islamized. The religious elements of Pakistan and the establishment were allies for a long time. Under Zia, laws were passed to attract the support of the Islamists. However, the 'sudden volte-face' under Musharraf weakened this alliance, and many of the extremist groups associated with the Taliban became disenchanted with the state.[133]

As statutory bodies (per Articles 199 and 207 respectively), the A-CII and its sister institution, the Islamic Research Institute, were only meant to give advice. The 1973 Constitution further provided that Islam would be the state religion (Article 2); that the president as well as the prime minister would be Muslim; and that the new oath for public office holders would confirm belief in the finality of prophethood with Islam. The new repugnancy clause (Article 29) changed sect to school of law as the source of differences in jurisprudence, thereby opening space for innovation (*ijtihad*). The 1973 Constitution also provided for the CII. However, its impact on Islamic legislation generally remained minimal, which often surfaced as a source of frustration for Islamists.

The martial law ordinances relating to Islamic legislation were a major source of extra-parliamentary input in law-making. Ayub's 1961 Family Ordinance sought to address the issue of the subordination of women in family matters relating to divorce, polygamy, and inheritance. It continues to invite the wrath of the ulema after six decades. They consider it un-Islamic as per the provisions of Sharia and therefore demand its annulment, most often from the pulpit of the mosque. Conversely, the most controversial series of Islamic ordinances was issued by President Zia's martial-law government, ranging from the 1979 Hudood Ordinances to the 1984 Evidence Act as well as amendments in the Blasphemy Law, providing the death sentence for several offences relating to desecration of the exalted personalities of Islam and the holy scriptures. The Hudood Ordinances have been criticized regularly by liberal opinion inside the country. It is interesting that a critique of these ordinances emerged from within the heartland of the Islamic establishment inside the state. The CII claimed that the definition of *Hadd* in the ordinance was neither derived from the Qu'ran and Sunna nor indeed in agreement with the definition of classical Islamic jurists.[134]

The CII has no direct role for legislation. Nor is it serving as an Islamic lobby in policy making circles. However, it remains a necessary adjunct institution of the government, to mollify Islamists. Its deliberations sometimes alienated the public through its religious injunctions. For example, it declared that DNA testing could not be used as a primary proof in rape cases.[135] It observed that sex-change operations were un-Islamic.[136] It asked the government to amend the law so as to facilitate polygamy.[137] It sought to remove the constraints over under-age marriage for girls.[138] The liberal intelligentsia sometimes demanded elimination of the institution for its allegedly medieval ideas about women, which were considered out of sync with the modern world.

The authors of the Penal Code, enforced in 1860 in India, strongly opposed laws against adultery since it would expose Indian women to wrongful accusations. They opined: 'To make laws for punishing the inconsistency of the wife, while the law admits the privilege of the husband to fulfil his *zenana* with women, is a course which we are most reluctant to adopt.'[139] The legal thinking in British India about adultery was based on maximum caution. However, a century later, several cases initially brought into the courts for rape were converted into *zina* allegations due to the courts' perception of the alleged (female) victims' conduct.[140]

Zia's Islamization programme, upheld by his successor Ghulam Ishaq, led to intense controversy over the role of women. Modernists, in this case the Commission on the Status of Woman, challenged the 1990 Qisas and Diyet Ordinance. It argued with reference to classical Islamic jurists that the *diyet* (blood money) for woman is equal to man's and not half, and that the consensus (*ijma*) on this issue is consensus by silence only. Similarly, the Law of Evidence that provided for one male or two female witnesses was challenged. It was argued that the second women's company was a privilege and not a compensatory provision for lack of sound judgement on the part of the female witness. Section 17 of the Law of Evidence was also challenged for going beyond the test of the Qur'an. The Commission raised several objections. Section 9 of the Prohibition (Enforcement of Hadd) Order 1979 provided for proof of only two male witnesses, whereby female witnesses were not catered for. Offence against property (theft) required two male witnesses (only). The Offence of Qazf (Enforcement of Hadd) Ordinance 1979 provided for two male witnesses while no women were admissible; offence under the Zina Ordinance 1979 required four male witnesses, which was unwarranted by the injunctions of the Qur'an.[141] A dissenting opinion came from the JI member of the Commission, Nisar Fatima. She took the position that the real place for women was at home; that a woman's basic responsibility was obedience to her husband and the raising of her children; that the greatest reason for rape was that women were out of purdah and intermixture of the two genders; and that co-education should end.[142]

The sentencing of a young couple to twenty lashes was noticed by diplomats as opposed to the government's claim that the Law of Evidence would not let such sentences to be carried out.[143] Indeed, the JUI-F proposed a ministry of ecclesiastical affairs that would remain immune to changes in government.[144] Various objections were raised to the passage of the Second Amendment that declared Ahmadis infidel: (1) parliament was not an ecclesiastical institution and could not therefore interfere in religious matters; (2) 16 MNAs and 14 out of 63 senators did not vote for the amendment; (3) parliament should equally determine who was not a Hindu, Sikh or Christian.[145]

Parliament was obliged to incorporate Islamic laws in the process of the indemnification of martial law regulations and ordinances in the 1985 8th Amendment. The 1949 Objectives Resolution was made a substantive part of the constitution, thereby rendering its Islamic injunctions justiciable. Amendments to Articles 62 and 63 were considered 'constitutional irritants', widely criticized as a manipulative and controlling mechanism meant to exclude people from politics at will.[146] In 2017, Prime Minister Nawaz Sharif was dismissed under Article 62(1) (f). No civilian government passed any Islamic laws on this scale before or after Zia, with the possible exception of the 2nd Amendment (1974) that declared Ahmadis outside the pale of Islam. Even that move took two decades to mature after the 1953 anti-Ahmadiya movement.[147] In *Zahir-ud-din* vs *The State*, the majority judgment concluded that 'certain religious terms are peculiar to Islam' and could not be appropriated by other religious communities; that the 'Islamic state is under the obligation to protect Islam', which may include preventing 'religious communities [like Ahmadis] from claiming that they are Muslims'; that the courts should decide 'the integral and essential elements of a religion'; and that any freedom of religion is subservient to Islamic law, 'which is the positive law of the land'.[148] In September 2018, Atif Mian, a leading Ahmadi scholar from Princeton, was removed from the newly formed Economic Advisory Council due to the opposition of clerics.[149] Under Nawaz Sharif (1990–3), the 15th Amendment – popularly known as the Sharia Act – was passed by the National Assembly, but it did not become law because it did not pass the Senate.

Islamic laws deepened the controversy as the 'liberals' and 'conservatives' fought intellectual battles on various fronts, including scholarly debates, the media's projection of rival positions, critical reports on textbook material for schools and colleges, and various civil society forums in general. The 'liberal' response to Islamic legislation after the turn of the twenty-first century was limited to issue-based legislation. This included the 2006 Hasba Bill, which was meant for putting in place an Ombudsman in KP for moral policing. It was passed by the MMA government in Peshawar but was not signed into act by the governor. The Elections Bill 2017 was amended due to pressure from the clerics. In this case, the replacement of the phrase 'I solemnly swear' with 'I believe' in the *Khatm-e-Nabuwwat* (finality of prophethood) clause caused an uproar in parliament as a result of which the change was reverted.[150] Minister for Law and Justice Zahid Hamid came under fire for what he later defended as a 'clerical error'. He pointed out that the parliamentary committee held 125 meetings in three years to reach the consensus document.[151]

Laffan describes how Islamic activists in the late colonial period presented Sharia as more than a 'rigid system of laws', by arguing how it encapsulated all the 'hallmarks of modern civilization such as democracy'. In this way the 'reformist vision of Sharia has more commonly coexisted rather than clashed with the authority of the day'.[152] Article 203-B(c) of the constitution provides for the establishment of a Federal Shariah Court (FSC) that essentially represents a parallel judicial system. However, its jurisdiction did not extend to constitutional law, Muslim personal law, or procedural as well as fiscal law for ten years after 1985 (Article 203-B). Case law indicated that the Sharia judicial system was obliged to address an Islamic legal perspective that was at variance with the traditional interpretation of the constitution.[153] The verdict in a case about implementation of the 1991 Enforcement of Sharia Act that addressed the plea that Sharia should be the supreme law of Pakistan rendered Section 3 (2) of that act invalid 'insofar as it relates to the curtailment of the jurisdiction of the FSC'.[154] However, more typically, the FSC itself declined jurisdiction on the issue of adjudicating the supremacy of Sharia over the constitution partially or fully, and for examining the substantive parts of the constitution.[155] The court's verdict acknowledged the lack of potential of Article 203-B to supersede all other provisions of the constitution, thereby confirming the FSC's limited jurisdiction in the context of Shariatization of the judicial system as enjoined by Article 2-A.

In 2012, the FSC favoured a petitioner seeking mandatory inclusion of the Arabic language in school curricula,[156] relying on Article 31(2) (a) of the constitution. However, it had been argued long ago that this article was not justiciable since it belongs to the Principles of Policy chapter of the constitution.[157] The Supreme Court vacated the FSC order in 2018 due to its lack of jurisdiction and justiciability of the matter.[158]

The issue of the purported supremacy of Islamic law over all other constitutional provisions continued to appear in various petitions against official measures allegedly involving repugnance to Islam, for example, appropriation of *waqf* (reserved properties of shrines and other religious places) and restriction of trade union activities. Justice Kaikaus sought an injunction from the Lahore High Court under Article 199 to declare the entire legal system under the constitution un-Islamic and to declare its adherents – ranging from the president to

MNAs and MPAs – non-Muslims. It is obvious that the Sharia judicial system assumed a tremendous moral potential that sought to ask Muslims to be faithful to Islam over and above the constitution, whose Islamic character was at best open to question in courts.[159] In the post-8th Amendment (1985) era, the insertion of 'moral' clauses in Articles 62 and 63 operated as a strategy of the state elite to weaken the political elite.[160] The CII reportedly responded to a query from the army that 'an officer did not need permission if he wanted to keep a beard', as had been the practice. It suggested that the government should make it compulsory for both public and private sector employees to pray and also advised 'posting of [a] religious attaché in Pakistan embassies abroad'.[161] Similarly, the mosque in the locality emerged as an arena for a sectarian fight. In one Masjid Noor in Lahore the imam publicly impugned Ahl-e-Hadith and welcomed Tahlighis in what was a Barelvi stronghold. The latter in turn cast shadows on the former's alleged religious inclinations towards Shias and identified him as a hypocrite and his mosque as Masjid Zarar (mosque of hypocrites at the Prophet's time).[162] Naveeda Khan in her study of *qabza* mosques quoted the chairman of the Lahore Development Authority (LDA) to the effect that 90 per cent of the mosques in the city were built illegally.[163]

One can mention the legislative moves toward passing the 9th Amendment in 1986 in favour of both the supra-constitutional character of Sharia and its implementation through the courts. General Zia's 'swan song' in this context, the 1988 Enforcement of Sharia Ordinance, purportedly sought to meet both demands – but obviously not to the satisfaction of Islamists. Similarly, the 1991 Sharia Act was more a formal than a substantive move in this direction. The court petitions in favour of Islamization incessantly relied on Article 2-A to deliver on the issues of eliminating interest-based banking, court fees that allegedly restricted access to justice to the rich only, and the perceived un-Islamic provisions of the 1961 Family Ordinance.[164] Similarly, the Sharia courts took up the issue of repugnance to Islam relating to the 1913 Punjab Pre-emption Act that would have denied thousands of landless tenants the right to purchase land.[165] Indeed, the high tide of judicial Islamism in the early 1990s was symbolized by a court verdict that lower courts were not obliged to follow the Supreme Court if that court transgressed Islamic laws.[166] In this way, the repugnancy clause(s) played a major role in re-shaping the constitutional discourse covering both legislative and judicial activity.

If the two periods before and after the 1985 8th Amendment are compared, the legal landscape of Pakistan in the second period appears to be far more opaque constitutionally than in the first period. As Martin Lau has argued, the situation was further complicated by the introduction of Islamic jurisprudence as an authoritative reference point in cases in which no legal guidance was available within the framework of the nation's constitutional law. Here, Islam emerged as a residual law whenever there was no recourse available to the state's codified law. In British India, the formula of 'justice, equity, and good conscience' operated to fill the legal vacuum (if any) usually with English Law, except in cases of personal law. In Pakistan, and occasionally in India whenever it was needed, a legal lacuna in some cases pushed the courts to Islamic jurisprudence as a residual step, although this practice remained unlikely to become a legal principle per se.[167]

In this context, one needs to mention a militant version of the extra-constitutional input. During the early 1990s, a millenarian movement called Tehrik Nifaz Shariat Mohammadi (TNSM), led by Sufi Mohammad, became active in Swat and other districts of the Malakand division and sought to establish Islamic law in that region. It represented two new approaches: demand for Sharia within a bounded space, i.e. a region that comprised the princely state of Swat until 1970; and militant action from outside parliament in pursuit of constitutional change. The Nawaz Sharif government felt obliged to issue the 1994 Nizam-e-Shariat Regulation to meet this demand. It was followed by the 1999 Sharia Nizam-e-Adl Regulations. Liberal opinion interpreted these responses to TNSM demands as adopting Islamic law under pressure.

In 2009, in the wake of the Taliban's incursion into Swat led by Sufi Mohammad's son-in-law, Fazlullah, who later became leader of the Tehrik Taliban Pakistan in October 2013 after Hakeemullah Mehsud was killed in a US drone attack, President Zardari signed the Sharia Nizam-e-Adl Regulations to establish the Islamic judicial system in Malakand Division. Article 247(3) served as the constitutional point of departure for this move. It provided that no Act of the national or provincial assemblies would have jurisdiction over the adjoining

FATA (Federally Administered Tribal Areas) or PATA (Provincially Administered Tribal Areas) respectively unless the president, or governor at the behest of the president, so directed. Article 247(4) opened the window for the governor, with the prior approval of the president, to make regulations for peace and good government for PATA that included Swat.

The 2009 Regulations provided for a three-tier court system for 'the said area' with local and district courts and a final appellate court, Dar-ul-Qaza, the PATA equivalent of the Supreme Court. The local judicial officer, *ilaqa qazi*, would be duly trained in Sharia through a recognized institution such as the Sharia Academy of the International Islamic University in Islamabad. All laws repugnant to Islam would cease to exist. It is curious that the 2009 Regulations included a list of ninety-four acts currently in force that 'shall apply to the said area' as before.[168] That was especially symbolic of the way the modernist state met with Islamic pressures on the ground through tough bargaining with the other party and yet conceding legal territory more symbolically than otherwise.

However, in the long run this was a classic example of the state retreating in the face of an extra-constitutional movement seeking a constitutional change for a specific area, while at the same time struggling to safeguard as much of the legal status quo as possible. Thus, the government reserved the right to select officials for the new set-up and kept a significant part of the current legal space from encroachment by the Taliban and proto-Taliban groups. In October 2013, when the issue of negotiations with the Taliban arose following a resolution of the National Assembly in this regard, the mainstream political forces insisted that these should be conducted within the constitution. However, the Taliban had already termed the electoral process, the judiciary, the army, parliament, and other structures and processes of the government un-Islamic. Liberal elements within and outside the state wondered how far the government would accommodate the Taliban's extra-constitutional demands. What was clear was the mounting challenge from Islamic discourse in legal, economic, political, judicial and educational domains, which had a crucial impact on the conception and application of state authority. The May 2013 elections marginalized the 'liberal' parties, the PPP, ANP and MQM, and returned the 'rightist' parties, the PML-N and PTI, to power with the former at the centre and in Punjab, and the latter in KP. There was a feeling that the PML-N government's quest for a deal with the Taliban could lead to deviation from the constitution. However, constitutionalism per se as an activity pursued within legal, judicial, and legislative circles gradually exhibited a loss of ultimate moral authority in favour of ideology in a supra-legal sense.

We have observed that the sources of jurisprudence in Pakistan have been shifting away from European legal philosophy and institutional practices in the direction of Islamic law. Islamization initially emerged out of the new state's quest for legitimacy. Civil–military tension led to what has been termed garrison–mullah alliance, which allowed Islamization a big leap forward in 1985. The Zia regime professed its desire for Pakistan to remain distant from any great power camp and instead lead the bloc of Islam.[169] Generational transition weakened the legal and institutional ties with the moral and philosophical universe of British India, and thus provided legitimacy to Islamization as a 'rational' expression of the desire for a Muslim homeland.

Islamization has been intermittent and sporadic in nature, corresponding to the power struggle on the ground. A 'tug-of-war' appears to exist between modernists and traditionalists in the formulation and interpretation of Islamic law. The latter made significant gains over time, but the turf was still in the hands of the former. The presence of two parallel judicial systems based on the mainstream constitutional tradition on the one hand and the FSC operating after the 1985 8th Amendment on the other created rival patterns of jurisprudential thought and practice. The former adhered to the superordinate legal position of the postcolonial state while the latter sought to demolish it.

A Religious Sub-system

Pernau observes the position of Islam in British India in the nineteenth century as a religious sub-system.[170] I want to argue that religion has assumed the character of a sub-system in the larger state system of Pakistan in both structural and operational terms. Structurally, Islamic institutions within the official framework as well as outside it in the form of madrassahs (more than 26,000 in 2019 and increasing), Islamic schools and universities, Islamic media and Islamic banking, point to a systemic dynamism. Operationally, the denominational organizations such as TLP have carried out their activities ostensibly with the establishment's support. However, there has been no large-scale party-based mass mobilization for an Islamic constitution, apart from examples of single-issue orientated street activity. A century of British Common Law, as it operated in the parts of India now included in Pakistan, carried the message of representative rule, whereby the local elite enjoyed access to district courts on the way to providing patronage to voters. The writ jurisdiction provided legal protection to citizens against arbitrary rule, although in a degenerative mode of operation after independence. Continuation of the constitutional source of legitimacy at one end and the space for Islamic legal and institutional activities at the other provide the key to preservation of the status quo.

Islamic finance is an area that has been conceived, conceptualized, operationalized and variously applied to banking practices from the 1980s onwards. By 2010, Islamic banking claimed 5 per cent of the banking operations in the country, with prospects for further growth. Some find Islamic banking and conventional banking practically the same while using different idioms.[171] Indeed, Islamic banking is caught in a 'vortex' where piety and operational feasibility are on opposite sides, leading to the use of Sharia-compliant phraseology such as 'profit-and-loss' sharing, even with additional transaction costs.[172] Profit rates of Islamic banking are benchmarked to the prevalent rates of interest in mainstream banking.

I want to argue that Islamic constitutionalism has advanced in theory rather than practice, in text rather than context, in scholarly and polemical studies rather than in adopting an original, innovative or revolutionary manifesto about an alternative financial system. The incursion of Islamism into the constitution has the effect of providing legitimacy, symbolism, deflection from the persistent crisis of governance, and reiteration of the importance of moral principles over practices. The neoliberal framework of the economy encapsulates whatever goes on by way of Islamic transactional activities just like mainstream banking. Similarly, the FSC remains the subsidiary system of adjudication in the context of its limited jurisdiction. The state manipulates the judicial process by shifting cases from the mainstream courts to the FSC or vice versa. It sometimes packs the FSC with modernists (judges from the courts) to outnumber the ulema to reverse a judgment that could become a source of embarrassment.[173]

The state managers continue to have the final authority in terms of their ability to define and implement law. However, their modernism is tempered by expediency. The modernists have high stakes in the maintenance of the constitutional state as it is. They have generally aligned themselves with Islamists. The clue to the latter's cooperation with the system lies in their accommodation by the state managers in more than one way. During the last several decades, they have been accommodated in statutory institutions such as the CII, federal and provincial textbook boards, jobs in the mosques and shrines run by the Auqaf department, TV and radio programmes as televangelists, and the Ruet-e-Halal Committee (moon-sighting committee). The PTI government allocated millions of rupees for funding the Madrassah Haqqania in Akora Khattak. The ulema parties got a firm foothold in the system after the 2002 elections when they formed the MMA government in Peshawar. Most of them upheld the cause of the Taliban who fought the NATO forces in Afghanistan after 9/11. The MMA government was instrumental in opening the way to thousands of Taliban fighters into the tribal areas and Swat valley. There have been several military operations against the Taliban, instigated by such events as the lashing of a 17-year-old girl in Swat in 2009 and the attack on the Army Public School in Peshawar in 2014. In other words, the state was able to clearly demarcate the red line beyond which the pursuit of the Islamic agenda was not permissible.

The religious sub-system of Pakistan has specialized itself in functional terms, which is distinguished from other social sub-systems such as economics, politics, science and law.[174] The Islamic 'establishment' in Pakistan has demonstrated its capacity for self-reproduction in the face of social, political and technological changes in wider society. This is possible because it has developed an internal complexity that can challenge the complexity of other sub-systems which operate with considerable autonomy, such as culture, art, economy, law and the health sector.[175] In the end, 'religious entrepreneurs',[176] much like ethnic entrepreneurs or business entrepreneurs operating in their respective sub-systems, are obliged to function in a pragmatic way by weighing their gains and losses in any engagement with the state machinery in pursuit of their demands. Speculations about seeing the religious sub-system evolve into the system per se, by displacing the constitution and subjugating the state apparatuses to its writ, are far from realistic.

Conclusion

The legal and institutional structures, ranging from habeas corpus to an elaborate system of magistracy, served as a safeguard against the authoritarian policies and practices of governments, especially the military regimes. In this process, the opposition ultimately, even unwittingly, raised the public profile of the judiciary as a bulwark against state oppression. As opposed to this, the executive implemented various initiatives pursuant to its own definition of the requisite constitutional provisions to establish its writ. This led to parallel interpretations of the constitution between the treasury and opposition benches, between the executive and the judiciary, and even between the bar and the bench such as under Chief Justice Iftikhar Chaudhry (2005–7, 2009–13).

I have argued that the chequered history of constitutionalism in Pakistan has been shaped by several unresolved conflicts among the rival contenders for power. These conflicts often fell outside the domain of law, essentially because the prevalent constitutional framework was unable to mediate between the competing forces struggling for influence and privilege. In other words, legal transformation of society by way of adoption of the jurisprudential definition of the claims to power remained incomplete. The state in British India was a limited instrumentality. The withdrawal of the British can be defined in terms of the inability of the current constitutional set-up to meet the demands of a rapidly expanding mobilized public that sought further expansion in the available political and legal space. Law remained underdeveloped in Pakistan in terms of its capacity to integrate society, a role that had been successful in the historical West.[177] Constitutionalism in Pakistan moved half-way to defining the mechanism for the distribution of power among institutions, departments and offices. It followed a top-down approach while delineating the hierarchy of state authority, whereby society at large remained at the receiving end. Throughout the post-independence period, legal socialization of the citizens of the new state remained marginal to both instruction through textbooks and rule-based behaviour patterns in the family, locality and community. Societal input into constitutionalism has been typically expressed through the challenge from the Islamic lobby and its institutional expression through the FSC, CII, and the training format of the Judicial Academy.

Despite all this, the law of the land is still the most authoritative source of the state's writ. In that capacity, it provides the supreme source of legitimacy for argumentation and decision-making in the courts, for the operational dynamics of the bureaucracy as well as for electoral democracy including party activity, public mobilization, and legislation in parliament. Although the power dynamics moved towards supplanting the existing body of laws to an ideological source of legitimacy, governments typically sought power and privilege and a change in the rules of the game and sanctions against political adversaries from within the prevalent constitutional framework. This pattern points to 'the political origins of constitutional reforms',[178] whereby the state elite and the political elite resorted to constitutional engineering corresponding to their capacity and will.

In the context of constitutional uncertainty, especially in situations of transition from military to civilian rule, judicial review indirectly indulged in constitution-making by 'rebuilding the ship at sea'.[179] The courts sought to resolve the conflict without recourse to legislators and by flowing with the current of public opinion. The different verdicts in the court cases against Nawaz Sharif and Imran Khan for corruption in late 2017 prompted a barrage of criticism against Articles 62 and 63. The Human Rights Commission of Pakistan (HRCP) claimed that the state had 'virtually given a blanket licence to fundamentalism and militancy in the name of religion' after the Faizabad incident in November 2017.[180] All this empowered not only the militant groups to openly target religious minorities such as Ahmadis, Christians and Shias but also judges and lawyers engaged in pursuit of the court cases.[181] There were violent demonstrations by far-right religious political parties and clerics after Asia Bibi's acquittal, calling for the heads of her lawyer and the supreme court justices.[182] Naveeda Khan argues that the 'Muslim becoming' reflected a continual struggle to be better Muslims through private or public disputations dotted by examples of a 'sudden eruption' of religious sentiment in a person.[183] Although the constitution is still at the centre of the power struggle among rival social and political forces, its potential to resolve conflicts within its jurisprudential limits is effectively constrained. In the absence of a continuing tradition of the legal socialization of the rulers and the ruled, the rival pattern of all-encompassing ideological socialization has contributed to a steady erosion of the crucial space for discourse on constitutionalism.

6

MASS PUBLIC

Introduction

In this chapter, I focus on the mass public in Pakistan, i.e. the section of society that carries relatively developed citizen orientations, and that responds to wider issues of policy and profile through various means of expression ranging from writing and teaching to street demonstrations. Habermas defined the public sphere in terms of the discursive space where private people came together and collectively behaved as public and articulated the interests of the society with the state.[1] Ideally, public space operates as an arena for the production and distribution of discourse, which is shared by those operating outside home at common social places and increasingly through the internet at home or in the office. The phenomenon relating to the perceived common good has led to various expressions such as 'public opinion', 'public conscience', 'public responsibility' and 'public attitude'. The public is a collection of individuals who develop a group consciousness around a problematic situation and act to resolve it by individual means.[2] Public not only taps into a set of subjectivities, but it also creates social textures and configurations where successive layers of social experiences and idea systems are built up.[3] Public is truly self-creating and self-organizing. Often it is a sub-set of the set of stakeholders at the higher levels.[4]

Pakistan inherited its state structure from the most developed imperial system in the world as compared to the French, Italian, Dutch, Spanish and Portuguese imperial systems. The 2011 Arab Spring sought political freedoms and civil liberties that had already become a part of the constitutionally protected public space in British India, not withstanding such murderous cases as the Jallianwala Bagh massacre in 1919. Violation of this space in post-independence India and Pakistan – for example, during the Emergency in India (1975–7) and under military governments in Pakistan – represented the gap between design and practice. However, a host of constitutional provisions, ranging from writ jurisdiction and habeas corpus to freedoms of expression, association and enterprise, ensured that public space existed de jure if not always de facto. For example, public demonstrations under late colonialism reflected the elite's 'quest for people' to build pressure in pursuit of independence and, more specifically, partition in the case of the Muslim League. After independence, public space was often taken over by street politics inasmuch as parliamentary deliberations were considered ineffective in the context of meeting public demands. The military governments of Ayub, Zia and Musharraf sought to bring 'stability' at the expense of participatory politics, political freedoms and civil liberties. Correspondingly, public space shrank after a military takeover that led to the declaration of political parties as defunct, the dissolution of elected assemblies and the implementation of an agenda of constitutional engineering. But the relative loss of public space was not accepted by society for long, even after the coup makers 'civilianized' their governments through elections in 1962, 1985 and 2002 respectively. Public space typically expanded during an election campaign as well as through street action of the mobilized sections of society. This chapter deals with the mass public as shaped and framed in three fields of public policy, i.e. civil society, education, and media.

A Marketplace of Ideas and Actions

For long, and for a variety of reasons, scholarly analysis has lavished attention and energy on the outermost structure of the social formation that defined the state. The result is a skewed picture of politics rooted in a misplaced priority attached to hegemonic and authoritative institutions carrying the potential for control. I want to argue that there is a need to investigate the off-stage players' input into politics. This may not fit with the script of power play. Joel Migdal has argued against the general understanding of the state as 'a unitary actor' operating from outside society: in his view, state is one of several forces in society that compete for domination economically, politically, and ideologically. He prefers to understand the state in the context of a 'society as a mélange of social organisations'.[5] He sees the public arena as the scene of a clash over the right to set the rules of the game, make coalitions and seek domination. This view projects a series of interminable conflicts taking place in public arenas that grossly overlap each other. Here, state operates as one of the organizations competing with others, often reflecting the pressures of the rival contenders for power. In this formulation, the state is far from a monolithic and all-encompassing entity.[6] Public space operates as a defining variable for understanding the nature, direction and limit of the state's authority. Indeed, the state is conceived as one sphere that exists apart from another sphere composed of all other associations, which can be defined for our purpose as the 'mass public', at the core of which lies 'civil society'. The latter keeps the state in check by keeping it within its limits and not allowing it, by its alertness, to encroach on activities not legitimately falling within its sphere.[7] Civil society is a structure of secure and reliable legality which leaves citizens relatively free to pursue their vocations.[8]

Public Space: Expansion and Contraction

As discussed earlier, Gilmartin dwelt at length on the way the local community in British India performed in public arenas as it increasingly drew upon religiously inspired symbols. These activities were generally autonomous of the state system, not least because they were locally rooted, culturally framed and typically not directly hostile to the principle and practice of the colonial state. Word of the mouth was replaced by public gatherings and rallies as well as by the printed word. This can be called the pre-history of what became a robust public space in India and Pakistan. One can point to four aspects of the emergent space: legislature, elections, law, and the street.

Firstly, legislative bodies brought the state and society closer to each other, one operating through an English-based, alien legal-institutional framework and the other representing public awakening rooted in primordial loyalties of caste and creed geared to carving out a niche in the political system. As legislative powers expanded, the state institutions also gained a higher level of relevance as sources of patronage and privilege in the locality.

Secondly, electoral dynamics provided a visible, activist, mobilizing and, ultimately, game-changing role for politicians who pursued public life as a career with all its uncertainties, gimmickry, ideology-laden discourse and identity-forming impact on the masses. Separate electorates from 1919 onwards provided a mechanism for Muslims and other minorities to stay afloat in the sea of the Hindu majority, where they could continue to maintain a presence of a sort on the basis of a transcendental identity which became operative in the currently expanding vote-based politics.[9]

Thirdly, law defined public space in British India from the mid-nineteenth to mid-twentieth century. By this reckoning, the 'first war of independence' in 1857 was actually the last war of independence. After that, it was no more a matter of two political entities competing for domination of India. The British side emerged as the state itself while the other side slipped into the status of a passive recipient of value from what became a transformative mechanism for the exercise of power. The new public space was thus born out of an interface between the two sides whereby the emergent rules of the game were charted out by the legal space available for expression of people's dissatisfaction, disgust and distrust with the 'system'. Legal provisions for writ jurisdiction, preservation of human rights and magistracy as a guardian of citizens' rights as opposed to the police as the armed wing of the state, defined and shaped the public space.

Finally, political space under late colonialism can be understood in the context of street politics that represented a negative response to the ruling dispensation from the public and revealed the latter's potential to impress its will on the authority structure. The street is a place for extraordinary political participation. The 'crowd' is generally understood as a source generating massive strength in the public arena to change the course of events in one or multiple contexts of mass activity.[10] We can find hundreds of examples of collective action out in the public before and after partition that can be located to street demonstrations. Mass agitation brought down the Unionist government in Punjab in 1947.[11] The marauding hordes of Hindu, Muslim and Sikh killers and arsonists sought to annihilate one another at partition. Bengali nationalist students were killed in Dhaka on 22 February 1951. Labour unionists on strike faced bullets in Karachi in 1972.[12] There were nationwide demonstrations against Ayub (1968–9), Bhutto (1977), Zia (1983) and Musharraf (2007–8). There have been scores of rallies protesting against the government, such as the peasant movements in Toba Tek Singh (1969),[13] in Hashtnagar in KP (1972)[14] and in Okara (2010–17).[15]

Demonstrations addressed economic and religious-cum-foreign policy issues. The former included price hikes on commodities such as petrol, wheat, sugar or vegetables and shortages of electricity and gas. The latter included the demolition of Babri Masjid (1992) and the Gujarat riots in India (2002), the religiously provocative cartoons in Denmark (2005), and later France (2020), Salman Rushdie's book *Satanic Verses* (1988), the trial and sentence of Dr Aafia Siddiqui in the USA on terrorism charges (2010), and Israel's bombardment of Hamas and the killing of Palestinians in 2014 and 2021. There were protests against the death sentence for Mumtaz Qadri for the murder of the Governor of Punjab Salman Taseer in 2011 for proposing procedural safeguards against the misuse of the blasphemy law. Other demonstrations aimed at a show of power, such as Benazir Bhutto's rally in Karachi on 18 October 2007 after her return from self-exile after eight long years, which came under murderous attack involving hundreds of casualties.

The definition of democracy expanded by default to include non-institutionalized public activity carried out outside the confines of parliament. In 2016, PTI agitation in Islamabad and Lahore was carried out in the name of its 'democratic' right to launch a mass movement against corruption and thus ask for Prime Minister Nawaz Sharif's resignation in the wake of the Panama Leaks revelations. In 2020–1, the joint leadership of the Pakistan Democratic Movement (PDM) exercised its 'democratic' right to topple what it considered an illegal government elected through the rigged 2018 election. Street politics often led to outright repression such as in 1968–9, 1977 and 2007–8, or otherwise to a change of regime. Even apart from agitational politics, it is common to mobilize people for religious marathons to celebrate the Prophet's birthday (Eid Milad-un-Nabi) or Yom

Ashura (the anniversary of martyrdom of Imam Hussain). There is a tremendously high level of commitment of time, attention, energy and finance by people for religious causes, sometimes involving a pattern of contestation with other religious and sectarian communities.

The mass public generally represented the self-consciously disenfranchised sections of the people through multiple means of expression. Ideally, the arena for a fight-out on public issues was expected to shift to the national and provincial assemblies after each election. But Pakistan does not provide a central role for parliament as a forum for conflict resolution. Public space has been used as a testing ground for power. In some cases, a civilian government took a step back from acting decisively to thwart a challenge to its lawful authority because it feared a backlash from the military establishment. Nawaz Sharif (2013–17) shied away from using force against the combined street demonstrations of the PTI/PAT/PAP in 2014 and the Defence Council of Pakistan, which were generally understood to be the establishment's protégés.

In 2020–1, Pakistan had people on the street in large numbers for various causes. A classical Huntingtonian scenario of political mobilization at a level that far exceeded the state's institutional potential to handle it had come into play. Kohli argued that this situation had rendered India ungovernable in the last quarter of the twentieth century.[16] The question is whether Pakistan had similarly become ungovernable a quarter of a century later. There were no institutional links between the haves and have-nots and, therefore, pressure from below could not influence policy at the top. In fact, policy had been conspicuous by its absence from the public arena for decades. An election campaign has typically been geared to patronage rather than policy. How to make sense of street politics if it has not contributed to social justice, political freedoms or representation of the grievances of the public in the corridors of power? We need to look for an answer in the utility of public space for political purposes.

One can ask whether political events create the public or the public creates political events. Public space is bounded by a given legal, moral, and political framework. We can examine the ingredients of an event as regards: (1) the prior announcement of a public meeting by a party leader; (2) the use of the media for spreading the news; (3) a formal application for permission tendered to a state functionary, carrying information about the time and venue of the proposed event; (4) the government grudgingly issuing permission at one end but politically opposing the move as an irresponsible and reckless act at the other; and (5) cultivated civility as the norm for law enforcement agencies responding, which could be matched by handling the mob with an iron hand.

Examples of brutal police handling of protestors or supporters of opposition parties and groups in the first quarter of the twenty-first century are legion. Fourteen people were killed by police shooting in April 2014 outside the main offices of the Minhaj-ul-Quran and the Pakistan Awami Tehreek (PAT) in Model Town in Lahore, both led by maverick cleric Tahir-ul-Qadri. Several supporters of the PPP's dissident leader, Zulfiqar Mirza, were manhandled by police in and outside the Sindh High Court in 2015. As mentioned earlier, the Nawaz Sharif government was extremely careful about not letting the PTI leader Imran Khan play politics over dead bodies, holding back its fire in 2014 and again in 2016. In this way, the mass public in Pakistan stamped its presence in the form of a non-institutional engagement with the state.

While the electronic media is a great maker and shaper of a collective understanding of issues, policies, leaders and parties, the concept of the public transcends the deterministic power of the media, as well as other influences such as educational curricula and the pulpit of the mosque. The public in Pakistan acquired its publicness not only late but also slowly during the last one hundred years. It is built on deeper cultural foundations, characterized by a shared legacy of colonial rule and the experiences and norms accumulated after independence. Together, these are transformed into a cluster of subjectivities, which defines a stable and resilient mass public in Pakistan beyond a mere situational and organizational expression of a problematized issue and mobilized group of people at any given time.

One can argue that the birth of the mass public in British India was indeed the point of departure for colonialism and the arrival of independence for the two successor states. The mobilizing potential of the two leading political parties, the Congress and the Muslim League, only meant that the state could no more operate from outside Indian society. Nor did the emerging 'Muslim public' in British India generally accept the idea of a Hindu-dominated state system after independence. The mass public has been expanding ever since.

One can interpret the successive military takeovers in Pakistan as attempts to control the perceived dysfunctional role of the mass public. For example, the 1958 coup took place before the dreaded moment of the general elections scheduled for February 1959 that were expected to bring the Bengali leader Sohrawardi to power. General Yahya and General Zia imposed military rule in the face of the mass rejection of the Ayub system by the nation in 1969 and the mass denial of the legitimacy to Bhutto's election victory in 1977 respectively. While the study of politics in Pakistan has generally focused on the contenders for power at the top, I want to argue that it is the mass public that has informally, indirectly and non-obtrusively – but in the end decisively – impacted the course of events. This includes not only the acceptance of military coups by the public but also the fear of non-acceptance of a coup, which has kept the military from a much-dreaded Bonapartist move as discussed elsewhere in this book.

For the army, the envisioned public response to its intervention in politics has been a matter of great importance. The army did not intervene after the retirement of forty-three generals by Z. A. Bhutto after taking over (1971), or after his dismissal of the army chief General Gul Hasan and Air Marshal Rahim (1972), or after the dismissal of General Jehangir Karamat (1997) by Nawaz Sharif. The 2011 US operation in the garrison town of Abbottabad that killed Osama bin Laden sparked rumours about a military takeover that did not happen. Similarly, the build-up of COAS General Raheel Sharif's profile as saviour of the nation under Nawaz Sharif during the anti-terrorist operation, Zarb-e-Azb in 2015, failed to mobilize the mass public in favour of an extension for, or takeover by, the former.

We can also look at the ambiguous attitude of the mass public towards the Taliban, at least for a decade and half. Was the group a bunch of thugs, terrorists, ruthless misogynists, sectarian killers, bank robbers and abductors for ransom? Or was it a band of defenders of Pakistan against penetration of Indian influence in Afghanistan, modern-day crusaders against the Christian West or a bunch of young self-righteous enthusiasts who had gone astray? Is the mass public of Pakistan a passive recipient of information and value, or a self-generating, self-perpetuating social entity? Is there one public in

Pakistan or several publics? Given an ethnic hierarchy operative in Pakistan whereby Mohajirs, followed by Punjabis, have a relatively higher level of education and urbanization, can we describe their input in public space as higher than input from other communities?

A major determinant of people's engagement in public activity, its mode of expression and its political idiom has been whether the region was ruled directly or indirectly under colonialism. Provinces that constituted British India displayed a propensity to operate within the prevalent institutional–constitutional framework because of their internalization of the dynamics of modern statehood for a century as defined by the role of the district courts, political parties, legislatures and local government. However, the princely states, such as Bahawalpur, Khairpur, Swat, Dir, Chitral, Kalat, Lasbela and others, operated under a 'feudal' system in British India.[17] These areas fell far short of providing public space where cultural and political activities could take place and group thinking could develop independent of dynastic patronage or tribal leadership. Bahawalpur state showed a measure of integration with mainstream politics only after partition, followed by Khairpur state as a poor second. The Balochistan states continued to be restive after accession to Pakistan because of stirrings of Baloch nationalism that acquired momentum at various times. Here, the regular paraphernalia of the district administration – ranging from police, revenue, education and health, industrial and agricultural departments to district courts – remained underdeveloped to varying degrees. FATA and PATA moved ahead at a snail's pace towards party-based electoral politics after the turn of the twenty-first century; however, they remained far behind the settled districts of KP in terms of the penetration of the state's institutional and constitutional structure in local society and the emergence of a viable public space. The merger of FATA with KP in 2018 was expected to start the process of creating some kind of public space in these areas.

One can also point to the difference between the urban and rural sectors. The mass public has typically been an urban phenomenon led by the provincial capital cities Karachi, Lahore, Peshawar and Quetta. These cities are not only the centres of political and cultural activity per se but also the foci of larger province-wide movements of people, ideas and ideologies for the purposes of street agitation in general. Karachi has attracted more scholarly research in recent years than all other major cities combined.[18] At the heart of it lay ethnic violence. The MQM was the leading actor on the political stage, enjoying vote power, street power and fire power.[19] Laurent Gayer argued that Karachi was a city of 'ordered disorder'.[20] He pointed to the eerie phenomenon of self-restraint of the city's population where politics resumed immediately after the guns fell silent.[21] On the other hand, the city raised 54 per cent of tax revenues and 70 per cent of income tax; contributed a quarter of GDP; and handled more than 90 per cent of the country's exports.[22] The author refers to the two dimensions of social life. One is defined by fear of moving around the locality, thus leading to disempowerment and humiliation. The second is an 'architecture of security' comprising social exclusion in the form of ever-expanding ghettos, both ethnically divided and mixed.[23]

Hyderabad, Peshawar and Quetta are focal points of Sindhi, Pakhtun and Baloch nationalisms, and Multan is a magnet for incipient Siraiki nationalism. Provincial capitals continue to operate as centres of higher education, entertainment, health facilities, clubs, sports, literary and artistic production and as meeting points of a cross-section of leaders, cadres, and workers of political parties. These cities represent two parallel centres of networking, use and abuse of authority, and links with the federation above and the district below: one is 'political' and the other is 'governmental'. The former is identified with the provincial assemblies of Punjab, Sindh, KP and Balochistan, where individual and collective bargaining takes place or contestation is played out between the ruling party or coalition and the opposition. At the other end, cabinet ministers in the secretariats provide the link between the public representatives and the state machinery. Access to their offices, and through them to the bureaucracy working under them, is a measure of the power and prestige of the social, political, economic, cultural, intellectual, landed and tribal elites as public office holders. Politicians in turn play out a brokerage function, thus mediating between the English-based, remote, and 'neutral' state and the patronage-seeking masses at large.

Concentration of authority in the provincial capitals vis-à-vis districts and their own perceived weakness vis-à-vis Islamabad in the context of the continuing hold of a centralist bureaucracy over administration and finance has resulted in a massive exercise in the political uses of the available public space. Politics in the provinces has remained a largely untapped area of research in Pakistan. This has led to reliance on identity and party leadership as explanatory variables. Identity represented a focus on the ethnic dimensions of the Baloch, Pakhtun, Sindhi and Mohajir nationalisms. Leadership represented a party identification model whereby the gap of policy orientation and ideological commitment was filled by dynastic leadership to project and maintain the hold of the party's appeal over its constituency. Ethnic publics have been considered problematic for the national project in terms of their demands for equanimous distribution of resources. As opposed to the process of homogenization of culture across ethnic and linguistic differences in the historical West, the exclusive cultural expressions of the constituent units of Pakistan and the communities therein have sometimes been reinvigorated and redefined in recent decades. Lower down, there are scores of towns where the pattern of life is slowly changing but the local power structures and customary practices rooted in social and cultural conservatism do not allow much public space.[24]

District is a unique legacy of British rule. It provides the clue to the constrained public space in the locality, especially in a rural milieu. Here, the 'subaltern classes' typically exit from the power play while the local 'dynasts' manage to keep the ball rolling through their electoral activity and relations with the revenue department and the courts. The local power structure plays a significant role in procedural matters of litigation, which include the recording of witnesses, the postponement of dates of hearing, grants of unnecessary adjournments, and the transfer of cases. Courts and votes represent the state-in-the-field and local politics, respectively. From the DC's office down to the lower staff of the magistracy and police, the district administration is fully responsive to the local string pullers.

Law is the strongest legitimizing force behind the district administration. In addition to the formal body of laws, there has emerged a large mass of subsidiary legislation enforced in the form of executive orders. In fact, the Law Commission stressed the need for 'pruning of the dead wood from the legislative forest from time to time'. But this 'forest' has provided the arena for a power struggle at the local level.

There is a whole army of para-professionals in the field of litigation operative around the office of lawyer, who is thus placed at the centre of a two-way traffic between the law-enforcing agencies of the state and the litigant public. The structural changes in property ownership have led to a large rise in litigation over the last century about inheritance, shares, transfers, mortgages, redemption of mortgages, sales, leases, boundaries, revenue-free grants, irrigation supplies, tenancy and pre-emption.

Civil Society

How to define civil society in Pakistan? Is it a collection of structures mediating between the government and citizens, a watchdog over official performance, a network of secondary associations in a Tocquevillian sense, or an '(un) civil society' that can undermine the system?[25] As noted earlier, civil society was accredited the role of agency in opening up the Eastern European communist societies, especially Poland.[26] The question is: how could civil society erode the legitimacy of a government in an East European country while it has hardly been able to do so in countries such as Pakistan, India, Sri Lanka, Bangladesh and a host of countries from Africa and Latin America? Actually, civil society as a non-state actor could undermine democracy – for example, by representing vested interests for blocking reform, or through citizens' militias, which in the USA posed a challenge to the system at large.[27] A similar danger could come from the institutionalization of interaction between government and non-government organizations representing interest groups – for example, the Chamber of Commerce and the Textile Millowners' Association, which were able to tilt policy to the right in the USA, as demanded by proponents of the public choice theory.[28] This would indeed result in expansion of the state contrary to the much-touted understanding of civil society's role as reduction of the state. Moving from rural to urban areas, we notice an increasing role for the mass public. In this context, I want to discuss the input of civil society in pursuit of social, educational, and cultural causes.

Apart from the 'money right' that could benefit from co-operation with the state, as mentioned above, the 'religious right' could, and in fact did, manage to exert a great influence on policy in Pakistan. This 'Islamic civil society' operated through relief organizations such as Jamat ud Dawah (JuD) in the context of natural disasters, i.e. the

2005 earthquake and the 2010 floods. Organizations such as Al-Huda, working for the religious training of Muslim women, had an extra-systemic input as far as the means and ends of democracy were concerned.[29] Various faith-based organizations in Pakistan collected *zakat* on behalf of voluntary organizations responsible for humanitarian work such as the Alkhidmat network affiliated with JI.[30]

In Pakistan, the concept of civil society became popular at the time of the emergence of NGOs in and around the 1980s. Civil society has impacted the way certain issues have surfaced and become part of the prevalent public discourse. In particular, the donor-funded NGO sector has contributed to public awareness about the need for resource input in the locality in pursuit of the goal of social and economic uplift. In the following discussion, I define and analyse the role of civil society with reference to three factors.

First, there is the leadership factor that steers the process of resource input. Its catchment area lies in the urban middle class. The 'progressive' urban-based intellectuals and activists who lead the NGOs operate in the apparently non-political space of the 'development sector', which often encompasses villages and small towns. They are billed as agents of change. They pursue the agenda of NGOs in the fields of community development, public health and infrastructural projects relating to roads, schools and wells. They have pro-poor, pro-woman and pro-minority agendas, straight out of the concept notes of the projects funded by the German, American, Canadian, British, Dutch and other Western donors. These projects often produce in NGO bosses a self-perception of being progressive intelligentsia with or without the appellation of the 'left'. This phenomenon defines the way they display an 'anti-establishment' stance on various issues relating to class, gender, and religion. Apparently, this perception reflects the goals and objectives of the donor community belonging to the capitalist states of the West. Donors seek to mitigate the absolute levels of alienation of various sections of the population living on the margins of Third World societies due to poverty, religious persecution and fossilized cultural practices in the context of gender-based oppression. In other words, NGOs typically eschew the need to analyse their role as agents of the principal, i.e., the 'world establishment'. This is a reflection of the contradiction between the self-perception of NGOs as upholders of the socially and culturally progressive agenda of the West and the implicit but substantive ideological framework of the 'Washington Consensus' couched in neo-liberalism at the donor's end.

NGO activity and civil society's role in general has contributed to a dilution if not elimination of class politics. Civil society is increasingly understood as a 'means to an end', be it democracy, economic growth or political development. Its contribution to the 'public political space' as a check on the state has been considered a beneficial outcome.[31] Civil society is also understood as an effect of social capital. But social capital can have a negative effect as well, because cohesiveness within a group often comes at the cost of pushing away its marginal section.[32] The inbuilt complexity of civil society, especially the leadership of the NGO community, poses a challenge to understanding its role in the larger society.

The second factor is the relatively non-political orientation of civil society. The middle-class 'progressive' leadership of NGOs operates in the context of 'new social movements' dealing essentially with non-economic issues that did not play a significant role in the electoral framework of the politics in the country. In this context, neo-liberalism has functioned as the dominant ideological framework as opposed to the social welfare state model along with its service structure. The popular argument about the crucial role of civil society for democracy does not hold ground against the evidence to the contrary: some sections of civil society joined General Musharraf's military government in 1999 that had displaced the elected government of Prime Minister Nawaz Sharif. Indeed, the middle-class ethos in Pakistan has been far from orientated toward the rule of public representatives. Instead, it has a prior commitment to the rule of law and the accountability of public institutions for inefficiency, corruption, and malpractice. The political system has afforded a role for civil society within the legal framework of the state. As argued by Pasha, civil society is a manifestation of the public space provided by the constitution and, accordingly, the legally accepted norms of political behaviour.[33] While the two power centres of Pakistan represented by the state elite and political elite have collided, coalesced and compromised, a clash of institutions typically reflected their conflict in the legal space operationalized through the higher courts. Conversely, civil society, especially the NGOs, operated within a relatively inconspicuous area of activity that did not provoke state authority and may even have filled the gap in development activity in certain localities.

The state in Pakistan, however, as elsewhere in the Third World, is extremely apprehensive about the inroads made by the donor community into its public sphere. It has sought to streamline the activities of the donor-funded NGOs that were required to be channelled and approved through the Economic Affairs Division of the federal government in Islamabad. Indeed, Nisar Chaudhary, minister of interior under the Nawaz Sharif government (2013–17), tightened the noose around NGOs and International Non-Governmental Organizations (INGOs).[34] The NGO community in Pakistan has been constrained to operate within the state system, thus shying away from taking up political issues in public. It has no significant input into the public discourse about electoral outcome, civil–military relations or ethnic bargaining. As Jalal argues, the class and ideological composition of civil society have been a great impediment in the struggle to create democratic institutions.[35]

Social and cultural issues and practices, but not economic and political issues and policies, have been at the heart of NGO activity. Starting in the 1980s as relief operations in the context of the Afghan war, the charitable NGOs later assumed advocacy functions underscored by the general feeling that the official planning for development had failed to deliver over time. The international donor community got increasingly involved in funding and setting policy frameworks for NGOs, which looked at their own role in the context of community development from the 1990s onwards.[36] This included such 'parastatal organizations' as the Rural Support Program in Gilgit-Baltistan, where the government and NGOs struggled to work together – for example, in the Working Group on Poverty Alleviation and the National Environment Action Plan.[37] On the one hand, the state was sceptical about the issue of the autonomy of NGOs and sought to regulate their activity. On the other hand, NGOs formed forums such as the Advocacy Development Network and tried to connect with the wider society, including the media. These organizations experienced tensions with the state, for example, on the issue of women-related legal reforms in the context of the aborted 1991 15th Amendment, and attacks on, and fatwas and death threats against, NGO personnel belonging to the Aurat Foundation, the Applied Socio-economic Research Resource Centre (ASR), Shirkat Gah and the Human Rights Commission of Pakistan among others.[38]

Thirdly, civil society has been accredited with participating in the 2007 lawyers' movement, and not without reason. At that time, both Nawaz Sharif and Benazir Bhutto at the top of the PML-N and PPP respectively were in exile. Suspension of Chief Justice Iftikhar Chaudhry by President Musharraf was not exactly a political showdown involving political parties or their leaders and workers, or a matter of parliamentary legislation, or even a law-and-order issue. It directly and immediately hit the bar as a natural constituency of the bench. Most typically, lawyers belong to the category of the middle and lower middle classes. In the event, it was the organizational expression of the lawyer community through the bar associations at the federal, provincial and district levels that carried the day.

A crucial role was played by the presence of lawyer's forums in the 4 provinces and 136 districts, along with individual lawyers' clientele, which spread to cities, towns and villages. The legal fraternity spread its tentacles all around, both vertically from the Supreme Court Bar Association and high court bar associations to the district bar associations, and horizontally through litigants to both rural and urban sectors. The lawyers operated as civil society in pursuit of the agenda of reinstating Chief Justice Chaudhry. In time, the movement gained momentum and became a fully-fledged agitation for the restoration of democracy and the removal of the military president, Musharraf. Benazir Bhutto arrived in Pakistan after her self-exile on 18 October 2007 and registered her support for the cause, as did other political parties and leaders. The 2007 lawyers' movement also produced Islamist and nationalist idioms as 'cultural and ideological frames' to praise Justice Iftikhar Chaudhry as an icon of justice, as well as YouTube videos as 'informational cascades'.[39]

One can draw two conclusions from this episode. First, civil society was represented by a relatively amorphous lawyers' community, whose leadership was nonetheless organized at the federal, provincial and district levels. The personnel from NGOs typically joined hands with the lawyers. Second, the electronic media broadcast political rallies live and thus played a political role in favour of democracy. The fact that civil society went back to its isolationist stance after this and has not been visible on the political scene for more than a decade points to its quintessentially non-political role.

While one generally finds a positive view of civil society being a contributor to democracy, Pasha has argued that the military–bureaucratic oligarchy has far from guaranteed its emergence.[40] He saw a 'nativized' civil society rooted in an indigenized middle class, which he traced to Zia's institutionalization of vernacular political interests. In Pasha's view, the postcolonial state in Pakistan was not 'overdeveloped' as per Alavi, who focused on the state's capacities in terms of its institutional powers; it was actually 'underdeveloped', in terms of moral leadership, public consent and legitimacy.

Not surprisingly, society has looked at the state as 'an external agency', something like a tax collector.[41] In Qadeer's view, civil society in Pakistan developed in three phases: (1) 'Civil Society of Clans and Welfare Associations 1947–68' was based on ethnic background; (2) 'The Ideological State and Divided Civil Society 1969–88' represented ethnicity, class and ideology that overpowered the earlier rural versus urban and traditional versus modern struggles; (3) there was a nexus of 'Civil Society, Community Development and Collective Goods'.[42] The problem with this formulation is that it is lumpy in character and only tenuously related to the political context, especially in the second and third phases. It generally lacks explanatory potential by way of conceptual or empirical analysis. Democratization does not necessarily benefit from the activity of a vibrant civil society. In the South African context, some analysts maintained that different sectors of civil society demonstrated completely opposite attitudes towards democratization.[43] The civil society movement under the apartheid regime did not demand the abolition of the system of racial segregation.[44] In Pakistan civil society was unable to offer resistance to governments that embarked on a one-dimensional state-building process. Coercion, rather than consent, repression rather than legitimacy, and administration rather than politics have been the order of things.[45]

However, some progressive legislation came out of civil society's efforts, including the 2011 Prevention of Anti-Women Practices Bill and the 2011 Acid Control and Acid Crime Prevention Bills. Civil society has advocated action on many other issues including the passage of the Minimum Wages for Unskilled Workers (Amendment) Bill for capital territory in the Senate, and the campaign for protection of UNHCR-declared heritage sites during the construction of the Orange Line Metro Train project in Lahore in 2017–18.

In Arjumand Kazmi's view, the modern conception of civil society considers it as functioning in an idealized counter-image to the coercion of state.[46] For example, democratization in Pakistan did not involve grassroots mobilization, volunteerism or ideological persuasion. The 'projectized' democratization has been a 'balancing act' by which NGOs have navigated the space in Pakistan's elitist political edifice. Instead of strengthening civil society, the elite NGOs could actually weaken it. Since 9/11, closer interaction between aid, foreign policy and the security agendas of the international funding agencies has led to 'securitisation of aid'.[47] Indeed, like the long-existing political, military and bureaucratic elites in Pakistan, a new sub-group of elites has emerged in the form of internationally funded NGOs in pursuit of democratization, whose intimacy with politics has been considered an asset. The movement of NGOs in the 1980s led by the Women's Action Forum along with others operating in the social sector diverged into 'projectized' democratization programmes supported by international funding in the early 2000s. Away from people demanding democracy 'on the streets', the projectized democratization operated through a 'corporate model', 'salaried people' and 'technocrats'. Activism was transformed into professionalism.[48] Kazmi has argued that democratization through NGOs is a de-politicized project operating usually, if not always, far from engagement with the masses.[49] Since a majority of the NGO people belonged to the middle class, their 'progressive' causes reflected the ideals of their own class, which typically shied away from mass politics. Politicians have been critical of the NGO's capacity-building projects and training programmes in the absence of adoption of political means in pursuit of political ends, for example by ignoring patronage politics as the very substance of electoral democracy. They consider these programmes essentially a 'hit and run exercise' because there is no substantive connection with the way the political class operates.[50]

In Akbar Zaidi's view, the prevalent justification for the role of NGOs is state failure, which manifests as a persistent crisis of governance.[51] He argues that due to the large financial input, 'the intellectual basis of NGOs remains essentially donor driven' underscored by the patron–client relationship between the two sides.[52] While NGOs are obliged to demonstrate efficiency for receiving funds, they tend to overstate the impact of their projects and even fudge data.[53] In view of NGOs' dependence on foreign donors' money, their accountability moves 'upwards' rather than downwards to the grassroots. If the donors' interests change, NGOs change accordingly. It is obvious that the input of the donors is time bound and project specific. NGOs are agents to a principal, i.e. an INGO, political party or a government in a Western country. In this way, accountability remains the hazy end of a process that is marked by arbitrariness and a self-propelled egalitarian agenda.[54] In a majority of cases, rather than becoming innovative, participatory and creative platforms for action and thought, NGOs operate as project implementers, as 'technical transfer agents', and as contractors for donors and governments.[55] In December 2017, Islamabad ordered twenty-one INGOs to leave the country after they failed to re-register under tough regulations introduced a few years before.[56] In December 2018, Pakistan kicked out eighteen INGOs after rejecting their final appeals to stay in the country. Another twenty organizations were also on the hitlist of the government after it singled out thirty-eight aid groups for closure. The idea was that the USA and European countries secretly brought spies into the country under the guise of aid workers. The CIA sting operation, in which a Pakistani doctor, Shakeel Afridi, posed as an international aid worker and used a fake hepatitis vaccination programme to try to get the DNA samples from Osama bin Laden's family, only added to the deficit of trust.[57]

Negative sentiment against NGOs is directly related to the enhanced sense of insecurity shared by the developing countries, which jealously guard their sovereignty. In the security establishment's view, INGOs contribute to a 'hybrid war' against Pakistan, promote a foreign agenda, support hostile spy agencies, collect confidential data and operate illegally.[58] In early 2018, the NAB decided to check the record of all NGOs and INGOs, as they were accused of not only misusing but also misappropriating funds. The government became especially active in regulating the NGO sector after Pakistan was placed on the Financial Action Task Force (FATF) grey list, as per allegations that some aid groups were involved in terror financing. The Securities and Exchange Commission of Pakistan (SECP) framed new regulations for NGOs and INGOs in pursuit of concerns over money laundering and terror financing.[59] In fact, the SECP cancelled the registration of 3,000 NGOs and NPOs (non-profit organizations) during 2017–18 on suspicions of money laundering. However, it had no jurisdiction to regulate and monitor around 15,000 NPOs registered under provincial laws across the country.[60] It is widely understood that the state was inimical to all voices and avenues that offered a narrative different from the official discourse. The idea was that NGO work was not their right but a privilege bestowed on them by the government in Islamabad.[61] It was argued that the Pakistani state never recognized civil society and only tolerated NGOs because of international pressures, mainly due to some UN conventions on allowing civil society's input on policy issues.[62] Ironically, the clamp-down on INGOs was enforced in the name of compliance with the latest conditions imposed by the FATF, since many religious organizations and charities were registered under the same law that governed NGOs.[63]

Pakistan's standing on the issue of controlling terror financing moved forward at a snail's pace. As opposed to the PTI government's expectations to move away from the grey list of FATF, it had failed to do so in February 2021 and again in June 2021. At the top of the FATF demands was improvement in investigation and prosecution, as well as demonstration of the effectiveness of court judgments in the form of proportionate and dissuasive sanctions against the designated 1,267 and 1,373 terrorists and their partners or facilitators respectively.[64] An analyst looked at all of this in terms of the impugned link of the FATF with the IMF in the context of the 'imperial' dictation of the colonial era. He pleaded for the right of Pakistan to be removed from the grey list that had brought the country to the brink of economic collapse.[65] He accused India of establishing terrorist training camps, twenty-one in the country and sixty-six in Afghanistan. At the other end, Dr Ikram ul Haq stressed the need to put one's own house in order.[66] He criticized various asset-whitening schemes and tax amnesties under the prime minister's package for the construction sector exactly when the FATF regime exerted its pressure in 2020. No significant measures were taken by the PTI government in terms of bringing the real estate agents, jewellers, accountants, NPOs and political parties under the net of tax filers.

It is difficult to understand civil society in Pakistan as a potential contributor to democracy. Non-NGO civil society lacks the institutional capacity to splash its message to the wider public. Being essentially urban-based and middle class in its origin, thinking and behaviour, civil society has a thin presence among the working classes in the urban and rural sectors, ethnically mobilized communities, sectarian groups, trade unions and other politically relevant sections of the population. In the erstwhile communist Eastern Europe, transition to liberal democracy has often been attributed to civil society.[67] But this is an exception that proves the rule. First, the relatively secure working class, along with the emergent middle-class sections, was never a part of the statecraft under the workers–state model that operated through the Communist Party's stranglehold over the general masses. There was no legal space for upwardly mobile and politically ambitious sections of the public to penetrate the state system. The politically restive groups operated against the communist system in an essentially non-violent way, through trade union activity, the media, bilateral negotiations with the state functionaries, and street demonstrations. The protagonists of the movement in pursuit of extra-systemic goals such as democracy in the East European framework generally fell under the rubrics of civil society.

A postcolonial state such as Pakistan, on the other hand, has a civil society that is politically conservative in terms of its means and ends. As for the means, there is a legally sanctioned public space in the form of media outlets, party activities, street demonstrations that sometimes become violent, and the widely operative court system for redress of public grievances. As for the goals, these are generally conceptualized and operationalized in overtly non-political contexts relating to the environment, religious persecution, child labour, and women's issues ranging from honour killing, expropriation from inheritance, divorce, domestic violence, discrimination in jobs and sexual harassment. State coercion can in part be explained by the underdevelopment of civil society. The capitalist nature of the colonial impact, expansion of the social division of labour and the market, and the system of accumulation under colonialism fell considerably short of securing the prerequisites for the emergence of civil society.[68] All this, however, does not preclude the possibility of civil society taking up a political role. This happened at least once before 2007, when the middle class actively participated, organized and financed the movement against Z. A. Bhutto after the 1977 elections.[69] It is possible that civil society may find a role for itself in future in the same mould, and exercise a significant input in shaping the new publicness by raising awareness about social, cultural, and political issues.

Education: Reproduction of the Ideological Matrix

While civil society is a relatively amorphous product of legal provisions and public space, education is somewhat planned, targeted, and directed either directly or indirectly by the state. In this section, I plan to deal with education at two levels. First, I want to explore the policy-making level in order to understand the process of formulation of educational objectives. Second, I want to focus on the textbook level so as to bring out the ideological framework that defines the worldview of youth. The public in Pakistan, like elsewhere, is the product of the national educational system. It reflects the social, cultural and ideological views of the nation that have shaped policy and practice at various levels of the hierarchy in the state apparatus. My argument is that young minds in Pakistan have been effectively geared towards a combative framework of nationalism, religion and civilization in general.

Making an Education Policy

According to Pierre Bourdieu, education is the process of the transmission of the cultural capital of the dominant classes and the characteristics which appropriate the dominant culture.[70] In Pakistan, education has become both a cause and effect of the state's ideological agenda since partition. Education as cause represents the national project that pushed the policy makers into shaping young minds along thinking in an atmosphere of acute insecurity and developmentalism in general. Education as effect points to the adversarial framework of thinking inculcated through textbooks, which has created gross inwardness among students, who operate in a binary of loving the best (Pakistan) and hating the rest (outside Pakistan).

I first look at the nature and direction of education policy in terms of input and then examine the curricula as output in the context of imparting knowledge to the younger generation. I point to a narcissist streak that ran through various intellectual endeavours, especially in the immediate post-independence years. Writers claimed that the eyes of the world, especially the Islamic bloc, were focused on Pakistan.[71] Moreover, education policies have been crafted to serve the interests of the ruling elite at the cost of cognizable ethnic identities.[72] The 2006 national curriculum policy virtually prescribed the curriculum for the provinces, thereby nullifying the purpose of devolutionary federalism.[73] Every education policy was preoccupied with creating 'the nation', right from the 1959 Sharif Report, the 1979 policy under Zia, the 1998 policy of Nawaz Sharif, and the 2009 policy of the PPP government under Zardari.[74]

It is interesting to see the change from policy to ideology in the educational context over the three generations after partition.[75] In the 1947 and 1951 policies there was a focus on the civilizational dimension of religion. The way to social justice was defined through Islamic socialism. Precedence was given to being citizens of Pakistan over religious identity. But the 1959, 1970 and 1972–80 policies increasingly invoked Islam for national unity, while expression of Islamic socialism was discounted. In 1970, the government's policy was essentially a statement of national goals and basic guidelines.[76] These goals included the introduction of Islamic values as 'an instrument of national unity', 'scientific, technical and vocational education' and 'decentralization of educational administration'.[77] The 1979 policy brought Islam into the classroom. The 1998 policy document defined education as the 'key to moral, cultural, political and socio-economic development'.[78] It also mentioned decentralized management as well as community mobilization as the two objectives of the policy, which, however, remained part of the rhetoric that accompanied most policy documents. As with other policy dossiers about education, this document also traced the history of policy formulation after independence, emphasized the importance of 'the right type of education' 'suitable to the genius of our people' and pointed to the need 'to build the character of our future generations' by instilling in them 'the highest sense of honour, integrity, responsibility and selfless service to the nation'.[79] Hyperbole remained a constant feature of what should have been a reasonable and well-argued expression of aims and objectives. Morality reigned supreme as an educational goal. The report is full of clichés such as education being a 'capital investment' and a great source 'for the socio-economic and cultural development'.[80]

Under Zia, the 1979 education policy promoted the idea of inculcating faith in youth by teaching Islamic Studies and even Arabic. As for academic activity, Shahid Siddiqui points to the state of research in Pakistan as miserable, with syllabi far from suitable for the new millennium and 'dull and drab teaching dynamics' unlikely to promote creativity.[81] The 2009 education policy argued for 'the imperative of uniformity' with a renewed vigour, and considered the presence of parallel education systems as violative of the spirit of nationalism.[82] It noted that, as per its position at 104 in the Global Competitive Index (GCI), Pakistan compared poorly with India at 49, Malaysia at 32 and Sri Lanka at 81. There was a lack of general understanding about educational inequality between the public and the private sector institutions, about well-articulated minimum standards of education, and integration of past initiatives. Political influence operated through the recruitment and the posting of teachers and giving textbook contracts without merit. The 2009 education policy document referred to the Economist Intelligence Unit, which described Pakistan's education system as the most deficient and backward in Asia.[83] Amazingly, in a rare moment of self-introspection, the document acknowledged that education could lead to both a vicious and a virtuous circle in the context of income distribution.[84]

In a move away from the practice of successive governments in the past, Imran Khan's government (2018–) decided to engage the madrassah federations in the formulation of the new education policy. It focused essentially on meeting the ideological dimension of education rather than addressing the pedagogical objectives.[85] The initiative applied to the whole of Pakistan in contravention of the provisions of the 18th Amendment, which made education a provincial subject. The government intended to provide thousands of jobs for madrassah graduates to teach the Qur'an in government schools, barring the private sector. It wanted to consolidate its ties with the Islamic lobby through appeasement.

Thus, piety and morality continued to dominate the ideals and aims of educating the students. There was criticism that this policy would lead to 'a mono-visual', coercive and 'jihadist' culture.[86] In a comparison with the Indian educational policy of 2020, which is exclusionary towards the Muslim past and driven by the postcolonial instinct for eliminating the colonial vestiges, Hoodbhoy sees Pakistan as creating a religious society, ultimately pushing the two neighbouring countries further apart.[87] Nayyar criticizes the misplaced priorities by ignoring the 22.8 million children out of school, the abysmal quality of textbooks and an over-emphasis on provision of the same curriculum for the whole country, which reflects the continuing hold of the cult of unity over the minds of policy-makers.[88] All this carried the grim prospect of turning the wheel of education away from the contemporary world, both in spatial and temporal terms, in the absence of exposure to global civilization and human history respectively. It was feared further that insularity would find a hospitable space in the country. Nadeem Farooq Paracha found the new education policy a retrogressive step as a close follow-up to the policy mainstreaming radical outfits in electoral politics.[89]

The PTI government's education policy in 2020 took the cumulative thinking of the establishment and the conservative middle class to new heights in the direction of nationalism rooted in the cult of unity and Islam as the ideological framework of learning. Some saw in it the 'construction of a majoritarian religious nationalism', with ideology shaping pedagogy, political objectives superseding educational ends and the dominant Sunni sectarian perspective sowing the seeds of division in a multi-sectarian and multi-religious society.[90] There was a clear class bias in the policy whereby the elite private schools were exempted from employing madrassah teachers while public sector schools would be obliged to hire them.[91] The policy aimed at the 'guidance' of young minds. Constitutionally speaking, the federal government transgressed the domain of the provincial governments, which controlled education as one of the forty transferred subjects as per the 2010 18th Amendment.[92] The expanded quantum of religion as part of the new curriculum meant that thousands of teachers and millions of students of madrassahs were brought into mainstream education along with their ideological commitments.[93] It seemed that the government was trying to integrate radical (madrassah-based) elements into the mainstream as it had earlier tried to mainstream jihadist elements into electoral politics.[94] The major themes in the curricula in Pakistan typically excluded non-Muslims from the national identity following the dictum that Pakistan was meant only for Muslims.[95] This was a clear violation of Articles 20 and 25 of the constitution, which guaranteed religious freedom and equality of citizens.[96]

HEC's Vision 2025

I want to analyse a policy statement of the Higher Education Commission (HEC) as part of the Vision 2025 of the Government of Pakistan issued in 2017. This document lays bare a cluelessness about higher education underscored by an unbridled flight of imagination and hollowness of argument. Vision 25 seeks to redesign the thirty universities in the top tier of the three-tiered model of tertiary education 'to serve as global centres of trans-disciplinary scholarship'.[97] However, there is not even one university from Pakistan in the loop of the leading universities of the world after decades of educational development. The HEC plans to develop human capital that is 'ethically committed to creating a just and democratic social order'.[98] But the document does not highlight the problem areas, for example, the current corrupt practices and unethical behaviour patterns that students must be warned against, or a programme of creating consciousness about what a just social order is. There is nothing on the larger makeup of society, its inbuilt injustices, and the patterns of oppression in terms of class, caste, gender, religion and generation.

Again, higher education is defined as an engine of 'socio-economic development of Pakistan', along with equitable access and culture of research. But the goal of equitable access during the last two generations has been put upside down. There was never so much inequitable access to quality education in the history of Pakistan as there is now in the context of a flourishing private sector incorporating elite schools, colleges and universities, along with a declining public school system.

Culture of research is a goal that has created much controversy in terms of the increasing trend of fake publications, plagiarism, and a forbidding financial burden. The draft vision adopts an unscientific methodology rooted in utopian imagination and unrealistic goals. It wants to prepare 'a critical mass of constructive, creative, competent and contributing human capital' and transform Pakistan from' 'an old agrarian society to a knowledge producing society'.[99] The HEC's claim that universities are crucibles to refine the talents of the young is anything but a scientific assertion of its institutional goals. The report relies heavily on bullet points as foci of discussion, based on bland aspirational goals mixed with data, often as unrelated variables, but together serving as a vision that has feet of clay. The data, phrases and the actual text are repeated multiple times. It is a depressing statement of action coming from the most highly self-aware guardian of higher education in the country.

The humanities and social sciences are almost absent from Vision 2025. It only mentions that 'more attention is needed in performing arts and design, humanities, social, regional and cultural studies'.[100] There is no policy but only a felt need to 'develop a sense of and commitment to social responsibility' and nurture an 'enlightened soft global image of our society'.[101] 'Our cultural renaissance demands bridging the gap between natural sciences and social sciences'.[102] As for Pakistan's cultural renaissance, one needs to look at the HRCP's annual reports on human rights to judge the real situation in this regard. No ways and means are suggested to bridge the gap between the natural and social sciences. These statements smack of a heavy moral air hanging over the policy makers' imagination at the cost of a clear, goal-orientated, disciplined and argumentative approach to the social sciences. Indeed, in the list of challenges, needs and new major programmes for 2016–25 – eleven items in total, including energy, CPAC, gas pipelines, water resource management and healthcare – the social sciences are part of only one programme. For the purposes of the document, the social sciences do not include the classical disciplines of history, political science, anthropology and sociology. Instead, the social sciences are defined as management sciences, ethics, public policy and international corporate law, apart from economics. Pakistan's education bureaucracy continues to look at fields of higher learning other than hard sciences as marginal and insignificant.

The report mentions an increase in the number of universities from 59 to 178 in the previous decade, the establishment of institutions and cells for quality enhancement and 'programmatic accreditation councils' to upgrade the curricula.[103] It takes it for granted that these and other measures in the past would have improved the quality of education. But there is no information on any analysis or survey carried out by independent evaluators about improvements in quality due to these initiatives. The whole document is riveted on input by way of initiatives of various kinds taken by the HEC, without any critical analysis of the output at any level.

It is interesting to see the imaginary world of the three tiers of universities. TIER I universities are 'the highest seats of learning', which would produce the best students and engage 'the most accomplished and productive faculty involved in pioneering highest quality educational and research programmes'.[104] TIER II universities provide education to the 'qualified masses'. It is difficult to decipher the meaning of this statement, except that these universities 'prepare creative, competent and credentialed specialists'.[105] All this is a dreamworld for scholars and professors who have operated in the system for decades. TIER III, the affiliated colleges – 3,600 of them – would bring education 'at the doorsteps of the learners'.

At the heart of this vision for higher education lies a highly ambitious wish list that mentions technological developments in the most advanced countries as part of the HEC's agenda. There is no mention of the reality at home, i.e. the poverty-stricken, overpopulated, and massively illiterate society in Pakistan. Vision 2025 aims at the 'new fourth industrial revolution' that characterizes contemporary digital technology, without even having brought about the first industrial revolution that took place in eighteenth-century England. It mentions five key enablers and seven pillars of development. These include what can only be considered unattainable targets. Vision 2025 wants expenditure on education at 4 per cent of GDP. It plans to make Pakistan one of the 'upper middle economies of the world'. One has only to take into account Pakistan's economy at per capita income of less than $1,500 as compared to Australia and Switzerland at $65,000 and $78,000, respectively.

The Vision seeks 'prosperity for all through quality education', and the building of new information and skills superhighways in the form of higher education institutions in such underdeveloped areas as Balochistan, KP, FATA and Gilgit-Baltistan. All this becomes questionable in the face of the proliferation of scores of substandard universities, corruption scandals relating to fake degrees, rampant plagiarism in research, and the widespread practice of copying in the examination halls as well as the notorious hate-based curricula. Vision 2025 aims at creating a new breed of visionary leaders as vice chancellors, world-class scholarship, and a rigorous system for accountability of faculty.[106] Continuing in the same vein, it mentions 'a judicious blend of comprehensive universities', smart sub-campuses, and a well-prepared middle class that can be internationally competitive. The HEC's goals are sky high. It wants to 'replace paucity of opportunities with abundance'.[107] The way out seems to be to open more universities and enrol more students, whereby quantity is defined as development and numbers mean growth.

Vision 2025 does not address the issue of stopping current universities from becoming dens of ignorance, bigotry and violence, as frequently reported by the media. It follows a method of not touching on the major flaws in the current education system, thus de-acknowledging its lack of productivity, extremely low standards and students' lack of capacity for rational thinking. It insists that the assessment of students will be done under the supervision of 'master craftsmen', who remain unidentified. Few among the leading academics, scholars and researchers know about these master craftsmen. One shudders at the idea that the 2025 visionaries are planning to open an additional 105 private sector 'comprehensive' universities to provide quality education. There is much about student enrolment, universities, gender, sub-campuses, curriculum review committees, monitoring arrangements, research publications, the ranking of universities and establishing a data-gathering authority. This thinking is called 'innovative reconceptualization', whereby 'visionary' leaders would 'recalibrate their institutional mission' as team leaders. This idiom represents one-dimensional optimism.

This apparently data-based document lacks in great measure any theoretical or methodological framework. Indeed, there are no data about failures of teaching and research programmes, cases of corruption with or without disciplinary action, and identification of low-quality research. One can argue that the HEC is galloping before walking. A US–Pakistan Knowledge Corridor is expected to prepare 10,000 PhD scholars, which would make universities value 'ethical entrepreneurship'. The hope is that Pakistan will move up from its position at 146 out of 187 countries, according to the Human Resource Development index, to a medium-level country. Vision 2025 assumes that Pakistan would suddenly start overtaking other Third World countries. The estimated development expenditure of this vision for the next decade is Rs 465 billion, as compared to the whole CPEC budget of $65 billion – i.e. Rs 11,050 billion – to be spent by China in Pakistan. There is no information about the level of equitable access to education at present, especially by class, by rural and urban sectors, by the poverty level of the envisioned students and their families, as well as by ethnicity. What is missing in the document *HEC Vision 2025* is scientific thinking and planning. During the first two decades of the twenty-first century, this institution moved very fast only to stay put.

The colossal expenditure of resources on the 'digital revolution' was grossly disproportionate to the commendable scholarly production. After the top leadership of the HEC changed in 2018, one could hope for moving beyond the status-quo orientation that underscored institutional life in Pakistan. However, the new chairman Tariq Banuri was dispensed with after two-and-a-half years of tension between the PTI government and the HEC. No new vision was made public in this period.

Textbooks: A Pedagogical Disaster

The prevalent official narrative and the worldview of the dominant groups is aptly reflected in Pakistani textbooks. The concept of identity plays a huge role in understanding social conflict. The school curriculum in Pakistan has all along aimed at creating a single identity based on Islam and anti-Indian and anti-Western sentiments out of the myriad imagined pasts of citizens.[108] In Rubina Saigol's view, new states are formed by 'amalgamating diverse regional entities into a single and centralized one' by developing hatred not only against the 'other' but, as in Pakistan, towards the self that was part of the latter before partition.[109]

The social studies textbooks define the Indo–Pakistan wars as wars between Hindus and Muslims.[110] In Roser's view, the defining features of Pakistan's social sciences textbooks are anti-Indianism, hostile references to Hindus, imagining the country's history through early Muslim conquests and an anti-democratic attitude by way of denying the perspectives of ethnicities other than Mohajir or Punjabi.[111] From the outset, the major themes in the curricula excluded non-Muslims from the national identity. The Hindu contribution to resistance in the 1857 war and Hindu heroes such as Mangal Pandey or Nana Saheb have been selectively erased. History books only mention the Muslim contribution to the 1857 war and depict Hindus as 'timid and womanly'.[112] Pakistan was only for Muslims; internalization of the faith-based ideology of Pakistan was the norm; and students were encouraged to take part in jihad and *shahadat*.[113]

Historically, the course of curriculum formulation moved from a focus on the spirit of the Pakistani movement (1947–55) to the One Unit politics that made the state more centralized (1955–70) to the 'civilian period' that described the four provinces as four brothers (1971–7).[114] The state's selection of specific incidents from history and deliberate removal of some others simply endorsed George Orwell's view that 'history is palimpsest scraped clean and re-inscribed'.[115] The 'textbook culture' in both India and Pakistan makes it hard to incorporate other educational resources in the build-up of young people's minds, which gives more power to the text.[116] In the texts about partition, opposite narratives are created from a single source of data. There is 'deliberate misrepresentation' to cater to a specific purpose such as nation-building.[117] Historians on both sides of the border avoid the traumatic experiences of the event, perhaps to maintain the 'celebratory character of independence'.[118]

Class dynamics underscored the level of hate internalized by students. Students from the lower middle class and the working classes in the fast-dwindling public sector schools were influenced direly by textbooks. Students from the private sector schools, however, had additional exposure to extra-curricular input by way of games, school and college debates, participation in drama clubs, watching Indian and Western movies, travelling within the country as well as abroad, hosting – or going to – parties and dinners in restaurants, often in gender-wise mixed company. At the other end, the dysfunctional government school system indirectly promotes child labour and crime due to the high dropout rate.[119] A study on religious tolerance, gender equality and bellicose attitude emanating from Pakistan's education system found that students from English medium schools scored highest on religious tolerance and gender equality and lowest on hostile narratives, while madrassah students scored lowest in religious tolerance and gender equality and highest in hostile attitude directed against other religions and countries.[120]

The language and substance of history textbooks are dependent on those who write and approve the books.[121] The textbook boards have been selected after careful screening for exactly that purpose. Indeed, Zia's education policy (1979) Islamized the science subjects.[122] Not surprisingly, modernists sought to endorse ideology through science. Educated in English, introduced to Western intellectual and philosophical traditions and professionally trained in various fields of development administration including a stint abroad, bureaucrats, military personnel and technocrats often took what they termed a 'scientific approach to ideological commitment'.[123] A member of the higher bureaucracy argued that the scientific method of enquiry in its functional aspect represented the axiological base of Islamic culture. In this way, understanding of social science research generally included a 'moral' as well as 'spiritual' framework of thought.[124] In this way, modernists continued to produce a bubbled-up logic, trying to understand apples through oranges and using 'scientific jargon' to explain the 'inner self' of the people. As opposed to this, the Taliban were at least clearer in their condemnation of what they considered the 'un-Islamic' nature of the whole political system, including parliamentary elections, university education and the role of women in public life. Marie Lall argues that textbooks were state-controlled mechanisms to control society at large.[125] Textbooks expressly carried the message that democracy was a Western system that had no history in Islam, and that politicians did not carry moral authority and were, therefore, unfit to lead the country.[126]

The policy of standardization of language made language an instrument to achieve an elitist status: it contributed to further inequality inasmuch as the standardized language of Pakistan and India remained the English language.[127]

It is intriguing to note examples of the foundational postulate of the education system. Textbooks promote gender inequality by using Urdu novels from the nineteenth century that promoted 'the well-mannered daughter-in-law' from the Deputy Nazir Ahmed's *Meerat ul Uroos*.[128] In 2007, the MMA protested against the teaching of pre-Islamic history.[129] In this context, the newly charted history provides a feeling of permanence to the currently cultivated identity. Any proliferation of memories that challenge one's newly created identity are quelled.[130] For example, one is struck by the textbook misinformation that Maulana Maudoodi, who was the ultimate nemesis of Jinnah, was the latter's right-hand man.[131] The complex nexus of education, religion and national identity served as a boundary between the self and the other, social polarization and eventually the ground for militancy.[132] Indeed, an overwhelming majority in Pakistan does not consider religious and non-religious education a zero-sum game.[133] The discourse of hate literature does not remain fixed within the discursive boundaries of a particular text: instead, there is a multiplication effect as stories from these books are carried into everyday conversation, political protest and sectarian slogans.[134]

I want to argue that Pakistan's preoccupation with following the functionalist approach to education as means to an end has led to a gross decline in the state's interest in the social sciences. A neo-liberal approach circumscribes education's realm, and views it only in corporatist terms.[135] For example, the donor-driven privatization of education focuses on the neo-liberal doctrine of quantity and expansion without promoting intellectual discourse.[136] In Akbar Zaidi's view, one cannot simply hold the lack of space for free debate, or the lack of democracy, responsible for the dismal state of the social sciences, because the country has had an active social science community even in the face of severe opposition from the government.[137] One can, however, argue that the first generation of the educated elite had its roots in British India whereas latter generations have been the product of a post-partition regimentation of education and intellectual activity. The political system discourages innovative thinking, non-ideological pedagogy and non-doctrinaire education in general. The ideological orientation based on religion, culture and nationalism largely underscores the curricula of the social sciences at the primary, secondary and university levels. A development orientation focuses on expansion of educational institutions instead of creativity. A quantitative orientation is responsible for a statistical approach to the rising number of universities instead of improving the quality of the curriculum. The official perception about the destabilizing role of the social sciences has resulted in the lack of funds allocated for them as compared to natural sciences.

Meanwhile, postcolonialism continues to represent a significant perspective in educational pursuits. A study of British ideological colonization through an analysis of the teaching of English literature at the International Islamic University Islamabad focused on Shelley's poem *Ode to the West Wind* and Shakespeare's play *Macbeth*. It considered the teaching methodology and course outline as the means of cultivating Anglicism and creating 'submissive subjects', and thus pointed to the need for deconstructive pedagogy to erase the binary between the colonists and the colonized created by the British.[138] It claimed that the colonial university created an unquestioning mind, a tradition that was maintained by the rulers after independence in order to confine people to an ideological framework, and thus there was need to alter the students' subjectivities.[139] The study aimed at the decoding of a literary text that imposed an ideological closure and at subjectivizing the 'desubjectivized subjects'.[140] We can see that the colonial impact and the continuing project of decolonization brought about an extremely opaque analysis that was more political than intellectual. Intriguingly, the new ideology operates to de-legitimize the old ideology by keeping the system going.

While a lot has been written about madrassahs in terms of their militant orientation, in pedagogical terms madrassahs focus on refuting the views of 'heretics', which reflects their core purpose for a thousand years. The Deobandi curriculum includes five books solely designated for the refutation of Ahmadi beliefs.[141] Some madrassahs also teach astronomy and medicine, but the curriculum is based on the medieval period. Teaching of medicine goes back to Ibn Sina (980–1037).[142] For Islamists, madrassahs and mosques in Pakistan have become places for expression of frustration with the way things are, because they find a 'repressive atmosphere' out in the society.[143] A Deobandi scholar in India, Maulvi Hamidi Qasmi, declared modern education strictly prohibited for women. First, while being in purdah, women should be confined to the private sphere such as the home. Second, modern education should be discouraged because it is a tool of the West to lead women to a path of 'disbelief and immorality'.[144]

Electronic and Social Media

Education shapes public opinion in a comprehensive way, socially, culturally and politically, over a long period of time. It builds a worldview, identity, cultural framework as well as biases and prejudices. Media shapes public opinion in terms of policy preferences within a short-term perspective. In recent decades, the influence of media-shaped communication in Pakistan has portrayed the underlying patterns of conflict, ranging from foreign policy issues to local phenomena. What the media says and how it says it, i.e. both the content and the frame, carries enormous social and political consequences.[145] Zamir Niazi documented an investigative study of control mechanisms, vis-à-vis the print media, operating through laws, the administrative machinery of the government, and street power exercised by political parties such as the MQM.[146] By the 1980s, there was already a generation of journalists who had not experienced freedom of expression as the bane of their profession. There was speculation that the English press was 'finished'.[147]

It has been argued that 'media practices as transactions might contribute to a dispersed form of communicative rationality'.[148] That implies a dimension of gradual change in relations between producers and consumers of the news and views as well as the disaggregated nature of the whole media activity. The idea is that the media could 'open up new performative spaces that may help constitute an urban public', along with the possibility of distorted communication in which media can serve the interests of the capitalist or bureaucratic elites.[149] The transactional infrastructure represents the way that everyday practices start to mediatize the communication, which includes the potential to contribute to democratic processes.[150] Often, Pakistanis' enquiry about the effect of the media draws on the 'hypodermic needle' model, which presupposes the media's impact on the receivers of the message as they decode it at their end. Similarly, the 'magic bullet theory' finds the media a great shaper and maker of public opinion.[151] As media research moved away from source-dominated theories to uses and gratifications theories, the audience emerged as active recipients of value. They felt qualified to behave like that for various reasons, including the emotional ground for fulfilment of expectations and the instructive content of the message.[152] However, this understanding about the media's impact on consumers has not gone unchallenged. For example, studies of the impact of TV on village life in India found no evidence of a major effect on social change.[153]

The turn of the twenty-first century saw a proliferation of new TV channels in the private sector in Pakistan. Many of these channels set an increasing trend of denigrating politics for being a dirty game and rendered politicians as 'untrustworthy, corrupt, hostile and divided'.[154] Liberalization of the media in 2002 had a great impact on the content and circulation of news. In 2007, the 'cross-media ownership rules' thoroughly expanded the industry. The number of people working as journalists increased from 2,000 to 17,000 between 2002 and 2010.[155] The idea behind Musharraf's liberalization of the media was to counter the growing influence of India's satellite channels and to strengthen national identity.[156] Social media further allowed the public landscape to become hydra-headed, following Musharraf's suspension of the constitution in 2007.[157] Students at Lahore University of Management Sciences and other universities and colleges participated in the protest against the state of emergency, declared by Musharraf on 3 November 2007, through SMS messages, blogging and emails, to distribute information about ongoing events.[158] The lawyers' movement of 2007 generally sparked a protest through electronic media. While it was initiated by lawyers, soon activists, professionals and students demonstrated their power through text messaging and 'user-generated websites' to organize protests. The use of Facebook played a significant role in it.[159] Later, the TV splashed conspiracy theories by creating 'national hysteria' against the USA on various occasions, ranging from the 'friendly' attack on Silala military checkpost (2011) to the Abbottabad Operation (2011). US President Trump's tweets reprimanded Pakistan's double-speak by helping terrorists while getting US aid for fighting terrorists. Washington was accused of 'micromanaging Islamabad's affairs'.[160]

In Pakistan there is a gap between the English press and the Urdu press. While the English press is relatively more objective and dispassionate, the Urdu press is in some ways led by the right-wing intelligentsia, including ideologues. Accordingly, it is more closely supervised by the state.[161] The Sindhi press has a sustained anti-establishment orientation. Talk shows have a political, social and psychological impact on their viewers. Studies show that the more the people are hooked on TV talk shows, the more they stick to their views and the less space they give to opposite views.[162] The 'national interest myth' promotes the idea that what the state does is always for the 'public good' as opposed to the multiple interests at stake.[163] The propaganda model of Edward Herman and Noam Chomsky suggests that the government used advertising money to promote its positive image and reduce the level of critical content.[164] In 2018–21 this model was enthusiastically employed in Pakistan under Imran Khan's government. Earlier, the PPP government (2008–13) received critical content from both the leading English-language dailies, *The News* and *Dawn,* despite itself being the major advertiser. The government was not pressed to react to its negative image because of the limited circulation of the English language newspapers, which made it an elite affair. Political satire on the electronic media has been a popular way of political communication. TV shows like *Hasb-e-Hal* and *Ham Sab Umeed Say Hain* generally focused on public office holders and party leaders as dark horses. It is revealing that the establishment – the army, the judiciary and even the bureaucracy – has not been a target for satire.[165]

By the time the Afghan war ended, militants were fully aware of the role and importance of the media in disseminating their narrative and in mainstreaming their ideologies.[166] By 1989 the number of publications propagating militant narratives in Pakistan had exceeded 100. Published in Urdu, Persian and Pashto, from Peshawar and Quetta, the militant media operated as a profitable business in the 1990s.[167] One medium of these publications was poetry and the pictorial romanticizing of the cause of jihadists.[168] Publications relating to jihad for Kashmir increased during the period 1980–9. Some of the famous publications on Kashmir included the JI's *Jihad e Kashmir* and the LeT's *Jihad Times*.[169] Jihadist publications focused on Afghanistan and Kashmir, onwards to 'global jihad'. They condemned East Germany, Poland, the USA, Russia and the West in general for their policies, and termed them 'infidels'.[170] In 2002, the government banned seventeen publications produced in Karachi, Lahore and Muzaffarabad.[171] The major publication of JuD included *Voice of Islam*, in which 'anti-social evils' like television were targeted.[172] Sectarian groups topped by the Sipah Sahaba Pakistan brought out their own publications.[173] The major source of finance for these publications was Islamic charity and funds. These publications mandated a 'call and march for Jihad'.[174] Several Islamic publications, including *Khawateen ka Islam* (Women's Islam) and *Tayyebat* (The Sacred) targeted female audiences in which 'mothers and sisters' were encouraged to send their sons and husbands to save the 'mothers and sisters' in Kashmir and Palestine from 'atrocities' committed against them.[175] There was the common narrative that natural disasters were the wrath of god.[176]

Some private TV channels also provided space to the Taliban-like jihadi groups. Glorification of an Islamic cause through television has been both a commitment and a complaint depending on which side of the fence you are on vis-à-vis the war on terror.[177] Over time, the media created a market for anti-American hate material. Indeed, the market set the media in motion for competition in attacking America.[178] The Western media did not miss the hostility spewed day and night against the USA by some Pakistan TV channels, and sought to seek higher ratings for themselves by catering to the local market.[179] The anti-American media's constituency included the ulema, dozens of Islamic parties and groups, the lower middle class in general, conspiracy-orientated middle-of-the-roaders, the intelligence community – the erstwhile supporter and supplier of the Taliban – and sophisticated high-ranking officers.[180] The controversial Kerry-Lugar Bill, which made provision for financial transfer to Pakistan for its war against terror, was condemned. Raymond Davis was declared an American spy and later a double agent for Washington and the Taliban, along with other Americans who were held responsible for launching attacks on the Pakistan army.[181] After the Abbottabad operation against Osama bin Laden on 2 May 2011, the immediate euphoric response in the electronic media turned against the USA. The 22 May 2011 attack on the naval base in Karachi led to a turf war between the army and PEMRA at one end and the TV channels, especially Geo, at the other on the issue of locating who was to blame for the breach of national security.[182] As the Taliban perpetrated violence on the soil of Pakistan, the idiom of war on terror was duly domesticated by the Pakistani media to make it palatable for local readers and viewers. This happened by slowly transforming the ownership of the war from 'theirs' to 'ours' as terrorist attacks gradually reached the doorsteps of people.[183]

Social Media

At the start of the third decade of the twenty-first century, a vibrant social media was at the heart of all mediated communication in Pakistan. Network agenda-setting became widely prevalent in the digital media. A specific use of language was adopted by the anchor-persons, to set a particular trend for the show.[184] The PTI government's restrictions over the print and electronic media provided an escape for members of the activist public in the form of social media. The enormous rise in the use of social media was generally analysed in the light of the political changes that followed. After the Arab Spring, Tunisia saw the manifestation of a conflict between religious and cultural platforms on social media. The growing virtual media sphere became an ideological battleground between the Islamist and the 'liberal' camps.[185] In Pakistan, the social media has been relatively anarchic and fragmented along different profiles, ranging from personal, trivial, cynical, aggressively nationalistic, religious, sectarian, anti-establishment and pro-establishment to anti-Indian, anti-Western and anti-liberal. It has not shown any capacity to rally the nation around a certain cause, especially a revolt against the system. A major reason can be the establishment's penetration deep into the social media through trolls, blogs and intermittent political threats against critics who were declared enemies of the nation.

Social media smacks of cynicism since the typical message is critical of an incident, of a political leader, or of the 'system'. It has operated through various platforms: Facebook, Twitter, threads of ongoing messages from members of a group, i.e. a family, a corporation, or like-minded people orientated to 'progressive', religious or ethnic causes. Messages can be part of a continuing thread parcelled into small interjections and quips. Most typically, these messages are disjointed and fragmented, because often other messages are placed between the two otherwise thematically related comments. Not surprisingly, these observations are devoid of concerted effort and a focused discussion because the messages are crisscrossed by jokes, pieces of Urdu poetry, strong personal rebukes or Islamic texts. There are scattered 'pearls of wisdom' that point to comments and opinions of those who retired from high positions in the civilian bureaucracy or the military. Others accumulated experience in a profession and then followed their incorrigible instinct to express it through the digital media.

The paragraphs that follow cover the select entries on Marvi Sirmad's thread, *The Dialogue*, on a single day, 24 July 2016.[186] One contributor wanted to resolve issues of religion in politics, civil–military relations, empowerment of local bodies, reforms in the judiciary and bureaucracy, all in one breath. Otherwise, he warned, the nation must wait for another 100 years. This cumulative approach to the perceived downward spiral of political conflict reflects the collective depression of society. The idea that the 'system' should be functional remained a constant concern. 'System' represents the status quo in an ultimate sense, which operates as an ideological construct for those on the wrong side of status and privilege. In the 1950s, it was understood as a capitalist system against which the progressive forces were obliged to join hands, led by the left. Around the 1970 elections, the 'system' referred to the broad category of the privileged classes and institutions, ranging from the bourgeoisie, the landed elite and the bureaucracy to the army. They were put together as hostile forces by the leftists and working classes in general from within and outside the PPP. All along, Islamic forces struggled to bring down the 'system', which was allegedly run by Western stooges along liberal and secular lines. In particular, the 1977 anti-Bhutto campaign was launched to establish the 'Prophet's System' (*Nizam-e-Mustafa*). Musharraf's coup in 1999 professedly aimed at cleansing the 'system' of its corrupt political class. When Zardari took over as president in 2008, he promised to change the 'system'. Imran Khan (2018–) consistently harped on changing the 'system' by moving from dynastic rule to people's democracy, from corruption to a clean society, and from a class-based pedagogy to a uniform education system. While the system as it existed was condemned as evil incarnate in the thread of *The Dialogue,* it carried the promise of a visionary future – 'the promised land' – be it a communist, Islamic, democratic or 'honest' system.

Largely echoing historical criticism of the dominant families in parliamentary politics and the twenty-two richest families in the economy made famous by Mahbubul Haq in the 1960s, there was talk about the 500 families that produced public representatives in 2016. Intriguingly, somebody, while referring to the American scholar Christine Fair for talking about the strategic culture of the middle class in Pakistan, discredited her for committing 'not less than a blasphemy'. The cumulative effect of decades of Islamization reached a new height with the murder of Salman Taseer in 2011. The word blasphemy was increasingly used as a warning and a threat against 'liberal' or 'Westernized' elements. Murderous attacks were carried out, such as that against 'liberal' intellectual and journalist, Raza Rumi, in March 2014. The accusation of blasphemy was similarly hurled against the five 'liberal' bloggers who were abducted in late 2016. Conversely, the consequences of jihad in Afghanistan were criticized ad nauseum in the thread, along with Zia's arbitrary changes in the education system, the mushrooming of madrassahs and the weaponization of society. Some warned of a replay of Zia in contemporary Turkey, apparently referring to Erdogan. The way out, it was suggested, was to reduce xenophobic paranoia. Every now and then, conspiracy crept in, mainly in the context of Indian and Soviet influences in Afghanistan in the 1970s, insurgency in Balochistan, the allegedly 'nefarious designs' of Sindhi and Pakhtun nationalists, and the smuggling of arms from India.

The next theme related to the controversial appointment of members of the Election Commission of Pakistan (ECP) who had been appointed without a hearing by the parliamentary committee. The other entry confirmed that the committee had just met, but apparently no 'hearing' was arranged. It was taken as a sad commentary on the parliamentarians for not taking their role seriously. Several contributors criticized the 2016 Pakistan Electronic Crimes Act (PECA), which threatened to erode human rights protection for people because it provided an opportunity for official abuse. They bemoaned the fact that already under the Protection of Pakistan Act (POPA) and the Fair Trial Act, agencies enjoyed enormous powers to investigate. There was a fear of unfettered censorship, violation of privacy and surveillance by the intelligence network and a concern that 'anybody can be booked under anything'. One entry mentioned a cleric who was considered 'most vocal and anti-state' in terms of speaking against the prevalent constitutional order. Another entry read: 'their volcano would erupt sooner or later'. That was followed by the comment: 'If the Generals stop meeting these guys…they'll lose all their steam.' One entry carried Imran Khan's 13-point agenda announced on the previous day, which included new police reforms, lower judiciary reforms, a mass transit system for Peshawar and a Swat expressway. There was a quick response: 'Wait a second, mass transit?', 'motorway?' Was it the PTI that had constantly condemned Nawaz Sharif's pursuit of infrastructural development and had instead pointed to what Imran thought was the real thing, i.e. human resource development? Was the PTI defeated in the battle of agendas by borrowing the vision of Imran Khan's nemesis, Nawaz Sharif?

The thread of messages on *The Dialogue* revealed three dimensions of the so-called 'citizen journalism'. First, the thread was well-knit in a web of conspiracy that remained the staple for messaging. That explained the lack of any ground-breaking news, revelations, or agenda, and thus the absence of a grand potential for a political initiative such as the 2011 Arab Spring. Second, the messages crossed the limits of time and space. These were carried by what is known in literary criticism as 'stream of consciousness'. It was perfectly normal to jump from one topic to another, from the current landscape of macro-politics to a humorous satirical anecdote from the private life of a leading personality in the past. The social media communication operated in the domain of catharsis, the need to spill the beans, and the urge to unburden oneself of the pressure emanating from personal, family, social, moral, ideological, institutional, or political life. The disaggregated mass of issues and concerns only meant that there was no organized effort to make a political or ideological effort to change the 'system'. Thirdly, many threads came from serving or retired 'establishment' people who served as guardians of the status-quo, thus discouraging out-of-the-box thinking. Their input served as a corrective to the misgivings of lesser mortals and injected a message of 'All is well' against what they considered negative viewpoints all around. One could argue that these characteristics of the digital interaction couched in a routine non-agitational framework end up de-politicizing the public.

On 27 July 2016, quite a bit of cyberspace was taken up with the issue of the perceived incarceration of the Geo television channel at the hands of the establishment ever since it had openly aired the accusation that ISI was responsible for the murderous attack on its leading anchor-person, Hamid Mir, in Karachi in 2014. The channel used for Geo News broadcasts was pushed out of the bouquet of news channels despite its generally accepted position at the top. One messenger commented that whatever wrong happened in the media houses, the 'army and its affiliate institutions have no right to curb media freedom'. The counter argument was that changing a channel number did not amount to a curb on press freedom. The reply to this message wondered why state institutions got so irked by 'every slight diversion'. The next message carried the question: what had the army to do with the task of allocating a position to a news channel? A strong rejoinder reminded of love and respect that people gave to that institution because of 'its selfless services and unparalleled sacrifices'. Intriguingly, Geo was held responsible for glorifying terrorists in Balochistan. A respondent pointed instead to Geo's leading position in initiating a debate on human rights violations in that province. An opposite view accused Hamid Mir and his colleagues of doing a great service to India by falsely propagating against Pakistan and the army in the context of Kashmir, by patronizing the Baloch guerrilla, Allah Nazar, as a hero. The commentator objected to Mir's alleged portrayal of Balochistan in the same category as Kashmir as well as wrong and exaggerated coverage of the situation in the province. A further comment in this line said that those publications that ridiculed Pakistan, its army or its ideology got huge US or Indian funding that would pave the way for their 'success'. This was followed by another conspiratorial observation that even sincere writers who wanted to improve Pakistan had become part of the defaming activities. There was an incessantly ultra-nationalist argument denouncing those who did not follow the establishment's line. Conspiracy reigned supreme. A critical view was that the establishment just wanted all to be the echo chamber for what it considered to be in the national interest after having lost the media war to its eastern neighbour after the Kargil conflict in 1999.[187] One entry lambasted liberals for being taken for a ride by Musharraf by way of praising him or silently supporting him after his coup in 1999. The question was asked: were liberals then able to stop mullahs from misogyny and bigotry after joining Musharraf?

Away from all this, the two-nation theory remained an active subject for discussion even seven-and-a-half decades after partition, mainly upholding the following positions. The theory failed in 1971. If the theory was to be defined in the name of religion, it would further divide Pakistan. The theory continued to be based on civilization. Islamic civilization was a secular civilization. Jinnah's speech on 11 August 1947 reflected the spirit of Islamic secularism. No, Islamic secularism is a sexy oxymoron. The theory united us in 1947 but was a divisive idea now. It was indeed the 1973 Constitution that was keeping us united. The two-nation theory just played the role of midwife to the birth of Pakistan, and it was not needed anymore. Pakistan could not afford to continue to project itself as a communal state and would do better with a territorial frame such as the Indus civilization.

Another string of opinions on the same day related to the hangings of some leading Islamists in Bangladesh who were on the wrong side of the 1971 war nearly four-and-a-half decades ago. One comment claimed that those being executed in Bangladesh for their support for the Pakistan army were our heroes. The opposite comment refused to call 'criminals, murderers and rapists' war heroes. All along, the debate was generally characterized by contrived civility. One commentator would call the ongoing argumentation senseless and bow out of what he sarcastically described as an 'enlightened discussion' by apologizing for being an 'illiterate brainwashed person'. The other prayed that God bless him 'for calling us all senseless'.[188] The rule of the thumb was to put words in the other person's mouth and repudiate the latter's impugned position.

Internet communication has reached staggering proportions in Pakistan, covering nearly 20 per cent of the adult population. It is worthwhile analysing its political impact. In the context of the 2011 Arab Spring, digital activism was defined in terms of its potential to exacerbate conflict. However, in Pakistan the social media has emerged as a populist 'corrective' vis-à-vis the mainstream media because the latter is dominated by the large media conglomerates. As a 'pull-medium', in the sense of looking for media applications as per one's individual interest, the internet has 'democratized' access to information and interpretation, which is known as 'citizen journalism'.[189]

The extremist and militant groups have found the internet massively useful in spreading their message.[190] Interestingly, however, the mainstream political parties have shied away from reaching out to the masses for the fear of radicalizing them and thus disturbing the enclaves of their tied vote in the context of the clientele structures at the constituency level. In fact, the expansion of social media outlets had an inverse relationship with the already underdeveloped role of political parties in shaping public opinion, providing solutions to the conflicts and giving a policy line to their constituents. The inequality of access to the public for political parties with their varied constituencies in rural and urban areas was further exacerbated by the intrusive role of the social media. For example, the unequal outreach of the mainstream media to the urban and rural sectors – 69 per cent and 11 per cent respectively in 2011 – was reflected through the internet outreach at 99 per cent and 1 per cent respectively.[191] In the absence of a robust filtering system, access to most websites was available by default. That paved the way for religious vigilantes to label any politically challenging material as blasphemous.[192] The blocking of websites was exercised in the case of Danish cartoons in 2006, in 2008, and again in 2010.

In terms of actual political uses of the internet, the PTI was the front runner in the 2013 and 2018 elections. Militant non-state actors such as the Taliban and Hizb ut-Tahrir have been active in using the internet for their radical propaganda against the state at home and with their allies among the expatriates in the West. Islamic militants have amply used hate mail against 'liberal' bloggers and have often subjected them to accusations of heresy. However, unlike the Arab Spring, the anti-government agitations, such as the 2007 lawyers' movement, crucially did not draw on the internet. Could web activity contribute to democracy as an alternative means for the use of freedom of expression for creating an awareness of human rights? The internet-based mobilization of some students against the 2007 state of emergency in Pakistan had only mixed results in this regard, especially as the law enforcement agencies tapped their communications and soon packed them up.[193]

Facebook is the most frequently used social network in Pakistan, with more than four million people in the age bracket 18–24, or 51 per cent of all users. In theory, the social media could aid in promoting better governance, but there have been several limitations to its use. Yasir Hussain documents the role Facebook played as an additional channel of communication to enhance e-government services in Gilgit-Baltistan, especially to disseminate information on the actions of the local government.[194] Implementing e-government requires time and priority. Both were lacking in Pakistan. It also involves the real threat of a breach of security.[195] Social media had been one of the potent platforms to mobilize people against Musharraf. It also crossed boundaries of space and involved overseas Pakistanis. The internet made everyone a source as well as a consumer.[196]

For Kugelman, one reason why social media tools in Pakistan have not been able to produce large-scale social change is because it was co-opted by the traditional media.[197] Nothing yet has been able to dismiss print media.[198] Twitter has provided a conversational medium between citizens and government. A survey conducted by Insight Express showed that almost 40 per cent of people prefer the internet as a source of media compared to the collective preference of 39 per cent given to radio, television and the newspapers.[199] The suspension of the constitution by Pervez Musharraf in 2007 was a watershed moment: people turned to virtual space, making cyber activism an important aspect of politics in Pakistan.[200] In one case, electronic media totally swayed public opinion on domestic affairs, such as the Taliban's lashing of a 17-year-old girl in public in Swat in 2009 that was followed by a military operation.[201] Ahmed and Skoric illustrate that the PTI and Imran Khan not only enjoyed a much larger number of followers on Twitter as compared to other parties but also got heavily engaged in interaction with users.[202] Huma Yusuf explored whether a prominent mass media group felt the need to include citizen journalists in the process of news gathering. Her work investigated why this evolution occurred, and how it was facilitated by both the old and new media.[203]

Open access to the internet in the West has become almost a democratic value. Policies regarding freedom of expression, equal access and education have all become part of the internet infrastructure.[204] In Pakistan, however, access to the internet is fast becoming problematic because of the tightening of the noose around users via PEMRA's rules, especially under the PTI government (2018–). In 2011, the Committee to Protect Journalists (CPJ) had ranked Pakistan as the 'deadliest country in the world' for the second time in a row.[205] Social media became a platform for victims of human rights violations and minorities to express themselves. Families of disappeared people from Balochistan, for example, used social media to communicate with the state and the public at large.[206]

The extent to which the state intervenes in digital networks can vary. It can completely shut down certain websites or deny access to the website's content. On the ground, the government has practised censorship by arresting content producers, and even by targeting internet service providers. The most common reason quoted for blocking access to sites or content was 'preserving cultural and religious morals'. In 2009 in Pakistan, more than 450 websites including YouTube and Facebook were blocked due to public pressure against drawings of the Prophet of Islam.[207] In the political realm, the killing of journalist Saleem Shehzad and the disappearance of other investigative journalists continued to be the practice under the post-military set-ups after Musharraf.[208] The media was used to shred the Sharifs' reputation. Of the 2018 elections Fahd Hussain wrote: 'Journalism had to die in order for Khan to resurrect.' 'Did he [Khan] win fair, though? We are an open enough society to know the shenanigans of the high and the mighty and a closed enough society not to talk about them openly.'[209] Pointing to media censorship on discussing the military's influence and unfair elections, he said on a TV show that all that was being declared as election results was fake, but media platforms avoided telling the truth.[210]

There is a strategy of smart censorship applied to the media. While there were no legal or formal directives, everybody knew about the fate of the two major TV channels, Geo and Dawn, which operated under considerable constraint. Thus others were scared of crossing the red line.[211] The state media did not even air Prime Minister Shahid Khaqan Abbasi's press conference after the National Security Committee's meeting on Nawaz Sharif's statement on the Mumbai attacks.[212] In Farooq Sulehria's view, the establishment was the main manipulator of the media in Pakistan, whether it was in direct or indirect control.[213] A treason case was filed against the newspaper columnist Cyril Almeida following his interview with Nawaz Sharif, which mentioned the role of a Pakistani militant organization (LeT) in the 2008 Mumbai terror attacks. This, along with his 'support' for the Pashtun Tuhaffuz Movement (PTM), was considered a threat to the state.[214] Islamabad bureau chief of Capital TV, Murtaza Solangi, told Reuters: 'Self-censorship has hit new heights.'[215] A seminar of the Lahore Literary Festival was cancelled at the eleventh hour.[216] Waqas Goraya was kidnapped and tortured because he ran a satirical Facebook page.[217] After a campaign was run in support of disappeared people, a counter campaign accused them of blasphemy. This was used to justify the enforced disappearances.[218] Salman Haider, a professor, poet, and known campaigner against enforced disappearances in Balochistan, and editor of the online magazine *Tanqeed,* was beaten with pipes and given electric shocks.[219] Those who favoured 'progressive' social values and practices, and criticized religious intolerance, were condemned as 'liberal fascists'. While grossly outnumbered by their opponents, they still managed to produce a discourse about modernity, the separation between religion and politics, and opposition to widespread misogyny.[220]

Pakistan has increasingly put in place strict laws to curb media freedom. In the field of social media, Pakistan's 2016 PECA, passed under the Nawaz Sharif government, has been an instrument for curbing freedom of expression. A show of dissent in internet messages became liable to criminal proceedings. In 2020, PECA was expanded to ban platforms such as Facebook, Twitter and YouTube for online criticism of the government, and it asked for decrypted data from messaging apps such as WhatsApp.[221] The new regulations also required social media companies to establish local offices, allowed the government to fine them up to $3.14 million, and even to block online platforms.[222] In retaliation, Facebook, Twitter, Google and other companies warned that they would withdraw from Pakistan if no amendments were made in the regulations. The companies later rejected the new regulations called Removal and Blocking of Unlawful Online Content (Procedure, Oversight and Safeguards) Rules. One of the social media companies warned that the government could not blanket-ban things.[223] The Asia Internet Coalition (AIC) was alarmed at what it considered violation of freedom of expression underscored by the use of police cases. The law was also criticized on constitutional grounds because it was a decree of the executive rather than a legislative measure. This led to the arrest of several journalists and the filing of court cases against them under the PTI government. A *Dawn* editorial criticized the media rules as a 'dark chapter in the digital history of Pakistan'.[224] Section 37 of PECA focused on content regulation. Not surprisingly, these rules were suspended, if not de-notified, under pressure from General Nutrition Centres (GNC), AIC, internet companies and civil society at home. The internet companies showed an unwillingness to open local offices given the weak rule of law in Pakistan and low freedom of expression indices. In 2021, the PTI government issued a concept note for establishing the Pakistan Media Development Authority (PMDA). The government empowered itself to issue policy directives to PDMA, cancel declaration of media outlets, determine their circulation and ratings, investigate and adjudicate complaints, and confiscate equipment and make arrest. The four leading media bodies APNS, CPNE, PDA and PFUJ rejected PDMA as a draconian body of laws and institutions.[225] Meanwhile, the independent journalists launched their programmes on YouTube led by Raza Rumi's Naya Daur, Imtiaz Alam's Badlo and Amir Mir's Googly, among others.

Apart from the official 'legal' route to controlling dissent, the PTI trolls were extremely active in the vilification of opposition leaders. In the case of female leaders, such as Maryam Nawaz, abusive language was augmented by misogynist remarks. According to the Coalition for Women Journalists, 42 per cent of the online abuse relating to female media persons came from PTI trollers, as compared to 3 per cent from the PML-N and around 1 per cent from the PPP.[226] Imran Khan's cult of personality led to the demonization of others across the fence almost by default.[227] Khurram Hussain located media violence to the PTI's 2014 container politics, which produced a regular flow of abuse.[228] Increasingly, however, trolls from the PML-N, PPP and other parties castigated the government, its leadership and its foot-soldiers in a similar jargon.

Militant groups often used social media for recruitment to their hate brigade.[229] The online public space has been relatively unchecked in Pakistan. It has now become a 'breeding ground for extremism, intolerance and hate' through Twitter and Facebook.[230] Part of the hate narrative on social media categorized democracy as a 'western system of control' operating under Jewish, American and Indian influence.[231] In one survey, a TV discussant topped the list of hate speech mongers on Twitter at 11.2 per cent.[232] The top five were all personalities related to the media. In religion-related hate speech on social media, 70 per cent were against Shias, 61 per cent against Ahmadis, 43 per cent against Hindus and 45 per cent against Muslims. For hate speech relating to ethnic groups in Pakistan, those targeting Pakhtuns were highest at 38 per cent, followed by those targeting the Baloch at 31 per cent. For the categories of race and nationality, most of the hate speech was directed against Jews (57 per cent), followed by Americans and Indians at 51 per cent each.[233] Hate speech online was 42 per cent about religion, followed by 23 per cent about nationalism.[234] A systematic campaign was launched to place the Beaconhouse School System in disrepute on WhatsApp whereby the 'hashtag BoycottBeaconHouse' became the top campaign with many fake accounts coming to the forefront and spreading false news.[235] In 2018, the PTI government reported 3,004 profiles for 'inciting violence' and 'spreading hate material', which placed Pakistan as one of the top three countries producing hatred.[236]

While the media users in the West generally connected to traditional media, those in Pakistan preferred social media per se as an escape route in their quest for 'freedom of expression'.[237] The government's ban on a satirical website that catered for a mature class of youthful readers reflected the nervous attitude of 'a paranoid state'.[238] Several laws addressed the issue of hate speech.[239] New legislation on hate speech, such as the National Counter Terrorism Authority (NACTA) 2013 and the Protection of Pakistan Act 2014, focused on extreme cases of hate speech but often overlooked its simpler everyday forms.[240]

The question remained as to why the bustling internet activity that engaged with disasters such as floods, assassinations of leaders such as

Salman Taseer (2011) and Benazir Bhutto (2007), and with recruitment drives such as those for anti-Musharraf agitation (2007), did not produce sustainable mass mobilization in Pakistan. It was argued that the mainstream media was still very strong vis-à-vis the social media, that the internet had a relatively low penetration level and that every move of liberal civil society was countered by a ferocious thread of hate messages against the West and the Westernized local elite.[241] How, then, to define the role of social media in Pakistan? Is it a dumping ground of cumulative frustration over the persistent inability of the system to deliver, an instrument to serve social and progressive causes, or the means to an extreme rightist end? Apparently, the emergent blogosphere is all this and much more. How does it materialize in terms of its impact? One can argue that the contradictory trends of opinion on the social media developed into an autonomous, self-sustaining, and self-regulating arena for a battle of narratives. This does not have an everyday fallout on political parties, civil society, militants, or the general public. Not surprisingly, there is a low level of efficacy of digital connectivity to put a dent in the prevalent attitudes to religion, politics, morals and manners, as well as foreign policy relating to the West, India, China and Saudi Arabia. Social media operated essentially in an urban milieu and represented civil society's aspirations and frustrations. In Pakistan, there is a disconnect between the constituency-based electoral politics dominated by the local elite and the expectations of the younger, more educated, and urbanized population with no electoral constituency of its own.[242]

Conclusion

My argument in this chapter has dealt with the state as one player among others on the political stage, although characterized by a quantum of potential and legitimacy unrivalled by others. This situation presupposed the existence of a visible public space that was increasingly filled by the media, party dynamics, electoral mobilization, legislative activity, and street power. The new public space shaped life after partition through the mobilization of the disenfranchised sections of the public and the alienated – even persecuted – intelligentsia who professed and projected a rights-based discourse. The street often resonated with the noise of the politically disgruntled elements, and sectarian and sub-sectarian groups. There were poor people squeezed by inflation, non-payment of salaries and police torture. Sugar cane cultivators asked for a rise in the purchase price of their produce, female health workers sought promotion to the next grade and young doctors demanded a higher salary. Public space took a new turn after the digital revolution and the shift from print to electronic media and onwards to social media. And yet, the new public remained captive of a host of old subjectivities, characterized by its ambiguous attitudes for and against the Taliban. It had its commitment to a globality of its own which was tantamount to an intellectual exit from the transnational flow of discourses based on rights, religious tolerance and peace. More than simply an issue-based public mobilized at will, there were other publics carrying longer-term moral and ideological commitments in Pakistan, including the Islamic public and the military public.

A significant part of the public space is attributed to civil society. I took issue with the replicability of the Polish experience in other contexts of regime change. Apart from voter-training and voter-registration, and various functions overseeing the casting of ballots, and the occasional brush with dialogue with political parties, civil society stayed clear of democracy as agenda, vocation, system of representation and source of legitimate authority. As agents of change in pursuit of progressive causes, NGOs operationalized their activities without any clear class dimension. The urban middle-class leadership of civil society and the agenda-setting role of the donor community, combined with official surveillance of the funding system, discouraged the emergence of a new publicness. Ideally, it would have represented the presence of the world outside in the world inside Pakistan, through a reformist vision and a programmatic framework pumped into a status quo orientated social milieu. Civil society has been full of goodwill for progressive causes but unable to activate them and take them forward.

While civil society is passively active in some sense, in terms of encouraging projects for the amelioration of public grievances, the role of education takes much longer to bear fruit. Education is not explosive in its impact like the media. Instead, it is transformative in nature. Media shapes opinion, education shapes the mind. In this chapter, I have analysed the education system at the two levels of policy-making and textbook orientation. Policy-making has been haphazard, bland, full of hyperbole and geared to a compilation of non-substantive and effervescent observations that cannot stand any scientific scrutiny as guidance for pursuit of educational excellence. The impact of the textbook has been far more lethal. It is full of hate messages against other nations, religions and faith-based communities. Education has all along cultivated a message of a potential exit from the world in pursuit of an introverted model of nationalism.

The media is potentially more relevant for a study of political conflict than education, due to its immediate effect. The official instinct worked to control it due to its much-feared impact on public opinion. Successive governments introduced legislation to tighten the noose around the media and media people, to streamline the public narrative in its own favour. The media asserted its power to fully utilize the public space provided by 'institutional design', especially Article 19 of the constitution dealing with freedom of expression, which often led matters to the courts. Media control is a rabid form of what is known as 'primitive accumulation of power'.[243] I analysed the role of the social media in its various incarnations, ranging from individual messages in a thread, to blogs, trolls and the use and abuse of political idiom that has incrementally vitiated the debate, especially under the PTI government (2018–). Some of the adverse effects of using social media are the deterioration of family ties and isolation, except when it is used for education.[244] There is a need for research on whether information communication technologies (ICTs) are connecting society, or otherwise creating another digital divide in Pakistan, which seems more likely.[245] I have brought out three significant dimensions of the social media: a variety of social concerns and corresponding cynicism over the non-resolution of public issues; the lack of potential of the social media to mobilize the public for collective action in the direction of regime change or a grand change of policy; and the increasingly harsh rules that seek to suppress independent public opinion in the name of curbing hate speech.

7

THE OUTSIDER

Introduction

In this book, I have discussed various patterns of conflict that encompassed the institutional structures and operational strategies of various contenders for power, including the state that controlled the public goods and its distributional frameworks. The state-initiated policies, agendas and projects led to responses of various kinds in the form of parliamentary debates, street politics and political violence based on identity politics, mass mobilization or otherwise ideological procrastination. This action–reaction cycle operated along multiple dimensions that divided the nation into insiders and outsiders. The insiders often had their own patterns of endemic conflict: for example, civil–military tension, the modernist–traditionalist dichotomy, and a series of unresolved issues relating to gender, class, rural and urban sectors as well as clash of institutions. At the other end, the functioning of the state system led to the emergence of communities that were relegated to the status of 'outsiders' irrespective of regime change. It was accompanied by the state's overtures to meet the demands of those on the other side of power and privilege through legal and financial measures as well as cultural and ideological co-optation. The 'outsider' is a necessary part of our analysis of political conflict because of the tenacity of the patterns of alienation from mainstream politics of ethnic and sub-ethnic as well as religious and sectarian minorities.

The outsider is not necessarily the one lacking resources, privilege, education, respect, status and recognition on an individual basis. A large majority of people suffer from all that and much more. The outsider can be defined with reference to the insider. Typically, people have been unable to challenge the power of the capitalist or the landed elite and make class a defining variable in a revolutionary situation or in terms of class struggle of a lesser magnitude such as the Sindh Hari movement (1950s and 1960s), the Hashtnagar movement (1970) or the Okara peasant movement of more recent times. There would be many among the Baloch, Sindhis, Pakhtuns and Hazaras who would have resources beyond the imagination of the working classes from amongst insiders such as Punjabis and Mohajirs. I aim at deconstructing the power structure of the state in the context of a persistent conflict between the gatekeepers and those who are struggling to get in but whose credentials are constantly scrutinized, found satisfactory, or otherwise rejected. The state plays a pivotal role in the insider–outsider conundrum.

Of course, the categories of insider and outsider do not have fixed boundaries. As Yogesh Atal analyses, successive waves of migrants into India created outsiders who became insiders over generations, though not as part of a 'melting pot' but rather as part of a 'salad bowl'.[1] Atal not only sees communities ranging from Anglo–Indians to Christian and Muslim converts as outsiders to their parent religions but also finds a sub-group of outsiders within a larger group of outsiders defined by their ethnic and caste identities.[2] What is more relevant for our purposes is Oommen's perspective that the mainstream social sciences essentially served the mainstream society of the insiders.[3] This is in line with Merton's perspective, which looks at the phenomenon of social polarization in the context of ideologization of knowledge – 'the barely concealed *ad hominem* innuendos' – that leads to insider truths that counter outsider truths.[4] In this context, movements emerge from the periphery that affirm pride and solidarity among those groups that have been for long 'socially and culturally downgraded, stigmatised or otherwise victimised in the social system'.[5] According to the doctrine of the insider, the outsider is incapacitated, unable to be in step with the insider because the latter does not share the former's group socialization and priority structure.[6]

In this book, we have noted that the Mohajir–Punjabi combine has dominated the state's agenda, master narrative, policy structure and cultural edifice, as well as the ideological orientation splashed through the education and the media. In the present chapter, we endeavour to locate the genesis of the outsider and analyse the state's strategies to deal with the phenomenon of the outsider either by accommodation or by repression. Of course, the insider–outsider dichotomy is fluid inasmuch as one can belong to one or both cognate statuses by exclusion or inclusion respectively.[7] The alienation of Mohajirs from the process of Punjabization of the state, and the incorporation of Pakhtuns in selected fields of mainstream public life, typically represent the phenomenon of fluidity. I shall first discuss the ethnic mosaic of Pakistan in the context of locating the outsider – Bengalis, Sindhis, Pakhtuns and the Baloch. My second category of outsiders belongs to religio-sectarian minorities, which experienced discrimination and infringement of their individual and collective rights at the hands of what has become a majoritarian state par excellence, much as India in the second decade of the twenty-first century.[8] The increasingly Islamic content of law and public policy placed Hindu, Christian and Ahmadi as well as Shia, Zikri and other denominational communities at the receiving end of the exclusionary practices of the mainstream social and political forces. I shall analyse the way the state has dealt with the issue of alienation of ethnic and religious minorities in the face of criticism from the liberal intelligentsia and the human rights regime at home and abroad.

Ethnic Outsider

As per the Cambridge school of history, which includes J. A. Gallaghar, Gordon Johnson, Anil Seal and others, anti-colonial movements have been understood as elite projects rather than national movements per se.[9] In order to understand these sub-national groups, I need to bring in the comparative strengths and weaknesses of ethnic elites in the constituent parts of the postcolonial state of Pakistan. In the historical West, the dominant states developed print capitalism and founded 'national languages', assimilated their weak neighbours militarily or otherwise, and founded nations at the cost of the latter's language, culture and identity.[10] As opposed to this, dozens of sovereign states and hundreds of princely states were placed together under the British imperial system in India, which fossilized their ethno-cultural and linguistic identities. When the British left, both India and Pakistan inherited the sovereign states-turned-provinces – and statelets such as Swat, Dir, Chitral, Patiala, Nabha and Kashmir – which became candidates for a fair share in the new power structure riding the wave of identity-based movements. The emergent ethnic imbalance sowed the seeds of internecine conflict all over. Lahore, as capital of Punjab, was now part of Pakistan, along with its cultural richness, commercial activity and administrative machinery.[11] Urban Sindh and urban Punjab soon recovered from the vacuum created by Hindu migration to India, due to the influx of mostly non-Punjabi and Punjabi migrants respectively. The fact that the former, now called Mohajirs, were the major architects of the Pakistan project and had established a 'migrant state' in Pakistan put them at the top of the new ethnic hierarchy. As discussed earlier, the Mohajir–Punjabi 'establishment' has been at the heart of a power structure that clearly sought to centralize state authority through legal, administrative, and military means.

On the Periphery

The ethnic 'outsider' is the most typical feature of the postcolonial states in Asia and Africa. In South Asia, both India and Pakistan represent ethnic federalism. In Gurharpal's formulation of ethnic conflict in India, there have been 'outside' ethnic movements, i.e. Punjab, Kashmir and northeast India, along with 'inside' movements such as Bengal and Tamil Nadu.[12] By contrast, there emerged ethno-nationalist movements in all the provinces of Pakistan except Punjab, i.e. in East Pakistan, KP, Balochistan and Sindh. Indeed, in the province of Sindh alone there have been two rival nationalist movements of Sindhis and Mohajirs. This is by no means an indication of a successful project of nation-building.

In Pakistan, much like in India, the ethnic issue can be traced back to British India. The areas under direct rule enjoyed precedence over those under indirect rule in terms of modern statecraft characterized by rational-legal bureaucracy, rule of law, establishment of universities and colleges, irrigation canals, industrialization and railroad networks. Areas under indirect rule of the paramountcy system remained underdeveloped by a large margin. In other words, Pakistan was born with an unequal pattern of growth among its constituent parts. Even more than seven decades later, yesterday's princely states continue to remain grossly underdeveloped, including Balochistan (except Quetta, which was leased to the government in British India), Bahawalpur, Khairpur, Swat, Dir, Chitral and the erstwhile FATA.

In the case of Pakistan, the separatist framework of ethnic politics pre-dated partition wholly or partially. The Bengali leadership, both Hindu and Muslim, represented by Sarat Chandra Bose and Suhrawardy respectively, had toyed with the idea of a separate and united Bengal – Free State of Bengal – outside the partition agenda. Balochistan raised the ambition of enjoying the status of a state that had treaty arrangements directly with Britain and which would not be obliged to join one or other dominion. Indeed, it declared independence on 15 August 1947. Pakhtun nationalism took a turn to Pakhtunistan as a separate entity, which, of course, remained ill-defined. Sindhi nationalism was in a strident mode after attaining the status of a province separate from Bombay only a decade before partition. Migrants operated as the new hegemon in the province. As discussed earlier, the 'migrant state' entered the new country with a bang by dismantling governments in the federating units.

Mohajirs have generally maintained the position that they were the creators of Pakistan. This reflects the fact that the progenitors of the Pakistan project belonged to those areas of British India that lay outside the 'promised land'. Muslims of UP, Bombay and other minority provinces had overwhelmingly voted for the Muslim League in the 1937 elections. The Muslim majority provinces, however, presented a different picture, with the Unionist Party government in Punjab, the Congress-KK government in KP, and coalition governments in Sindh and Bengal. It took another decade for Muslims of the 'majority provinces' to convert to the cause of Pakistan in the 1946 elections. The KP government was still in the hands of the Congressite Pakhtun leadership at partition, and the Sindh Muslim League leader, G. M. Syed, had fallen out with Jinnah and opposed the project of Pakistan. Partition transformed the division between the early and late converts to the cause of Pakistan into a new dichotomy between 'insiders', who became state managers, and 'outsiders', who were now 'managed' by them.

This led to the assumption of a higher level of legitimacy by the migrant elite of both Mohajir and Punjabi extraction and the attribution of a lower level of legitimacy to the 'local' political leaderships, who were now identified with their respective provinces. In this way, the Pakistan project set the pattern of a new ethnic hierarchy with migrants from the Muslim minority provinces at the top, and then a downward scale that represented migrants from East Punjab, followed by West Punjab proper and then others further below.

As we noticed in our discussion of the two power centres in Chapter 3, migrants from all over India, along with a strong contingent of migrants from Hyderabad Deccan, initially led the middle class in Pakistan, which was the catchment area for the state elite. They emerged as the ultimate insiders in the new state while the 'locals' from East Bengal, Sindh, KP and Balochistan, which had a weak middle class and therefore a relatively insignificant representation in the state elite, were relegated to the status of 'outsiders'. In Burki's formulation, the dichotomy between insiders and outsiders corresponded to their geographical origins, i.e. as locals and migrants respectively; he finds the latter relatively modern and liberal and the former traditional and paternalistic.[13] I argue that since the migrants were in control of the new state, they were the real insiders, while their counterparts from the Pakistan areas (except Punjab) became outsiders in the political system.

Indeed, partition and migration increased the power differential between insiders and outsiders in another crucial sense. Partition tremendously weakened the two 'outsider' provinces of Pakistan, robbing them of their urban sectors and thus turning them into headless entities. First, Bengal's cosmopolitan centre, Calcutta, along with its bourgeois culture, artistic and literary heritage, and industrial and commercial activity – presided over by the *bhadralok* community – became part of India. Only the vast rural hinterland of Bengal fell to Pakistan. For a generation after partition, the ruling elite in Karachi and later Islamabad maintained that East Bengalis were under West Bengal's literary and cultural influence, which was considered harmful for its own agenda of national integration.[14] The fact that the two Bengals shared a language as well as its script and that ethnic identity often overtook religious identity in pursuit of demands for provincial autonomy – most prominently in the 1954 elections – sowed the seeds of mistrust between the two wings. The Bengalis' outsider status was reflected through their persistently underprivileged position in the establishment, for example, at 10 per cent in the army and 13 per cent in the bureaucracy.[15]

Parallel to East Bengal's loss of urban sector by territory, Sindh's loss was caused by the migration of Hindus, who had dominated the urban sector. In this way, Sindh lost its Hindu nascent bourgeoisie, intelligentsia and professional middle class, leaving behind a decadent rural sector. While communal tension had characterized relations between the Hindu and Muslim social and political elites, especially after Sindh separated from Bombay in 1936, it did not lead to the mass killing of Hindus or to their exodus at the hands of Sindhi Muslims in 1947. In fact, the nationalist zeal of the new ruling elite led by Mohajirs and Punjabis created the opposite effect on Sindhis in the form of a nostalgia for their pluralist past, which was remembered for inter-religious harmony. This did not fit well with the insiders' ideological framework, and gradually pushed Sindhis to the status of outsiders.

It is intriguing to see the actual outsiders in geographical terms turning into insiders in political terms and geographical insiders becoming political outsiders. As Sarah Ansari has noted, Sindhi Muslims were already conscious of the increasing domination of, first, local Hindus, who opposed the separation of Sindh from Bombay in 1936, then non-Sindhis from Gujarat and Bombay seeking employment in Sindh, then Punjabi settlers in the newly irrigated lands, and then millions of Mohajirs. Together they alerted the 'locals' about 'the extent of outsider ambitions' because they were being 'replaced by outsiders'.[16]

Partition-related migration created huge concerns about the increasing number of non-Sindhis, and about Urdu's replacement of Sindhi as an educational and professional language, which was termed 'cultural genocide'. Separation of Karachi from Sindh in 1948 gave a new life to the simmering ethno-nationalist feelings of Sindhis. The establishment of One Unit in 1955 was the last nail in the coffin of Sindhi ambitions for provincial autonomy. The national project of the centre at Karachi and later Islamabad encouraged the narrative of Islamic unity, Urdu as the national language, and anti-Indianism as the dominant discourse. However, as Asma Faiz has comprehensively analysed, the Sindhi nationalist idiom championed by G. M. Syed and his followers upheld the agenda of 'secularism', socialism, quotas for Sindhis, recognition of Sindhi as the official language of Sindh and friendly relations with India.[17] The emergence of the 'migrant state' in Pakistan transformed insiders into outsiders, and outsiders into insiders in Sindh.

The Pakistani segment of the two provinces of Bengal and Sindh – divided by partition and migration respectively – experienced nostalgia for the other half in India and struggled to keep their cultural links across the border as well as with Hindus within the country. This rendered their commitment to the state of Pakistan suspicious in the eyes of the establishment. This official mistrust was not confined to these two communities. The Pakhtun and Baloch communities suffered the same fate at the time of their entry into Pakistan because of their historic divide across the borders of Afghanistan and Iran respectively. Especially in KP, Pakhtun nostalgia for their co-ethnics in Afghanistan was a formidable factor in keeping them socially, culturally and often politically engaged with those on the other side. Abdul Ghaffar Khan's party, KK (Khudai Khidmatgars), had led the Pakhtun nationalist movement from the 1930s onwards, joined the Congress and formed the government in Peshawar in 1937 and again in 1946. However, following a referendum on the issue of joining Pakistan, won by the Muslim League in the face of the KK's boycott, this government was dismissed soon after partition.[18] Thus, the KK's Congressite affiliation and opposition to the Pakistan project created a huge distance between the central government and the Pakhtun nationalist leadership. Moreover, the latter's Pakhtunistan project was considered a proxy for Afghanistan's historical irredentism about the Pakhtun areas across the Durand Line.

The state's suspicion about the federating units of Pakistan related even more intensely to Balochistan. Unlike the cases of East Bengal, Sindh and KP, it was Balochistan's controversial accession to Pakistan itself that sparked its ethnic movement. We do not need to reiterate the history of the political struggle and ethnic idiom of the Baloch nationalist movement: much scholarly research has been produced about it that has addressed its origin, philosophy and methodology of resistance.[19] Baloch nationalist literature as well as Western scholarship have generally focused on the 'original sin' of accession by the Khan of Kalat. Balochistan comprised the Khanate of Kalat, which included the tribal areas administered under the Sandeman System based on tribal chiefs' indirect rule and 'British Balochistan', which included the areas leased to the British, including Quetta. In June 1947, a Shahi Jirga referendum was reportedly held among a few dozen *sardars* and members of the Quetta Municipal Committee, which declared accession to Pakistan. Inayatullah Baloch has given a critical view of the whole process of accession dotted by strategically important points of contention.[20] These included declaration of independence by the Khan of Kalat on 15 August 1947 followed by promulgation of a written constitution, formation of a council of ministers, election of a bicameral parliament and negotiations for accession initiated by the government of Pakistan that dragged on for several months, couched in an atmosphere of increasing distrust on both sides. Meanwhile, accession of Kharan, Las Bela and Makran to Pakistan took away a large chunk of the Khanate's territory and cut it off from Iran and Afghanistan at one end and from the route to the sea at the other.

All this led to the Khan's accession to Pakistan 'under duress' on 30 March 1948, recourse to armed rebellion by Prince Karim against the accession, and hostility towards the people of Pakistan, who were accused of 'non-fraternity, inequity, injustice and repression' along with 'Punjabi fascism'.[21] Even a fatwa was issued by Maulvi Mohammed Afzal that Liaqat Ali Khan was *Rafizi* (heretic), Nishtar was an atheist and Zafarullah was a 'Qadiani pagan'.[22] As Martin Axmann explains, the process of the integration of Balochistan moved on through various legislative measures. These brought the tribal and leased areas under the jurisdiction of Pakistan, and established the Balochistan States Union (BSU) in 1952, incorporating the four princely states, as well as realizing the merger of the BSU first with the rest of Balochistan in 1954, and then with One Unit in 1955.[23] The long, complex and essentially one-sided process of accession left a legacy of hostility, warfare and tension that has served as a source of motivation for Baloch nationalists for three generations carrying demands ranging from provincial autonomy to independence.

Federation *sans* Federalism

The process of Balochistan's accession to Pakistan, KP's merger with the new country not through its elected government but through a referendum of dubious quality, and the diminution of Bengalis and Sindhis to lesser partners in the scheme of things, left the project of nation-building in tatters. It was not until the 1970 elections that the long-awaited societal input into the state materialized. This election turned out to be a milestone in the country's history, especially as new players emerged on the political stage who wrote a new script in the form of the 1973 Constitution.

For the first quarter of a century after independence, no elections were held at the national level based on adult franchise. The federal government had dismissed nine provincial governments between 1947 and 1958, a phenomenon that has been called 'constitutional terrorism' in India.[24] The demographic imbalance among provinces, reflected through the phenomenon of one-province-dominates-all – first, in the case of East Pakistan and then Punjab – made the federalization project a constitutional nightmare. We have discussed in Chapter 5 how the design of the federation was immersed in centralist practice and alienated various provinces that struggled for autonomy. Maryam Khan has discussed the 'federal design' that defined the contours of the project, whereby provinces got acknowledged as legal and legitimate entities carrying the stamp of the ethnic identity of their respective majority communities – Punjabis, Pakhtuns, Sindhis and the Baloch.[25] We have discussed how the new ethno-regional vigour was enshrined in the sense of alienation of the three smaller provinces – sometimes represented by groups such as the SBPF (Sindhi Baloch Pushtoon Front, 1985) and the PONM (Pakistan Oppressed Nations Movement, 1998). Christophe Jaffrelot explained Pakistan's national project as 'a case of nationalism without a nation'.[26] The SBPF focused on re-defining the federal formula on the basis of the 1940 Lahore Resolution that would reserve only three subjects for the centre.[27] The PONM opposed the construction of the Kalabagh dam, which was allegedly meant to serve only Punjab. It also wanted to consider Siraiki-speaking people as a separate nationality entitled to provincial status. I have analysed the 2010 18th Amendment in Chapter 5 as a step forward in the direction of meeting the demands of provinces for making federalism in Pakistan meaningful by transferring the legislative subjects included in the Concurrent List to provinces. While this step was generally hailed as a progressive step by the political class in general, and ethnic parties in particular, this left the minority communities of provinces in the lurch – Siraikis in Punjab, Mohajirs in Sindh, Hindko-speakers in KP and Pakhtuns in Balochistan.

Khan has discussed the emergent issues of 'minorities within minorities' whereby the minority communities in the three 'minority provinces' of Pakistan looked for recognition in terms of government formation in the areas of their concentration and thus for the creation of new provinces.[28] She elaborates on the theme of Sindh being a 'de jure' province as per the 1973 Constitution whereas Mohajirs were a minority community living in the province, which thus 'belonged' to Sindhis.[29] Curiously, the Mohajir movement was never considered by the Sindhi, Pakhtun and Baloch movements as one of them. They felt distant from it because Mohajirs were not recognized as sons of the soil. Indeed, the MQM was considered the product of intelligence agencies, and thus a proxy for the establishment. Furthermore, they were a privileged community not an underprivileged one, and in most cases not an oppressed community. While there was a military operation against the MQM (1992–5) and a police-cum-rangers anti-terrorism campaign against the militant section of that party for the following two decades, the Mohajir elite remained part of the establishment in a fundamental sense. The MQM often raised demands for the repatriation of Biharis left in Bangladesh in 1971, for the division of Sindh, and for the elimination of the quota system that was detrimental to the Mohajir community's chances of admission to the institutions of higher learning and jobs. However, the state's fear of pushing Sindhis to a demand for Sindhudesh prevailed over any significant accommodation of the Mohajirs' grievances.

Mohajirs took pride in creating Pakistan. Others in turn identified the whole project of a Muslim homeland with Mohajir and Punjabi imperialism. Indeed, the three ethnic minorities traditionally claimed their glorious history in their respective areas as a source of their current movement against the perceived tyranny of the state. For Mohajirs, it was their sacrifices rendered in the creation of the state that remained the main source of inspiration.[30] Despite the frequent encounters with the state, the MQM's Mohajir constituency did not qualify for the status of 'outsider'. Despite the much-touted plan of creating a Jinnahpur or Urdu Nagar in Karachi, or Altaf Hussain's pronounced agenda of changing the geography of Pakistan, Mohajirs have been able to enjoy insider status as a community, barring some of the MQM's militant members who were traced to having relations across the border.

Whilst Mohajirs' demand for a Karachi or Mohajir province entailed the division of Sindh, an extremely explosive issue for Sindhi nationalists, the Siraikis' demand for a separate province has been a relatively low-pitched issue. The Siraiki ethnic struggle is an 'inside' movement in the context of Gurharpal's typology of inside and outside ethnic movements. The Siraiki area in south Punjab represents a mosaic of speakers of Punjabi, Urdu and Sindhi languages overlapping the urban and rural sectors. Its political leadership has been typically ambitious to enjoy privilege and status in Lahore rather than Multan. The intelligentsia and the incipient middle class remain the core constituency of the Siraiki movement. However, a new province to be carved out of Punjab for those who have been outsiders amongst the insiders for a long time is not expected to pose a challenge to the state. In fact, the 2013 elections had seen both the PPP and the PML-N promising the formation of one and two provinces out of the Siraiki region respectively, the latter adding a separate Bahawalpur province. Again, prior to the 2018 elections, the MNAs from the Siraiki region broke away from the PML-N and joined the PTI as per the latter's promise of creating a separate province of South Punjab. In the absence of a Siraiki nationalist party capable of winning elections in the area, the electoral route to formation of a Siraiki province remains a tall order. The social, cultural and economic backwardness of the Siraiki people makes them a depressed community by default rather than outsiders per se.[31]

Studies of ethnicity in Pakistan generally point to the assimilation of Pakhtun nationalism into mainstream politics,[32] mainly because of the community's integration into the national economy as well as its visible representation in the army and the bureaucracy. While the decline of the arch-Pakhtun nationalist party, ANP, created a vacuum that was partially filled by the PML-N, PML-Q, PPP, JUI-F and PTI parties, a resilient ethno-nationalist ideological thinking continued to operate at the intellectual level. Some interpreted even the MMA's ascendency in the first decade of the twenty-first century as Pakhtun nationalism by other means.[33] In 2019–20, the PTM thrived on the grievances of millions of internally displaced persons who had left their homes and hearths in the wake of military operations against the Taliban in Swat and the former FATA from 2009 onwards. Their anger related to loss of property and business, alleged high-handedness of the security forces in the process of their rehabilitation, and destabilization of their community networks in general.[34] The ISPR condemned the party and its leader, Manzoor Pashteen, and its MNAs, Mohsin Dawar and Wazir Ali, for drawing support from the Research and Analysis Wing (RAW) of India. This group emerged on the political scene from the periphery of not only Pakistan but also KP. Indeed, the leader of the Pakhtun nationalist party, ANP, threw its core members, Afrasiab Khattak and Bushra Gohar, out of the party for supporting the PTM. The PTM had only a tiny electoral base from 2018 onwards. It showed unwillingness to opt for militant means in pursuit of political ends, especially under the heavy military presence in the region. Whether it could develop into an ethnic movement or would remain a low-scale, issue-orientated party depends on the larger ideological orientations of Pakhtuns from KP down to Karachi.

The presence of the insider–outsider dichotomy on the political stage of Pakistan has a great explanatory potential. The push for tackling the outsiders has contributed to the state's agenda of securitization of vision, military operations, ideologization of the master narrative through education and the media, and reliance on extra-constitutional means to control dissent. All along, the state took into consideration the potential of the outsider groups to challenge its writ or to potentially create hurdles in pursuit of its longer-term objectives and weaken the national bond among the constituent parts of the country. Sometimes, the state had to balance the agenda of appeasement of an insider group with its negative impact on an outsider group, whereby it chose not to alienate the latter. This happened with the Mohajirs' demands for the repatriation of Biharis, the elimination of the quota system, and the division of Sindh, all of which would have alienated Sindhis. In the case of the Baloch outsiders, the state opted for co-opting some nationalists into mainstream politics, struggling to deal with fence-sitters – the ideologically motivated Baloch activists – and, thirdly, fighting the armed bands.[35]

In 2020, the status of a separate province for south Punjab seemed to be a multi-tier project whereby the Punjab would have two subsidiary secretariats, one in Multan – the epicentre of the Siraiki movement – and the other in Bahawalpur, the home of a 'Riyasti' nationalism. A third secretariat in D. G. Khan was also mooted. All this reflected the old official thinking about not acknowledging the politics of ethnic identity and considering the whole problem as one of administrative and territorial devolution. In March 2021, the bureaucracy made a move to wrap up its operations in the three sub-secretariats in south Punjab. The old dichotomy continued: while the insiders have been more drawn to adopting the prevalent political, administrative, and economic strategies to pursue their agenda, the outsiders dwelled essentially on identity, culture, language and history as sources of mobilization.

Minority Outsider

In the contemporary world, debate about the situation of religious minorities in political, economic and cultural terms is located in the national context whereby the numerical majority is able to transform its will into the national will and then into the writ of the state. The open-ended character of a pluralist society comprising numerical entities – one majority and one or more minorities – changes into a hierarchy of wills, ultimately reflecting the former's deterministic hold over policy initiatives vis-à-vis the latter. The modern state plays a central role in elevating one community to potentially 'sovereign' status and subjugating other communities to its 'sovereign' will. Concern about minority rights in the West has moved forward from the principle of equal citizenship to the current focus on cultural rights of minority communities, most importantly their language and tradition.[36] However, the minorities' status in the predominantly religious societies of South Asia remains far from settled. Several studies have focused on the increasingly vulnerable Christian, Hindu and Ahmadi communities of Pakistan and the state's lack of will or capacity to meet the challenge of religious intolerance. It has been argued that these and other minority groups have their life-worlds shaped by social, cultural, professional and ethnic ties with the larger society and should not therefore be studied as intrinsically isolated and inward-looking entities.[37]

Because of the pervasive current of nationalism in the postcolonial world, the status of religious minorities was considered problematic for the supreme cause of national integration, and attempts were made to secure their well-being through constitutional and political means.[38] In the long run, however, as nations developed their narratives on the basis of their history and territory, minorities gradually dropped out of the collective memory of the past and became potentially de-historicized and de-territorialized. Minorities were defined by their religion as an a priori identity marker at the cost of other aspects of their existence, such as social, economic and cultural ties and multiple non-religious identities.[39] This was bound to de-humanize religious minorities and reduce them to one-dimensional beings.

Minoritization of Communities

When the colonial state withdrew, the founders of the two nations of India and Pakistan never planned to change the 'secular' nature of the state, even during and after partition when religious emotions ran high and, at least in Pakistan, religion was considered the genesis of the state itself. Jinnah's famous statements about not mixing religion with the business of the state and not allowing Pakistan to become a theocracy meant that the constitutional provisions of the British Indian state would remain the basis of legislation for determining the status of minorities. The postcolonial state of Pakistan struggled to adhere to an agenda of protection of non-Muslims through constitutional provisions. That was the first step towards the minoritization of communities whereby the function of numbers shifted from representing a quantitative index of the strengths and weaknesses of groups to a qualitative deficit in their status and privilege.

Pakistan's emergence as a Muslim homeland defined the majority as insiders by default and minorities as outsides by design. The 1973 Constitution gave the citizen 'the right to profess, practice and propagate his religion' and 'the right to establish, maintain and manage the religious institutions' (Article 20). It acknowledged the right not 'to take part in any religious ceremony or attend religious worship, if such instructions, ceremony or worship relates to a religion other than his own' (Article 21). It also recognized the right not to 'be denied admission to any educational institution receiving aid from public revenue on the ground only of race, religion, caste or place of birth' (Article 22). However, it has been argued that, beyond the provisions of the constitution, minorities' equal citizenship was described as conditional to their loyalty to Pakistan, which was not the case with the majority.[40]

The most fateful move towards the minoritization of communities came with the much-celebrated 1949 Objectives Resolution passed by the Constituent Assembly, which divided the house – and therefore the nation it represented – along religious lines. All ten non-Muslim members voted against it. One of the minority members, Prem Hari Barma, pointed to the need for circulating the resolution to the public at large, accommodating dissent if there was any, and thus avoiding 'hot haste'.[41] Another Hindu member, Sri Chandra Chattopadhyaya, questioned the need for a resolution of this kind while the nation was already on its way to making the constitution.[42] When Prime Minister Liaqat Ali Khan pointed to minority members as a party, Chattopadhyaya clarified that 'there is no party of mine' and the prime minister explained that he meant 'the non-Muslim Members' of the house.[43] The new 'other' was thus clearly identified. Only one Muslim member, Mian Iftikharuddin, opposed the resolution.

In contemporary Pakistan, with the number of Christians ranging from 1.6 per cent to 2 per cent of the population, closely followed by Hindus, their combined low demographic strength has been socially and culturally a negative factor in terms of broad-based cross-communal communication. Worse still, two factors have kept the two leading minorities away from each other. First, Christians are mostly Punjabis while Hindus are almost wholly Sindhis. This pointed to an absence of social, cultural, ethnic, and linguistic ties across minority communities. Second, Christians live in ghettos such as Yuhannabad in Lahore and Christian villages in canal colony districts in Punjab, while Hindus are concentrated in Umarkot, Tharparker, Sanghar and Mirpur Khas in Sindh. This meant that the former lacked the social and political leverage that the latter enjoyed to a limited extent, for example for electoral purposes.

A lack of interaction between the majority and minority communities, especially after the migration of the bulk of Hindus to India after partition, has all along kept them far from a pattern of recurrent communal riots. This is unlike India where communal conflict was both a cause and effect of a gradual decline of Muslims as a minority.[44] In Pakistan, minorities have been abjectly depressed communities at the receiving end of social and cultural violence. The annual electronic media coverage of 'our Hindu biradri' celebrating Diwali and Holi, or 'our Christian biradri' celebrating Christmas, was both paternalistic and reflective of a fossilized image of the depressed 'other'. Educational textbooks have been a lethal instrument of minoritization of non-Muslims.[45] This phenomenon has been expressed through the minorities' informal exclusion from the 'public', especially in the context of making a collective profile on national and international, social and cultural as well as moral and ideological issues. Hindus, Christians and Ahmadis were not part of the master narrative. It was not the quality of their argument, soundness of their judgement and sincerity of their purpose but their identity as non-Muslims that mattered and de-legitimized their role as part of the 'public'.[46] It virtually reduced them to the abstract notion of the plain white strip on the national flag that symbolized their presence on the soil of Pakistan but nothing else. They remained 'the (un)imagined citizens of the state'.[47] Even the symbolism of tolerance for minorities in the immediate post-partition years was pushed out of the national memory. For example, Jinnah opted for the Dalit leader Jogendranath Mandal as the first honorary chairman of the Constituent Assembly of Pakistan and, more astonishingly, as minister of law in a country that was purportedly poised at a juncture of establishing the rule of Sharia. It looked surreal three generations later. As opposed to the sects and sub-sects of the Muslim majority that became part of the public discourse, the internal differentiation of religious minorities along sectarian, caste, ethnic and linguistic identities was submerged in their larger composite identity. A good example is the way the identity of Mandal and his Dalit followers, along with their struggle against caste-Hindus in East Bengal, was merged with their overall Hindu identity per se.[48]

Christians in Pakistan, unlike Hindus and Sikhs, have no history of power and privilege – no 'golden age' – except a few persons occupying elite positions and thus enjoying a requisite level of social status. There are few references to antiquity. There is only a legend that Jesus's Apostle, St Thomas, visited south India in the first century AD, and perhaps stopped at Taxila on his way. Here, a cross was discovered in 1935 that now serves as the symbol of the Church in Pakistan.[49] The first Portuguese archdiocese was established in Goa in 1533, which provided leadership to Catholics in India and further east. A large majority of Christians now living in Pakistan were converted mainly by three American missionaries in the late nineteenth century. Though racist but not colonialist, Americans in their egalitarian spirit converted some who converted many, sometimes whole castes.

During the colonization of land before and after partition, Christian villages were allotted land – forty-seven in Punjab and six in Sindh. The lands were usually at the tail-end of irrigation canals and had a low productivity level. Many Christians moved to cities after a generation and established their ghettos. The two Christian members of the Punjab Assembly had voted for Pakistan in 1947 and urged their fellow Christians to migrate from East to West Punjab. While a vast majority of Christians belonged to the untouchables at the bottom of Hindu society, the idea was that life would be much better in West Punjab, which would not adhere to religiously sanctioned inequality among people. Soon, it was a dream turned sour. Indeed, within the community there were low-caste Christians and upper–middle caste Goans in Karachi who pursued their separate social and professional activities.[50] There were no Muslim converts to Christianity, who would have served as a bridge with the majority community.[51] Indeed, the Protestant leadership would not countenance the idea of reaching out to Muslims, as initiated by the Christian Study Centre Rawalpindi, largely drawing on 'a non-sequitur of the paradox between evangelical and ecumenical'.[52]

Christians at the bottom of society had one thing common with the West: the faith along with its infrastructural expression in the form of the church. That rendered the community into 'agents' of the West in the eyes of extremist Muslims, and churches into targets for Muslim anger. Christians outnumbered other communities as victims of blasphemy cases. Several factors accounted for this state of affairs: the abject insecurity of the poor-income strata, and a lack of support mechanisms for family and *biradari* networks due to the relatively recent migration from village to city in many cases. The Zia government's drive towards Islamization indirectly provided 'legitimacy' to mob justice before court conviction.

While minoritization was a social, political and symbolic process about non-Muslims, for Ahmadis it was quintessentially legal and religious in nature, rooted in a long gestation period. There was a prolonged movement of ulema parties, led by the Majlis-e-Ahrar, for pushing Ahmadis out of Islam, spread over four decades before the 2nd Amendment that declared them a minority in 1974. This is a surrealistic story of how an insider group turned into an outsider and an outsider became an insider. On the one hand, the government incorporated the Ahmadi elite in the modern state apparatus, as a foreign minister, as bureaucrats, and as generals in the army. On the other hand, the Islamic lobby declared the whole Ahmadi community apostate. Indeed, the Majlis-e-Ahrar, the arch-champion of the anti-Ahmadi movement and a former ally of the Congress, had itself been considered an outsider before partition. It had opposed the Pakistan project and held Jinnah 'responsible for Muslim genocide in East Punjab'. It called 'Begum Liaqat Ali Khan and other women who did not observe purdah as prostitutes'. It attributed the abduction of Muslim women by Hindus and Sikhs to Jinnah's 'desire to become the Governor-General of Pakistan'.[53]

Back in the 1930s, the atrocities committed against Kashmiri Muslims had mobilized Muslims of British India to campaign against the maharaja. It was led by Majlis-e-Ahrar as well as the All-India Kashmir Committee, which included Allama Iqbal, Mirza Bashiruddin – the head of the Ahmadi sect – and Abdur Rahim Dard, another Ahmadi, as secretary. Jinnah appointed a leading member of the Ahmadi community, Sir Zafrullah, as a member of the Punjab Boundary Commission in 1947, and later appointed him as foreign minister of Pakistan. Indeed, the Muslim League also gave some party tickets to Ahmadis to fight elections in 1951.[54] However, the ulema continued to build street power against the Ahmadis, who were variously held responsible for killing Liaqat Ali Khan, for spying for India,[55] and even for air crashes.[56] The ulema wanted Ahmadis to be declared infidels and for Sir Zafrullah to be ousted as foreign minister along with other Ahmadis in elite positions. However, the government was firm that its function was not 'to coerce any group into becoming a minority community', and that no government servant could be removed 'because of the religion he professes'.[57] Indeed, the 1954 Munir Report observed that the ulema had been emboldened to put up religious demands by those at the helm of the state 'who had during the last several years been crying themselves hoarse over their intention to establish in Pakistan an Islamic state'.[58] In this way, the issue of the Ahmadis sharpened the dichotomy between modernists and traditionalists. Unlike the issue of other minority communities, whose outsider status was non-controversial, the issue of the Ahmadis involved a basic question of who was the insider and who was the outsider. When responding to Jinnah's speech of 11 August 1947, which referred to the irrelevance of personal faith for the business of the state, freedom of worship, and equal citizenship for all religious communities, the JI's Amin Ahsen Islahi claimed that such a state 'is the creature of the devil'. Other ulema also 'replied in an unhesitating negative' manner.[59]

Minorities: (non-)Representation

The state in Pakistan inherited the constitutional provisions and humanitarian concerns for religious minorities as a colonial legacy. The issue of representation of these communities in the constitutional framework often cropped up in the context of elections for assemblies, and legal safeguards to be handled through the courts. The modernists referred to the classical Islamic positions of tolerance and pluralism and sometimes gave the example of the Charter of Medina signed by the Muslim and Jewish communities under the direct tutelage of the Prophet of Islam. The ulema, for their part, would argue for the imposition of *jizya* (tax) on minorities and delineation of their status as *dhimmis*, which would deprive them of equal citizenship.[60] However, constitutional development in British India had gone too far for the issue of representation of minorities in the state system as equal citizens to be rolled back. Indeed, Muslims were direct beneficiaries of the constitutional provisions for their representation in the emergent legislatures from 1909 onwards, in the form of separate electorates in the teeth of opposition from the Congress.

After partition, the Indian Constitution provided for the preservation of the language, culture, rituals and personal laws of religious minorities but scrapped the system of separate electorates for religious communities. Only the Scheduled Tribes and Scheduled Castes were provided reserved seats in various legislatures. In

Pakistan, unlike the Muslim minority in British India, which sought the cushion of separate electorates against the perceived tyranny of Hindu majority, minorities led by Christians and Hindus generally sought accommodation in mainstream politics through a joint electorate.[61] Previously, the government in British India, as a supra-national entity, was not bound by the (Hindu) majority's will whereas the government in Pakistan was inextricably linked with the Muslim majority in the new state. Minorities struggled to join hands with it.

Indeed, the issue of separate electorates for religious minorities in Pakistan was not only a matter for minorities: separate electorates were important for the mainstream politicians. The ulema parties gave Islamic reasons for supporting separate electorates inasmuch as politics was required to be distinctly based on an understanding between communities of faith. The JI regarded the joint electorate as a negation of the two-nation theory. However, these ideological positions were underscored by political considerations, which pushed various contenders for power to win a majority in the national and provincial assemblies. The minority communities, including Hindus, Christians and later Ahmadis, were not the constituency of Islamic parties. The more the latter stressed their Islamic agenda to define the national destiny of Pakistan, the more it pushed the minorities to seek security elsewhere. It resulted in a net loss of votes for Islamic parties in favour of the 'liberal', leftist, and ethno-regional parties, including the Awami League, ANP and PPP. Islamists wanted to bring in separate electorates and thus prevent the minority vote from going to the 'liberal' parties under a joint electorate system.

The Muslim League, however, along with other mainstream parties, kept changing its stance on this issue. In the early 1950s, it typically though not wholly supported separate electorates, but in the late 1950s and the 1960s it upheld the cause of a joint electorate. The Hindu-led minority communities had opposed the second Basic Principles Committee report in the early 1950s for its provision for separate electorates. The matter came to a head in 1952 when the federal government amended the electoral law under the 1935 India Act as amended in 1947 to make provision for separate electorates for the Scheduled Castes, ostensibly to divide the Hindu voters. The East Bengal Minority Conference at Comilla in 1952 condemned the idea as inherently divisive and as opposed to national integration. The minority leadership in East Pakistan supported the joint electorate along with the reservation of seats for under-represented minorities such as the Scheduled Castes and Christians. People in East Pakistan comprehensively voted out the Muslim League in the 1954 elections, along with the dominant party line on separate electorates. Later, the responsibility for legislating on that issue shifted to provincial assemblies as per the 1956 Constitution, whereby the bill for the joint electorate was passed by East Pakistan Assembly.

By 1957, after five years of bitter controversy, the joint electorate became the basis of the election system in whole of Pakistan. General elections were held in 1962, 1965, 1970 and 1977 on the basis of the joint electorate. While the 1956 Constitution was unequivocal on the issue, the 1962 and 1973 Constitutions clearly provided for a joint electorate. In other words, none of the three constitutions provided for separate electorates.

Under Zia, Islamic parties mounted a campaign for separate electorates once again. They believed that they had failed at the polls in the 1970 and 1977 elections because of the joint electorates. The military junta also believed that religious minorities would vote for the PPP if it went ahead with elections under a joint electorate system. Consequently, the local bodies elections in 1979, 1983 and 1987, and the national elections in 1985, were held according to separate lists of voters and candidates for faith-based communities. In the face of severe criticism from liberal opinion at home and abroad, the 1985 8th Amendment enshrined the provision for separate electorates that became the rule for the general elections in 1988, 1990, 1993 and 1997.

Procedurally, the election of minority candidates became a farce because their constituencies spread out to the whole country or a whole province or otherwise extremely large areas not to be handled easily by single candidates. In one case, as few as 248 polled votes returned a candidate for the National Assembly as successful.[62] The system was considered akin to religious apartheid. Human rights organizations condemned it as a virtual disenfranchisement of minorities. However, the Islamic lobby all along argued that minorities would indeed get more seats under this system than they would otherwise. For example, when elections were held based on separate electorates in 1955, there were 11 minority members in the (second) Constituent Assembly:

9 from East Bengal, 1 from Punjab and 1 from Sindh. Later, under the joint electorate, there was no minority member in the National Assembly and only 4 members in the East Pakistan Assembly of 155 members as compared to the large minority population in that province.

But for minorities, the issue was larger than formal representation on the floor of parliament. In their view, separate electorates infested the polity with religious hostility and reinvigorated communal disaffection in social, cultural, and residential contexts. Separate electorates provided legitimacy to discriminatory practices in various fields of public activity such as education, employment and social interaction. While Muslims enjoyed territorial representation in legislatures, minorities were tied down to the colonial baggage of communal representation. Separate electorates effectively barred a minority group from access to the local administration, especially the police, while their 'representatives' lived far away in a different district or province.[63] Certain Christian leaders – especially Joshua Fazluddin – had supported separate electorates in the past, the idea being to placate the majority community and hope for some generosity on its part. But electoral politics and parliamentary activity took away that dream from the minority section of the Christian intelligentsia because of the perceived irrelevance and powerlessness of the minority legislators, in addition to the brutalization of inter-communal relations in the society.

The second Benazir Bhutto government (1993–6) proposed an electoral reform package that included the right of a double vote for non-Muslims as part of affirmative action for the underprivileged minority population. Various Islamic groups and rightist parties opposed the move as unconstitutional and un-Islamic, being ultra vires of Articles 51 and 106, and Articles 2A and 227 respectively. The anomalous character of supra-territorial constituencies for minorities meant that voters and their representatives belonged to different regions and different segments of minority communities. For example, the Kalash and Buddhist representatives came from central Punjab whereas these communities were concentrated in Gilgit-Baltistan. In all these cases, political interaction with the majority community remained absent.[64]

A basic principle underlining the system of separate electorates was that citizens were barred from voting for contestants belonging to faiths other than their own. This directly affected minorities who lived in all regions of the country in varying numbers but who were excluded from voting for their territorial representatives. This virtually de-citizenized individuals belonging to minority communities by violating constitutional guarantees about equality of all citizens before law.[65] Under these circumstances, minorities showed general unwillingness to register themselves as voters. Only 50 per cent of Christians eligible for voting had registered themselves and only 10 per cent had voted in the 1993 and 1996 elections.[66] Under Musharraf, all minority communities adopted a strategy of boycott in the context of the 2000–2001 local bodies' elections. In the first phase of these elections, 97 per cent of minority seats were boycotted in Balochistan, 91 per cent in KP, 73 per cent in Sindh and 70 per cent in Punjab.[67] This meant that only 88 out of 957 minority seats were contested, while candidates returned unopposed in 146 seats and 723 seats remained vacant.[68] Finally, the Musharraf government read the writing on the wall and restored the joint electorate for the 2002 general elections.

Social and Cultural Violence

The in-group/out-group dichotomy based on the religion of majority and minority communities not only restricted the latter's entry into the public space but also subjected them to social, cultural, and physical violence. The judiciary typically abdicated the role of the protection of minorities from oppression. The outsider gradually became de-citizenized in the face of a court system that seemed to favour only the insider as a legitimate petitioner seeking justice. As far as the state system was concerned, the legal and judicial protection of outsiders deteriorated over time. Courts failed to entertain their cases on an equitable basis. Nor was the government able to provide them with physical safety and economic security, as in the form of quotas for jobs. In one study, in twenty-five years following the amendments to the blasphemy laws in the 1980s, 38 Christians, 21 Hindus and 454 Ahmadis were arrested and charged under them.

The reason why Christians outnumbered Hindus in this context related to the radicalization of Punjab society as opposed to the relatively syncretic and pluralist framework of Sindhi society. A report by the Movement for Solidarity and Peace in Pakistan found that at least 1,000 girls belonging to Christian and Hindu communities were forced to marry Muslim men every year.[69] Examples of anti-Hindu attitudes related to revenge attacks on temples after the 1992 demolition of the Babari Mosque in Ajodhya in India, opposition to celebration of Diwali and other Hindu festivals, and barring Hindus from visiting renovated temples such as Katas Raj.[70] In 2020, a Hindu temple was burnt to ashes by Muslim zealots in KP. The court ordered the rebuilding of the temple by the imam of the local mosque who had initiated the mob attack.[71] Moreover, the Christian ghettos were interspersed across large Muslim areas, which rendered them vulnerable. The Hindu population was densely located in the rural districts of Sindh, which made them somewhat secure from the wrath of the majority.[72]

In 1972, the nationalization of elite private schools and colleges, including the Christian institutions, dealt a severe blow to a credible source of social leverage to that community. However, in Charles Amjad-Ali's view, the Christian community did not benefit from missionary schools and colleges, where the children of the Muslim elite mainly studied.[73] In the 1960s, the media launched preposterous allegations that 300,000 Muslims had been converted to Christianity, which created a wave of contempt for the latter community.[74] At the other end, the Hindu religion was subjected to vilification through such publications of the JuD as *Hindu Religion: Murderer of Humanity*, where outcast Hindus were promised deliverance from their awful plight through acceptance of Islam.[75] In fact, even Hindus would speak 'the language of the hegemon' in public by praising the majority's religion, obviously as a strategy for their survival.[76]

The issue of the forced abduction, conversion and marriage of Hindu girls often got confused with the issue of minimum age for marriage in the absence of a law covering a minimum age for conversion. When the PPP government introduced a bill in the Sindh Assembly to that effect in 2016, it led to an outcry in the Islamic lobby. The government felt obliged to withdraw the bill. Forced conversions were at 52 per cent in Punjab and at 44 per cent in Sindh; 54.3 per cent Hindu girls and 44.44 per cent Christian girls; 46.3 per cent minor girls and 16.67 adult women.[77]

The forced conversion of Hindu girls to Islam at the hands of Muslim men – forty-one girls in six months and hundreds in a decade as per a Hindu member of the Sindh Assembly – was generally attributed to the heads of two Muslim shrines, Mian Mithu of Dargah Barchundi Shareef Ghotki and Pir Mohammad Ayub Jan of Sarhandi shrine.[78] Apart from conversions, the proscribed Deobandi outfits – LeJ, JuD and ASWJ among others – established madrassahs in areas of Hindu concentration in Sindh, such as Tharparkar, Umarkot, Jacobabad and Shikarpur.[79] These included both registered and unregistered madrassahs, 6,503 and 2,987 respectively. Many people, ranging from a Sufi folk singer, Manjhi Faqir, to the principal of a private school, have been targets of allegations of blasphemy.[80]

In cases of abduction and forced conversion of young Hindu women, a Hindu would blame outside forces trying to divide the community rather than point directly to the culprit.[81] Sometimes, the perspective of scholars dealing with the issue of minorities was criticized for lumping together different caste-based, sect-based, locality-based and class-based segments of minority communities as a 'mass of oppressed people suffering from the same fate'.[82] This de-personalization of the followers of minority religions was tantamount to their de-humanization. This cost them their multiple identities tied with their engagements within and outside their respective communities.

Christians have been subjected to allegations of blasphemy more often than others, including Muslims. Defenders of the blasphemy laws often point to their origin in Sections 295, 296, 297 and 298 of Chapter 15 of the Indian Penal Code of 1860, which provided for a jail sentence of two years and a fine. However, under these laws only six cases were registered from 1947 to 1982. New amendments include Sections 298-A, 298-B, and 298-C in 1984, 295-C in 1986 involving the sentence of death, and, later, elimination of the option of a life sentence from 295-C in 1990 by the Federal Shariah Court (FSC). Lower courts were prone to sentencing the accused to death. However, they were typically released by the higher courts. Some of the accused were whisked away to another country, as with Asia Bibi, landing in Canada in 2019 after years of confinement. There was mob violence, as in the case of a Christian couple who were pushed into the burner of a kiln for blasphemy. Barring HRCP, Human Rights Watch and some other NGOs, the issue of violence against minorities has yet to occupy a significant place in the activities of the organized intellectual or activist groups in civil society, such as student bodies, writers' forums, political parties, bar associations, or lobbyists in and around the country's legislatures.

Sectarian Outsider

Has Muslim society in Pakistan been moving towards integration or disintegration? One sect, the Ahmadi, has already been declared non-Muslim and subjected to social and cultural persecution. Is the other sect – the Shia – bound to face the same fate eventually? There have been periodic waves of Sunni anger against that community, characterized by targeted killings and attacks on the Muharram processions and *imambarghas*. Apart from Ashna Ashari and Ismaili Shias, Hazaras in Balochistan have been the target of both sectarian and ethnic hatred. In addition, Zikris, who are the followers of one Syed Mohammad Jaunpuri in Balochistan, have been condemned as heretics. Islamic parties such as the JUI-F and the conservative middle-class elements within and outside the province have an agenda of declaring some or all of them beyond the pale of Islam. The more the state moved in the direction of conflation between religion and politics, the more the large Sunni majority sought to define the route to state authority in terms of its own sect-based Islamic theology and rituals.

Shias

There are some uncomfortable facts relating to Shias. Pakistan, as a predominantly Sunni country has a Shia father of the nation: Jinnah. Indeed, the three most prominent leaders of the All-India Muslim League in British India – Sir Agha Khan, Raja Sahib of Mahmudabad and Jinnah – were all Shia. The last major state of UP was ruled by a Shia dynasty for a hundred years before it was annexed by the British in 1856. Like other minorities, Shias have been generally shy of projecting their sectarian identity, except when they converged on the federal secretariat in Islamabad in 1980 to protest against Zia's Sunni-based project of Islamization.[83] The Shia sect is committed to the public display of grief over the martyrdom of Imam Hussain. The perception of Sunni diehards, however, is that a sectarian minority assumes a kind of street power that is disproportionate to its numerical or political strength. Among Sunnis, a large majority of the Barelvi sect shared Shia sentiments against the persecution of Imam Hussain. Andreas Rieck calls Barelvis 'crypto-Shia'.[84]

From the early twentieth century onwards, Sunnis started to cleanse their sect of Shia beliefs and practices, which had been accommodated by them under the Shia ascendancy in UP and elsewhere, such as in Jhang in Punjab. In Lucknow, Sunnis started to conduct processions of Madh-e-Sahaba in praise of the Prophet's companions on the day of Ashura. It was banned under the recommendations of the Piggot Committee in 1909. However, the ban was lifted from areas outside Lucknow following the 1938 Allsop Committee Report. Later, the Congress government of UP (1937–9) allowed the Madh-e-Sahaba rallies on the birthday of the Prophet, followed by reimposition of the ban from 1940 till after partition. During the Pakistan Movement, Shia–Sunni conflict was overridden by Hindu–Muslim conflict. The All India Shia Conference (AISC) was bypassed by Shias, who supported Pakistan instead. Indeed, the AISC leader, Husseinbhai Laljee, got only 127 votes against Jinnah's 3,601 votes from the Bombay Urban Muslim Constituency for the Central Legislative Assembly in 1946.[85] In Pakistan, two rival organizations, the All Pakistan Shia Conference and Idaret-e-Tahaffuz-i-Huquq-i-Shia, remained active on the sidelines of mainstream politics. There was controversy about whether Shias should raise their visibility and whether that would demote them to a pariah status.[86] For a generation, the Mohajir ulema took the lead in Shia activities.[87] In 1957, rising Sunni bigotry engulfed Sufi-orientated Barelvis. One Qamaruddin Sialvi of the JUP issued a fatwa to declare Shias infidel.[88] The decade of the 1960s exposed Shias of Pakistan to news about the repression of their counterparts in Iraq under the Ba'thist regime in the name of Arab socialism. The 1970 election set the main trend among the Shia electorate to vote for the relatively liberal party, PPP, as a safeguard against the Islamic parties that campaigned for a (Sunni-based) Islamic rule in the country. Under Zia, the Shia leadership got a new cause to pursue, i.e. resisting the imposition of Sunni jurisprudence on Shias. This included the Zakat and Ushr Ordinance 1980 and the establishment of Shariah benches in high courts and the Supreme Court and later the Federal Shariah Court. In August

2020, a First Information Report (FIR) was filed against a Shia cleric, Alvi, under Article 295-A (blasphemy law), and another Shia person was arrested for reciting Ziarat-e-Ashura.[89] During the last quarter of 2020, several Shias were killed or embroiled in blasphemy cases. Anti-Shia hashtags trended. It was estimated that 22,000 Shias had been killed since 1968. The militant Sunni party, SSP, considered Shias spies for Iran. An important development in this period was radicalization of Barelvis led by the Tehreek Labbaik Pakistan (TLP). It was widely speculated that the perpetrators of anti-Shia hatred and violence would eventually push for a constitutional amendment to declare Shias beyond the pale of Islam. Indeed, it was argued that the continuing economic and political downslide obliged the PTI government to rely on 'Sunni majoritarian populism' to stem the tide of public reaction to bad governance.[90]

The Shia–Sunni conflict in the locality emerged as a part of larger phenomena such as partition and the specific context of electoral politics. In this context, the city of Jhang in Punjab presents an ideal case study. Before partition, the city and the surrounding rural areas were dominated by the Shia landed elite. A large number of refugees from East Punjab and further east and south settled in the city, which brought about a demographic change. Sunni-ization of the population shattered the 'peace' that had operated within a 'putative negotiation space'.[91] The old Shia aristocracy and the new Sunni middle and lower middle classes sought to redefine the political space in the framework of expansion of franchise. The Shia elite faced the challenge of keeping their vote base intact across the emergent multiple identities, while the incoming Sunnis dwelt on the sectarian divide to produce a new boundary.[92] Religion became a contested territory.[93]

It is argued that religion is a second-order concept and not a prime mover and therefore cannot be considered an independent variable. We need to understand the Shia–Sunni conflict within a social constructionist framework whereby religion lent legitimacy to identity formation along exclusive lines. While Shia clerics in Pakistan continued to organize themselves in the form of political parties, the general Shia public eschewed the need for projecting and profiling its sectarian identity. Not surprisingly, its majority typically ended up voting for the PPP, the perceived liberal and tolerant party in a mode of electoral behaviour shared by other religious and sectarian minorities.

After independence, Sunnis got increasingly stronger. Milestones on the route to the Islamic project were formally inclusive but substantively Sunni, for example, the 1949 Objectives Resolution, the 1952 Basic Principles Committee Report, the periodic recommendations of the Council of Islamic Ideology (CII) and, most blatantly, the 1980 Zakat and Ushr Ordinance. Meanwhile, the returnees from Saudi Arabia and other Gulf countries were half-converted to Wahhabism. All this further distanced the two communities as followers of two exclusive models of a sacred cosmos.

A gradual process of minoritization of Shias set in under Zia. Divination of the political landscape through the project of Islamization failed to accommodate different exegetical articulations of the religion. The 1978 Iranian revolution signified the first major leap forward to sectarian intolerance among Sunnis. The state's religio-sectarian agenda, underscored by vote politics, contributed to the mobilization of activists on both sides with violent clashes. In Gilgit-Baltistan, where the combined Ashna Ashari and Ismaili population enjoyed a clear majority, the state took up the project of Sunnification by facilitating the settlement of migrant Pakhtun and Punjabi professional and commercial elements from outside.

The decades of the 1980s and 1990s saw the worst period of sectarian violence in Jhang and Gilgit-Baltistan. Similarly, Shia Turis faced incoming Sunni Afghan mujahideen in Kurram agency in the erstwhile FATA. In Karachi, the Shia–Sunni riots of Lucknow from the first half of the twentieth century were periodically re-enacted, topped by the target killing of Shia doctors. It can be argued that Islamization paved the way for a journey back in time across a millennium-and-half to the classical, original and authentic sources of the divide in the Islamic *umma*. The gruesome past, full of sectarian hostility and sedimented feelings of otherness, shaped the present. The past became an imaginary world of reified symbols of presentation sublimated as sacrifice. Even as the Shia elite was gradually losing its edge in urban professional and business life, it was unlikely that Sunni clerics would win their battle to declare the community infidel in constitutional terms any time soon, given the Shia's demographic and historic importance. However, the decline of Shia power vis-à-vis its Sunni counterpart was the cost that the state was willing to pay in pursuit of its agenda of creating national unity through the Islamic project.

Hazaras

The Hazara community of Balochistan has been the worst hit section of the Shia community. Shias in general, numbering approximately 30 million in a country of more than 200 million, were ostensibly attacked to punish them for their religious practices, such as Ziarat-e-Ashura, or to stop their public display of grief about the martyrdom of Imam Hussain. However, attacks on Hazaras are ostensibly part of a project to oust them from Balochistan.[94] It was a tiny community of 95,000 living on the outskirts of Quetta, the capital of Balochistan, and according to some estimates is now reduced to 65,000.

Hazaras had fled their brutal persecution under King Abdur-Rehman of Afghanistan in the 1890s.[95] The commander-in-chief of British Indian forces, Lord Kitchener, ordered the formation of a Hazara Pioneers Battalion. However, Hazaras found themselves on the wrong side of local society a century later, caught in the midst of sectarian terrorism. While Hazaras were given citizenship rights in 1963, by 2015 the National Database and Registration Authority (NADRA) blocked 45,000 national identity cards of the community.[96] Litigation continued over the issue for years.

Apart from legal issues of citizenship, Hazaras were neither institutionally represented in the national or provincial assemblies nor considered politically important by way of finding a role for them in political parties. No official or unofficial organization championed the issue of their security, their jobs and a decent living. They have often been the target of bomb blasts. They have been indirect victims of a proxy war between Iran and Saudi Arabia, which supported their Shia and Sunni henchman on the soil of Pakistan respectively. Ostensibly, the Zainabiyoun Brigade of Iran recruited Shias from Kurram and from the Hazara community of Pakistan, which fought in Iraq against ISIS in 2014 and in Syria against the Turkish army in 2019–20. Sunni insurgents from Sistan–Balochistan in Iran and the Khorasan segment of ISIS were also involved in attacks on Hazaras. In the post-9/11 scenario, many Taliban of Afghanistan who settled in Quetta targeted Hazaras as fifth columnists. There was pressure on Hazaras to sell their property at throwaway prices and flee the area.[97]

Hazaras have been massacred several times from 2003 onwards, for which the Sunni militant outfit Lashkar Jahngvi (LJ) has claimed responsibility. In Behryab's view, Hazaras questioned the way the state provided space to LJ for these attacks, even while it had come down heavily on the TTP and other terrorist groups elsewhere in the country.[98] He located the origin of the hatred for Hazaras in the Islamic literature taught in Sunni madrassahs, which equated Shias to Ahmadis.[99] The killing of one Shia person was declared to be the route to paradise.[100]

When the Karzai government in Afghanistan released Taliban militants belonging to Pakistan from 2002 onwards, these returnees were full of anger over the post-9/11 change in Islamabad's foreign policy. They brought back stories of cruelty and violence perpetrated against them in the jails of Kabul and massively ignited feelings of revenge among Sunni militants in Pakistan. There was a gruesome attack on the Moharram procession of Hazaras in Quetta in 2004.[101] In 2011, LJ militants killed Hazara pilgrims travelling to Iran after carrying out an identity parade to separate them from others. In January 2021, eleven miners of the Hazara community were beheaded in the Mach coalfield area and a video of this heinous act was put online by the Islamic state (IS) group, the self-proclaimed killers. Hazaras staged a protest on the road at sub-zero temperatures and demanded that Prime Minister Imran Khan come to console them and ensure their safety. The prime minister first brushed it aside as blackmail but then came, but only after the Hazaras had buried the dead bodies.

Zikris

While Hazara killings made the headlines, the other sectarian minority in Balochistan – the Zikris – has been a silent victim of increasing bigotry and hatred. The origin of the faith of the Zikri community living in Makran, along the coastline of south Balochistan, is usually located to Syed Mohammad Jaunpuri of Gujrat Kathiawar in India in the fifteenth century. Zikris believe in remembering God, which distinguishes them from those who perform rituals (*namazis*). Their annual pilgrimage to Koh-e-Murad in Turbat on 27th Ramadhan is similarly considered repugnant to Islam. Some placed Zikris between Sunnis and Shias in terms of their faith and practice.[102]

The Baloch population has a history of tolerance towards Zikris, except under the rule of Nasir Khan (1749–95). Under Zia, mainstream religious elements exerted public pressure to declare Zikris non-Muslims. In this way, their vote would have been registered in the separate electorates for minorities and would thus have cost the Baloch nationalists contesting elections from Makran. Minoritization of communities served the Sunni majority's electoral purposes, as in the case of Hindu Bengalis discussed earlier. Baloch nationalists obviously resisted the move.

Zikris emerged into the limelight in the early twenty-first century when the city of Gawadar became a kingpin of the China–Pakistan Economic Corridor project. Zikris had lived in the region for centuries when infrastructural projects such as the Gawadar-Hashab East of Turbat motorway and the Gawadar-Lasbela-Awaran highway were begun. Caught in the crossfire between the security forces and the Baloch militants, the former have often distrusted Zikris for being on the latter's side. Under these circumstances, Zikris adopted the strategies of other minorities, i.e. migration from rural to urban areas and from Makran to Karachi and abroad, as well as reducing their visibility personally, culturally and politically. Zikris were reduced to a mere one-third of the population of Makran division, where they had once accounted for an absolute majority.[103]

The year 2014 was extremely bad for Zikris. A Zikri pilgrims' bus was hit by a bomb blast whilst returning from Koh-e-Murad. An attack on a shrine in Awaran killed six people. A wave of anti-Zikri bigotry swept Makran. An earthquake that hit Awaran brought in Islamic relief agencies from the militant outfits, which played havoc with inter-communal harmony and put Zikris under renewed pressure.[104] In Shah Mohammad Marri's words, the clue to anti-Zikri onslaught lay in the agenda to divide the Baloch community along religious lines.[105]

Keeping the Outsider Inside

In terms of dealing with conflict, there are various fault lines that define the issues and policies of successive governments in Pakistan. In Paul Brass's view, government policy and ethnic elites are the two independent variables that defined and shaped ethnic conflict in India.[106] Frequently, these policies led to a reaction from the federating units of the new state against what was understood as encroachment by the legislative and administrative powers, and infringement of their cultural and linguistic heritage. I have argued in this book that we need to bring into consideration something more generic and archetypical than official policies as the prime mover of ethnic nationalism. In this context, I want to focus on the 'national project' that was considered a canonical necessity by the ruling elite in pursuit of national integration. While the elite felt obliged to follow these policies, this pursuit created disaffection, alienation, and disillusionment with the state managers amongst various ethnic communities.

The first quarter of a century after partition was characterized by a roller coaster strategy whereby the project of state-building dominated all other functions. According to the prevalent policy and discourse, ethnicity was a curse, demand for provincial autonomy was tantamount to parochialism, leftism was atheism, and politics was dirty business. The state ended up not listening to the electoral representatives of the underprivileged ethnic communities and thus not holding national elections on the basis of adult franchise. While a thousand conflicts were brewing, the state had neither the means nor the will of knowing the situation on the ground. However, in the face of the more obvious dangers to the project of national integration and the need to limit the potential of disgruntled elements for conflict, the state was constrained to roll back some of its policy measures that ate into its plans to keep the country united. Often it was too little too late inasmuch as the damage had been done in terms of the destabilizing potential of an issue at hand. It was not uncommon to see the establishment reverse its policy after considering the harm done to what it considered to be the national interest. As per Oomen's argument, the postcolonial states most typically raised the notion of 'nationalist expectancy' whereby the 'centre' believed that the 'periphery' had only 'temporarily' desacralized its primordial ties of caste, language, ethnicity and region in its struggle against the alien rulers. Subsequently, re-sacralization of primordial ties in the periphery in countries such as India led to the dichotomy of insiders and outsiders representing the centre and periphery respectively.

The policies of exclusivism questioned the very bonding of the outsiders with the state.[107] Pakistan and other postcolonial states have consistently experienced this 'primordial collectivism'[108] of those considered outsiders to mainstream politics. One of the most consistent pursuits of policy for the centre in this regard was to weigh the cost of being inclusive on specific issues vis-à-vis outsiders for its own political or ideological objectives. In this section, I plan to map out the way this option was applied to outsiders on various contentious matters. Here, I shall take up those cases where the state compromised with those on the other side of the fence with a view to avoiding pressure on its hegemonic control and thus avoiding a crisis of major proportions.

Separation of Karachi from Sindh

A lot has been written about the fateful decision of the federal government at Karachi to separate the capital of the new country from the province of Sindh in 1948.[109] At the bottom of the issue lay three potential areas of conflict. First, after superimposition of the federal capital over the provincial capital, the division of property, financial allocations and the scope of the writ of administration between the two governments became problematic, including the handling of government buildings, expenditure of day-to-day governance and overlapping areas of jurisdiction. Second, concerning the resettlement of refugees from India, there was a crucial difference in policy between the Pakistan government struggling to rehabilitate as many of them as possible and Chief Minister Khuhro trying to restrict their numbers to manageable limits. Third, Mohajirs from India pushed for the exodus of Sindhi Hindus out of Pakistan but Sindhi Muslims wanted to keep them in their homes and hearths. Ultimately, the federal government sent the Sindh government packing to a non-descript provincial capital, Hyderabad, in the teeth of opposition from the Sindhi political leadership and intelligentsia.[110]

In the political imagination of the new state managers, demography was up, territory was down. In the face of the hundreds of thousands of migrants who converged on Karachi and turned it into a Mohajir city overnight, territory was considered disposable and dispensable. The lack of sensitivity about the position of Karachi as part of Sindh — historically, politically, administratively and culturally — reflected the territorial agnosticism that characterized the policy orientations of the ruling elite. The 'migrant state' took away the most cherished and the richest part of Sindh. The battle for the city was directly related to the issue of 're-peopling' the state by bringing in those who were left on the wrong side of the border but who deserved a place under the sun in their new homeland as its makers. In Hamida Khuhro's view, Prime Minister Liaqat had been 'arbitrarily' elected from a seat in East Bengal vacated for him by a sitting member, and he wanted to build an electoral constituency for himself in Karachi, which pushed the Sindh government to Hyderabad.[111]

The loss of Karachi was the most visible and negative reflection of the federation's encroachment on both the territory and the seat of government of Sindh. In this context, the Sindh government's resolution of February 1948 against the separation of Karachi and the transfer of its jurisdiction to the federal government was overruled, along with the former's argument that it violated the 1940 Resolution.[112] Protest against the separation of Karachi from Sindh started even before the Constituent Assembly had turned it into a reality. For twenty-two years, this issue inspired the Sindhi nationalist agenda. There was a widespread feeling that whatever Sindhis had gained out of separation from Bombay, they had lost at the hands of Pakistan. The loss of Karachi crystallized Sindhi nationalism in terms of grievances, demands and street action against the profile of a '"second class" status of the province, its inhabitants, its language and its culture'.[113] Later, when Sindh lost its identity altogether after merger with One Unit in 1955 along with other provinces of West Pakistan, the alienation of Sindhis knew no bounds.[114] In 1970, Yahya's martial law government restored the four provinces and reunited Karachi with Sindh, as its capital. The move was facilitated by the fact that the federal capital had meanwhile moved to Islamabad in 1960.

Bengali as a National Language

The dominant feature of the Pakistan project was the creation of a faith-based umbrella Muslim identity as opposed to the mega-identity of Hindus. Regional identities were down but not out. These acquired a new significance — as political resources in pursuit of political interests. Later, the Bengali language provided an idiom of regeneration for the community, which had been recently cut off from its ethnic cohorts in West Bengal and which now felt grossly alienated by its religious cohorts in West Pakistan.

The contrast with the narrative of the ruling elite at the top was indeed forbidding. The latter's iconography included: the Mughal imperium; Urdu language; Perso–Arabic script of local languages; and condemnation of all language-based politics as antinational. Indeed, Maulvi Abdul Haq claimed that 'neither Jinnah nor Iqbal had made Pakistan: rather Urdu made Pakistan'.[115] East Bengal plunged into a language war between Bengali and Urdu. One finds this phenomenon in Europe, especially Germany in the 1920s, where Hebrew was promoted by Zionists for educational, unificatory and 'regenerative' purposes – 'the womb of the nation'[116] – while Yiddish, as the vernacular of Jews in exile, lagged behind in community formation. The language-based cultural nationalism of the former won the day[117]. While the two cases belong to two different trajectories, in both cases language fashioned the nation by representing, in Herder's terms, 'the soul of a people' expressed through the mother tongue.[118]

For a hundred years under British rule Urdu was generally known as Hindustani and served as a lingua franca. By the late nineteenth century, identification of Urdu and Hindi with Muslims and Hindus respectively was an established fact. For Muslims in Bengal, the Bengali language operated in a grey area where it was religiously Muslim but ethnically Bengali. There were efforts to create a binary opposition between a Hindu and a Muslim Bengali language. On the eve of independence, the policy of making Urdu the language of instruction in Pakistan was termed by Bengalis 'political slavery'.[119] Within months of partition, the demand for making Bengali a national language spread all around East Bengal. Jinnah believed firmly in the one-nation-one-language formula as a guarantee of national unity, in step with men of his generation such as Nehru and scores of others who ruled over the new nations. On 21 February 1952, the tragic incident of the shooting and killing of Dhaka University students represented a milestone on the march of Bengalis to acquiring national status for their language. The East Bengal Assembly passed a resolution to that effect against a background of province-wide turmoil in intellectual and activist circles. The defeat of the ruling Muslim League party in the 1954 elections in East Bengal finally paved the way for providing Bengali with the status of the national language. Demonstration of the influence and popularity of the cause contributed enormously to a change of policy with the purpose of keeping the outsider inside. However, as later events showed, it was too late because the language issue had blown up into a fully-fledged movement for provincial autonomy that led further to a separatist agenda.

One Unit

While constitutional negotiations were often stuck on the issue of the proper representation of the provinces in the national legislature, given the situation of one-province-dominates-all, the establishment supported the political class from Punjab, which gradually moved to the idea of inter-wing parity. The idea was that, instead of various provinces – East Bengal, KP, Sindh and Balochistan (as a chief minister's province) – which already operated as outsiders, joining hands against Punjab and, by default, against the establishment, it was better to merge the provinces, princely states and federally and provincially administered areas of West Pakistan into a mega-province called One Unit. This would represent an effective counterweight against the most populous province of East Bengal and secure Punjab's position as the power base of Pakistan. The defeat of the Muslim League in East Bengal in the 1954 elections that led to a massive victory of Bengali nationalist coalition, Jugto Front, further signalled the prospects of that province making an alliance with smaller provinces of West Pakistan.

One Unit was designed to stop the majority in the Eastern wing from attaining political power. It also provided an opening, in the hands of Punjab, to grabbing the thousands of acres of agricultural lands brought under cultivation through the Kotri barrage in Sindh. With Lahore established as the capital of One Unit in 1955 and Islamabad as the capital of the federation in 1960 – both in Punjab – the Punjabization of Pakistan took great strides forward. The central government dismissed chief ministers of the erstwhile provinces who opposed One Unit and installed those in favour of the merging of their provinces with the new mega-province through their respective assemblies.

The project of One Unit had a long gestation period. Iqbal's famous presidential address to the Muslim League session at Allahabad in

1930 mentioned the need for Punjab, Sindh, KP and Balochistan to be 'amalgamated' into a 'consolidated northwest Indian Muslim state'. Later, Iqbal purportedly clarified his position: he meant 'a Muslim province' within the fold of the 'proposed Indian federation'.[120] After partition, the thinking about uniting all the provinces and states of West Pakistan into one province continued to emerge from the political spectrum on the right.[121] A 'secret' document circulated in 1954 claimed that this region already had one culture, one economy and one railway system. It was suggested that the way to the formation of One Unit required suppression of opposition for some time, approval of the provinces through their assemblies and use of religious people for spreading the narrative of unity of Pakistan. It was argued that West Pakistan was divided into 'unnatural' provinces and princely states, and there was need for removal of the fear of Punjab's domination. The document argued for keeping the service structure as it was — but opening low-grade jobs for local people, removing 'provincial consciousness', and changing people's opinion, which should not be difficult because of their 'backwardness'.[122]

In the years that followed, opposition to One Unit gave rise to a long series of street demonstrations, public rallies, critical speeches on the floor of the West Pakistan Assembly, articles and editorials in the newspapers, student boycott of classes and a general alienation among intellectuals, party cadres and leaders from the smaller provinces. They bemoaned the loss of their identity and the diminution of their status vis-à-vis Punjab's demographic preponderance. By G. M. Syed's reckoning, the newly irrigated lands from the Kotri barrage were allocated to non-Sindhis; officers from Punjab superseded their counterparts from Sindh; the 1945 water accord between Sindh and Punjab was tampered with; and smaller nationalities were suppressed in the name of Islam, Pakistan and nationalism.[123] Various political groups, forums and parties emerged, ranging from the Anti-One Unit Front, the Pakistan National Party and the National Awami Party, to the Sindh Students Federation, the Sindhi Adabi Sungat and the Sindh Muttahida Mohaz, that relentlessly opposed One Unit. The West Pakistan Assembly passed a resolution to abolish One Unit in 1957 but to no avail. Between 1955 and 1970 the popular movement against One Unit continued to build. A large part of the nationwide movement against Ayub (1968–9) related to the grievances of Sindh, Balochistan and KP in this regard. Finally,

Yahya scrapped One Unit and restored the four provinces in 1970, and thus took away a major source of conflict that fed the boiling cauldron of hatred against the centre.

Presidential Form of Government

Pakistan was born in insecurity at the hands of India. Karachi faced recalcitrant provincial leaderships that demanded autonomy in the face of the centralization of bureaucracy and the financial control of the federal government. The training of army officers in the USA in the mid-1950s exposed them to the US presidential system, which they were enamoured of as a principle of unity of command. Similarly, the making and breaking of coalition arrangements in the centre and provinces convinced the civil and military officers that the parliamentary form of government was unsuitable for Pakistan. However, whilst the army and Punjab – the core insiders – opposed parliamentarism, all other provinces supported parliamentarism.

After Ayub's takeover, the die was cast in favour of a presidential constitution, which was promulgated in 1962. Ayub considered parliamentarism opposed to the genius of the nation, which was purportedly tuned to the rule of kings. People at large, however, and the political class in general, thought otherwise. The Ayub system was overthrown along with its presidential system in 1969, and the new military ruler, Yahya, was obliged to restore the parliamentary system as the basis for the 1970 elections. However, the middle class in general and the state elite in particular continued to prefer presidentialism to parliamentarism. Not surprisingly, both Zia and Musharraf inserted Article 58(2)(b) into the constitution whereby the president could dissolve the National Assembly, a power that was exercised four times between 1988 and 1996. This article introduced a semi-presidential system by default.

While the post-Musharraf civilian governments of the PPP (after the 2010 18th Amendment), PML-N and PTI have not been straitjacketed by Article 58(2)(b), the military establishment has been able to influence the parliamentary parties in terms of legislation – for example, on the issue of establishing military courts for two years and later extending them by another two years. The vote of the three mainstream parties, PPP, PML-N and PTI, along with smaller parties in favour of the extension of COAS General Qamar Javed Bajwa's term for three years in 2019 was tantamount to accepting the tutelary role of the army. The loss of parliamentary sovereignty by means other than Article 58(2)(b) has thus kept the political system open to pressures from supra-parliamentary forces. However, the shift back to a presidential system was unlikely after a short-lived but disastrous experience from 1962 to 1969. Indeed, COAS General Bajwa declared in his speech in the Senate in 2019 that the presidential system would be disastrous for the nation.

The Quota System

In the face of rising demands from underprivileged communities, the state in Pakistan devised ways and means of securing appropriate representation of ethnic communities in jobs and institutes of higher learning.[124]

Three major aspects of affirmative action policies in Pakistan can be identified. First, for Pakistan ethnicity is what race is for the USA, and what caste is for India as far as policies of preference for underprivileged communities are concerned. Second, unlike the USA and India, where laws make a provision for positive discrimination in favour of the black community and backward castes and Other Backward Classes (OBCs) respectively and not according to their regional location, laws in Pakistan covering these policies are generally based on provinces rather than on neatly defined groups. Third, these policies were selectively implemented along sectoral lines in the province of Sindh to help the relatively underprivileged community of Sindhis, that was typically represented by the rural sector.

The fact that the state is the largest employer in the country has made the issue of jobs a public issue of dire proportions. Development activity expanded the margin of inequality between regions defined in terms of districts. In one study, Karachi scored 26.0147 on the scale of social development including education, health and water supply, while Lahore scored 15.8617, Hyderabad 4.8612, Peshawar 1.3097 and Jhang 0.6348.[125] In Pakistan, three major quota systems have been in operation. The first system, introduced in September 1948, provided for a regional/provincial model of recruitment (see Table 7.1).

Table 7.1 Quota system, 1948

Region/Province	Quota (%)	Population (%)
East Bengal	42	56.75
(West) Punjab	24	28.00
Karachi	2	1.50
Other provinces and states of (W) Pakistan	17	13.75
Potential migrants from India	15	(9.80) included in the above

While a substantial portion of the federal bureaucracy located in Karachi belonged to the migrant group, the new policy guaranteed an additional 15 per cent share in services for potential migrants from India. In the face of criticism from locals, the provision for the quota of intending migrants was abolished but a provision for introducing a principle of merit was brought in with a revised quota system in November 1949 (see Table 7.2). It curtailed the quota for East Bengal by 2 per cent, Punjab by 1 per cent and all other areas of West Pakistan by 2 per cent.

Table 7.2 Quota system, 1949

Category	Quota (%)
Merit	20
East Bengal	40
Punjab (including Bahawalpur)	23
Karachi	2
All other provinces and princely states	15

The provision for merit almost guaranteed jobs for candidates from Punjab and the Mohajir community. The 1956 Constitution extended the quota system by fifteen years. The 1962 Constitution extended it by another ten years. Yahya (1969–71) further extended the quota system to urban and rural sectors within the province of Sindh to 60 per cent and 40 per cent respectively. The 1973 Constitution consolidated this provision under the PPP government. The new policy served Sindhis well inasmuch as it opened up doors for their entry into educational institutions and services. This created a widespread feeling of despair among Mohajir youth, who later took to a militant form of nationalism from the platform of the MQM. The 1973 Constitution not only kept the quota system intact but also extended it by another ten years. It also scaled down the provision of seats to be filled on merit from 20 per cent to 10 per cent, which further hurt Mohajirs (see Table 7.3).

Table 7.3 Quota system, 1973

Category	Quota (%)
Merit	10
Punjab	50
Sindh	19 (rural 11.4, urban 7.6)
KP (formerly NWFP)	11.5
Balochistan	3.5
Northern Areas GB and FATA	4
Azad Kashmir	2

It can be observed that the shares of Sindh, KP and Balochistan along with GB, FATA and Azad Kashmir were neatly defined for the first time only in 1973, mostly at the expense of urban Sindh (see Table 7.3). The premier Mohajir party, MQM, demanded a new quota according to the latest population figures and claimed that the censuses held in 1972 and 1982 were grossly tampered with in order to reduce the number of Mohajirs.[126] Mohajirs had the same reservations about the 1998 and 2017 censuses. Policies of ethnic preference, combined with the relatively lax conditions for getting a local domicile involving all kinds of corrupt practices, created an explosive situation at the cost of representation of Mohajirs in the services. Between 1973 and 1983, all ethnic groups identified with their respective provinces increased their representation in the services with the only exception being Mohajirs, whose share declined from 30.1 per cent to 17.4 per cent for all grades and from 33.5 per cent to 20.2 per cent for senior grades.[127] However, even though recruitment into services on the quota basis might have benefited candidates from the underdeveloped regions in the long run, the dominant power in the short run remained in the hands of the deeply entrenched bureaucratic elements from the traditionally privileged communities of Punjabis and Mohajirs.

An offshoot of affirmative action policies was the provision for relaxation of the rules relating to age, qualification, and experience for candidates from the underdeveloped regions. The upper age limit in the case of tribal candidates was relaxed by three years in 1968. The 'recognized tribes' for this purpose in (W) Pakistan were residents of Quetta and the Kalat divisions of Balochistan, Lasbela district and Nasirabad sub-division of Khairpur division in Sindh as well as parts of the FATA, D. G. Khan district in Punjab and Hazara district in KP. In 1984, the upper age limit was relaxed for the whole of Balochistan, rural Sindh, FATA and GB.[128] This was an obvious response to the 1983 MRD agitation, which had taken a violent turn in Sindh. Mohajirs failed to keep their relatively strong position in the services from constantly declining. Within Sindh, the official policy of positive discrimination in favour of Sindhis according to the 60:40 ratio for rural and urban sectors, combined with the increasing number of the domiciled upcountry migrants eating into the urban quota, produced a high level of accumulated anger among Mohajir youth. It is not surprising that students belonging to these communities emerged in leadership positions in their respective nationalist movements. The Mohajir political party, MQM, was established by the founder leader of a student organization, the All Pakistan Mohajir Student Organization (APMSO), led by Altaf Hussain in both cases. In the case of the Sindhi nationalist movement, students provided the cadre and core constituency of G. M. Syed's Jiye Sindh Mohaz and later formed its breakaway factions.

In a judgment dated 14 June 1989, the FSC held that the quota system could not be challenged in view of Article 203-B(C) of the 1973 Constitution, which had taken the constitution as well as Muslim personal law out of its jurisdiction. Later, the FSC declared (in a judgment dated 23 April 1992) that the Establishment Division Office memorandum dated 31 August 1973, which provided provincial quotas under rule 14 of Civil Servants (Appointment, Promotion and Transfer) Rules, was repugnant to the injunctions of the Qur'an and Sunnah.[129] In 1994, the Lahore High Court bench at Rawalpindi also declared that, in addition to being repugnant to Islam, the memorandum in question had in any case lapsed after the expiry of a period of twenty years on 15 August 1993. The FSC decided that continuation with the quota system after this date was unconstitutional, illegal and without any lawful authority.[130] On 22 October 1997, the Lahore High Court stayed the holding of the Central Superior Services (CSS) examination scheduled for 15 November on the plea that admission forms issued to the CSS candidates specified provision for various quotas that violated Article 27 of the constitution. In 1999, the Senate passed the 16th Amendment, which amended Article 27 clause (1) of the constitution to extend the quota system by another forty years. However, the government of Nawaz Sharif, which enjoyed a majority in the National Assembly, extended the quota by twenty years. Later, the share of merit was reduced to 7.5 per cent and the share of Balochistan was raised to 6 per cent.

Mohajirs resisted extension of the quota system all along. One study observed that the current provision left a large number of vacancies unfulfilled not only for the whole of Sindh, ranging from 20 out of 25 in 2005 to 31 out of 95 in 2015, but also for urban Sindh, which lost seats ranging from 13 seats in 2005 to 19 seats in 2019.[131] From 2007 onwards, a 10 per cent quota for women was to be adjusted against the provincial quota.

The quota system continued to be a major source of resentment among Mohajirs, who produced graduates in far greater numbers than commanded by their requisite quota for jobs and admissions and who referred to the principle of liberal democracy as enshrined in the constitution against discrimination among citizens. On the other hand, Sindhis felt that they would be permanently disadvantaged without protection against merit. The state finally opted to keep the outsiders inside by sticking to the quota system.

Kalabagh Dam

The centre and the core insider province of Punjab have been engaged for decades in a low-intensity conflict with the three smaller provinces on the issue of building a dam at Kalabagh on the River Indus. With all the political power, expertise and support of the World Bank and other potential donors, the project has still not seen the light of day, nor is it likely to do so in the foreseeable future. On the one hand, both civil and military governments – with the Water and Power Development

Authority (WAPDA) as the hatchet man – often pushed the case vehemently in public and through the media. One the other hand, the Sindh, Balochistan and KP Assemblies passed resolutions against construction of the Kalabagh dam. Sindh has taken the lead in opposing the building of the dam on the plea that it should not repeat past mistakes by opening up lands for irrigation and thus invite colonization of the land by Punjab. Out of 1.48 million acres of land brought under irrigation by the Kotri barrage, 0.87 million acres had been allotted to serving and retired civil and military officers, the vast majority of whom belonged to Punjab.[132] Not surprisingly, Sindhi nationalists considered Punjabis to be grabbers of vast agricultural lands along the River Indus and accused them of expansionist designs.

Successive governments have felt obliged to keep the outsider inside and not to alienate it further by going ahead with the project. However, Islamabad has continued to express its support for the dam periodically in an effort to keep the issue alive. Chief Justice Saqib Nisar (2016–19) warned the nation about the absolute scarcity of water looming large and urged the construction of the Kalabagh dam, in addition to two other dams, Dymer-Bhasha and Mohmand, for which he ambitiously initiated fund-raising. Two decades ago, in the midst of euphoria subsequent to the testing of a nuclear device by Pakistan on 28 May 1998, Prime Minister Nawaz Sharif called for the construction of the Kalabagh dam, which was immediately rejected and which later led to the emergence of the Pakistan Oppressed Nations Movement to oppose it.[133] In 2010, a PML-N MNA, Abid Sher Ali, said that 'those Provincial Assemblies which oppose the construction of Kalabagh Dam should be abolished and people who are against the construction of Kalabagh Dam are Indian agents'.[134] In response, the Sindh Assembly passed another resolution: 'This assembly once again categorically rejects the construction of the buried Kalabagh Dam'.[135]

Much debate followed the move to construct the dam. The 'developmentalists' supported it, drawing upon government officials, engineers and Punjab-based politicians. Environmentalists – as in India – warned against an ecological disaster and the displacement of people. Ethno-nationalists found it an encroachment on their water supply that would render a large number of people unemployed and leave whole communities rudderless. The official argument all along focused on the storage of excess water that fell into the sea, which could be tapped for generating 3,600 megawatts electricity and for irrigating 2.4 million acres of land, apart from flood control. The media found the opponents of the dam irrational in the face of a clear technical situation that had been politicized. The opponents in turn objected to the veracity of the numbers about the water flow, which varied from year to year, and the changing period of time for calculating the average flow, ranging from 186 million acre feet to 97 million acre feet for the 'western' rivers according to the Indus Water Treaty about the lands that would be irrigated. Other issues related to matters such as 'ungauged civil canals' in KP – where water flow was not measured at the rim stations – system losses, alleged wrong figures for water outflow into the sea, and arbitrary water availability figures expected after the construction of the dam, ranging from 5.56 million acre feet in 1992 to 16.7 million acre feet in 1994.[136]

Hydropolitics emerged as a source of conflict in the context of the perceived injustice that would privilege some – in this case the upper riparian region of Punjab – at the cost of others. This 'hydro hegemony'[137] pointed to social power relations. In Daanish Mustafa's view, 'resource scarcity and security are all socially constructed'.[138] He traced the conflict back to the 1945 water treaty between Punjab and Sindh, which gave 75 per cent of the Indus water to Sindh and 94 per cent of the water of its eastern tributaries to Punjab. The 1960 Indus Water Treaty gave the water of three eastern rivers to India and compensated Punjab for its loss through link canals and storage facilities from the Indus and Jhelum rivers, allegedly at the cost of Sindh. The 1991 Water Accord under Nawaz Sharif fell a victim to charges of lack of transparency in negotiations, the artificially arranged – and therefore unrepresentative – coalition government in Karachi, and manipulation of the figures of water flow (on the higher side).

Hydropolitics in Sindh was popularized by Sindhi nationalists, who mixed it with identity politics. Hydropolitics in Punjab was a more elite affair.[139] Tariq Niazi discusses the whole debate between the pro-dam and anti-dam lobbies in the context of Habermas's concepts of instrumental rationality based on technocratic expertise – 'scientisation of politics' – and communicative rationality operative in the public sphere through meet-the-people exercises respectively.[140] The pro-dam system sought to optimize its gains through bureaucratic and economic rationality based on 'instrumental logic'. The anti-dam 'life-world' experienced cultural reproduction and identity formation among 'farmers, fishers, families and communities' affected by 'the damming of the Indus'.[141] One finds reference to the spiritual aspect of the Sindhi resistance to the dam as well, such as worshippers of the Indus (Daryapanthis) who dread the prospects of seeing their land turn into a 'spiritual desert'.[142] Sindhi nationalists find the Kalabagh dam project to be 'upstream colonialism', and thus 'combine love of terra with love of aqua', thereby combining territorial and water nationalisms.[143] In addition to Sindh, KP feared the grim prospects of the rehabilitation of those affected by the proposed dam.

The Kalabagh dam symbolizes a six-decades long conflict between the centre–Punjab and the smaller provinces. One can question whether it is the cause of disaffection between the two sides or indeed the effect of a persistent gap of trust between insiders and outsiders that needs to be filled prior to taking up such projects. For those against it, politics, culture and micro-economics have precedence over governance, data – allegedly contrived at best – and macro-economics. Intriguingly, the issue of the Kalabagh dam has divided political parties. The Sindhi members and leaders of the PPP typically opposed the project while the party members and leaders from Punjab favoured the project. Community preceded party in this matter, which reflected the chasm between the political commitments of the outsiders and insiders. The puzzle is that the insiders have upheld the cause of the dam for half a century and kept the agenda alive, but they have not taken it up in earnest. The power of ethnic outsiders, as reflected through their political will represented by the resolutions of the three provincial assemblies and their narrative against Punjab and the centre, became a deterrent factor in this matter. Nor has the establishment sought to tackle the issue indirectly, i.e. by eliminating various other sources of alienation, or to win the trust of Sindhis and others to get them on board. Non-pursuit of the dam project is part of the strategy of keeping the outsiders inside.

Repatriation of Biharis

The post-1971 situation of 'stranded Pakistanis' in Bangladesh created the issue of repatriation of Biharis to Pakistan, who had cooperated with the army in its operation against Bengalis. Some escaped through the land route via India and Nepal, others by sea or by air. During the two decades following the fall of Dhaka, 178,096 Biharis were repatriated to Pakistan.[144] Half a century later, more than a quarter of a million Biharis still lived in Bangladesh, mostly in settlements-cum-camps turned into urban slums. In Pakistan, the strong Mohajir lobby and right-wing politicians such as Nawaz Sharif and the ulema parties favoured an agenda of bringing back the stranded Pakistanis. The latter's support for the Pakistan army in 1971, their life in misery and their stateless and status-less position in Bangladesh kept their kith and kin in Karachi and urban Sindh tied to the cause of their repatriation to Pakistan, especially from the platform of the MQM. In other words, the establishment and pro-establishment social, religious and political groups and communities acknowledged the bona fides of Biharis who had defended their country in 1971, and who fully qualified to be repatriated to Pakistan.

But Sindhis did not want them. Karachi was a constant reminder of the prevalent pattern of dwarfing of the Sindhi population. The prospect of repatriation of Biharis was expected to upset a cart that was already tilting in the direction of non-Sindhis. Sindhis got a new cause after the causes of restoring Karachi as the capital of Sindh, ending One Unit and safeguarding the quota system. The state's fear of losing Sindh and Sindhis after East Bengal and Bengalis was real enough to stop the repatriation of Biharis after the initial inflow. Keeping the outsiders inside was considered the only option. Sindhis were out there as part of everyday life while Biharis were far away from what was the territory of Pakistan and increasingly farther from the hearts and minds of most Pakistanis in the following generations.

The MQM struggled for a quarter of a century for repatriation of Biharis but the state managers did not want to take the risk of alienating Sindhis any further. This is an anomalous case of accommodating those outside the inner circle of the ruling elite even at the cost of alienating the Mohajir community, which had been a core group of the establishment in ethnic terms. The loss of Mohajir clout in the 1970 elections, the revival of the Sindhudesh movement in the 1970s and 1980s, and the military operation against the MQM in the 1990s all dampened the issue of the repatriation of Biharis. This is a classic case of a state abandoning its citizens after they helped it in their 'patriotic' war, essentially because of an ethnic conflict that would not allow another wave of migrants. Biharis largely belonged to non-elite sections of East Pakistan's population and had no formal and institutionalized networking relationships with their counterparts in Pakistan except divided families. This meant that no powerful lobby existed to fight for their return. The Biharis' last hope was the MQM, which emerged as a militant organization on the political scene of Sindh. The state's counterterrorism operations against the party cost the latter in terms of moral ground to pursue the cause of a Bihari comeback.

Keeping the Outsiders at Bay

In some cases, the state withdrew from such policy agendas, which proved to be counterproductive as in the cases of One Unit, which had alienated the smaller provinces of West Pakistan, and Kalabagh dam, which was likely to create even more alienation. In other cases, the state stuck to its policies, which did not accommodate the demands of various sections of society and thus alienated them still further, as it pursued what it considered the national agenda.

The Baloch Outsiders

Among ethnic outsiders, the Baloch present the worst-case scenario in terms of neglect of their grievances, persistent pressure on their politically active elements, and the bypassing or bending of the rule of law in the province. Frederic Grare maintained that the Supreme Court had not been able to convince the security establishment 'to respect the law'.[145] Mainstream 'insiders' would not agree with his position that many Pakistanis now considered the security forces part of the problem rather than the solution.[146] This was because separatists – at one-third as opposed to the provincial autonomists at two-thirds – were an abject minority anyway.[147] While there were small guerrilla groups such as the Baloch Liberation Army (BLA) and the Baloch Republican Army (BRA), led by Hyrbyair Marri and Brahamdagh Bugti respectively, other nationalist groups – the National Party (NP), the Balochistan National Party (BNP) and the Baloch Students Organization (BSO) – opted for playing mainstream politics. Grare also pointed to the shift of the nationalist movement to the middle class and from rural to urban areas.[148] His other findings pointed to

Musharraf's attempted devolution plan as a negation of the political leadership and a demand for provincial autonomy.

Massive rigging of the elections in 2002 included 65 per cent fake registered Baloch voters leading to a manufactured assembly, all of whose members (except one) were part of the cabinet.[149] The Islamization project was used as a weapon to break the Baloch ethnic project. It smacked of Islamabad's strategy adopted during the East Pakistan insurgency in 1971, whereby the latter had rejected Islamization as centralization of state authority.[150] This strategy included expansion of space for sectarian groups such as Lashkar-e-Jhangvi (LJ) among the 'secular Baloch'.[151] On the pattern of Merton's use of the term 'insiderism',[152] I would argue for 'outsiderism' of Balochistan, which continues unabated in the absence of policies that would focus on cooperation and not co-option, building consensus and not imposing control, and a strategy for peace not war.

From 2006 onwards, after the killing of Nawab Akbar Bugti when the Baloch nationalist movement entered the fifth stage of resistance, the issue of enforced disappearances emerged as the leading humanitarian issue. Views about the scale of abduction, torture and disappearance of Baloch nationalists varied. The old Baloch hand, Selig Harrison, described it as a 'slow-motion genocide'.[153] However, there is a difference in the figures claimed for the actual number of missing people in 2016, ranging from 621 according to the Commission on the Inquiry of Enforced Disappearances (constituted by the PPP government in 2010) to the Baloch claims of more than 24,000 casualties.[154] The 2010 Human Rights Watch report summarized the theory, methodology, extent and nature of the whole issue, which threw light on the political stage, the dramatis personae and the message of the gruesome drama.[155] In 2018, the Commission on the Inquiry of Enforced Disappearances identified 153 state officials who were responsible for more than 4,000 disappeared people. However, none of them was charged.[156] The captors belonging to the security apparatuses made it clear that they were bound not by what the president or chief justice said but only by what the military chief said. This reflected the bland reality on the ground about civil–military relations. President Zardari found this issue worth his attention due to public demonstrations by the families of the abductees and the criticism of human rights activists at home and abroad. The logic of disappearance lay in denial of responsibility and therefore accountability. It was a step outside the operational dynamics of the constitutional state, which would have required that detention should be followed by legal action. The Peshawar High Court bench, which had acquitted 196 people convicted by military courts for terrorism, ruled that those courts had violated the Pakistan Army Act and rules by not providing the accused with the counsel of choice.[157]

Often, abductions were not carried out secretly, at night or in far off places: people were picked up in broad daylight in front of potential witnesses. In other words, the reality of the act of disappearance – not the issue of legality – mattered for abductors, apparently to make an example of the person(s) who dared operate politically in pursuit of 'nationalist' goals. Beating and dragging the people on the floor, as well as blindfolding them, aimed at communicating the message effectively. The principal–agent relationship between the state that carried the ultimate legal authority and one of its armed wings was traditionally expressed through the uniform in order to distinguish the latter from society at large, as a symbol of the former's legitimate authority.

But the disappearances were often carried out by plainclothes men. The unlawfulness of the act of disappearance, thus unsupported by the legitimacy and sovereignty of the state, gave a wrong message that 'Might is right'. Such acts were ruefully damaging for the 'rule of law'. Even when the government disclosed the number of detainees under court order or under public pressure from within or outside parliament, charged them for various crimes and transferred them to police custody, the question of the accountability of the unlawful action of enforced disappearance was not raised. This happened at various levels: no registration of cases with the police; no police investigation; reluctance of the courts to prosecute security agencies; and an unwillingness of high government officials to control the field officers.[158] When the Supreme Court under Justice Iftikhar Chaudhry took up the cases of the disappeared it incurred the wrath of President Musharraf. Balochistan has been the prime target of this pattern of governance, not least because large areas of this province have been ruled indirectly through Frontier Corps (FC), comprising military units under the command of administrative authority. Public reporting of incidents of disappearance were either 'cloaked in euphemisms' or not published at all.

The Census Controversy

The holding of the national census has been a great source of conflict, which has often led to the exercise being postponed for several years at a stretch. The smaller provinces have shown great distrust in the whole exercise and accused the centre and by default Punjab for undercounting their population so as to keep intact the hold of 'big brother' over the structural dynamics of the federation. The conflict has had a devastating effect on the way the state managers have carried out the planning of the national agenda for development, which, in the eyes of Sindh, Balochistan and KP, was based on concocted figures relating to the population.

The 1981 census was followed by a huge gap of seventeen years, when the 1998 census was conducted. The next census took another nineteen years and was again mired in controversy. Indeed, the enumerators in the 2017 census were accompanied by men in uniform when they visited people's houses for the purpose of filling in the census forms. Adversarial relations among communities, especially among Sindhis and Mohajirs in Sindh, as well as feelings of alienation among the Hazaras, the Baloch and Pakhtuns in Balochistan, vitiated the atmosphere for a headcount in the context of a perceived conspiracy of the state.

A leading issue in the 2017 census was undercounting urban or urbanizing areas. Thus, Karachi showed an increase of 2.2 per cent annual growth in nineteen years, i.e. less than the 2.4 per cent for the whole country even though it had traditionally been a land of migration from other provinces and from within Sindh for seventy years. A related controversy was about considering rural areas as urban areas, which turned Sindh into an urban-dominated province, with 52 per cent now living in cities and towns. Islamabad, which hardly had a rural patch left, showed more than 6 per cent rural population, as a result of classifying the elite farmhouses of Chak Shehzad and Bani Gala and the luxury suburban areas as 'rural'.[159] Similarly, as compared to the 60 per cent growth rate of Karachi, i.e. from 9.34 million to 15.91 million for the period 1998–2017, Lahore and Peshawar showed growth rates of 116 per cent and 200 per cent respectively. This difference was interpreted as a great conspiracy against the province of Sindh, which rejected it outright. The census was criticized for reducing the number of Mohajirs and for committing socio-economic murder of people in Karachi, which would ruin the city and turn it into Mohenjo-Daro. It was strongly alleged that the establishment was pushing the country towards another Bangladesh.[160]

Controversy over the population census contributed a great deal to the demographic nationalism of ethnic communities. After all, population determined the allocation of seats in the National Assembly as well as provincial shares in the NFC Award, where 82 per cent of allocations were tied to numbers. As per Schedule IV of the Federal List Part II, the census was originally the responsibility of CCI, but was shifted to the federal government where it stayed even after the 18th Amendment.[161] Various studies of the unsatisfactory nature of the 2017 census point to procedural deficiencies leading to undercounting and overcounting. Sindh protested against the loss of numbers as a whole, and against the deficit in Karachi in particular, which had been a haven for a large number of intending migrants from upcountry. One reason could have been counting on a de jure basis, i.e. relating to the permanent address, which often belonged to the area of origin before migration to Karachi.

The requirement of an identity card issued by National Database and Registration Authority (NADRA) for the registration of voters cost Karachi heavily, where 'aliens' including Bengalis, Afghans, Rohingyas and others were not counted. In Mehtab Karim's analysis of the annual household sample survey conducted by the Pakistan Bureau of Statistics, 7.9 million people were undercounted in Sindh, along with 0.6 million in Balochistan, as opposed to an overcounting of 5.7 million and 2.8 million in Punjab and KP respectively.[162] In his view, the population of Sindh should have been about 4 per cent higher and Punjab's share should have been around 3 per cent lower.[163] It was claimed that, as opposed to more than 400 NADRA offices in Punjab, there were only 34 offices in Balochistan out of which 10 were located in Quetta alone; this left a large number of people unregistered and therefore uncounted.[164] Anne Goujon has indicated several missing points in the census: no reliable estimate of migration flows; no use of both de jure and de facto enumeration of people, i.e. by including the period of local stay; and no post-enumeration survey (PES) to corroborate the findings of the census through a limited sample.[165]

The net result of the persistent controversy about the undercounting of people, with its centre of gravity in Sindh, alienated both communities of Sindhis and Mohajirs. They implicated the Punjab-based power structure of Pakistan in a conspiracy to keep the latter's own demographic preponderance intact. It is unlikely that the situation would have changed in the near future. The MQM threatened to resign as a coalition partner after the PTI government in Islamabad formally approved the 2017 census in late December 2020. In April 2021, the government approved the issuance of revised census results with a promise to hold a new census in 2023 prior to elections.

Ahmadis: 'Heretic outsiders'[166]

A series of movements, laws, court cases and militant activities pushed Ahmadis not only beyond the pale of Islam but also from their status as equal citizens of Pakistan that would have given them a right to the state's protection against social, cultural and physical violence. They experienced shrinking access to jobs and businesses, and sometimes public display of disgust and hatred for them, such as notices hanging on shop doors barring their entry.[167] In 1974, parliament passed the Second Amendment, declaring Ahmadis a minority. The military dictator Zia's Ordinance XX stopped them from 'posing' as Muslims. The judiciary gradually moved from protecting their human rights to endorsing their position as imposters, which obliged them to adopt non-Muslim paraphernalia, ranging from re-naming their places of worship to their virtual disappearance from social and cultural life.

Qasmi has discussed the way that Ahmadis were legally ostracized in 1974 while still continuing to live their normal life as a minority.[168] Later, they were obliged to create a whole new infrastructure for themselves in terms of the public performance of their rituals around their place of worship – not to be called a mosque anymore – and their cultural, social and educational activities. In a 1978 court case, the judiciary did not entertain the idea that Ahmadis' ritualistic practices and iconography perpetrated any damage to Muslim property rights. In a 1988 case, the judge had moved on to Zia's doctrine: since the Coca Cola company would not allow its produce to be bottled and sold as fake products, so Muslim property rights should also not be violated by others. Islamists also succeeded in forcing the government to make provision for including religion on passports – ostensibly to disable Ahmadis from going for their pilgrimage to Makkah. They later targeted ID cards for that purpose also.

Intriguingly, Musharraf's electoral reforms that put an end to separate electorates for all religious minorities in 2002, were followed by an exception for Ahmadis, even as a minority. In the 2018 elections, Ahmadis refrained from voting under the separate electorate provided for them. Neither Muslims nor a minority for the purposes of the election system for minorities, Ahmadis could be considered the ultimate outsiders because the political, legislative, judicial, and electoral systems of Pakistan discriminated against them. Ironically, Ahmadis were refused membership of the Minorities Commission that was established in 2019. Such 'heretic otherness', defined as an 'organicist religious subjectivity', was most unlikely to be incorporated into a typical modern liberal state.[169] In 2018, Islamabad High Court demanded a separate database for Ahmadis. In another case, it asked for details of the travel of Ahmadis, a step that allegedly exposed them to persecution. This is a glaring example of the gap between the 'design' and the practice of statehood in the country. On the one hand, Article 18 ensured the right of freedom of religion for everyone: 'this right includes freedom to change his religion or belief, and freedom, either alone or in community with others and in public or private, to manifest his religion or belief in teaching, practice, worship and observance'. On the other hand, the electoral and institutional alienation of the Ahmadi community brought to light the social and cultural violence against it.

In this context, we need to draw on Tayyab Mahmud's analysis of the courts' abdication of the protection of religious minorities. He traced various steps about dwindling judicial even-handedness and the corresponding rise in ostracization of Ahmadis. Mahmud analyses the first phase of the 'principled and unequivocal protection' of minorities with reference to the decision in a case in the Chief Court of Sindh in 1952 that declared that it was not up to a court to adjudicate the sincerity or otherwise of a religious belief.[170] Later, the 1954 Munir Report criticized the 1949 Objectives Resolution for being 'nothing but a hoax' that carried out not even 'a semblance of the embryo of an Islamic state'.[171] The second phase, which started with rendering Ahmadis infidel in 1974, was ambivalent towards the issue of minorities. The court accepted the validity of the Second Amendment but did not bar Ahmadis from practising their religion as they liked. In the third phase, after the promulgation of Zia's Ordinance XX in 1984, the court acknowledged and accepted the fact of the 1973 Constitution being in abeyance and the authority of martial law to operate beyond the human rights provisions of the constitution. Later, the FSC forbade Ahmadis from 'posing' as Muslims, from calling their place of worship a mosque and from issuing *azan* (call for prayer). The court rendered various international regimes dealing with human rights irrelevant in this matter. The judicial ostracization of the outsider as a religious minority was sealed for the foreseeable future.

Conclusion

This chapter is an attempt at laying bare the reality of the outsider as well as the relative obscurity of the outsider in public forums. Outsiders, ranging from ethnic groups to religious and sectarian communities, got only miniscule coverage from the print and electronic media, on the floor of the parliament, or in mainstream academic research. They suffered from double jeopardy. First, they were the target of social, cultural and political discrimination. Second, their issues were barred from the public eye and were therefore far less addressed in the media — much less resolved as a matter of policy — than the issues of 'insiders'. I have mentioned how insider truths were different from outsider truths. I have traced outsider status to British India, where indirect rule in large areas had already created proto-outsiders. I have noted that partition and migration reduced both Bengali and Sindhi communities to rural hulks; their nostalgia for the other half across the border, for at least a generation, further pushed them to the outgroup category. I have analysed ethnic minorities from the perspective of the one-province-dominates-all syndrome whereby demographic nationalism played a crucial role in the conflict among and between ethnic communities and the state. Some constant features of the insiders' thinking and policies have had the capacity to remain potential sources of conflict with outsiders, such as the cult of unity often expressed through presidentialism, prefectural federalism and the closing of individual and group contacts across the borders with India and Afghanistan. However, the state opted for reversal of policy when the outsider phenomenon threatened social disorder, a drift towards separatism and an increase in the cost of governance.

At the other end, the state has grossly alienated certain outsiders, especially the Baloch among ethnic minorities and the Ahmadis among religious minorities. The cost for the former played out in the form of political violence, extreme restiveness among Baloch youth, human rights violations and political instability. That kept the establishment heavily involved in the province not only militarily by way of periodical operations but also politically by the formation of parties such as the Balochistan Awami Party and putting together ruling coalitions in Quetta such as in 2018. I have argued that religious minorities suffered from what can be described as minoritization by way of providing 'protection' to them in the constitution in a paternalistic mode, thus potentially circumscribing their 'equality' of status as citizens. The state treated them as communities rather than citizens who would have carried individual rights and duties and multiple identities based on caste, class, profession, habitat, and gender. This policy rendered people from the religious minorities into one-dimensional persons. The cost of the policy to Ahmadis was far more nuanced because of their dwindling numbers as a result of their outmigration for decades in the face of the rising tide of hatred and violence against them. However, the liberal intelligentsia at home, the world media and international human rights organizations persistently criticized Pakistan's policies of discrimination against religious minorities. The 'insiders' pursued their agenda of state-building and nation-building in a way that alienated and thus 'created' outsiders, who then refused to be pushed under the carpet. In that sense, this chapter has revealed far more about the insiders than the outsiders.

CONCLUSION

The focal point of this book is political conflict in Pakistan, its genealogy, its cultural codification, and its spatial and temporal dimensions
in terms of regional variations and periodic transformations. In a way,
all politics is about conflict. In F. G. Bayley's formulation, politics is a
game defined by a set of rules that covers competition between rivals
who roughly match each other.[1] There are normative rules of the
game, such as the electoral agenda to serve the people, and pragmatic
rules that are understood to be either effective or ineffective no matter
whether these are just or unjust. Competition can become fight, and
then a different set of rules mediates through a military coup or revolution. There is a reward at the end. Conflict is writ large throughout
this process. For the current study of political conflict in Pakistan, the
set of rules was couched in the institutional design of the state. Normative rules that covered elections were often overruled by pragmatic
rules that discounted ethics in favour of the coveted rewards. In this
book, I have tried to unravel the story of conflict between the two sets
of rules as reflected through the agendas and actions of the political
competitors in the country.

In Pakistan, partition operated at various levels: as a game changer,
by way of taking some communities up the scale, such as Mohajirs
and Punjab, and pushing others downhill, such as East Pakistan, Sindh
and Balochistan, in terms of their share in the national resources.
Partitioning of hearts and minds between the two successor states
of British India became the national agenda. I have analysed the way
in which the 're-sizing' of the state in geographical terms and the
're-peopling' of the state in demographic terms created new sources

of conflict in the form of ethnic and linguistic tensions. Migrants, who amounted to 20 per cent of the population of (W) Pakistan as compared to 1 per cent in India, vehemently influenced national politics. Partition of India, as in the cases of Palestine, Korea and Ireland, remained the ultimate source of contention. India all along served as the ultimate symbol of the 'other', which rendered any peace initiative to normalize relations between the two countries susceptible to charges of treason at the hands of successive civil and military governments. The political elite is permanently under surveillance. During the 'retreat' in Daman Koh — a hilltop restaurant — in Islamabad, where the SAARC summit conference was held in 1989, Benazir Bhutto and Rajiv Gandhi strolled around for a few minutes. For years after that, Benazir was condemned as a security risk for the country because she had allegedly walked away beyond the range 'covered' by Inter-Services Intelligence (ISI).

In his book, *Hostility: A Diplomat's Diary of Pakistan–India Relations*, Abdul Basit, a former high commissioner of Pakistan to India, reveals the extent of the establishment's mistrust of Prime Minister Nawaz Sharif in the context of his interaction with India and Indian leaders.[2] Basit objects to Nawaz Sharif's unilateral gesture of goodwill towards India by freeing Indian fisherman on the eve of his visit to Delhi in 2014. In his view, Pakistan negotiated poorly the joint statement signed on 9 December 2015 on the occasion of Modi's visit to Lahore. He even accuses Nawaz Sharif of showing an emotional attachment to the Indian state and society. He objects to Nawaz Sharif's meeting with Indian journalists of his own choosing. Basit accuses the prime minister of keeping him away from his Indian contacts and withholding information from him as per instructions issued to the junior staff of the foreign office. He claims that he did not resign in protest at this insult and humiliation, in order to protect Pakistan's 'principled position'. The PTI's government (2018–) excelled its predecessors by a large margin in declaring opposition figures as traitors.

At the other end, partition consolidated the military province of Punjab, divided Sindh along communal lines, alienated East Bengal, rendered Pakhtun nationalism rudderless and ignited Baloch nationalism after its accession to Pakistan in 1948. Partition and migration created several unresolved conflicts, which led to a narrative that divided the nation into insiders and outsiders.

CONCLUSION

Methodologically speaking, it is very important to ask questions that address directly the subject of enquiry and do not prejudge the answer. This happened, for example, when we discussed certain questions in Chapter 2 that were deliberately asked in a way that led to preconceived conclusions. Asking wrong questions can lead to wrong answers. This applies to Anatol Lieven's tendency to ask questions as to why the state in Pakistan did not (and would not) collapse and why Islamic revolution was not round the corner.[3] In his view, if Pakistan 'eventually collapses, it will be not Islamic extremism but climate change'.[4] He asks the question whether the Taliban's terrorist movement had the potential to dismantle the state and take over.[5] Lieven's thesis of a 'weak state' in Pakistan is based on the argument that this state does not affect people's lives very much. Policemen, judges and officials are 'working – and sometimes killing – on their own account';[6] but he finds the society strong, with kinship as its central glue. He finds the cultural system strong that makes a father kill his own daughter. Kinship reigns supreme over the party and the state. This is the key to dynastic politics. Kinship barred the way to radical change despite rapid urbanization. Feudals are powerful not because of their large landholdings but because they are chiefs of large tribes. Their world would look familiar to fifteenth-century English landlords.[7]

This is a skewed picture of the power of the landed elite in Pakistan, which operates in a world of the written state, electoral politics, district and higher courts and black letter law defining major areas of public policy. Lieven refers to several attempts to radically change Pakistan by leaders ranging from Ayub, Bhutto, Zia and Musharraf. 'And they all failed'; none of them was 'able to find a new mass party'.[8] It required a high level of ingenuity on his part to attach the grand purpose of a military coup not to status quo orientation but to radical change, and then give the credit to patronage politics for failing them all. In reality, the military rulers rendered political parties defunct as a reflection of their abhorrence for any organized expression of public opinion in society. Other observations are no less interesting: 'In Pakistan, only the armed forces work'; democracy reflects not so much the electorate but 'the distribution of social, economic, cultural and political power'; and there are two modernizing impulses operating in the country, the 'Western modernizers' and the 'Islamic modernizers'.[9] It is hard to find any explanatory potential in these observations.

As the national project of Pakistan displayed an incessant commitment to shape the master narrative, it steered a regional transition from South Asia to the Middle East as the source of a faith-based identity. However, it was a tremendous task by any stretch of imagination because it sought to disassociate the new nation from the 2,000-year-old cultural, linguistic and geographical heritage of the Indian subcontinent and associate it with the core Islamic lands across cultural, linguistic and geographical differences. The two rival projects remained incomplete. The cultural practices, ranging from the customary laws, music, dance, theatre, and folk literature to the wedding rituals and herbal medicine of India, remained widely operative. Similarly, the impact of the Gulf states was limited to the religious domain in the context of Wahhabism. The master narrative focused on Islam as ideology, nationalism as anti-Indianism, dichotomy between Islam and the West as the dominant worldview, and conspiracy as the leading methodology for understanding others.

Benedict Anderson's delineation of the three archetypal concerns of the newly independent states – census, map and museum – played a defining role in shaping the national discourse in Pakistan.[10] Only three years after partition, Mortimer Wheeler published a book, *Five Thousand Years of Pakistan*,[11] and thus 'museumized' the new homeland in an effort to lend it the historical depth that it lacked. The territorial foundations of the state were laid not by geography but by demography in the form of Muslim majority areas. Pakistan turned 'map' into an ambition by extending its borders to Indian Kashmir. The gap between geography and demography, mapping and un-mapping Kashmir as part of one country or the other, together with museumizing the ancient past for a freshly born country, continued to pose the challenge of profiling Pakistan as a historical and mythical country. In this context, postcolonialism emerged as the new paradigm in pursuit of the project to decolonize the hearts and minds of the nation. This led to a quest for identity in the pre-colonial period, all the way back to the early period of Islam.[12] All along the dominant elite wrote the large text over the small text written by ethnic and religious minorities to define the cultural landscape.

This book has traced the roots of the mega conflict in Pakistan as a sustained and long-term clash between two power centres: the middle class and what can, for want of a better word, be called the political class. I have argued that the two classes have drawn on different historical trajectories. The middle class sought to direct society's forward march to such goals as national unity, economic development, accountability for corruption and Islamic destiny. The political class was constituency bound. It was geared to public interest, patronage politics and party-based mobilization. I have analysed the civil–military conflict, the recurrent crises of democracy and the persistence of ethno-nationalist movements, in terms of the tension between these two power centres. I discussed the party system of Pakistan as a subsidiary system vis-à-vis the political system at large. I have defined the politics of Pakistan as an establishmentarian democracy. The idea is to analyse the building blocks of electoral democracy by locating the initiative at different levels, i.e. in the hands of electoral candidates rather than voters, the party leadership rather than the contestants, and the establishment rather than political parties. I have argued for the need to go beyond the generic model of hybrid regimes, which is indeed an effect of an underlying cause whereby the establishment as the overarching power structure operates as political agency, both directly and more frequently indirectly. Pakistan in the third decade of the twenty-first century represents a discursive democracy representing various interests and identities, making them public and evaluating them as politically relevant. Through the end of 2020 and the beginning of 2021, Nawaz Sharif was able to put a dent in the dynamics of discursive democracy by openly criticizing the all-but-visible role of the army from the platform of the Pakistan Democratic Movement (PDM).

Pakistan's experience with democracy took a different route from India because of the weaker participatory culture of its constituent units, the shift in initiative to the 'military province' of Punjab and the migratory elite that occupied the seat of power and thus had no incentive to hold elections in the absence of a 'local' constituency. Indeed, India is an exception that proves the rule that an absolute majority of the postcolonial states were not the 'imagined' communities at the time of their independence riding on the shoulders of print capitalism and military power.[13] Multiple imaginations first contributed to the struggle against the colonial 'other', but later became instruments of an identity-based contestation for power. Unlike in India, where the state establishment sought to guide the political establishment from within the system, in Pakistan it assumed the role of an entity parallel to the institutional design. The military governments typically resorted to constitutional engineering, manipulation of elections and co-option of political parties. This model of democracy drew on a military metaphysics which thoroughly distrusted the potential of the political class and the 'unguided' rule of public representatives.[14] It sought to make alignments outside electoral politics, such as with Islamists of various shades. In this endeavour, the judiciary continued to pander to the middle-class ethos, which often tilted in favour of the establishment even as it struggled to maintain the profile of its formally autonomous triadic role. All this led to a continuing tug of war between the institutional apparatuses of the state.

While the constitutional source of legitimacy in the form of mass mandate remained at the heart of the controversy, law became an instrument of politics. The constitutional history of Pakistan has been characterized by rival interpretations of legal provisions as well as massive interpolations in the constitution as a result of successive unresolved conflicts. These conflicts drew upon social, cultural, religious and ethnolinguistic causes. In the absence of legal socialization of the citizenry at large, as well as contradictory provisions for equality before the law and equal protection by the law in the constitution, the domain of law remained unspecified in several areas of jurisdiction. This included a host of issues ranging from the distribution of resources among the federating units and preservation of the principle of separation of powers to protection of individual citizens from the tyranny of the state and non-implementation of the provisions against abrogation or suspension of the constitution. After independence, British common law gradually lost its moral authority, especially as the Islamic lobby expanded its influence and redefined the prevalent bond between legality and legitimacy that had existed for more than a century. However, the constitution remained the ultimate source of state authority in Pakistan as a powerhouse of 'normative rules', even as it has been subjugated to manipulation by the practitioners of 'pragmatic rules'. In this context, the judicial review served to fill the gap between the two sets of rules exercised by various players on the political stage. A persistent and comprehensive pattern of ideological socialization at the cost of legal socialization has grossly contributed to the erosion of constitutionalism per se. The clue to resilience of the legal order, and the continuing practice of utilization of the legal space by the opposition and social activists such as students, women, labourers, peasants and low-paid employees among others, lies in the mass public.

Pakistan and other ex-British colonial societies saw the emergence of an incipient mass public on the eve of independence. Indeed, I have argued that this phenomenon was responsible for the exit of the colonial rulers in the first place, because they could no longer stop the demand for national self-determination in British India. After independence, we see a state-meets-the-society model operating in the two successor states. A tangible public space had come into existence defined by street demonstrations, print and electronic media, electoral mobilization, and the rights-based discourse of the progressive intelligentsia. Of course, the mass public was active in a limited sense in terms of its outreach by way of mediated communication, at least before the digital revolution took place during the second decade of the twenty-first century.

I have offered a reappraisal of the role of civil society in Pakistan in the context of its much-lauded contribution to democracy. I have pointed to various caveats in this regard, including the un-representative character of the NGO-led civil society, its middle-class leadership and its obligation to stay away from politics as the contractual requirement of donor-driven activity. Despite the espousal of 'progressive' causes relating to the elimination of poverty, women's emancipation and putting an end to bonded labour among others, the method and scope of civil society remained limited as far as its contribution to democracy is concerned.

Perhaps education could have brought about a new publicness due to the mushrooming of schools, colleges and universities in the private sector. However, the new pedagogical framework led to two widely ignored consequences. First, the focus on merit-based competition and the hierarchy of excellence-related educational institutions led to a reckless pursuit of individual careerism and lack of a public-spirited approach among youth. Second, as Bourdieu has argued, the transfer of 'cultural capital' to the students of these institutions widened their distance from larger society and contributed to elite formation at a higher pedestal.[15] I have discussed how education policy has become intellectually barren over the years and how textbooks have widely spread the hate message against other nations and religions as well as against domestic 'liberals', who talked of peace and tolerance and were thus condemned as traitors and infidels. I have discussed the way in which the press and TV expanded their coverage of the political leadership and its activities. There was a stringent move towards tightening the noose around journalists and media owners. After Ayub's Press and Publication Ordinance, successive governments sought to control the voice of the media. After censorship under Zia's martial law strangulated the press, repression of the media under the establishmentarian democracy of Imran Khan (2018–) was the most horrendous attack on freedom of expression. Only the social media, including Facebook, Twitter, YouTube and a few other platforms, continued to operate relatively freely, especially for covering the opposition's rallies, such as the PDM's public meetings in Gujranwala, Karachi, Quetta, Peshawar, Multan and Lahore in the last quarter of 2020. There emerged a repressive legal regime to control the media through PEMRA that put extreme pressure on the media houses, culminating in the arrest of Mir Shakilur Rehman, the owner of the largest media network, Jang-News-Geo, for a year and a half on flimsy charges. The sacking of dozens of leading journalists from their jobs caused widespread insecurity in the profession. Instead of creating what is described as a new publicness, the state in Pakistan under Imran Khan moved towards a model of deliberative democracy that was set to control the process of opinion formation itself.[16]

On the other hand, while the public space has been squeezed and manipulated, political activism often put the state on the defensive and forced it to retrace its steps. Indeed, Pakistan is a state in permanent crisis management. In this book, I have outlined various ethnic and religious groups in terms of their position as outsiders who perceived state policy as discriminatory towards them and struggled to overturn it. Whenever the conflict assumed crisis proportions, the state obliged and opted for a reversal of policy. Sustained public pressure made the state shift from presidentialism back to parliamentarism, restore Karachi as capital of Sindh, accept Bengali as a national language along with Urdu, bar the repatriation of Biharis from Bangladesh, dither over going ahead with the Kalabagh dam project, and keep the quota system intact despite opposition from Mohajirs. However, this kind of conflict management did not apply to certain other communities such as the

Baloch and Ahmadis, who remained on the margins of the 'political society' of Pakistan.

While a lot has changed in the country during the past several decades, Pakistan was reported in the 2020s — as in the 1950s — as a place where prices were rising, development projects were slow to move, politicians were corrupt, democracy was discounted as a viable system, elections were rigged, and a coup was feared.[17] One can argue that Pakistan is the prototype of a postcolonial state characterized by perpetual sources of instability. The purpose of writing this book would be amply served if it has mapped the domain of political conflict in Pakistan credibly and comprehensively. I must reiterate that all politics is about conflict, and it depends on the capacity of state managers to be sensitive to the pre-conflict stage of a potentially combative situation and use soft power instead of hard power to tackle the contentious issues. I hope that the present endeavour sets the stage for future research on the patterns of conflict and conflict management in Pakistan and other postcolonial states.

NOTES

INTRODUCTION

1. Roedad Khan, *Pakistan: A Dream Gone Sour,* Oxford University Press, Karachi, 1997; Sartaj Aziz, *Between Dreams and Realities: Some Milestones in Pakistan's History,* Oxford University Press, 2010; Maleeha Lodhi, ed., *Pakistan Beyond the 'Crisis State',* Oxford University Press, Karachi, 2011.

2. Lewis A. Coser, 'Social Conflict and the Theory of Social Change', *British Journal of Sociology,* Vol. 8, No. 3, September 1957, 197–207.

3. Edward I. Steinhart, *Conflict and Collaboration,* Princeton University Press, 2019, 260.

4. Riaz Hasan and Taghi Azadarmaki, 'Institutional Configuration and Trust in Muslim Societies', *Islamic Studies,* Vol. 42, No. 1, 2003, 98.

5. Harsh Sethi, ed., *State of Democracy in South Asia,* Oxford University Press, New Delhi, 2008, 36–7.

6. Ibid., 337.

7. Ibid., 38.

8. Ibid., 45–6.

9. Kevin A. Clarke and Randall W. Stone, 'Democracy and the Logic of Political Survival', *American Political Science Review,* Vol. 102, No. 3, 2008, 387.

10. Houston A. Baker, Jr, Teresa Dovey, Rosemary Jolly and Herbert Deinert, 'Colonialism and Postcolonial Condition', *PMLA (Journal of the Modern Language Association of America),* Vol. 110, No. 5, October 1995, 1,047.

11. Ibid., 1,048.

12. Partha Chatterjee, *The Nation and Its Fragments: Colonial and Post-Colonial Histories,* Princeton University Press, 1993, 158–9.

13. Vivek Chibber, *Postcolonial Theory and the Specter of Capital,* Verso Books, New York, 2013, 155.

14. Ibid., 250.

15. Joel Migdal, 'Integration and Disintegration: An Approach to Society-formation', in Kumar Rupesinghe, Paul Sciarone and Luc van de Goor, eds, *Between Development and Destruction: An Enquiry into the Causes of Conflict in Post-colonial States,* Palgrave Macmillan, London, 1996.

16. Richard Jackson, 'Violent Internal Conflict and the African State: Towards A Framework of Analysis', *Journal of Contemporary African Studies,* Vol. 20, Issue 1, 2002, 38.

17. Ibid., 37–8.

18. Ibid., 39.

19. See Mohammad Waseem, Fauzia Yazdani and Susan Loughhead, 'The Role of the UK and the International Community 2000-2008', DFID, October 2008.

20. Myron Weiner, 'Political Change: Asia, Africa and the Middle East', in Myron Weiner and Samuel Huntington, *Understanding Political Development,* Little Brown, Boston, MA, 1987, 36–7.

21. See Mohammad Waseem, 'Ethnic and Islamic Militancy in Pakistan', in Paul Brass, ed., *Routledge Handbook of South Asian Politics: India, Pakistan, Bangladesh, Sri Lanka, and Nepal*, Routledge, London, 2010.

22. Armando Salvatore, *Islam and the Political Discourse of Modernity,* Ithaca Press, New York, 2000, 20.

23. Steve C. Caton, 'Anger Be Now thy Song: Anthropology of an Event', Occasional Paper Number 5, Harvard University, November 1999, 10, available at https://www.ias.edu/sites/default/files/sss/papers/paperfive.pdf (accessed 18 December 2020).

24. Mohammad Waseem, 'Dilemmas of Pride and Pain: Sectarian Conflict and Conflict Transformation in Pakistan', Working Paper No. 48, University of Birmingham, 2010, 24.

25. Tayyab Mahmud, 'Protecting Religious Minorities: The Courts' Abdication', in Charles H. Kennedy and Rasul Baksh Rais, eds, *Pakistan 1995,* Routledge, London, 1995, 83–102.

26. For the emergence of alternative globalities in the Muslim world, see Dietrich Reetz, '"Alternate Globalities": On the Cultures and Formats of Transitional Muslim Networks for South Asia', in Ulrike Freitag and Achim von Oppen, eds, *Translocality: The Study of Globalising Processes from a Southern Perspective'*, Brill, Leiden, 2010, 291–334.

27. Melanie Meirotti, 'Introduction', in Melanie Meirotti and Grant Masterson, eds, *State Capture in Africa: Old Threats, New Packaging,* EISA Publications, Johannesburg, 2.

28. Ibid., 5.

29. Tom Lodge, 'State Capture: Conceptual Considerations', in Melanie Meriotti and Grant Masterson, eds, *State Capture in Africa,* 14–15.

30. Ibid., 18.

31. Anthoni van Nieuwkerk, 'Africa Australis: Imperium in Imperio?', in Melanie Meriotti and Grant Masterson, eds, *State Capture in Africa*, 44.

32. Ibid., 44–6.

33. Ibid., 50.

34. Olufunto Akinduro and Grant Masterson, 'Encoding the Rules: Capturing the State through Electoral Process', in Melanie Meriotti and Grant Masterson, eds, *State Capture in Africa*, 59.

35. Ibid., 61.

36. This is a South Asian phenomenon. See Inge Amundsen, 'Democratic Dynasties: Internal Party Democracy in Bangladesh', *Party Politics*, Vol. 10, 2013, 1–10.

37. See Ali Cheema, Hassan Javaid and Mohammad Farooq Naseer, 'Dynastic Politics in Punjab: Facts, Myth and their Implication', IDEAS Working Paper, 2013, 1–13.

38. See Stephen Lyon, *Political Kinship in Pakistan: Descent, Marriage and Government Stability,* Rowman & Littlefield, Lanham, MD, 2019.

39. See Kamran Asdar Ali, *Surkh Salam: Communist Politics and Class Activism in Pakistan, 1947-1972*, Oxford University Press, Karachi, 2015.

40. See Karamat Ali, *Raah Guzar to Dekho*, (Look at the pathway, Urdu text), Institute of Historical and Social Research Karachi, 2020.

41. See Leela Fernandes and Patrick Heller, 'Hegemonic Aspirations: New Middle-Class Politics and India's Democracy in Comparative Perspective', *Critical Asian Studies,* Vol. 38, No. 4, 2006.

42. Yogendra Yadav, 'Electoral Reforms: Beyond Middle Class Fantasies', *Seminar* 440, April 1996, 59.

43. Eric Goodfield, 'Postmodern Paper Tiger: Lyotard, Baudrillard, and the Contemporary Politics of Poststructuralist Subversion', *Cultural Politics*, Vol. 16, No. 2, 2020, 238.

44. See Ivor Goodson, 'The Rise of the Life Narrative', *Teacher Education Quarterly*, Vol. 33, No. 4, 2006, 7–8.

45. John B. Thompson, *The Media and Modernity: A Social Theory of the Media,* Polity Press, Cambridge, 236–7, 246.

46. Asma Faiz, 'Populism of the Right: The Rise of Imran Khan in Pakistan', in Christophe Jaffrelot and Elise Massicard, eds, *Populismes au Pouvoir*, Sciences Po Press, Paris, 2019, 77.

47. Kenneth Roth, 'The Dangerous Rise of Populism: Global Attacks on Human Rights Values', *Journal of International Affairs.* Special 70th Anniversary issue: The Next Order, 2017, 79.

48. Ibid., 80.

49. Jean Luc Racine, '"Pakistan and the India Syndrome": Between Kashmir and the Nuclear Predicament' in Christophe Jaffrelot, ed., *Pakistan: Nationalism Without a Nation*, Zed Books, London, 2002.

50. Stephen Cohen, *The Idea of Pakistan*, Brookings Institution Press, Washington, DC, 2004, 108; Robert Wirsing, 'Introduction: Religion, Radicalism, and Security in South Asia', in Robert Wirsing and Mohan Malik, eds, *Religious Radicalism and Security in South Asia*, Asia-Pacific College of Security Studies, Hawaii, 2004, 1–17.

51. Ministry of Law and Justice (Legislative Department), New Delhi, 12 December 2019.

52. 'Jinnah Has Completely Won in India: Shashi Tharoor's Adoration of Jinnah's Vision', GVS (Global Space Village), 1 February 2020, URL: https://www.globalvillagespace.com/jinnah-has-completely-won-in-india-shashi-tharoors-adoration-of-jinnahs-vision/

53. Partha Ghosh, 'Region without regionalism: Cooperation in South Asia', *Economic and Political Weekly*, Vol. 51, Issue 32, 6 August, 2016 https://www.epw.in/journal/2016/32/special-articles/region-without-regionalism.html.

1. SEVENTY YEARS OF PARTITION

1. See Ayesha Jalal, *The Sole Spokesman*, Cambridge University Press, 1985; Mushirul Hasan, *India's Partition: Process, Strategy and Mobilization*, Oxford University Press, New Delhi, 1994.

2. See Ian Talbot, *Divided Cities: Partition and its Aftermath in Lahore and Amritsar 1947–1957 (The Subcontinent Divided: A New Beginning)*, Oxford University Press, 2007; Vazira Fazila-Yacoobali Zamindar, *The Long Partition and the Making of Modern South Asia: Refugees, Boundaries, Histories*, Columbia University Press, New York, 2007.

3. I owe this expression to Professor Dipankar Gupta of Jawaharlal Nehru University, New Delhi.

4. Swarna Aiyar, '"August Anarchy": The Partition Massacres in Punjab, 1947, South Asia', *Journal of South Asian Studies*, Vol. 18, Special Issue, 1995, 13–36.

5. For controversy about Urdu being a Pakistani language, see Tariq Rahman, *From Hindi to Urdu: A Social and Political History*, Oxford University Press, Karachi, 2011, 92–6. For an alternative view that claims Urdu to be a Pakistani language, see Hafiz Mahmood Khan Sherani, *Urdu in Punjab* [in Urdu], Sang-e-Meel Publications, Lahore, 2005, 27, 74–8, 105–10.

6. Khaled Ahmad, *Word for Word*, Oxford University Press, Karachi, 2010, 12–14.

7. Leon Festinger, 'Cognitive Dissonance', *Scientific American*, 1962, Vol. 207, No. 4, 93.

8. Jaswant Singh, *Jinnah: India–Partition–Independence*, Rupa & Co., New Delhi, 2009, 498.

9. The analysis usually focuses on Muslim refusal to assimilate into the local population that culminated in a 'perilous triumph'. I. H. Qureshi, *The Muslim Community of the Indo-Pakistan Subcontinent, 610–1947*, Renaissance Publishing House, Delhi, 1996, 112–13.

10. For the latest expose of this thesis, see Sikandar Hayat, *A Leadership Odyssey: Muslim Separatism and the Achievement of the Separate State of Pakistan*, Oxford University Press, 2021, 24-41.

11. Harjot Oberoi, *The Construction of Religious Boundaries: Cultures, Identity, and Diversity in the Sikh Tradition*, University of Chicago Press, 1994, 9–12.

12. Peter Hardy, 'Modern European and Muslim Explanations of Conversion to Islam in South Asia', in Nehemia Levtzion, ed., *Conversion to Islam*, Holmes & Meier, New York, 1979, 179.

13. Ibid., 180–1.

14. Ibid., 191.

15. Ibid., 195–7.

16. Ibid., 199.

17. Richard Eaton, 'Approaches to the Study of Conversion to Islam in India', in Richard C. Martin, ed., *Approaches to Islam in Religious Studies*, Oneworld Publications, London, 2001, 111–12.

18. Ibid., 113–14.

19. Ibid., 114.

20. Ibid., 121.

21. Shail Mayaram, 'Rethinking Meo Identity: Cultural Faultline, Syncretism, Hybridity or Liminality', *Comparative Studies of South Asia, Africa and the Middle East*, 1997, Vol. 17, No. 2, 40–2.

22. Harjot Oberoi, *The Construction of Religious Boundaries*, 158.

23. Richard Eaton, 'Approaches to the Study of Conversion', 117.

24. M. Mujeeb, *The Indian Muslims*, George Allen & Unwin, London, 1967, 12–16.

25. For details on thuggee, see Maire ni Fhlathuin, '"That Solitary Englishman": W. H. Sleeman and the Biography of British India', *Victorian Review*, Vol. 27, No. 1, 2001.

26. Shahnaz Rouse, 'The State of Lahore under Colonialism: A Political Economic Analysis', Lahore School of Economics, Economic History Pakistan Studies Working Paper No. 03-19, 2019, 40.

27. David Gilmartin, 'Partition, Pakistan, and South Asian History: In Search of a Narrative', *The Journal of Asian Studies*, Vol. 57, No. 4, 1998, 1,074.

28. Pashaura Singh and Louis E. Fenech, eds, *The Oxford Handbook of Sikh Studies*, Oxford University Press, Oxford, 2014, 29, 73.

29. Christophe Jaffrelot, *The Hindu Nationalist Movement and Indian Politics, 1925 to the 1990s: Strategies of Identity-building, Implantation and Mobilisation*, Hurst & Co., 1996, 11.

30. R. K. Ghai, 'Hindu–Muslim Relations during the 1920s with Special Reference to Shuddhi and Tabligh', *Proceedings of the Indian History Congress*, Vol. 46, 1985, 526, 533.

31. I. H. Qureshi, *The Muslim Community of the Indo-Pakistan Subcontinent*, 60.

32. Justice Muhammad Muneer, *From Jinnah to Zia*, Vanguard Books, Lahore, 1979, xv; Beena Sarwar, 'Advani: Jinnah Created History,' *The Hindu*, 5 June 2005.

33. *The Pioneer*, quoted in Venkat Dhulipala, *Creating a New MEDINA: State Power, Islam, and the Quest for Pakistan in Late Colonial North India*, Cambridge University Press, 2014, 484.

34. Ranabir Samaddar, 'Introduction', in Stefano Bianchini, Sanjay Chatarvedi, Rada Ivekovik and Ranabir Samaddar, eds, *Partitions: Reshaping States and Minds*, Frank Cass, Abingdon, 2005, 1.

35. Pippa Virdee, 'Partition in Transition: Comparative Analysis of Migration in Ludhiana and Lyallpur', in Anjali Gera Roy and Nandi Bhatia, eds, *Partitioned Lives: Narratives of Home, Displacement and Resettlement*, Pearson, New Delhi, 2007, 24–5, 31–2.

36. Mohammad Waseem, 'Dilemmas of Pride and Pain: Sectarian Conflict and Conflict Transformation in Pakistan', Working Paper No. 48, University of Birmingham, 2010, 14.

37. Mohammad Asad, *The Principles of State and Government in Islam*, University of California Press, 1961, 31.

38. Katherine Adeney, *Federalism and Ethnic Conflict Regulation in India and Pakistan*, Palgrave Macmillan, London, 2007, 138, 145.

39. Katherine Adeney and Andrew Wyatt, 'Democracy in South Asia: Getting Beyond the Structure–Agency Dichotomy', *Political Studies*, 2004, Vol. 52, No. 1, 1–18.

40. See Farzana Shaikh, *Community and Consensus in Islam: Muslim Representation in Colonial India, 1860–1947*, Cambridge University Press, 1989.

41. Ira Bhaskar and Richard Allen, *Islamicate Cultures of Bombay Cinema*, Tulika Books, New Delhi, 2009, 6–8.

42. Tariq Rahman, *Language, Ideology and Power: Language-learning among the Muslims of Pakistan and North India*, Oxford University Press, Karachi, 2002, 222–4.

43. See Raza Rumi, *Delhi By Heart*, Harper Collins, India, 2013.

44. Henry Vincent Hodson, *The Great Divide: Britain-India-Pakistan*, Oxford University Press, 1997.

45. Ranabir Samaddar, 'Introduction', 1.

46. Ibid., 5–6.

47. Ibid., 6.

48. Rada Iveković, 'Partition as a Form of Transition', in Stefano Bianchini et al., eds, *Partitions*, 11.

49. Ibid., 15.

50. Ibid., 18–19.

51. Ibid., 20.

52. Yasmin Khan, *The Great Partition: The Making of India and Pakistan*, Yale University Press, 2007, 5.

53. Ranabir Samaddar, 'The Undefined Acts of Partition and Dialogue', in Stefano Bianchini et al., eds, *Partitions*, 2005, 89.

54. Ibid., 92.

55. Ibid., 97.

56. Sanjay Chaturvedi, 'The Excess of Geopolitics: Partition of "British India"', in Stefano Bianchini et al., eds, *Partitions*, 100.

57. Quoted in Shaikh Mujibur Rehman, 'Cleaning up the Kashmir Mess', *The Hindu*, 1 November 2019.

58. Sanjay Chaturvedi, 'The Excess of Geopolitics', 106.

59. For the agenda of the great powers, see Ishtiaq Ahmed, *The Garrison State: Origins, Evolution, Consequences*, Oxford University Press, 2013, 37–38.

60. Sanjay Chaturvedi, 'The Excess of Geopolitics', 108.

61. Ibid.

62. Ibid., 109.

63. Ibid.

64. Ibid., 116.

65. Ibid., 121.

66. Ibid., 126.

67. Jinnah, Muhammad Ali. *Annexure II. Extract from a Statement by Mr. Jinnah Dated 6th December 1945*. The National Archives of the UK, CAB – Records of the Cabinet Office, Cabinet Office: Private Collections of Ministers' and Officials' Papers Sir Stafford Cripps. Personal correspondence: Mohammad Ali Jinnah, 01/02/1946-31/10/1948, CAB 127/136.

68. K. B. Sayeed mentioned this a few times in his lectures at SOAS, where he was a visiting fellow in 1974.

69. Hamid Khan, *Constitutional and Political History of Pakistan*, Oxford University Press, Karachi, 2001, 83.

70. Ibid., 75.

71. Ibid., 81.

72. Keith Callard, *Pakistan: A Political Study*, Allen & Unwin, London, 1957, 266.

73. See, for example, The Citizens Archive of Pakistan – Oral History Project, http://www.citizensarchive.org/projects/the-oral-history-project/ (accessed 26 August 2019).

74. Arvind-Pal Singh, 'Interrogating Identity: Cultural Translation, Writing and Subaltern Politics', in Gurharpal Singh and Ian Talbot, eds, *Punjabi Identity: Continuity and Change*, Manohar, New Delhi, 1996, 204–5.

75. This section comprehensively draws on Mohammad Waseem, 'Partition, Migration and Assimilation: A Comparative Study of Pakistani Punjab', *Journal of Punjab Studies*, 1997, Vol. 4, No. 1.

76. Lord Mountbatten's broadcast on All-India Radio, 3 June 1947, National Documentation Centre, *The Partition of the Punjab, 1947: A Compilation of Official Documents*, Vol. I, Sang-e-Meel Publications, Lahore, 1993, 1–2.

77. *The Pakistan Times*, 19 August 1947.

78. Alastair Lamb, *Birth of a Tragedy*, Oxford University Press, Karachi, 1994, 37–40.

79. Victoria Schofield, *Kashmir in the Crossfire*, I. B. Tauris, London, 1996, 125–30; Mushtaqur Rahman, *Divided Kashmir: Old Problems, New Opportunities for India, Pakistan, and the Kashmiri People*, Lynne Rienner, Boulder, CO, 1996, 57–60.

80. Hasan Askari Rizvi, *The Military and Politics in Pakistan*, Progressive Publishers, Lahore, 1986, 39.

81. Mushtaqur Rahman, *Divided Kashmir*, 56.

82. National Documentation Centre, *The Partition of the Punjab*, Vol. III, 230.

83. Ibid., 231.

84. Gurharpal Singh, *Communism in Punjab*, Ajanta, New Delhi, 1994, 90–1.

85. Mosarrat Sohail, *Partition and Anglo-Pakistan Relations, 1947–51*, Vanguard Books, Lahore, 1991, 72–4.

86. Ibid.

87. Swarna Aiyar, 'August anarchy', 23–4.

88. Ibid.

89. Ibid., 28.

90. Clive Dewey, 'The Rural Roots of Pakistani Militarism', in D. A. Low, ed., *The Political Inheritance of Pakistan*, Palgrave Macmillan, London, 1991, 265.

91. Sir E. Jenkins to Lord Wavell, 17 March 1947, OIOC Cat. No. R/3/1/176; National Documentation Centre, *Disturbances in the Punjab 1947*, Islamabad, 1995, 100.

92. Punjab Police Abstract of Intelligence for the week ending 22 March 1947, National Documentation Centre Accession No. S 415, *Disturbances in the Punjab*, 107.

93. Punjab Police Abstract of Intelligence for the week ending 29 March 1947, 113.

94. Gurbachan Singh Talib, *Muslim League Attack on Sikhs and Hindus in the Punjab 1947*, Voice of India, New Delhi, 1991, 20.

95. Ibid., 114.

96. Christophe Jaffrelot, *The Hindu Nationalist Movement*, 14.

97. Darshan Singh Tatla and Ian Talbot, eds, *Punjab*, World Bibliographical Series, Clio Press, Totnes, UK, 1995, xxi.

98. Note by E. Jenkins, 9 April 1947, OIOC Cat. No. R/3/1/176, NDC-MFU Accession No. 34, *Disturbances in the Punjab*, 136.

99. Message from Prime Minister of Pakistan to Prime Minister of the United Kingdom, 10 September 1947; FO 371/65574.

100. Sir E. Jenkins to Lord Wavell, *Disturbances in the Punjab*, 101.

101. Gyanesh Kudaisya, 'The Demographic Upheaval of Partition: Refugees and Agricultural Resettlement in India 1947–67', *South Asia: Journal of South Asian Studies*, Vol. 18, No. 001, 1995, 86.

102. Vazira Fazila-Yacoobali Zamindar, *The Long Partition*, 2.

103. Mushirul Hasan, *India's Partition*, 173.

104. Vazira Fazila-Yacoobali Zamindar, *The Long Partition*, 22.

105. Akeel Bilgrami, 'Two Concepts of Secularism: Reason, Modernity and Archimedean Ideal', *Economic and Political Weekly*, Vol. 29, No. 28, 1994, 1,749.

106 See Ayesha Jalal, *The Sole Spokesman*.

107 Waheed Ahmed, ed, *The Nation's Voice: Vol VII: Launching the State and the End of the Journey*, Quaid-i-Azam Academy, Karachi, 2003, 243–58.

108. G. W. Choudhary, *Constitutional Development in Pakistan*, Ideal Book House, Karachi, 1995, 36–42.

109. Christophe Jaffrelot, *Dr Ambedkar and Untouchability*, Columbia University Press, 2005; Faisal Devji, *Muslim Zion: Pakistan as a Political Idea*, Hurst & Co., London, 2013.

110. Subrata K. Mitra, *Citizenship as Cultural Flow: Structure, Agency and Power*, Springer Science & Business Media, Berlin, 2013, 4.

111. See Francis Robinson, *Separatism among Indian Muslims: The Politics of the United Provinces' Muslims, 1860–1923*, Cambridge University Press, 1975.

112. Asma Barlas, *Democracy, Nationalism and Communalism: The Colonial Legacy in South Asia*, Westview Press, Boulder, CO, 1995, 162.

113. Ibid., 19, 21.

114. Ibid., 8–9.

115. Brendan O'Leary, 'The Elements of Right-sizing and Right-peopling the State', in Brendan O'Leary, Ian S. Lustik and Thomas Callaghy, eds, *Right-sizing the State: The Politics of Moving Borders*, Oxford University Press, 2001, 56.

116. Radha Kumar, 'The Troubled History of Partition', *Foreign Affairs*, Vol. 76, No. 1, January/February 1997, https://www.foreignaffairs.com/articles/europe/1997-01-01/troubled-history-partition.

117. Jean Gottmann, 'Spatial Partitioning and the Politician's Wisdom', *International Political Science Review*, Vol. 1, No. 4, 1980, 433.

118. Brendan O'Leary, 'The Elements of Right-sizing', 15.

119. Ibid., 26.

120. Ibid., 54.

121. Ibid., 56.

122. Chaim D. Kaufmann, 'When All Else Fails: Ethnic Population Transfers and Partitions in the Twentieth Century', *International Security*, Vol. 23, No. 2, 1988, 123–5.

123. Ibid., 132.

124. Ibid., 141–3.

125. See Mushirul Hassan, *Legacy of a Divided Nation: India's Muslims from Independence to Ayodhya*, Westview Press, Boulder, CO, 1997, 13–18.

126. Abul Kalam Azad, *India Wins Freedom*, Orient Black Swan, Hyderabad, 1989, 164–5.

127. Author's discussion with Hamza Alavi at Manchester University in 1996.

128. Mushirul Hassan, *Legacy of a Divided Nation*, 83 footnotes 144, 145.

129. Farzana Sheikh, *Community and Consensus in Islam*, 4, 9, 194.

130. Christophe Jaffrelot, 'India and Pakistan: Interpreting the Divergence of Two Political Trajectories', *Cambridge Review of International Affairs*, Vol. 15, No. 2, 2002, 260–1.

131. David Gilmartin, 'Partition, Pakistan, and South Asian History', 1,088.

132. Ibid., 1,074.

133. Sanjay Chaturvedi, 'The Excess of Geopolitics', 130.

134. Faisal Devji, *Muslim Zion*, 137–8.

135. Marvin G. Weinbaum and Gautam Sen, 'Pakistan Enters the Middle East', *Orbis*, Vol. 22, No. 3, 1978, 595–612.

136. Constitution (Second Amendment) Act, 1974, Article 106, clause 3, Article 260, clause 2.

137. Ishtiaq Ahmed, *The Punjab Bloodied, Partitioned and Cleansed: Unravelling the 1947 Tragedy through Secret British Reports and First Person Accounts*, Rupa & Co., New Delhi, 2011.

138. Swarna Aiyar, '"August anarchy"', 23–4.

139. Ian Talbot and Gurharpal Singh, *The Partition of India*, Cambridge University Press, 2009, 61.

140. Ibid., 66–7.

141. Venkat Dhulipala, *Creating a New MEDINA*, 474.

142. This is a variation of Brendan O'Leary's terms. See Brendan O'Leary, 'The Elements of Right-sizing', 15.

143. The peripheral situation of West Pakistan areas was described by Abdul Qayum Khan before partition in depressing terms. See Mushtaq Ahmed, *Before and After Independence*, Royal Book Company, Lahore, 1989, 37.

144. For a detailed discussion, see Mohammed Waseem, *Politics and the State in Pakistan*, Progressive Publishers, Lahore, 1989, 113–14.

145. C. N. Vakil, *Economic Consequences of Divided India*, Vora & Co., Mumbai, 1950, 13.

146. Migrants in Pakistan numbered 7.2 million. Migrants in India numbered 4.4 million. East Bengal accounted for only 9 per cent of migrants in Pakistan. The rest went to West Pakistan. See E. H. Slade, *Census of Pakistan, 1951*, Government of Pakistan, 1951.

147. 'Leave Out Migrants and You Undercount Population', *The Friday Times*, 31 March 2017, https://www.thefridaytimes.com/leave-out-migrants-and-you-undercount-population/ (accessed November 20, 2019). See also Anita Weiss, 'Much Ado about Counting: The Conflict over Holding a Census in Pakistan', *Asian Survey*, Vol. 39, No. 4, 1999.

148. See Ian Talbot and Gurharpal Singh, *The Partition of India*.

149. Mohammad Waseem, 'Pakistan's India Policy and Elite Perceptions of the Status of Indian Muslims,' in E. Sridharan, ed., *International Relations Theory and South Asia*, Vol. II, Oxford University Press, New Delhi, 2011, 20–3.

150. See Prakash Tandon, *Punjabi Century, 1857–1947*, University of California Press, 1969; Pran Neville, *Lahore: A Sentimental Journey*, Penguin, 2006; and Ian Talbot and Tahir Kamran, *Colonial Lahore: A History of the City and Beyond*, Oxford University Press, Karachi, 2017.

151. Arvind-Pal Singh, 'Interrogating Identity', 208.

152. Conversation with Professor Mehtab Ali Shah, Oxford, 1997.

153. Yasmeen Khan, *The Great Partition: The Making of India and Pakistan*, Yale University Press, 2007, 172–3.

154. Ibid., 200–4.

155. Ian Talbot, *Divided Cities*, 49–56.

156. *Census of Pakistan, 1951,* Vol. I, Table 19-A; Vol. VI, 65.

157. Brendan O'Leary, 'The Elements of Right-sizing', 15.

158. *Census of Pakistan, 1951*, Vol. I, 30.

159. Ibid., Vol. VI, 65.

160. Ibid., Vol. I, 31.

161. Sarah Ansari, 'Punjabis in Sind: Identity and Power', in Gurharpal Singh and Ian Talbot, eds, *Punjabi Identity: Continuity and Change*, Manohar, New Delhi, 1996, 93–7.

162. Ibid., 100–2.

163. *Census of Pakistan, 1951*, Vol. VI, 36.

164. Ibid., Vol. I, 87.

165. David Gilmartin, *Empire and Islam: Punjab and the Making of Pakistan*, University of California Press, 1988, 199-204.

166. Ian Talbot, 'The Unionist Party and Punjab Politics 1937–1947', in Anthony Low, ed., *The Political Inheritance of Pakistan*, Palgrave Macmillan, London, 1991, 88.

167. Ayesha Jalal, *The Sole Spokesman*, Cambridge University Press, 1985, 110–13.

168. Dr Hatim Jatoi, ed., *Statement of the Accused: Baba-e-Sindh Haider Bakhsh Jatoi,* Hyderabad, Pakistan, 1997, 30.

169. R. F. Mudie, Governor West Punjab, 'Rehabilitation of Refugees', in Government of Pakistan, Cabinet Secretariat, Cabinet Division, *The Journey to Pakistan: A Documentation on Refugees of 1947*, National Documentation Centre, Islamabad, 1993, 78–9.

170. *The Statesman* newspaper, 18 September 1947.

171. Mohammed Ahsen Choudhry, 'Evacuee Property in India and Pakistan', *Pakistan Horizon*, Institute of International Affairs, Karachi, Vol. 10, No. 2, June 1957, 96–109.

172. Ibid., 98–9, 102.

173. Joseph B. Schechtman, 'Evacuee Property in India and Pakistan', *India Quarterly*, Vol. 9, No. 1, March 1953, 84.

174. Ibid., 85.

175. Mohammed Ahsen Choudhry, 'Evacuee Property in India and Pakistan', 102.

176. Ibid., 96–7.

177. These observations draw on Mohammad Waseem, 'Pakistan's India Policy and Elite Perceptions of the Status of Indian Muslims', 199–202.

178. Joseph B. Schechtman, 'Evacuee Property', 32-3.

179. Yunas Samad, 'Pakistan or Punjabistan: Crisis of National Identity', in Gurharpal Singh and Ian Talbot, eds, *Punjabi Identity*, 61.

180. Ayesha Jalal, *The State of Martial Rule*, Vanguard Books, Lahore, 1991, 79.

181. Tariq Rahman, 'The Siraiki Movement in Pakistan', *Language Problems and Language Planning*, Vol. 19, No. 1, 1995, 19.

182. Ibid., 16–17.

183. Asma Faiz, 'Building Language, Building Province: Civil Society and Ethnic Nationalism in Pakistan, *Journal of Civil Society*, Vol. 17, Issue 1, 2021, 92–3.

184. Constituent Assembly of Pakistan (CAP) Debates, 20 May 1948, 713.

185. Ayesha Jalal, *The State of Martial Rule*, 79.

186. Constituent Assembly of Pakistan Debates, 12 March 1953, 48.

187. For a detailed study, see Mohammad Waseem, *Politics and the State in Pakistan*, National Institute of Historical and Cultural Research, Islamabad, 1994, 110–11.

188. Constituent Assembly of Pakistan Debates, 23 March 1954, 405.

189. *Census of Pakistan*, Vol. I, 44.

190. Ilyas Chattha, 'Competition for Resources: Partition's Evacuee Property and the Sustenance of Corruption in Pakistan', *Modern Asian Studies*, Vol. 46, Issue 5, September 2012, 1192.

191. Ibid., 1193–5, 1198.

192. Ibid., 1200.

193. Ibid., 1203.

194. For a detailed discussion on the pattern of refugee resettlement in Punjab, see Mohammed Waseem, *Politics and the State in Pakistan*, 109-10.

195. Darshan Singh Tatla and Ian Talbot, *Punjab*, xxx–xxxi.

196. For a detailed discussion of AISSF, see Hamish Telford, 'The Political Economy of Punjab: Creating Space for Sikh Militancy', *Asian Survey*, Vol. 32, No. 11, 1992, 970.

197. Ajay K. Mehra, 'Ethnicity, Democratisation and Governance: The Case of India', *Ethnic Studies Report*, Colombo, 1993, 230.

198. Shinder Singh Thandi, 'Fighting Sikh Militancy: Counter-insurgency Operation in Punjab', in Iain Hampsher-Monk and Jeffrey Stanyer, eds, *Contemporary Political Studies*, Political Studies Association, Belfast, 1996, 550–4.

199. Gurharpal Singh, 'The Punjab Crisis Since 1984: A Reassessment', *Ethnic and Racial Studies*, Vol. 18, No. 3, 476–93.

200. Mohammad Waseem, 'Mohajirs in Pakistan: A Case of Nativization of Migrants', in Crispin Bates, ed., *Community, Empire and Migration: South Asians in Diaspora*, Palgrave, London, 2001, 245–260.

201. M. Rafique Afzal, *Political Parties in Pakistan: 1947-1958*, Vol. 1, National Commission on Historical and Cultural Research, Islamabad, 1976, 36–7, 1998, 481.

202. Charles Kennedy, 'Managing Ethnic Conflict: The Case of Pakistan', *Regional Politics and Policy*, Vol 3, No. 1, 1993, 138–9.

203. See Gustav Papanek, *Pakistan's Development: Social Goals and Private Incentives*, Harvard University Press, 1967; Stanley Kochanek, *Interest Groups and Development: Business and Politics in Pakistan*, Oxford University Press, 1983; Rashid Amjad, *Private Industrial Investment in Pakistan*, Cambridge Books, 2008; Akbar Zaidi, *Issues in Pakistan's Economy: A Political Economy Perspective*, Oxford University Press, 2015.

204. Waqar Zaidi, 'Pakistani Civil Aviation and US Aid to Pakistan, 1950 to 1961', *Journal of the Research Institute for the History of Global Arms Transfer*, 8, 2019, 85.

205. Don Mitchell, *Cultural Geography: A Critical Introduction*, Blackwell Publishers, 2000, 30.

206. See Mohammad Waseem, *Politics and the State in Pakistan*, Chapter 3.

207. See Mahbub-ul-Haq, 'Seven Sins of Economic Planners', in Moin Baqai and Irving Brecher, eds, *Development Policy and Planning in Pakistan, 1950–1970*, National Institute of Economic and Social Research, Karachi, 1973.

208. Abdul Rahman Siddiqi, *Partition and the Making of the Mohajir Mindset: A Narrative*, Oxford University Press, 2008, 127.

209. Mohammad Waseem, 'Ethnic and Islamic Militancy in Pakistan', in Paul Brass, ed., *Routledge Handbook of South Asian Politics: India, Pakistan, Bangladesh, Sri Lanka, and Nepal*, Routledge, Abingdon, UK, 2010, 281–3.

2. MASTER NARRATIVE

1. Edward Said, *Culture and Imperialism,* Chatto & Windus, London, 1993, xiii.

2. Barbara Weinstein, 'History without a Cause? Grand Narratives, World History, and the Postcolonial Dilemma', *International Review of Social History*, Vol. 50, No. 1, 2005, 72.

3. Jean-François Lyotard, *The Postmodern Condition: A Report on Knowledge*, University of Minnesota Press, 1984, xii.

4. Jean Luc Racine, '"Pakistan and the India Syndrome": Between Kashmir and the Nuclear Predicament', in Christophe Jaffrelot, ed., *Pakistan: Nationalism without A Nation*, Zed Books, London, 2002, 195.

5. Marvin Weinbaum and Gautam Sen, 'Pakistan Enters the Middle East', *Orbis*, Vol. 22, No. 3, 1978, 595–612.

6. Saroosh Irfani, 'Pakistan's Sectarian Violence: Between the "Arabist Shift" and Indo–Persian Culture', in Satu P. Limaye et al., eds, *Religious Radicalism and Security in South Asia*, Asia–Pacific Center for Security Studies, Honolulu, 33, 2004, 147.

7. Anjum Altaf, 'India's Pakistan Policy?', The South Asian Idea, Weblog, 21 April 2011.

8. Jennifer Frost, 'Using "Master Narratives" to Teach History: The Case of the Civil Rights Movement', *The History Teacher*, Vol. 45, No. 3, 2012, 437–8.

9. Gary Baines, 'The Master Narrative of South Africa's Liberation Struggle: Remembering and Forgetting', *International Journal of African Historical Studies*, Vol. 40, No. 2, 2007, 285.

10. Afrasiab Khattak, quoted in *Dawn*, 3 May 2003.

11. *Dawn*, 17 December 2006.

12. See Gearóid Ó Tuathail, 'Thinking Critically about Geopolitics', in Gearóid Ó Tuathail, Simon Dalby and Paul Routledge, eds, *The Geopolitics Reader*, Routledge, London & New York, 1998, 1–12.

13. Gertjan Dijkink, *National Identity and Geopolitical Visions: Maps of Pride and Pain*, Routledge, Abingdon, UK, 2002, 4–5.

14. Ibid., 8.

15. See Rashid Amjad and Farooq Ali, eds, *Pakistani Adab* [Pakistani Literature, text in Urdu], Federal Government Sir Syed College, Rawalpindi, 1981, for a colloquium held on 5 November 1954 at Radio Pakistan Lahore. Henceforward *PL*. The colloquium included Khalifa Abdul Hakim, Justice S. A. Rehman, Abdul Majeed Salik, Mazharuddin Siddiqui, Dr Burhanuddin Ahmed and Hamid Ali Khan, among others.

16. Ibid., 27, 35, 40.

17. Ibid., 31, 32, 37.

18. Ibid., 36.

19. Jamil Jalibi, 'Quest for a New Meaning', *PL*, 127–30.

20. Ibid., 131–4.

21. Syed Mohammad Taqi, 'Pakistan Nationalism', *PL*, 156,159, 162–3.

22. Sajjad Naqvi, Colloquium on the Identity of Pakistani Culture, *PL*, 183.

23. Ibadat Barelvi, Colloquium on the Identity of Pakistani Culture, *PL*, 184.

24. Dr Wazir Agha, Colloquium on the Identity of Pakistani Culture, *PL*, 200.

25. Ibid., 203–4.

26. Saleem Ahmed, 'Iqbal and Indo–Muslim Civilization', *PL*, 215–16, 222.

27. Sheema Majeed, ed., *Essays of Muhammad Hasan Askari* (Maqallat Muhammad Hasan Askari, MMHA) [in Urdu], Vol. II, Ilm-o-Irfan Publishers, Lahore, 2001, 47–8.

28. Muhammad Hasan Askari, 'Muslim Proselytizing Delegations in the West', in *Collected Works* [Majmua, Urdu text], Sang-e-Meel Publications, Lahore, 2008, 175.

29. Sheema Majeed, *Essays of Muhammad Hasan Askari*, 50.

30. Ibid., 66–7.

31. Dr Anwar Sadeed, 'The Issue of Pakistanism in Literature', *PL*, 556–7.

32. A. R. Siddiqi, *Partition and the Making of the Muhajir Mindset: A Narrative*, Oxford University Press, Karachi, 2008, 108.

33. Syed Mohammad Taqi, 'Pakistani Nationalism', 157.

34. Jamil Jalibi's contribution to the colloquium 'Identity of Pakistani Culture', *PL*, 196.

35. Dr Syed Abdullah, 'Cultural Motives of the Pakistani Movement', *PL*, 66.

36. S. M. Ikram, 'Introduction', in S. M. Ikram and Percival Spears, eds, *The Cultural Heritage of Pakistan*, Oxford University Press, Karachi, 1955, iii.

37. Abdulsalam Khursheed, 'Culture of Pakistan', *PL*, 71.

38. Brigadier Syed Naseeurddin, 'A Discussion from the Perspective of the Pakistan Movement with Reference to Aligarh', *PL*, 81.

39. Ibid., 133–4.

40. Ibid., 151.

41. Ibid., 162.

42. Ibid., 189–90.

43. Muhammad Hasan Askari, 'Muslim Proselytizing Delegations in the West', 114.

44. S. M. Ikram, 'The Spiritual Heritage', in S. M. Ikram and Percival Spear, eds, *The Cultural Heritage of Pakistan*, 171–4.

45. Hafiz Mahmud Shirani, *Urdu in Punjab* [in Urdu], Sang-e-Meel Publications, Lahore, reprinted 2005, 71–6.

46. Kamran Asdar Ali, 'Progressives and "Perverts": Partition Stories and Pakistan's Future', *Social Text*, Vol. 29, No. 3, 2011, 3.

47. The British High Commission, Dispatch No. 90 (522), Dated 27 March 1948, File No. 6203/47 Commonwealth Relations Office, British Library.

48. Sajjad Zaheer, *The Light: The History of the Movement for Progressive Literature in the Indo-Pakistan Subcontinent*, Oxford University Press, 2006, 96.

49. Ibid., 129.

50. Kamran Asdar Ali, *Surkh Salam: Communist Politics and Class Activism in Pakistan, 1947–1972*, Oxford University Press, Karachi, 2015, 106.

51. Ibid., 135.

52. Ibid., 141.

53. Ibid., 148.

54. Ali Raza, 'An Unfulfilled Dream: The Left in Pakistan ca. 1947–50', *South Asian History and Culture*, Vol. 4, No. 4, 2013, 503–4.

55. The British High Commission, Letter No. 90 (522), Dated 27 March 1948, IOR L/P&J/ 12/772, British Library.

56. Ibid.

57. Mohammad Waseem, 'Anti-Americanism in Pakistan', in Tony Judt and Denis Lacrone, eds, *With US or Against US: Studies in Global Anti-Americanism*, Palgrave Macmillan, New York, 2005, 184.

58. Ibid.

59. For a detailed discussion on the level of mass mobilization during the anti-Ayub movement, see Lal Khan, *Pakistan's Other Story: The 1968-9 Revolution*, Aakar Books, New Delhi, 2009.

60. Mohammad Waseem, *Pakistan Under Martial Law, 1977–1985*, Vanguard Books, Lahore, 1987, 196–202.

61. Jamil-ud-Din Ahmad, *Speeches and Writings of Mr Jinnah*, Sheikh Muhammad Ashraf, Lahore, 1942, 98.

62. Ibid., 103–4.

63. I. H. Qureshi, *The Muslim Community of the Indo–Pakistan Subcontinent, 610–1947*, Renaissance Publishing House, New Delhi, 1962, 348.

64. Ghulam Abbas, 'The Cultural Perspective of Sir Syed's Movement', *PL*, 84–5.

65. Syed Abdullah, 'Cultural Motives of the Pakistan Movement', *PL*, 61–2.

66. Nazia Majid, *The Creation*, Vol. IV, Issue III, 2013, n.p.

67. Firoz Khan Noon, 'The Position in Pakistan and India', enclosed in telegram no. 298 (579/30/47) from Ambassador Sir David Kelly, the British Embassy, Ankara, 13 November 1947, Public Record Office, UK, FO371/63572, 153672, 1.

68. Ibid.

69. Ibid.

70. Ibid.

71. Ibid, 5.

72. Ibid.

73. Ibid.

74. I. H. Qureshi, *The Muslim Community of the Indo–Pakistan Subcontinent*, 114.

75. Ibid., 117.

76. Ibid., 118.

77. Ibid., 134.

78. Ibid., 135.

79. K. K. Aziz, *The Murder of History: A Critique of History Textbooks Used in Pakistan*, Vanguard Books, Lahore, 1993, 13.

80. Ibid., 76.

81. Ibid., 99.

82. Ibid., 111.

83. Ibid., 69.

84. A. H. Nayyar and Ahmed Salim, *The Subtle Subversion: The State of Curricula and Textbooks in Pakistan Urdu, English, Social Studies and Civics*, Sustainable Development Policy Institute, Islamabad, 2005, 21.

85. Ibid., 61.

86. Ibid., 83.

87. Ibid., 21.

88. Ibid., 21.

89. Ibid., 59.

90. Ibid., 61.

91. Ibid.

92. For a detailed study of Choudhary Rahmat Ali's book, see Alyssa Ayres, *Speaking Like a State: Language and Nationalism in Pakistan*, Cambridge University Press, 2009, Figure 8–23, 107–22.

93. Choudhary Rahmat Ali, *Pakistan: The Fatherland of the Pak Nation,* Book Traders, Lahore, 1935 (reprinted 1978), 181–201.

94. Ashok K. Behuria and Mohammad Shehzad, 'Partition of History in Textbooks in Pakistan: Implications of Selective Memory and Forgetting', *Strategic Analysis*, Vol. 37, Issue 3, Manohar Parrikar Institute for Defense Studies and Analyses, New Delhi, May 2013, 358.

95. Qazi Javed, *Indo–Muslim Civilization* [Urdu text], Vanguard Books, Lahore, 1983, 160–1.

96. Ali Usman Qasmi, 'Identity Formation through National Calendar: Holidays and Commemorations in Pakistan', *Nations and Nationalism*, Vol. 23, No. 3, 2017, 620–3.

97. Arnaud De Borchgrave, UPI Editor at Large, 'Commentary: Paranoidistan', retrieved from https://www.upi.com/Commentary Paranoidistan/87111265041190/#ixzz5dPhW2ZPs.

98. Ibid.

99. John. W. Anderson, 'Conspiracy Theories, Premature Entextualization and Popular Political Analysis', *The Arab Studies Quarterly*, Vol. 4, No. 1, 1996, 97.

100. Ibid.

101. Husain Haqqani, *Reimagining Pakistan: Transforming a Dysfunctional Nuclear State*, HarperCollins, 2018, 146–55.

102. Huma Yusuf, 'Conspiracy Fever: The US, Pakistan and its Media', *Survival*, Vol. 53, No. 4, 2011, 95–118.

103. Husain Haqqani, *Reimagining Pakistan*, 3–14.

104. Orya Maqbool Jan, 'Birth Control: Pakistan Main Kyun?', *Awaz Today*, 10 December 2018.

105. Neo TV, 'Orya Maqbool Loses Temper | Zainab Incidence | Harf E Raz | Neo News', *YouTube*, 11 January 2018.

106. Khadija Khan, 'Extremism Is Entering Pakistan Again – Albeit through a Different Door this Time Around', *The News*, 7 November 2016.

107. Rawal TV, 'Ansar Abbasi's Hate Speech against Dr Abdus Salam', *YouTube*, 11 November 2017.

108. Bol TV, 'Hate Speech by Aamir Liaquat?', *YouTube*, 2 August 2017.

109. Husain Haqqani, *Reimagining Pakistan*, 146–58.

110. Ibid., 149.

111. Ibid., 152.

112. Shafqat Tanveer Mirza, 'Punjabi Themes', *Dawn*, 20 November 2011.

113. Mirza Kashif Ali, *I Am not Malala: I Am Muslim, I Am Pakistani*, All Pakistan Private School Federation (APPSF), Lahore, 2015, 1–6, 26, 51, 329.

114. Anthony Smith, 'Culture, Community and Territory: The Politics of Ethnicity and Nationalism', *International Affairs*, Vol. 72, No 3, 1996, 453–5.

115. Alain Dieckhoff, *The Invention of a Nation: Zionist Thought and the Making of Modern Israel*, London: Hurst & Co., 1993, 99–105.

116. For example, Matthew A. Cook, *Annexation and the Unhappy Valley: The Historical Anthropology of Sindh's Colonization*, Brill, Leiden, 2015; Olaf Caroe, *The Pathans*, Oxford University Press, Karachi, 1983; Winston Churchill, *The Story of the Malakand Field Force*, Courier Corporation,

North Chelmsford, MA, 2012; Reginald Bosworth Smith, *Life of Lord Lawrence*, Smith, Elder, & Company, London, 1885.

117. Sudipta Kaviraj, 'Imagined History', Occasional Papers on History and Society, Nehru Memorial Museum and Library, Second Series, 1988, No. 7, 23.

118. Ibid., 23, 28.

119. Ibid., 28, 36–7, 46, 49, 59.

120. Faisal Devji, *Muslim Zion: Pakistan as a Political Idea*, Hurst & Co., 2013, 89.

121. Ibid., 95–100.

122. Ibid., 105.

123. Ibid.

124. Tariq Rahman, *From Hindi to Urdu: A Social and Political History*, Oxford University Press, Karachi, 2018, 136–40.

125. Christopher King, 'The Hindi–Urdu Controversy of the North-Western Provinces and Oudh and Communal Consciousness', *Journal of South Asian Literature*, Vol. 13, No. 1/4, 1977–98, 111–13.

126. Tariq Rahman, 'How Urdu Got Associated with Muslims in India? – I', *The Express Tribune*, 20 August 2011, https://tribune.com.pk/story/235805/how-urdu-got-associated-with-muslims-in-india--i/.

127. Mohammad Waseem, 'Pakistan's India Policy and Elite Perception of the Status of Indian Muslims', in E. Sridharan, ed., *International Relations Theory and South Asian Regional Cooperation*, Oxford University Press, New Delhi, 2010, 14.

128. See M. Mujeeb, *The Indian Muslims*, George Allen & Unwin, London, 1967, 560–1.

129. See C. Shackle and Javed Majeed, *Hali's Musaddas: The Flow and Ebb of Islam*, Oxford University Press, 1997.

130. See Anil Seal, *The Emergence of Indian Nationalism: Competition and Collaboration in the Later Nineteenth Century*, Cambridge University Press, 1971, 308–20.

131. K. K. Aziz, *The Murder of History*, 96.

132. See Aftab A. Kazi, *Ethnicity and Education in Nation-building: The Case of Pakistan*, Vanguard Books, Lahore, 1987, 120.

133. Ibid., 118–19.

134. Ayesha Jalal, 'The Past as Present', in Maleeha Lodhi, ed., *Beyond the 'Crisis State'*, Columbia University Press, 2011, 9.

135. Ibid., 11.

136. For details, see Fakhar Zaman, *Punjab, Punjabi aur Punjabiat* [in Urdu], Alhamad Publications, Lahore, 2003, appendices 3–8, 285–310.

137. Muhammad Haneef Ramay, *Punjab Ka Muqadma* (The Case of Punjab, Urdu text), Jang Publishers, Lahore, 1988, 53.

138. Ibid, 61.

139. Ibid.

140. R. E. M. Wheeler, *Five Thousand Years of Pakistan*, Royal India and Pakistan Society, London, 1950, http://asi.nic.in/asi_books/17045.pdf (accessed 27 August 2019).

141. Sarah Ansari, *Life After Partition: Migration, Community and Strife in Sindh, 1947–1962*, Oxford University Press, Karachi, 2005, 108.

142. Hamida Khuhro, 'The Capital of Pakistan', in Hamida Khuhro and Anwer Mooraj, eds, *Karachi: Megacity of Our Times*, Oxford University Press, Karachi, 1998, 95–111.

143. Ibid., 379.

144. Alyssa Ayres, *Speaking Like a State*, 10.

145. Aitzaz Ahsan, *The Indus Saga and the Making of Pakistan*, Oxford University Press, Karachi, 2000, xv.

146. Dr Syed Abdullah, 'The Issue of Pakistanism in Urdu Literature', in *PL*, 541–2.

147. I. H. Qureshi, *The Muslim Community of the Indo-Pakistan Subcontinent*, 82–3.

148. See General Zia's speech quoted in *Dawn*, 6 September 1977.

149. The migrant phenomenon and *longue durée* of collective memory were reflected in Paul's work. See Jogindar Paul, *Sleepwalkers* [Urdu novel translated into English], Katha Perspectives, New Delhi, 1991.

150. Ian S. Lustick, 'Hegemonic Beliefs and Territorial Rights', *International Journal of Intercultural Relations*, Vol. 20, No. 3/4, 1996, 486.

151. Alia Amirali, *Balochistan: A Case Study of Pakistan's Peacemaking Praxis*, Sage Publications, New Delhi & Thousand Oaks, CA, 2015, 108–11.

152. Discussion with Inayat Ullah Baloch, Heidelberg University, 1992.

153. See Tariq Rahman, *Language and Politics in Pakistan*, Oxford University Press, Karachi, 1996; Sabiha Mansoor, *Language Planning in Higher Education: A Case Study of Pakistan*, Oxford University Press, Karachi; Alyssa Ayres, *Speaking Like a State*; Farina Mir, *The Social Space of Language: Vernacular Culture in British Colonial Punjab*, University of California Press, 2010; Lars O. Dyrud and Carla F. Radloff, *A Sociolinguistic Survey of Punjab, Pakistan*, National Institute of Pakistan Studies, Quaid-i-Azam University Islamabad, 2011; Asma Faiz, 'Building Language, Building Province: Civil Society and Ethnic Nationalism in Pakistan', *Journal of Civil Society*, Vol. 17, Issue 1, 2021.

154. Feroz Ahmed, *Ethnicity and Politics in Pakistan*, Oxford University Press, Karachi, 1998, 101.

155. Quoted from a school textbook by K. K. Aziz, *The Murder of History*, 109.

156. Alain Dieckhoff, *The Invention of a Nation*, 110.

157. John Hutchinson, 'Cultural Nationalism', in John Breuilly, ed., *The Oxford Handbook of History of Nationalism,* Oxford University Press, 2013, 76–94.

158. Quoted in Alyssa Ayres, *Speaking Like a State,* 16.

159. Alain Dieckhoff, *The Invention of a Nation,* 98–127.

160. For efforts in this regard, see Tariq Rahman, *Language and Politics in Pakistan,* 88–9.

161. Ibid., 84.

162. Sabiha Mansoor, *Punjabi, Urdu, English in Pakistan,* Vanguard Books, Lahore, 1993, 16, 27.

163. See Farina Mir, *The Social Space of Language,* 59–60.

164. Katherine Adeney, *Federalism and Ethnic Conflict Regulation in India and Pakistan,* Palgrave Macmillan, London, 2007, 161–2, 179–80.

165. Quoted by Carl W. Ernst, *Refractions of Islam in India: Situating Sufism in India,* Sage Publications, New Delhi, 2016, 116.

166. Conversation with the author at his residence in Aligarh, 2003.

167. For the following observations, see 'Injunction of Apostasy against Quaid-e-Azam' [Quaid e Azam par kufar ka fatwa, in Urdu], *Lail-o-Nehar,* April 1970.

168. Inamur Rehman, *Public Opinion and Political Development in Pakistan, 1947–1958,* Oxford University Press, Karachi, 1982, 4–9.

169. Iftikhar H. Malik, *Islam, Nationalism and the West,* Palgrave Macmillan, London, 1999, 21–2.

170. Farzana Shaikh, *Making Sense of Pakistan,* Oxford University Press, 2009, 5.

171. Andreas Rieck, *The Shias of Pakistan: An Assertive and Beleaguered Minority,* London, Hurst & Co., 2015, 51.

172. Faisal Devji, *Muslim Zion,* 65–7.

173. Ibid.

174. Ibid., 9.

175. Husain Haqqani, *Pakistan: Between Mosque and Military,* Carnegie Endowment for International Peace, Washington DC, 2010, 2–3.

176. The British High Commission, Opdom no. 31, Letter dated 30 April 1948, File No. IOR E/P&J/8/798, DO 142/423.

177. The British High Commission, Letter No. 6, Dated 5 May 1948, DO 142/345, IOR L/7/13864, British Library.

178. H. E. Stephenson's letter dated 15 April 1948, The British High Commission, File No. IOR L/PJ/7/13864, DO 142/345, British Library.

179. Letter from U.K. High Commission, Stephenson, File No. DO 142/345 BNA.

180. A. K. Brohi, *Islam in the Modern World,* United Publishers, Lahore, 1975, 53.

181. Ibid., 54.

182. Ibid., 60.

183. Ibid., 60.

184. Ibid., 61.

185. Ibid., 66.

186. Ibid., 84.

187. Ibid., 215.

188. Ibid., 216.

189. Louis D. Hayes, *The Islamic State in the Post-modern World: The Political Experience of Pakistan*, Ashgate, Farnham, UK, 2004, 95.

190. Aziz Talbani, 'Pedagogy, Power, and Discourse: Transformation of Islamic Education', in Stephen Lyon and Iain R. Edgar, eds, *Shaping a Nation: An Examination of Education in Pakistan*, Oxford University Press, 2010, 61–2.

191. M. Iqbal Chaudhry, *Pakistan Society*, Aziz Publications, Lahore, 1984, 518.

192. Vartan Gregorian, *Islam: A Mosaic, Not a Monolith*, Brookings Institution Press, Washington, DC, 2003, 94–5.

193. Aziz Talbani, *Shaping a Nation*, 64.

194. Sabeeha Hafeez, *The Changing Pakistani Society*, Royal Book Company, Karachi, 1991, 9.

195. Iftikhar Malik, *Islam, Nationalism and the West*, 106.

196. Ibid., 257–8.

197. Ali Usman Qasmi, *The Ahmadis and the Politics of Religious Exclusion in Pakistan*, Anthem Press, London, 2014, 218.

198. Ibid., 217.

199. Gurharpal Singh, 'India as an Ethnic Democracy', Conference paper, CEIAS/MSH Conference on Democracy, Ethnicity and Conflicts in South Asia, Paris, 2004, 8.

200. Ibid., 15.

201. 'How the Islamabad Protests Happened', *Dawn*, 27 November 2017.

202. Mohammad Waseem, 'Patterns of Conflict in Pakistan: Implications for Policy', Working Paper No. 5, Brookings Project on US Relations with the Islamic World, 2011, 2.

203. See Masooda Bano, *The Rational Believer: Choices and Decisions in the Madrassas of Pakistan*, Cornell University Press, 2012.

204. Scott W. Hibbard and David Little, *Islamic Activism and US Foreign Policy*, United States Institute of Peace Press, Washington, DC, 1997, xvii–xviii.

205. S. M. Ikram, 'The Patterns of Pakistan's Heritage', in S. M. Ikram and Percival Spear, *The Cultural Heritage of Pakistan*, 1-7.

206. Zaigham Khan, 'The Day of the TLP', *The News*, 5 November 2018.

207. For the glorification of war, See K. K. Aziz, *The Murder of History*, 192–3.

208. Noman Baig, 'God and Greed: Money and Meditation in Karachi's Marketplace', PhD thesis, University of Texas at Austin, 2014, available at https://repositories.lib.utexas.edu/bitstream/handle/2152/28317/BAIG-DISSERTATION-2014.pdf?sequence=1,.

209. Umair Javed, 'Profit, Piety and Patronage: Bazaar Traders and Politics in Urban Pakistan', PhD thesis, London School of Economics and Politics, 2018, available at http://etheses.lse.ac.uk/3843/1/Javed__profit-piety-and-patronage.pdf (accessed 8 September 2020).

210. *Dawn*, 2 January 2020.

211. Akeel Bilgrami, 'The Clash within Civilizations', *Daedalus*, Vol. 132, No. 3, Summer 2003, 91.

212. Sadaf Aziz, 'Making a Sovereign State: Javed Ghamidi and "enlightened moderation"', *Modern Asian Studies*, Vol. 45, No. 3, 2011, 615.

213. Graham E. Fuller, *The Future of Political Islam*, Palgrave Macmillan, London, 2003, 195.

214. Samina Yasmeen, 'Narratives of Jihad and Islamic Identity: JUD/LeT and the Gulf Connection(s)', in Christophe Jaffrelot and Laurence Louer, eds, *The Islamic Connection: South Asia and the Gulf*, Penguin Random House, 2017, 74.

215. Ibid., 74.

216. Ibid., 80.

217. Tariq Rahman, *Interpretations of Jihad in South Asia: An Intellectual History*, Walter de Gruyter, Berlin, 2018, and Husain Haqqani, *Reimagining Pakistan*, 134–6.

218. Husain Haqqani, *Reimagining Pakistan*, 146.

219. Dietrich Reetz, 'Alternate Globalities? On the Cultures and Formats of Transnational Muslim Networks from South Asia', 2010, available at https://www.researchgate.net/publication/290951112_'Alternate'_globalities_On_the_cultures_and_formats_of_transnational_Muslim_networks_from_South_Asia (accessed 25 August 2020).

220. Ejaz Ahmed Farooqi, *Pakistan: A Crisis in the Renaissance of Islam*, Sang-e-Meel Publications, Lahore, 1991.

221. Malik Zafrul Hasan, *Educating Pakistan*, Sheikh Muhammad Ashraf, Lahore, 1948, 14.

222. Anwar S. Dil, ed., *Perspectives on Pakistan*, Book Services Abbottabad, Pakistan, 1965, 25.

223. Hassaan Faizi, *PL*, 8–9, 19.

224. Zulfikar Ali Bhutto, *Thoughts on Some Aspects of Islam*, Sheikh Mohammed Ashraf, Lahore, 1976, 10.

225. J. R. Patersons' Letter to the Commonwealth and Foreign Relations Office, Dated 21 September 1972, The British High Commission, File No. FCO 37/1138, British Library.

226. Alastair Lamb, *Asian Frontiers: Studies in a Continuing Problem*, Frederick A. Praeger, New York, 1968, 41.

227. Ronald G. Suny as quoted in Alyssa Ayres, *Speaking Like a State*, 28.

228. S. M. Burke, *Pakistan Foreign Policy: A Historical Analysis*, Oxford University Press, London, 1973, 3–11.

229. P. R. Kumaraswamy, *Beyond the Veil: Israel–Pakistan Relations*, Jaffee Center for Strategic Studies, Tel Aviv, Israel, 2000, 68.

230. Huma Yusuf, 'Conspiracy Fever', 96.

231. Sigrid Faath, ed., *Anti-Americanism in the Islamic world*, Markus Wiener Publishers, Princeton, NJ, 2006, 189–90.

232. Mohammad Waseem, 'Perceptions about America in Pakistan', *International Journal of South Asian Studies*, Vol. 50, No. 2, 2004, 35.

233. See Mohammad Waseem, 'Pakistan's Perceptions of the Impact of US Politics on its Policies towards Pakistan', in Noor Hussain and Leo Rose, eds, *Pakistan–US Relations*, University of California Press, 1988.

234. Ayesha Jalal, 'The Past as the Present', 9.

235. Armando Salvatore, *Islam and the Political Discourse of Modernity*, Ithaca Press, New York, 2000, 77.

236. Dennis Kux, *The United States and Pakistan, 1947–2000: Disenchanted Allies*, Johns Hopkins University Press, Baltimore, MD, 2001, 360.

237. See Ziauddin Sardar and Meryl Wyn Davies, *Why Do People Hate America?*, Icon Books, Cambridge, 2000, 116.

238. Usaama Makdisi, 'Anti-Americanism in the Arab world: An Interpretation of a Brief history', *Journal of American History*, Vol. 89, No. 2, 2002, 557.

239. Mohammad Waseem, 'The Dialectic between Politics and Foreign Policy', in Christophe Jaffrelot, ed., *Pakistan: Nationalism without a Nation*, Manohar Publishers, New Delhi, 2002, 271.

240. Richard Rose, '"Russia" as an Hour-glass Society: A Constitution without Citizens', *East European Constitutional Review*, Vol. 4, No. 1, 1995, 35.

241. Marvin Weinbaum and Gautam Sen, 'Pakistan Enters the Middle East,' *Orbis*, Vol. 22, No. 3, 1978, 595–612.

242. For a detailed discussion on the trajectory of anti-Americanism in Pakistan see Mohammad Waseem, 'Islam and the West: A Perspective from Pakistan', in James L. Peacock, Patricia M. Thornton and Patrick B. Inman, eds, *Identity Matters: Ethnic and Sectarian Conflict*, Berghahn Books, New York & Oxford, 2007, Chapter 10.

243. Andre Gunder Frank, *The Underdevelopment of Development*, Stockholm, Sweden, Bethany Books, 1991.

244. See Frank C. Darling, *The Westernization of Asia: A Comparative Political Analysis*, Rochester, VT, Schenkman, 1980.

245. Joseph-Ernest Renan, *La Réforme intellectuelle et Morale*, 1871, (Source Wikipedia; 'Post colonialism'.)

246. Armando Salvatore, *Islam and the Political Discourse of Modernity*, 67.

247. Frantz Fanon, *The Wretched of the Earth*, Grove Press, New York, 1963, 48–51.

248. Thomas Hardy, *The Return of The Native*, Belgravia, 1878.

249. Ashish Nandy, *Intimate Enemy: Loss and Recovery of Self under Colonialism*, Oxford University Press, Oxford, 1989.

250. Ibid., ix.

251. Ibid., x.

252. Ibid., xi, xii.

253. Ibid., xvii.

254. Ibid., xiii.

255. Ibid., xvi.

256. Ibid., xvi.

257. Jorge Luis Andrade Fernandes, 'Return of the Native: Postcolonial Migrancy and the (Im)Possibility of the Nation', PhD thesis, University of Hawaii, 2002, 1.

258. Ibid., 1–2.

259. Ibid., 12.

260. Ibid.,14.

261. This is a borrowing from Fanon's work. See Frantz Fanon, *Black Skin, White Mask*, Grove Weidenfeld, New York, 1991.

262. See Talal Asad, *Formations of the Secular: Christianity, Islam and Modernity*, Stanford University Press, 2003, 5.

263. Ibid., 7.

264. Ibid., 11.

265. Ibid., 181–3.

266. Ibid., 187.

267. Ibid., 195, 198, 200.

268. Ibid., 193.

269. For a prime example of 'apologetic' scholars of Islam, see Syed Ameer Ali, *History of Saracens*, facsimile edition, Darf, London, 1984 [1899].

270. Akbar S. Ahmed, *Islamic Anthropology: Definition, Dogma and Directions*, International Institute of Islamic Thought, Herndon, VA, 1986, 13.

271. Ibid., 50.

272. Ibid., 56.

273. Ibid., 56, 58.

274. Ibid., 63.

275. Humeira Iqtidar, *Secularizing Islamists: Jamaat-I-Islami and Jamaat-U-Daawaa in Urban Pakistan*, University of Chicago Press, 2011, 1.

276. Ibid.

277. Ibid., 8.

278. Ibid.

279. Ibid.

280. Ibid.

281. Ibid.

282. Constituent Assembly of Pakistan (CAP) Debates, March 1949, 2.

283. Ibid.

284. Ibid., 4.

285. 'Report of the Court of Inquiry constituted under Punjab Act II of 1954 to enquire into Punjab Disturbances of 1953', Government Printing Press, Lahore, 1954, 186.

286. Mohammad Waseem, *Democratization in Pakistan: A Study of the 2002 Elections*, Oxford University Press, Karachi, 2006, 121, 126.

287. Humeira Iqtidar, *Secularizing Islamists*, 22.

288. See Sadaf Ahmad, *Transforming Faith: The Story of Al-Huda and Islamic Revivalism among Urban Pakistani Women*, Syracuse University Press, 2009.

289. Saba Mahmood, *Politics of Piety: The Islamic Revival and the Feminist Subject*, Princeton University Press, 2012, 7.

290. Ibid., x.

291. Ibid., xi.

292. Ibid., 189.

293. Ibid., 190.

294. Saba Mahmood, 'Secularism, Sovereignty and Religious Difference: A Global Genealogy', *Society and Space*, Vol. 35, No. 2, 2018, 200–1.

295. Saba Mahmood, *Politics of Piety*, 191.

296. Ibid., 192.

297. Gayatri Spivak, 'Can the Subaltern Speak?', in Cary Nelson and Lawrence Grossberg, eds, *Marxism and the Interpretation of Culture*, Macmillan, London, 1988, 24.

298. Don Mitchell, *Cultural Geography: A Critical Introduction*, Blackwell Publishers, Oxford, 2000, 5.

299. See Christopher Tilley, *A Phenomenology of Landscape: Places, Paths and Monuments*, Berg Publishers, Oxford, 1997.

300. Ibid., 26.

301. Tariq Rahman, *Interpretations of Jihad in South Asia*, 217.

302. See Syeda Abida Hussain, *Power Failure: The Political Odyssey of a Pakistani Woman*, Oxford University Press, 2015.

303. Ali Usman Qasmi and Megan Eaton Robb, eds, *Muslims against the Muslim League: Critiques of the Idea of Pakistan*, 'Introduction', Cambridge University Press, Cambridge, 2018, 17–19.

304. See Farzana Shaikh, *Community and Consensus in Islam: Muslim Representation in Colonial India, 1860–1947*, Cambridge University Press, 1989.

305. Clifford Geertz, *The Interpretations of Culture: Selected Essays*, Basic Books, New York, 1973, 90–1.

306. See Carl. H. Bolton and Francisco Soto, 'A Semiotic Approach to the Internal Functioning of Publics: Implications for Strategic Communication and Public Relations', *Public Relations Review*, Vol. 24, Issue 1, 1998, 21–44.

307. Stephen M. Lyon, *An Anthropological Analysis of Local Politics and Patronage in a Pakistani Village*, Edwin Mellen Press, Lewiston, NY, 2004, 13.

308. Ibid.

309. Gellner brought in the notions of 'high' and 'low' cultures denoting differences between urban literate societies and the culture of folk societies. See Ernest Gellner, *Nations and Nationalism*, Cornell University Press, 1983, 35–8.

310. S. M. Ikram, 'The Pattern of Pakistan's Heritage', in S. M. Ikram and Percival Spears, eds, *Cultural Heritage of Pakistan*, Oxford University Press, 1955, 15.

311. Saadia Toor, *The State of Islam: Culture and Cold War Politics in Pakistan*, Pluto Press, London, 2011, 79.

312. Dr. Ahmed Hasan Dani, 'Identity of Pakistan', *PL*, 53–4.

313. Abdussalam Khurshid, 'Pakistani Culture', *PL*, 75.

314. Qudratullah Fatimi, 'Foundation of Pakistani Culture', *PL*, 144–5, 153.

315. Aitzaz Ahsen, *The Indus Saga and the Making of Pakistan*, Oxford University Press, Pakistan, 1996, 251–3.

316. For a detailed discussion on the objectives of the progressive writers' movement see Sajjad Zaheer, *The Light*, 96–109.

317. M. Yusuf Abbasi, *Pakistani Culture: A Profile*, National Institute of Historical and Cultural Research, Islamabad, 1992, 51.

318. Faiz's poem 'This Moth-eaten Morning' remains the classic symbol of this sentiment.

319. Yusuf Abbasi, *Pakistani Culture*, 71–2.

320. Sheema Majeed, *Culture and Identity: Selected Writings of Faiz*, Oxford University Press, Karachi, 2005, 31, 45, 84.

321. David Gilmartin, *Empire and Islam: Punjab and the Making of Pakistan*, I. B. Tauris, London, 1988, 212–18.

322. Inamur Rehman, *Public Opinion*, 162.

323. Saadia Toor, *The State of Islam*, 26–8.

324. Sheema Majeed, *Culture and Identity*, 44–7.

325. Joginder Paul, *Sleepwalkers*, 14–18.

326. Tariq Rahman, *Language and Politics in Pakistan*, 95.

327. Maryam Khan, 'Politics of Ethnic Federalism in Pakistan', in Asma Faiz, ed., *Making Federation Work: Federalism after the 18th Amendment in Pakistan*, Oxford University Press, Karachi, 2015, 168.

328. T. S. Subramaniam, 'Rakhigarhi, the Biggest Harappan Site', *The Hindu*, 27 March 2017, available at https://www.thehindu.com/features/friday-review/history-and-culture/rakhigarhi-the-biggest-harappan-site/article5840414.ece (accessed 21 August 2020).

329. Tony Joseph, 'Who Built the Indus Valley Civilization?' *The Hindu*, 23 December 2017.

330. Yusuf Abbassi, *Pakistani Culture*, 207.

331. Ibid., 215–16.

3. TWO POWER CENTRES

1. Fred Riggs, *Administration in Developing Countries: The Theory of Prismatic Society*, Houghton Mifflin, Boston, MA, 1964, 134–8.

2. Clive Dewey, 'The Rural Roots of Pakistani Militarism', in D. A. Low, ed., *The Political Inheritance of Pakistan*, Macmillan, London, 1991, 260–2.

3. Hamza Alvi, 'The State in Post-colonial Societies: Pakistan and Bangladesh', *New Left Review*, No. 74, July/August 1972.

4. Najam Sethi, 'Miltablishment's End Game', *The Friday Times*, 15 August 2014. https://www.thefridaytimes.com/miltablishments-end-game/ (accessed 25 August 2019).

5. Niloufer Siddiqui, Mariam Mufti and Sahar Shafqat, 'Introduction: Pakistan's Political Parties in an Era of Transition', in Mariam Mufti, Sahar Shafqat and Niloufer Siddiqui, eds, *Pakistan's Political Parties: Surviving Between Dictatorship and Democracy*, Georgetown University Press, Washington, DC, 2020, 11–15.

6. Egger Report, *Report of the Commission for Improvement of Public Administration in Pakistan*, Karachi, 1953, para. 115.

7. For landlord-*pirs*, see David Gilmartin, '"Divine Displeasure" and Muslim Elections: The Shaping of Community in Twentieth-century Punjab', in D. A. Low, ed., *The Political Inheritance of Pakistan*, 1991, 106–29; for Deobandis, see Barbara D. Metcalf, *Islamic Revival in British India: Deoband, 1860–1900*, Princeton University Press, 1982.

8. Jurgen Habermas, *The Structural Transformation of the Public Sphere: An Inquiry into a Category of Bourgeois Society Studies in Contemporary German Social Thought*, MIT Press, Cambridge, MA, 1991 edition, 175–6.

9. Jurgen Habermas, *Legitimation Crisis*, Heinemann, London, 1976, 93.

10. Yogendra Yadav, 'Electoral Reforms: Beyond Middle Class Fantasies', *Seminar* 440, April 1996, 61.

11. See Hasan Habib, *Babus, Brahmans and Bureaucrats: A Critique of the Administrative System in Pakistan,* Peoples Publishing House, Lahore, 1973.

12. Hamza Alavi, 'The State in Post-colonial Societies', 59–81.

13. S. Akbar Zaidi, 'In Pakistan, It's Middle Class Rising', *The Hindu*, 28 February 2017.

14. Arif Hasan, 'Emerging Urbanisation Trends: The Case of Karachi', Working paper No. C-37319-PAK-1, International Growth Centre, London, 2016, 6.

15. Sabeeha Hafeez, *The Changing Pakistani Society*, Royal Book Company, Karachi, 1991, 22–35.

16. K. B. Sayeed, *Politics in Pakistan: The Nature and Direction of Change*, Frederick A. Praeger, New York, 1980, 195.

17. Pierre Bourdieu, 'Cultural Reproduction and Social Reproduction', in Richard K. Brown, *Knowledge, Education and Cultural Change: Papers in the Sociology of Education,* Tavistock Publications, London, 1973, 56.

18. Ibid., 67.

19. Homi Bhaba, *The Location of Culture*, Routledge, London, 1994, 1.

20. Leela Fernandes and Patrick Heller, 'Hegemonic Aspirations: New Middle-class Politics and India's Democracy in Comparative Perspective', *Critical Asian Studies*, Vol. 38, No. 4, 2006, 496–7.

21. Ibid.

22. Asim Sajjad Akhtar, 'The Overdeveloped Alavian Legacy', in Matthew McCartney and S. Akbar Zaidi, eds, *New Perspectives on Pakistan's Political Economy: State, Class and Social Change*, Cambridge University Press, Cambridge, 2019, 57–8.

23. Edward Shils, 'Intellectuals in the Political Development of New States: The Political Significance of Intellectuals in Underdeveloped Countries', *World Politics*, Vol. 12, No. 3, 1959–60, 330–3.

24. Leela Fernandes and Patrick Heller, 'Hegemonic Aspirations', 500.

25. S. Akbar Zaidi, 'The Improbable Future of Democracy in Pakistan', paper prepared for the project State of Democracy in South Asia, Lokniti (Programme of Comparative Democracy), Centre for Study of Developing Societies, 2004, 6; also see Sridharan, 'The Political Economy of the Middle Classes in Liberalizing India', ISAS Working paper, 22 September 2008, 3: Leela Fernandes and Patrick Heller, 'Hegemonic Aspirations', 499–501.

26. Ammara Maqsood, *The New Pakistani Middle Class*, Harvard University Press, 2017, 2–7.

27. Ali Usman Qasmi, 'Making Sense of Naya Pakistan', *The Friday Times*, September 2018, available at https://www.thefridaytimes.com/making -sense-of-naya-pakistan-i/ (accessed 10 September 2020).

28. Ayesha Siddiqa, *Military Inc.: Inside Pakistan's Military Economy*, Oxford University Press, Karachi, 2007, 1–4.

29. Gulf remittances are an important component of Pakistan's foreign exchange reserves. In 2018–19, Pakistan received US$21 billion in remittances from the Gulf. For details see Arhama Siddiqa, 'Pakistan and the Foreign Remittance Sector', *Asia Dialogue*, 23 March 2020, available at https://theasiadialogue.com/2020/03/23/pakistan-and-the-foreign -remittance-sector/ (accessed 2 September 2020).

30. S. Akbar Zaidi, 'The Improbable Future of Democracy in Pakistan', 11.

31. I. A. Rehman, 'A Galloping Religiosity', *Dawn*, 30 July 2020.

32. A. H. Nayyar, 'Dissecting the Single National Curriculum', *Dawn*, 31 July 2020.

33. Shahrukh Rafi, Aasim Sajjad Akhar and Foqia Khan, 'Local Body Elections: Need for Improvement', in Mohammad Waseem, ed., *Electoral Reform in Pakistan*, Friedrich Ebert Stiftung, Islamabad, 2002, 115.

34. Durr-e-Nayab, 'Estimating the Middle Class in Pakistan', Working paper, Pakistan Institute of Development Economics, Islamabad, 2011, https:// www.pide.org.pk/pdf/Working%20Paper/Middle_Class_Nayab.pdf (accessed 9 September 2020).

35. E. Sridharan, 'The Political Economy of the Middle Classes in Liberalizing India', 8.

36. *The Growth of the Middle Class in Pakistan*, National Institute of Social and Economic Research, Karachi, 1971, 23.

37. Ibid.

38. Mohammad Qadeer, 'An Assessment of Pakistan's Urban Policies', *Pakistan Development Review*, Vol. 35, No. 4, Part II, Winter 1996, 444–5.

39. Durr-e-Nayab, 'Estimating the Middle Class in Pakistan', 7.

40. Jawaid Abdul Ghani, 'The Emerging Middle Class in Pakistan: How it Consumes, Earns, and Saves', conference paper, International Conference on Marketing, Institute of Business Administration (IBA), Karachi, 2014, available at http://iba.edu.pk/testibaicm2014/parallel_sessions/ConsumerBehaviorCulture/TheEmergingMiddleClassPakistan. pdf (accessed 12 November 2020).

41. Adnan Adil, 'Our Middle Class', *The News*, 15 June 2017.

42. Umair Javed, 'Pakistan's "Middle-class" Future', *Dawn*, 20 November 2017.

43. For a discussion of the class structure of Pakistan with reference to the modes of production debate, see Taimur Rahman, *The Class Structure of Pakistan*, Oxford University Press, Karachi, 2012.

44. Dror Wahrman, *Imagining the Middle Class*, Cambridge University Press, Cambridge, 1995, 5.

45. Ibid., 11.

46. Ibid., 18.

47. S. Ambirajan, *Classical Political Economy and British Policy in India*, Cambridge University Press, Cambridge, 1971, 15.

48. Philip Woodruff, *The Men Who Ruled India: The Guardians*, Jonathan Cape, London and St Martin's Press, New York, 1954, 76.

49. K. B. Sayeed, 'Political Leadership and Institution Building under Jinnah, Ayub and Bhutto', in Lawrence Ziring, Ralph Braibanti and W. Howard Wriggins, eds, *Pakistan: The Long View*, Duke University Press, 1977, 251–2.

50. Paul Brass, *The Politics of India since Independence*, Cambridge University Press, 1994, 74.

51. Vali Nasr, *The Vanguard of Islamic Revolution: The Jama'at-i-Islami of Pakistan*, University of California Press, 1994, 171.

52. See Muneer Ahmed, *The Civil Servant in Pakistan*, Oxford University Press, Karachi, 1964, 43–4.

53. S. J. Burki, *Pakistan under Bhutto, 1971–1977*, Macmillan Press, London, 1980, 11–35.

54. Rajmohan Gandhi, *Punjab: A History from Aurangzeb to Mountbatten*, Aleph Books, New Delhi, 2013, 132.

55. Najmul Ghani Khan, *Tarikh-e-Awadh* [A History of Awadh, in Urdu], Vol. 2, Nawal Kishore, Lucknow, 1919, 267–8.

56. Elie Kedourie, 'Introduction', in Elie Kedourie, ed., *Nationalism in Asia and Africa*, Meridian Books, New York, 1970, 28–30.

57. Margrit Pernau, *Ashraf into Middle Classes: Muslims in Nineteenth-century Delhi*, Oxford University Press, New Delhi, 2013, 63–5.

58. For a detailed description of the way that British officials of the East India Company travelled in India largely in the footsteps of the Mughal princes, see William Dalrymple, *White Mughals: Love and Betrayal in Eighteenth-century India*, Penguin Books, London, 2003.

59. Margrit Pernau, *Ashraf into Middle Classes*, 95; Eric Stokes, *The English Utilitarians and India*, Oxford University Press, 1959, 89.

60. Margrit Pernau, *Ashraf into Middle Classes*, 103–4; Shamsur Rahman Farooqi, *Kai Chand Thay Sar-e-Aasman* [There Were Many Moons on the Horizon, novel, in Urdu], Scheherazade, 2006, 500–20.

61. Margrit Pernau, *Ashraf into Middle Classes*, 116–19.

62. David Gilmartin, 'Partition, Pakistan and South Asian History: In Search of a Narrative', *Journal of South Asian History*, Vol. 57, No. 4, 1998, 1,073.

63. Ibid., 162.

64. Ibid., 1,075–6.

65. For a good account of *qasbas*, see Mushirul Hasan, *From Pluralism to Separatism: Qasbas in Colonial Awadh*, Oxford University Press, New Delhi, 2004.
66. Margrit Pernau, *Ashraf into Middle Classes*, 190, 196.
67. Ibid., 247.
68. Ibid., 256.
69. Ibid., 264–6.
70. Ibid., 276–7.
71. Ibid., 146–8.
72. Ibid., 358–9.
73. See Tariq Rahman, *From Hindi to Urdu: A Social and Political History*, Oxford University Press, Karachi, 2011, 167–71.
74. Margrit Pernau, *Ashraf into Middle Classes*, 431.
75. Najmul Ghani Khan, *Tarikh-e-Awadh*, 15.
76. See Barbara Metcalf, *Perfecting Women: Maulana Ashraf Ali Thaanvi's Bihishti Zewar*, University of California Press, 2011, 992.
77. Margrit Pernau, *Ashraf into Middle Classes*, 424–5.
78. Mirza Mohammad Hadi Ruswa, *Umraojan Ada* [novel, in Urdu], Sang-e-Meel Publications, Lahore, 2007, 201.
79. Ibid., 201–2.
80. Mohammad Waseem, 'Constitutionalism in Pakistan: The Changing Patterns of Dyarchy', *Diogenes*, Vol. 53, No. 4, 2006, 102–15.
81. Markus Daechsel, *The Politics of Self-Expression: The Urdu Middle-Class Milieu in Mid-Twentieth Century India and Pakistan*, Routledge, April 21, 2009, 13.
82. Ibid, 14.
83. Ibid, 25.
84. Ibid, 52.
85. S. J. Burki, 'The Middle-Class Debate', *The Express Tribune*, 1 April 2012.
86. Marta Bolognani, 'A Community Criminology: Perceptions of Crime and Social Control amongst Bradford Pakistanis', PhD thesis, University of Leeds, 2006, 190.
87. S. J. Burki, discussions with the author at various occasions.
88. Shahid Kardar, 'The Growing Middle Class', *Dawn*, 28 October 2014. For an earlier study, see Mohammad Waseem, *Politics and the State in Pakistan*, National Institute of Historical and Cultural Research, Islamabad, 1994, 290–2.
89. Ibid.
90. Ayesha Siddiqa, 'The Narrative of the Middle Class', *The Express Tribune*, 16 April 2011.
91. Niaz Murtaza, 'Middle-class Ethos', *Dawn*, 24 May 2016.

92. Ammara Maqsood, *The New Pakistani Middle Class*, 9–10.
93. See Vali Nasr, *Forces of Fortune: The Rise of the New Muslim Middle Class and What It Will Mean for Our World*, Simon & Schuster, New York, 2009, 24–6.
94. Ibid., 231.
95. Ibid., 1.
96. Adnan Rafiq, 'New Politics of the Middle Class', in Ishtiaq Ahmad and Adnan Rafiq, eds, *Pakistan's Democratic Transition: Change and Persistence*, Routledge, Abingdon, UK, 2017, 72.
97. Ibid., 73.
98. Ibid., 73–6.
99. Altaf Gauhar, *Ayub Khan: Pakistan's First Military Ruler*, Oxford University Press, Karachi, 1996, 116.
100. For an excellent analysis see Nadeem Farooq Paracha, 'Student politics in Pakistan: A celebration, lament & history', *Dawn*, 3 July 2014.
101. Hassan Javid, 'Patronage, Populism and Protest: Student Politics in Pakistani Punjab', *Samaj*, special issue on student politics in South Asia, available at https://journals.openedition.org/samaj/6497 (accessed 24 August 2020).
102. Marie Lall and Tania Saeed, *Youth and the National Narrative: Education, Terrorism and the Security State in Pakistan*, Bloomsbury, London, 2020, 32, 38–9, 45–6, 50, 55.
103. Ibid., 86.
104. For a detailed discussion, see Charles Kennedy, *Bureaucracy in Pakistan*, Oxford University Press, Karachi, 1987.
105. Osama Siddique, 'The Judicialization of Politics in Pakistan', in Mark Tushnet and Madhav Khosla, eds., *Unstable Constitutionalism: Law and Politics in South Asia*, Cambridge University Press, 2015, 159–91.
106. Sameen A. Mohsin Ali, 'Party Patronage and Merit-based Bureaucratic Reform in Pakistan', *Commonwealth and Comparative Politics*, Vol. 58, No. 2, 2020, 184–201.
107 See Imran Khan, *Pakistan: A Personal History*, Bantam Press, London, 2011.
108. Yogendra Yadav, 'Electoral Reforms: Beyond Middle-class Fantasies', *Seminar* 440: The Election Carnival, April 1996, 59.
109. Myron Weiner, *State Politics in India*, Princeton University Press, 2015, 39.
110. See Fred M. Hayward et al., *Elections in Independent Africa*, Westview Press, Boulder, CO, 1987, 276.
111. Yogendra Yadav, 'Electoral Reforms', 60.
112. Ibid.
113. Ibid.

114. Myron Weiner and Mary Fainsod Katzenstein, *Indian Preferential Politics: Migrants, the Middle Class, and Ethnic Equality*, University of Chicago Press, 1982, 131.

115. Asma Barlas, *Democracy, Nationalism and Communalism: The Colonial Legacy in South Asia*, Westview Press, Boulder, CO, 1995, 143.

116. Edward I. Steinhart, *Conflict and Collaboration*, Princeton University Press, 2019, 260.

117. David Gilmartin, *Empire and Islam: Punjab and the Making of Pakistan*, London, I. B. Tauris, 1998, 115–17.

118. See A. L. P. Tucker, *Sir Robert G. Sandeman: K.C.S.I., Peaceful Conqueror of Baluchistan*, Society for Promoting Christian Knowledge, London, and Macmillan, New York, 1921.

119. Giovanni Sartori, *Parties and Party System: A Framework for Analysis*, Cambridge University Press, New York, 1976, 125.

120. Ibid., 171, 173, 273, 240.

121. Steve Patten, 'The Evolution of the Canadian Party System', in Alain-G. Gagnon and A. Brian Tanguay, eds, *Canadian Parties in Transition*, Broadview Press, Peterborough, Canada, 2007, 55–81.

122. See Milan Vaishnav and Jamie Hinston, 'The Dawn of India's Fourth Party System', Carnegie Endowment for International Peace, 2019, available at https://carnegieendowment.org/files/201909-VaishnavHintson.pdf (accessed 1 June 2020).

123. Ibid., 3–8.

124. Ibid., 12–13.

125. See Mariam Mufti, Sahar Shafqat and Niloufer Siddiqui, eds, *Pakistan's Political Parties*.

126. Mariam Mufti, 'What Do We Know about Hybrid Regimes after Two Decades of Scholarship', *Politics and Governance*, Vol. 6, No. 2, 2018, 112–19.

127. Mohammad Waseem, 'The Operational Dynamics of Political Parties in Pakistan', in Christophe Jaffrelot, ed., *Pakistan at the Crossroads: Domestic Dynamics and External Pressures*, Columbia University Press, 2016, 69–75.

128. Robert Rohrschneider, 'Mobilizing Versus Chasing: How Do Parties Target Voters in Election Campaigns?', *Electoral Studies*, Vol. 21, No. 3, 2002, 379–82.

129. Mohammad Waseem and Mariam Mufti, *Political Parties in Pakistan: Organization and Power*, Lahore University of Management Sciences, Lahore, 2013.

130. See Ergun Ozbudun, 'Institutionalizing Competitive Elections in Developing Societies', in Myron Weiner and Ergun Ozbudun, eds, *Competitive Elections in Developing Countries*, Duke University Press, 1987, 398.

131. The British High Commission, Letter from W. L. Allison to MVO, Dated 8 August 1962, File No. DO 134/29 F, British Library.
132. Hamza Alavi, 'The State in Post-colonial Societies, 59–81.
133. Christophe Jaffrelot, 'The Indian–Pakistani Divide: Why India is Democratic and Pakistan Is Not', *Foreign Affairs*, Vol. 90, No. 2, March/April 2011, 259–60. Also see Maya Chadda, *Building Democracy in South Asia: India, Nepal, Pakistan*, Lynne Rienner Publishers, Boulder, CO, 2002.
134. The British High Commission, Opdom 28, Dated 7 April 1948, File No. DO 142/423, British Library.
135. Rajni Kothari, 'The "Congress System" in India', *Asian Survey*, Vol. 14, No. 2, 1964, 1,161–2.
136. Zahid Hussain, 'Dynastic Politics', *Dawn*, 24 July 2012.
137. The candidature of Shahbaz Sharif and Nawaz Sharif was rejected by the Lahore High Court via ex parte proceedings in 2009. The court had contested the terms of the presidential pardon granted to them. This was later overturned by the Supreme Court. See *The News*, 27 May 2009.
138. See *Dawn,* 24 May 2020. Also see *Dawn*, 4 November 2019.
139. See, Hassan Javaid and Mariam Mufti, 'Candidate–Party Linkages in Pakistan: Why Do Candidates Stick with Losing Parties', in Mariam Mufti, Sahar Shafqat and Niloufer Siddiqui, eds, *Pakistan's Political Parties*, 144–62.
140. See Bruce Bueno de Mesquita et al., *The Logic of Political Survival*, MIT Press, Cambridge, MA, 2003.
141. Doug McAdam, 'What Are They Shouting About?', in Doug McAdam, Sidney Tarrow and Charles Tilly, eds, *Dynamics of Contention*, Cambridge University Press, 2001, 7.
142. Tabinda M. Khan, 'Pakistan Tehreek-e-Insaf: From a Movement to a Catch-all Party', in Mariam Mufti, Sahar Shafqat and Niloufer Siddiqui, eds, *Pakistan's Political Parties*, 60–75.
143. Vali Nasr, *The Vanguard of the Islamic Revolution*, 33–4.
144. Fred M. Hayward, 'Introduction', in Fred M. Hayward, ed, *Elections in Independent Africa*, Westview Press, Boulder, CO, 1987, 14.
145. Kausar Parveen, *The Politics of Pakistan: The Role of the Opposition, 1947–1958*, Oxford University Press, Karachi, 2013, 132.
146. M. Rafique Afzal, *Political Parties in Pakistan, 1947–1958*, Vol. 1, National Institute of Historical and Cultural Research, Islamabad, 1998, 335–8.
147. Ibid., 2.
148. See Tahir Naqvi, 'What Remains of the Muttahida Quomi Movement?', in Mariam Mufti, Sahar Shafqat and Niloufer Siddiqui, eds, *Pakistan's Political Parties*, 81–3.
149. *Dawn*, 24 August 2016; *Dawn*, 27 August 2016.

150. See Free and Fair Election Network (FAFEN), 'A Tribute to Women Legislators: National Assembly and Senate of Pakistan, 2017–18', FAFEN, Islamabad, 2018, available at https://fafen.org/wp-content/uploads/2018/03/FAFEN-Women-Legislators-Performance-Report-2017-18.pdf (accessed 6 August 2020).

151. Nicolas Martin, 'The Dark Side of Patronage in the Pakistani Punjab', in Anastasia Piliavsky, ed., *Patronage as Politics in South Asia*, Cambridge University Press, 2014, 327–8.

152. Mohammad Waseem, 'Operational Dynamics of Political Parties', 80–2.

153. *The Nation*, 29 January 2014.

154. Mohammad Waseem, 'Operational Dynamics of Political Parties', 81.

155. *The News*, 6 May 2013.

156. *Dawn*, 11 November 2013.

157. *The News*, 2 January 2015.

158. *Dawn*, 23 March 2015.

159. Letter from M. J. Lyall Grant on student politics, Dated 11 July 1982, File No. FCO 37/2922, British National Archives London.

160. Ayesha Siddiqa, 'Jihadism in Pakistan: The Expanding Frontier', *Journal of International Affairs*, Vol. 63, No. 1, 2009, 60–1.

161. *The Express Tribune*, 28 February 2014.

162. Mohammad Waseem, 'Operational Dynamics of Political Parties', 82.

163. *Dawn*, editorial, 'Height of Denial', 8 May 2013.

164. *The News*, 12 January 2014.

165. *The News*, 20 May 2014.

166. For a detailed study of the evolving nature of the JUI's politics, see Sayyid A. S. Pirzada, *The Politics of the Jamiat Ulema-i-Islam Pakistan*, Oxford University Press, 2000.

167. Saeed Shafqat, 'From Official Islam to Islamism: The Rise of Dawat-ul-Irshad and Lashkar-e-Taiba', in Christophe Jaffrelot, ed., *Pakistan: Nationalism without a Nation?*, 132.

168. M. S. Lodhi, Karachi Tour Report, 23–29 May 1982, Dated 3 June 1982, File No. FCO 37/2922, The British National Archive, London.

169. Ibid.

170. The British High Commission, Despatch from J. D. Copleston, Dated 29 April 1982, File No. FCO 37/2922, The British National Archives, London.

171. The British High Commission, Letter from M. J. Lyall Grant, Dated 6 December 1983, File No. FCO 37/3331, The British National Archives, London.

172. The British High Commission, Letter from M.J. Lyall Grant, Dated 1 August 1983, File No. FCO 37/3330, The British National Archives, London.

173. Mohammad Waseem, *Pakistan Under Martial Law 1977–1985*, Vanguard Books, Lahore, 1987, 30–34.

174. The British High Commission, Letter from M. J. Lyall Grant, Dated 6 December 1983, File No. FCO 37/3331, The British National Archives, London.

175. Ashfaq Yusufzai, 'A Party under Siege', *Dawn*, 22 April 2013.

176. Gareth Nellis and Niloufer Siddiqui, 'Secular Party Rule and Religious Violence in Pakistan', *American Political Science Review*, Vol. 112, No. 1, 2007, 1.

177. Ibid, 4.

178. *The News*, 14 May 2013.

179. *The News*, 17 June 2014.

180. *The News*, 24 November 2014.

181. Mohammad Waseem, 'Operational Dynamics of Political Parties', 82.

182. *The News*, 18 June 2013.

183. Ibid, 74–75.

184. Mohammad Waseem, 'Operational Dynamics of Political Parties', 64, 66.

185. Charles H. Franklin and John E. Jackson, 'The Dynamics of Party Identification', *The American Political Science Review*, Vol. 77, No. 4, 1983, 962.

186. The British High Commission, Letter No. 147/60/1, Dated 30 July 1957, File Number, 298/6/8, British National Archives, London.

187. The British High Commission, Despatch No. 20, Dated 14 April 1958, File No. 321/2, British National Archives, London.

188. The British High Commission, Opdom No. 26, Dated 9 April 1948, File No. 142/423, British Library.

189. The Conduct of General Elections Order, 2002, Chief Executive's Order no. 7 of 2002, February 27, 2002, 8A

190. Cynthia Bottern, 'Striking at the Heart of Democracy: Leadership Education Requirements in Musharraf's Constitutional Order', conference paper, New Perspectives on Pakistan: Contexts, Realities, and Visions for the Future, School of International and Public Affairs (SIPA), Columbia University, April 2003, 6.

191. S. Akbar Zaidi, 'Elected Representatives in Pakistan: Socio-Economic Background and Awareness of Issues', *Economic and Political Weekly*, Vol. 39, No. 45, 2004, 4,935–41.

192. Ibid., 4,938–9.

193. Robert Eric Frykenberg, 'Introduction', in Robert Eric Frykenberg, ed., *Land Control and Social Structure in Indian History*, Manohar, New Delhi, 1979, 7.

194. See the Annual Reports of the Human Rights Commission of Pakistan throughout the period 2010–20 and beyond.

195. Maya Chadda, *Building Democracy in South Asia*, 8.

196. Mohammad Waseem, 'Political Parties in an Establishmentarian Democracy', in Mariam Mufti, Sahar Shafqat and Niloufer Siddiqui, eds, *Pakistan's Political Parties*, 273.

197. The British High Commission, File No. 581, D 1147, 15 June 1966, British National Archives, London.

198. The British High Commission, Letter from O. G. Forster, Dated 24 September 1965, File No. DO 196/320, British Library.

199. Letter from W. K. K. White, Dated 8 June 1979, File No. FCO 37/2196, British National Archives, London.

200. Ibid.

201. The British High Commission's Letter to Lord Carrington, File No. FCO 37/2196, Dated 9 May 1979, British National Archives, London.

202. Rafi Raza, *Zulfikar Ali Bhutto and Pakistan, 1967–1977*, Oxford University Press, Karachi, 1997, 383.

203. The British High Commission, Letter from A. P. Fabian, Dated 11 August 1980, File No. FCO 37/2358, British National Archives, London.

204. Mohammad Waseem, 'Operational Dynamics of Political Parties', 63.

205. *The Nation*, 7 January 2012.

206. Mohammad Waseem, 'Operational Dynamics of Political Parties', 64.

207. Robert Michels, 'Iron Law of Oligarchy', in Martin Slattery, ed., *Key Ideas in Sociology*, Nelson Thornes, Oxford, 2003, 52–5.

208. Pakistan Institute of Legislative Development and Democracy (PILDAT), *Assessment of the Quality of General Election 2018*, Lahore, September 2018, 6.

209. Syed Wiqar Ali Shah, 'Pakistan People's Party', in Subrata Mitra, et al., eds, *Political Parties in South Asia*, Frederick A. Praeger, London, 2004, 3.

210. Hasan Askari Rizvi, 'Political Parties and Fragmented Democracy in Pakistan,' in Heinrich Boll Foundation, ed., *Pakistan: Reality, Denial and the Complexity of its State*, Schriften zur Demokratie series, Vol. 16, Henrich Boll Stiftung, Berlin, 2010, 6.

211. Ernesto Calvo and Juan Manuel Abal Medina, 'Institutional Gamblers: Majoritarian Representation, Electoral Uncertainty, and the Coalitional Costs of Mexico's Hybrid Electoral System', *Electoral Studies*, Vol. 21, No. 3, 2002, 469–71.

212. M. Rafique Afzal, *Political Parties in Pakistan, 1958–1969*, Vol. II, National Institute of Historical and Cultural Research, Quaid-i-Azam University, 2000, 174, 212–13.

213. For an analysis of the different patterns of electoral alliances, see Mohammad Waseem, *Democratization in Pakistan: A Study of the 2002 Elections*, Oxford University Press, Karachi, 2006, 137–9.

214. Anastasia Piliavsky, ed., *Patronage as Politics in South Asia*, Cambridge University Press, 2014, 3.

215. Ibid., 4–5.
216. David Gilmartin, 'The Paradox of Patronage and People's Sovereignty', in Anastasia Piliavsky, ed., *Patronage as Politics in South Asia*, 125.
217. Ibid., 130–1.
218. Ibid., 139.
219. Shandana Khan Mohmand, *Crafty Oligarchs, Savvy Voters: Democracy Under Inequality in Rural Pakistan*, Cambridge University Press, 2019, 120–25.
220. Ibid, 155–58.
221. Nicolas Martin, 'The Dark Side of Patronage in the Pakistani Punjab', in Anastasia Piliavsky, ed., *Patronage as Politics in South Asia*, 327.
222. Ibid., 327–8.
223. Mohammad Waseem, 'Political Parties in an Establishmentarian Democracy', 273.
224. Mohammad Waseem, 'Operational Dynamics of Political Parties', 65.
225. PILDAT and Canadian High Commission, 'Election 2007: Challenges and Prospects with Special Focus on NWFP and Balochistan', PILDAT and Canadian High Commission, Islamabad, 2007.
226. Naveed Siddiqui and Haseeb Bhatti, 'Gen. Bajwa to Stay on for 6 More Months: SC', *Dawn*, 28 November 2019.
227. The social media parodied Faiz Ahmed Faiz's epic song: 'Hum daikhen ge' (We look forward to the bright morning after dark night) into 'Hum laitein gay' (We will serve as a doormat).
228. Sarah Birch, 'Electoral Management Bodies and Electoral Integrity: Evidence from Eastern Europe and the Former Soviet Union', Working paper No. 2, University of Essex Project on Electoral Malpractice in New and Semi-Democracies, 2008, 3.
229. M. Mahfuzul Huq, *Electoral Problems in Pakistan*, Asiatic Society of Pakistan Publication, 1966, 65.
230. The British High Commission, Lahore Report no. 8, Dated 8 May 1957, File No. CON 298/ 6/8, British Library.
231. Mohammad Waseem, *Politics and the State in Pakistan*, National Institute of Historical and Cultural Research, Islamabad, 146–8.
232. Ministry of Law, Government of Pakistan, 'Report of the Franchise Commission 1963', 1964, 9.
233. Yogendra Yadav, 'Electoral Reforms', 60.
234. Human Rights Commission of Pakistan (HRCP), 'Attempts to Maneuver Polls Unacceptable', 16 July 2018, available at http://hrcp–web.org/hrcpweb/attempts–to–maneuver–polls–unacceptable–hrcp/ (accessed 15 September 2020). Also see *Financial Times*, 'Pakistan Heads for Dirtiest Elections in Years', 18 July 2018, available at https://www.ft.com/content/4572d7f4-89c1-11e8-bf9e-8771d5404543 (accessed 10 July 2020).

235. Comments by Sir Cyril Pickard on 1970 Elections in Pakistan, Dated 22 December 1970, File No. FCO 37/684, The British High Commission, British National Archives, London.

236. Mohammad Waseem, 'Operational Dynamics of Political Parties', 67.

237. Richard Rose, 'Electoral Systems: A Question of Degree or of Principle?' in Arend Lijphart and Bernard Grofman, eds, *Choosing an Electoral System: Issues and Alternatives*, Frederick A. Praeger, 1984, 73.

238. Ibid.

239. Centre for Civic Education, 'Country Report Based on Research and Dialogue with Political Parties', Islamabad, 2006, 4.

240. The term for these 'donors' for the PTI in the 2018 elections was ATM. Both Jahangir Tareen and Aleem Khan were satirically called the PTI's ATMs.

241. *Dawn*, 15 July 2015.

242. Kenneth Benoit, 'The Endogeneity Problem in Electoral Studies: A Critical Re-examination of Duverger's Mechanical Effect', *Elsevier Science (Electoral Studies)*, Vol. 21, No. 1, 2002, 35.

243. Myron Weiner, 'Empirical Democratic Theory', in Myron Weiner and Ergun Ozbudun, eds, *Competitive Elections in Developing Countries*, 5.

244. *Dawn*, 11 June 2013.

245. *Dawn*, 2 December 2018.

246. Maurice Duverger, 'What Is the Best Electoral System', in Arend Lijphart and Bernard Grofman, *Choosing an Electoral System: Issues and Alternatives*, Frederick A. Praeger, 1984, 31–5.

247. Sarah Birch, 'Single-member District Electoral Systems and Democratic Transition', *Electoral Studies*, Vol. 24, No. 2, 2005, 284, 296.

248. *Pakistan Today*, 21 May 2013; 'How PML-N Won 2013 Elections', *The News*, 8 August 2014.

249. Aqil Shah, 'Voting under Military Tutelage', *Journal of Democracy*, Vol. 30, No. 1, 2019, 130; Kriti M. Shah and Sushant Sareen, 'Pakistan General Elections 2018: Analysis of Results and Implications', Observer Research Foundation (ORF), December 2018, 5.

250. *Dawn*, editorial, 'Undemocratic Poll', 13 January 2018.

251. R. J. Johnson, C. J. Pattie and J. G. Allsopp, *A Nation Dividing? The Electoral Map of Great Britain, 1979–1987*, Longman, London, 1988, 55.

252. Theodore P. Wright, 'Biradaris in Punjab Elections', *Journal of Political Science*, Vol. 14, No. 2, 1991, 82.

253. Cees Van Der Eijk, 'Design Issues in Electoral Research: Taking Care of (Core) Business', *Electoral Studies*, Vol. 21, No. 2, 2002, 8.

254. Norman Nie, Sidney Verba and John R. Petrocik, *The Changing American Voter*, Harvard University Press, 1976, 137, 158.

255. Hameed Haroon, 'A Dirty War on the Freedom of Press in Pakistan', *Washington Post*, 11 July 2018.

256. *Dawn,* 9 May 2017. Only 8 out of 23 party accounts had been declared to the ECP.

257. 'PTI Delay Funding Case: ECP', *Dawn*, 8 February 2018.

258. *Dawn*, 10 October 2019.

259. *Dawn*, 24 October 2019.

260. Ibid.

261. *Dawn*, 24 November 2019.

262. Ayesha Siddiqa, 'Of Kings, Queens, and Pawns: Civil–Military Relations in Pakistan', in Bilal Zahoor and Raza Rumi, eds, *Rethinking Pakistan: A 21ˢᵗ Century Perspective*, Folio Books, Lahore, 2019, 227.

263. Ali Cheema and Asad Liaqat, 'Elections 2018: The Battle of Narratives', *Herald*, July 2018.

264. European Union Election Observation Mission (EUEOM), 'Final Report: Islamic Republic of Pakistan General Elections', 25 July 2018, 5 available at http://www.eods.eu/library/PR%20PAKISTAN%20 10.07.2013_en.pdf (accessed 26 September 2020).

265. Ibid.

266. Ibid., 10.

267. *Dawn*, 16 April 2018.

268. Shashank Bengali and Aoun Sahi, 'As Pakistan Prepares for Elections, Its Powerful Military Appears to Be Meddling', *Los Angeles Times*, 20 July 2018 available at https://www.latimes.com/world/asia/la-fg-pakistan-elections-20180720-story.html (accessed 20 August 2020).

269. C. Christine Fair, 'Pakistan's Sham Election: How the Army Chose Imran Khan', *Foreign Affairs*, 2018, available at http://www.christine-fair.net/pubs/ShamElections.pdf (accessed 8 September 2020).

270. PILDAT, 'General Election 2018: Comparative Analysis of Election Manifestos of Major Political Parties in Pakistan', August 2018, 14, available at https://pildat.org/wp-content/uploads/2018/09/ComparativeC-MRAnalysisofElectionManifestoes.pdf? (accessed 20 September 2020).

271. *The Guardian*, editorial, 'The Guardian View on Pakistan's Elections: Imran Khan's Real Test is Coming', 26 July 2018.

272. Asif Shahzad, 'Pakistan Army Pushed Political Role for Militant-linked Groups', *Reuters*, 16 September 2016.

273. EUEOM, Final Report, 11.

274. Ibid., 12.

275. Ibid.

276. Ibid., 17.

277. FAFEN, 'Election Observation Report: 1.67 Million Ballots Excluded from the Count', Islamabad, 3 August 2018, 1.

278. Ibid., 2.
279. FAFEN, 'Preliminary Election Observation Report', Islamabad, 27 July 2018, 8.
280. Ibid., 13.
281. Roshaaneh Zafar, 'Beyond Women Voter Turnout in Elections,' *The Express Tribune*, 11 September 2018.
282. Hanif Samoon, 'Thari Women Set Example for All with Nearly 73% Turnout in 2018 Elections', *Dawn*, 29 July 2018, https://www.dawn.com/news/1423671.
283. FAFEN, 'Election Observation Report: Voter Turnout in GE–2018', 12 August 2018, 6.
284. *Pakistan Today*, 28 July 2018.
285. Mohammad Waseem and Mariam Mufti, *Political Parties in Pakistan*, 31.
286. Umair Javed, 'How Candidates Have Cracked the Code for Winning Elections', *Herald*, August 2018.
287. Ibid.
288. UNDP, 'Summary: Pakistan National Human Development Report – Unleashing the Potential of a Young Pakistan', 2017, 1.
289. PILDAT, 'Assessment of the Quality of Democracy in Pakistan 2017', July 2018, 11.
290. Mumtaz Alvi, 'Daska Election Declared Void', *The News*, 26 February 2021.
291. URL: https://www.focus-economics.com/countries/pakistan
292. These observations draw on S. Akbar Zaidi, 'Destroying Livelihoods', *Dawn*, 11 February 2020.
293. Ibid.
294. Transparency International, *Corruption Perception Index (CPI) Report*, 2020, 3.
295. These observations draw on Myra Ahmed, 'What Is the Economic Impact of the Pakistani Diaspora', *Dawn*, 19 December 2020.
296. For a variety of perspectives from expatriates, see Virinder S. Kalra, ed., *Pakistani Diasporas: Culture, Conflict, and Change*, Oxford University Press, Karachi, 2009, and Avtar Brah, ed., *Cartographies of Diaspora: Contesting Identities*, Routledge, 2003.
297. Ibid.

4. AN ESTABLISHMENTARIAN DEMOCRACY

1. Stephen Levitsky and Lucian Way, 'The Rise of Competitive Authoritarianism', *Journal of Democracy*, Vol. 13, No. 2, 2002, 55–6.
2. Tisaranee Gunasekara, 'A Garrison State', *Himal Southasian*, 13 October 2014, available at https://www.himalmag.com/garrison-state/ (accessed 16 August 2020).

3. See Smruti S. Pattanaik, 'Re-emergence of the Military and the Future of Democracy in Bangladesh', *Strategic Analysis*, Vol. 32, No. 6, 2008, 975–95.

4. Philip Oldenburg, *India, Pakistan, and Democracy: Solving the Puzzle of Divergent Paths*, Routledge, Abingdon, UK, 2010, 1.

5. Sumit Ganguly and C. Christine Fair, 'The Structural Origins of Authoritarianism in Pakistan', *Commonwealth & Comparative Politics*, Vol. 51, No. 1, 2013, 122.

6. Maya Tudor, *The Promise of Power: The Origins of Democracy in India and Autocracy in Pakistan*, Cambridge University Press, 2013, 4, 11–13; Christophe Jaffrelot, 'India and Pakistan: Interpreting the Divergence of Two Political Trajectories', *Cambridge Review of International Affairs*, Vol. 15, No. 2, 2002, 252; Maya Chadda, *Building Democracy in South Asia: India, Nepal, Pakistan*, Lynne Rienner Publishers, Boulder, CO, 2000, 2–3, 68, 70.

7. Maya Chadda, *Building Democracy in South Asia*, 14.

8. Ibid., 12–13.

9. Ibid., 22–3.

10. Ibid., 35.

11. Ibid., 6, 17.

12. Ibid., 28.

13. See K. B. Sayeed, *The Political System of Pakistan*, Houghton Mifflin, Boston, MA, 1967; G. W. Choudhury, *Constitutional Development in Pakistan*, Ideal Book House, Karachi, 1995; Hamza Alavi, 'The State in Postcolonial Societies: Pakistan and Bangladesh', *New Left Review*, Vol. 74, No. 1, 1972; Mohammad Waseem, *Politics and the State in Pakistan*, National Institute of Historical and Cultural Research, Islamabad, 1994.

14. Mohammad Waseem, 'Democracy and Pluralism in Pakistan', in John Rex and Gurharpal Singh, eds, *Governing Multicultural Societies*, Ashgate, Basingstoke, UK, 2004, 188.

15. Mohammad Waseem, *Politics and the State in Pakistan*, 51–4; Christophe Jaffrelot, 'India and Pakistan', 253–4.

16. Munir Ahmed, *The Civil Servant in Pakistan*, Oxford University Press, Karachi, 1964, 43–4.

17. Christophe Jaffrelot, 'India and Pakistan', 257.

18. Anil Seal, *The Emergence of Indian Nationalism: Competition and Collaboration in the Later Nineteenth Century*, Cambridge University Press, 1971, 298–340.

19. See Rajni Kothari, *State against Democracy: In Search of Humane Governance*, Ajanta Publications, New Delhi, 1988.

20. K. B. Sayeed, 'Political Leadership and Institution-building under Jinnah, Ayub and Bhutto', in Lawrence Ziring, Ralph Braibanti and Howard Wriggins, eds, *Pakistan: The Long View*, Duke University Press, Durham, NC, 1977, 251–2.

21. Yogendra Yadav, 'Politics', in Marshall Bouton and Philip Oldenburg, eds, *India Briefing: A Transformative Fifty Years*, M. E. Sharpe, Armonk, NY, 1999, 130.

22. Philip Oldenburg, *India, Pakistan, and Democracy*, 27.

23. Hamza Alavi, 'Authoritarianism and Legitimation of State Power in Pakistan', in Subrata Kumar Mitra, ed., *The Post-colonial State in Asia: Dialectics of Politics and Culture*, Sang-e-Meel Publications, Lahore, 1998, 32.

24. Ayesha Jalal, *Democracy and Authoritarianism in South Asia: A Comparative and Historical Perspective*, Sang-e-Meel Publications, Lahore, 1995, 29–30.

25. Ibid., 28, 40.

26. Ibid., 249, 256.

27. Ibid., 4.

28. Christophe Jaffrelot, 'India and Pakistan', 261; Philip Oldenburg, *India, Pakistan, and Democracy*, 225.

29. Christophe Jaffrelot, 'India and Pakistan', 263.

30. Maya Chadda, *Building Democracy in South Asia*, 8–9.

31. Ibid., 223–4.

32. Hamza Alavi, 'Authoritarianism and Legitimation of State Power in Pakistan', 42.

33. Imran Ali, *The Punjab under Imperialism: 1885–1947*, Oxford University Press, New Delhi, 1989, 62.

34. Ibid., 84, 91.

35. See Hassan Javaid, 'Class, Power and Patronage: The Landed Elite and Politics in Pakistan', PhD thesis, London School of Economics, 2012, available at http://etheses.lse.ac.uk/468/

36. E. H. Slade, *Census of Pakistan, 1951*, Government of Pakistan, 1951, 30.

37. For 'illiberal hybrid regime', see Katharine Adeney, 'How to Understand Pakistan's Hybrid Regime: The Importance of a Multidimensional Continuum', *Democratization*, Vol. 24, No. 1, 2017, 119–37.

38. See Samuel Huntington, *The Third Wave: Democratization in the Late Twentieth Century*, University of Oklahoma Press, 1991.

39. See Fareed Zakaria, *The Future of Freedom: Illiberal Democracy at Home and Abroad*, Norton, NY, 2004.

40. For a critique of the Freedom House Index, see Mohammad Waseem, 'Functioning of Democracy in Pakistan', in Zoya Hassan, ed., *Democracy in Muslim Societies: The Asian Experience*, Sage, London and Thousand Oaks, CA, 2007, 177–218.

41. For the two schools of thought relating to rule of law, see David Gilmartin, 'The Strange Career of the Rule of Law in Punjab', *Pakistan Vision*, Vol. 10, No. 2, 2009, 1–21.

42. For a detailed study see Partha Ghosh, *BJP and the Evolution of Hindu Nationalism: From Periphery to Center*, Manohar, New Delhi, 1999.

43. See, for example, V. S. Naipaul, *India: A Wounded Civilization*, Knopf, NY, 1977.

44. Faisal Devji, *Muslim Zion: Pakistan as a Political Idea*, Hurst & Co., London, 2013, 97.

45. *Dawn*, 6 May 2018.

46. Owen Jones, *The Establishment: And How They Get Away with It*, Allen Lane, London, 2014, 85–6, 296.

47. Ibid., 86.

48. Ibid., 3.

49. Ibid., 12.

50. Ibid., 293.

51. Ibid., 12, 295.

52. Ibid., 17.

53. Ibid., 27, 32.

54. Despatch from Sir Cyril Pickard, Dated 21 May 1971, File No. FCO 37/870, British Archives London.

55. Mohammad Waseem, 'Constitutionalism in Pakistan: The Changing Patterns of Dyarchy', *Diogenes*, Vol. 53, No. 4, 2006, 111.

56. 'Faizabad Sit-in Ends as Army Brokers Deal', *Dawn*, 28 November 2017.

57. Abdul Majid Abid, 'The General We Deserved', *The Nation*, 31 August 2015, available at https://nation.com.pk/31-Aug-2015/the-general-we-deserved (accessed 15 September 2020).

58. For details of this incident, see 'General (retd.) Zaheerul Islam: The Shadow Warrior', *Herald*, 6 October 2015, available at http://herald.dawn.com/news/1153259 (accessed 15 September 2020).

59. The British High Commission, Letter from O. G. Forster, Dated 1 March 1982, File No. FCO 37/2922, British National Archives London.

60. Wendy McElroy, 'Military Metaphysics: A Military Definition of Reality', *The Bell*, 5 February 2015, available at https://www.thedailybell.com/all-articles/editorials/wendy-mcelroy-military-metaphysics-a-military-definition-of-reality/ (accessed 16 July 2020).

61. For discussion see Mehtab Ali Shah, *The Foreign Policy of Pakistan: Ethnic Impacts on Diplomacy, 1971–1994*, I. B. Tauris, 1997.

62. C. Wright Mills, *The Power Elite*, Oxford University Press, New York, 1956, 205–8.

63. Lt. Col. Abdulqadir, *Be-tegh-Sipahi: Jang 71 aur Qaid ki Rudad* [Soldier Fighting without Sword: The 1971 War and the Story of Imprisonment],

Ilm-o-Irfan Publishers, Lahore, 2011, 20, as quoted by Manuel Uebersax, 'The Other Battlefield: Construction and Representation of the Pakistani Military "Self" in the Field of Military Autobiographical Narrative Production', PhD thesis, University of Bern, 2017, 97, https://boristheses.unibe.ch/1253/.

64. Ibid., 103–4.

65. Ibid., 150–1.

66. Maria Rashid, *Dying to Serve: Militarism, Affect and the Politics of Sacrifice in the Pakistan Army*, Stanford University Press, 2020, 29–33.

67. 'The Bajwa Doctrine', *Dawn*, 29 March 2018.

68. Maj. Gen. Akbar Khan, *Raiders in Kashmir*, National Book Foundation, Islamabad, 1975, 10, 171.

69. Maj. Gen. Sher Ali Pataudi, *Soldering and Politics in India and Pakistan*, Syed Mobin Mahmud & Co., Lahore, 1988, iii–iv, 342.

70. Maj. Gen. Hakeem Arshad Qureshi, *The 1971 Indo–Pak War: A Soldier's Narrative*, Oxford University Press, Karachi, 2002, 26–7.

71. Ikram Sehgal, *Escape from Oblivion: The Story of a Pakistani Prisoner of War in India*, Oxford University Press, Karachi, 2012, 1.

72. General K. M. Arif, *Working with Zia: Pakistan's Power Politics, 1977–1988*, Oxford University Press, 1995, 13.

73. Siddiq Salik, *State and Politics: A Case Study of Pakistan*, Al-Faisal Nashran, Lahore, 1997, 20.

74. Ata Rabbani, *I was the Quaid's ADC*, Oxford University Press, 1996, 1.

75. Ibid., 3.

76. Ibid., 37.

77. Pervez Musharraf, *In the Line of Fire: A Memoir*, Simon & Schuster, New York, 2006, 71.

78. Ibid., 84.

79. Admiral Iftikhar A. Sirohey, *Truth Never Lies*, Jang Publishers, Lahore, 1995.

80. Maj.-Gen. Syed Wajahat Hussain, *Memoirs of a Soldier 1947: Before, During, After*, Ferozsons Ltd, Lahore, 2010, 284.

81. Ibid., 285.

82. Brigadier Z. A. Khan, *The Way It Was*, Ikram ul-Majeed Sehgal (pvt) Ltd, 1998, 365.

83. Major Aftab Ahmed, *General! I Accuse You*, Jumhoori Publications, Lahore, 2004, 152.

84. Manuel Uebersax, 'The Other Battlefield', 9.

85. Ibid., 10. For a detailed discussion, see Pierre Bourdieu, *Distinction: A Social Critique of the Judgement of the Taste*, Harvard University Press, 1984.

86. Christine Fair, *Fighting to the End: The Pakistan Army's Way of War*, Oxford University Press, 2014, 35.

87. Aqil Shah, 'Institutions Matter: The State, the Military and the Social Class', in Matthew McCartney and S. Akbar Zaidi, eds, *New Perspectives on Pakistan's Political Economy: State, Class and Social Change*, Cambridge University Press, Cambridge, 2019, 76.

88. Maria Rashid, *Dying to Serve*, 10–12.

89. Ibid., 24.

90. Ibid., 36, 115.

91. Ibid., 182.

92. Manuel Uebersax, 'The Other Battlefield'.

93. Ibid., 39.

94. As quoted in Manuel Uebersax, 'The Other Battlefield', 44.

95. Shahid Hamid's autobiography, Manuel Uebersax 'The Other Battlefield', 45.

96. Ibid., 84.

97. General Shahid Hamid's account of the perceived Hindu–British collusion after 1857, Manuel Uebersax, 'The Other Battlefield', 83.

98. Ibid., 79.

99. Ibid., 80.

100. General Gul Hasan, Manuel Uebersax, 'The Other Battlefield', 87.

101. Ibid., 88.

102. Ibid., 92.

103. Siddiq Salik, quoted in Manuel Uebersax, 'The Other Battlefield', 106.

104. Admiral Sirohey, quoted in Manuel Uebersax, 'The Other Battlefield', 120.

105. Ibid., 122

106. Ibid., 125.

107. Ibid.

108. Sajjad Haider's *Flight of the Falcon*, Manuel Uebersax, 'The Other Battlefield', 139. A local expression, 'played on sand' means something like making a castle on shifting sands, i.e. on a slippery ground.

109. Maria Rashid, *Dying to Serve*, 96.

110. Cyril Almeida, 'Retaking Bomb Project', *Dawn,* 23 April 2008.

111. Stephen Cohen, *The Idea of Pakistan*, Brookings Institution Press, Washington, DC, 2004, 98.

112. Aqil Shah, *The Army and Democracy: Military Politics in Pakistan*, Harvard University Press, 2014, 165.

113. Mohammad Ayoob, 'The Security Predicament of the Third World State: Reflections on State-making in a Comparative Perspective', in Brian L. Job, ed., *The Insecurity Dilemma: National Security of Third World States*, Lynne Rienner Publishers, Boulder, CO, 1992, 65.

114. Barry Buzan, 'Third World Regional Security in Structural and Historical Perspective', in Brian L. Job, ed., *The Insecurity Dilemma*, 174.

115. Veena Kukreja, *Civil–Military Relations in South Asia: Pakistan, Bangladesh and India*, Sage, London and Thousand Oaks, CA, 1991, 231.

116. Ibid., 80.

117. Ibid., 99–100.

118. Roedad Khan, *A Dream Gone Sour*, Oxford University Press, Karachi, 1997, 7.

119. Ibid.

120. Conversation with Hamza Alavi, who had served as one of the whizz kids of Nur Khan's reformist team in the Yahya government (1969–71) for six months. University of Manchester, 1988.

121. *The Telegraph*, 18 August 2008.

122. Stephen P. Cohen, *The Idea of Pakistan*, 319.

123. Nancy de Wolf Smith, 'The Idea of Pakistan', *Far Eastern Economic Review*, Vol. 168, No. 2, 2005, 72.

124. Stephen P. Cohen, *The Idea of Pakistan*, 97.

125. Ibid., 108.

126. Henri J. Barkey, 'Why Military Regimes Fail: The Perils of Transition', *Armed Forces & Society*, Vol. 16, No. 2, 1990, 3.

127. Shahid Siddiqui, 'Political–Military Discourse', *Dawn*, 13 February 2008.

128. Jean-Luc Racine, 'Pakistan and the India Syndrome: Between Kashmir and Nuclear Predicament', in Christophe Jaffrelot, ed., *Pakistan: Nationalism Without a Nation*, Manohar, New Delhi, 2002, 197.

129. Ayesha Siddiqa, 'Pakistan's Political Economy of National Security', in Veena Kukreja and M. P. Singh, eds, *Pakistan: Democracy, Development and Security Issues, Sage,* London and Thousand Oaks, CA, 2005, 124.

130. Vali Nasr, *The Vanguard of the Islamic Revolution: The Jama'at-i Islami of Pakistan,* I. B. Tauris, London, 1994, 171.

131. *The Daily Times*, editorial, 'Pakistan Army and the Nation', 30 September 2007.

132. Mazhar Aziz, *Military Control in Pakistan: The Parallel State*, Routledge, Abingdon, UK, 2007, 41.

133. Ahmed Rashid, *Pakistan on the Brink: The Future of Pakistan, Afghanistan and the West*, Allen Lane, London, 2012, 27.

134. Charles Kennedy, 'A User's Guide to Guided Democracy: Musharraf and the Pakistani Military Governance Paradigm', in Charles Kennedy and Cynthia Botteron, eds, *Pakistan 2005,* Oxford University Press, 2006, 122–38.

135. Mohammad Waseem, Constitutionalism in Pakistan, 69–74.

136. Veena Kukreja, *Civil–Military Relations in South Asia*, 59.

137. Jendayl Frazer, 'Conceptualizing Civil–Military Relations during Democratic Transition', *Africa Today*, Vol. 42, No. 1/2, 1995, 39.

138. Katharine Adeney, 'What Comes after Musharraf?', *The Brown Journal of World Affairs*, Vol. 14, No.1, 2007, 49–51.

139. A. M. Goodenough, 'Pakistan: Internal Disturbances – August/September 1983', M. St. E. Burton, Esq., South Asian Department, FCO, FSP 014/1, 25 September 1983.

140. Ishtiaq Hossain, 'Pakistan's October 1999 Military Coup: Its Causes and Consequences', *Asian Journal of Political Science*, Vol. 8, No. 2, 2000, 40.

141. Interview with Hasan Askari Rizvi, *Herald*, October 2004, 67.

142. *The News*, 7 October 2009; see Shuja Nawaz, *The Battle for Pakistan: The Bitter US Friendship and a Tough Neighborhood*, Liberty Publishing, Karachi, 2019, 231–35.

143. *The Nation*, 9 October 2009.

144. *Daily Times*, 15 October 2009.

145. *The Post*, 2 November 2009.

146. *Dawn*, 3 May 2011.

147. *The News*, 3 May 2011.

148. *Daily Times*, 3 May 2011.

149. *Dawn*, 5 May 2011, 14 May 2011.

150. *The News*, 12 May 2011.

151. *The Express Tribune*, 9 July 2013.

152. *Dawn*, 9 September 2011.

153. *The News*, 29 February 2012.

154. *The Nation*, 12 February 2015.

155. *Dawn*, 19 November 2011.

156. *The Nation*, 2 December 2011.

157. Amir Mir, 'Between Memo and Military', *The News*, 27 November 2011.

158. *Dawn*, 22 December 2011.

159. Ibid., 49.

160. *The News*, 30 August 2014.

161. Ayesha Siddiqa, 'Mapping the "Establishment"', in Ishtiaq Ahmed and Adnan Rafiq, eds, *Pakistan's Democratic Transition: Change and Persistence*, Routledge, London, 2016, 55.

162. *Dawn*, 26 January 2017.

163. M. S. Lodhi, Karachi Tour Report, 23–29 May 1982', Dated 3 June 1982, File No. FCO 37/2922, The British High Commission, British Archives, London.

164. Ibid.

165. Ayesha Siddiqa, 'Of Kings, Queens, and Pawns: Civil–Military Relations in Pakistan', in Bilal Zahoor and Raza Rumi, eds, *Rethinking Pakistan: A 21st Century Perspective*, Folio Books, Lahore, 2019, 226.

166. Ayesha Jalal, 'The Past as Present', in Maleeha Lodhi, ed., *Beyond the 'Crisis State'*, Columbia University Press, 2011, 7–8.

167. Ayesha Siddiqa, 'Mapping the "Establishment"', 63.

168. Hein G. Kiessling, *Faith, Unity, Discipline: The ISI of Pakistan*, Hurst & Co., 2010, 135–6.

169. Hassan Abbas, *Pakistan's Drift into Extremism: Allah, the Army and America's War on Terror*, Pentagon Press, New Delhi, 2005, 203.

170. Ibid.

171. Husain Haqqani, 'The Role of Islam in Pakistan's Future', *The Washington Quarterly*, Vol. 28, No. 1, 2004, 85.

172. Bidanada Chengappa, 'The ISI Role in Pakistan's Politics', *Strategic Analysis*, Vol. 23, No. 11, 2000, 1,868.

173. Mazhar Aziz, *Military Control in Pakistan*, 94.

174. Cyril Almeida, 'Exclusive: Act Against Militants or Face International Isolation, Civilians Tell Military', *Dawn*, 6 October 2016.

175. *Dawn*, 11 October 2016.

176. *Dawn*, 29 October 2016.

177. *Dawn*, 29 April 2017.

178. *Dawn*, 10 May 2017.

179. *The News*, 13 December 2013.

180. *Dawn*, 16 June 2016.

181. Zeenia Shaukat, 'The Anguish Caused by Enforced Disappearances', *Herald*, November 2017.

182. Ibid.

183. Aysha Shafiq, 'The War on Terror and the Enforced Disappearances in Pakistan', *Human Rights Review*, Vol. 14, No. 4, 2013, 390.

184. Ibid., 392.

185. *The News*, 13 April 2014, 20 August 2014, and 18 December 2015.

186. Hamid Khan, 'Military and Judiciary in Pakistan October 1999 Onwards', *Journal of South Asian and Middle Eastern Studies*, Vol. 26, No. 4, 2003, 45.

187. See Adam Dolnik and Khuram Iqbal, *Negotiating the Siege of the Lal Masjid*, Oxford University Press, 2015.

188. *Dawn*, 11 November 2013.

189. Stephen Tankel, *Storming the World Stage: The Story of Lashkar-e-Taiba*, Hurst & Co., 2011, 257.

190. Ayesha Jalal, 'The Past as Present', 15–17.

191. Saeed Shafqat, 'Pakistan Military: Sustaining Hegemony and Constructing Democracy?', *Journal of South Asian and Middle Eastern Studies*, Vol. 42, No. 2, 2019, 32, 33, 34, 35.

192. Ibid., 43, 45, 49.

193. This section draws on Mohammad Waseem, 'Judging Democracy in Pakistan: Conflict between the Executive and Judiciary', *Contemporary South Asia*, 2012, 20 (1), 19–31.

194. Pratab Bhanu Mehta, 'India's Judiciary: The Promise of Uncertainty', in Devesh Kapur and Pratab Bhanu Mehta, eds, *Public Institutions in India: Performance and Design*, Oxford University Press, New Delhi, 172–3.

195. Harris Gazder, 'Judicial Activism vs Democratic Consolidation in Pakistan', *Economic and Political Weekly*, Vol. 44, No. 52, 8–14 August 2009, 10.

196. Alec Stone Sweet, 'Judicialization and the Construction of Governance', *Comparative Political Studies*, Vol. 32, No. 2, 1999, 147–84.

197. Paula R. Newberg, *Judging the State: Courts and Constitutional Politics in Pakistan*, Cambridge University Press, 1995, 236.

198. *Dawn*, 10 March 2011.

199. Joel Verner, 'The Independence of Supreme Courts in Latin America: A Review of the Literature', *Journal of Latin American Studies*, Vol. 16, No. 2, 1984, 478–88.

200. The British High Commission, Letter from P. R. Fearn, Dated 9 May 1979, File No. FCO 37/2196, British National Archives London.

201. Ibid.

202. Paula R. Newberg, *Judging the State*, 247.

203. Charles Kennedy, 'Presidential–Prime Ministerial Relations: The Role of the Superior Courts', in Charles Kennedy and Rasul Bakhsh Rais, eds, *Pakistan, 1995*, Westview Press, Boulder, CO, 1995, 17–30.

204. Owen Bowcott, Ben Quinn and Severin Carrell, 'Johnson's Suspension of Parliament Unlawful, Supreme Court Rules,' *The Guardian*, 24 September 2019, https://www.theguardian.com/law/2019/sep/24/boris-johnsons-suspension-of-parliament-unlawful-supreme-court-rules-prorogue (accessed 10 November 2020).

205. Stephen P. Nicholson and Robert M. Howard, 'Framing Support for the Supreme Court in the Aftermath of Bush v. Gore', *Journal of Politics*, Vol. 65, No. 3, 2003, 676–95.

206. *The Daily Times*, 22 July 2009.

207. Christopher M. Larkins, 'Judicial Independence and Democratization: A Theoretical and Conceptual Analysis', *American Journal of Comparative Law*, Vol. 44, No. 4, 1996, 621.

208. Ibid., 618–24.

209. Civil Miscellaneous Application no. 244 of 2017 before the Supreme Court of Pakistan, para. 8.

210. *Ishaq Khan Khakwani* vs. *Mian Muhammad Nawaz Sharif*, PLD 2015 SC 275, para. 3.

211. Ibid., para. 3

212. *Dawn*, 13 April 2018.

213. Saeed Ahmed Rid, 'The Popular Mandate and Courts in Pakistan', paper presented at the LUMS Annual Humanities and Social Sciences (HSS) conference, LUMS, 15 March 2018.

214. Waris Hussain, 'Avoiding the Judicialization of Politics in Pakistan's Supreme Court: A Comparative Study of Self-restraint Justiciability Doctrines and Procedures for Judicial Review in India, the United States, and Pakistan', PhD thesis, American University, Washington DC, 2017, 36–7.

215. Ibid., 47.

216. Ibid., 70.

217. Ibid., 94.

218. Ibid., 99–100.

219. *Dawn*, 10 March 2011.

220. Paula R. Newberg, *Judging the State*, 31.

221. Najam Sethi, 'Will Musharraf Withdraw Reference against CJP', *Daily Times*, 2007.

222. 'Iftikhar Muhammad Chaudhary Speaks', *The Post*, 2008.

223. Nasim Hasan Shah, 'Judiciary in Pakistan: A Quest for Independence', in Craig Baxter and Charles Kennedy, eds, *Pakistan, 1997*, Westview Press, Boulder, CO, 1998, 62–3.

224. Krishnadas Rajagopal, 'The Validity of the Collegium System', *The Hindu*, 25 June 2014, available at https://www.thehindu.com/news/national/the-validity-of-the-collegium-system/article6148870.ece (accessed 10 September 2020).

225. Hamid Khan, 'Military and Judiciary in Pakistan October 1999 Onwards', 41.

226. Azaz Syed, 'A Well-planned Action', *The Post*, 2007.

227. See Leslie Wolfe-Phillips, 'Constitutional Legitimacy: A Study of the Doctrine of Necessity', *Third World Quarterly*, Vol. 1, No. 4, 1979.

228. Mohammad Waseem, 'Constitutionalism in Pakistan,' 211–12.

229. *Mahmood Khan Achakzai* vs *Federation of Pakistan*, PLD, 1997 SC 426.

230. *Sindh High Court Bar Association* vs *Federation of Pakistan*, PLD 2009 SC 879.

231. *Sindh High Court Bar Association* vs *Federation of Pakistan*, PLD 2009 SC 879.

232. Mohammad Waseem, 'The NRO Revisited', *The Express Tribune*, 18 April 2010.

233. Osama Siddique, 'The Jurisprudence of Dissolutions: Presidential Power to Dissolve Assemblies under the Pakistani Constitution in its Discontents', *Arizona Journal of International and Comparative Law*, Vol. 23, No. 3, 2006, 713.

234. Waqar Gillani, 'First after the 18th Amendment', *The News on Sunday*, special report, 13 January 2019.

235. See Diva Rai, 'Golaknath I. C. v State of Punjab (1967): Overview and Analysis', available at https://blog.ipleaders.in/golaknath-c-v-state-punjab-1967-overview-analysis/#Identification_of_Parties_including_the_name_of_the_judges (accessed 16 September 2020).

236. *Kesavananda Bharati* v. *State of Kerala*, AIR 1973 SC 1461. On the Kesavanada case, see Arvind P. Datar, 'The Case that Saved Indian Democracy', *The Hindu*, 24 April 2013, available at https://www.thehindu.com/opinion/op-ed/the-case-that-saved-indian-democracy/article12209702.ece (accessed 16 September 2020).

237. Pratap Bhanu Mehta, 'India's Judiciary', 171–2.

238. *Mahmood Khan Achakzai* vs *Federation of Pakistan*, PLD 1997 SC 426; *Zafar Ali Shah and others* vs *Pervez Musharraf*, PLD 2000 SC 869.

239. Nauman Asghar, 'In Favour of Judicial Review', *Dawn*, 27 April 2010.

240. Feisal Naqvi, 'Not a New Debate', *Dawn*, 23 April 2010.

241. *Federation of Pakistan* vs *Saeed Ahmed Khan*, PLD 1974 SC 151; *Federation of Pakistan* vs *United Sugar Mills*, PLD 1977 SC 397.

242. *Pakistan Lawyers' Forum and Others* vs *Federation of Pakistan and Others*, PLD 2005 SC 719.

243. Pratap Bhanu Mehta, 'India's Judiciary', 169.

244. Nasim Hasan Shah, 'Judiciary in Pakistan', 73–4.

245. Alec Stone Sweet, 'Judicialization and the Construction of Governance,' 155–6.

246. Ibid., 161.

247. Pratap Bhanu Mehta, 'India's Judiciary', 170–3.

248. *Dawn*, 6 May 2008.

249. *Mahmood Khan Achakzai* vs *Federation of Pakistan*, PLD 1997 SC 426.

250. *The News,* 14 February 2010.

251. *The Express Tribune*, 5 March 2011.

252. Feisal Naqvi, 'Not a New Debate'.

253. *The News*, 5 March 2010.

254. Ayaz Amir, 'Their Lordships Overstep the Mark', *The News*, 10 July 2009.

255. Ansar Abbasi, 'Courts Bound to Help People', *The News*, 13 July 2009.

256. Usman Manzoor, 'Billions Saved from Loot by Restored Judges', *The News*, 9 March 2010.

257. Babar Sattar, 'Fading Romance', *The News*, 31 July 2010.

258. *The News*, 18 September 2010.

259. *Dawn*, 8 September 2018.

260. Moeen Cheema and Ijaz Gilani, *The Politics and Jurisprudence of the Chaudhry Court, 2005–2013*, Oxford University Press, 2015, 57–61, 85–93, 263–270, 157.

261. *The Express Tribune*, 8 September 2017.

262. *ARY News*, 16 December 2017.

263. *The News*, 28 February 2018.

264. *The Express Tribune*, 26 June 2018.

265. *The Express Tribune*, 29 June 2018.

266. *Dawn*, 16 September 2018.

267. *Dawn*, 17 November 2018.

268. *Dawn*, 16 October 2018.

269. *Dawn*, 01 February 2018.

270. *Barrister Zafarullah Khan and others* vs. *Federation of Pakistan and others*, 2018 SCMR 1621, para. 2.

271. *The Express Tribune*, 15 September 2018.

272. *Dawn*, editorial, 'A Controversial Investigation', 6 June 2017.

273. *Mian Muhammad Nawaz Sharif* vs. *The State through Chairman NAB*, PLD 2018 Islamabad 148, para. 6.

274. Mohammad Waseem, 'When Courts Define Politics', *The News*, 6 August 2017.

275. *Dawn*, 13 September 2017.

276. *Dawn*, 13 September 2017.

277. *Dawn*, 16 March 2011.

278. Alefia T. Hussain, 'Here There Is No Consensus on Democracy: An Interview with Dr Mohammad Waseem', *The News on Sunday*, 23 July 2017.

279. *The Guardian*, 6 July 2018.

280. Alefia T. Hussain, 'Here There Is No Consensus on Democracy'.

281. Pratap Bhanu Mehta, 'India's Judiciary', 170–1.

282. International Crisis Group (ICG), *Bringing Judicial Independence in Pakistan*, Asia Report, November 2004, 10–11.

283. *The Muslim*, 22 April 1994.

284. *Dawn*, 9 November 2012.

285. *Business Recorder*, 9 May 2018.

286. *Federal Government of Islamic Republic of Pakistan* vs *General (R) Pervez Musharraf*, Special Court, Islamabad, Complaint No. 1 of 2013.

287. Ibid., para. 66.

288. Ibid.

289. Ibid.

290. *Dawn*, 19 December 2019.

291. Ali Sultan, 'Rule of Law and Judicial Efficiency', *Development Advocate Pakistan*, Vol. 4, No. 3, UNDP, 2018, 13.

292. *Dawn*, 4 May 2009.

293. *Dawn*, 21 January 2018.

294. *The News,* 20 June 2010.

295. Harris Gazdar, 'Judicial Activism vs. Democratic Consolidation in Pakistan', *Economic and Political Weekly*, Vol. 44, No. 32, 2009, 10–11.

296. Paula R. Newberg, *Judging the State*, 240.

297. Reema Omer, tweet via account @reema_omer, Twitter, 6 February 2019.

298. Supreme Court of Pakistan Suo Motu Case No. 7 of 2017, para. 53 (12).

299. Ibid., para. 53 (15).

300. Ibid., para. 45, 33–4.

301. Ibid., para. 21, 15–16.

302. *Dawn*, 21 April 2019.

303. *Dawn*, 23 April 2019.

304. *Dawn*, 1 June 2019.

305. *Dawn*, 30 May 2019.

306. *Dawn*, 19 July 2019.

307. Pratap Bhanu Mehta, 'India's Judiciary', 172–3.

5. CONSTITUTIONAL DYNAMICS

1. This chapter is a revised version of Mohammad Waseem, 'Constitutionalism and Extra-constitutionalism in Pakistan', in Mark Tushnet and Madhav Khosla, eds, *Unstable Constitutionalism: Law and Politics in South Asia,* Cambridge University Press, New York, 2015, 124–158.

2. Mohammad Waseem, 'Constitutionalism in Pakistan: The Changing Patterns of Diarchy', in Gilles Tarabout and Ranabir Smaddar, eds, *Conflict, Power and the Landscape of Constitutionalism*, Routledge, London, 2008, 223–4.

3. Yogendra Yadav, 'Electoral Reforms: Beyond Middle Class Fantasies', *Seminar* 440, 1996, 2.

4. Madhav Khosla and Mark Tushnet, eds, *Unstable Constitutionalism: Law and Politics in South Asia*, Cambridge University Press, 2015.

5. See Chanchal Kumar Sharma, '*A Situational Theory of Pork-Barrel Politics: The Shifting Logic of Discretionary Allocations in India*', GIGA German Institute of Global and Area Studies, GIGA Working Papers, February 2017.

6. The following observations on FPTP draw on Mohammad Waseem, '*Democratization in Pakistan: A Study of the 2002 Elections*', Oxford University Press, 2006, 108.

7. Ahmed Bilal Mehboob, 'Ordinances Over the Years', *Dawn*, 8 December 2019.

8. For details, see the Web Desk of Geo TV: 'The Ordinances Route: Since 2018 Over 55% Laws Have Been Ordinances', 9 February 2021, URL: https://www.focus-economics.com/countries/pakistan

9. Joel Migdal, 'Integration and Disintegration: An Approach to Society-formation', in Kumar Rupesinghe, Paul Sciarone and Luc van de Goor, eds, *Between Development and Destruction: An Enquiry into the Causes of Conflict in Post-colonial States*, Palgrave Macmillan, London, 1996, 94–6.

10. Gulmina Bilal, 'Constitutional Fallacies of Pakistan', *Liberal Times*, Islamabad, Vol. 11, No. 4, 2003, 25.

11. *Mahmood Khan Achakzai* vs *Federation of Pakistan*, PLD 1997 Supreme Court 426, 480.

12. Constitutional Petition No. 12 of 2010 (Before the Supreme Court of Pakistan), para. 23, 100.

13. Ishtiaq Ahmad and Adnan Rafiq, 'Introduction', in Ishtiaq Ahmad and Adnan Rafiq, eds, *Pakistan's Democratic Transition: Change and Persistence*, Routledge, Abingdon, UK, 2017, 1–13.

14. Rannabir Smaddar, 'Introduction', in Gilles Tarabout and Rannabir Smaddar, eds, *Conflict, Power and the Landscape of Constitutionalism*, 5.

15. Keith Callard, *Pakistan: A Political Study*, Allen & Unwin, London, 1958, 285.

16. Hamza Alavi, 'Constitutional Changes and the Dynamics of Political Development in Pakistan', *Collection of Seminar Papers on Constitutional Changes in the Commonwealth Countries*, Institute of Commonwealth Studies, University of London, 1973, 65–6.

17. Mohammad Ayoob, 'The Security Predicament of the Third World State: Reflections on State-making in a Comparative Perspective', in Brian L. Job, ed., *The Insecurity Dilemma: National Security of Third World States*, Lynne Rienner, Boulder, CO, 1992, 64–6.

18. Granville Austin, 'The Expected and the Unintended in Working a Democratic Constitution', in Zoya Hasan, E. Sridharan and R. Sudarshan, eds, *India's Living Constitution: Ideas, Practices, Controversies*, Permanent Black, Delhi, 2002, 320.

19. Ibid., 320–5, 329.

20. Mohammad Waseem, 'Judging Democracy in Pakistan: Conflict between the Executive and Judiciary', *Contemporary South Asia*, Vol. 20, No. 1, 2012, 19–31.

21. Mushtaq Ahmed, *Government and Politics in Pakistan*, Space Publishers, Karachi, 1970, 211.

22. George M. Platt, 'Basic Democracies: The Experiment in Local Government', in S. H. Hashmi, ed., *The Governing Process in Pakistan, 1958-69*, Aziz Publishers, Lahore, 1987, 230–8.

23. Charles Kennedy, 'Presidential–Prime Ministerial Relations: The Role of the Superior Courts', in Charles Kennedy and Rasul Bakhsh Rais, eds, *Pakistan, 1995*, Westview Press, Boulder, CO, 1995, 19–27.

24. Osama Siddique, 'The Jurisprudence of Dissolutions: Presidential Power to Dissolve Assemblies under the Pakistani Constitution in its Discontents', *Arizona Journal of International and Comparative Law*, Vol. 23, No. 3, 2006, 32–72.

25. Paula R. Newberg, *Judging the State: Courts and Constitutional Politics in Pakistan*, Cambridge University Press, 1995, 2.

26. Ibid., 7, 13.

27. *Federation of Pakistan* vs *Maulvi Tamizuddin*, PLD 1955 Federal Court 240.

28. *Yusaf Patel* vs *The Crown*, PLD 1955 Federal Court 387.

29. Paula R. Newberg, *Judging the State*, 13.

30. *The State* vs *Dosso*, PLD 1958 Supreme Court 533.

31. *Asma Jilani* vs *Government of Punjab*, PLD 1972 Supreme Court 139.

32. Leslie Wolf-Phillips, *Constitutional Legitimacy: A Study of the Doctrine of Necessity*, Third World Foundation Monograph 6, London, 1980, 8, 11, 17, 22.

33. Hamid Khan, *Constitutional and Political History of Pakistan*, Oxford University Press, Karachi, 2001, 936.

34. Ibid., 937.

35. Naseem Zehra, *From Kargil to the Coup: Events that Shook Pakistan*, Sang-e-Meel Publications, Lahore, 2018, 195–9.

36. *Imran Ahmed Khan Niazi* vs *Mian Muhammad Nawaz Sharif and others*, PLD 2017 Supreme Court 265, para. 78.

37. Mohammad Waseem, *Politics and the State in Pakistan*, National Institute of Historical and Cultural Research, 1994, 448–9.

38. Heather K. Gerken, 'Federalism as the New Nationalism: An Overview', *Yale Law Journal*, Vol. 123, No. 6, 2014, 1,891.

39. Ibid., 1,892.

40. Ibid., 1,892, 1,909, 1,907.

41. Katharine Adeney, *Federalism and Ethnic Conflict Regulation in India and Pakistan*, Palgrave Macmillan, London, 2007, 101.

42. F. Boni, and Katharine Adeney, 'The Impact of the China–Pakistan Economic Corridor on Pakistan's Federal System', *Asian Survey*, Vol. 60, No. 3, 2020, 441–65.

43. Ibid.

44. NFC Award, 18th Amendment.

45. *Dawn*, editorial, 'Sindh–Centre Tensions', 6 May 2020.

46. Ibid., 2 May 2019.

47. *The News*, 1 March 2021.

48. Will Kymlicka, 'Multicultural Citizenship within Multination States', *Ethnicities*, Vol. 11, No. 3, 2011, 281–303.

49. Ian Talbot, 'The Growth of the Muslim League in the Punjab, 1937–1946', *Journal of Commonwealth & Comparative Politics*, Vol. 20, No. 1, 1982, 20–1.

50. Inamur Rehman, *Public Opinion and Political Development in Pakistan, 1947–1958*, Oxford University Press, Karachi, 1982, 65.

51. Ibid., 70.

52. Alfred Stepan, 'Federalism and Democracy: Beyond the US Model', *Journal of Democracy*, Vol. 10, No. 4, 1999, 22–3.

53. H. M. Rajashekara, 'The Nature of Indian Federalism: A Critique', *Asian Survey*, Vol. 37, No. 3, 1997, 246.

54. Imtiaz Sheikh, 'Making the NFC Award Fair', *Dawn*, 31 May 2002.

55. Balveer Arora, 'Multiple Identities and Diverse Majorities: India's Federal Democracy', paper for the Conference on Democracy and Federalism, All Souls College, University of Oxford, 5–7 June 1997, 6–9.

56. *Dawn,* 'PM Choudhary Mohammad Ali's Broadcast', 15 October 1955.

57. M. Rafique Afzal, *Political Parties in Pakistan*, Vol 1, National Institute of Historical and Cultural Research, Islamabad, 1998, 47–58, 238–42.

58. Ali Cheema and Asad Liaqat, 'Elections 2018: Does Regional Inequality Matter?', *Herald*, July 2018, available at https://herald.dawn.com/news/1398609 (accessed 8 September 2020).

59. G. W. Choudhary, *Constitutional Development in Pakistan*, Ideal Book House, Karachi, 1995, 36–42.

60. Letter from R. E. Escritt, General Elections in Pakistan, Dated 14 April 1970, British National Archives London.

61. Ibid.

62. The British High Commission, Opdom No. 35 for the period April 29th – May 5th 1948, File No. DO 142/423, British Library, London.

63. Telegram No. 133 dated 9 November 1954, The British High Commission, File No. DO 35/5405, British National Archives, London.

64. United Kingdom High Commission, Pakistan Fortnightly Report, File No. DO 35/5406, June 1955, British National Archives, London.

65. Telegram No. 1660, The British High Commission, Dated 6 October 1958, File No. 321/2, British Archives London.

66. Memorandum by the United Democratic Front presented to The British High Commission, Received on 20 December 1974, File No. FCO 37/1496, British National Archives, London.

67. The following observations draw on Mohammad Waseem, 'Pakistan Resolution and Ethnonationalist Movements', in Kaniz Yusuf, Saleem Akhtar, and Razi Wasti, eds, *Pakistan Resolution Revisited*, National Institute of Historical and Cultural Research, Islamabad, 1990.

68. Ayesha Jalal, *The Sole Spokesman*, Cambridge University Press, 1985, 111-12.

69. Text of the Lahore Resolution, in S. Sharifuddin Pirzada, ed., *Foundations of Pakistan: All-India Muslim League Documents, 1906–1947*, National Publishing House, Karachi, 1970, Vol. 11, 341.

70. Mohammad Waseem, 'Pakistan Resolution and the Ethnonationalist Movements', 516–20.

71. Ian Talbot, 'The Growth of the Muslim League', 20–1.

72. For a discussion of the Awami League and the Six Points, see *The Bangladesh Papers*, Vanguard Books, Lahore, n.d., 23–8.

73. Vali Nasr, 'The Negotiable State: Borders and Power Struggles in Pakistan', in Brendan O'Leary, Ian S. Lustik and Thomas Callaghy, eds, *Right-sizing the State: The Politics of Moving Borders*, Oxford University Press, 2001, 190.

74. Farhan H. Siddiqui, *The Politics of Ethnicity in Pakistan: The Baloch, Sindhi and Mohajir Ethnic Movements*, Routledge, London, 2012, 59–60.

75. Ibid., 68–70.

76. Alfred Stepan, 'Federalism and Democracy', 22–3.

77. Mohammad Waseem, 'Pakistan: A Majority-constraining Federalism', *India Quarterly*, Vol. 67, No. 3, 2011, 218.

78. Juan J. Linz, 'Democracy, Multinationalism and Federalism', paper for the Conference on Democracy and Federalism, All Souls College, Oxford, 5–7 June 1997, 22–30.

79. Mohammad Waseem, 'Pakistan: A Majority-constraining Federalism', 220.

80. Lawrence Saez, 'India's Economic Liberalization, Interjurisdictional Competition and Development', *Contemporary South Asia*, Vol. 8, No. 3, 1999, 323.

81. Maryam S. Khan, 'Ethnic Federalism in Pakistan: Federal Design, Construction of Ethno-Linguistic Identity and Group Conflict', *Harvard Journal on Racial and Ethnic Justice*, Vol. 30, 2014, 5, 6, 14.

82. Ibid.

83. Selig Harrison's interview of Zia, *Jang*, 13 April 1982.

84. *Dawn*, 16 May 2006.

85. The 18th Constitutional Amendment, 2010. http://www.pakistani.org/pakistan/constitution/amendments/18amendment.html

86. Shahid Javed Burki, 'The 18th Amendment: Pakistan's Constitution Redesigned', ISAS Working Paper No. 112, 2010, 18.

87. Sania Nishtar, 'Health and the 18th Amendment: Need for a National Structure', *Heartfile Organization*, Islamabad, 2011, 7–9.

88. This provision had no impact on practice. In 2019, the PTI government issued two presidential ordinances in one go, squarely violating the provision.

89. Shabbir Cheema and Dennis A. Rondinelli, eds, *Decentralizing Governance: Emerging Concepts and Practices*, Brookings Institution Press, Washington DC, 2007, 8.

90. 'Election Celebrations Turn Deadly in Khyber-Pakhtunkhwa', AFP And *Newsweek Pakistan*, 1 June 2015. https://www.newsweekpakistan.com/election-celebrations-turn-deadly-in-khyber-pakhtunkhwa/

91. Farrukh Moriani, 'The Circularity of Public Policy Reforms in Pakistan: The Case of the 18th Amendment', in *Development Advocate Pakistan, Five Years of the 18th Amendment: Lessons Learnt, Milestones Achieved*, Vol. 2, No. 1, United Nations Development Programme Pakistan, Islamabad, April 2015, 21.

92. Maryam S. Khan, 'Ethnic Federalism in Pakistan', 77.

93. Parliamentary Committee for Constitutional Reforms (PCCR), 'Parliamentary Committee on Constitutional Reforms Report', 2 April 2010, Annexure D-VIII (no page).

94. Farrukh Moriani, 'The Circularity of Public Policy Reforms in Pakistan', 22.

95. Suhail Warraich, 'The Bajwa Doctrine: From Chauvinism to Realism', *The News*, 18 March 2018, https://www.thenews.com.pk/print/293885-the-bajwa-doctrine-from-chauvinism-to-realism

96. Khurram Husain, 'Reversing the 18th Amendment?', *Dawn*, 22 March 2018.

97. Colin Cookman, 'The 18th Amendment and Pakistan's Political Transitions', *Centre for American Progress*, 2010, available at https://www.americanprogress.org/issues/security/news/2010/04/19/7587/the-18th-amendment-and-pakistans-political-transitions/ (accessed 19 January 2019).

98. For an incisive and comprehensive analysis of this region, see Nosheen Ali, *Delusional States: Feeling Rule and Development in Pakistan's Northern Frontier*, Cambridge University Press, 2019.

99. Mohammad Waseem, 'Dilemmas of Pride and Pain: Sectarian Conflict and Conflict Transformation in Pakistan', Working Paper No. 48, University of Birmingham, 2010, 24.

100. Rubina Saigol, *The Pakistan Project: A Feminist Perspective on Nation and Identity*, Women Unlimited, New Delhi, 2013, 50.

101. Nasra M. Shah, 'Pakistani Women', Pakistan Institute of Development Economics (PIDE), Islamabad, 1986, 26–7.

102. The British High Commission, Opdom 24 for the period March 18th to 24th, 1948.

103. Mohammad Waseem, *Politics and the State in Pakistan*, 30–7, 43–4, 48–51.

104. Vali Nasr, 'The Rise of Sunni Militancy in Pakistan: The Changing Role of Islamism and the Ulama in Society and Politics', *Modern Asian Studies*, Vol. 34, No. 1, 2000, 142.

105. Ibid., 146.

106. Keith Callard, *Pakistan*, 200–1.

107. Inamur Rehman, *Public Opinion*, 4.

108. Keith Callard, *Pakistan*, 274.

109. Report from J. D. Murray, 'Pakistan: Provisional Assessment of New Government', Dated 28 October, 1954, File No. DO 35/5406, The British High Commission, British Library.

110. See Olivier Roy, *The Failure of Political Islam*, I. B. Tauris, London, 1994; Graham E. Fuller, *The Future of Political Islam*, Palgrave Macmillan, London, 2003; Frederic Grare, *Political Islam in the Indian Subcontinent*, Manohar, Delhi, 2001; K. B. Sayeed, *Western Dominance and Political Islam: Challenge and Response*, State University of New York Press, 1995.

111. Letter from A. P. Fabian to Richard G. Simmons MVO, Karachi, Dated 9 October 1980, The British High Commission, File No. FCO 37/2358, British National Archives, London.

112. Letter from A. P. Fabian, Dated 6 November 1979, File No. FCO 37/2189, British National Archives, London.

113. Bobby Sayyid and Sign O'Times, 'Kaffirs and Infidels Fighting the Ninth Crusade', in Ernesto Laclau, ed., *The Making of Political Identities*, Verso, London, 1994, 265.

114. Opdom No. 18, Dated 6 May 1949, File No. DO 142/424, British National Archives, London.

115. Opdom No. 31 for the Period 15 to 21 April 1948, File No. DO 142/423, British National Archives, London.

116. Naveeda Khan, *Muslim Becoming: Aspiration and Scepticism in Pakistan*, Duke University Press, 2012, 206.

117. Gunes Murat Tezcur, 'Constitutionalism, Judiciary and Democracy in Islamic Societies', *Polity*, Vol. 39, No. 4, 2007, 480–5.

118. Ibid., 489–90.

119. Louis D. Hayes, *The Islamic State in the Post-modern World: The Political Experience of Pakistan*, Ashgate, Farnham, UK, 2014, 96.

120. Keith Callard, *Pakistan*, 200–1.

121. Glenn E. Robinson, 'Can Islamists be Democrats? The Case of Jordan', *Middle East Journal*, Vol. 51, No. 3, 1997, 373.

122. Leonard Binder, *Religion and Politics in Pakistan*, University of California Press, 1961, 149.

123. Fazlur Rehman, 'Islam and the Constitutional Problem of Pakistan', *Studia Islamica,* No. 32, 1970, 285.

124. Martin Lau, 'The Legal Mechanism of Islamization: The New Islamic Criminal Law of Pakistan', *Journal of Law & Society*, Vol. XI, No. 18, 1992, 45–6.

125. Ibid.

126. Fazlur Rehman, 'Islam and the Constitutional Problem of Pakistan', 35.

127. Ibid., 40–1.

128. Mohammad Waseem, *Politics and the State in Pakistan*, 290–1.

129. Farzana Shaikh, 'From Islamization to Shariatization: Cultural Transnationalism in Pakistan', *Third World Quarterly*, Vol. 29, No. 3, 2008, 593.

130. Syed Abdul Quddus, *Local Self-government in Pakistan*, Vanguard Books, Lahore, 1981, Chapter 4.

131. Afzal Iqbal, *Islamization of Pakistan*, Vanguard Books, Lahore, 1986, 66–8.

132. Rubiya Mehdi, *The Islamization of the Law in Pakistan*, Routledge, London, 1994, 85–6.

133. Aqil Shah, 'Democracy on Hold in Pakistan', *Journal of Democracy*, Vol.13, No.1, 2002, 69.

134. The Council of Islamic Ideology (CII), 'Hudood Ordinance 1979: A Critical Report', Islamabad, 2007, 2.

135. *Dawn*, 'CII Rules Out DNA as Primary Evidence in Rape Cases', 23 September 2013.

136. Kalbe Ali, 'CII Against Cloning, Sex Change', *Dawn*, 6 November 2013.

137. Peer Muhammad, 'CII Chief Opposes Laws Against Polygamy', *The Express Tribune*, 10 March 2014.

138. Kalbe Ali, 'CII Endorses Underage Marriage', *Dawn*, 22 May 2014.

139. Asma Jahangir and Hina Jillani, *The Hudood Ordinances: A Divine Sanction?*, Rhotas Books, Lahore, 1990, 86–7.

140. *Ihsan Ahmed alias Nanna* vs *State*, 1980 P. Cr. L. J 1037, 3.

141. '*Report of the Pakistan Commission on the Status of Women*', See Commission, Islamabad (n.d.), 140, 142, 146–9.

142. Ibid., 168–69.

143. Letter from S. J. Hiscock, Dated 19 April 1982, File No. FCO 37/2922, The British High Commission, British National Archives, London.

144. Inamur Rehman, *Public Opinion*, 4.

145. *Muslim Herald*, editorial, 'The Qadiyanies: A Non-Muslim Minority in Pakistan', April 1975, 3–5.

146. Faqir Hussain, 'Electoral Reforms: A Legal Perspective', in Mohammad Waseem, ed., *Electoral Reform in Pakistan*, Friedrich Ebert Stiftung, Islamabad, 2002, 39.

147. David Taylor, 'The Politics of Islam and Islamization in Pakistan', in James P. Piscatori, ed., *Islam in the Political Process*, Cambridge University Press, 1983, 181–97.

148. Eugene Cotran, and Shibli Malat, *Yearbook of Islamic and Middle Eastern Law: Vol. 1, 1994*, Kluwer Law International, Alphen aan den Rijn, The Netherlands, 1995, 569.

149. *Dawn*, 7 September 2018.

150. *Dawn*, 20 December 2017.

151. *Business Recorder*, 6 October 2017.

152. Michael Laffan, 'The Tangled Roots of Islamist Activism in Southeast Asia', *Cambridge Review of International Affairs*, Vol. 16, No. 3, 2003, 1.

153. See Jeffrey A. Redding, 'Constitutionalizing Islam: Theory and Pakistan', *Virginia Journal of International Law*, Vol. 44, No. 3, 2004, 784–8.

154. *Mohammad Ismail Qureshy vs Federal Government of Pakistan Through Secretary Law and Parliamentary Affairs*, Islamabad, PLD 1992 Federal Shariat Court 445.

155. *Muhammad Saifullah* vs *Federal Government*, PLD 1992 Federal Shariat Court 376.

156. *Dr. Zahoor Ahmad Azhar* vs *Federation of Pakistan*, PLD 2013 Federal Shariat Court 1.

157. J. S. Bains, 'Some Thoughts on Pakistan's New Constitution', *Indian Journal of Political Science*, Vol. 23, No. 1/4, 1962, 209–24.

158. *Dawn*, 20 September 2018.

159. See Martin Lau, *The Role of Islam in the Legal System of Pakistan*, Martinus Nijhoff, Leiden, The Netherlands, 2005, 32–4.

160. Mohammad Waseem, 'When Courts Define Politics', *The News*, 6 August 2017.

161. Khaled Ahmed, 'Council for Islamic Ideology: Our Divorce from Reality', *The Friday Times*, 2002, 1–5.

162. Naveeda Khan, *Muslim Becoming*, 52.

163. Ibid., 13.

164. Charles Kennedy, 'Presidential–Prime Ministerial Relations', 98–9.

165. Martin Lau, *The Role of Islam in the Legal System of Pakistan*, 189.

166. Ibid., 196.

167. Ibid., 35, 39–41.

168. *The Daily Times*, 15 April 2009.

169. I. A. Rehman, 'Zia-ul-Haq: The Master of Illusion', *Herald*, 23 August 2016, available at http://herald.dawn.com/news/1153499 (accessed 22 September 2020).

170. Margrit Pernau, *From Ashraf into Middle Classes: Muslims in Nineteenth-century Delhi*, Oxford University Press, New Delhi, 2013, 274.

171. Faisal Khan, *Islamic Banking in Pakistan: Sharia-compliant Finance and the Quest to Make Pakistan More Islamic*, Routledge, Abingdon, UK, 2015, 114.

172. A. W. Dukuki and Abdulazeem Abuzaid, 'A Critical Appraisal on the Challenges of Realizing *Maqasid al Sharia* in Islamic Banking and Finance', *Journal of Economics and Management*, 2007, Vol. 15 No. 2, 143–165.

173. Mohammad Waseem, *Politics and the State in Pakistan*, Institute of Historical and Cultural Studies, Islamabad, 1994, 381.

174. Enzo Pace, 'System's Theory and Religion', *Civitas*, Vol. 17, no. 2, 2017, 357.

175. Ibid., 350.

176. Ibid, 355.

177. Ran Hirschl, 'The Political Origins of the New Constitutionalism', *Indiana Journal of Global Legal Studies*, Vol. 11, No. 1, 2004, 75.

178. Ibid., 84.

179. Ibid., 89–90.

180. Human Rights Commission of Pakistan (HRCP), *State of Human Rights in 2017*, 2017, 82.

181. Gabriela Knaul, 'Report of the Special Rapporteur on the Independence of Judges and Lawyers', UN General Assembly, A/HRC/23/43/Add.2, 2013, 13.

182. *Dawn*, 3 November 2018.

183. Naveeda Khan, *Muslim Becoming*, 204.

6. MASS PUBLIC

1. Jurgen Habermas, *The Structural Transformation of the Public Sphere: An Inquiry into a Category of Bourgeois Society* [English translation], MIT Press, Cambridge, MA, 1991, 176.

2. Gabriel M. Vasquez, 'A Homo Narrans Paradigm for Public Relations: Combining Bormann's Symbolic Convergence Theory and Gruing's Situational Theory of Publics', *Journal of Public Relations Research*, Vol. 5, No. 3, 1993, 201–16.

3. Samuel Mateus, 'The Public as Social Experience', *Comunicação e Sociedade*, Vol. 19, 2011, 275–86.

4. Brad Rawlins, 'Prioritizing Stakeholders for Public Relations', Institute of Public Relations, University of Florida, Gainesville, FL, 2006, 2, available at https://www.instituteforpr.org/wp-content/uploads/2006_Stakeholders_1.pdf (accessed 28 July 2020).

5. Joel Migdal, 'Integration and Disintegration: An Approach to Society-formation', in Kumar Rupesinghe, Paul Sciarone and Luc van de Goor, eds, *Between Development and Destruction: An Enquiry into the Causes of Conflict in Post-colonial States*, Palgrave Macmillan, London, 1996, 94.

6. Ibid., 94–6.

7. Sudipta Kaviraj, 'In Search of Civil Society', in Sudipta Kaviraj and Sunil Khilnani, eds, *Civil Society: History and Possibilities*, Cambridge University Press, 2001, 293.

8. Ibid., 296.

9. David Gilmartin, 'Partition, Pakistan and South Asian History: In Search of a Narrative', *Journal of South Asian History*, Vol. 57, No. 4, 1998, 1079.

10. Ian Talbot, *Freedom's Cry: The Popular Dimension in the Pakistan Movement*, Oxford University Press, Karachi, 1996, 23–5.

11. Ian Talbot, 'The Unionist Party and Punjabi Politics, 1937–1947', in D. A. Low, ed., *The Political Inheritance of Pakistan*, Palgrave Macmillan, London, 1991, 99–100.

12. Kamran Asdar Ali, *Surkh Salam: Communist Politics and Class Activism in Pakistan, 1947–1972*, Oxford University Press, Karachi, 2015, 249–56.

13. Christophe Jaffrelot, *The Pakistan Paradox: Instability and Resilience*, Random House India, Gurgaon (Gurugram), Haryana, India, 2015, 319.

14. Noaman G. Ali, 'Agrarian Class Struggle and State Formation in Postcolonial Pakistan, 1959–1974: Contingencies of Mazdoor Kisan Raj', *Journal of Agrarian Change*, Vol. 20, No. 1, 2019, 9.

15. Aasim Sajjad Akhtar, 'When a Movement Stops Moving: The Okara Peasant Struggle Twenty Years On', *Critical Asian Studies*, 19 November 2019, https://criticalasianstudies.org/commentary/2019/11/19/201923-aasim-sajjad-ahktar-when-a-movement-stops-moving-the-okara-peasant-struggle-twenty-years-on

16. See Atul Kohli, *Democracy and Discontent: India's Growing Crisis of Governability*, Cambridge University Press, 1995.

17. See Diwan Singh Maftoon, *Naqabil-e-Faramosh* [Unforgettable, Urdu text], Ilmo-Irfan Publishers, Lahore, 1957.

18. For example, Steve Inskeep, *Instant City: Life and Death in Karachi*, Penguin Viking, 2011 & Nichola Khan, *Mohajir Militancy in Pakistan: Violence and Transformation in the Karachi Conflict*, Routledge, 2010.

19. See Mohammad Waseem, 'Ethnic Conflict in Pakistan: Case of Mohajir Nationalism', in G. Peiris and SWR Samarasinghe eds, *Millennial Perspectives: Essays in Honour of Kingsley de Silva*, Law and Society Trust Colombo, 1999.

20. Laurent Gayer, *Karachi: Ordered Disorder and the Struggle for the City*, New Delhi: Hurst & Co., 2014, 9.

21. Ibid., 10.

22. Ibid., 5.

23. Ibid., 250–8.

24. See Fareeha Zafar et al., 'A Tale of Two Towns: Pakpattan and Arifwala', and Anila Nadeem, 'Shikarpur: Experience of a City under the Shadow of a Glorious Past', in Pervaiz Vandal, ed., *Life in Small Towns*, Trust for History, Art & Architecture, Pakistan, Thaap Publications, Lahore, 2013.

25. Daanish Mustafa, 2005. '(Anti) Social Capital in the Production of an (Un) Civil Society in Pakistan', *Geographical Review*, Vol. 95, No. 3, 2005, 328.

26. Juan Linz and Alfred Stepan, *Problems of Democratic Transition and Consolidation: Southern Europe, South America and Post-communist Europe*, Johns Hopkins University Press, 1996, 233.

27. Antoaneta Dimitrova and Tony Verheijen, 'Revitalizing Civil Society in Central and Eastern Europe: Turning the Fish Soup into an Aquarium', conference paper, Conference on Democracy and Development, Bucharest, 1997, 6–7.

28. Ibid., 8–9.

29. Sadaf Ahmad, *Transforming Faith: The Story of Al-Huda and Islamic Revivalism among Urban Pakistani Women*, Syracuse University Press, 2009.

30. Nida Kirmani and Sarah Zaidi, 'The Role of Faith in the Charity and Development Sector in Karachi and Sindh, Pakistan', DFID Working Paper No. 50, Religions & Development Research Programme, University of Birmingham, UK, 2010, 31–8.

31. Nira Wickramasinghe, 'The Idea of Civil Society in the South: Imaginings, Transplants, Designs', *Science & Society*, Vol. 69, No. 3, 2005, 458.

32. Francis Fukuyama, *Social Capital and Civil Society*, International Monetary Fund, Washington, DC, 2000, 3–4.

33. Mustapha Kamal Pasha and David L. Blaney, 'Elusive Paradise: The Promise and Peril of Global Civil Society', *Alternatives: Global, Local, Political*, Vol. 23, No. 4, 1998, 421–4.

34. *The Express Tribune*, 12 June 2015.

35. Ayesha Jalal, 'Ideology and the Struggle for Democratic Institutions', in Victoria Schofield, ed., *Old Roads, New Highways: Fifty Years of Pakistan*, Oxford University Press, Karachi, 1997, 124.

36. Omar Asghar Khan, 'Critical Engagement: NGOs and the State', in Victoria Schofield, ed., *Old Roads, New Highways*, 283.

37. Ibid., 288.

38. Ibid., 289–91.

39. Rauf Arif, 'Social Movements, YouTube and Political Activism in Authoritarian Countries: A Comparative Analysis of Political Change in Pakistan, Tunisia and Egypt', PhD thesis, University of Iowa, 2014, abstract, available at https://ir.uiowa.edu/etd/4564/ (accessed 21 May 2020).

40. Mustapha Kamal Pasha, 'Savage Capitalism and Civil Society in Pakistan', in Anita Weiss and Syed Zulfiqar Gilllani, eds, *Civil Society and Political Change in Asia*, Oxford University Press, Karachi, 2001, 32.

41. Ibid., 35–7.

42. Mohammad Qadeer, 'The Evolving Structure of Civil Society and the State in Pakistan', *Pakistan Development Review*, Vol. 36, No. 4, 1997, 747.

43. Lorenzo Fioramonti, 'Civil Societies and Democratization: Assumptions, Dilemmas and the South African Experience', *Theoria: A Journal of Social and Political Theory*, Vol. 52, No. 107, 2005, 70, 72.

44. Ibid., 75.

45. Mustapha Kamal Pasha, 'The "Hyper-extended" State: Civil Society and Democracy', in Rasul Baksh Rais, ed., *State, Society and Democratic Change in Pakistan*, Oxford University Press, Karachi, 1997, 197.

46. Arjumand Kazmi, 'Democratisation in Context: A Phenomenological Inquiry into the Role of Internationally Funded non-Governmental Organizations (NGOs) in Pakistan', PhD thesis, University of Warwick, UK, 2017, 43.

47. Ibid., 49.

48. Ibid., 150–1.

49. Ibid., 157.

50. Ibid., 160.

51. Akbar Zaidi, *The New Development Paradigm: Papers on Institutions, NGOs, Gender and Local Government*, Oxford University Press, Karachi, 1999, 206.

52. Ibid., 210.

53. Ibid., 211.

54. Ibid., 212–13.

55. Ibid., 215.

56. *Dawn*, 15 December 2017.

57. *Dawn*, 6 December 2018.

58. *Dawn*, 9 October 2018.

59. *Dawn*, 12 June 2018.

60. *Dawn*, 23 November 2018.

61. Tahir Mehdi, 'Why NGOs in Pakistan Are at the Brink of Extinction', *Herald*, 19 November 2018.

62. Arjumand Kazmi, 'The Dissenter – Asma Jahangir on the Role of NGOs in Democratizing Pakistan', *Dawn*, 16 February 2018.

63. Ibid.

64. *Dawn*, 25 February 2021.

65. Senator Rehman Malik, 'FATF Discrimination and Indian Terrorist Financing', *The Nation*, 19 February 2021.

66. Ikram ul Haq, 'FATF: FBR's Challenges', *The Daily Times*, 14 March 2021.

67. Marcia A. Weigle and Jim Butterfield, 'Civil Society in Reforming Communist Regimes: The Logic of Emergence', *Comparative Politics*, Vol. 25, No. 1, 1992, 1–2.

68. Mustapha Kamal Pasha, 'The "Hyper-extended" State', 199.

69. K. B. Sayeed, *Politics in Pakistan: The Nature and Direction of Change*, Frederick A. Praeger Publishers, New York, 1980, 157–8.

70. Pierre Bourdieu, 'Cultural Reproduction and Social Reproduction', in Richard K. Brown, ed., *Knowledge, Education, and Cultural Change: Papers in the Sociology of Education*, Tavistock, London, 1973, 58.

71. Malik Zafrul Hasan, *Educating Pakistan*, Sheikh Mohammed Ashraf, Lahore, 1948, 14.

72. Aftab A. Kazi, *Ethnicity and Education in Nation-building: The Case of Pakistan*, Vanguard Books, Lahore, 1987, 3–4.

73. Mariam Chughtai, 'What Produces a History Textbook?' PhD thesis, Harvard University, 2015, 131.

74. Rubina Saigol, 'Curriculum and the Constitution', in Bilal Zahoor and Raza Rumi, eds, *Rethinking Pakistan: A 21ˢᵗ Century Perspective*, Folio Books, Brisbane, 2019, 102–3.

75. See Mariam Chughtai, 'What Produces a History Textbook?'

76. Government of Pakistan, Ministry of Education and Scientific Research, *New Education Policy of the Government of Pakistan*, Islamabad, March 1970, 1.

77. Ibid., 1–2.

78. Government of Pakistan, Ministry of Education, *National Education Policy, 1998–2010*, Islamabad, 1998, iii.

79. Ibid., 5.

80. Ibid., 65.

81. Shahid Siddiqui, *Education Policies in Pakistan: Politics, Projections and Practices*, Oxford University Press, Karachi, 2016, 112.

82. Government of Pakistan, Ministry of Education, *National Education Policy, 2009*, Islamabad, revised 1 August 2009, 10.

83. Ibid., 12–15.

84. Ibid., 17.

85. Neelam Hussian and Dr Rubina Saigol, 'Policy: Education for One and All', *Dawn*, 6 September 2020.

86. Ibid.

87. Pervez Hoodbhoy, 'How Does India's New Education Policy Compare with Pakistan's Recent Single National Curriculum?', Scroll.in, 11 August 2020, available at https://scroll.in/article/969972/how-does-indias-new-education-policy-compare-with-pakistans-recent-single-national-curriculum (accessed 12 October 2020).

88. A. H. Nayyar, 'Dissecting the Single National Curriculum', *Dawn*, 31 July 2020.

89. Nadeem Farooq Paracha, 'A Regressive National Curriculum', *Dawn*, 16 August 2020.

90. Neelam Hussain and Dr Rubina Saigol, 'Policy: Education for One and All', *Dawn*, 6 September 2020.

91. Ibid.

92. A. H. Nayyar, 'Dissecting the Single National Curriculum'.

93. Ibid.

94. Nadeem Farooq Paracha, 'A Regressive National Curriculum'.

95. A. H. Nayyar and Ahmed Salim, *The Subtle Subversion: The State of Curricula and Textbooks in Pakistan*, Sustainable Development Policy Institute (SDPI), Islamabad, 2003, 11–22.

96. See Benjamin Yousaf et al., *Education versus Fanatic Literacy: A Study on the Hate Content in the Textbooks in Punjab and Sindh Provinces*, National Commission for Justice and Peace, Lahore, 2013, available at http://csjpak. org/publications_with_other_organizations/Education_vs_Fanatic_ Literacy_English.pdf (accessed 1 September 2020).

97. Higher Education Commission (HEC), *HEC Vision 2025*, HEC, Islamabad, 2017, foreword.

98. Ibid.

99. Ibid., 3.

100. Ibid., 14.

101. Ibid.

102. Ibid.

103. Ibid., 3.

104. Ibid., 6–7.

105. Ibid., 7.

106. Ibid., 70.

107. Ibid., 69–72.

108. Naureen Durrani and Máiréad Dunne, 'Curriculum and National Identity: Exploring the Links between Religion and Nation in Pakistan', *Journal of Curriculum Studies*, Vol. 42, No. 2, 2010, 215.

109. Rubina Saigol, 'Enemies Within and Enemies Without: The Besieged Self in Pakistani Textbooks', *Futures,* Vol. 37, No. 9, 2005, 1,005.

110. Naureen Durrani and Máiréad Dunne, 'Curriculum and National Identity', 226.

111. See Yvette Claire Roser, *Islamization of Pakistani Social Sciences Textbooks*, quoted by Yoginder Sikand, Book Review, countercurrents.org available at https://www.countercurrents.org/sikand260309.htm (accessed 11 November 2020).

112. Rubina Saigol, 'A Tale of Two Communities: Pakistani Textbook Representations of 1857', in Stephen Lyon and Iain R. Edgar, eds, *Shaping a Nation: An Examination of Education in Pakistan*, Oxford University Press, 2010, 116.

113. A. H. Nayyar and Ahmed Salim, *The Subtle Subversion*, 11–22.

114. Aftab A. Kazi, *Ethnicity and Education in Nation-building*, 138.

115. Mubarak Ali, 'History, Ideology and Curriculum', in S. Akbar Zaidi, ed, *Continuity and Change: Socio-political and Institutional Dynamics in Pakistan*, City Press, Karachi, 2003, 57.

116. Krishna Kumar, 'Partition in School Textbooks: A Comparative Look at India and Pakistan', in S. Settar and Indira B. Gupta, eds, *Pangs of*

Partition: The Human Dimension, Volume II, Manohar Publishers, New Delhi, 2002, 17–28.

117. Ibid., 22.

118. Ibid., 24.

119. International Crisis Group, *Pakistan: Reforming the Education Sector*, Asia Report, October 2004, 8–10, available at https://d2071andvi-p0wj.cloudfront.net/84-pakistan-reforming-the-education-sector.pdf (accessed 22 July 2020).

120. Nazia Nazar, Österman Karin and Björkqvist Kaj, 'Religious Tolerance, Gender Equality and Bellicose Attitudes: A Comparative Study of Three Educational Systems in Pakistan', *European Journal of Social Sciences Education and Research*, Vol. 11, No. 1, 2017, 126.

121. Mariam Chughtai, 'What Produces a History Textbook?', 63.

122. Marie Lall, 'Educate to Hate: The Use of Education in the Creation of Antagonistic National Identities in India and Pakistan', *Compare: A Journal of Comparative and International Education*, Vol. 38, No. 1, 2008, 110.

123. A. Salam Ansari, ed., *Social Research in National Development: Conference Proceedings*, Pakistan Academy for Rural Development, Peshawar, 1963, 99.

124. M. Basharat Ali, 'Scientific Enquiry and the Quran', in A. Salam Ansari, ed., *Social Research in National Development*, 72.

125. Marie Lall, 'Educate to Hate', 103–10.

126. K. K. Aziz, *The Murder of History: A Critique of History Textbooks in Pakistan*, Sang-e-Meel Publications, Lahore, 1993, 187–94.

127. Tariq Rahman, *Language, Education, and Culture*, Oxford University Press, Karachi, 1999, 163–5.

128. Rubina Saigol, *The Pakistan Project: A Feminist Perspective on Nation and Identity*, Women Unlimited, New Delhi, 2013, 58.

129. Ibid., 10.

130. Ibid.

131. Durdana Najam, 'Textbooks Breeding Extremism and Hatred in Society', *News Lens Pakistan*, 4 January 2016, http://www.newslens.pk/textbooks-breeding-extremism-in-society/.

132. Naureen Durrani and Máiréad Dunne, 'Curriculum and National Identity', 215.

133. Matthew J. Nelson, 'Dealing with Difference: Religious Education and the Challenge of Democracy in Pakistan', *Modern Asian Studies*, Vol. 43, No. 3, 2009, 595.

134. Deepak Mehta, 'Words that Wound: Archiving Hate in the Making of Hindu–Indian and Muslim–Pakistani Publics in Bombay', in Naveeda Khan, ed., *Beyond Crisis: Re-evaluating Pakistan*, Routledge, London, 2010, 315.

135. Rubina Saigol, 'The State of Educational Discourse in Pakistan', in Inayatullah, Rubina Saigol and Pervez Tahir, eds, *Social Sciences in Pakistan*, Council of Social Sciences, Pakistan, Islamabad, 2005, 81–2.

136. Ibid., 88–9.

137. S. Akbar Zaidi, 'The Dismal State of Social Sciences in Pakistan', in S. Akbar Zaidi, ed., *Social Science in Pakistan in the 1990s*, Vol. 2, Council of Social Sciences Pakistan, Islamabad, 2003, 289.

138. Asma Mansoor and Samina Malik, 'Deconstructive Pedagogy and Ideological Demystification in Post-colonial Pakistan', *Curriculum Inquiry*, Vol. 46, No. 5, 2016, 493.

139. Ibid., 494–5, 497.

140. Ibid., 497–8.

141. Ibid., 69.

142. Tariq Rahman, 'Madrasas: The Potential for Violence in Pakistan?', in Jamal Malik, ed., *Madrasas in South Asia*, Routledge, London, 2007, 66.

143. Mamoun Fandy, 'Enriched Islam: The Muslim Crisis of Education', *Survival*, Vol. 49, No. 2, 2007, 92.

144. Yogi Sikand, 'Modern Education of Girls Is Opposed: A Deobandi Mullah's Diatribe against "Modern" Education for Girls', Islamic Research Foundation International (IRFI), article 428, https://www.irfi.org/articles/articles_401_450/modern_education_of_girls_is_opp.htm (accessed 4 June 2020).

145. John Zaller, 'The Statistical Power of Election Studies to Detect Media Exposure Effects in Political Campaigns', *Electoral Studies*, Vol. 21, No. 2, 2002, 323.

146. For pioneering work in this field, see Zamir Niazi, *Press in Chains*, Karachi Press Club, Karachi, 1986.

147. Letter from J. S. Hiscok, Dated 8 June 1982, File No. FCO 37/2922, British National Archives London.

148. Gary Bridge, 'Reason in the City? Communicative Action, Media and Urban Politics', *International Journal of Urban and Regional Research*, Vol. 33. No. 1, March 2009, 237.

149. Ibid., 238.

150. Ibid., 239.

151 Shearon Lowery, *Milestones in Mass Communication Research: Media Effects*, Longman Publishers, White Plains, New York, 1995, 400.

152. Mohammed Ali Shaikh, *Satellite Television and Social Change in Pakistan: A Case Study of Rural Sindh*, Orient Books Publishing House, Karachi, 2004, 89–90, 93.

153. Ibid., 98.

154. See interview of Mohammed Waseem by Alefia T. Hussain, 'Here There Is No Consensus on Democracy', *The News on Sunday*, 23 July 2017.

155. Huma Yusuf, *Mapping Digital Media: Pakistan*, Report by Open Society Foundations, 2013, 7–8, available at https://theasiadialogue.com/wp-content/uploads/2018/06/mapping-digital-media-pakistan-20130902.pdf (accessed 5 September 2020).
156. Marcus Michaelsen, *New Media vs. Old Politics: The Internet, Social Media and Democratisation in Pakistan*, Fesmedia Asia Series, Friedrich Ebert Stiftung, Berlin, 2010, 36.
157. Huma Yusuf, *Old and New Media: Converging during the Pakistan Emergency (March 2007–February 2008)*, MIT Centre for Future Civic Media, 2015, 3, available at https://civic.mit.edu/index.html%3Fp=1178.html (accessed 2 December 2020).
158. Marcus Michaelsen, *New Media vs. Old Politics*, 55.
159. Huma Yusuf, *Mapping Digital Media*, 6.
160. Huma Yusuf, 'Conspiracy Fever: The US, Pakistan and Its Media', *Survival*, Vol. 53, No. 4, 2011, 98.
161. Suhail Warraich, 'A Critical Evaluation of Vernacular Press', paper for the News South Asian Media, Islamabad, 2000, 1–2.
162. Abid Ali Butt, 'The Role of TV Talk Shows in the Political Orientation of Youth', MPhil. dissertation, Department of Communication Studies, Punjab University, Lahore, 2017, 39.
163. I. A. Rahman, 'Towards a People-centric Media', paper for the News South Asian Media Conference, Islamabad, 2000, 1.
164. Jeffrey Klaehn, 'A Critical Review and Assessment of Herman and Chomsky's "Propaganda Model"', *European Journal of Communication Studies*, Vol. 17, No. 2, 2002, 151–2.
165. Abida Eijaz, 'Articulation of Political Discourse through the Prism of Mass Media in Pakistan', *European Journal of Business and Social Sciences*, Vol. 1, No. 3, 2012, 1–21.
166. Pakistan Institute of Peace Studies (PIPS), 'Understanding the Militant Media in Pakistan: Outreach and Impact', Islamabad, 2010, 32.
167. Ibid., 34.
168. Ibid., 27–9.
169. Ibid., 41.
170. Ibid., 42–3.
171. Ibid., 47–8.
172. Ibid., 57–8.
173. Ibid., 79–80.
174. Ibid., 122.
175. Ibid., 176.
176. Richard Schumack, 'The Pakistan Floods and the Mystery of Suffering', ABC News, 2 September 2010, available at https://www.abc.net.au/

religion/the-pakistan-floods-and-the-mystery-of-suffering/10102136 (accessed 8 July 2020).

177. Kiran Hassan, 'The Role of Private Electronic Media in Radicalizing Pakistan', *Round Table*, Vol. 103, No. 1, 2014, 66–8.

178. Ibid., 2014, 70.

179. Huma Yusuf, 'Conspiracy Fever', 96.

180. Huma Yusuf, *Mapping Digital Media*, 6–7.

181. Huma Yusuf, 'Conspiracy Fever', 98–9.

182. Ibid., 100–1.

183. Ali Qadir and Pertti Alasuutari, 'Taming Terror: Domestication of the War on Terror in the Pakistan Media', *Asian Journal of Communication*, Vol. 23, No. 6, 2013, 582–3.

184. Nasreen Amanat, 'The Role of the Media in Promoting Network Agenda Setting', MPhil. Dissertation, Department of Communication Studies, Punjab University, Lahore, 2017, 136.

185. Noureddine Miladi, 'Social Media as a New Identity Battleground: The Cultural Comeback in Tunisia after the Revolution of 14 January 2011', in Noha Mellor and Khalil Rinnawi, eds, *Political Islam and Global Media*, Routledge, Abingdon, UK, 2016, 34.

186. The following discussion covers the input of social media activists on the thread. The dialogue was led by Marvi Sirmed and others, 24–6 July 2016.

187. See Kiran Hassan, 'Why Did a Military Dictator Liberalize the Electronic Media in Pakistan?', in Sahana Udupa and Stephen D. McDowell, eds, *Media as Politics in South Asia*, Routledge, Abingdon, UK, 2017, 79.

188. See Twitter discussion involving Marvi Sirmed and others, 24–6 July 2016.

189. Marcus Michaelsen, *New Media vs. Old Politics*, 15, 17.

190. Ibid., 16.

191. Ibid., 33.

192. Ibid., 41.

193. Maqsood Ahmad Shaheen, 'Use of Social Networks and Information-seeking Behaviour of Students during Political Crises in Pakistan: A Case Study', *International Information & Library Review*, Vol. 40, No. 3, 2008, 2–3, 6.

194. Yasir Hussain, 'Social Media as a Tool for Transparency and Good Governance in the Government of Gilgit-Baltistan', Crossroads Asia Working Paper Series, No. 22, 2014, 3.

195. Fiaz Hussain and Bushra Qureshi, 'Social Media and Policy Making in Pakistan', *Pakistan Administrative Review*, Vol. 2, No. 1, 2018, 208–11.

196. Hena Khursheed Bajwa, 'Pakistani Media, Public Opinion, and the Downfall of Pervez Musharraf: News Attribute, Agenda-setting, and Cognitive Liberation in the Lawyers' Movement', PhD thesis, University of Texas, Austin, 2016, 12-14, available at https://repositories.lib.utexas.edu/bitstream/handle/2152/39462/BAJWA-DISSERTATION-2016.pdf?sequence=1&isAllowed=y (accessed 27 June 2020). See also 'Trend in News Coverage and Public Opinion of Musharraf', Table 11, 144, available at https://repositories.lib.utexas.edu/bitstream/handle/2152/39462/BAJWA-DISSERTATION-2016.pdf?sequence=1&isAllowed=y (accessed 27 June 2020).

197. Michael Kugelman, *Social Media in Pakistan: Catalyst for Communication, not Change*, Norwegian Peacebuilding Resource Centre (NOREF), NOREF Report, August 2012, 1.

198. Dileep Padgoankar, 'The Information Revolution and the Print Media', paper for the News South Asian Media Conference, Islamabad, 2000, 1.

199. Abida Eijaz, 'Articulation of Political Discourse', 115.

200. Saqib Saeed, Markus Rhode and Volker Wulf, 'ICTs, an Alternative Sphere for Social Movements in Pakistan: A Research Framework', paper available at https://www.wineme.uni-siegen.de/paper/2008/saeed-rohde-wulf--ict--2008.pdf (accessed 22 July 2020).

201. Huma Yusuf, 'Conspiracy Fever', 107.

202. Saifuddin Ahmed and Marko M. Skoric, 'My Name is Khan: The Use of Twitter in the Campaign for the 2013 Pakistan General Election', conference paper, 47th Hawaii International Conference on System Sciences, 2014, 2,243, 2,246.

203. Huma Yusuf, *Old and New Media*, 3.

204. Phillip Howard, Sheetal D. Agarwal, and Muzammil M. Hussain, 'The Dictators' Dilemma: When Do States Disconnect their Digital Networks?', *Issues in Technology Innovation No. 13*, Center for Technology Innovation at Brookings, Washington DC, 2011, 8.

205. Huma Yusuf, *Mapping Digital Media*, 9.

206. Ibid., 43.

207. Ibid., 225–7.

208. Mohammad Hanif, 'Censorship under Military Dictators Was Bad. It May Be Worse in Democracy', *The New York Times*, 17 October 2018.

209. Fahd Hussain, 'A New Beginning', *The Express Tribune*, 29 July 2018.

210. See 92 News [TV channel], 'Fahad Hussain Exposed Media Censorship, Elections and Military Influence', YouTube, 30 July 2018, available on https://twitter.com/fahdhusain/status/1023841016678367232?lang=en

211. Daud Khattak and Frud Bezhan, 'Every Body is Scared: Pakistan Media Fighting and Losing Battle with Extreme Censorship', Radio Free

Europe, 3 June 2018, available at https://www.rferl.org/a/every-body-is-scared-pakistani-media-fighting----and-losing----battle-with-extreme-censorship/29268374.html (accessed 4 September 2020).

212. Kanwar Khuldune Shahid, 'Self-censorship Descends on Pakistani Media as Polls Loom', *Asia Times*, 30 May 2018, available at https://asiatimes.com/2018/05/self-censorship-descends-on-pakistani-media-as-polls-loom/ (accessed 4 September 2020).

213. Farooq Sulehria, 'From Overdeveloped State to Praetorian Pakistan: Tracing the Media's Transformation', in Matthew McCartney and S. Akbar Zaidi, eds, *New Perspectives on Pakistan's Political Economy: State, Class and Social Change*', Cambridge University Press, Cambridge, 241–55.

214. Madiha Afzal, *Pakistan's Censorship Model: An Image- and Identity-obsessed Country*, Brookings Institution, Washington DC, 30 May 2018, https://www.brookings.edu/blog/order-from-chaos/2018/05/30/pakistans-censorship-model/

215. Saad Sayeed, 'In Pakistan's Once Vibrant Media, Some Journalists View Intimidation as the New Normal', Reuters, 9 October 2018, https://www.reuters.com/article/pakistan-media/in-pakistans-once- vibrant-media-some-journalists-view-intimidation-as-the-new- normal-idINK-CN1MJ0DZ (accessed 4 September 2020).

216. Two scheduled panellists of a seminar claimed that their invitation to speak at the Lahore Literary Festival was rescinded at the last minute allegedly because state authorities ordered the organizers to remove the panellists and threatened to revoke the festival's No Objection Certificate (NOC) if they did not comply, *Dawn*, 20 November 2018.

217. BBC, 9 March 2017.

218. Ibid.

219. Ibid., 28 January 2017; Fahd Hussain, 'A New Beginning', *The Express Tribune*, 29 July 2018.

220. *Dawn*, 10 January 2017.

221. The following observations draw on Asad Hashim, 'Pakistan's New Regulations Aim to "silence the internet"', *Al Jazeerah*, 2 December 2020.

222. Ibid.

223. Ibid.

224. *Dawn*, editorial, 'Social Media Rules', 21 November 2020.

225 Imtiaz Alam, 'Pakistan: Censoring Journalism in the Name of "Media Development"', *TheWire*, 6 September, 2021.

226. Raza Habib Raja,' Dissecting the Actions of PTI's Online Brigade', *The Tribune*, 30 December 2020.

227. Ibid.

228. Khurram Hussain, 'Trolls and Hate', *Dawn*, 13 August 2020.

229. Huma Yusuf, 'Mapping Digital Media', 45.

230. Jahanzaib Haque, 'Hate Speech: A Study of Pakistan's Cyberspace', report by Bytesforall, Lahore, June 2014, 1.

231. Ibid., 14–15.

232. Ibid., 29.

233. Ibid., 50.

234. Ibid., 59.

235. Ramsha Jahangir, 'A Battle of Ideas: How Social Media Has Become a War Zone for Competing Narratives', *Herald,* December 2018, 38.

236. *Dawn,* editorial, 17 December 2018.

237. Dhiraj Murthy and Scott A. Longwell, 'Twitter and Disaster: The Uses of Twitter during the 2010 Pakistan Floods', *Information, Communication and Society*, Vol. 16, No. 6, 2013, 838, 852.

238. *Dawn*, editorial, 4 February 2017.

239. For examples, see the Pakistan Penal Code Section 153-A and Sections 295–8 as amended under the 1985 8th Amendment; Maintenance of Public Order Ordinance 1960; Anti-Terrorism Act 1997; The Protection of Pakistan Act 2014; and Pakistan Electronic Media Regulatory Authority (PEMRA) Ordinance 2002.

240. Centre for Social Justice, Association of Women for Awareness and Motivation, 'Combating Hate Speech beyond Administrative Measures', Sanjh Publications, Lahore, 2–4, http://csjpak.org/pdf/analysis_hate_speech_laws_CSJ.pdf (accessed 22 July 2020).

241. Michael Kugelman, *Social Media in Pakistan*, 4–6.

242. Daanish Mustafa and Amiera Sawas, 'Urbanisation and Political Change in Pakistan: Exploring the Known Unknowns', *Third World Quarterly*, Vol. 34, No. 7, 2013, 1,302.

243. Here I refer to the concept of 'primitive accumulation of power' in a Marxian sense. For details, see Mara Loveman, 'The Modern State and the Primitive Accumulation of Power', *American Journal of Sociology*, Vol. 110, No. 6, 2005, 1,651–83.

244. Rabia Ali, 'Social Media and Youth in Pakistan: Implications on Family Relations', *Global Media Journal*, Vol. 14, No. 26, 2016, 2.

245. Ibid.

7. THE OUTSIDER

1. Yogesh Atal, 'Managing Multiplicity: The Insider–Outsider Duality', *Economic and Political Weekly*, Vol. 36, No. 36, 2001, 3,460.

2. Ibid., 3,463.

3. Ibid., 3,465.

4. Robert K. Merton, 'Insiders and Outsiders: A Chapter in the Sociology of Knowledge,' *American Journal of Sociology*, Vol. 78, No. 1, 1972, 10–11.

5. Ibid., 11.

6. Ibid., 15.

7. Ibid., 22.

8. See Angana P. Chatterji, Thomas Blom Hansen and Christophe Jaffrelot, eds, *Majoritarian State: How Hindu Nationalism is Changing India*, Harper Collins, London, 2019.

9. See John Gallaghar, *The Decline, Revival and Fall of the British Empire*, Cambridge University Press, 1982; Gordon Johnson, *Provincial Politics and Indian Nationalism: Bombay and the Indian National Congress, 1880–1915*, Cambridge University Press, 1974; and Anil Seal, *The Emergence of Indian Nationalism: Competition and Collaboration in the Later Nineteenth Century*, Cambridge University Press, 1969.

10. Benedict Anderson, *Imagined Communities: Reflections on the Origin and Spread of Nationalism*, Verso, London, 1983, 44–5.

11. Tai Yong Tan and Gyanesh Kudaisya, *The Aftermath of Partition in South Asia*, Routledge, London & New York, 2000, 175–9.

12. Gurharpal Singh, 'Resizing and Reshaping the State: India from Partition to the Present', in Brendan O'Leary, Ian Lustick and Thomas Callaghy, eds, *Right-sizing the State: The Politics of Moving Borders*, Oxford University Press, 2001, 153–4.

13. S. J. Burki, *Pakistan under Bhutto*, Palgrave MacMillan, London, 1980, 14–15.

14. Siddik Salik as quoted by Manuel Uebersax, 'The Other Battlefield: Construction and Representation of the Pakistani Military "Self" in the Field of Military Autobiographical Narrative Production', PhD thesis, University of Bern, 2017, 114.

15. M. Anisurrehman, *East and West Pakistan: A Problem in the Political Economy of Regional Planning*, Cambridge University Press, MA, 1970, 15.

16. Sarah Ansari, 'Identity Politics and Nation-building in Pakistan: The Case of Sindhi Nationalism', in Roger D. Long, Gurharpal Singh, Yunas Samad and Ian Talbot, eds, *State and Nation-building in Pakistan: Beyond Islam and Security*, Routledge, Abingdon, UK, 2015, 107.

17. Asma Faiz, *In Search of Lost Glory: Sindhi Nationalism in Pakistan*, Hurst & Co., London, 2021, 65–7.

18. For the politics of referendum see Syed Wiqar Ali Shah, *Ethnicity, Islam and Nationalism: Muslim Politics in the North-West Frontier Province, 1937–1947*, Oxford University Press, Karachi, 1999, 220–1.

19. See Robert G. Wirsing, *The Baluchis and Pathans*, Minority Rights Group, London, 1981; Selig Harrison, *In Afghanistan's Shadow: Baluch Nationalism and Soviet Temptations*, Carnegie Endowment for International Peace, Washington, DC, 1981; Inayatullah Baloch, *The Problem of 'Greater Baluchistan': A Study of Baluch Nationalism*, Beiträge zur Südasienforschung series, Vol. 116, Südasien Institut, University of Heidelberg, Franz

Steiner Verlag, Wiesbaden, 1987, published online by Cambridge University Press, 24 December 2009; Rajshree Jetly, 'Resurgence of the Baluch Movement in Pakistan: Emerging Perspectives and Challenges,' in Rajshree Jetly, ed., *Pakistan in Regional and Global Politics*, Taylor & Francis, London, 2012; Frédéric Grare, 'Pakistan: The Resurgence of Baluch Nationalism', Carnegie Papers No. 65, Carnegie Endowment for International Peace, Washington DC, 2006; Martin Axmann, *Back to the Future: The Khanate of Kalat and the Genesis of Baluch Nationalism, 1915–1955*, Oxford University Press, Karachi, 2012; Farhan Hanif Siddiqi, *The Politics of Ethnicity in Pakistan: The Baloch, Sindhi and Mohajir Ethnic Movements*, Routledge, London & New York, 2012; Alia Amirali, *Balochistan: A Case Study of Pakistan's Peacemaking Praxis*, Sage Publications, New Delhi, 2015.

20. Inayatullah Baloch, *The Problem of 'Greater Baluchistan'*, 178–97.

21. Ibid., 192.

22. Ibid., 194.

23. Martin Axmann, *Back to the Future*, 263–7.

24. The comment of a former Supreme Court judge, V. R. Krishna Iyer, about Article 356 as quoted in H. M. Rajashekara, 'The Nature of Indian Federalism: A Critique', *Asian Survey*, Vol. 13, No. 3, 1997, 250.

25. Maryam S. Khan, 'Politics of Ethnic Federalism in Pakistan', in Asma Faiz, ed., *Making Federation Work: Federalism in Pakistan after the 18th Amendment*, Oxford University Press, Karachi, 2015, 167–76.

26. Christophe Jaffrelot, *A History of Pakistan and its Origins*, Anthem Press, London, 2004, 38.

27. For discussion, see Mohammad Waseem, *Pakistan under Martial Law: 1977–1985*, Vanguard Books, Lahore, 1987, 63, 184.

28. Maryam Khan, 'Politics of Ethnic Federalism in Pakistan', 187–90.

29. Ibid.

30. Tahir Naqvi, 'What Remains of the Muttahida Quomi Movement', in Maryam Mufti, Sahar Shafqat and Niloufer Siddiqui, eds, *Pakistan's Political Parties: Surviving Between Dictatorship and Democracy*, Georgetown University Press, 2020, 81–4, 86.

31. Asma Faiz, 'Building Language, Building Province: Civil Society and Ethnic Nationalism in Pakistan', *Journal of Civil Society*, Vol. 17, No. 1, 2021, 93.

32. Shahid Kardar, 'Polarisation in the Regions and Prospects for Integration', in S. Akbar Zaidi, ed., *Regional Imbalances and the National Question in Pakistan*, Vanguard Books, Lahore, 1992, 314.

33. Vali Nasr, 'Military Rule, Islamism and Democracy in Pakistan', *Middle East Journal*, Vol. 58, No. 2, 2004, 205.

34. Interview with Afrasiab Khattak, formerly associated with the ANP, Islamabad, 10 December 2019, Islamabad.

35. Asma Faiz, 'Building Language, Building Province', 95.

36. D. L. Sheth and Gurpreet Mahajan, eds, *Minority Identities and the Nation State*, 'Introduction', Oxford University Press, New Delhi, 1999, 1–2.

37. Maria-Magdalena Fuchs and Simon Wolfgang Fuchs, 'Religious Minorities in Pakistan: Identities, Citizenship and Social Belonging', *South Asia: Journal of South Asian Studies*, Vol. 43, No. 1, 2020, 7.

38. Ibid., 9–10.

39. Ibid., 11.

40. Ajay K. Raina, 'Minorities and Representation in a Plural Society: The Case of the Christians of Pakistan', *South Asia: Journal of South Asian Studies*, Vol. 37, No. 4, 2014, 688.

41. Constituent Assembly of Pakistan Debates (CAP), Vol. 5, 7–12 March 1949, fifth session, 8.

42. Ibid., 9.

43. Ibid., 10.

44. Christophe Jaffrelot and Laurent Gayer, *Muslims in Indian Cities: Trajectories of Marginalization*, Harper Collins Publishers, Noida, Uttar Pradesh, India, 2013, 2–4.

45. See, for example, A. H. Nayyar and Ahmed Salim, *The Subtle Subversion: The State of Curricula and Textbooks in Pakistan Urdu, English, Social Studies and Civics*, Sustainable Development Policy Institute, Islamabad, 2005.

46. Jürgen Schaflechner, 'Betwixt and Between: Hindu Identity in Pakistan and "Wary and Aware" Public Performances', *South Asia: Journal of South Asian Studies*, Vol. 43, No. 1, 2020, 101–18.

47. Anushay Malik, 'The (un)Imagined Citizens of the Islamic Republic of Pakistan', *Herald*, 15 August 2016, https://herald.dawn.com/news/1153493.

48. Ghazal Asif, 'Jogendranath Mandal and the Politics of Dalit Recognition in Pakistan', *South Asia: Journal of South Asian Studies*, Vol. 43, No. 1, 2020, 119–35.

49. Charles Amjad-Ali, 'From Dislocation to Dislocation: The Experience of the Christian Community in Pakistan', *International Review of Modern Sociology*, Vol. 41, No. 1, Spring 2015, 4.

50. Ibid., 12–13.

51. Ibid., 21.

52. Ibid., 23–4.

53. 'Report of the Court of Inquiry constituted under Punjab Act II of 1954 to enquire into Punjab Disturbances of 1953' (Munir Report), Government Printing Punjab, Lahore, 1954, 14–15, available at https://www.thepersecution.org/dl/report_1953.pdf (accessed 10 September 2020).

54. Ibid., 29.

55. Ibid., 37.

56. Ibid., 125.

57. Ibid., 147.

58. Ibid., 186.

59. Ibid., 203.

60. Sean William White, 'Medina Charter and Pluralism', *Fountain Magazine*, July 2011, available at https://www.metpdx.org/images/METpdf/Medina_Charter__Pluralism.pdf (accessed 17 September 2020).

61. M. Mahfuzul Huq, *Electoral Problems in Pakistan*, Asiatic Society of Pakistan, Dhaka, Bangladesh, 1966, 78.

62. Mohammad Waseem, *The 1993 Elections in Pakistan*, Vanguard Books, Lahore, 1994, 218.

63. Charles Amjad-Ali, 'From Dislocation to Dislocation', 21.

64. See Dominic Moghal and Jennifer Jagjivan, 'Major Issues Confronting the Religious Minorities Especially the Christians in Pakistan', *Al-Mushir*, Vol. 42, No. 2, Rawalpindi, Pakistan, 2000, 71–3.

65. Article 25 of the Constitution provides that: 'All citizens are equal before law and are entitled to equal protection of law.'

66. Human Rights Commission of Pakistan, *Survey of Human Rights*, HRCP Publications, Lahore, 1998, 38.

67. Farzana Bari, *Local Government Elections December 2000 (Phase-I)*, PATTAN (NGO), Islamabad, 2001, 43.

68. *Human Rights Monitor*, International Service for Human Rights, New York and Geneva, 2001, 78.

69. Ashfaq Yusufzai, 'Minorities in Pakistan Fear "forced conversion" to Islam', Movement for Solidarity and Peace in Pakistan, 19 May 2014, available at http://www.ipsnews.net/2014/05/minorities-pakistan-fear-forced-conversion-islam/ (accessed 18 July 2020).

70. For details see Haroon Khalid, *A White Trail: A Journey into the Heart of Pakistan's Religious Minorities*, Westland, New Delhi, 2013.

71. 'Mob Vandalises, Burns Down Shrine of Hindu Saint in KP's Karak', *Dawn*, 30 December 2020.

72. Ajay K. Raina, 'Minorities and Representation in a Plural Society', 691.

73. See Charles Amjad-Ali, 'From Dislocation to Dislocation', 17–18.

74. Anushay Malik, 'The (un)Imagined Citizens of Pakistan', 10.

75. Jürgen Schaflechner, 'Betwixt and Between', 101–18.

76. Ibid., 114.

77. *Dawn*, editorial, 'Forced Conversion', 4 November 2020.

78. Hafeez Tunio, 'Decade in Review: From the Land of Sufis to the Land of Fear', *The Express Tribune*, 3 January 2020, https://tribune.com.pk/story/2129387/1-decade-review-land-sufis-land-fear/ (accessed 11 September 2020).

79. Ibid.

80. Ibid.

81. Ibid.

82. Maria-Magdalena Fuchs and Simon Wolfgang Fuchs, 'Religious Minorities in Pakistan', 7.

83. The following observations draw on Andreas T. Rieck, *The Shias of Pakistan: An Assertive and Beleaguered Minority*, Hurst & Co., London, 2015, xi.

84. Ibid., 60.

85. *Dawn*, 5–6 December 1945.

86. Rieck, *The Shias of Pakistan*, 60–3.

87. Ibid., 80.

88. Ibid., 97.

89. The following observations draw on Jaffar Mirza, 'The Changing Landscape of Anti-Shia Politics in Pakistan', *The Diplomat*, 28 September 2020.

90. Shah Meer Baloch and Hannah Ellis-Petersen, 'Pakistani Shias Live in Terror as Sectarian Violence Increases', *The Guardian*, 21 October 2020.

91. Ibid., 16.

92. See G. Djinck, *National Identity and Geopolitical Visions: Maps of Pride and Pain*, Routledge, 1996, 5.

93. Muhammad Waseem, 'Dilemmas of Pride and Pain: Sectarian Conflict and Conflict Transformation in Pakistan', Working Paper No. 48, University of Birmingham, 2010, 16.

94. For a comprehensive analysis of Hazaras, see Shahid Ali, 'The Specter of Hate and Intolerance: Sectarian-Jihadi Nexus and the Persecution of Hazara Shia Community in Pakistan', *Contemporary South Asia*, Vol. 29, No. 2, 2021, 198-211.

95. Sarfraz Khan and Noor ul Amin, 'Minority, Ethnic, Race and Sect Relations in Pakistan: Hazara Residing in Quetta', *Journal of Humanities and Social Sciences*, Vol. xxvii, No.2, 2019, 81–108.

96. Ibid., 85.

97. Ibid., 92.

98. Rahmatullah Behryab Hazara, *Tragic Incidents* [Saanihat, Urdu text], 2012. No publisher or place given.

99. Ibid., 296.

100. Ibid., 297.

101. Ibid., 355.

102. For an excellent study of Zikris, see Inayatullah Baloch, 'Islam, The State and Identity: The Zikris of Balochistan', in Magnus Marsden, ed., *Islam and Society in Pakistan*, Oxford University Press, Karachi, 2010, 259-82.

103. *The Friday Times*, 30 September 2016.

104. *The Express Tribune*, editorial, 31 August 2014.

105. Saher Baloch, 'Zikris under Attack in Balochistan', *Dawn*, 2 January 2015.

106. Paul Brass, *Ethnicity and Nationalism*, Sage, New Delhi, 1991, 8.

107. T. K. Oommen, 'Insiders and Outisder in India: Primordial Collectivism and Cultural Pluralism in Nation-building', *International Sociology*, Vol. 1, No. 1, 1986, 53–5.

108. Ibid.

109. See Hamida Khuhro, *Mohammed Ayub Khuhro: A Life of Courage in Politics*, Ferozsons, Lahore, 1998; Sarah Ansari, *Life after Partition: Migration, Community and Strife in Sindh, 1947–1962*, Oxford University Press, 2005; Suranjan Das, *Kashmir and Sindh: Nation-building, Ethnicity and Regional Politics in South Asia*, K. P. Bagchi & Co., 2001; Feroz Ahmed, *Ethnicity and Politics in Pakistan*, Oxford University Press, 1998; Mehtab Ali Shah, 'Ethnic Tensions in Sindh and their Possible Solutions', *Contemporary South Asia*, Vol. 6, No. 3, 1997; and Yunas Samad, *A Nation in Turmoil: Nationalism and Ethnicity in Pakistan, 1937–1958*, Sage Publications, India, 1995.

110. For a detailed analysis of the contention over control of Karachi and the accompanying ethnic dichotomy, see Asma Faiz, *In Search of Lost Glory: Sindhi Nationalism in Pakistan*, Hurst & Co., London, 2021, 55–9.

111. Hamida Khuhro, *Mohammad Ayub Khuhro*, 383.

112. Ibid., 379.

113. Sarah Ansari, 'Identity Politics and Nation-building in Pakistan', 113.

114. Aijaz Qureshi, *One Unit and Sindh* [Urdu text], Fiction House, Lahore, 2016, 216–45.

115. Quoted in Alyssa Ayers, *Speaking Like a State: Language and Nationalism in Pakistan*, Cambridge University Press, 2009, 16.

116. Alain Dieckhoff, *The Invention of a Nation: Zionist Thought and the Making of Modern Israel*, Hurst & Co., 2003, 110.

117. Ibid., 113–18.

118. Ibid., 115.

119. Quoted in Tariq Rahman, *Language and Politics in Pakistan*, Oxford University Press, Karachi, 1996, 84.

120. Quoted from a letter from Iqbal to one Edward Thompson, in Aijaz Qureshi, *One Unit and Sindh*, 20–1.

121. Akmal Shehzad Ghumman, *Media Mandi*, Jamhoori Publications, Lahore, 2016, 19–38: interviews with Majeed Nizami and Arif Nizami.

122. See appendices in Aijaz Qureshi, *One Unit and Sindh*, 319–35.

123. Asma Faiz, *In Search of Lost Glory*, 129–31.

124. The following observations and tables draw on Mohammad Waseem, 'Affirmative Action Policies in Pakistan', *Ethnic Studies Report,* Vol. 15, No. 2, July 1997.

125. A. F. Aisha Ghaus, Hafiz A. Pasha, Rafia Ghaus and M. Aslam Chaudhary, 'Social Development Ranking of Districts of Pakistan', *The Pakistan Development Review*, Vol. 35, No. 4, Papers and Proceedings PART II. Twelfth Annual General Meeting of the Pakistan Society of Development Economists Islamabad, 14–16 December 1996, 601–2, Table 3.

126. MQM, Constitutional Petition in the Supreme Court of Pakistan, Part 1, 1994, 4–5.

127. Charles H Kennedy, *Bureaucracy in Pakistan*, Oxford University Press, Karachi, 1988, 132.

128. National Documentation Centre (NDC), O. M. No. 4/9/83 - R. 2, Dated 2 February 1984, Establishment Division, Islamabad.

129. *Mohammed Kamran Khan* vs *Secretary Establishment and Federal Public Service Commission Islamabad*, Lahore High Court Bench at Rawalpindi, No. 21109/94, lit 3, para. J.

130. Ibid., paras K, N.

131. Abdul Wajid Rana, 'Quota System in Pakistan', *The Express Tribune*, 9 November 2017.

132. Abbas Rashid and Farida Shaheed, *Pakistan: Ethno-politics and Contending Elite*, United Nations Research Institute for Social Development, Geneva, 1993, 16.

133. Moonis Ahmer, 'Conflict Dynamics of Kalabagh Dam', *The Daily Times*, 15 June 2018, https://dailytimes.com.pk/253725/conflict-dynamics -of-kalabagh-dam/ (accessed 2 September 2020).

134. Quoted in 'Sindh Rejects Construction of Kalabagh Dam', *Dawn*, 17 June 2010, https://www.dawn.com/news/969905.

135. Ibid.

136. Munir Ghazanfar, 'Kalabagh Dam and the Water Debate in Pakistan', *Lahore Journal of Policy Studies*, Vol. 2, No. 1, 2008, 154–9.

137. Mark Zeitoun and Jeroen Warner, 'Hydro-hegemony: A Framework for Analysis of Trans-boundary Water Conflict', *Water Policy*, Vol. 8, No. 5, 2006, 435–6.

138. Daanish Mustafa, 'Social Construction of Hydropolitics: The Geographical Scales of Water and Security in the Indus Basin', *Geographical Review*, Vol. 97, No. 4, 2007, 488.

139. Ibid., 493–4.

140. Tarique Niazi, 'Contesting Instrumental Knowledge with Communicative Action: Why Kalabagh Dam (Pakistan) Remains Unbuilt', *Organization & Environment*, Vol. 32, No. 4, 2019, 3.

141. Ibid., 6–7.

142. Ibid., 11.

143. Ibid., 16.

144. Eric Paulsen, 'The Citizenship Status of the Urdu-speakers/Biharis in Bangladesh', *Refugee Survey Quarterly*, Vol. 25, No. 3, 2006, 55.

145. Frederic Grare, 'Balochistan: The State Versus the Nation', Carnegie Papers, Carnegie Endowment for International Peace, Washington, DC, April 2013, 1.

146. Ibid.

147. Ibid., 3, 13.

148. Ibid., 6.

149. Ibid., 7–8.

150. Ibid., 11.

151. Ibid., 12.

152. Robert K. Merton, 'Insiders and Outsiders', 13.

153. Quoted in Shakoor Ahmad Wani, 'The Changing Dynamics of the Baloch Nationalist Movement in Pakistan', *Asian Survey*, Vol. 56, No. 5, 2016, 813.

154. Ibid., 816.

155. 'We Can Torture, Kill, or Keep You for Years: Enforced Disappearances by Pakistan Security Forces in Balochistan', Human Rights Watch, New York, July 2011, 1–6.

156. Sulema Jahangir, 'Forced Conversions', *Dawn*, 12 April 2020.

157. 'Terror Conviction by Army Courts in 196 Cases Against Law', *Dawn*, 11 July 2020.

158. Human Rights Watch, 'We Can Torture, Kill, or Keep You for Years', 58–66.

159. Safiya Aftab, 'Census 2017 Controversies', *Daily Times*, 31 August 2017.

160. Majid Rajput, 'Politicians Smell Controversy in 2017 Census', *Daily Times*, 30 August 2017.

161. Sanaullah Baloch, 'Census Controversies', *The News*, 5 April 2017.

162. Mehtab Karim, 'Missing People in Census', *Dawn*, 17 October 2017.

163. Ibid.

164. Sanaullah Baloch, 'Census Controversies'.

165. Muhammad Asif Wazir and Anne Goujon, 'Assessing the 2017 Census of Pakistan Using Demographic Analysis: A Sub-National Perspective', working paper, Vienna Institute of Demography, Austrian Academy of Sciences, Vienna, June 2019, 35–6, available at https://www.econstor.eu/bitstream/10419/207062/1/1667013416.pdf (accessed 21 August 2020).

166. Michael Nijhawan, '"Today, We Are All Ahmadi": Configurations of Heretic Otherness between Lahore and Berlin', *British Journal of Middle Eastern Studies*, Vol. 37, No. 3, 2010, 430.

167. 'Shop Owner Held for Putting Up "Hate Notice"', *Dawn*, 14 December 2015.

168. Ali Usman Qasmi, 'The Ahmadis and the Politics of Religious Exclusion in Pakistan' in, *Anthem Modern South Asian History*, 2014.

169. Michael Nijhawan, 'Today, We Are All Ahmadi', 434–6.

170. Tayyab Mahmud, 'Protecting Religious Minorities: The Courts' Abdication', in Charles Kennedy and Rasul Bakhsh Rais, eds, *Pakistan 1995*, Westview Press, Boulder, CO, 1995, 86.

171. Quoted in Tayyab Mahmud, 'Protecting Religious Minorities', 87.

CONCLUSION

1. F. G. Bayley, *Stratagems and Spoils: A Social Anthropology of Politics*, Schocken Books, New York, 1969, 1–18.

2. The following observations are based on Indian TV anchor Karan Thapar's interview with Abdul Basit about his forthcoming book. Interview, *The Wire*, 23 March 2021, 'Nawaz Sharif Pandered to India Unilaterally and Unconditionally as PM', URL https://www.youtube.com/watch?v=KNlcpIyK5jY. See also Abdul Basit, *Hostility: A Diplomat's Diary of Pakistan-India Relations*, HarperCollins, London, 2021.

3. Anatol Lieven, *Pakistan: A Hard Country*, Allen Lane, London, 2011, 5, 7, 10.

4. Ibid., 5.

5. Ibid., 6.

6. Ibid., 13.

7. Ibid., 14–20.

8. Ibid., 23.

9. Ibid., 26–9.

10. Benedict Anderson, *Imagined Communities: Reflections on the Origin and Spread of Nationalism*, Verso, London, 1983, 163–86.

11. Mortimer Wheeler, *Five Thousand Years of Pakistan*, Christopher Johnson (Publishers), London, 1950.

12. After coming to power in 2018, Imran Khan often referred to his project to establish the state of Medina in Pakistan.

13. Benedict Anderson, *Imagined Communities*, 18, 36, 96.

14. For example, see Ayub Khan, *Friends not Masters: A Political Autobiography*, Oxford University Press, 1967.

15. Pierre Bourdieu, 'Cultural Reproduction and Social Reproduction', in Richard K. Brown, ed., *Knowledge, Education and Cultural Change: Papers in the Sociology of Education*, Tavistock, London, 1973, 59–60.

16. John Thompson, *The Reinvention of Publicness: The Media and Modernity*, Polity Press, Cambridge, 1999, 255.

17. Ibid., 38, 82–8.

GLOSSARY

Ad hominem	Directed against a person rather than the position they are maintaining.
Ahimsa	Non-violence
Ahmadi	A heretical sect of Islam
Aiyas	Governesses
Ajlaf	Indians converted to Islam
Aman ki Asha	Hope for peace
Ameen	Honest
Ashraf	Nobility (of non-Indian descent)
Ashram	Spiritual hermitage
Athna Ashri	The Twelver (Shia) sect of Islam
Azan	Call for prayer
Bangla	The Bengali language
Bhadralok	Well-mannered, elite, well-educated
Bibis	'Native' housewoman
Biraderi	Kinship network
Daryapanthis	Worshippers of river (god)
Devi	Goddess
Dharna	Sit-in
Dhimmi	Non-Muslims ('protected' by the Islamic state)
Diyet	Blood money
Eid Milad-un-Nabi	Celebration of the birthday of Prophet Mohammed (Peace Be Upon Him)
Faqih	Islamic jurist
Fatwa	Religious injunction

Fawad	Heart
Ganga-Jamuni	Belonging to the land between rivers Ganges and Jamuna
Gharanas	Families
Ghuzwa-e-Hind	Holy war of India
Gurdwara	Sikh place of worship
Guzara	Sustenance
Hadd	Divinely ordained punishment
Hanafi	An Islamic Sect, followers of Imam Abu Hanifa
Hazara	Shia community in Balochistan (originally from Hazara, Afghanistan)
Hindutva	Hindu nationalism
Hundi	Informal transfer of money
Ijma	Consensus
Ijtihad	Innovation
Imam	The prayer leader
Imambarghas	Places of congregation for Twelver Shias
Intifada	Uprising
Ismaeli	A subset of Shias
Jathas	Armed bands
Jialas	Party activists (PPP)
Jihad	Holy war
Jihadi group	Holy warrior
Jirga	A Pakhtun tribal assembly of elders (for dispute settlement)
Jizya	Tax on non-Muslims under an Islamic state
Kafis	A genre of classical Punjabi poetry
Karokari	Honour killing (in Sindh and Balochistan)
Khaki	Belonging to army (wearing uniform)
Khasadar	Paramilitary forces (in erstwhile FATA)
Khatm-e-Nabuwwat	Finality of prophethood
Khoja	A caste in the Gujrati-speaking community
Kurta	A loose shirt worn in India and Pakistan
Levies	Paramilitary law enforcement agency (Balochistan)

Locus standi	The right of a party to be heard before a court of law
Lok Mela	Public festival
Longue durée	Long duration
Madh-e-Sahaba	In praise of the Prophet's companions
Madrassah	Islamic seminary
Mai-baap	Mother–father (expression of respect for the elderly/authority)
Majlis-e-Shura	Advisory Council
Mandal	B. P. Mandal, Chairman of the Second Backward Classes Commission 1979
mandi	Market, privatization of economy by Manmohan Singh 1999
Mandir	Hindu temple (Babri masjid/Ram Janmabhoomi demolished 1992)
Maran barat	Fast unto death
Melas	Festivals
Mirasi	Folk singer
Mujahideen	Holy warriors
Mullahs	Local cleric/Imam in a mosque
Nafs	Instinct
Namazi	One who says his prayers
Nazim	(District) administrator
Nizam-e-Adl	Justice system
Nizam-e-Mustafa	Prophet's system
Non sequitur	A statement not logically following the previous statement
Panchayat	Assembly of five elders (for dispute settlement under Customary Law)
Pirs	Sufi spiritual guides
Purba	Eastern
Purdah	Veil
Qabza	Forceful occupation
Qasba	Small town
Qawwali	Islamic devotional singing (in South Asia)
Qazf	False accusation of adultery
Qisas	Retaliation in kind, eye for an eye
Rafizi	One who abandons belief

Ragas	Melodic framework for Indian classical music
Raj	Rule
Ramadhan	The fasting month in Islamic calendar
Regere imperio populos	Rule people with your power
Riyasti	Belonging to (Bahawalpur) state
Sadiq	Truthful
Salafi	A sect of Islam (also called Wahhabi)
Salus populi suprema lex	The health of the people is the supreme law
Sans	Without
Sardar	Tribal leader; one belonging to the family of tribal leadership
Satyagraha	Holding on to truth
Sawara	Giving minor girls in marriage as compensation for dispute settlement in KP
Shahadat	Martyrdom
Shariah	Islamic Law
Shia	A sect of Islam
Shuddhi	Purification among Hindus/reconversion of the erstwhile Hindus
Sunni	Main sect of Islam
Suo motu	On the court's own initiative
Swadeshi	Boycott of foreign goods
Tabligh	Proselytization
Takht	Powerhouse (Throne)
Talukdar	Estate holder
tammadun	Culture
Tariqa	Sufi Islam
Tehsil	The basic unit for revenue extraction
Thuggee	Murder and robbery (in mid-nineteenth century UP, India)
Ulema	Muslim theologians
Ultra Views	Acting beyond the legal authority
Umma	Islamic community

Vani	Giving minor girls in marriage as compensation for dispute settlement in Punjab
Ver sacrum	Sacred spring, a religious practice of ancient Italic people, concerning the deduction of colonies
Waqf	An Islamic endowment of property
Yom Ashura	Anniversary of martyrdom of Imam Hussain
Zakat	Islamic tax
Zamindar	Landlord
Zenana	Pertaining to women
Ziarat-e-Ashura	Islamic salutatory prayer to Allah (Shia)
Zikri	A heretical sect of Islam (Balochistan)
Zina	Adultery

INDEX

Notes: Page numbers followed by "*t*" refer to tables.

INDEX